A History of the Inquisition of Spain: Volume II
By Henry Charles Lea, LL.D.
Edited by Anthony Uyl

Woodstock, Ontario, 2017

A History of the Inquisition of Spain: Volume II
By Henry Charles Lea, LL.D.
Edited by Anthony Uyl

Originally Published by:
New York The MacMillan Company London: MacMillan & Co., Ltd. 1922; Copyright, 1906

The text of A History of the Inquisition of Spain - Volume II is all in the Public Domain. The layout is not in the Public Domain and is Copyright 2017© Devoted Publishing a division of 2165467 Ontario Inc.

Let us hear your philosophies and thoughts!

Contact us at: devotedpub@hotmail.com
Visit us on Facebook at: @DevotedPublishing
Visit our website for a full selection of print products: www.devotedpublishing.com

Published in Woodstock, Ontario, Canada 2017.

ISBN: 978-1-988297-80-4

Henry Charles Lea, LL.D.

Table of Contents

BOOK III - JURISDICTION 5
   CHAPTER I - HERESY...5
   CHAPTER II - THE REGULAR ORDERS 16
   CHAPTER III - BISHOPS 21
   CHAPTER IV - THE EDICT OF FAITH 41
   CHAPTER V - APPEALS TO ROME...46
BOOK IV - ORGANIZATION 70
   CHAPTER I - THE INQUISITOR-GENERAL AND SUPREME COUNCIL 70
   CHAPTER II - THE TRIBUNAL 87
   CHAPTER III - UNSALARIED OFFICIALS 110
   CHAPTER IV - LIMPIEZA...119
BOOK V - RESOURCES 131
   CHAPTER I - CONFISCATION 131
   CHAPTER II - FINES AND PENANCES 162
   CHAPTER III - DISPENSATIONS 167
   CHAPTER IV - BENEFICES 173
   CHAPTER V - FINANCES 180
BOOK VI - PRACTICE 190
   CHAPTER I - THE EDICT OF GRACE..190
   CHAPTER II - THE INQUISITORIAL PROCESS 193
   CHAPTER III - ARREST AND SEQUESTRATION 201
   CHAPTER IV - THE SECRET PRISON 210
   CHAPTER V - EVIDENCE..222
   CHAPTER VI - CONFESSION 236
APPENDIX OF DOCUMENTS..244
   I. EDICT OF FAITH. 244
   II. CONFESSIONAL LETTER OF ABSOLUTION ISSUED BY THE PAPAL PENITENTIARY, DECEMBER 4, 1481. 245
   III. REVOCATION OF LETTERS OF ABSOLUTION AND OF EXEMPTIONS, MAY 17, 1488. 246
   IV. PETITION OF GERONIMO ZURITA 246
   V. DETAILS OF THE ORGANIZATION OF THE INQUISITION OF MURCIA, AS REPORTED TO THE SUPREMA IN 1746. 247
   VI. COMMISSION OF AN INQUISITOR 247
   VII. PERSONNEL OF THE INQUISITION IN 1746..248
   VIII. CERTIFICATE OF LIMPIEZA. 248
   IX. RECEIPT, MARCH 30, 1524, BY THE WIFE OF A RECONCILED HERETIC FOR HER DOWER, FROM THE CONFISCATED ESTATE..248
   X. ABSTRACT OF PARTIAL STATEMENT OF RECEIPTS CHARGED AGAINST THE CANON JOAN DE ASTORGA, RECEIVER OF CONFISCATIONS IN VALENCIA FOR THE YEAR 1493.[1763] 249
   XI. KING FERDINAND TO TORQUEMADA, MARCH 30, 1498.............................250

XII. CEDULA OF KING FERDINAND, FEBRUARY 23, 1510, ON THE DIMINISHED RECEIPTS FROM CONFISCATIONS. 250

XIII. RECITAL OF EDICT OF GRACE IN CIUDAD REAL, 1483. 251

XIV. CONFESSION UNDER EDICT OF GRACE, OCTOBER 9, 1483, OF MARIA GONSALES, SUBSEQUENTLY BURNT IN AUTO DE FE OF FEBRUARY 23, 1484. 251

XV. REFUSAL OF A REQUEST FOR A COPY OF THE INSTRUCTIONS. 252

XVI. CARTA ACORDADA OF FEBRUARY 26, 1607, ENFORCING SECRECY. 252

XVII. FINANCES OF THE INQUISITION IN 1731. 253

FOOTNOTES: 254

BOOK III - JURISDICTION

CHAPTER I - HERESY

The Inquisition was organized for the eradication of heresy and the enforcement of uniformity of belief. We shall have occasion to see hereafter how elastic became the definition of heresy, and we have seen how far afield its extinction led the operations of the Holy Office but, to the last, the suppression of unorthodox belief remained the ostensible object of its existence.

It is not easy at the present day, for those accustomed to universal toleration, to realize the importance attached by statesmen in the past to unity of belief, or the popular abhorrence for any deviation from the standard of dogma. These convictions were part of the mental and moral fibre of the community and were the outcome of the assiduous teachings of the Church for centuries, until it was classed with the primal truths that it was the highest duty of the sovereign to crush out dissidence at whatever cost, and that hatred of the heretic was enjoined on every Christian by both divine and human law. The heretic was a venomous reptile, spreading contagion with his very breath and the safety of the land required his extermination as a source of pestilence.[1]

In the earlier periods of the Inquisition, moreover, when the hierarchy was filled with New Christians of doubtful orthodoxy, it was essential to know that the sacraments necessary to salvation were not vitiated by the apostasy of the ministrant, for his intention is indispensable to their validity. No man could tell how many priests there were like Andrés González, parish priest of San Martín de Talavera, who, on his trial at Toledo, in 1486, confessed that for fourteen years he had secretly been a Jew, that he had no intention when he celebrated mass, nor had he granted absolution to the penitents confessing to him. There was also a classical story, widely circulated, of Fray Garcia de Zapata, prior of the Geronimite monastery of Toledo, who, when elevating the Host, used to say "Get up, little Peter, and let the people look at you" and who always turned his back on the penitent to whom he pretended to grant absolution.[2]

CONDITIONS OF JURISDICTION

The merciless zeal of the Holy Office might gradually relieve the people of this danger, but it intensified by its methods the unreasoning abhorrence of heresy. The honest cavalier Oviedo, about the middle of the sixteenth century, merely phrases the current opinion of the time when he says that all possible punishments prescribed by the canons and admitted by the laws should be visited on the persons and property of heretics; they eat the bread of the good, they render the land infamous, by their conversation they lead souls to perdition and, with their marriages and kinships, they corrupt the blood of good houses.[3] As time wore on this increased rather than diminished. Galceran Albanell, Archbishop of Granada, who had been tutor of Philip IV, wrote to his former pupil April 12, 1621, to express his horror at learning that the English ambassador had been allowed to have divine service performed in his house, after the rites of his sect. The king should not allow it; it is the greatest of sins and unless it is remedied we shall all perish. It is an accursed reason to allege that that accursed king permits the Spanish ambassador to have mass celebrated in London. The English ambassador should be dismissed and the English king can send away the Spanish ambassador; if the Council of State interferes, let Philip show them the way of God. The Licenciado de Angulo should have a bishopric because he resigned his office as fiscal of the Council rather than affix his name to a paper in which the English king was styled Defender of the Faith and Albanell declares his readiness to resign his own see in Angulo's favor.[4] To a population sedulously trained in such sentiments the awful ceremonies of the auto de fe were a triumph of the faith, of which they felt proud, and they were filled with pious exultation when the flames of the brasero consumed the bodies of heretics who passed through temporal to eternal fire. It was a vindication of the honor of God, and it is necessary to understand and bear in mind this temper when considering the performance by the Inquisition of its allotted task.

***

The jurisdiction of the Holy Office over heresy was confined to the baptized, for baptism is a condition precedent to heresy; the unbaptized are outside of the Church and it has no spiritual authority over them. In the auto de fe of 1623, at Valladolid, a woman taken out to be relaxed for Judaism, declared that she was not baptized, whereupon the proceedings respecting her were stopped and she was remanded for investigation.[5] Although baptism can be validly administered by a heretic, yet in the trial of foreign Protestants, minute inquiry was made as to the details of their baptism in their sects, so as to be assured that they were truly baptized; in the case of Jacques Pinzon, at Toledo, in 1598, his advocate ingeniously but vainly argued that this could not be assumed, because it could not be proved that the minister had the proper intention, without which the rite was invalid.[6]

Age placed slender limits on inquisitorial jurisdiction. Children were considered capable of committing heresy as soon as they were doli capaces, at six or seven years, but were not held responsible until they reached years of discretion. This was fixed by Torquemada at twelve for girls and fourteen for boys, below which they were not to be made to abjure in public,[7] but the limit was frequently infringed. In 1501, Inesita, daughter of Marcos Garcia, between nine and ten years old and Isabel, daughter of Alvaro Ortolano, aged ten, were sentenced to appear in an auto de fe. They had confessed to fasting once or twice and the latter had been told by her father not to eat pork.[8] In 1660, at Valladolid, Joseph Rodríguez, aged eight, accused of Judaism, was regularly tried, with all the complicated formalities of procedure, occupying a year, and was made to give evidence against his father and brother; he was absolved secretly and placed in the penitential prison for instruction.[9] Of course there was no maximum limit of age. In 1638, at Valladolid, María Díaz, a hundred years old, was thrown into the secret prison for Judaism and her trial went forward.[10]

Responsibility to the Inquisition varied with the grade of heresy, which was carefully classified by the theologians. Material heresy is error in a baptized person arising from ignorance and, if the ignorance is inculpable, it is scarce to be considered as true heresy deserving of punishment.[11] Formal or mixed heresy is voluntary and pertinacious error, pertinacity being adherence to what is known to be contrary to the teachings of the Church. This formal heresy is again distinguished into internal, or mental, and external. Internal, or mental, heresy is that which is secretly entertained and is not manifested by either word or act. External heresy is subdivided into occult and public. Occult external is that which is manifested by words or signs, either in secret or to one or two persons only--as though a man in the solitude of his chamber should say "There is no God," or should utter his thought in the presence of another. Public external is that which is manifested openly, either in public or to more than two persons.[12] The bearing of these distinctions on the work of the Inquisition will be apparent hereafter.

EPISCOPAL JURISDICTION

There was still another definition of even greater importance. Heresy was both a sin and a crime. As a sin it was subject to the forum internum, or forum of conscience; as a crime, to the forum externum or judicial forum. A penitent in sacramental confession, admitting heretical belief, might receive sacramental absolution and be pardoned in the sight of God, but the crime, like that of murder or any other violation of human laws, would still remain to be punished in the judicial forum. We shall see that in the Inquisition the penitent, who confessed and repented and received absolution, was still subject to penalties ranging, according to circumstances, from slight penance to death.

***

Prior to the organization of the Inquisition in the thirteenth century, the cognizance of heresy was a natural attribute of the episcopal office. The duty of persecution was negligently performed and, when the Catharan and Waldensian heresies threatened the predominance of the Latin Church and the Albigensian Crusades left it master of the situation, the Inquisition gradually sprang up as an assistance to the bishops. There was some rivalry, but the bishops, as a rule, did not share in the confiscations and, as few of them had persecuting zeal sufficient to induce them to perform this gratuitous service, the field was virtually abandoned to the new organization, in the lands where it was introduced. Still the episcopal rights were undisputed. Jurisdiction over heresy was recognized to be cumulative--that is, it was enjoyed by both tribunals, either of which was entitled to any case in which it had taken prior action. Finally, in 1312, the Council of Vienne, in response to complaints of the cruelty of inquisitors, formulated a settlement under which the combined action of both jurisdictions was required in all commitments to harsh detentive prison, in all sentences to torture and in all final sentences, unless the one called upon to coöperate failed to come within eight days.[13] This, embodied in the acts of the council, technically known as the Clementines, remained the law of the Church. The bishops, however, remained indifferent and rarely took independent action. The inquisitorial districts were large, comprehending a number of dioceses; the episcopal jurisdiction was limited to the subjects of a single diocese. It was impossible for the bishops to assemble at the seat of the tribunal, and when an auto de fe was in preparation they would usually delegate their Ordinaries to represent them or commission an inquisitor to act.

Such was the somewhat cumbrous combination of episcopal and inquisitorial jurisdiction which the founding of the Holy Office brought into Spain. Independent action by bishops still continued occasionally, of which we have seen example (Vol. I, p. 167) and it was recognized, though subordinated to the inquisitorial jurisdiction in a brief of Innocent VIII, September 25, 1487, conferring on Torquemada appellate power in cases before episcopal courts, whether they were acting separately or in conjunction with inquisitors, provided appeal was made before sentence was rendered.[14] The popes of the period, moreover, were careful to maintain the assertion of episcopal participation in inquisitorial proceedings, as is manifested in the superscription of their letters addressed "Ordinariis et Inquisitoribus," or assuming that inquisitors acted under episcopal as well as papal authority.[15] Theoretically, this continued throughout the sixteenth century. The writers of highest authority treat bishops and inquisitors as possessing cumulative jurisdiction, so that both could prosecute, either separately or conjointly and the old canons were still cited threatening with deposition the bishop who was negligent in purifying his diocese of heresy.[16]

CLAIM OF EXCLUSIVE JURISDICTION

Thus there was no legislation depriving the episcopal order of its traditional jurisdiction over heresy, yet the Inquisition claimed, and made good the claim, that its cognizance was exclusive and that the Clementines merely gave to the bishops a consultative privilege in the three sentences specified. No such privative right was conferred in the papal commissions to the inquisitors-general and the only source of such right is to be looked for in Ferdinand's masterful determination that nothing should interfere with the swift operation of his favorite institution, and no claim be admitted to a share in its pecuniary results. It was natural that he should favor the Inquisition, for procedure in the spiritual courts was public and was much less likely to result in conviction than the secrecy of the tribunals, and by 1500 he seems to have established the matter to his satisfaction for, in a letter of August 19th of that year to the Archbishop of Cagliari, he expresses surprise that the prelate, without his licence, or a commission from the inquisitor-general, should have meddled with matters belonging to the Inquisition and have collected certain pecuniary penances, although he had already been forbidden to do so. This prohibition is now emphatically repeated; he is to have nothing to do with the affairs of the Inquisition, except to aid the inquisitor when called upon, and he is at once to hand over his collections to the receiver, Pedro López, who is going to Sardinia.[17] Nothing can be more peremptory in tone than this missive, although the Sardinian tribunal was thoroughly disorganized and was about to be reconstructed by sending a full corps of officials. We may assume from this that if there had been any resistance on the part of the Castilian episcopate it had by this time been overcome.

That this concentration of exclusive jurisdiction in the Inquisition was the work of the royal power and was not universally admitted, even by the middle of the sixteenth century, is manifest from the remark of Bishop Simancas, himself an experienced inquisitor, when he says that it is the duty of bishops to enquire into cases of heresy, but they ought to send the prisoner and the testimony to the inquisitor, for otherwise their inexperience is apt to result in failure, as he had often found; there ought to be a papal decree prescribing this and, in default of it, the king is accustomed to order it of the bishops.[18] Of this we have an example, in 1527, when the vicar-general of the Archbishop of Toledo was required by Inquisitor-general Manrique to surrender a cleric whom he had arrested and was prosecuting.[19]

Simancas still recognizes the duty of the bishop to make preliminary inquiries into heresy, but even this had long before been forbidden, although there was a prolonged struggle before it was surrendered. In 1532 the Ordinary of Huesca issued an Edict of Faith, modelled on that of the Inquisition, calling for denunciation of heretics, for which the empress-regent sharply rebuked him, in a letter of March 23d, calling it an innovation unknown since the Inquisition had been introduced, and threatening him with fitting measures for the repetition of such intrusion on the jurisdiction of the Inquisition.[20] In spite of this, Archbishop Ayala of Valencia, in 1565, and his successor the Blessed Juan de Ribera, in 1576, and another bishop in 1567 repeated the indiscretion for which they were promptly called to account. When, in 1583, the Bishop of Tortosa committed the same offence, the Suprema wrote, January 14, 1584, that the popes had given the Inquisition exclusive jurisdiction over heresy and had prohibited its cognizance by others and that he must not in future intervene in such matters.[21] Undeterred by this, the Council of Tarragona, in 1591, reasserted the ancient episcopal jurisdiction by ordering all bishops to be vigilant in watching their flocks and, if they found any disseminators of heresy, to see to their condign punishment according to the canons.[22] How completely justified was the council in this and how false was the assertion of the Suprema, was manifested in 1595, when the Archbishop of Granada complained to Clement VIII that the inquisitors had forbidden him to issue an edict on the subject of heresy and the pope forthwith wrote to the inquisitor-general that this must not be allowed, for the faculties delegated to inquisitors in no way abridged episcopal jurisdiction.[23]

EXCLUSIVE JURISDICTION ENFORCED

After this, at least, the Suprema could not plead ignorance and yet it persisted in the assertion that it knew to be false. A savage quarrel broke out in Guatimala between the bishop, Juan Ramírez, and the commissioner of the Inquisition, Phelipe Rúiz del Carral, who was also dean of the chapter. Ramírez imprisoned him and undertook to organize a sort of inquisitorial tribunal of his own, whereupon, in 1609, the Suprema presented to Philip III for signature a letter which it describes as drawn in the form customary for cases where bishops interfere in matters concerning the faith. This describes how the pope, in instituting the Inquisition, evoked to himself all cases connected with heresy and committed them to the inquisitor-general and his deputies, inhibiting all judges and Ordinaries from intervening in them, in consequence of which they have ceased to take cognizance of such matters and have referred to the inquisitors whatever came to their knowledge. As the bishop has laid his hand on things beyond his jurisdiction, he is ordered in future not to meddle with anything touching the Inquisition, as otherwise fitting measures will be taken.[24] The only foundation for this mendacious assertion was, as we shall see hereafter, that, in the struggle made by Ferdinand and Charles V to prevent appeals to Rome from the Inquisition, briefs were sometimes obtained from popes evoking to themselves all cases pending in the tribunals and committing them to the inquisitor-general, with inhibition to any one, including cardinals and officials of the curia, to entertain appeals from him. In this there is absolutely nothing that relates to original jurisdiction and nothing to limit the traditional functions of the episcopate, but the Suprema held the records and could assert what it pleased concerning them.

Still the bishops did not wholly abandon their rights and cases continued occasionally to occur, in which of course they were worsted. They were frequent enough to justify, in a Formulary of 1645, the insertion of a formula framed to meet them. It is addressed to the provisor of Badajoz and recites that the fiscal complains of him as having commenced proceedings against a certain party for heretical propositions; as this is a matter pertaining exclusively to the Inquisition, he is commanded to surrender it under the customary penalties of excommunication and fine. The fiscal also demands that the provisor be prosecuted so that in future neither he nor any one else shall dare to usurp the jurisdiction of the Inquisition and the document ends with a statement that the prosecution has been commenced.[25] Such methods were not easily resisted. When, in 1666, the Barcelona tribunal learned that the Bishop of Solsona, on a visitation, had taken considerable testimony against some parties in a matter of faith, it at once claimed the papers, which he promptly surrendered. It had the audacity to propose to prosecute him, but the Suprema wisely ordered it to take no action against him.[26] Yet Benedict XIV repeated the assertion of Clement VIII that the popes, in delegating powers to inquisitors, had never intended to interfere with episcopal jurisdiction or to relieve bishops from responsibility.[27]

Not content with thus depriving the episcopate of its immemorial jurisdiction over heresy, inquisitors sought to obtain cognizance of a class of cases clearly belonging to the spiritual courts, on the ground of inferential heresy--bigamy, disregard of church observances, infractions of discipline and the like. In 1536 the tribunal of Valencia created much excitement by including in its Edict of Faith a number of matters of the kind but, on complaint from the vicar-general, the Suprema ordered the omission of everything not in the old edicts.[28] The attempts continued and, in 1552, a decision was required from the Suprema that eating pork on Saturdays was not a case for the Inquisition,[29] and the Concordia of 1568 contains a clause prohibiting inquisitors from entertaining cases belonging to the Ordinaries.

EPISCOPAL CONCURRENCE

In a carta acordada of November 23, 1612, the Suprema made an attempt to define the boundaries of the rival jurisdictions, in which it allowed to the spiritual courts exclusive jurisdiction only over ecclesiastics in matters touching their duties as pastors, the ministry of the Church, simony and cases relating to Orders, benefices and spiritual affairs, while it admitted cumulative jurisdiction in usury, gambling and incontinence.[30] Restricted as were these admissions, the Suprema itself did not observe them. In 1637, Sebastian de los Rios, cura of Tombrio de Arriba, who met with one or two accidents in handling the sacrament and feared accusation, by his enemies, of irreverence, denounced himself to the provisor of Astorga and was fined in four thousand maravedís. In spite of this he was prosecuted, in 1640, by the tribunal of Valladolid; he vainly pleaded his previous trial; the Suprema assumed its invalidity in ordering his incarceration in the secret prison, where he died.[31] This process of encroachment continued and towards the end, when there was little real heresy to occupy its energies, its records are full of cases which, even under its own definitions, belonged unquestionably to the spiritual courts--inobservance of ecclesiastical precepts of all kinds, irregularities in the celebration of mass, taking communion after eating, eating flesh on fast days, working and inattendance at mass on feast days and other miscellaneous business, wholly foreign to its original functions.[32] It does not argue favorably for the Spanish episcopate that they seem to have welcomed this relief from their duties and strenuously resisted the abolition of the Inquisition in 1813, which restored to them, under limitations, their original functions. After the Restoration, the Archbishop of Seville, in 1818, gathered evidence to show that the cura of San Marcos had not confessed for many years and then, in place of punishing him, handed the papers over to the tribunal. This was probably fortunate for the peccant priest, as the Suprema ordered that nothing should be done except to keep him under surveillance and that the archbishop should be warmly thanked and assured that the necessary steps had been taken.[33]

***

There was one formality preserved which recognized the episcopal jurisdiction over heresy. We have seen that, in the Clementines, the concurrence of both bishop and inquisitor was requisite in ordering severe detentive incarceration, in sentencing to torture and in the final sentence. No allusion was made to this in the bull of Sixtus IV authorizing the appointment of inquisitors for Castile. No allusion, in fact, was necessary, as it had been for nearly two centuries a matter of course in inquisitorial procedure, but the earliest inquisitors took no count of it and Sixtus, in his brief of February 11, 1482, called forth by complaints of their cruelty, insisted on the concurrence of episcopal officials in all judgements.[34] Ferdinand was indisposed to anything that threatened interference with the autonomy of the Inquisition and his experience in Valencia with the representatives of Rodrigo Borgia, the absent archbishop, showed him how this episcopal right could be exercised to obstruct proceedings and compel division of the spoils. He doubtless represented to Sixtus that there were many of Jewish blood among the bishops and their officials, whom it would not be safe to trust, for Sixtus, with Borgia behind him, met such objection with a brief of May 25, 1483, addressed to all the Spanish archbishops. In this he ordered them to warn any of their suffragans of Jewish extraction not to meddle with the business of the Inquisition but to appoint an Old Christian, approved by the archbishop, who should have exclusive powers over all such matters. In case this was not done the archbishop was to make the appointment for each diocese and the appointee was to be wholly independent of the bishop.[35] Then a question arose whether Torquemada's appellate jurisdiction, as inquisitor-general, could override judgements in which bishops participated, but this was settled in Torquemada's favor by a brief of Innocent VIII, September 25, 1487, thus completely subordinating episcopal to inquisitorial jurisdiction.[36]

Ferdinand was not satisfied, but he had to acquiesce and adopt the device of the bishops delegating one of the inquisitors as their representative--an expedient for which precedents can be found in the early Inquisition of Languedoc. That this soon became common is indicated in the Instructions of 1484, which warns the inquisitor holding the commission that he is not to deem himself superior to his colleagues.[37] Another plan was to require the bishops to issue a commission as vicar-general to whomsoever the inquisitors might designate, as Ferdinand ordered the bishops of Aragon to do, in a letter of January 27, 1484. The individual thus selected became an official of the tribunal and was borne on its pay-roll for a salary to be paid out of the confiscations for which he might vote. Of this we have examples in Martin Navarro thus serving at Teruel, in 1486, on a yearly stipend of two thousand sueldos and in Martin Garcia, included as vicar-general at a salary of three thousand sueldos, in the Saragossa pay-roll of the same year.[38]

***

It is possible that the bishops grew restive under this absorption of their powers and that they remonstrated with the Holy See for, in 1494, when Alexander VI issued commissions to the four new inquisitors-general there appeared a new condition requiring them to exercise their functions in conjunction with the Ordinaries of the sees or their vicars or officials, or other persons deputized by the Ordinaries.[39] Ferdinand, however, was not accustomed to brook opposition to his will. The most efficient and economical expedient was the episcopal delegation to an inquisitor and this he enforced by whatever pressure was necessary. Thus when, in 1498, the Bishop of Tarazona demurred to do this, Ferdinand, in a letter of November 21st, brushed aside his reasons and imperatively ordered the delegation to be sent at once. Still the bishop recalcitrated and Ferdinand wrote, January 4, 1499, that he must do so at once; no excuse would be admitted and nothing would change his determined purpose, but it was not until March that he learned the bishop's submission. In this same year, 1499, he broke down, in similar rude fashion, the resistance of two other bishops and when, in 1501, the Archbishop of Tarragona notified the tribunal of Barcelona not to hear, without his participation, certain cases committed to them on appeal, Ferdinand expressed his indignant surprise; the archbishop must remove the obstruction at once and not await a second command.[40]

Ferdinand's resolve was to render episcopal concurrence a mere perfunctory form and, when bishops presumed to act or their vicars-general were distasteful to him, there are various cases which attest his imperious methods of dealing with them. He had some trouble, on this account, with his son, Alfonso Archbishop of Saragossa, who, in 1511, obtained the perpetual administratorship of Valencia and who persisted in retaining as his delegate the vicar-general of Valencia, Micer Soler, against the commands of his father, so that in 1512 and again in 1513, there was delay in the celebration of autos de fe, greatly to Ferdinand's annoyance.[41] These occasional obstructions explain why, as he wrote November 27, 1512, he endeavored to reduce it to a rule that the Ordinary should confer his powers on the inquisitors and should not be allowed to see the cases.[42]

The people did not view the matter in the same light and regarded the participation of the bishop or his representative as some guarantee against the arbitrary proceedings of the inquisitors. Among the complaints of the prisoners of Jaen, in 1506, to Philip and Juana, is one reciting that the inquisitors act independently of the episcopal provisor and communicate nothing to him, so as to be able to work their wicked will without interference.[43] Similarly the Córtes of Monzon, in 1512, included among the abuses requiring redress the royal letters concerning episcopal concurrence, the delegation of powers to inquisitors and other methods by which the participation of the bishops was evaded, and when Leo X, in 1516, confirmed the Concordia, he ordered that the Ordinaries should resume their functions.[44] It was the same in Castile, where, as we have seen (Vol. I, p. 217) one of the petitions of the Córtes of Valladolid, in 1518, was that the episcopal Ordinaries should take part in the judgements.

***

While the petitions of Valladolid for the most part received scant attention, this one at least bore fruit for, with the removal of Ferdinand's pressure, the bishops had an opportunity to reassert themselves. In 1520, a decision of Cardinal Adrian required the presence of both inquisitors and Ordinary at abjurations and confessions under Edicts of Grace and, in 1527, Manrique and the Suprema declared that the Ordinary concurred in the cases required by the law--an ambiguous phrase which seems to have been variously construed.[45] This was not conducive to harmony, the inquisitors grudging any intrusion on their jurisdiction and the Ordinaries insisting on their rights under the Clementines. In 1529, when the Suprema chanced to be at Toledo, the matter was brought before it by Diego Artiz de Angulo, fiscal of the local tribunal, in a memorial arguing that to require the presence of the Ordinary would entail great delay, as he often could not attend when summoned; besides, he was always in contradiction with the tribunal, as was notorious to all connected with the trials, objecting to pecuniary and light penalties and endeavoring to acquire jurisdiction at the expense of the Holy Office. At Angulo's request, the Suprema had a number of witnesses examined, of whom the most important was Martin Ximenes, who had been occupied for forty years in the tribunals of Barcelona, Toledo, and Seville. He testified that the Ordinaries were only called in for the three acts specified in the Clementines, but in explaining details he showed that the inquisitors construed them in a fashion to exclude the Ordinary from much of his functions, for, in place of participating in all sentences, he was allowed to join only in convictions for heresy and bore no part in the lighter cases, the object being to prevent his claiming a share in the pecuniary penalties, although he was summoned to the consulta de fe in which they were voted on. Other witnesses bore the same testimony and it is not difficult to understand why the Ordinaries took little interest in the exercise of the jurisdiction thus arbitrarily limited.[46] It was probably owing to this discussion that the Suprema, January 25, 1530, told the tribunals that differences with the Ordinary must be avoided. In the same year it notified Valencia that all cases sent up to it must have been voted on by him and, in 1532, it sent similar orders to Barcelona, adding that the presence of the Ordinary was requisite at all abjurations.[47] Evidently the tribunals were jealous, the Ordinaries were rebuffed and discouraged, and the coöperation of the two jurisdictions was little more than a formal recognition of a virtually obsolete right.

The routine practice and its working are exemplified in the report of a summons served, August 8, 1534, on Blas Ortiz, then vicar-general of Toledo. It cited him to come and assist in despatching the accumulation of cases since the last auto de fe, held nearly four years before. He was to lay aside all other business and present himself daily at the morning audience to witness the torture in nine specified cases and, at the afternoon audience, to vote on ten of which the trials had been completed. He was notified that, if he did not come, the inquisitors, after the delay specified by law (eight days) would proceed without him. The summons was borne by the fiscal, accompanied by a notary, who made a formal act of the service. When the fiscal stated his errand, Blas Ortiz negligently told him that there was no necessity of reading the paper; he was not well but, if he were able, he would be present at all the cases; if he did not come he committed his powers to the two inquisitors, or to either of them who was willing to accept the commission.[48] Apparently Ortiz did not come, for in several sentences rendered this year at Toledo the inquisitors styled themselves "apostolic inquisitors holding the powers of the Ordinary."[49]

10

From some motive, not clearly apparent, a custom arose to some extent of appointing episcopal Ordinaries or provisors as inquisitors. This was frequent enough to lead the Córtes of Madrid, in 1552, to complain of the combination of the two offices, because when a provisor arrested a layman, which he could not do legally, he claimed that he acted as inquisitor, with the result that many persons were subjected to infamy. They therefore petitioned that no provisor should also be inquisitor, to which the answer was returned that in such cases royal cédulas had been issued and that this would be continued.[50] Discouraging as was this reply, the petition seems to have made an impression for, in 1556, both Charles V and Philip II rebuked Inquisitor-general Valdés, who was also Archbishop of Seville, because his provisor was also inquisitor in that tribunal. His defence was that this had been the case in Seville for half a century, owing to the poverty of the tribunal, which paid only one-third the customary salaries and that he himself defrayed the stipend of the provisor.[51]

***

During the remainder of the century we generally find the participation of the Ordinary carefully recorded, whether it was by a special representative or by delegation to the inquisitors. In 1561, Inquisitor Cervantes takes the Barcelona tribunal to task for not keeping record of this and he orders the fiscal to observe it sedulously for, without the concurrence of the Ordinary, the sentence is invalid.[52] A carta acordada of October 15, 1574, reminds the tribunals that he must sign all sentences of torture and all final sentences on which he has a vote, but there was a rule that he did not sign sentences of acquittal, even though he had voted on them.[53] Yet how purely perfunctory was his participation appears in the case of Fray Hieronimo de la Madre de Dios, at Toledo, in 1618. In the consulta de fe, Melgoso, the provisor, agreed with one of the inquisitors and a consultor on a certain punishment; another inquisitor voted for a heavier penalty and, when the matter was submitted to the Suprema, it adopted the latter, but Melgoso obediently signed the sentence.[54] The inquisitorial jurisdiction, for all practical purposes, had absorbed the episcopal.

As the inquisitorial districts usually embraced several dioceses and it was impossible for the bishop or provisor of those at a distance from a tribunal to be personally present when their subjects were tortured or sentenced, it became customary for them to delegate their powers to some resident of the city which was the seat of the tribunal. That they were not always careful in their selection would appear when the tribunal of Sicily was obliged, in 1574, to notify an archbishop that he must appoint ecclesiastics and not laymen to sit in judgement on matters of faith.[55] Taking advantage of this carelessness the Inquisition undertook to control the character of appointees and it issued, August 17, 1637, instructions to bishops that their provisors must be graduates in canon law but, as canonists proved to be scarce, it was obliged, October 12, to modify this and permit the appointment of theologians. In accordance with this there is an entry by the tribunal of Valencia, that it will recognize Don Luis Crispi as Ordinary of Tortosa, although he is a theologian.[56]

Thus a further encroachment was made on episcopal jurisdiction by the Inquisition in claiming and exercising the right to determine whom it would recognize as a fit representative of the bishop. How offensively this was sometimes used was manifested in 1752, in Lima, when the inquisitors Amusquibar and Rodríguez were involved in a prolonged quarrel with the secular and ecclesiastical organizations. To annoy the inquisitors, Archbishop Barroeta notified them that in view of their bitter competencia with the viceroy, he withdrew the faculty of Don Fernando de la Sota as his representative and appointed Padre Francisco Larreta, S. J. To this they replied that they recognized his right to withdraw the faculty, but as for Larreta he was incapacitated by his profession from exercising the functions; if the archbishop would appoint some one in accordance with the statutes of the Holy Office and possessing the necessary qualifications, he would be received. The assumption that they would recognize only whom they pleased staggered the archbishop and he asked them to explain the disqualification of Larreta, to which they insolently replied that they had already stated what was sufficient for his guidance. He submitted and appointed the Franciscan Thomas de la Concha, who was accepted, but when the archbishop transmitted the correspondence to Inquisitor-general Prado y Cuesta and asked for reparation he obtained none.[57]

Episcopal concurrence had never been more than a bare formality in recognition of the immemorial jurisdiction of bishops over heresy and, as time wore on, the Inquisition became careless even of this. In a number of trials by the tribunal of Madrid, between 1703 and 1710, the inquisitors are recorded as acting sometimes with and sometimes without the episcopal representatives and, in the latter half of the century, a writer informs us that the concurrence of the Ordinary is unusual; it depends on the will of the inquisitors, who sometimes summon him and sometimes do not.[58] Still there were some bishops, zealous for the claims of their order, who persisted in asserting this remnant of jurisdiction. Antonio Tavira, Bishop of Canaries, and subsequently of Salamanca, expressed their feelings when, in 1792, he complained to Carlos IV of the treatment of the episcopal order by the Inquisition, saying that they had ceased to vote in cases of faith in order to escape the humiliation and degradation to which they were exposed; they sent their vicars, although this was indecorous and wholly useless, but they felt that they must preserve this little shadow of a jurisdiction which was rightly theirs.[59]

THE FORUM OF CONSCIENCE

Under the Restoration greater attention seems to have been paid to episcopal concurrence and the adherence to strict formalities is shown in a duplicate trial of Juan Antonio Manzano, a physician of Lumbrales in the diocese of Ciudad-Rodrigo and inquisitorial district of Llerena. In 1817 he was tried for heretical propositions by the tribunal of Logroño, which inquired of the Suprema whether the Ordinary of its own diocese could act and was told that the authority of the culprit's own bishop was imperative and that the Bishop of Ciudad-Rodrigo must appoint a representative. The next year Manzano was again arrested, for the same offence, by the tribunal of Llerena and was transferred to Seville because Llerena had no prison. April 17, 1819, the Seville tribunal asked whether its own Ordinary could join in the sentence and received the same answer--that it must apply to the Bishop of Ciudad-Rodrigo to make an appointment.[60] It was all the merest technicality, for by this time the Suprema decided all cases, irrespective of how the consulta de fe might vote and thus the incontestable episcopal jurisdiction over heresy was practically abolished.

***

As regards the internal forum, or forum of conscience, the Inquisition claimed and enjoyed a still more absolute jurisdiction than in the external forum for which it had been primarily instituted. While in a formal and perfunctory manner it recognized the episcopal claims in the judicial forum, it so employed its delegated papal authority as to vindicate with the utmost jealousy exclusive control over the forum of conscience in matters of heresy. Bishops, in fact, had long before been ousted from this by the invention of papal reserved cases--cases in which sacramental absolution could only be had from the Holy See, thus creating a profitable market for its indulgences, confessional letters and the absolutions of its Penitentiary. Heresy was the chief sin anathematized in the early form of the bull, subsequently known as in Coena Domini, from its annual publication on Holy Thursday and, in 1364, Urban V placed all the offences enumerated in it under the jurisdiction of the papal chamberlain.[61] The papacy thus assumed exclusive control over the sin of heresy, for which no absolution could be granted save by papal delegation, and Paul II, in 1469, and Sixtus IV, in 1478, issued further decrees to the effect that special licence was necessary for this, as no general commissions were held to cover it.[62] The Council of Trent, in 1563, timidly endeavored to revendicate a fraction of episcopal rights by asserting that bishops, in the forum of conscience only, could personally absolve for secret or occult heresy, but the Roman Inquisition, by repeated decisions based on the utterances of St. Pius V and Gregory XIII, overrode the conciliar decree and deprived them of that slender remnant of their functions.[63]

This strict reservation of the sin of heresy was imperfectly understood in Spain and so little was known of the laws of persecution that at first the New Christians, who apprehended arrest, endeavored to escape by sacramental confession and absolution, ignorant that already in the thirteenth century it had been decided that the pardon of the sin, in the forum of conscience, did not cover the crime in the judicial forum. This method of evasion could not be allowed and yet the Inquisition was uncertain how to act. A brief was therefore procured, November 10, 1487, from Innocent VIII, addressed to all the inquisitors and Ordinaries in Spain, reciting their doubts about proceeding against those who assert that they have secretly confessed and abjured to their confessors. To overcome this it was asserted that the decrees of the fathers required such abjurations to be accompanied by an oath, taken before an Ordinary, in presence of a notary and witnesses, never to return to the abjured heresy, wherefore the inquisitors were empowered to proceed against all who had not observed this rule.[64] If such a rule had ever existed, which is doubtful, it had long been forgotten and was wholly unknown in Spain, so that all who had had recourse to this device were brought under the jurisdiction of the Inquisition.

OCCULT HERESY

The New Christians were not long in realizing the futility of such attempts and we hear little of them in the later periods. Yet there were cases of occult heresy concerning which the functions of the Inquisition seem to have varied. In the earlier times the Edicts of Grace brought these to the tribunals and the Instructions of 1484 permit the inquisitor to admit them to secret reconciliation and abjuration and do not contemplate his delegating his power to another.[65] There must have been doubts as to his faculties for this, since, in 1530, Clement VII delegated powers to inquisitors to absolve and reconcile for occult heresy, with the imposition of appropriate penance.[66] This evidently contemplates his administering sacramental absolution and yet not long afterwards he was told that he was judge in the external and not in the internal forum and that it was not his business to hear sacramental confessions.[67] In fact, the inquisitor was by no means necessarily in priests' orders and, when acting in his judicial capacity, sentencing a culprit and hearing his abjuration, he simply granted licence to any approved confessor to absolve him from excommunication and to impose salutary penance.[68]

There was, however, a class of cases, by no means infrequent, demanding sacramental rather than judicial ministration, which gave rise to some debate before their treatment was settled. These consisted of good Christians, who were assailed by secret doubts or indulged in erroneous speculations and who brought their spiritual troubles to the confessional. Over these, priest and bishop had been deprived of jurisdiction, and to make sure of this there was a clause in the annual Edict of Faith prohibiting confessors from granting absolution in any case touching the Inquisition and ordering the penitent to be sent to the tribunal.[69] If he refused to go, the only alternative was for the confessor to obtain from the inquisitor a licence to absolve him, for the confession was covered by the seal and prosecution was out of the question, but as to this, even in the middle of the sixteenth century, there were doubts. Bishop Simancas says that the power of the inquisitor to grant licences is doubtful and he can only suggest reference of each case to the Suprema.[70] A body of practice, of uncertain date, asserts that when a confessor reports that a penitent has confessed heresies and asks for a licence to absolve him, it cannot be given. He must be ordered to induce the penitent to come to the tribunal; in case of necessity, or of persons in high station, the inquisitor may go with a notary to receive the confession, which is examined in the tribunal and the consequent absolution or abjuration is performed in secret. In the case of nuns, who could not be induced to discharge their consciences before a commissioner and a notary, there was a concession that the confessor might reduce the confession to writing and send it to the tribunal which would consult the Suprema, and frailes were to be compelled to seek the tribunal, where they were treated as espontaneados, or spontaneous self-denouncers and were absolved or reconciled secretly with spiritual penances.[71]

The indisposition to license confessors to absolve for heresy in the forum of conscience is easily explicable. By compelling the penitent to come to the tribunal, a record was made for use in case of relapse; if he had accomplices he could be forced to reveal them and their prosecution followed, and there was an opportunity of inflicting pecuniary penances, although confiscation was waived in such cases.[72] These same reasons operated in a contrary sense with the penitent, besides the horror which all men felt as to falling into the hands of the Inquisition. When he was obstinate, the tribunal was powerless, for the seal of confession shielded his identity; it finally yielded the point and no longer pretended that licenses could not be given to confessors. In 1562 a case was referred to the Suprema of a person who had confessed sacramentally to certain heresies, without having been taught them by any one, when the inquisitor-general empowered the inquisitors to absolve him in such way as they thought best and they empowered the confessor.[73] Finally it became the rule that the confessor sought to induce the penitent to apply to the Inquisition; if he resolutely refused the confessor applied for a faculty, which was granted or not, according to the temper of the tribunal.[74]

***

A case in 1754 shows the Inquisition in a favorable light and has interest also as illustrating the tortures of a soul which rejects belief and yet holds belief to be essential to salvation. Fray Thomas de Sos reported to the Toledo tribunal that, while on a mission at Ajofrin, a penitent had asked him to obtain a commission to absolve her for heresies internal and external, which yet were occult, as she had never expressed them except to her aunt. She said that, on a previous occasion, a confessor had done this for her and she wished to avoid the disgrace of personal appearance before the Inquisition. He was ordered to ascertain all details and reported that the penitent was a poor woman named María Lara, living with an aunt aged eighty. Her heresies were only of a few months' standing, occasioned by intense grief at the ingratitude of one whom she had benefited; she disbelieved in the Trinity, the Incarnation, the Law of God, the Virgin, hell and the devil and at the same time felt herself lost beyond the hope of salvation. She could not say how much of this she had uttered to herself or before her aunt and the importance attached to this point indicates the weight attributed to the distinction between internal and external heresy. The aunt was examined, the cura of Ajofrin was called in, the registers were searched and finally, after six weeks had been consumed, a commission was issued which the good fraile, eager to heal a despairing soul, at an hour's notice bore to Ajofrin and absolved her.[75]

These cases gave the Inquisition considerable concern and, in 1772, the Suprema called upon all the tribunals to report what was their practice. After carefully weighing their answers, it issued, November 9, 1772, instructions that, when a confessor reported such a case, he was to be ordered to use every effort to induce the penitent to denounce himself, assuring him of merciful treatment and showing him that he would thus be saved in case of denunciation by others. He could make this denunciation to the tribunal or to a commissioner, or could even authorize the confessor to denounce him, giving all details under oath. If, however, the penitent obstinately refused, then the confessor could absolve him, explaining that it was only in the forum of conscience.[76] If we may believe Lorenzo Villanueva, however, this liberal concession was by no means put in practice, at least by all tribunals.[77]

Confession of formal heresy was not so leniently treated and, as it inferred accomplices, every effort was made to secure their denunciation. The confessor was ordered to persuade, if possible, the penitent to come to the Inquisition and confess as to himself and others, promising secret absolution without confiscation. This was virtually the offer made to those who came forward under an Edict of Grace and did not exclude arbitrary pecuniary penance; it was not likely to attract self-denunciation, especially as it included betraying kindred and friends, although power to absolve was not granted in case of refusal. This led to a dead-lock and possibly in such cases the confessor was expected to violate the seal of confession under the old rule that it did not cover heresy. At least this may be inferred from a case occurring in Lima about 1580, when Padre Luis López, S. J. reported that a penitent in confession had admitted to have Judaized and on being told to go to the Inquisition had refused. The matter was regarded as so grave that it was referred to the Suprema which sent orders to deliver López to the viceroy for shipment to Spain--apparently one who would not violate the seal was too dangerous to be left in Peru.[78] Simancas, however, characterized this as a most pernicious doctrine and argues that infraction of the seal is much worse than allowing a heretic to escape punishment.[79]

When the Inquisition was re-established in 1814, under the Restoration, it recognized the impossibility of investigating and punishing the innumerable heresies disseminated in the licence of years of warfare and exposure to foreign armies. In its zeal for the salvation of souls it therefore, by edict of January 2, 1815, granted for a year, to all confessors, faculties to absolve for heresy external or mixed. The confessor, in fact, was made a quasi-inquisitor and the procedure formidably resembled that of the tribunals. The penitent had a pledge of secrecy, but his confession had to be minute and comprehensive; it was reduced to writing, signed and sworn to, and was then forwarded to the tribunal to be filed among its records. This relieved him from prosecution in case of denunciation by others, while, if he refused to do this, he was to be absolved, but only in the forum of conscience; he was to be reported to the tribunal and remained liable to the external forum.[80]

***

CRUZADA AND JUBILEE INDULGENCES

In view of the recognized principle that sacramental absolution does not affect the external forum, it shows the watchful jealousy with which the Inquisition guarded its jurisdiction that it remonstrated against the papal indulgences of the Santa Cruzada and the jubilee. The former granted an indulgentia plenissima; it was a state affair, managed by the Government and bringing in a large revenue of which a portion accrued to the Holy See; its sale was pushed in every quarter with the utmost vigor and the Inquisition punished severely any utterances calculated to diminish the demand. Only extreme sensitiveness as to its jurisdiction could have led the Inquisition to cast any doubt as to the unlimited efficacy of the indulgence but, when St. Pius V, in 1571, after an interval of five years, renewed the concession of the Cruzada, it took the alarm. In cartas acordadas of May 30 and June 13, 1572, the Suprema informs the tribunals that in some places it is asserted that the Cruzada bulls grant faculties for the absolution of heresy; this is not the case and, if it were, the pope would be asked to withdraw them; the assertion must be contradicted everywhere and the prelates are to be asked to give corresponding instructions to confessors.[81] A more effective step was taken, in 1576, by procuring from Gregory XIII a brief declaring that it never was the papal intention that the indulgence should include heresy and to make this known he authorized the Commissioner of the Cruzada to translate the brief into the vernacular and publish it wherever the Cruzada was preached. The Suprema did not trust the Commissioner, but sent copies of the brief to all the tribunals, with instructions to notify the Ordinaries and the prelates of the Orders, so that confessors might be duly informed. A month later, in January, 1577, it ordered the brief to be published in all the churches.[82] Eventually, however, its anxieties were removed by a clause in the bulas of the Cruzada specifically excepting heresy from the faculties granted to confessors, a form which they have retained to the present day, long after the extinction of the Holy Office.[83]

The Cruzada indulgence was a special financial favor to the Spanish monarchy which it could virtually control, but it was otherwise with the jubilee indulgences which, about this period, the popes began to publish--plenary remissions of sins such as were obtainable by pilgrimage to Rome at the jubilees celebrated every twenty-five years. St. Pius V set the example of this, on his accession in 1566, which has since been followed by his successors, together with special jubilees decreed at decreasing intervals. The jubilee published in 1572, on the accession of Gregory XIII, excepted heretics and readers of prohibited books and added a positive declaration that in it and all that might be subsequently issued the absolution was only in the forum of conscience and did not affect the judicial forum.[84] Taking advantage of this, when another jubilee indulgence appeared, in 1578, the Suprema ordered it to be published with the omission of all that concerned the Inquisition, in accordance with the declarations of Gregory.[85] Subsequent jubilees, however, of 1589, 1592 and 1595 included heresy and called forth unavailing protests from Spain until finally, in the latter year, preachers were ordered to declare, as of their own motion, that, under the general clause of the jubilee, absolution could not be had for heresy.[86] While the Roman Inquisition made no protest against these indulgences, the Spanish persistently objected to them and it seemed impossible to harmonize the conflict. When Alexander VII, on his accession, in 1655, published a jubilee, it contained the obnoxious clause; Cabrera, the agent of the Suprema in Rome, warmly remonstrated with him and he promised in future to except heresy; this did not satisfy Cabrera who asked for a constitution excepting heresy from all jubilees. Alexander promised to investigate the matter, but apparently his investigations were resultless for the subject continued till the end of the century to furnish occasion for repeated discussion.[87]

***

SECRECY AND EXCLUSIVENESS

Heresy was an elastic term and the Inquisition stretched it to extend its exclusive jurisdiction in all directions. It did the same to shield itself from investigation and restraint. We are told that, in the numerous cases of appeal to the throne for injustice suffered at its hands, if the king ordered the inquisitor-general to report on the subject so that it might be submitted to a junta composed of members of the Suprema and Royal Council, the first business of the Suprema was to examine whether the question arose from a matter of faith, or was in any way dependent upon faith, or concerned the free exercise of the duties of the Holy Office. There were not many things that could not be brought within this charmed circle and then a consulta was addressed to the monarch protesting that he could not refer it to a junta, because its nature precluded its consideration by laymen and it would be a violation of the secrecy of the Inquisition, so that it had to be submitted to the Suprema alone, which would make a verbal report to him. It was on record that, in a case of this kind, Philip II pledged his royal word that he and Don Cristóval de Mocera alone should be admitted to the confidence and, in 1645, Philip IV could only obtain from Arce y Reynoso a verbal explanation.[88] Thus between exclusive cognizance and inviolable secrecy the Inquisition realized the ideal of spiritual jurisdiction--it judged all and was judged by none.

CHAPTER II - THE REGULAR ORDERS

Over the laity the jurisdiction of the Inquisition was complete. No one was so high-placed as to be exempt, for heresy was a universal leveller. Theoretically the king himself was subject to it, for it was based on the principle of the supremacy of the spiritual over the temporal power. The piety of the Spanish monarchs prevented occasion for putting this to the test, for we may safely reject as fables the stories concerning Juana la loca and Don Carlos, but no station exempted him who was suspect in the faith from prosecution and from punishment if he was found guilty. In Valencia, nobles who sought to protect their Morisco vassals from the raids of the Inquisition were tried as fautors of heresy, the most conspicuous of these being Don Sancho de Córdova, Admiral of Aragon and allied to the noblest blood of Spain. At the age of 73 he was compelled to abjure for light suspicion of heresy, he was fined and confined in a convent, where he died.[89] We shall have occasion to consider in detail the still more remarkable case of Don Gerónimo de Villanueva, Prothonotary of Aragon and favorite of both Olivares and of Philip IV and, even when the Inquisition was far gone in its decline, we shall see how it took steps to assail Don Manuel de Godoy, Prince of the Peace and all powerful favorite of Carlos IV.

With the exception of bishops, of whom more hereafter, the secular clergy were equally at the mercy of the Holy Office. Even when, as we have seen, in the bitter quarrels between the tribunal of Majorca and the clergy of the islands, the latter obtained the protection of special papal briefs, these exempted them only from the royal jurisdiction of the Inquisition and did not affect their liability in matters of faith, against which they raised no protest. The regular clergy, however--the members of the religious Orders--made long and persistent struggles to escape subjection, preferring the milder discipline of their own prelates. In the twelfth and thirteenth centuries, the monastic establishments had, for the most part, obtained exemption from episcopal jurisdiction and were amenable only to the Holy See. When the Mendicant Orders were organized, in the thirteenth century, they were likewise subject immediately to the pope. It is true that, in 1184, Lucius III, in his Verona decree, had abolished this immunity in matters of faith and had remanded, in so far, the regulars back to episcopal jurisdiction, for as yet the Inquisition had not been thought of,[90] but, when the Mendicants claimed that this did not apply to their subsequently founded Orders, Innocent IV, in 1254, subjected them to the Inquisition, which by that time was in full operation. Boniface VIII emphatically confirmed this, even declaring that for heresy they were to be punished more severely than laymen, as the Spiritual Franciscans found to their cost under John XXII.[91] As inquisitors acted under delegation from the pope, there would be no question as to their jurisdiction over the regulars, but, in the case of the Dominican Master Eckart, tried, in 1327, by the Archbishop of Cologne, it was settled that the episcopal Inquisition also had cognizance.[92] Yet, about 1460, Pius II granted to the Franciscans the privilege of being tried only by the vicar-general of their Order and, in 1479, Sixtus IV, in view of the inveterate hostility between Franciscans and Dominicans, from which Orders nearly all inquisitors were drawn, prohibited those of one Order from prosecuting members of the other.[93]

FLUCTUATING POLICY

Such was the situation when the Spanish Inquisition was founded. Conversos were numerous in the Orders and many were prosecuted. Under Torquemada, himself a Dominican, the inquisitors were largely Dominicans and the Franciscans naturally claimed the privileges of the papal decrees of 1460 and 1479; when, in 1487, some Observantine Franciscans were prosecuted, Innocent VIII ordered their release and repeated the provisions of 1479.[94] In the following year, however, by a motu proprio of May 17, 1488, he declared that none of the Orders were exempt and specially mentioned the Cistercians, Dominicans and Franciscans.[95] Even before this, Torquemada had treated the regulars as under his jurisdiction for, though he had granted to the Geronimite prelates power to try some of their frailes he revoked this, May 3, 1488, and commissioned the inquisitors of Toledo to prosecute them.[96] In Rome the influence of the regular Orders was great; that of the growing Spanish power was steadily increasing, and the contest between these opposing forces is seen in the fluctuating policy of the Holy See. The motu proprio of 1488 remained in force for a considerable time, but, after the death of Ferdinand, the Franciscans in 1517 obtained from Leo X the renewal of their old privileges, which probably also included the Dominicans.[97] The Augustinians soon followed, for a letter of the Suprema, May 7, 1521, directs the tribunals, in view of their privileges to be tried by their prelates, to obtain from the superiors delegated power to act in their cases, or to get a fraile assigned to sit as assessor, or to remit the cases to the Suprema as they may deem best.[98] Apparently these exemptions were not always respected, for Clement VII, by a brief of January 18, 1524, emphatically confirmed the Franciscan privileges and ordered all their cases pending in the tribunals to be transferred within six days to the prelates of the accused.[99] So when, in a brief of March 19, 1525, he prohibited descendants of Jews and heretics from acquiring dignities in the Observantine branch of the Order, he gave as a reason that the provincials are judges of their subjects.[100]

It required but a few months to change all this. The Inquisition was restive under this restriction on its jurisdiction. Inquisitor-general Manrique, in a letter of June 30, 1524, asserted that a revocation of the Augustinian privileges would be procured and he proved a true prophet.[101] The services of Charles V in stemming the tide of the Lutheran revolt were indispensable and his demands could not be refused. A brief of April 13, 1525, subjected the frailes again to the Inquisition, but softened the blow by providing that the provincials should appoint assessors to sit with the tribunals in their cases. This did not satisfy Spain and, two months later, a brief of June 16th subjected them absolutely to the inquisitor-general.[102] That the Inquisition thus obtained and exercised jurisdiction over the regulars is seen in an order by the Suprema, July 18, 1534, requiring that it should be consulted and the testimony be submitted to it, before proceedings were instituted against a fraile--an order repeated, June 10, 1555, and subsequently extended to all ecclesiastics.[103]

JURISDICTION OBTAINED

In issuing this the Suprema evidently was unaware that some three weeks earlier there had occurred another shifting of the scales. The frailes had not been idle; the Franciscans, and presumably the other Orders, had won a victory. A brief of Clement VII, June 23, 1534, recites the various exemptions granted by preceding popes to the Franciscans, while numerous complaints showed that some inquisitors continued to prosecute them, to their great perturbation and scandal, wherefore it was ordered that whenever any of the frailes were suspected of heresy they must be remitted to their superiors for punishment, notwithstanding all privileges granted to the Holy Office. Confirmation of this was procured from Paul III, November 8th of the same year, but apparently these commands received slender attention, for another confirmation was obtained, December 15, 1537, with the addition that all cases pending in the Inquisition must be surrendered to the superiors of the Order within six days and all sentences in derogation of this were declared invalid.[104] Even this did not keep the Inquisition in check and Paul issued, March 6, 1542, another decree reciting cases in contempt of his orders, wherefore all inquisitors, in every part of the world, were commanded, under penalty of excommunication, deprivation of benefice and disability for preferment, not to proceed against the frailes and to deliver up any who might be imprisoned. All bishops and prelates were made executors of the brief, with power to invoke the aid of the secular arm.[105]

The rigor of these provisions is the measure of the resistance encountered and, in singular contrast to them is the fact that, but a fortnight later, Paul, by a brief of March 21st, annulled all the exemptions of the Mendicant Orders in Upper Italy and the Island of Chios, and subjected their members, with the exception of bishops, to the Inquisition, in matters of faith.[106] This put the Spanish Inquisition at a disadvantage in comparison with the newly organized Roman Congregation, although its order of June 10, 1555, above referred to, would indicate that it paid but little attention to the papal utterances. It fully recovered its lost ground, however, when the Holy See recognized that it was the only tribunal that could be relied upon to check the prevalent vice of "solicitation" or seduction in the confessional--the principal offenders being frailes. When, as an experiment, Paul IV, in 1559, empowered the tribunal of Granada to prosecute these cases, he withdrew all privileges and exemptions, not only in this offence but in all heretical crimes; he authorized the inquisitors to degrade the culprits and to deliver them to the secular arm for execution and the provisions of this brief were extended by Pius IV, in 1561, to all the tribunals in the Spanish dominions.[107] This rendered the Inquisition master of the situation, while, at the same time, the inclusion of solicitation among heretical crimes made the regular Orders still more solicitous to escape from its jurisdiction.

The development of the Society of Jesus and the unbounded favor which it enjoyed with the Holy See introduced a new factor in the struggle. In 1587 the Inquisition discovered that the Jesuits claimed exemption. The Compendium of their privileges stated that Gregory XIII, vivæ vocis oraculo, on March 18, 1584, had conferred on their General, with power of subdelegation, faculty for absolving his subjects from heresy, even in cases of relapse; any one knowing the heresy of another was therefore to denounce him to his superior and not to the Inquisition and it was broadly asserted that the members were subject to no judge, episcopal or inquisitorial.[108] It was impossible for the Inquisition to overlook such denial of its authority and it promptly ordered the suppression of the Compendium and of all regulations incompatible with its jurisdiction, giving rise to considerable correspondence with Rome.[109]

The case which led to this proceeding is too suggestive not to deserve relation in some detail.

Solicitation being subjected to the exclusive jurisdiction of the Inquisition it became, under the Edict of Faith, the duty of every one, under heavy penalties, to denounce to the nearest tribunal any case coming to his knowledge. In 1583, the Jesuits of the college of Monterey, in Galicia, learned that one of their number, the Padre Sebastian de Briviesca, had been guilty of it with certain beatas and also of some Illuminist practices. Padre Diego Hernández was sent to Segovia to report the matter to Antonio Marcen, the Provincial of Castile. To avert from the Society the disgrace of the prosecution of a member, Hernández was ordered to return and get the evidence in legal shape, so that Briviesca could be secretly tried and punished, but Marcen warned him that all consultation and action must be under pretext of confession, so as to be covered by the seal. Hernández went back to Monterey and consulted with Padres Francisco Larata and Juan López, who said it was a dangerous business; the case belonged to the Inquisition and but for the seal of confession, they would be bound to denounce Briviesca, however damaging it might be to the Society. Profound secrecy was enjoined on the beatas; Hernández took the evidence to Marcen, gave it to him under the seal and was sent with it to Salamanca, where it was submitted, without names, to the theologians of the Jesuit college. They reported that the culprit must be denounced to the Inquisition and that the beatas could not be absolved unless they denounced him but, on being told that the Society was involved, they reversed their opinions. Hernández was sent to Monterey, where he absolved the beatas, while Marcen imprisoned Briviesca, obtained a partial confession, gave him dismissory letters and the habit of a secular priest, and sent him with a companion to Barcelona, where he was shipped to Italy. He had previously been guilty at Avila of the same practices.

EFFORTS TO EVADE IT

Hernández had dutifully obeyed orders, but he was becoming thoroughly frightened. He begged Marcen to allow him to denounce the matter to the Inquisition and was told that if through him harm came to the Society he would be imprisoned for life in chains. He persisted and then reports were spread that he was insane and possessed by the devil; he was sent to the college at Oviedo, where there was no Inquisition and no means of communicating by post, and for a year he was unable to discharge his conscience, for the confessors were forbidden to absolve him unless he pledged submission to his superiors. Then promises were tried and he was told that whatever he asked for would be obtained for him from the General, and he was further informed that the beatas had retracted their testimony.

How the Inquisition obtained knowledge of the affair is not stated, but it was probably through the garrulousness of the beatas who could not be kept from talking. As soon as it obtained sufficient evidence it acted vigorously. Marcen, Larata and López were imprisoned and put on trial, in 1585; in the progress of the case it was found that this was by no means the first time that Marcen had defrauded the Inquisition of its culprits. Padre Cristóbal de Trugillo had been guilty of the same offence and Marcen had simply dismissed him from the Society. Also Padre Francisco de Ribera had repeatedly uttered heretical propositions for which some of the brethren demanded that he should be denounced to the Inquisition, but Marcen dismissed him from the Society and gave him money to betake himself to Italy, for all of which his defence was that he only obeyed the orders of the General.[110]

The case was a clear one; Marcen and his colleagues were convicted, but the Inquisition had not the satisfaction of punishing them. The Society did not venture to question the jurisdiction of the Inquisition, but its influence at Rome was great and it probably had little difficulty in convincing Sixtus V that the interests of religion required the suppression of the scandal, for which he had only to exercise his right of evoking the case to himself. He did so, in 1587, and when the Suprema tried its usual dilatory tactics, the impetuous pontiff notified Cardinal Quiroga that, if the prisoners and the papers were not surrendered forthwith, he would be deprived of both the cardinalate and the inquisitor-generalship. Sixtus was not a man to be trifled with and the surrender was made.[111] The treatment of Briviesca, Trugillo and Ribera serve to explain why the frailes were so anxious to avoid the inquisitorial jurisdiction of which the familiars were so eager to avail themselves.

The ascription to the Inquisition of the crime of solicitation naturally stimulated the desire of the frailes to recover their exemption and Marcen's case rendered the Jesuits especially active. A prolonged agitation in Rome was the result, which finally took the shape of submitting to the Congregation of the Inquisition the question whether, in this crime, the jurisdiction of the Holy Office was exclusive or whether it was cumulative with that of the prelate, depending on the first possession of a case. The decision was made, December 3, 1592, in the presence of Clement VIII, declaring that the jurisdiction of the Inquisition was exclusive, that the prelates could not exercise it and that all members of the Orders were bound to denounce offenders to the tribunals. The victory of the Inquisition was complete, but the pope expressed to the Suprema, through a cardinal, his desire that the inquisitors would exercise their functions with the prudence, circumspection and moderation that would preserve the cult due to the sacrament of penitence and, at the same time, the good repute of the frailes.[112]

Still the regulars could not be brought to submit to the jurisdiction of the Inquisition and Paul V, by a brief of September 1, 1606, evoked to himself all pending cases and committed them to it, at the same time decreeing that it should have exclusive jurisdiction in all cases of suspected heresy; whenever, during a visitation, any member of an Order was found to be suspected he was at once to be denounced and any superior refusing obedience was threatened with deprivation and perpetual disability. Moreover this decree was to be read in all chapters of the Orders. Even this was deemed insufficient and was supplemented, November 7th, with another prohibiting superiors, under any pretext or custom, from receiving denunciations or taking cognizance in any way of cases pertaining to the Inquisition. Every member, whether superior or subject, was required, without consulting any one, to denounce to the Inquisition or to the Ordinary all who were suspected, however lightly, of heresy.[113]

JURISDICTION CONFIRMED

Some details in this would seem to point to the Society of Jesus as the chief recalcitrant and this is confirmed by a brief of Alexander VII, July 8, 1660, which condemns, as pernicious and rash, opinions calling in doubt the obligation to denounce and the pretexts employed of fraternal correction to prevent denunciation. Even the Company of Jesus is ordered to obey the constitution of Paul V; no superiors are to molest or oppress their subjects for performing this duty but must exhort them to it. Disobedience is threatened not only with the penalties provided by Paul V but with deprivation of office, the right of voting and being voted for, perpetual disability and other punishments at the discretion of the pope and removable only by him. The decree is to be read annually on March 1st at the public table and notarial attestation of the fact is to be sent to the nearest tribunal or to Rome and a copy is to be posted where all can read it. The Inquisition lost no time in publishing this and the decree of November 7, 1606, in an edict commanding their observance and pointing out that the alternative of denunciation to the Ordinary was invalid in Spain, where the Inquisition had exclusive jurisdiction. It further ordered that in all books where contrary opinions were taught there should be noted in the margin "This opinion is condemned as pernicious and rash by our Holy Father, Alexander VII."[114]

No further papal utterances seem to have been asked for; indeed there was nothing that the Holy See could add to these comprehensive decrees. In time, however, they seem to have been conveniently forgotten for, in 1732, Inquisitor-general Juan de Camargo reissued them in an edict saying that some persons were ignorant, or affected ignorance, of the doctrines expressed in them, wherefore he ordered them to be posted in the sacristies of all churches, with the announcement that all contraventions would be punished with the utmost rigor.[115] Of course it is impossible to say how many frailes may have escaped prosecution through the indisposition of the Orders to recognize the jurisdiction of the Inquisition, but, from the numbers who appear in the registers of the tribunals, it is charitable to assume that evasion in this way was exceptional.

***

The completeness of the domination assumed by the Inquisition over the religious Orders is illustrated by its intervention in a matter which would appear wholly beyond any possible definition of its jurisdiction. The internecine strife between the different bodies had long been an inextinguishable scandal. The old hatred between Franciscans and Dominicans was inflamed to white heat by the quarrel over the Immaculate Conception. The immense success of the Jesuits brought upon them the virulent enmity of the older communities, which regarded them as upstarts and were repaid with interest. The new Moral Philosophy of the Probabilists was a fresh source of active discord. These mutual antagonisms found free expression in the press, the pulpit and the professorial chair, where the rivals derided and insulted each other, to the grief of the faithful and the amusement of the godless. The Inquisition appeared to be the only authority that could restrain the expression of the mutual wrath of the good fathers, though it might not be easy to define on what grounds it could claim authority on such a matter. Scruples as to this, however, rarely gave it concern and it undertook to effect what popes had repeatedly failed to accomplish.

March 9, 1634, the Suprema issued a decree which it printed and sent to all superiors with instructions to publish and make it known. This recited the evils arising from the discord and rivalry between the Orders, scandalous to the Christian people and dangerous as arising from the difference in the manners and customs of the various organizations. To bring about peace and concord the inquisitor-general proposed to assemble a council of the superiors of all the Orders and meanwhile rigorous proceedings were threatened against all who should provoke or foment these discords. Any religious who, by writing or words or in sermons or lectures, should insult another Order, or any of its members, would incur major excommunication and be recluded in a convent in another district, for a time proportioned to the gravity of the offence and moreover be incapable of holding any position in the Holy Office. Superiors were charged to expurgate all offensive expressions in books written by their subjects, before according the necessary licence to print or, if they had not authority to do this, they must refer the objectionable matter to the Suprema, and this was binding on those deputed to examine the MSS. The decree closed with a threat of rigorous punishment for all contravention of its provisions.[116]

QUARRELS BETWEEN THE ORDERS

Whether the council indicated was ever assembled or whether any offender was ever punished under this decree does not appear, but any effect which it may have produced was transient. The old passions and hatreds remained as vehement as ever and the controversy over the claims of the Carmelites to have been founded by Elijah furnished fresh material for acrimonious debate. In spite of this failure, the Inquisition maintained its claim to intervene and Inquisitor-general Valladares, June 24, 1688, issued another edict, incorporating that of 1634 and deploring that the old quarrels had become more virulent than ever. It was doubtful, he said, whether the previous utterances had been communicated to the Orders outside of Madrid, so a copy was ordered to be sent to every convent in Spain, with orders to be posted in a conspicuous place and the threat that it would be rigidly enforced. The belligerent ebullitions of the holy men were as little checked by this as by its predecessor and Inquisitor-general Rocaberti, October 19, 1698, took a further step by an edict in which he reprinted the previous ones and sent it to the tribunals with orders to publish it in all towns and have it posted on all church doors, thus taking the public into confidence and proclaiming to it not only the disreputable conduct of the frailes but the powerlessness of the Inquisition to reduce them to order and decency.[117] In fact, the Inquisition eradicated Judaism, it virtually expelled the Moriscos, it preserved Spain from the missionary zeal of Protestantism, but it failed ignominiously when it undertook to restrain the expression of aversion and contempt mutually entertained by Dominican and Franciscan, Jesuit and Carmelite.

CHAPTER III - BISHOPS

There was, in Spain, but one class over which the Inquisition had no jurisdiction. Boniface VIII, at the close of the thirteenth century, had decreed that, when a bishop was suspect of heresy, the inquisitor could not prosecute. The most that he could do was to gather evidence and send it to the Holy See, which reserved to itself judgement on the episcopal Order.[118] This was embodied in the canon law and remained in force, although of course the pope could delegate his power or could enlarge inquisitorial commissions, as when, in 1451, Nicholas V responded to the request of Juan II and included bishops among those subjected to the inquisitors whom he appointed.[119] During the middle ages the question was one of scarce more than academic interest, but in Spain, where the conversos had attained so many lofty positions in the Church and where all of Jewish blood were regarded with suspicion, it might at any moment become of practical importance.[120] The influence and power of the Inquisition would manifestly be increased if it should be granted faculties to prosecute bishops and Torquemada seems to have applied for this, in 1487, intimating that there were suspects among the bishops. Innocent VIII, however, was not disposed to subject the whole episcopate of Spain to the Holy Office and replied, September 25th, reciting the decree of Boniface and telling him to examine carefully all the evidence collected by the inquisitors and, if in it he found what incriminated prelates or showed that they were defamed or suspected of heresy, he should send it in legal shape and carefully sealed to Rome, where it would be duly weighed and proper action be taken.[121]

THE ACCUSED SENT TO ROME

If Torquemada failed in obtaining the desired jurisdiction over the Spanish episcopate, he could at least strike terror by accusing some of them to the Holy See, where their condemnation would be followed by that of their ancestors and large confiscations would result. Two of those of Jewish blood, Dávila of Segovia and Aranda of Calahorra, were selected for attack. In the existing popular temper it could not have been difficult to collect evidence that they were regarded as suspect and were defamed for heresy. Presumably this was sent to Rome and the matter was regarded as of sufficient moment to induce the despatch of Antoniotto Pallavicini, then Bishop of Tournay, as a special nuncio to confer with Torquemada.[122] He returned to Rome with evidence deemed sufficient to justify their summons thither. In 1490, Dávila went to Rome, in his eightieth year. Since 1461 he had been Bishop of Segovia and, in spite of Jewish descent, his family was one of the most influential in Castile, intermarried with its noblest blood.[123] He had given ample proof of pitiless orthodoxy, in 1468, when, at Sepúlveda, the rabbi, Solomon Pico and the leaders of the synagogue were accused of crucifying a Christian boy during Holy Week. Bishop Dávila promptly arrested sixteen of those most deeply implicated, of whom seven were burnt and the rest were hanged, except a boy who begged to be baptized--although this did not satisfy the pious Sepúlvedans, who slew some of the remaining Jews and drove the rest away.[124] He had given cause of offence, however, for, when the Inquisition was introduced in Segovia, he drove the inquisitors from his diocese and remonstrated boldly with the sovereigns and, when this proved fruitless, it was in evidence that he dug up at night, from the cemetery of the convent of la Merced, the bones of his ancestors and concealed them, in order to destroy the proof of their interment in the Jewish fashion.[125] In Rome he seems to have found favor with Alexander VI who, in 1494, sent him to Naples in company with his nephew, the Cardinal of Monreale. His case was protracted and he died in Rome, October 28, 1497; the result is not positively known, but it must have been favorable as otherwise his pious legacies would have been fruitless and Colmenares, the historian of Segovia, would not have dared to call him one of the most useful prelates that the see had enjoyed, nor would Galindez de Carvajal have said that his errand to Rome was merely to defend the bones of his father.[126]

Pedro de Aranda of Calahorra was a man of equal mark who, in 1482, acquired the high position of President of the Council of Castile. His father, Gonzalo Alonso, had been baptized with the famous Pablo de Santa María and had been ennobled. The Valladolid tribunal prosecuted his memory, with the result of a discordia, or disagreement, and the bishop went to Rome in 1493, where he gained papal favor and procured a brief transferring the case to the Bishop of Córdova and the Benedictine Prior of Valladolid. He remained in Rome, when Alexander VI, in 1494, sent him to Venice as ambassador and subsequently made him Master of the Sacred Palace. Since 1488, however, Torquemada had been collecting evidence against him. It was sent to Rome and, on the night of April 21, 1498, he was ordered to keep his room in the palace as a prison; on the 26th he was brought before the pope and had a hearing, after which he was taken to other rooms and kept under guard until September. Meanwhile Alexander seized his property and Sanuto intimates that his real crime was his abundance of ready money, while Burchard tells us that he was accused of heresy and marrania and that he had many enemies. Three bishops of the curia were commissioned as his judges; they heard many witnesses presented by the fiscal and a hundred and one by the accused, but all of these testified against him. The points against him were that he said the Mosaic Law had one principle, the Christian three; in praying he said Gloria Patri, omitting Filio et Spiritui Sancto; he celebrated mass after eating; he ate meat on Good Friday and other prohibited days; he declared that indulgences were useless and had been invented by the Fathers for gain; that there was neither hell nor purgatory but only paradise, and much more of the same nature. On November 16th the judges laid the evidence before the pope in secret consistory when, by the advice of the cardinals, Aranda was deposed and degraded from Orders; he was confined in the Castle of Sant' Angelo, where he was given a good room and he died there, apparently in 1500.[127]

Pope Alexander seems to have felt that it was necessary to guard his jurisdiction against the encroaching tendencies of the Spanish Inquisition, for in granting to the Bishop of Avila appellate powers, in his brief of November 4, 1594 (Vol. I, p. 179), he was careful to except the venerable brethren, the archbishops and bishops, whose cases by law were reserved to the Holy See.[128] It was well understood by this time, however and, in the case of Archbishop Talavera of Granada, it will be remembered that Lucero made no attempt to do more than gather evidence to be sent to Rome and, when papal authority was obtained, it was granted not to the Inquisition but to prelates specially commissioned.[129]

TEMPORARY JURISDICTION GRANTED

Half a century was to elapse before there was another case involving the episcopal Order. It has been sometimes thought that the Inquisition was concerned in the trial and execution of Antonio de Acuña, Bishop of Zamora, but such was not the fact, although the case illustrates the difficulty of holding a bishop accountable for his misdeeds. That turbulent prelate, somewhat absurdly styled a second Luther by Leo X, was an active leader in the Comunidades, who, after the defeat at Villalar, April 21, 1521, fled in disguise but was caught at Villamediana, on the Castilian border. Episcopal immunity rendered him a doubtful prize; Charles V was resolved on his death, but there was considerable doubt as to how he was to be punished. The Inquisition was not brought into play but, after some negotiation, Leo X was induced to issue a commission to Cardinal Adrian and the nuncio to take testimony and forward it for judgement by the pope in consistory. On Adrian's accession to the papacy he transferred the commission to the Archbishop of Granada and the Bishop of Ciudad-Rodrigo, but gave no authority to employ torture. Then Clement VII, by a brief of March 27, 1524, granted faculties to proceed to extremities, under which the trial went on, but apparently died out when carried to Rome. Wearied with five years' confinement in the castle of Simancas, Acuña made a fruitless attempt to escape, in which he killed the alcaide, Mendo Noguerol. Charles then sent to Simancas his alcalde de casa y corte, Rodrigo Ronquillo, with instructions to torture Acuña and put him to death--instructions faithfully executed, March 23, 1526. This violation of the immunities of the Church caused no little scandal. Charles speedily obtained for himself, from Clement, absolution from the ipso facto excommunication incurred, but that which he had promised to procure for his subordinates was granted with difficulty and only after delay of more than a year, the final ceremony not taking place until September 8, 1527. At Valladolid a tradition was long current that Ronquillo came to an evil end, being carried off by demons.[130]

As the Lutheran revolt grew more threatening and the dread of its extending to Spain increased, a certain limited jurisdiction over bishops was conferred on Cardinal Manrique by a brief of Clement VII, July 15, 1531. He was empowered to inquire against them if suspected of favoring Lutheran doctrines or of aiding those who held them; he was not permitted, however, to arrest and imprison, although he could punish them according to the canons and he was granted the fullest faculties of absolving and rehabilitating those who abandoned their errors and asked for forgiveness.[131] It is not likely that any occasion arose for the exercise of these faculties, but if there was it has left no trace.

This evidently was a personal delegation, expiring with Manrique, for no reference to it was made in the next case--that of Bartolomé de Carranza, Archbishop of Toledo. This was, perhaps, the most important affair during the career of the Inquisition. It attracted the attention of all Catholic Europe and illustrates in so many ways, not only inquisitorial methods but the conflict between orthodoxy and reform that it merits consideration in some detail.[132]

VALDÉS OUT OF FAVOR

Henry Charles Lea, LL.D.

Inquisitor-general Valdés, who was also Archbishop of Seville and whose name often comes before us, was perilously near disgrace in 1557. Philip II was in desperate straits for money; the glories of Saint-Quentin and Gravelines were not acquired cheaply and the war forced upon him by Paul IV was exhausting his Italian possessions. From Flanders he sent Count Melito to Spain with orders to raise forced loans from nobles and prelates, and the Princess Juana, then Governor, called among others on Valdés for a hundred and fifty thousand ducats. The Bishop of Córdova when approached, promptly furnished a hundred thousand and promised more if he could raise it: the Archbishop of Saragossa, who was asked for a hundred thousand, only gave twenty thousand. Valdés was even more niggardly, and supplied nothing, although it was observed about this time that six loads of money reached Valladolid for him. Charles V, from his retirement of Yuste, wrote to him, May 18th, expressing surprise that he, the creature of imperial favor, should hesitate to repay the benefits conferred, especially as he could have what security he desired for the loan. This letter, with one from Juana, was conveyed to him by Hernando de Ochoa, whose report to Charles, May 28th, of the interview, showed how little respect was felt for the man. Ochoa reproached him with having promised to see what he could do, in place of which he had gone into hiding at San Martin de la Fuente, fourteen leagues from the court at Valladolid, where he had lain for two months, hoping that the matter would blow over. "He said to me, before a consecrated host, that the devils could fly away with him if ever he had 100,000 or 80,000, or 60,000, or 30,000 ducats, for he had always spent much in charities and had made dotations amounting to 150,000." Ochoa pressed him hard; he admitted that his archbishopric, which he had held since 1546, was worth 60,000 ducats a year and Ochoa showed that, admitting his claims for charities and expenses, he had laid aside at least 30,000 a year "which you cannot possibly have spent, for you never have any one to dine in your house and you do not accumulate silver plate, like other gentlemen; all this is notorious, and the whole court knows it.... This embarrassed him, but he repeated with great oaths that he had no money, that it was not well thus to oppress prelates, nor would money thus obtained be lucky for war; God would help the king and what would Christendom say about it." The honest Ochoa still urged him to return to the court and save his honor, intimating that the king might take action that would be highly unpleasant, but it was to no purpose. Valdés was obdurate and clung resolutely to his shekels.[133]

Philip had sent instructions as to the treatment of recalcitrants--probably relegating bishops to their sees and nobles to their estates--but there was hesitation felt as to banishing Valdés from the court, although the continued pressure of Charles and Juana only extorted a promise of fifty thousand ducats. Yet it was desired to remove him and plans were tried to offer him a pretext for going. In March, 1588, Juana ordered him to accompany the body of Queen Juana la loca to Granada for interment, from which place he could visit his Seville church; he made excuses but promised to go shortly. Then, when she repeated the order, he offered many reasons for evading it, including the heresies recently discovered in Seville and Murcia; the translation of the body could wait until September and everybody, he said, was trying to drive him from the court. She referred the matter to the Royal Council, which decided that his excuses were insufficient and that, even if the interment were postponed he could properly be ordered to reside in his see.[134]

It was evident to Valdés that something was necessary to strengthen his position and he skilfully utilized the discovery of a few Protestants in Valladolid, of whom some were eminent clerics, like Augustin Cazalla and Fray Domingo de Rojas, and others were persons of quality, like Luis de Rojas and Doña Ana Enríquez. We shall have occasion to note hereafter the extraordinary excitement caused by the revelation that Protestantism was making inroads in court circles, the extent of which was readily exaggerated, and it was stimulated and exploited by Valdés, who magnified his zeal in combating the danger and conjured, at least for the moment, the storm that was brewing. Philip wrote from Flanders, June 5, 1558, to send him to his see without delay; if he still made excuses he was to be excluded from the Council of State and this would answer until his approaching return to Spain, when he would take whatever action was necessary. Ten days later, on receiving letters from Valdés enumerating the prisoners and describing the efforts made to avert the danger, he countermanded the orders.[135] Still, this was only a respite; we chance to hear of a meeting of the Council of State, in August or September, in which Juan de Vega characterized as a great scandal the disobedience of a vassal to the royal commands, in a matter so just as residence in his see, and he suggested that, when the court moved, no quarters should be assigned to Valdés, to which Archbishop Carranza replied that it was no wonder that the orders of the king were unable to effect what the commandments of God and the Church could not accomplish.[136]

Something further was necessary to render him indispensable--something that could be prolonged indefinitely and if, at the same time, it would afford substantial relief to the treasury, he might be forgiven the niggardness that had resisted the appeals of the sovereign. He had for some time been preparing a scheme for this, which was nothing less than the prosecution of the Primate of the Spanish

Church, the income of whose see was rated at from 150,000 to 200,000 ducats. To measure the full audacity of this it is necessary to appreciate the standing of Archbishop Carranza.

ARCHBISHOP CARRANZA

Bartolomé de Carranza y Miranda was born in 1503. At the age of 12 he entered the university of Alcalá; at 18 he took the final vows of the Dominican Order and was sent to study theology in the college of San Gregorio at Valladolid, where, in 1530, he was made professor of arts, in 1533 junior professor of theology and, in 1534, chief professor as well as consultor of the tribunal of Valladolid. In 1540 he was sent as representative of his Order to the General Chapter held in Rome, where he distinguished himself and was honored with the doctorate, while Paul III granted him a licence to read prohibited heretic books. On his return to Spain his reputation was national; he was largely employed by the Suprema in the censorship of books, especially of foreign Bibles, while the Councils of Indies and Castile frequently submitted intricate questions for his judgement. In 1542 he was offered the see of Cuzco, esteemed the wealthiest in the colonies, when he replied that he would willingly go to the Indies on the emperor's service but not to undertake the cure of souls.[137] On the convocation of the Council of Trent, in 1545, Charles V selected him as one of the delegates and, during his three years' service there, he earned the reputation throughout Christendom of a profound theologian. When, in 1548, Prince Philip went to join his father in Flanders, they both offered him the position of confessor which he declined, as he did the see of Canaries which was tendered to him in 1550. In this latter year he was elected provincial of his Order for Castile and, in 1551, he was sent to the second convocation of the Council of Trent by Charles and also as the representative of Siliceo, Archbishop of Toledo. As usual, he played a prominent part in the Council and, after its hasty dissolution, he remained there for some time employed in the duty of examining and condemning heretical books. In 1553 he returned to his professorship at Valladolid and when, in 1554, Prince Philip sailed for England to marry Queen Mary and restore the island to the unity of the Church, he took Carranza with him as the fittest instrument for the work.[138]

Carranza subsequently boasted that, during his three years' stay in England, he had burnt, reconciled, or driven from the land thirty thousand heretics and had brought two million souls back to the Church. If we may believe his admiring biographers he was the heart and soul of the Marian persecution and Philip did nothing in religious matters without his advice. When, in September, 1555, Philip rejoined his father in Flanders, he left Carranza as Mary's religious adviser, in which capacity he remained until 1557. Regarded by the heretics as the chief cause of their sufferings he barely escaped from repeated attempts on his life by poison or violence.[139] It is true that English authorities of the period make little mention of him, but the continued confidence of Philip is ample evidence that his persecuting zeal was sufficient to satisfy that exacting monarch.

When, in 1557, Carranza rejoined Philip in Flanders he was probably engrossed in the preparation and printing of his large work on the Catechism, of which more hereafter, but he still found time to investigate and impede the clandestine trade of sending heretic books to Spain.[140] That he had completely won Philip's esteem and confidence was seen when Siliceo of Toledo died, May 1, 1557, and Philip appointed him as successor in the archbishopric. He refused the splendid prize and suggested three men as better fitted for the place. Philip persisted; he was going to a neighboring convent to confess and commune prior to the opening of the campaign and ordered Carranza to obey on his return. When he came back he sent the presentation written in his own hand; Carranza yielded, but on condition that, as the war with the pope would delay the issue of the bulls, the king in the interval could make another selection. This effort to avoid the fatal gift was fruitless. On his return from the campaign, Philip in an autograph letter summoned him to fulfil his promise and made the appointment public. So high was Carranza's reputation that, when the presentation was laid before the consistory in Rome, on December 6th, it was at once confirmed, without observing the preconization, or the customary inquiry into the fitness of the appointee, or a constitution which prohibited final action on the same day.[141]

***

The elevation of a simple friar to the highest place in the Spanish Church was a blow to numerous ambitions that could scarce fail to arouse hostility. Valdés himself was said to have aspirations for the position and to be bitterly disappointed. Pedro de Castro, Bishop of Cuenca, had also cherished hopes and was eager for revenge. Carranza, moreover, was not popular with the hierarchy. He was that unwelcome character, a reformer within the Church and, while everyone acknowledged the necessity of reform, no one looked with favor on a reformer who assailed his profitable abuses. As far back as 1547, while in attendance on the Council of Trent, Carranza had preached a sermon on one of the most crying evils of the time, the non-residence of bishops and beneficiaries, and had embodied his views in a tractate as severe as a Lutheran would have written on this abuse and the kindred one of pluralities, to which possibly the stringent Tridentine provisions on the subject may be attributed.[142] Such an outburst was not calculated to win favor, seeing that the splendor of the curia was largely supported by the prelacies and benefices showered upon its members and that in Spain there was scarce an inquisitor or a fiscal who was not a non-resident beneficiary of some preferment.

Carranza had, moreover, a peculiarly dangerous enemy in a brother Dominican, Melchor Cano, perhaps the leading Spanish theologian of the time when Spanish theology was beginning to dominate the Church. Learned, able, keen-witted and not particularly scrupulous, he was in intellect vastly superior to Carranza; there had been early rivalry, when both were professors of theology, and causes of strife in the internal politics of the Order had arisen, so that Cano could scarce view without bitterness the sudden elevation of his brother fraile.[143] His position at the time was somewhat precarious. When, in 1556, Paul IV forced war on Philip II, that pious prince sought the advice of theologians as to the propriety of engaging in hostilities with the Vicegerent of God, and the parecer, or opinion which Cano drew up, was an able state paper that attracted wide attention. He defended uncompromisingly the royal prerogatives, he virtually justified the German revolt when the Centum Gravamina of the Diet of Nürnberg, in 1522, were unredressed and he described the corruption of Rome as a disease of such long standing as to be incurable.[144] This hardy defiance irritated Paul in the highest degree. April 21, 1556 he issued a brief summoning that son of perdition, Melchor Cano, to appear before him within sixty days for trial and sentence, but the brief was suppressed by the Royal Council and Cano was ordered not to leave the kingdom. The Spanish Dominicans rallied to his defence; in the chapter of 1558 he was elected provincial and deputy to the general chapter to be held in Rome, but Paul ordered the election to be annulled and Cano to be deprived of his priorate of San Esteban. Cano complained of lukewarmness in his defence on the part of both Philip and Carranza and it is easy to understand that, feeling keenly the disgrace inflicted on him, he was in a temper to attack any one more fortunate than himself.[145]

***

At this inauspicious moment Carranza presented himself as a fair object of attack by all who, from different motives, might desire to assail him. If we may judge from his writings, he must have been impulsive and inconsiderate in his speech, given to uttering extreme views which made an impression and then qualifying them with restrictions that were forgotten. He was earnestly desirous of restoring the Church to its ancient purity and by no means reticent in exposing its weaknesses and corruption. He had been trained at a time before the Tridentine definitions had settled points of faith which, since the twelfth century, had been the subjects of debate in the schools, and even in his maturity the Council of Trent had not yet been clothed with the awful authority subsequently accorded to it, for the inglorious exit of its first two convocations, in 1547 and 1552, gave little promise of what lay in the future. The echo of the fierce Lutheran controversies had scarce penetrated into Spain and comparatively little was there known of the debates which were shaking to its centre the venerable structure of the Church. Carranza's very labors in condemning heretic books and converting heretics had acquainted him with their doctrines and modes of expression; he was a confused thinker and his impulsive utterances were liable to be construed in a sense which he did not anticipate. As early as 1530 he had been denounced to the Inquisition by Fray Juan de Villamartin as a defender of Erasmus, especially in the matter of confession and the authorship of the Apocalypse and, during his persecuting career in England, he more than once gave opportunity, in his sermons, to unfavorable comment.[146] It was also in evidence that when in Rome, in 1539, he had written to Juan de Valdés in Naples, asking what authors should be studied for understanding Scripture, as he would have to teach that subject, and that Valdés replied in a letter which Carranza circulated among his students in Valladolid--a letter highly heretical in its teachings which Valdés subsequently included in his "One hundred and ten Divine Considerations."[147] It is true that, in 1539, Juan de Valdés was not reckoned a heretic, but, if the letter was correctly identified with the "Consideration" in question its circulation was highly imprudent, for it asserted that the guides for the study of Scripture are prayer inspired by God and meditation based on spiritual experience, thus discarding tradition for private interpretation, and it further dwelt upon the confidence which the soul should feel in justification through Christ. In the death-struggle with Protestantism the time had passed for easy-going latitude of opinion and, in the intricate mazes of scholastic theology, it was necessary to walk warily, for acute censorship could discover heresy in any unguarded expression. The great services rendered by Cardinal Morone and Cardinal Pole did not save them from the prosecuting zeal of Paul IV and Contarini and Sadoleto were both suspect of heresy.[148] Under such conditions a rambling inconsequential thinker like Carranza was peculiarly open to attack.

He had unquestionably been more or less intimate with some of the prominent personages whose arrest for Lutheranism, in the spring of 1558, produced so immense a sensation. It was not unnatural that, on their trials, they should seek to shield themselves behind his honored name, but the detached fragments of conversation which were cited in support of vague general assertions, even if correctly reported, amount to nothing in the face of the emphatic testimony by Fray Domingo de Rojas, for the discharge of his conscience, a few hours before his execution, that he had never seen in Carranza anything that was not Catholic in regard to the Roman Church and all its councils, definitions and laws and that when Lutherans were alluded to he said their opinions were crafty and deceiving; they had sprung from hell and the incautious could easily be deceived by them.[149] The credence due to the evidence of the Lutherans, on which so much stress was laid, can be gauged by a subsequent case illustrative of the tendency to render Carranza responsible for all aberrations of belief. A certain Gil Tibobil (de Bonneville) on trial in 1564 for Lutheranism, in Toledo, sought to palliate his guilt by asserting that he had heard Carranza preach, in the church of San Agustin, against candles and images and that confession was to be made to God and not to the priest. This was too crude to be accepted and he was sternly told that it cast doubt on the rest of his confession for, if Carranza had thus preached publicly, it would have come to the knowledge of the Inquisition and he would have been punished.[150]

Whether the testimony acquired in the trials of the Lutherans was important or not, Inquisitor-general Valdés lost no time in using it to discredit Carranza in the opinion of the sovereigns. As early as May 12, 1588, in a report to Charles V at Yuste, his assistance is asked in obtaining the arrest of a fugitive, whose capture would be exceedingly important; he had been traced to Castro de Urdiales, where he was to embark for Flanders to find refuge with Carranza or with his companion Fray Juan de Villagarcia, where he was sure of being well received. That the real motive was to injure Carranza with Charles appears from Valdés repeating the story to him in a report of June 2, adding that the fugitive had escaped and that information had been sent to Philip in order that he might be captured.[151] It is reasonable to assume that whatever incriminating evidence could be obtained from the prisoners was promptly brought to the notice of the sovereigns and that inferences were unscrupulously asserted as facts.

***

At this critical juncture, Carranza delivered himself into the hands of his enemies. In England and Flanders he had employed the intervals of persecution in composing a work which should set forth the irrefragable truths of the Catholic faith and guard the people from the insidious poison of heretical doctrine. This was a task for which, at such a time, he was peculiarly unfitted. He was not only a loose thinker but a looser writer, diffuse, rambling and discursive, setting down whatever idea chanced to occur to him and wandering off to whatever subjects the idea might suggest. Moreover he was earnest as a reformer within the Church, realizing abuses and exposing them fearlessly--in fact, he declared in the Prologue that his object was to restore the purity and soundness of the primitive Church, which was precisely what the heretics professed as their aim and precisely what the ruling hierarchy most dreaded.[152] Worst of all, he did this in the vulgar tongue, unmindful of the extreme reserve which sought to keep from the people all knowledge of the errors and arguments of the heretics and of the contrast between apostolic simplicity and the splendid sacerdotalism of a wealthy and worldly establishment.[153] This he cast into the form of Commentaries on the Catechism, occupying a folio of nine hundred pages, full of impulsive assertions which, taken by themselves, were of dangerous import, but which were qualified or limited, or contradicted in the next sentence, or the next page, or, perhaps, in the following section.

No one, I think, can dispassionately examine the Commentaries without reaching the conviction that Carranza was a sincere and zealous Catholic, however reckless may seem many of his isolated utterances. Nor was his orthodoxy merely academic. He belonged to the Church Militant and his hatred of heresy and heretics breaks out continually, in season and out of season, whether apposite or not to his immediate subject. Heretic arguments are not worthy of confutation--it is enough to say that a doctrine is condemned by the Church and therefore it is heretical. The first duty of the king is to preserve his dominions in the true faith and to chastise those who sin against it. Even if heretics should perform miracles, their disorderly lives and corrupted morals would be sufficient to guard the people from listening to them or believing them. If they do not admit their errors they are to be condemned to death; this is the best theology that a Christian can learn and it was not more necessary in the time of Moses than it is at present.[154]

Even in that age, when theology was so favorite a topic, few could be expected to wade through so enormous a mass of confused thinking and disjointed writing, and it was easy for Carranza's enemies to garble isolated sentences by which he could be represented to the sovereigns as being at least suspect in the faith, and suspicion of heresy was quite sufficient to require prosecution. Carranza himself, after his book was printed, seems to have felt apprehension and to have proceeded cautiously in giving it to the public. A set of the sheets was sent to the Marchioness of Alcañizes and a dozen or more copies were allowed to reach Spain, where they were received in March, 1558. Pedro de Castro, Bishop of Cuenca, obtained one and speedily wrote to Valdés, denouncing the writer as guilty of heretical opinions. Valdés grasped the opportunity and ordered Melchor Cano to examine the work. Cano took as a colleague Fray Domingo de Cuevas and had no difficulty in discovering a hundred and one passages of heretical import. The preliminaries to a formal trial were now fairly under way, the result of which could scarce be doubtful under inquisitorial methods, if the royal and papal assent could be obtained, necessary even to the Inquisition before it could openly attack the Primate of the Spanish Church.

Despite the profound secrecy enveloping the operations of the Inquisition, it was impossible that, in an affair of such moment, there should not be indiscretions and Carranza in Flanders was advised of what was on foot. His friends urged him not to return to Spain but to take refuge in Rome under papal protection, but he knew that this would irrevocably cost him the favor of Philip, for exaggerated jealousy of papal interference with the Inquisition was traditional since the time of Ferdinand and Isabella, and he virtually surrendered his case at once by instructing his printer, Martin Nucio, not to sell copies of the Commentaries without his express orders, thus withdrawing it from circulation.[155]

***

But little adverse impression seems as yet to have been made on Philip. When Carranza was about to leave Flanders, the king gave him detailed instructions which manifest unbounded confidence. He was to go directly to Valladolid and represent the extreme need of money; then he was to see Queen Mary of Hungary, Charles' sister, and persuade her to come to Flanders; then he was to hasten to Yuste where Philip, through him, unbosomed himself to his father, revealing all his necessities and desires in family as well as in state affairs. In short, Carranza was still one whom he could safely entrust with his most secret thoughts.[156]

Carranza, with his customary lack of worldly wisdom, threw away all the advantages of his position. Landing at Laredo on August 1st, he passed through Burgos, where he was involved in an unseemly squabble with the archbishop over his assumed right to carry his archiepiscopal cross in public. He did not reach Valladolid until the 13th and there he tarried, busied ostensibly with a suit between his see and the Marquis of Camarasa over the valuable Adelantamiento of Cazorla, but doubtless occupied also with efforts to counteract the intrigues of Valdés. Then he performed his mission to Mary of Hungary and it was not until the middle of September that he set out on a leisurely journey to Yuste. Valdés had taken care to forestall his visit. An autograph letter of the Princess Juana to Charles, August 8th, says that Valdés had asked her to warn him to be cautious in dealing with Carranza, for he had been implicated by the Lutheran prisoners and would already have been arrested had he been anyone else. Charles was naturally impatient to see him, not only to obtain explanations as to this, but also to receive the messages expected from Philip, for which he was waiting before writing to Flanders. Carranza's delay, in spite of repeated urgency from Yuste, could not but create a sinister impression and all chance of justification was lost, for Charles was prostrated by his fatal illness before Carranza left Valladolid and the end was near when he reached Yuste about noon on September 20th. Charles expired the next morning at half-past two, Carranza administering to him the last consolations, his method in which formed one of the charges against him on his trial. He had thrown away his last chance and the unexpected death of Charles deprived him of one who might possibly have stood between him and his fate.[157]

The plans of Valdés were now sufficiently advanced for him to seek the papal authorization which alone was lacking, and his method to obtain this was characteristically insidious. The Suprema addressed, September 9th, to Paul IV a relation of its labors in discovering and prosecuting the Lutheran heretics. There was skilful exaggeration of the danger impending from a movement, the extent of which could not be known, and it was pointed out that sympathy with the sectaries might be entertained by officials of the Inquisition itself, by the Ordinaries and the consultors; so that extraordinary powers were asked to arrest and judge and relax those suspected or guilty, even though they were persons holding a secular or pontifical and ecclesiastical dignity or belonging to any religious or other Order.[158] As the Inquisition already had jurisdiction over all but bishops (it had not hesitated to arrest and try the Dominican Fray Domingo de Rojas) the self-evident object of this was to obtain surreptitiously, under cover of the word "pontifical," some general expression that might be used to deprive Carranza of his right to trial by the pope. The Dean of Oviedo, a nephew of Valdés, was sent to Rome as a special agent to procure the desired brief; whether royal sanction for this application was obtained does not appear, but it probably was not, at least at this stage.

***

Carranza meanwhile had been vainly endeavoring to get copies of the censures on his book in order to answer them. He appealed earnestly to his friends in Philip's court and in Rome but, without awaiting their replies, he pursued his policy of submission and, on September 21st, the day of Charles's death, he wrote to Sancho López de Otálora, a member of the Suprema, that he consented to the prohibition of his work, provided this was confined to Spain and that his name was not mentioned.[159] In this and what followed he has been accused of weakness, but it is difficult to see what other course lay open to him. He doubtless still considered his episcopal consecration a guarantee for his personal safety, while his reputation for orthodoxy could best be conserved by not entering into a fruitless contest with a power irresistible in its chosen field of action--a contest, moreover, which would have cost him the royal favor that was his main reliance.

In pursuance of this policy he even descended to attempting to propitiate Melchor Cano by offering to do whatever he would recommend. Cano subsequently asserted, with customary mendacity, that Carranza would have averted his fate had he adopted any of the means which he devised and advised to save him, but it is difficult to imagine what more he could have done.[160] Towards the close of November he wrote to Valdés and the Suprema and to other influential persons professing his submission. He explained the reasons which had led him to write his book in the vernacular after commencing it in Latin; it could readily be suppressed for, on reaching Valladolid, he had withdrawn the edition from the printer; there were no copies in the bookshops and what he had brought with him he would surrender, while the dozen or so that had been sent to Spain could easily be called in as the recipients were all known. Then, on December 9th, he proposed to the Suprema that the book should be prohibited in Spanish and be returned to him for correction and translation into Latin.[161] Had the real object of Valdés been the ostensible one of preserving the faith, this would have amply sufficed; the book would have been suppressed and the public humiliation of the Archbishop of Toledo, so distinguished for his services to religion, would have been an amply deterrent warning to all indiscreet theologians. It was a not unnatural burst of indignation when, in a letter to Domingo de Soto, November 14th, he bitterly pointed out how the heretics would rejoice to know that Fray Bartolomé de Miranda was treated in Spain as he had treated them in England and Flanders and that, after he had burnt them to enforce the doctrines of his book, it was pronounced in Spain unfit to be read.[162] Carranza's submission brought no result save to encourage his enemies, who put him off with vague replies while awaiting the success of their application to the pope.

Meanwhile he had reached Toledo, October 13th, and had applied himself actively to his duties. He was rigid in the performance of divine service, he visited prisons, hospitals and convents, he put an end to the sale of offices and charging fees for licences, he revised the fee-bill of his court, he enforced the residence of parish priests and was especially careful in the distribution of preferment--in short he was a practical as well as theoretical reformer. His charity also was boundless, for he used to say that all he needed was a Dominican habit and that whatever God gave him was for the poor. Thus during his ten months of incumbency, he distributed more than eighty thousand ducats in marrying orphans, redeeming captives, supporting widows, sending students to universities and in gifts to hospitals.[163] He was a model bishop, and the resolute fidelity with which the chapter of Toledo supported his cause to the end shows the impression made on a body which, in Spanish churches, was usually at odds with its prelate.

He had likewise not been idle in obtaining favorable opinions of his book from theologians of distinction. In view of the rumors of inquisitorial action, there was risk in praising it, yet nearly all those prominent in Spanish theology bore testimony in its favor. The general view accorded virtually with that of Pedro Guerrero, Archbishop of Granada, than whom no one in the Spanish hierarchy stood higher for learning and piety. The book, he said, was without error and, being in Castilian, was especially useful for parish priests unfamiliar with Latin, wherefore it should be extensively circulated. It was true that there were occasional expressions which, taken by themselves, might on their face seem to be erroneous, but elsewhere it was seen that they must be construed in a Catholic sense. To this effect recorded themselves Domingo and Pedro de Soto, men of the highest reputation, Garrionero Bishop of Almeria, Blanco of Orense, Cuesta of Leon, Delgado of Lugo and numerous others.[164] If some of these men belied themselves subsequently and aided in giving the finishing blow to their persecuted brother, we can estimate the pressure brought to bear on them.

***

Valdés speedily utilized the power of the Inquisition to check these appreciations of the Commentaries. When, at the University of Alcalá, the rector, the chancellor, and twenty-two doctors united in declaring the work to be without error or suspicion of error, save that some incautious expressions, disconnected from the context, might be mistaken by hasty readers, Valdés muzzled it and all other learned bodies and individuals by a letter saying that it had come to his notice that learned men of the university had been examining books and giving their opinions. As this produced confusion and contradiction respecting the Index which the Inquisition was preparing, all persons, colleges and universities were forbidden to censure or give an opinion concerning any book without first submitting it to the Suprema, and this under pain of excommunication and a fine of two hundred ducats on each and every one concerned.[165] It was impossible to contend with an adversary armed with such weapons. Not content with this, the rector of the university, Diego Sobaños, was prosecuted by the tribunal of Valladolid for the part he had taken in the matter; he was reprimanded, fined and absolved ad cautelam.

Similar action was taken against the more prominent of those who had expressed themselves favorably and who, for the most part, were forced to retract.[166] The Inquisition played with loaded dice.

Dean Valdés of Oviedo meanwhile had succeeded in his mission to Rome, aided, as Raynaldus assures us, by the express request of Philip, though this is more than doubtful. The brief was dated January 7, 1559; it was addressed to Valdés and recited that, as there were in Spain some prelates suspected of Lutheranism, he was empowered for two years from the receipt of the brief, with the advice of the Suprema, to make investigation and, if sufficient proof were found against any one and there was good reason to apprehend his flight, to arrest and keep him in safe custody, but as soon as possible the pope was to be informed of it and the prisoner was to be sent to him with all the evidence and papers in the case.[167] With the exception of the provision against expected flight, this was merely in accordance with the received practice in the case of bishops, but it was the entering wedge and we shall see how its limitations were disregarded.

The brief was received April 8th. In place of complying with it and sending Carranza to Rome with the evidence that had been collecting for nearly a year, a formal trial was secretly commenced. The fiscal presented a clamosa or indictment, on May 6th, asking for Carranza's arrest and the sequestration of his property, "for having preached, written and dogmatized many errors of Luther." The evidence was duly laid before calificadores, or censors, who reported accordingly and, on the 13th, there was drawn up a summons to appear and answer to the demand of the fiscal. Before proceeding further, in an affair of such magnitude, it was felt that the assent was required of Philip, who was still in Flanders.[168] As recently as April 4th he had replied encouragingly to an appeal from the persecuted prelate. "I have not wanted to go forward in the matter of your book, about which you wrote to me, until the person whom you were sending should arrive; he has spoken with me today. I had already done something of what is proper in this business. Not to detain the courier who goes with the good news of the conclusion of peace, I do not wish to enlarge in replying to you, but I shall do so shortly and meanwhile I earnestly ask you to make no change in what you have done hitherto and to have recourse to no one but to me, for it would be in the highest degree disadvantageous."[169] Philip evidently thought that only Carranza's book and not his person was concerned, that the affair was of no great importance and his solicitude was chiefly to prevent any appeal to Rome, a matter in which he fully shared the intense feeling of his predecessors. When Carranza ordered his envoy to Flanders, Fray Hernando de San Ambrosio, to proceed to Rome and secure an approbation of the Commentaries, he replied, April 19th, that all his friends at the court earnestly counselled against; it had been necessary to assure Philip of the falsity of the reports that he had done so, whereupon the king had expressed his satisfaction and had said that any other course would have displeased him.[170]

***

Advantage, for which Carranza foolishly offered the opportunity, was taken of this extreme jealousy to win him over. When the Dominican chapter met, in April, 1559, there was open strife between him and Cano, over a report that Cano had styled him a greater heretic than Luther and that he favored Cazalla and the other prisoners. Carranza demanded his punishment for the slander and sought to defeat his candidacy for the provincialate. In this he failed. Cano's assertion that he had been misunderstood was accepted; he was again elected provincial and Carranza unwisely carried his complaint to Rome.[171] There it became mixed up with the question of Cano's confirmation, for Paul IV naturally resented the repeated presentation of that "son of iniquity." Philip, on the other hand, could not abandon the protection of one whose fault, in papal eyes, was his vindication of the royal prerogative, and he interested himself actively in pressing the confirmation. Paul equivocated and lied and sought some subterfuge which was found in Cano's consecration, in 1552, as Bishop of Canaries (a post which he had resigned in 1553) which was held to render him ineligible to any position in his Order, and a general decree to that effect was issued in July.[172]

All this was skilfully used to prejudice Philip against Carranza. In letters of May 16th to him and of May 22nd and 25th to his confessor Bernardo de Fresneda, Cano with great adroitness and small respect for veracity represented himself as subjected to severe persecution. He had always been Carranza's friend; he had withheld for seven months his censure of the Commentaries and had yielded only to a threat of excommunication and now Carranza was repaying him by intriguing against the confirmation in Rome--the truth being that it was not until the end of June that Carranza's agent reached there. It was a terrible thing, Cano added, if the archbishop, through his Italian General, could thus wrong him and he could not defend himself. He was resolved to suffer in silence, but the persecution was so bitter that if the king did not speedily come to Spain he would have to seek refuge in Flanders.[173] What, in reality, were his sufferings and what the friendly work on which he was engaged, are indicated by a commission issued to him, May 29th, granting him the extraordinary powers of a substitute inquisitor-general and sending him forth on a roving expedition to gather evidence, compelling everyone whom he might summon to answer whatever questions he might ask.[174] The Suprema and

Valdés, moreover, in letters of May 13th and 16th to Philip, adopted the same tone; Cano's labors throughout the affair had been great and it was hoped that the king would not permit his persecution for the services rendered to God and his majesty; there need be no fear of injustice to Carranza, for the investigation was impartial and dispassionate.[175]

Philip had already been informed by Cardinal Pacheco, February 24th and again May 13th, that Carranza had sent to the pope copies of the favorable opinions of his book, asking that it be judged in Rome and that his episcopal privilege of papal jurisdiction be preserved.[176] Whatever intentions he had of befriending Carranza were not proof against the assertions that to his intrigues was attributable the papal interference with Cano's election. On June 26th he wrote to Cano, expressing his satisfaction and assuring him of his support in Rome and, on the same day, to the Suprema approving its actions as to the Commentaries and expressing his confidence that it would do what was right.[177] In thus authorizing the prosecution he ordered the archbishop's dignity to be respected and he wrote to the Princess Juana that, to avoid scandal, she should invite him to Valladolid to consult on important matters, so that the trial could proceed without attracting attention.[178]

***

Philip's letters were received July 10th, but there was still hesitation and it was not until August 3d that the princess wrote, summoning Carranza in haste to Valladolid, where she would have lodgings prepared for him. This she sent, with secret instructions, by the hands of Rodrigo de Castro, a member of the Suprema.[179] Carranza was at Alcalá de Henares, whither Diego Ramírez, inquisitor of Toledo, was also despatched, under pretext of publishing the Edict of Faith. Carranza, who suspected a snare, was desirous of postponing his arrival at Valladolid until Philip, on whose protection he still relied, should reach Spain. Accordingly he converted the journey into a visitation, leaving Alcalá on the 16th and passing through Fuente el Saz and Talamanca to Torrelaguna, which he reached on the 20th. On the road he received intimations of what was in store and at Torrelaguna Fray Pedro de Soto came with the news that emissaries had already started to arrest him, which elicited from him a despairing and beseeching letter to Fresneda, the royal confessor.[180]

De Soto's report was true. Valdés dreaded as much as Carranza desired Philip's arrival; the delay on the road risked this if the device of the invitation to Valladolid was to be carried out. For his plans it was essential that an irrevocable step should be taken in the king's absence--a step which should compromise Carranza and commit the Inquisition so fully that Philip could not revoke it without damaging the Holy Office in a way that to him was impossible. To allow Carranza to be at liberty while investigating the suspicion of his heresy, as Philip had ordered, would leave the door open to royal or papal intervention; to seize and imprison him would leave Philip no alternative but to urge forward his destruction, while his dilatory progress could be assumed to cover preparations for flight. Accordingly, on August 17th the Suprema issued a commission, under the papal brief of January 7th, to Rodrigo de Castro to act with other inquisitors in the case, while, as justice required Carranza's arrest, Valdés commissioned de Castro, Diego Ramírez and Diego González, inquisitor of Valladolid, to seize the person of the archbishop and convey him to such prison as should be designated, at the same time sequestrating all his property, real and personal and all his papers and writings. Simultaneously Joan Cebrian, alguazil mayor of the Suprema, was ordered to coöperate with the inquisitors in the arrest and sequestration.[181]

Cebrian started the same day for Torrelaguna, where he kept his bed through the day and worked at night. The inquisitors came together; a force of familiars and others was secretly collected and, by day-break on the 22nd the governor, the alcalde and the alguaziles of Torrelaguna were seized and held under guard, the house where Carranza lodged was surrounded, de Castro, Ramírez, Cebrian and a dozen men ascended the stairs and knocked at the door of the antechamber. Fray Antonio de Utrilla asked who was there and the dread response came "Open to the Holy Office!" It was the same at the door of Carranza's chamber; de Castro knelt at the bed-side, where Carranza had drawn the curtains and raised himself on his elbow; he begged Carranza's pardon with tears in his eyes and said his face would show his reluctance in performing his duty. Cebrian was called in and read the order of arrest. Carranza replied "These señores do not know that they are not my judges, as I am subject directly to the pope." Then de Castro produced the papal brief from the bosom of his gown and read it. Some say that Carranza fell back on his pillow, others that he remained imperturbable. He ordered out all the rest and remained for a considerable time alone with de Castro and Ramírez.[182]

He was at once secluded in the most rigid manner, all his people being excluded, except Fray Domingo Ximenes, who was required to assist in the sequestration and inventory. At table he was served by de Castro and Ramírez, who treated him with the utmost respect and endeavored to console him, for by this time his fortitude had given way and he was overwhelmed. His attendants were all dismissed and given money to find their way whither they chose and their grief we are told moved every one to compassion. Only the cook and steward and a muleteer were retained to serve the party. At nine in the evening proclamation was made throughout the town that until daylight no one was to leave his house or look out of a window. At midnight Cebrian assembled forty horsemen; de Castro and Ramírez brought Carranza down and stationed themselves on either side of his mule as the cavalcade rode forth in the darkness and then Salinas, the owner of the house, was allowed to come out to close his door. The heat was overpowering and when, by ten in the morning they reached Lozoya, they rested for a day and a night. On the 27th they arrived at Laguna del Duero, near Valladolid, where de Castro and Ramírez left the party and rode forward for instructions, returning the same day and, at two in the morning of the 28th, Carranza was brought to the city and lodged in the house of Pedro González de Leon, in the suburb of San Pedro beyond the walls, which had been taken by the Inquisition.[183]

***

Carranza thus disappeared from human sight as completely as though swallowed by the earth. It is a forcible illustration of inquisitorial methods, but conspicuous only by reason of the dignity of the victim, for it rested with the discretion of the officials whether thus to spirit away and conceal their prisoners or to cast them publicly into the secret prison. Morales tells us that it was years before the place of Carranza's incarceration was known, although every one said that he had been seized by the Holy Office. Even to say this, however, was not unattended with danger, for, in the trial, in September, by the tribunal of Toledo, of Rodrigo Alvárez, one of the charges against him was that, about September 5th, he had remarked to a casual fellow-traveller, that he came from Valladolid and was quite certain that the archbishop was imprisoned.[184]

There could be no doubt about it in Toledo, where the news of the arrest was received on the 24th. On the 26th the chapter assembled in sorrow to take what measures they could, in aid of their beloved prelate, but they were powerless save to delegate two of their number to reside in Valladolid and render such assistance as was possible. It amounted to little save a testimony of sympathy, for no communication was allowed, but they advised with his counsel and performed what service they were able. This faithful watch was kept up during the long and weary years of the trial and when it was adjourned to Rome they went thither and remained to the end. The chapter also, almost monthly, sent memorials to Philip praying for a speedy and favorable end of the case. The great Dominican Order also felt keenly the disgrace inflicted on its distinguished member and exerted itself in his favor as far as it could. The Spanish episcopate also was greatly perturbed, not knowing where the next blow might fall and the scandal throughout the land was general.[185]

Philip had disembarked at Laredo on August 29th. Valdés evidently felt that some excuse was necessary for action so much more decisive than that prescribed by the king and, in a letter of September 9th, explained to him that Carranza was delaying his movements in order to meet him on his arrival at Laredo; that he was working in Rome to impede the matter; that the infamy of his position was daily spreading and that the auto de fe prepared for the Lutherans could not take place while he was at liberty. Seeing that the effort to entice him to Valladolid had failed, it was resolved to bring him there, which was done quietly and without disturbance. He had been well treated and would continue to be so and the king might rely on the affair being conducted with all rectitude. An intimation, moreover, that all his property had been sequestrated indicates that the financial aspect of the matter was deemed worthy of being called to the royal attention and the whole tone of the letter shows that Carranza's imprisonment was predetermined. The allusion to his design of meeting the king at Laredo disposes of the plea that he was suspected of flight and the fact that the auto de fe of the Lutherans did not take place until October 8th is a test of the flimsiness of the reasons alleged.[186]

Carranza's treatment was vastly better than that of ordinary prisoners confined in the cells of the secret prison. He was asked to select his attendants, when he named six, but was allowed only two--his companion, Fray Alonso de Utrilla and his page, Jorje Gómez Muñoz de Carrascosa.[187] Two rooms were allotted to the party--rooms without provision for the needs of human nature, with windows padlocked and shutters closed, so that at times the stench became unendurable. The foul atmosphere brought on a dangerous illness in which Carranza nearly perished; the physicians ordered the apartment to be ventilated, morning and evening, but all that the Suprema would permit was a small grating in the door, though at times it was left ajar with a guard posted at it.[188] Communication with the outside world was so completely cut off that when, in 1561, a great conflagration ravaged Valladolid, raging for thirty hours, destroying four hundred houses and penetrating to the quarter where the prison stood, the prisoners knew nothing of it until after reaching Rome.[189] The inquisitorial rule that all consultation with counsel must be held in the presence of an inquisitor was rigidly observed and also that which denied to prisoners the consolation of the sacraments.

***

Diego González, one of the inquisitors of Valladolid, was assigned to the special charge of Carranza who, in a long and rambling memorial to the Suprema represents him as treating him without respect, insulting him, suppressing his communications with the Suprema, fabricating answers, throwing every impediment in the way of his defence and aggravating, with malicious ingenuity, the miseries of his position. Some details as to the parsimony with which he was treated are almost incredible when we reflect that the Inquisition and Philip were enjoying the enormous sequestrated revenues of their prisoner.[190]

Although the papal brief only authorized the collection of evidence and its transmission to Rome with the person of the accused, the trial was conducted as though the Inquisition had full jurisdiction. It was commenced September 4th; as Carranza could not be taken to the Inquisition, Valdés and the Suprema came to his place of confinement, administered the customary oath and, according to routine procedure, gave him the first monition to discharge his conscience and confess freely. He replied by recusing Valdés as his judge on the score of enmity, to whom he subsequently added two members of the Suprema, Andrés Pérez, Bishop of Ciudad-Rodrigo and Diego de Cobos, Bishop of Jaen.[191] This recusation excited no little debate. There were some who pronounced it frivolous, others that it should be referred to the pope and others again that it should be decided by arbitrators. The latter opinion prevailed; Carranza and the fiscal named their arbitrators who rendered a decision in Carranza's favor on February 23, 1560. A new judge thus became necessary; Carranza's friends and the Dominicans were busy in Rome to have the case transferred thither, but at that time Philip's will was substantially law to Pius IV and, on May 4th a brief was obtained authorizing the king to appoint one or more bishops, or other just and experienced ecclesiastics, to hear the case and bring it to a proper conclusion. This conferred full jurisdiction and placed Carranza in a worse position than before. Strenuous representations must have been made to Pius for, on July 3rd he issued another brief defining his intention to be that the judges should conduct the case up to the point of sentence and then send the papers under seal to Rome, where he, in secret consistory, would decide it as a matter specially reserved to the Holy See.[192] This revendicated the papal jurisdiction, but at the same time it confirmed the usurpation of Valdés in formally trying Carranza in lieu of merely collecting testimony for a trial in Rome.

***

Philip leisurely postponed for a year the nomination of new judges. It may seem harsh to attribute this to the repulsive motive of prolonging the trial in order to enjoy the benefit of the sequestrated revenues of Toledo, but his financial needs were extreme and the temptation was great. In violation of the rule of the Inquisition that sequestrations were held for the benefit of the owner, to be accounted for unless confiscation was imposed, Philip had appointed Tello Giron administrator of the archbishopric, had procured his confirmation from Pius IV, in spite of the earnest remonstrances of the chapter, and was quietly absorbing the revenues, except such portion as the Suprema claimed for the expenses of Carranza and of the trial.[193] We happen to have evidence of this in the promise of a pension of twelve thousand cruzados on the see of Toledo, by which he won over Cardinal Caraffa to the Spanish interest, during the long conclave which resulted in the election of Pius IV[194], and the acquiescence of that pope in his enjoyment of the revenues was probably purchased by the promise of a similar pension of twelve thousand crowns to his favorite nephew, St. Charles Borromeo--a promise which he neglected to fulfil although, in 1564, it was reckoned that he had already received from the see some eight hundred thousand crowns. When he quarrelled with Pius for deciding the question of precedence in favor of France, the pope threatened to make him disgorge, but without success.[195] It is therefore easy to understand why the case promised to be interminable. The two years of the original brief expired in April, 1561; Pius extended it for two years more; then, by a brief of April 4, 1563, he renewed it for another year, at the same time prescribing that Carranza should be more mercifully treated; then, August 12, 1564, it was extended until January 1, 1565, and for another year still before the matter passed into the sterner hands of St. Pius V.[196] These delays it was the fashion to impute to Carranza. Bishop Simancas, who hated him for the proverbial reason odisse quem læseris, asserts that he was constantly employing devices to prevent progress, but this is absurd.[197] It was Carranza's interest to be released from his dreary incarceration and to be sent to Rome, where he felt confident of favor; the cumbrous estilo of the Inquisition enabled it to retard action at will, while the accused could do little either to hasten or to impede.

When Philip at last acted on the power to name Carranza's judges he appointed, March 13, 1561, Gaspar Zuñiga, Archbishop of Santiago who, on May 2nd, subdelegated the work to Bishops Valtodano and Simancas, both members of the Suprema and hostile to the prisoner. Carranza, as the result of his recusation, thus found himself practically remanded to Valdés, who was moreover shielded from direct responsibility. Carranza naturally recused his new judges, on the ground that they had voted for his arrest, but Philip airily dismissed the recusation, saying that if this were just cause no judge could try a culprit whose apprehension he had ordered.[198] In the following June Carranza was allowed to select counsel--a special favor for, as a rule, the accused was restricted to one or two lawyers who held appointments under the tribunal. He chose Martin de Azpilcueta and Alonso Delgado and also Doctors Santander and Morales, though of these latter we hear nothing subsequently. Azpilcueta, known also as Doctor Navarro, was one of the leading canonists of the time and a man of the highest reputation. He served faithfully to the end and probably thereby ruined his career in Spain, for he remained in Rome as a papal penitentiary.

After nearly two years of imprisonment the formal trial began July 30th and proceeded in most leisurely fashion. The rules of the Inquisition required three monitions to be given within ten days after arrest, but Valtodano and Simancas administered the first monition to discharge his conscience by confession on July 30th, the second on August 25th and the third on August 29th. He replied that for two years he had been desirous of learning the cause of his arrest and begging to be informed, which showed how ignorant he was of inquisitorial practice, for this was sedulously concealed from the accused, who was sternly ordered to search his conscience and earn mercy by confession. Then, on September 1st, the fiscal presented the accusation, in thirty-one articles, to each of which the accused was required to make answer on the spot. After this a copy was given to him on which to frame a more formal defence and for this he asked to have access to his papers--a fruitless request, for it was not the style of the Inquisition to allow the accused to have means of justifying himself.[199]

The articles of accusation were drawn not only from the Commentaries but from the confessions of the Lutheran heretics, the gossip and hearsay evidence industriously collected, and from the mass of papers seized when he was arrested. Many of these were not his own, but essays of others. There were extracts from heretic books which he had made at Trent for the purpose of refuting them; there were essays written when as a youth he had entered the Dominican Order, forty years before; there were notes of sermons taken down for practice when he was a student, and sermons preached in the refectory as required by the Rule of his Order; scattered thoughts jotted down for consideration and development; memoranda made when examining heretic Bibles and their comments for the Inquisition--in short all the vast accumulation of a man who for forty years had been busily studying and teaching and preaching and writing and wrangling on theology.[200] All the intellectual sins of youth and manhood had been scrutinized by malevolent eyes and he was called upon to answer for them without being allowed to know from what sources the charges were brought. There was in this no special injustice inflicted on him--it was merely the regular inquisitorial routine.

***

Thus a year passed away and, on June 5, 1562, the fiscal presented a second accusation, for there was no limit to these successive charges, each of which could be made to consume time. These new articles were mostly based on rumors and vague expressions of opinion, for all who were inimical, secure in the suppression of their names, were free to depose as to what they thought or imagined and it was all received as evidence. These he answered as best he could and he succeeded in identifying the names of some of the adverse witnesses. Then he presented a defence, doubtless drawn up as customary by his counsel, for it was clear and cogent, bearing little trace of his discursive and inconclusive style. In support of this he handed in a long list of witnesses to be examined, including Philip II and the Princess Juana, but the fiscal, passing over the royalties, objected to the rest on the ground that they were friends of Carranza--hostile testimony was admitted from any source, but that which was suspected of favorable partiality was rejected. As a principle, this was recognized in inquisitorial practice, but it was not habitually applied with so much rigor.[201]

On August 31, 1562, Carranza addressed an earnest appeal to Philip, reminding him of his command, in April, 1559, to trust in him alone. Three years had passed in prison, his case had scarce more than begun and promised to be interminable. His judge, the Archbishop of Santiago, had not delegated full powers to Valtodano and Simancas; questions arose which they could not or would not decide and, when these were submitted to the archbishop, months elapsed before an answer was received. On January 19th his counsel had issued a requisition on the archbishop to come and hear the case personally or to grant full powers to his delegates, but up to the present time no reply had come. Never in the world, he said, was justice administered in this fashion, and he despairingly entreated Philip to expedite the case or to permit him to appeal to the pope.[202] Whether or not this cry from the depths reached Philip, it produced no effect.

By this time the affair had become a European scandal. The bishops assembled at the third convocation of the Council of Trent felt it acutely, both as an opprobrium to the Church and an attack on the immunities of their order. Philip was aware of this and, in letters of October 30th and December 15, 1562, to his representative at Trent, the Count of Luna, and to Vargas, his ambassador at Rome, he gave instructions to prevent its discussion and to ask the pope to order his legates to see that the Council kept its hands off from the Spanish Inquisition.[203] It was with difficulty that the council could be restrained. In the early months of 1563 the legates repeatedly reported that it ardently desired him to evoke the case and order the papers sent to Rome. In reply Pius earnestly disclaimed indifference; he had urged the matter until Philip's temper showed that further pressure would disrupt the concord so necessary to the universal good. This did not satisfy the bishops, who persisted till Pius assured them that he had seen the earlier papers in the case and could affirm that Carranza's imprisonment was not unjust; he promised that he would not permit delay beyond April, 1564, and that he would render a just judgement.[204] If the bishops could not help their captive brother, they could at least provide for their own safety and this they did by a decree which greatly strengthened a declaration adopted in 1551 concerning the exclusive papal jurisdiction over bishops.[205]

There was another way in which the council sought to aid Carranza. It had a standing congregation employed in compiling an Index of prohibited books. The Commentaries came legitimately before it and, after examination, it was pronounced, June 2, 1563, to be good and Catholic and most worthy to be read by all pious men. The secretary of the congregation, Fra Francesco Forerio, issued a certificate of this, conferring licence to print it, and Pius followed, June 23rd, with a papal licence to the same effect. The Count of Luna was greatly exercised at this and was aided by the celebrated scholar, Antonio Agustin, then Bishop of Lérida. Matters went so far that the Legate Morosini dreaded the disruption of the council and peace was only restored by withdrawing the certificate of approbation. A copy had been given to Carranza's friends which they were forced to surrender.[206] Philip's indignation at this, as expressed in a letter to Luna, of August 2nd, was too late to be of service and is important only from its statement that he considered the affair of Carranza to be the most momentous that he had in connection with the council.[207]

Meanwhile the case was dragging on, one series of charges being presented after another, until the aggregate was over four hundred, each of which furnished opportunity for discussion and procrastination.[208] Besides the financial motive for this delay, Philip was now engaged in a struggle with Rome to protect the Inquisition from the consequences of its own evil work. There was nothing in his eyes more important than to preserve and augment its privileges, and his jealousy of any attempt at interference by the Holy See was an overmastering passion. His secret object was to arrogate to it complete jurisdiction over bishops and prevent the final submission of the case to papal decision.

***

Pius IV, to do him justice, felt keenly the humiliating position in which he was placed by the overbearing determination of Philip, but each attempt at self-assertion only rendered more evident the contempt in which he was held. More than once he wrote to the Archbishop of Santiago rebuking him for the long delay which kept Carranza in prison while the case made no advance. He named January 1, 1564, as the limit of the archbishop's commission, after which the process, whether completed or not, was to be forwarded to Rome. The limit passed without obedience to his commands and he wrote again, expressing high displeasure at the contumacy which doomed such a man to grow old in the squalor of a prison without law or justice. Again he ordered the case, whether completed or not, to be sent to Rome; if there were delay, all concerned were ipso facto anathematized, deprived of all dignities and functions and rendered infamous and incapable of restoration; all letters granting jurisdiction were revoked and the case was evoked to Rome for decision. Carranza himself was to be delivered forthwith to the nuncio, who was empowered either to keep him in honorable custody or to liberate him on bail. These were brave words, but there was no heart to back them up with action and, when they were disregarded, he extended, on August 12th the Archbishop's commission until January, 1565, after which, as previously ordered, the case was to be transmitted to Rome, and there was a significant absence of the minatory tone so prominent in the previous briefs.[209]

Encouraged by this evidence of weakness, on November 24, 1564, Philip sent Rodrigo de Castro to Rome on a mission to have Carranza abandoned to the Inquisition, significantly instructing him not to disdain whatever means he might find necessary to win over everybody of influence. Even the unlimited bribery thus planned failed of success, although the secondary object of procrastination was effected. Castro commenced by demanding, in a private audience, that the case be abandoned to the Inquisition, but refused to put the demand in writing. Then he lowered his tone and the pope agreed to send a special legate to Spain to review the case and pronounce sentence, but Castro insisted that the Suprema and such prelates as the king might select should be adjoined to the legate. This the pope refused, but there was some misunderstanding about it, and when Castro saw the commission drafted for the legate he was furious. He sought an audience and accused the pope of breaking his word; Pius lost his temper and said that in this whole business he had been treated like an ass; the affair was his and he would do as he pleased. Thus rebuffed, Castro poured forth his griefs to Cardinal Borromeo and declared that, if the legate went to Spain with such a commission, he would not get a real. This assertion may seem enigmatical to modern ears, but it is explained by the remark of the shrewd French ambassador, when reporting to Charles IX the arrival of the legate, that the case of Carranza and the use of his legatine faculties would bring him much money.[210]

The Holy See has rarely sent abroad a body so distinguished as this legation, predestined to failure. The special legate A LATERE was Cardinal Buoncompagni, afterwards Gregory XIII, accompanied by Archbishop Rossano, subsequently Urban VII, Fra Felice Perretti, afterwards Sixtus V and Giovanni Aldobrandini, subsequently cardinal and brother of Clement VIII. The legate had been given discretional power as to admitting Spanish associates, but he found on arrival at Madrid, in November, 1565, that the demand made on him was the impossible one which Pius had refused to Castro--the whole Suprema and prelates, amounting in all to fifteen Spaniards. He offered to admit two as against two of his associates, but he would do no more. As he wrote to Pius, the terror inspired by the Inquisition was beyond belief; to admit a majority of Spaniards would be to invite injustice, for the acquittal of Carranza would be the conviction of the Inquisition and any one who had the courage to bring this about would be exposed to lifelong persecution.[211] Of course Philip was firm, as his object was to baffle the legate, but discussion was cut short when the news came of the death of Pius IV, December 9th. Buoncompagni departed in haste to participate in the conclave; he was met at Avignon with the intelligence of the election of Pius V, January 7, 1566, in spite of which he continued his journey to Rome.[212]

***

Pius IV had carried to an extreme his subservience to Philip. Pedro de Avila, one of Philip's agents, wrote, August 23, 1565, that Cardinal Borromeo assured him that the pope had done and was doing more than he had power to do in order to gratify the king; he had gone against the canons, the councils and the cardinals and, when recently he thought himself to be dying, nothing weighed on his conscience more heavily than this.[213] His successor was a man of different stamp. To few popes does Catholicism owe more than to St. Pius V, for, while pitiless in his persecution of heresy, his recognition of the need of reform and his unbending resolution to effect it, regained for the Church much of the respect which it had forfeited. The Spanish agents speedily found that in the matter of Carranza he was incorruptible and intractable. As the ambassador Zuñiga plaintively reported to Philip, February 23, 1566, "He is certainly well-intentioned but, having no experience in affairs of state and no private interests, which are the two things that ordinarily make popes yielding, he fixes his eyes on what he deems just and is immovable."[214] As cardinal-inquisitor and Dominican he had been favorably inclined to Carranza, whose friends received with hope the news of his accession. They conveyed this by means of an arrow aimed at one of his window-shutters and he responded by casting out a paper, picked up by a person stationed for the purpose, in which he addressed the new pope in the words of Peter, "Lord, if it be thou, bid me come unto thee on the water" (Matt. xiv, 28).[215]

Pius did not need urging. One of his first acts was to despatch a messenger to Buoncompagni ordering him to remain and bring the affair to a conclusion, but the legate's Spanish experience did not incline him to return from Avignon. Doubtless his report brought conviction that justice was not to be expected in Spain, for Pius speedily made a demand for the person of Carranza and the papers so that he might decide the case. Accustomed to browbeat popes, Philip replied that the demand was offensive and contrary to the royal prerogative, as an attempt to change a matter unalterably fixed by the Holy See, and that it would not be entertained; the pope could commit the case to such persons as he pleased, provided they were Spaniards, otherwise, if Carranza should linger in prison until he died, the responsibility would not be with those who had offered every possible alternative. This audacious answer only strengthened the determination of Pius, who summoned Zuñiga and told him to tell his master that he exposed himself to all the indignation of the Holy See, for the pope was resolved to carry the matter to a conclusion. Zuñiga was silenced and could only report to Philip the terrible earnestness of Pius, from which there was no hope of diverting him.[216]

That he was in deadly earnest is apparent in his brief of July 30th, which he caused to be privately printed and sent copies to the nuncio Rossano, with an autograph letter of August 3rd, commanding its rigid execution. After dwelling on the injustice and scandal of the treatment of Carranza, he deprived Valdés, the Suprema and all concerned of jurisdiction in the case. Under pain of excommunication and suspension of functions, Carranza was to be set at liberty and, after appointing a vicar for his see of Toledo, was at once to present himself to the pope for judgement. Under pain of the indignation of God and of the apostles Peter and Paul and of excommunication, all the papers in the case were to be delivered in Rome within three months, and any one impeding the execution of these commands incurred excommunication and suspension from office.[217]

By this time Pius was known as a man who was not to be trifled with, but Valdés and the Suprema were ready to risk a rupture with the Vicegerent of Christ rather than to remit their victim to his judgement. When Philip consulted them they urged him not to permit even a copy of the process to be sent to Rome, much less Carranza's person, lest he should impair his prerogatives. They asserted that the papal brief had given ample power both to prosecute and to sentence and that, having been granted, it could not be withdrawn; that, under the papal concessions to Ferdinand and Isabella, the Spanish Inquisition was wholly independent of Rome and that, if the episcopal character were successfully urged in this case, some other excuse would be found in other cases.[218]

***

Valdés might be willing to risk a schism, but Philip drew back; it was not to be thought of that the Catholic king should incur excommunication, and he recognized what strength the heretic cause throughout Europe would derive from such a quarrel in such a cause. Still he dallied, until Pius forced Valdés to resign and threatened to lay all Spain under interdict.[219] He had encountered a will stronger than his own and Antonio Tiepolo, the Venetian envoy, is doubtless correct in saying that no other pope but Pius could have carried his point.[220] The pressure became irresistible and he yielded. Carranza, under charge of the hated inquisitor Diego González and guarded by a body of troops, left Valladolid December 5th, reaching Cartagena on the 31st, where he was confined in the castle until April 27, 1567, awaiting the arrival of the voluminous papers of the case, when he was placed on the admiral's ship which was conveying the Duke of Alva on his fateful way to Flanders. Civita Vecchia was reached May 25th and Rome May 28th, where he was confined in the Castle of Sant' Angelo--a second imprisonment that was to last for nine years. It was much less harsh than the previous one; besides his two faithful attendants he was allowed two others; he was assigned apartments in the quarters reserved for archbishops, he was sometimes permitted to leave his room under guard and enjoy the landscape, and at the first jubilee he was admitted to confession, although communion was still denied.[221]

The case promised to be as interminable in Rome as it had been in Spain. The anxiety of Pius for a thorough investigation caused endless delays, which were skilfully improved by the agents of the Inquisition. The enormous mass of papers reached Rome in the utmost confusion and some portions were lacking which had to be sent for. Then they had to be translated, as well as the voluminous Commentaries, which consumed a year. Philip was frequently sending new opinions and statements and Pius ordered all of Carranza's writings, and even notes of his lectures taken by students, to be searched for and brought to Rome. He formed a special congregation of seventeen consultors, including four of the Spaniards who had been concerned in the case, with Ramírez as the fiscal. When all was ready the congregation met weekly under the presidency of the pope; the Spaniards insisted on his presence and, as his other duties frequently prevented this, the affair dragged on from year to year. Philip followed it with intense anxiety, as shown in his correspondence with Zuñiga. Thus a long letter of instructions, June 6, 1570, tells the ambassador to assure the pope that everything had been done in Spain with the most minute deliberation; there is an almost childish insistence on the opinions of some obscure theologians as to Carranza's guilt, and it is pointed out that, if he is acquitted, he will teach and preach with greater authority than before and the whole prosecution will have been a blunder. All this, he says, should have weight with the pope, who is moreover to be threatened with what the king may find it necessary to do if the sentence is warped by personal considerations. Foolish communications of this kind were reiterated until, August 12, 1571, Pius, in an autograph letter, alluded to the repetition of these insinuations, which he declared to be groundless and, in dignified terms, warned Philip not to let his pious zeal get the better of his discretion.[222]

***

The Spanish tactics of delay were successful. Pius V died, May 1, 1572, without having published a sentence. Whether one was framed or not is a disputed question. Salazar tells us that it was drawn up, but that Pius, before publication, desired to submit it to Philip and sent it by his chief chamberlain, Alessandro Casale, who was detained by bad weather and other accidents until after the death of the pope. Llorente gives the details of the sentence as absolving Carranza of the charges but maintaining the prohibition of the Commentaries in the vernacular, with permission to translate it into Latin after removing the doubtful expressions. Simancas, who was one of the inquisitors employed on the case in Rome, says positively that Pius died without framing a sentence; that when Carranza's friends claimed that he had done so, and urged his successor, Gregory XIII, to publish it, the latter offered twenty thousand crowns to any one who would produce it and thus save him the task of reviewing the case.[223] However this may be, Pius was convinced of Carranza's innocence. He allowed the Commentaries to be publicly sold in Rome; when the fiscal Salgado petitioned for its suppression, he made no answer and, when Salgado insisted upon it in the congregation, he replied angrily that he did not consider it subject to suppression and that they had better not by persistence force him formally to approve it by a motu proprio.[224]

Gregory XIII was not liable to the reproach bestowed by Zuñiga on Pius V of indifference to personal and worldly considerations. He was quite accessible to them and realized fully the importance to the Holy See of keeping on good terms with the Spanish master of Italy. His experience as the Legate Buoncompagni had sufficiently acquainted him with Philip's temper and, when Carranza's friends naturally expected him to take the matter up where the death of Pius had left it, he insisted on going over it personally from the beginning. As he could give but fragmentary attention to it he was thus able to postpone committing himself for some years. This gave Philip opportunity to gather fresh testimony. By means not the most gentle, the survivors of Carranza's friends, who had approved of the Commentaries, were induced to retract. The three bishops, Guerrero, Blanco and Delgado condemned propositions by the hundred, drawn from works submitted to them as Carranza's and they exculpated themselves from their approval of the Commentaries by saying that they had not then seen his MS. writings and, in view of his reputation, they had sought to give a Catholic sense wherever possible. Other opinions were industriously collected; Gregory made a decent show of resistance to admitting fresh testimony at this late day, but yielded to Philip's threats of what he might find necessary to do in case his desires were thwarted, and thus excuses, if not reasons, were afforded for reaching a different conclusion from that of Pius V.[225]

As the time approached at which it was understood that the long protracted case would be terminated, Philip's anxiety increased. An autograph letter of February 16, 1575, to Pope Gregory, strongly urged Carranza's speedy condemnation, in view of the dangers which he had represented to Pius, and asked the fulfilment of a promise to communicate to him the sentence before publication. Whether such promise was made or not, Gregory refused to submit it to him, but intimation of what it was to be reached him and, on April 20th, he wrote vigorously to Zuñiga expressing surprise that the pope did not keep his word. As for Carranza, he was so thoroughly convicted of heresy that, according to inquisitorial routine, he ought to be burnt, or at least reconciled after abjuring all kinds of heresy. To allow him to abjure for vehement suspicion of heresy, with temporary suspension from his see, assumes that in time he will return to occupy the primatial church of Toledo, which would cause disturbance and scandal impossible to contemplate. The pope can well conceive the dangers which may follow, in Spain and elsewhere, by the mere example of such a criminal in such a position. Even if the suspension were perpetual yet, if God should remove his Holiness, a successor might lift the suspension unless Carranza is wholly deprived.[226]

This was passion and eloquence wasted, for the sentence had been pronounced six days before, on April 14, 1576. Whatever promise Gregory had made was kept to the letter but not to the spirit by announcing it to him on April 11th. Its provisions were shrewdly framed to turn the whole affair to the advantage of the Holy See, by keeping Carranza as a potential sword of Damocles hanging over Philip's head and meanwhile absorbing the revenues of the see of Toledo. The tenor of the articles was, as communicated to Philip:--

The Archbishop of Toledo will be declared vehemently suspect of sundry errors and as such will be required to abjure them.

He will be suspended and removed from the administration of his church for five years and subsequently at the pleasure of the pope and the Holy See.

During this time he will be recluded in a monastery in Orvieto, and not allowed to depart without special licence of the pope and the Holy See.

The pope will appoint an administrator of the church of Toledo, with disposition of all the fruits since the date of sequestration and during the suspension, which he will convert to the benefit of the Church and other pious uses, after deducting pensions, expenses and debts.

For the support of the archbishop there shall be assigned a monthly allowance of a thousand gold crowns.

Some salutary penances will be imposed on him.

***

His Catechism will be prohibited to be possessed, read, or printed.[227]

The errors of which he was declared vehemently suspect amounted to sixteen, professedly drawn from his writings. As they were merely the peg on which to hang the sentence they need not be recapitulated here and it suffices to say that on April 12th they were taken, with the abjuration, by Giantonio Fachinetti (afterwards Innocent XI) to the Castle of Sant' Angelo, where Carranza obediently signed the abjuration.[228]

The publication of the sentence was made with a solemnity befitting the conclusion of a case which, for seventeen years, had occupied the attention of Christendom. On April 14th, Carranza was brought from his prison to the Hall of Constantine, where Gregory occupied the papal throne under a canopy, the cardinals sat on benches and about a hundred other spectators stood around. After the opening formalities, Gregory handed a roll containing the sentence to Alonso Castellon, the secretary in the case, who read it aloud. It was very long, reciting the vicissitudes of the affair from the beginning and concluded with the articles as stated above. Then Carranza read his abjuration, as Simancas tells us, with impassive indifference, as though it related to another, after which he was led to the feet of the pope who expatiated on the mercy shown to him and told him he might expect more if he lived as he ought. He was then handed to the captain of the guard to be conveyed to the Dominican convent of

Santa Maria sopra Minerva and, as he was led out, in passing Cardinal Gambara, he quietly asked him to have his effects transferred to the convent. Evidently there was no sense of guilt or humiliation.[229] It was a fitting end to Gregory's disgraceful part in the tragedy that when, on April 20th, he formally notified Philip and the chapter of Toledo of the result, he mournfully expressed his regret that he had been compelled to condemn in place of acquitting, as he had hoped.[230]

As a penance, the pope ordered Carranza to visit the seven churches on Saturday of Easter week (April 28th) and offered him his own litter and horses for his servants, which he declined. It was noised abroad and the whole population was stirred to accompany him, for the compassion felt for him was universal. To avoid such a demonstration Gregory changed the day to Monday the 23rd, but notwithstanding this the throng of coaches and crowds of people changed the penance into a triumph. In the churches he was received with all honor and at the Lateran he celebrated mass but, towards the end of the day, a strangury commenced and, on his return to the convent, he took to his bed, never to leave it. The disease made rapid progress, during which the pope repeatedly sent consolatory messages and, on April 30th, his apostolic benediction, with an indulgence a poena et a culpa. The same day Carranza made a solemn declaration before his secretaries, affirming his unbroken adhesion to the faith; he received with fervor the last consolations of religion and passed away at 3 A.M. on May 2nd. He had entered his prison a vigorous man of 56 and had left it to die, a broken old man of 73.[231]

***

That an autopsy should have been ordered indicates that immediately doubts had arisen whether the death had been natural. The physicians reported some slight ulcers in one kidney and three stones in the gall-bladder, but in a position to do no harm and they attributed the retention to some "carnosities."[232] If suspicions existed of poison, they found no public utterance that has reached us, yet, in an age when the removal of an impediment was a recognized resource of state policy, the opportune and sudden death of Carranza is at least suggestive. We have seen how energetically Philip remonstrated against his being left in a position in which his return to Toledo was possible. His resumption of his see would have inflicted an incurable wound on the authority and influence of the Inquisition and have covered the monarch with mortification; it would have led to complications which, in the temper of the age, would have been insoluble. The injustice meted out to Carranza had rendered his death a necessity, if he was not branded as a heretic or disqualified as a bishop. Philip and he could not exist together in Spain. Besides, so long as Carranza lived, he was a dangerous weapon, in the hands of the papacy, to thwart Spanish policy by threats of removing the suspension or to extort concessions as the price of maintaining it. To attribute his sudden death to the zeal of Spanish agents in Rome, or to secret orders sent in advance, would do no injustice to a prince who did not shrink from the executions of Montigny and Lanuza or the assassinations of Escobedo and of William the Silent. It suited him, however, to accept it piously as a special dispensation of Providence. June 11th he replied to Gregory's letter of April 11th and 16th conveying copies of the sentence and abjuration. To persons, he said, of great learning and experience in Spain, the sentence was too lenient, but he recognized the pope's holy zeal and that God's hand had applied the proper remedy to avert greater evils.[233] Yet subsequently Morales, writing by Philip's order, concludes his account "They say that he apparently died as a saint, which I believe and that it was really so.... The Lord reserved him for the other life, a signal mercy which he grants to those whom it pleases him."[234]

In one respect the Inquisition was triumphant. The Commentaries, which had been approved by the Council of Trent and by Pius IV and Pius V, was condemned and prohibited with a callous disregard of consistency. The work remained in the successive issues of the Spanish Index until 1747, but was dropped in the latest one of 1790. Rome was even more persistent and retained it until 1899, though it disappeared, with much other antiquated lumber, in the recension of 1900. Yet Carranza's reputation as an orthodox champion of the Church seems to have suffered little from his prosecution and condemnation. Cardinal Quiroga, the inquisitor-general, who in 1577 succeeded him in the see of Toledo, caused his portrait to be placed with those of his predecessors, erected a tomb to his memory and, in June, 1578, performed solemn obsequies for him which lasted for a fortnight.[235] Odoricus Raynaldus, the official annalist of the Holy See, and Cardinal Pallavicini, the official historian of the Council of Trent, unite in saying that nothing serious was found against him, only vehement suspicion, and that on his death-bed he gave evidence not only of uncorrupted faith but of singular piety.[236] Nicholás Antonio tells us that for some mere presumptions, in the absence of legitimate proof of admitted impiety, he was ordered by abjuration to purge all suspicion of guilt.[237] Balmés, the champion of Catholicism, while admitting that, on the delicate subject of justification, his expressions lacked clearness, asserts that beyond doubt, in his own conscience before God, he was wholly innocent.[238] The dispassionate judgement of posterity has condemned the Inquisition in acquitting its victim.

If Philip failed to blast the memory of Carranza he at least succeeded in one of his objects. For seventeen years he had wrongfully enjoyed Carranza's sequestrated revenues, which, allowing for all deductions, must have yielded him two or three millions of ducats. Much must have been spent in the endeavor to convict the rightful possessor but, when the case was concluded, outstanding engagements were repudiated. During the trial in Rome, Don Lope de Avellaneda had borrowed twenty-six thousand ducats to pay the salaries of the parties employed in the notoriously expensive litigation of the curia, but the bills of exchange drawn to satisfy the indebtedness were returned dishonored. The Roman bankers were too important an adjunct of the curia not to be efficiently protected; on April 10, 1577, Gregory wrote to the inquisitors (probably of Toledo) to collect the amount, with interest up to the date of payment, from the revenue of the archiepiscopal table of Toledo, enforcing the demand, if necessary, by excommunication, interdict and the invocation of the secular arm.[239] Philip evidently maintained his hold on the revenues until the consecration of Archbishop Quiroga, in December, 1577, and his administrator would allow no diversion of the funds. Gregory, in the sentence had endeavored to provide for an accounting to him of the accumulations, but the effort was a failure. Like Philippe le Bel, in the analogous case of the Templars, Philip had a grip on the spoils which nothing could loosen. When, in 1581, Gregory sought to stimulate him to undertake an expedition against Queen Elizabeth, and promised him financial assistance towards so pious an enterprise, it turned out that this aid was merely the mesne profits of the see of Toledo which he had collected and had long since consumed.[240]

JURISDICTION CLAIMED

The affair of Carranza seems to have been regarded as weakening the position of bishops and, with the customary audacity of the inquisitors in extending their jurisdiction, the tribunal of Cuenca boasted or threatened that it would arrest the bishop. The services of the incumbent, Pedro de Castro, in furnishing evidence against Carranza, had been too recent to permit him to be hoisted by his own petard and Valdés, in a letter of June 17, 1560, rebuked the tribunal for its superserviceable zeal.[241] We have seen how the bishops, at the Council of Trent, endeavored to protect themselves by reserving to the pope exclusive right to pronounce sentence, but this was of small avail when he assumed the right to delegate his power as he pleased. When Sixtus V, January 25, 1586, issued a commission to the Cardinal Archduke Albert of Austria, as inquisitor-general of Portugal, it specifically subjected archbishops, bishops and patriarchs to his jurisdiction and that of his subdelegates.[242] As Portugal was under the Spanish crown, this served as a precedent when in December, 1629, the Inquisition desired to prosecute Gavino Mallani, Archbishop of Oristano in Sardinia, against whom it had gathered evidence that, since his consecration, in 1627, he had never been to confession or had celebrated mass, that he was a blasphemer, that he had a familiar demon confined in a ring, etc. The Suprema submitted to Philip IV the Portuguese commission and asked him to instruct his ambassador to procure a similar one for Spain or, failing this, to obtain a special brief for the case of Mallani. Philip ordered the necessary letter to be drafted for his signature, but the effort failed. Mallani was probably sent to Rome with the evidence, for he was deposed, being succeeded, in 1635, by Pedro Vico, while he did not die until 1641.[243] In spite of this recognition of lack of jurisdiction over bishops, we have seen (Vol. I, p. 501) that, in the quarrel with Manjarre de Heredia, Bishop of Majorca, in 1668, Inquisitor-general Nithard claimed that the Inquisition could prosecute him criminally. He had the effrontery to assert, in a consulta of February 5, 1668, that its possession of this power was so notorious and so completely established in practice as to require neither argument nor demonstration, and the infatuated queen-regent sustained him in summoning the bishop to appear for trial. In spite of an adverse decision in Rome, the Inquisition continued the prosecution, even after the expulsion of Nithard, and proceedings ceased only with the death of the bishop.[244]

The next case in which the Inquisition had to deal with a bishop was one which attracted much attention at the time--that of José Fernando de Toro, Bishop of Oviedo. We shall have to consider it hereafter in its relation with Illuminism and Molinism and need only say here that he was an adept in the dangerous mysticism which mistook the promptings of the senses for divine impulses and taught that union with God conferred impeccability. There was no doubt of his guilt, for he confessed freely when arraigned, and the Inquisition raised no question as to the exclusive papal jurisdiction. After elaborate investigation, Inquisitor-general Ibañez de la Riva Herrera put the mass of testimony into shape and sent it to Clement XI, November 27, 1709. On June 7, 1710, Clement authorized the imprisonment of Toro and the prosecution of the case, the results to be sent to him. After the death of Ibañez, a fresh commission was sent to his successor Giudice; in 1714 Clement granted permission to Toro to come to Rome, but this was not carried out until 1716, when he was confined in the Castle of Sant Angelo and his trial dragged on until 1719. Sentence was pronounced July 27th, with the same ceremonies as that of Carranza, the records of which were examined for the purpose.[245]

JURISDICTION ASSERTED

While the Inquisition thus freely admitted its incompetence to sit in judgement on bishops yet, in the next case that occurred, it asserted complete jurisdiction. Manual Abad Queipo was bishop-elect of Mechoacan (Valladolid) in Mexico where, although not consecrated, he was accepted by the chapter and governed the diocese as bishop, fulminating, in 1810, excommunication against Hidalgo and his followers, which was confirmed by the archbishop, Ligama y Beaumont.[246] He was thus fully recognized as bishop and it was probably the disturbed state of the land, during the rebellion of Hidalgo and Morelos, that prevented the assembling of bishops for his consecration. In the turbulence of the period he made enemies and an anonymous denunciation was lodged against him with the Mexican tribunal. It collected evidence and forwarded it, August 31, 1814, to the Suprema which referred it to the Madrid tribunal for investigation and report.

  The question as to the liability of bishops-elect is rather intricate, dependent on whether there has been presentation by the king or election by the chapter and confirmation by the pope,[247] but it would seem that Queipo was not subject to the Inquisition, nor were the charges matters of heresy. The Madrid tribunal recognized this in its report, October 27, 1814, saying that he should be cited to answer, provided his office did not stand in the way, at the same time admitting that the charges were the work of enmity and that at most he had been careless in conduct and ministration. Queipo returned to Spain and, on February 12, 1816, the Suprema ordered the tribunal to proceed. He refused to acknowledge the jurisdiction; the tribunal, May 16th, pronounced his reasons invalid and the Suprema, September 2nd took the high ground that no one could question its acts; when it has once declared itself a competent judge no private person could dispute it or impede the execution of its decrees. This could only be done by an authority feeling its jurisdiction invaded and, as there was none such in the kingdom, he was only prejudicing his case, which otherwise he could expedite and preserve the right of maintaining his claims by a protest which would be admitted. Queipo offered to answer the charges extra-judicially, but this was refused and he was told that if he did not present himself to answer them fully within three days, he would be prosecuted in contumacy. He yielded under protest and was spared the humiliation of appearing in the Inquisition, for Inquisitor Zorilla was ordered to conduct the audiences in the convent where he was residing, but during them he was ordered not to leave it and when they were over he was set at liberty, under command to present himself at the house of the fiscal whenever summoned. Thus, at the end of its career, the Inquisition successfully asserted its jurisdiction over a bishop, but he had his revenge. It was evidently no accident that, in the revolution of 1820, Queipo was made a member of the Provisional Junta of March 9th which, on the same day, caused Fernando VII to decree the extinction of the Holy Office.[248]

CHAPTER IV - THE EDICT OF FAITH

Occasional allusions have been made above to the Edicts of Faith, whereby the tribunals obtained knowledge of offences coming within their jurisdiction. This was one of the most efficient methods by which that jurisdiction was exercised and was brought home to the consciences of the people as an ever-present power. It rendered every individual an agent of the Inquisition, bound under fearful penalties spiritual and temporal, to aid it in maintaining the purity of the faith and, at the same time, it made every man conscious that his lightest word or act might subject him to prosecution by that terrible court whose very name inspired dread. No more ingenious device has been invented to subjugate a whole population, to paralyze its intellect and to reduce it to blind obedience. It elevated delation to the rank of high religious duty, it filled the land with spies and it rendered every man an object of suspicion, not only to his neighbor but to the members of his own family and to the stranger whom he might chance to meet. Continued through generations, this could not fail to leave its impress on the national character. Even Mariana, in enumerating the results of the Inquisition, ventures to allude to the cautious reserve which it rendered habitual among Spaniards.[249]

A somewhat crude prototype of the Edict of Faith is found in the old Inquisition, when inquisitors visited their districts and, at each town, summoned an assembly of the people, preached to them and caused to be read an edict calling upon all the inhabitants to come forward within a specified time and reveal anything that might tend to the suspicion that any one was a heretic, under pain of ipso facto excommunication, removable only by them or by the pope.[250] While this was nominally preserved in the Aragonese Inquisition, that institution had become so inert that we may assume that the inquisitors no longer visited their districts or had occasion to issue edicts. In Castile, when the Inquisition was founded, this practice was evidently unknown, for the Instructions of 1484 merely order that when the inquisitors open their tribunal in any town, after the sermon they shall publish a monition with censures against all who resist or contradict them.[251] By 1500, however, the efficacy of what became known as the Edict of Faith had been discovered, and Inquisitor-general Deza, in ordering yearly visitations of the districts, specifies that, on arriving at every town or village, a general edict shall be issued, summoning those who know anything of heresy to come forward and reveal it.[252] The form of this was probably the same as that which, in the same year 1500, the inquisitors of Sicily, Dr. Sgalambro and Montoro Bishop of Cefalù, issued, requiring all cognizant of heresy to denounce it within fifteen days, promising secrecy to the informer and threatening with prosecution, as fautors of heresy, those who failed to do so.[253] In Catalonia, the Concordia of 1512, in alluding to the edict requiring the denunciation of all offences against the faith, shows that it was already an established custom,[254] while, in 1514, the Instructions of Inquisitor-general Mercader prove that the various offences included in the expanding jurisdiction of the Inquisition were specifically enumerated, for the general term of heresy no longer sufficed.[255] The effect on the people of these proclamations, with their threats and anathemas, is vividly expressed in the description of the terror excited by the publication of the edict, when the tribunal of Jaen made a raid on Arjona.[256]

DETAILS OF THE EDICT

As, in the course of time, new fields of activity were opened to the Inquisition the enumeration of offences requiring denunciation grew to be a long and detailed catalogue, in which all the acts by which they could be recognized were specified so that there could be no excuse for omission. The simplest and oldest formula which I have met is that published in Mexico at the installation of the Inquisition, in 1571, and, in view of its comparative brevity, it is given in the Appendix. Subsequently the edict grew to portentous dimensions, the purport of which can be gathered from an abstract of that of 1696.

It begins by reciting that the fiscal has represented that for some time there has been no visitation or inquest made in many places of the province, whereby numerous crimes against the faith remain unpunished. Seeing this complaint to be justified, the edict is addressed to every one individually, so that, if he has known or heard say that any one, living or dead, present or absent, has done or uttered or believed any act, word or opinion, heretical, suspect, erroneous, rash, ill-sounding, scandalous or heretically blasphemous, it must be revealed to the tribunal within six days. Then follows an enumeration of all Jewish rites and customs; then similar lists concerning Mahometanism, Protestantism and Illuminism; then, under the heading of "Diversas Heregias," follow blasphemy, with specimens of heretical oaths; keeping or invoking familiar demons; witchcraft; pacts tacit or expressed with the devil; mixing for this purpose sacred and profane objects and attributing to the creature that which belongs to the Creator; marrying in Orders; solicitation of women in confession; bigamy; saying that there is no sin in simple fornication, in usury, or perjury, or that concubinage is better than marriage; insulting or maltreating crucifixes or images of saints; disbelieving or doubting any article of faith; remaining a year under excommunication or despising the censures of the Church; having recourse to astrology, which is described at length and pronounced fictitious; being guilty of sorcery or divination, the practices of which are described with instructive profusion; possessing books condemned in the Index, including Lutheran and Mahometan works and Bibles in the vernacular; neglecting to perform the duty of denouncing what has been seen or heard, or persuading others to omit it; giving false witness in the Inquisition; concealing or befriending heretics; impeding the Inquisition; removing sanbenitos placed by the Inquisition; throwing off sanbenitos or non-performance of penance by reconciled penitents, or their saying that they confessed in the Inquisition through fear; saying that those relaxed by the Inquisition were innocent martyrs; non-observance of disabilities by reconciled penitents, their children or grandchildren; possession by scriveners or notaries of papers concerning the above-enumerated crimes. Confessors, moreover, were ordered, under the same penalties, to withhold absolution from penitents who had not denounced all offences coming to their knowledge.[257] This was a tolerably searching grand inquest in which the whole population was summoned to assist, and the ceremonies of its publication were designed to render it as impressive as possible.

On the Saturday previous, a proclamation was made by the inquisitors, requiring all persons over the age of twelve (or of fourteen in some texts) to assemble to hear the edict and, on the following Sundays to hear the anathema, under pain of excommunication and of fifty ducats.[258] In the smaller towns this proclamation was made by the town-crier or, if there were none, by house-to-house notification. The next day, at the offertory in the mass, the edict was to be read slowly, distinctly and in a loud voice, after which the priest was to explain the obligation to denounce whatever was known of the living and of the dead, of themselves or of others, and the peril of omitting it; it was not to be talked about but was to be done directly, even if it was known that others had done so, otherwise the penalty was incurred.[259]

In larger cities, especially the seats of tribunals, the ceremonies were more imposing. In Seville, for instance, on the afternoon of Saturday before the second Sunday of Lent, the familiars assembled on horseback at the castle of Triana, where they formed a procession with drummers and trumpeters and the town-crier to escort the alguazil mayor and one of the secretaries of the Inquisition. This wound through the city, stopping at eight principal places, to publish the proclamation and to order that there should be no sermons in other churches on the days of the publication and anathemas. Then, on those Sundays, other processions were timed to meet the inquisitors at the doors of the cathedral and San Salvador--the churches designated for the ceremonies. Inside, the secretary, at the proper time, mounted the pulpit and read the edict; the sermon followed and then the mass was resumed.[260]

THE ANATHEMA

When the six days allowed for denunciation or confession had elapsed, a second proclamation was made, reciting the former one and adding that the fiscal complained that many had not complied with it and he demanded the fulmination of the censures in the most aggravated form. An edict was therefore addressed to all priests requiring them at high mass, when the people were assembled, to denounce as publicly excommunicated and anathematized all who had not obeyed the first edict, sprinkling holy water to drive away the demons who kept them in their toils and praying Christ to bring them back to the bosom of the Church. If they persisted in contumacy, all faithful Christians were ordered within three days to withdraw from all intercourse with them, under pain of similar excommunication. Both those who should have confessed and those who should have denounced, but who continued contumacious, were involved in the anathema pronounced on the third Sunday.

This was an awe-inspiring solemnity. The clergy marched in procession; the cross was covered with black and two flaming torches were on the altar, where the priests stood in profound silence during the reading of the curse.--"We excommunicate and anathematize, in the name of the Father and of the Son and of the Holy Ghost, in form of law, all apostate heretics from our holy Catholic faith, their fautors and concealers who do not reveal them, and we curse them that they may be accursed as members of the devil and separated from the bosom and unity of the holy Mother Church. And we order all the faithful to hold them as such and to curse them so that they may fall into the wrath and indignation of Almighty God. May all the curses and plagues of Egypt which befell King Pharaoh come upon them because they disobey the commandments of God! May they be accursed wherever they be, in the city, or in the country, in eating and in drinking, in waking and in sleeping, in living and in dying! May the fruits of their lands be accursed and the cattle thereof! May God send them hunger and pestilence to consume them! May they be a scorn to their enemies and be abhorred of all men! May the devil be at their right hand! When they come to judgement may they be condemned! May they be driven from their homes, may their enemies take their possessions and prevail against them! May their wives and children rise against them and be orphans and beggars with none to assist them in their need! May their wickedness ever be remembered in the presence of God! May they be accursed with all the curses of the Old Covenant and of the New! May the curse of Sodom and Gomorrha overtake them and its fire burn them! May the earth swallow them alive, like Dathan and Abiram for the sin of disobedience! May they be accursed as Lucifer, with all the devils of hell, where may they remain with Judas and the damned forever, if they do not acknowledge their sin, beg mercy and amend their lives!" Then the people responded Amen! while the clergy again marched in procession, chanting the Psalms Deus laudem meam and Miserere, to the chapel or altar. The great bells tolled as for a death and the bearers of the torches extinguished them in the font of holy water saying "As these torches die in the water, so will their souls in hell!" and the procession was resumed to the sacristy. After this, the edict continues, any one knowing these things and not revealing them, and remaining contumaciously and persistently thus for a year, is held suspect in the faith and shall be prosecuted with all the rigor of the law.[261]

Thus all the resources of religious terrorism were exhausted to impress upon the popular conscience the supreme duty of denouncing kindred and friends for the slightest act or word which might be held to infer suspicion of heresy or of the varied classes of offences over which the Inquisition had succeeded in extending its jurisdiction. It is true that the constant abuse of anathemas in the pettiest quarrels with officials, lay and clerical, must have somewhat blunted their effect. It is also true that casuistry, early in the seventeenth century, had no difficulty in proving that, when the obligation to denounce involved danger to life or reputation, the natural law of self-protection overrode the positive law of denunciation, with its threat of excommunication.[262] Still, to those not trained in such subtilties and who piously believed in the power of the keys, it was impossible that this terrible cumulation of curses, temporal and spiritual, should not overcome natural affection and human kindliness. It was not the fault of the Inquisition if Spain was not converted into a nation of spies and informers, in which no man could trust those nearest and dearest to him.

ITS DISTRIBUTION

The Edict of Faith was published annually, on a Sunday in Lent, in cities which were the seat of a tribunal and, during the earlier times, elsewhere, when the inquisitors went on their visitations; indeed, we are told, in 1560, that it was of little service unless the inquisitors visited their districts, for people would not incur the labor and expense of coming from a distance and the publication was regarded as the chief object of the visiting inquisitor who was directed to see that it was made in the monasteries as well as in the churches.[263] Visiting their districts, as we shall see, was the duty most disliked by the inquisitors, which they shirked whenever possible, and, with the development of postal communication, it was easier and more speedy to send the printed edicts to commissioners for distribution. What was the total number thus annually showered upon the land we have no means of knowing, but it must have been large. In 1595, the Inquisitor Arevalo de Zuazo, reporting his visitation of the mountainous dioceses of Urgel, Vich and Solsona, states that he distributed six hundred copies among the parish churches, besides personally publishing it in all the towns. From a printer's bill of June 7, 1759, when the custom was declining, it appears that in Valencia the edition printed was four hundred and a list of churches in the city, in which it was posted, amounted to sixty-three.[264]

This device was not confined to Spain, though Rome was somewhat tardy in adopting it. The Congregation of the Inquisition issued, January 3, 1623 a brief edict, commanding the denunciation, within twelve days, of all heretics, under pain of excommunication removable only by it or by the pope.[265] This was followed, January 10, 1666, by one more in detail, specifying the offences to be denounced. It was universal in its character and therefore applied to Spain, but as usual the Spanish Inquisition maintained its independence and continued to employ its own more elaborate formulas.[266]

Although the annual publication remained the rule, there were occasional intermissions. In 1638, for instance, it was suspended without a reason being assigned and again in 1689 on account of the death of María Luisa, wife of Carlos II.[267] Local causes, also, sometimes interfered with it, especially when questions of etiquette arose, as that which we have seen at Valladolid, in 1635, over the point whether, at its reading, a bow should be made to the sacrament or to the inquisitors. Sixteen years later, we are told that since then there had been no reading of the edict at Valladolid and that in consequence, during the visitations of the inquisitors, other places refused to have it read, on the ground that this was not done in the city where there was a full tribunal.[268] A similar trouble arose at Quito, because the Audiencia refused to allow the commissioner of the Inquisition a seat with a cushion during the reading; for this, in 1699 and again in 1700, he appealed to the viceroy, stating that, in consequence of this, it had been many years since the edict had been published there.[269]

With the decline in the activity of the Inquisition, towards the close of the eighteenth century, there grew to be negligence in the annual publication. In 1775 the Suprema ordered that there should be no change with regard to it. A document of 1777 indicates that it was still customary, but on inquiry, in 1784, by the Suprema of the tribunals, whether or not it had been suspended, shows that it was falling into desuetude, and another of 1806, asking how long it had been since the publication ceased, indicates that it had become obsolete.[270]

ITS INFLUENCE

The efficacy of the Edict of Faith is incontestable, although, in 1578, the Inquisitor Francisco de Ribera, in reporting his visitation of the dioceses of Gerona and Elne and his publication of it in places which had never before been visited, complains that it did not render the people disposed to make denunciations, which he attributes to their limited intelligence.[271] In more enlightened centres its effectiveness is seen in the frequency with which accusers preface their charges with the statement that their attention has been called to the duty by the publication of the edict. It naturally set men to searching their memories for what they had seen or heard respecting the various offences so elaborately enumerated and described. For instance, the edict was published in Madrid on September 4, 1569 and, the next day, Hans de Evalo appeared before the inquisitor to denounce Hans Brunsvi and Costancio, two members of the royal Guarda Tudesca, for things which he had heard and known of them, but of which he had thought nothing until he heard the edict read.[272] It was the same in stimulating self-denunciation, whether through pricks of conscience or fear of accusation by others. Thus, in 1581 we have two cases following each other, in which Juan González and Bartolomé Benito accuse themselves of having, in conversation with their wives, asserted that fornication is no sin, for which both were duly penanced and fined. The wives were sent for and confirmed the confessions, which we may safely attribute to the fear that the spouses might be led to denounce them.[273]

The habit of delation in which the Spaniard was thus trained continued after the Edict of Faith ceased to be published and was stimulated by the assurance of immunity through the profound secrecy which denied to the accused all knowledge of his accuser. The records of the tribunals show how these were welcomed, no matter how flimsy was the evidence, nor through how many months it had passed. Thus, January 5, 1816, the Dominican Fray Vicente Manendo writes to the tribunal of Barcelona that he had heard Joseph Castellar of Manlleu say that, on Easter day, 1815, he had been discussing some pending suits with the advocate Balderich when the time came for hearing mass and he said "Let us go to mass" to which Balderich replied by a contemptuous expression. Instructions were therefore forthwith sent to the commissioner at Panelada to put the denunciation into formal legal shape for prosecuting Balderich. Informers thus were not put to the trouble of coming forward personally and facilities for delation were brought to every man's door. Thus on June 28, 1807 Dr. Pedro Reguart of Suria writes to the tribunal of Barcelona that he has a denunciation to make and asks that a commission be sent to some one in Suria to receive it. Full instructions were accordingly sent to the parish priest of Suria, when deposition was made to the effect that, eighteen months before, at the clinic in Barcelona, Reguart had seen, in the possession of a student named Pedro Sitzas, a book entitled Eusebio, which he understood to be prohibited, and a year ago he had also seen a copy in the hands of another student named Jaime Coll. In this case the tribunal, with rare moderation, only ordered its apparitor to seize the books in the hands of the students.[274] So carefully were accusers protected against recognition that when, in 1818, Don Francisco de Mora, a retired lieutenant of artillery, accused Don Thomas Sans, of the same corps, to the tribunal of Valencia, because, in a loose conversation between them, he had asserted that there was no sin in fornication, and when Mora found himself obliged to testify that another officer, Manuel Moreno was present, the tribunal dropped the case at his request because Moreno would have identified the source of the accusation.[275]

The very triviality of these cases is the measure of their importance. It was not merely the Judaizing converso or the secret Protestant, but the whole body of the Catholic nation that was exposed to prosecution and infamy for a thoughtless word, the denunciation of which was commanded by the Edict of Faith and invited by the impenetrable secrecy of the tribunal. The shadow of the Holy Office lay over the land and no one could feel sure that a trusted comrade might not at any moment become a spy and an informer, or might not repeat an incautious word until it reached some one who recognized the inexorable duty imposed on all--a duty more deeply felt by the conscientious than by those of easy morals.

***

There was, moreover, the fatal facility afforded for the safe gratification of malice, as in the case of Don Joseph del Campillo, whose merits raised him from obscurity to the position of finance minister under Philip V, in 1740. In 1726, when holding a responsible office in the administration of the navy, he had a quarrel with a Gerónimite fraile over the occupancy of a house. The fraile forthwith collected gossip about him, especially from a dissolute chaplain whom he had dismissed from the service, and all this was welcomed by the tribunal of Logroño, which commenced to gather testimony against him with a view to prosecution. It came to his ears through the boasts of the frailes as to what they had done, and the profound horror which seized him at the prospect of being dishonored for life, by the mere suspicion that he was liable to prosecution, shows how terrible a weapon the system placed at the service of malignity.[276]

***

In the life of a nation, outward calamities can be survived and recovery from their effects is but the work of time. Far more lasting and benumbing are the results of the perpetual and unrelaxing vigilance which seeks to penetrate into the secret heart of every man, to control his thoughts, to stifle their expression, to repress every effort to move out of a beaten and prescribed track, to destroy mutual confidence and to lead each individual to regard his fellows as the possible destroyers of his reputation and career. Such was the system imposed on Spain by the Inquisition, and its appropriate expression is found in the Edict of Faith.

CHAPTER V - APPEALS TO ROME

So long as the acts of the Spanish Inquisition were not final but were subject to revision by the Roman curia, its jurisdiction was incomplete. To emancipate itself from this it struggled for more than two centuries, aided unreservedly by all the power of the Spanish crown. This long-protracted and intricate contest is full of interest and merits a somewhat detailed investigation. Soon after the Inquisition commenced its work, complaints of its remorseless cruelty poured in upon the sovereigns. They sent around, as we are told, certain conscientious prelates to investigate and report, who informed them that four thousand houses had been abandoned in Andalusia, but this seems only to have inflamed Isabella's ardor and the business of vindicating the faith was prosecuted with undiminished energy.[277] The only refuge of the victims was the Holy See, which had always been open to appeals from the sentences of the Inquisition.

***

Papal predominance had its foundation in the universal supreme jurisdiction, original and appellate, of Rome in all matters of faith and the unlimited area of affairs contingent on faith. This had been gradually acquired during the dark ages and was strenuously upheld, as it was the source of wealth as well as of power, and without it the Bishop of Rome would speedily shrink to his original primacy of honor. That he should divest himself of it was not to be expected, especially for the benefit of inquisitors, whose jurisdiction was a delegation from him and whose claim to superiority over bishops was based on the functions of the latter being merely "ordinary" while theirs were "apostolic." It is true that Nicholas V, in his projected Castilian Inquisition of 1451, had granted jurisdiction without appeal, but this could have been withdrawn at any time and the whole attempt had been so soon forgotten that no allusion was ever made to it in the subsequent controversy. In the Old Inquisition, appeals to the pope were recognized, but it was an intricate and costly process, only possible to those familiar with canon law and, as the victims then were mostly peasants or ascetic missionaries, it was rarely employed and still more rarely successful.

Now, however, the situation was wholly different. The class assailed consisted largely of men of wealth or learning--merchants, bankers, lawyers, high officials, theologians and prelates, able to command the services of skilful canonists and ready to sacrifice a portion of their fortunes to save their persons from the stake and their estates from confiscation. The curia of the period, moreover, was notorious for shameless venality--a place where everything was for sale, from cardinalates to pardons, and where the supreme jurisdiction of the papacy was exploited to the utmost. It did not take long for the keen-witted Conversos to recognize that the mercy denied them in Spain could be bought in the open market of Rome and the curia, which had mourned the lost opportunity of sharing in the confiscations, welcomed the prospect of selling exemptions from confiscation.

Everything therefore pointed to an exercise of the supreme appellate jurisdiction of the Holy See which would seriously limit the activity of the Spanish Inquisition, or at least would confine it to those whose poverty rendered them unprofitable subjects of persecution. Ferdinand soon became alive to the situation and manifested little reverence for the papacy in his resolute resistance to the protection which it sold to all applicants.

CONFESSIONAL LETTERS

The earliest recourse was naturally to the papal Penitentiary. It had long been in the habit of selling confessional letters, empowering any confessor, whom the purchaser might select, to absolve him from all sins, including those reserved to the Holy See. Originally these were understood to be good only in the forum of conscience, but the further step was easily taken of making them effective also in the judicial forum, thus anticipating or annulling the action of the courts and selling immunity for crime as well as pardon for sin.[278] There was no difficulty in obtaining such letters for anyone, and they were sought by the Conversos as a means of protection in advance and of setting aside sentences after conviction. In the Appendix will be found a specimen, issued December 4, 1481, by the Major Penitentiary, to Francisco Fernández of Seville and his wife and mother. It purports to be granted by the direct command of the pope and authorizes the recipient to select any confessor who, after secret abjuration, can absolve him for all acts of heresy, apostasy, relapse and dogmatism and annul all sentences by whomsoever pronounced after trial and conviction, redintegrating him into the Church, removing all stain of heresy, restoring him to all his rights and releasing him from all punishment, only imposing on him salutary penance--which, at that period, was understood to be a money payment for the benefit of the poor, i. e. the Church or its members. A final clause grants the further faculty of overcoming all opposition by the use of censures under papal authority.

It was impossible for Ferdinand and Torquemada to allow the Inquisition to be reduced to impotence by the speculative activity of the curia in selling such exemptions, which were not only good for the future but had a retroactive effect in annulling its acts. No reverence for the Holy See could restrain them from visiting their wrath on all who were concerned in rendering effective this purchasable clemency. We have a glimpse at the methods adopted by both sides, in a notarial act, evidently part of a process to set aside a papal letter of a somewhat different kind, and to punish those engaged in its use, the narrative showing that all concerned felt that they were incurring serious perils. The notary, Anton Peláez, deposes that in Xeres de la Frontera he received from the Duke of Medina Sidonia a letter of April 16, 1482, calling him to San Lucar de Barrameda to draw certain business papers. He went and, while engaged on them in the house of Juan Matheos, on April 20th, at 2 P.M. a messenger summoned him to the duke, whom he found in company with the duchess, the Teniente de Bora, Fray Thomas, prior of the Order of Santa María de Barrameda, and others. Then entered Juan Ferrández of Seville, the duke's contador, or auditor, carrying a bull with a lead seal, said to be from the pope, Sixtus IV, and ordered Peláez to read it to the prior. He was alarmed and refused, but finally yielded to the entreaties of the duke and duchess. Then Fray Thomas refused to accept it, as he had been inhibited verbally by the inquisitors, and promised to produce the inhibition in writing within eight days. The duchess left the room in anger, but, in a quarter of an hour, Ferrández brought Fernando de Troxillo, prior of the universidad of Xeres and not of the church of San Salvador, as described in the bull. The duke told him that this made no difference and urged him to accept it, throwing his arms around him and promising that he would expose his whole rank and dignity to make good whatever he might suffer in person or property. Troxillo accepted the bull with the greatest reverence and kissed it. Then, as apostolic judge under it, he ordered Juan Matheos, cura and vicar of San Lucar, to absolve Ferrández and his wife of any sentence of excommunication, interdict, suspension etc. placed on him by the inquisitors, on his giving security, which was promptly furnished by Gonzalo Peráez, Ruy Perráez and Ferrand Riquel, swearing that Ferrández would stand to the mandates of the Church, as required in the bull. Thereupon Troxillo, as apostolic judge, ordered Juan Matheos to absolve Ferrández and his wife, which was duly performed. The duke's lawyers drew up an inhibition to the inquisitors, which the deponent engrossed; the duke wanted Troxillo to sign it, but the deponent privately advised him not to do so until he should consult his counsel at Xeres and, whether he did so or not, the deponent could not say.[279]

POWER OF THE PENITENTIARY

This gives us an inside view of the struggle to escape the Inquisition which was going on in every corner of the land. It was useless, for these papal letters were disregarded and the purchasers could look for no redress from the curia, for Pope Sixtus had no scruple in abandoning his customers. It was a lucrative business, this disposing of exemptions and then allowing them to be annulled for a consideration. Both sides thus contributed to the papal treasury and, as it all came from the Conversos in the end, the curia indirectly got its share of the confiscations, and the Inquisition was but nominally restricted. One device for accomplishing this is revealed in a cruzada indulgence, granted March 8, 1483, ostensibly in aid of the war with Granada, but, as Sixtus bargained for one-third of the proceeds, his share was sufficient inducement for sacrificing the purchasers of his confessional letters. A special clause of the indulgence empowered any confessor to absolve the possessor of it--the price being six reales--for killing or despoiling those seeking the Roman court, or for preventing the execution of papal letters, or for forbidding notaries to draw up acts concerning such letters, or for detaining them from those to whom they belonged,--all of which was evidently framed to allow the sovereigns to annul the papal briefs in any way they deemed best.[280]

Yet while Sixtus thus was content, for a moderate compensation, to permit those who were seeking his court to be detained or slain and to have his letters contemptuously annulled, yet when their market was threatened by the assertion that the Penitentiary was only a court of conscience and its absolutions were good only in the interior forum, his indignation burst forth in a bull of May 9, 1484, stigmatizing all such opinions as contumacious and sacrilegious. The Penitentiary, he declared, could grant absolutions good in either forum and those for the judicial forum were good in both spiritual and secular courts. This monstrous assumption, which claimed for the Penitentiary the power to anticipate or set aside the judgement of every criminal court in Europe, for the benefit of culprits who could pay the moderate fee demanded for its letters, was not merely a temporary policy adopted by Sixtus for this occasion. Having once been asserted, it was persisted in. Paul III, July 5, 1549, confirmed the bull of 1484 and subjected to the anathemas of the bull in Coena Domini all who called in question the validity of such letters; when confined to the forum of conscience they were sealed and addressed to the confessor, when intended for the judicial forum they were patent. As Paul died, November 10, 1549, before the publication of this brief, it was confirmed and issued, February 22, 1550, by Julius III.[281] It was the settled purpose of the Holy See of the period to continue this profitable business of selling pardons so long as purchasers could be found for them; they continued to plague the Inquisition and we shall see what stern measures Ferdinand found necessary for their suppression. Yet Ferdinand was justified and the curia was self-condemned for, when the Roman Inquisition was reorganized and found its operations similarly impeded by the letters of the Penitentiary, it ordered, September 26, 1550, its subordinates to pay no attention to them.[282]

Meanwhile the struggle continued in Spain. Isabella applied in 1482 to Sixtus to give her inquisitors power to pronounce final judgements that should not be subject to revision or appeal. He replied, February 23, 1483, that he would take counsel with the Sacred College, the result of which was a bull of May 25th, in which he conferred on Iñigo Manrique, Archbishop of Seville, appellate jurisdiction from the inquisitors, deputizing him in place of the pope for the Spanish dominions.[283] This expedient brought no relief to the Conversos. The inquisitors paid no respect to it and would-be appellants found that it was not safe to go to Seville for revision of their cases by the archbishop. It was the same with the letters of absolution that continued to be issued; they were disregarded and many fugitives who had procured them found on their return that they had been burnt in effigy during their absence and that the document on which they relied was of no avail. They needed something more and Sixtus was nothing loath to grant it. As early as August 2nd, he followed the bull of May 25th with another, for which we may safely assume that the Conversos paid roundly, for in it he evoked to Rome all pending cases of appeal, he ordered the Spanish bishops to protect at all hazards the bearers of papal letters of absolution, even to the invocation of the secular arm, and he entreated Ferdinand and Isabella to show mercy to their subjects as they hoped for mercy from God.[284]

STRUGGLES WITH THE CURIA

Whatever was paid for this was money vainly thrown into the bottomless sea of the curia. Eleven days later, with shameless effrontery, Sixtus wrote to the sovereigns that it had been issued without proper deliberation and that he suspended it. This reinstated Manrique as appellate judge, and Juan of Seville, who had carried the previous brief to the Bishop of Evora for multiplying, was brought, with his companions, before the archbishop, who condemned them.[285] The gold of the victims was vainly pitted against the unalterable will of the sovereigns, for the Holy See had no scruple in selling exemptions and abandoning the purchasers. The delegation to Archbishop Manrique by no means inferred that Sixtus relinquished his own profitable appellate jurisdiction and, to encourage appeals, it was necessary to manifest indignation when the inquisitors rated the papal action at its true value. How little they respected it is manifested in a brief of July 4, 1484, addressed to the inquisitors Miguel de Morillo and Juan de San Martin, reciting that the Dean of Mondoñedo, two canons of Seville and several others, whom they were prosecuting and whose property they had sequestrated, had appealed from them; that Sixtus had referred the cases to the Bishop of Terracina and some auditors of the Sacred Palace, at whose instance the inquisitors had been ordered to cease proceedings, to grant absolution ad cautelam and to lift the sequestration which deprived the parties of the means to carry on the appeal; that the inquisitors had not only flatly refused obedience and had kept possession of the property, but had constrained the appellants under oath and threat of censures not to prosecute the appeal or even to write to Rome, on the ground that they had the jurisdiction and would render judgement. Wherefore Sixtus now pronounces null and void all proceedings since the issue of the inhibitory order and prohibits further action under threat of excommunication; the sequestration is to be lifted and all the papers are to be sent to Rome.[286] There was no reason why this should command obedience more than the previous order and we may feel sure that the appellants fared no better in consequence. The case has interest only as a specimen of innumerable others which were bringing an abundant harvest to the officials of the curia, without affording relief to the victims, who were like a shuttlecock between two battledores, yielding sport to the players, as they were driven from one to the other.

Archbishop Manrique's position as appellate judge must also have been lucrative for, on his death in 1485, the succession was eagerly sought for and was obtained by the papal vice-chancellor, Rodrigo Borgia, but Ferdinand had had experience of him in Valencia and the sovereigns remonstrated so effectually that he was obliged to withdraw in favor of their nominee, Cardinal Hurtado de Mendoza, Bishop of Palencia.[287]

Sixtus IV had died, August 12, 1484, to be succeeded by Innocent VIII. The Inquisition might hope for an improvement, but was resolved to resist with greater energy than before, if the new pope should imitate his predecessor. In a series of instructions, issued December 6, 1484, Torquemada provided for a resident agent in Rome, whose expenses were to be defrayed from the confiscations; he complained of the extraordinary and illegal letters so profusely granted by Sixtus and announced that the sovereigns would suspend the operation of such letters, but that action would be withheld until it should be seen whether Innocent continued a practice so prejudicial.[288] Innocent must already have given evidence that his methods were the same as those of Sixtus, for, in less than ten days, Ferdinand issued, December 15th, a savage pragmática far more decisive than Torquemada had forecast, for it decreed death and confiscation for all who should use such letters, whether emanating from the pope or his subordinates, unless they should have received the royal exequatur, and all notaries and scriveners who should act under them or make transcripts of them were deprived of their offices.[289]

***

As a matter of course the change of pontiffs worked no change in the lucrative business, except that perhaps under Innocent the practice of taking money and betraying those who paid it became more unblushing than before and promises to both sides were made and broken with still greater facility. To this end, care was taken to maintain the papal jurisdiction, for when the new pope was asked to confirm or renew Torquemada's commission and power was asked for him to disregard the exemptions issued in blank for names to be filled in and absolutions granted on false confessions, and other abuses impeding in every way the Inquisition, Innocent turned a deaf ear and the commission was only renewed, not enlarged.[290] Then the sovereigns assumed the power denied to Torquemada and issued circular letters, July 29, 1485, addressed to all the ecclesiastical authorities, reciting how, to the scandal of religion, disregard of the royal pre-eminence and damage to the fisc, certain parties obtained bulls, rescripts, provisions and confessional letters, from Sixtus IV and Innocent VIII, to protect themselves in their crimes. As it is not to be supposed that the popes would do this knowingly, all such letters are suspended until the papal intention, after due information, can be ascertained and obeyed. Meanwhile no such briefs are to be enforced until after submission to the sovereigns for their approval.[291]

It is not easy to follow the rapid tergiversations of the pope, for the pledges given to either side were impartially violated almost as soon as given, the only explanation being that both sides could get what briefs they desired provided they were willing to pay what was demanded. For awhile the influence of Ferdinand and Isabella prevailed and, in a solemn repetition of Torquenada's commission, April 24, 1486, Innocent directed that all appeals should be made to him and not to the Holy See.[292] Still more emphatic was a disgraceful brief of November 10, 1487, by which he declared inoperative all the letters issued by the Penitentiary, whose purchasers he thus surrendered to the inquisitors, whom he authorized to proceed in spite of the inhibitions contained in them.[293] Possibly he may have recognized that this breach of faith was likely to damage the market by destroying confidence, for the ink was scarce dry on this brief when he issued another, November 27th, ordering that, when such letters were produced, they, or authentic copies of them, should be sent, with details of the case, and that, until his decision was announced, proceedings should be suspended.[294]

Ferdinand thereupon forbade the inquisitors to accept such letters, notwithstanding which their issue continued without intermission for, on May 17, 1488, Innocent declares that they should be invalid unless presented within a month of that date.[295] Simultaneous with this was an elaborate bull of the same date, doubtless procured by the Converses of Aragon, addressed to the Bishop of Majorca, reciting the daily appeals from the kingdoms of Aragon which were committed to judges in the curia who issued inhibitions to the inquisitors. As this impeded the Inquisition the pope evoked to himself all pending cases and committed them to the bishop to be decided without appeal, his commission continuing during the papal pleasure.[296] We may reasonably doubt whether Ferdinand permitted the bishop to exercise these functions; even if he did so the Conversos profited little, for the good bishop died in about six months and there is no trace of the appointment of a successor.

Yet when Ferdinand wanted to save those whom he favored from the Inquisition, he sometimes had recourse to procuring for them papal letters to which he granted his exequatur. He did this for his treasurer, Gabriel Sánchez and for the vice-chancellor of Aragon, Alonso de la Caballería; Gabriel Sánchez also obtained letters for his brothers Alonso and Guillen, which Ferdinand approved and had some difficulty, in 1498, in preventing the tribunal of Saragossa from seizing and suppressing them.[297] There was an even more significant recognition of the appellate power of the Holy See in the case of Gonsalvo Alfonsi, defunct, in 1493. The consulta de fe was unable to reach unanimity and, in place of referring it to the Suprema, the consultors referred it to Alexander VI, who, by brief of August 13th, appointed the Bishop of Córdova and the Benedictine Prior of Valladolid to decide the case, at the same time inhibiting the inquisitors from further cognizance.[298]

***

The year 1492 saw the conquest of Granada achieved and the death of Innocent VIII. The one event greatly increased the reputation and influence of Ferdinand and the other placed in the papal chair Rodrigo Borgia, better known as Alexander VI. Both men were unscrupulous, but the political situation brought them into close relations and the services rendered by the king to the pope--or still more, perhaps, the disservice which he could render--made the latter eager to gratify him. In 1494 he confirmed and enlarged the letters of Innocent VIII prescribing that appeals should be made to the inquisitor-general and not to the Holy See.[299] To render this effective he commissioned, as we have seen, one of the inquisitors-general, Francisco de la Fuente, as appellate judge to hear all cases. The brief of appointment, November 4, 1494, shows in what a tangled condition these matters had been brought by the shifting and shiftless papal policy, governed alone by the expectation of profit. It recites that Innocent VIII, at the instance of Spanish suspects of heresy, had committed their cases, both original and appellate, to various auditors of the Sacred Palace, where they remained pending for lack of evidence not obtainable in Rome, wherefore Innocent had evoked them all to himself, but had appointed no judge to hear them and no further progress was made. Besides, under their commissions, the said auditors had issued letters compulsory, inhibitory and citatory on inquisitors and other officials, in consequence of which they were under excommunication and against this they appealed. To put an end to these dangers and scandals, Alexander therefore evoked anew all these cases to himself and committed them to la Fuente, together with all arising in future, granting him full power for their final determination.[300]

Still the lucrative business of issuing letters of absolution and redintegration went on unchecked, until pressure from Spain, which was insufficient to restrain their manufacture and sale, at least induced Alexander to betray those who had bought them. On August 29, 1497, he issued a bull reciting how heretics, who had been burnt in effigy, had obtained from him absolution, rehabilitation and exemption from inquisitorial jurisdiction, to the scandal of the faithful, wherefore, at the request of Ferdinand and Isabella, he now withdraws and annuls all these letters, except in the forum of conscience.[301] Even this did not satisfy Ferdinand who, under the pretext that a papal secretary named Bartolommeo Florido had issued false ones, ordered the inquisitors to seize them when presented and send them to him in order that he might communicate with the pope about them. This was followed by decrees of the Suprema, January 8 and February 12, 1498, commanding all who had obtained absolutions and dispensations from Rome to deliver them within a given time to the inquisitors, who would forward them to the inquisitor-general for verification of their genuineness, thus obtaining possession of all letters, to the general terror of the owners. Ferdinand, as we have seen, was obliged to write to Saragossa to protect Alonso de la Caballería and the brothers Sánchez, while Isabella interceded, June 26th, for a servant of hers who had procured such a letter and could not produce it.[302] Then Alexander was called upon for a more absolute surrender of those who had dealt with him and, on September 17th, he addressed a brief to the Spanish inquisitors empowering them to proceed against all heretics, notwithstanding all letters of absolution and redintegration heretofore or hereafter issued, for all such letters were to be held as having been granted inadvertently.[303] What with Spanish fanaticism and papal faithlessness the Conversos were between the hammer and the anvil.

***

Their only recourse was exile. Many abandoned Spain and a portion of these found in Rome a refuge, for Alexander welcomed them in view of the heavy imposts which they paid for safety and toleration. They also furnished him with material for a speculative outburst of persecution when, in 1498, he was in need of funds to furnish forth the magnificent embassy of his son Cæsar, sent to bear to Louis XIII the bull of divorce from Queen Jeanne. He appointed as inquisitors Cardinal Pietro Isuali and the Master of the Sacred Palace, Fra Paolo de Monelia, who proclaimed a term of grace during which the Spaniards suspect of heresy could come forward. Two hundred and thirty presented themselves; the form of receiving and examining their confessions was gone through with; they were admitted to mercy and a salutary penance was imposed in lieu of the penalties that might have been inflicted in Spain. What was the amount of this cannot be known, but it must have been considerable, for the inquisitors could ransom them at discretion. A solemn auto de fe was celebrated in St. Peter's, July 29th, in the presence of Alexander and his cardinals. The penitents were marched thither in pairs, were reconciled to the Church, abjured their heresies and were sentenced to wear the sanbenito and to undergo penance, after which they were taken in procession to Santa Maria sopra Minerva, where they were relieved of the sanbenitos and discharged. The performance evidently was expected not to be pleasing to the Spanish sovereigns, for part of the penance assigned was to furnish a notarial attestation that they would not return to Spain without licence from the Catholic kings under pain of relaxation as relapsed.[304]

There were doubtless intimations of Ferdinand's displeasure which drew from these impromptu inquisitors a letter of September 10th to their Spanish brethren and one of October 5th from Alexander to the sovereigns, in which the provision respecting return to Spain was emphasized. Ferdinand however was not to be thus placated; indeed he had already, on August 2nd, issued an edict, designed to frustrate further attempts by the papacy to share in the profits of persecution. In this he ordered the execution, without trial, of all who had fled from condemnation by the Inquisition and who should venture to return, no matter what exemptions, reconciliations, safe-conducts or privileges they might allege. Any property they might possess was apportioned in thirds to the informer, the official and the fisc and any one harboring them and any official neglecting to execute the edict was threatened with confiscation.[305] The prevention of further speculative performances of the kind was doubtless the motive for the stringent regulations, which we have seen above, in 1499 and 1500, to prevent the escape of Conversos.[306]

Ferdinand sometimes recognized the papal letters as in the case of some parties named Beltram, in 1499, which he permitted to be heard by the commissioners appointed by the pope,[307] but there was too much at stake for him to abandon the struggle and the papacy followed its practice of sacrificing those who sought its protection, while never failing to promise it. Early in 1502, the sovereigns remonstrated forcibly as to the great damage to the faith resulting from these letters transferring cases to special commissioners, and Alexander promptly responded by a bull evoking to himself all such cases and committing them to Inquisitor-general Deza, to be decided by him personally or with assessors whom he might call in. To this Ferdinand objected, under pretext of the hardship which it would inflict on the appellants, as Deza had to follow the migratory court and Alexander, with his usual pliancy, empowered Deza, August 31st, to appoint deputies to decide cases. Deza availed himself of this to restore the cases to the tribunals, instructing them to proceed to final judgement without regard to any papal letters that might be presented, and thus again the unlucky appellants were delivered back to their persecutors without recourse.[308]

Julius II was elected November 1, 1503, and the next day, even before his coronation, he issued a motu proprio to Ferdinand and Isabella, confirming all graces and privileges granted by his predecessors and especially those to the Inquisition. Still, appeals to the Holy See continued to pour in and to be welcomed and, in 1505, Ferdinand remonstrated energetically, asking a recall of all commissions and drawing a doleful picture of the religious condition of Spain, which was saved only by the Inquisition from a schism worse than that of Arius.[309] Philip of Austria, however, in his eagerness to win papal support, abandoned the claims of the Inquisition and admitted to the Holy See that it could not refuse to entertain the appeals of those who sought its protection.[310] Julius had no intention of divesting himself of the supreme jurisdiction which was so profitable and he took care to assert it in the commissions issued, in 1507, to Ximenes and Bishop Enguera, as inquisitors-general respectively of Castile and Aragon, by evoking to himself all cases pending in the tribunals and committing them to the new incumbents and those whom they might deputize.[311]

***

Like his predecessors, Julius, with one hand, sold letters of absolution and inhibition while, with the other, he declared them invalid. A brief of November 9, 1507, recites that some persons, pretending to be aggrieved, have appealed to the Holy See, whereby the Inquisition is impeded; therefore he decrees that all appeals must be to the inquisitor-general, while those to Rome are to be regarded as null; the inquisitors are to disregard them and not to delay on account of them.[312] Still, the output of these letters was unchecked and for awhile Ferdinand fluctuated in his policy with regard to them. Sometimes, as in a Sardinia case, in 1508, he orders the inquisitor to arrest and punish severely those concerned in procuring them, assuring him of the royal protection against the indignation of Rome.[313] Sometimes, as in a Valladolid case, in 1509, he assumes the current convenient fiction that the letters are issued surreptitiously, that the pope, on better information, will withdraw them, and meanwhile they are held suspended; the trial is to go on and the sequestrations are not to be lifted.[314] Finally, in a pragmática of August 31, 1509, a definite policy was adopted combining both methods and based on the principle that, if the letters were surreptitious, those who obtained them deserved condign punishment. This required all such briefs to be submitted to the Suprema for examination and reference back to Rome; if found to be rightly issued, exequatur would be granted, but without this any one presenting such letters to inquisitors incurred, as in the pragmática of December 15, 1484, irremissible death and confiscation; notaries acting under them were deprived of office, while secular officials were commanded to execute the edict under pain of five thousand florins and ecclesiastics under seizure of temporalities and perpetual exile.[315]

The ferocity of this, after a constant struggle with the curia for twenty-five years, shows the importance attached by Ferdinand to the autonomy of the Inquisition and his determination to suppress all papal interference. Still that interference continued and Ferdinand could not but recognize that it was legal. In a case occurring in 1510, when a certain Augustinian Fray Dionisio, on trial before the tribunal of Seville, obtained letters committing the case to a judge who inhibited the tribunal, Ferdinand requested the pope to evoke the case and commit it to Cardinal Ximenes and further that all future cases of the kind should be similarly treated.[316]

In all this long wrangle the diplomatic reserve is observable which assumed that the Holy See was actuated by motives that, if mistaken, were at least disinterested. The financial element underlying its action was fully recognized, however, and, when the Spanish delegates were sent to the Lateran Council in 1512, among the instructions which they bore was one which said that Rome must not in future defend, as it had been defending, the apostates of Jewish race who were burnt in effigy at home while they purchased for money dispensations in the curia. In fact, Charles V, in a letter of April 30, 1519, to his ambassador Luis Carroz, openly asserted that the briefs issued in the time of Ferdinand had been obtained by the Conversos through the payment of heavy sums.[317]

The delegates to the Lateran council of course effected nothing, and Leo X, while his penitentiaries and auditors were as busy as ever, was even more regardless than his predecessors of the papal dignity, in annulling their acts after the fees had been paid. In a motu proprio of May 31, 1513, he alludes to the letters negligently granted by Julius II and himself, through which the business of the Inquisition was impeded, wherefore he empowers Ximenes to inhibit, under excommunication and other penalties, all persons, even of episcopal rank, from using such letters of commission to entertain appeals.[318]

***

In the kingdoms of Aragon, the Córtes of Monzon, in 1510, agreed that no one should appeal from the tribunals to the pope, but only to the inquisitor-general.[319] Possibly this may have led to the invention of a method of reprisals which was infinitely annoying and difficult to meet. A certain Baldiri Meteli procured from Rome a citation to appear addressed to Mossen Coda, the judge of confiscations in Barcelona, and some other officials. This completely nonplussed the tribunal and Ferdinand was driven to instructing, November 2, 1510, his Lieutenant-general of Catalonia to consult with Inquisitor-general Enguera as to the best mode of inducing Meteli to withdraw the citation. He was obstinate, especially as he had meanwhile procured citations on other officials, and Ferdinand could find no other remedy than notifying the diputados that the agreement of Monzon was a totality and that, if the clause respecting appeals was violated, Enguera would disregard the rest.[320] What was the result the documents fail to inform us, but an even more troublesome case occurred in Saragossa when Sánchez de Romeral on being prosecuted fled to Rome. March 11, 1511, Ferdinand wrote to his ambassador to request the pope to send him back to the inquisitor-general, but the pope declined and Ferdinand was moved to lively wrath, in 1513, on learning that Romeral, who had meanwhile been burnt in effigy, had procured citations on all the officials, from inquisitors down, including even the consultors who had acted in the consulta de fe, and that he had managed to get the citations published in Tudela and Cascante. Ferdinand wrote to Rome in terms of vigorous indignation and ordered the Archbishop of Saragossa, the Captain-general of Navarre and the inquisitors to consult with lawyers as to the best means of punishing this audacious attack on the Inquisition. Apparently there were no means of parrying such an attack save coming to terms with the other side, so long as the curia was willing to lend itself to this guerrilla warfare. This was seen in a somewhat similar case in Sicily, in 1511, when a certain Cola de Ayelo, condemned to perpetual imprisonment by Inquisitor Belorado, managed to escape; he took himself to Rome as a penitent and there commenced suit against Belorado and his colleague the Bishop of Cefalù. The bishop was obliged to obey a summons to Rome; the affair was protracted and gave so much trouble that, when Ayelo wanted to return to Sicily and offered to withdraw the suit, Ferdinand agreed to let him come back, pardoned his offences, including gaol-breaking, and gave him a safe-conduct against further prosecution. This method of fighting the Inquisition would probably have been more frequently adopted but for the risk to which were exposed the notaries and scriveners whose ministrations were essential. In the present case the one who sent the citation to the bishop was seized by the viceroy, tortured and probably punished severely.[321]

One or two cases will illustrate the chaotic condition produced by these contending elements, especially after the death of Ferdinand, January 23, 1516, had removed from the scene of action his resolute will and ceaseless activity. Miguel Vedreña, suspected of complicity in the murder of Bernardo Castelli, assessor of the tribunal of Balaguer, appealed to the pope from the prison of the tribunal of Barcelona. The Suprema of Aragon vainly instructed its Roman agent to make every effort to defeat the appeal. Leo X committed the case to the Bishop of Ascoli, who ordered the tribunal to release Vedreña on his giving security to constitute himself a prisoner in Rome. The inquisitors had lost all respect for papal letters and refused obedience, whereupon the bishop appointed certain local prelates as commissioners to prosecute them and inflict censures. The Suprema inhibited these commissioners from acting, but not before they had excommunicated the inquisitors, who applied to Leo for relief. Leo had already, at least in appearance, abandoned Vedreña, in a brief of May 5, 1517, addressed to Cardinal Adrian, then Inquisitor-general of Aragon, styling Vedreña "that son of iniquity," evoking the case to himself and committing it to Adrian. But accompanying this brief and of the same date was another of private instructions, in which Vedreña was alluded to as his dearest son and Adrian was told that the case was committed to him in order that his dexterity might compound it; the evidence was doubtful and Vedreña had purged it sufficiently; it would seem that he should rather be acquitted than condemned but if Adrian thought otherwise he was to send a statement, when Leo would give final orders. Some three months later there was another brief to Adrian about the excommunicated inquisitors; if the censures were subsequent to the withdrawal of the case from the Bishop of Ascoli, they were invalid, but the whole matter was left to Adrian.[322] We have no means of knowing what was the final outcome of the case, but it sufficiently indicates the entanglements caused by the conflicting jurisdictions and the contradictory actions of the pope as his officials were bought by one side or the other.

***

Another aspect of these affairs is exhibited in the case of the heirs of Juan Enríquez de Medina, whose bones were condemned, by the tribunal of Cuenca, to be exhumed and burnt. The heirs appealed to Ximenes, who commissioned judges to revise the sentence, but these refused to the heirs a copy of the proceedings, by which alone they could rebut the evidence. Then they appealed to Pope Leo, who appointed three commissioners to hear the case and communicate the proceedings to the heirs, on their giving security not to harm the witnesses. The parties appointed, doubtless fearing to incur the enmity of the Inquisition, declined to serve and the last we hear of the case is a brief of May 19, 1517, threatening them with excommunication for persistence.[323]

With the appointment of Cardinal Adrian, as inquisitor-general of Castile as well as of Aragon, Leo, in 1518, confirmed the decrees of Innocent VIII and Alexander VI, granting to him exclusive appellate jurisdiction and Adrian, when pope, repeated this in 1523, in favor of Manrique.[324] Yet this in no way interfered with the reception in Rome of the multitudinous applications, both appellate and in first instance, which Charles V, in a letter of October 29, 1518, to Cardinal Santiquatro, broadly hinted was accomplished by the free use of money.[325] How recklessly, indeed, the papal jurisdiction was prostituted at the service of the first comer, is evidenced in the case of a mill in Paterna, purchased by Juan Claver from the confiscated estate of Jufre Rinsech. The Infante Enrique laid claim to it; the tribunal of Valencia decided in favor of Claver and imposed perpetual silence on Enrique. On the death of Claver, Enrique brought suit against his heir before a judge of his own selection, whom the tribunal promptly inhibited. Enrique then procured a papal brief inhibiting the tribunal and committing the case to this judge. Then Charles V intervened, October 29, 1518, ordering Enrique to bring his suit before the tribunal.[326] Papal letters issued after such fashion had no moral weight and were lightly disregarded. The contempt felt for them was increased by Leo's perpetual vacillations. A brief of September 9, 1518, to Adrian states that, in view of the iniquity and injustice of the tribunal of Palermo and some others, he had placed all such matters in the hands of his vicar, the Cardinal of S. Bartolommeo in Insula, with faculties to decide them and coerce the inquisitors with censures and fines, but now he thinks it better that these affairs shall be confided to Adrian, to whom he commits them with full powers.[327]

***

A contemporary case, which attracted much attention at the time, shows Leo in a more favorable light. Blanquina Díaz was an octogenarian widow of Valencia, whose orthodoxy had never been suspected, but in 1517 she was denounced for Judaism and thrown into the secret prison. An appeal to the pope brought orders that she be released on good security, be allowed defence and the case be speedily tried. This brief never reached the tribunal, being apparently suppressed by the Suprema, whereupon Leo issued a second one, March 4, 1518, evoking the case to himself and committing it to two ecclesiastics of Valencia, Blanquina being meanwhile placed in a convent and Cardinal Adrian being especially prohibited from intervening, anything that he might do being declared invalid. It was probably before this was received that the tribunal submitted the case to Adrian, who assembled a consulta de fe and condemned Blanquina to perpetual imprisonment and confiscation. The papal intervention seems to have aroused much feeling; Charles was ready to sign anything drawn up for him by Adrian, and, in two letters, of May 18th and June 18th to his Roman agent Luis Carroz, he ordered the latter to disregard all other business in the effort to procure the withdrawal of the two briefs. If the safety of all his dominions had been at stake he could not have been more emphatic; such interference with the Inquisition was unexampled; unless the pope would revoke the briefs and promise never to issue similar ones, the Holy Office would be totally destroyed, and heresy would flourish unpunished, for every one would seek relief at the curia and the service of God would become impossible. He also wrote to the pope and the cardinals, while Adrian and the Suprema sent pressing letters. Leo, however, was firm in substance, though he yielded in form. In briefs of July 5th and 7th to Adrian he ordered that everything done since his letters of March 4th should be annulled, Blanquina being restored to her good fame, her sanbenito being removed and she being placed, under bail, in a convent or in the house of a kinsman. As the evidence against her consisted of trifles committed in childhood, he again evoked the case to himself and committed it to Adrian. There had been active work on both sides in Rome, for the brief of July 5th gave Adrian full power to decide the case while that of the 7th limited him to sending the results to Leo and awaiting instructions as to the sentence. Leo thus kept Blanquina's fate in his hands; Adrian was only his mouthpiece and the sentence pronounced her to be lightly suspect of heresy and discharged her without imprisonment or confiscation.[328]

A further instance of Leo's vacillation is the coincidence that the brief of March 4th in Blanquina's favor was dated the same day as Adrian's commission as inquisitor-general of Castile, in which Leo evoked to himself all pending cases, whether in the tribunals or the curia, and committed them to Adrian with full power to inhibit all persons from assuming cognizance of them.[329] With this before him it is scarce a subject of surprise that Charles V on April 30th instructed his ambassador to tell the pope that no letters prejudicial to the Inquisition would be admitted.[330] This threat he carried out in a contemporaneous case which for some years embroiled the Inquisition with the curia. Bernardino Díaz had been tried and discharged by the tribunal of Toledo, after which he had a quarrel with Bartolomé Martínez, whom he accused of perjury in his case, and killed him. Díaz fled to Rome, while the tribunal not only burnt him in effigy but seized his wife and mother and some of his friends as accomplices in his escape. In Rome he secured pardon in both the interior and exterior forum on condition of satisfying the kindred of Martínez, to the great indignation of Charles, who complained, not without reason, of this invasion of jurisdiction. Díaz also procured a brief ordering the liberation of the prisoners and the release of their property, but when the executors named in it endeavored to enforce it, the Toledo tribunal seized their procurator and compelled its surrender. This realization of Charles's threat exasperated the curia and the auditor-general of the Camera summoned the inquisitors to obey the brief or answer personally in Rome for their contumacy; they did neither and were duly excommunicated. Charles wrote repeatedly and bitterly about this unexampled persecution of those who had merely administered justice; the case dragged on for some three years and its ultimate outcome does not appear, but the family of Díaz were probably released for, in 1520, we hear of the removal of the excommunication in connection with the revocation by the inquisitors of their proceedings against Juan de Salazar, a canon of Toledo, residing in Rome in the papal service, whom they had deprived of citizenship and temporalities for some action of his in prejudice of the Inquisition.[331]

**

Another person who, about this time, gave infinite vexation to Charles and Adrian was Diego de las Casas of Seville, the agent who bore to Rome the contested proceedings of the Córtes of Aragon and labored for their confirmation. He was well supplied with funds and naturally was a persona grata to the curia. The Inquisition speedily attacked him, in its customary unscrupulous manner, by not only prosecuting him in absentia but by seizing his brothers, Francisco and Juan, and their wives. To meet this he procured a brief committing the cases to Adrian and to Ferdinand de Arce, Bishop of Canaries, with a provision that the parties should present themselves to Adrian and Arce and keep such prison as might be designated for them, and further permitting them to select advocates for their defence. Equitable as were these provisions, the brief excited hot indignation. When laid before the royal council it was pronounced scandalous and of evil example and its execution was refused. Charles wrote in haste to Leo, April 30, 1519, that it was scandalous and would destroy the Inquisition; he instructed his agents to procure its revocation to be forwarded by the next courier and he invoked by letters the cardinals in the Spanish interest to bring what pressure they could upon the pope. His urgency was fruitless and when, in September, he sent Lope Hurtado de Mendoza to Rome, as special ambassador in the quarrel with Aragon, his instructions were to represent to the pope the impropriety of harboring in Rome fugitives from the Inquisition, especially Diego de las Casas and his colleague Juan Gutiérrez, whose parents and grandparents and kindred had been reconciled or burnt; they should be expelled, and Mendoza was to labor for the revocation of their briefs and all other exemptions and commissions in favor of Conversos. Mendoza exerted all his diplomatic ability, but, although Leo admitted, in a brief of July 13, 1520, to Adrian that the evocation of cases to Rome, both on appeal and in first instance, led to delays, impunity for offenders and encouragement of offences, still he would not abandon Diego de las Casas. The grant by Sixtus IV of appellate jurisdiction to the inquisitor-general, he admitted had been beneficial and, in hopes that Adrian would use it with integrity and justice, he evoked to himself all cases pending in the Roman courts and committed them to Adrian with full powers, but he made no promises as to the future and he especially excepted his physician, Ferdinand de Aragon and his wife, Diego de las Casas, Juan Gutiérrez and the deceased Juan de Covarrubias, whose cases had long been in dispute.

To all these, and to their kindred to the third degree and their property, Leo granted letters exempting them from the jurisdiction of the Inquisition and committing them to the Archbishop of Saragossa and certain other ecclesiastical dignitaries. Complaints soon arose as to the manner in which these commissioners exercised their powers to the dishonor of the Inquisition; Leo yielded by a brief of January 8, 1521, in which he substituted Adrian and the nuncio Vianesio de' Albergati, with full power to inhibit their predecessors. Then, in a more formal brief of January 20th he deprecated the evil caused by the cases which were daily brought to Rome and committed them all to Adrian, saving those of the five exempts, in which the nuncio was to be conjoined with him, and at the same time he revoked the letters exempting them and their kindred and empowering them to select judges for themselves.[332] It was a practical surrender, although Leo distinguished las Casas and Gutiérrez by styling them his beloved children.

These cases will suffice to show how the traditional policy of the curia continued, of taking the money of the refugees and appellants for protecting briefs, and then abandoning them by revocations issued, without even a sense of shame, when their funds were exhausted in the protracted struggle. Yet, undeterred by this, there was a constant succession of new applicants, who had no other refuge on earth, and the valueless briefs were granted with unfailing readiness. It was a source of perpetual irritation and Charles was untiring in his efforts to counteract it, not always observing due courtesy, as when, March 25, 1525, he wrote to Clement VII, in violent language, to revoke and erase from the registers a brief granted to Luis Colon and to order his officials not to issue such letters, as they were scandalous.[333] He no longer had the excuse of his youthful tutelage under Adrian and yet his subserviency to the Inquisition was complete. This was manifested in the case of Bernardo de Orda, a servant of Cardinal Colonna, who had a suit against Doctor Saldaña about the treasurership of the church of Leon. Saldaña was a member of the Suprema and, when Orda came to Spain, it was not difficult to have him charged with heresy and arrested by the tribunal of Valladolid. He escaped to Rome and the prosecution was continued against him in absentia, whereupon Charles demeaned himself by writing to Colonna, July 30, 1528, asking him to prevent Orda from obtaining a brief of exemption, as it would be an injury to the faith, and also not to favor him in his suit with Saldaña.[334]

***

Meanwhile the popes continued to propitiate Charles's growing power by granting, with as much facility as ever, what was nominally exclusive appellate jurisdiction to the inquisitor-general. In 1523, Adrian VI, as we have seen, confirmed in favor of Manrique the bulls of Sixtus IV and Alexander VI. Clement VII went even farther for, in a bull of January 6, 1524, he not only evoked all pending cases and committed them to Manrique but decreed that any commissions which he might thereafter issue should be invalid without the express assent of Charles, while all appeals were to be made to the inquisitor-general and not to the Holy See, and this he repeated, June 16, 1525. Still appeals continued to be made to Rome and briefs to be granted requiring repeated confirmations of the bulls of 1524 and 1525 with inclusion of the letters obtained in the interval, of which we have examples in 1532 and 1534.[335] Charles was thus justified in enforcing Ferdinand's pragmática of 1509, as when, in 1537, he ordered the corregidor of Murcia to prevent the publication of certain letters understood to have been procured from the pope against the Inquisition; if presented they were to be sent to the Council of Castile for its action, and parties endeavoring to use them were to be arrested and dealt with as might be deemed most advantageous to the Holy Office.[336]

The position of Charles, as the master of Italy and the protagonist of the Church in its struggle with Lutheranism, had thus enabled him to obtain for the Inquisition virtual, though not acknowledged, independence of Rome. There is a very striking illustration of this, in 1531, when Clement VII intervened in favor of Fray Francisco Ortiz, a celebrated Observantine preacher, prosecuted for audaciously criticizing the Inquisition from the pulpit. He had lain in prison for more than two years, obstinately refusing to retract, when the interposition of Clement was sought. He did not evoke the case but, in terms of remarkable deference, July 1, 1531, he suggested to Manrique that, if nothing else was alleged against Ortiz, he might be held as sufficiently punished by his long imprisonment and might be restored to liberty, in view of his blameless life and the profit to souls to be expected from his preaching. This Clement asked as a favor, moved only by Christian charity and zeal for the salvation of souls.[337] To this carefully guarded request the Inquisition turned a deaf ear. If the trial of Ortiz came to an end in February, 1532, it was because he voluntarily submitted himself completely and his sentence was by no means light, including public penance, which was rarely inflicted on an ecclesiastic.[338] Paul III was more decided when his intervention was asked by Charles V, who, in spite of his bitter protests against papal interference, found himself obliged to appeal in behalf of his favorite preacher, Fray Alonso Virues. The Seville tribunal had prosecuted the latter on a charge of Lutheranism, had kept him imprisoned for four years and had sentenced him to reclusion in a convent for two years and suspension from preaching for two more. Charles, who had vainly sought to protect him during his trial, supported an appeal to the pope and obtained a brief of May 29, 1538, which not only annulled the sentence but forbade his future molestation.[339] When, in 1542, Paul III reorganized the moribund papal Inquisition by forming a congregation of cardinals as inquisitors-general for all Christendom, there was a not unnatural apprehension that this, even if not so intended, might interfere with the independence of the Spanish Holy Office. To representations of this he responded by a brief of April 1, 1548, in which he characterized such fears as baseless; he declared that it was not designed to interfere with the authority of inquisitors in Spain and he formally revoked anything to their prejudice that might be found in the decree establishing the Congregation.[340] This brief remained to the end the charter to which the Spanish Inquisition appealed in its frequent collisions with the Roman Congregation and, but for such a declaration, it would probably have been subordinated.[341]

This in no way affected the continual applications to Rome for relief, nor the effort of the Inquisition to suppress them. It was a singular departure from the settled policy of the government in this matter which led the Suprema, in 1548, to utter a bitter complaint to Charles V, setting forth the facility with which citations and inhibitions and commissions were granted in Rome and the daily royal cédulas despatched to prevent them, and yet when recently a Converso presented to the Royal Council a petition stating that he did not dare to notify the inquisitor-general of letters concerning a case which had been decided, the Council issued an order permitting any notary to serve the papers and testify to the service, with penalties for impeding it.[342] The popes were more consistent in their inconsistency. We have seen how Paul III, in 1549 and Julius III in 1551, confirmed the 1484 bull of Sixtus IV insisting on the validity of papal letters in both the interior and judicial forum and threatening the curses of the bull in Cæna Domini on all who should impede them, yet in 1550 a case in which papal letters were obtained led to vigorous remonstrance and Julius, by a brief of December 15, 1551, confirmed those of Clement VII and Paul III, besides evoking all pending cases and committing them to Inquisitor-general Valdés.[343]

***

Yet the very fact of doing this inferred the papal possession of supreme jurisdiction which it merely delegated, a point of which the Holy See never lost sight. The commissions to the successive inquisitors-general during the century contains a clause by which all unfinished business was evoked and committed to the appointee. It is true that there was also a provision that no appeals from the tribunals should lie except to the inquisitor-general, all other appeals, even to the Holy See, being invalid and referred back to him, who was empowered to use censures to prevent interference even by cardinals.[344] The popes could afford to be thus liberal in their grants, for their irresponsible power enabled them to disregard or to modify these delegated faculties at discretion, and these provisions never prevented them from entertaining appeals.

This was shown in the friction which continued throughout the long reign of Philip II, who was no less earnest than his father in maintaining the independence of the Inquisition, although his attitude was more deferential. In 1568 we find him complaining to his ambassador, Juan de Zuñiga, that appeals were made from Sardinia to Rome, not only in cases of faith, but in matters of confiscation and in civil cases concerning familiars and officials, all of which was damaging to the Inquisition and in derogation of the royal jurisdiction. Zuñiga was therefore ordered to supplicate the pope to refuse admission to all such appeals, while the viceroy of Sardinia was instructed to prevent testimony from being taken in such cases.[345] This effort was fruitless as likewise was that of Abbot Brizeño, sent in 1580 as special commissioner on the subject to Gregory XIII, to remonstrate with the utmost earnestness against the reception accorded in Rome to fugitives from the Inquisition.[346]

Soon after this a case occurred which strained the relations between the courts. Jean de Berri, a Frenchman on trial by the tribunal of Saragossa, managed to escape to Rome, whereupon he was condemned in contumacy and burnt in effigy. He presented himself to the Congregation of the Inquisition which admitted him to bail and he went to reside in Orbitello. The case must have been the subject of active recrimination for Juan de Zuñiga, at that time Viceroy of Naples, with superabundant zeal, kidnapped him and despatched him to Spain. Instantly the papal court was aflame; Zuñiga was promptly excommunicated, but the censure was suspended for four months to allow him to return the fugitive. A rupture seemed imminent and Zuñiga, conscious of his mistake, on learning that the galeasses had been driven back to Palermo, sent thither in hot haste, but his messenger was too late and Jean de Berri was carried to Spain. Papal despatches couched in vigorous language were forthwith sent to the nuncio, to Philip, to Inquisitor-general Quiroga and to the Saragossa tribunal, the nuncio being ordered to prosecute Quiroga if the prisoner was not remanded. Philip had no alternative; Quiroga, in a letter of September 12, 1582 to Gregory announced Berri's departure, at the same time remonstrating against the asylum to fugitives offered by Rome. Berri was duly delivered to the Roman Inquisition, but there was probably a secret understanding for, at a meeting of the Congregation, June 13, 1583, presided over by Gregory, it was decreed that he should be placed in the hands of Quiroga, who should judge his case. Quiroga did nothing of the kind; he was sent to Saragossa and the last we hear of him is a letter of the Suprema, August 3rd, to that tribunal ordering it to do justice--the customary formula for confirming a sentence.[347] As usual, the curia abandoned those whom it had undertaken to protect.

***

From 1582 to 1586, the nuncio, Taberna Bishop of Lodi, was largely occupied with the question of these appeals.[348] It formed one of several grievances arising from the exercise of papal jurisdiction in Spain--a jurisdiction which was becoming an anachronism in the development of absolute monarchy, but, as the faculties of the Inquisition were solely a delegation from the Holy See, papal control of its operations was unassailable and had to be endured. Philip gained nothing by instructing his ambassador Olivares, November 10, 1583, that it was highly important to represent to the pope that appeals should not be entertained but should be remitted back to the inquisitor-general.[349] We have seen how little ceremony was used by Sixtus V, in 1585, when he evoked the case of the Jesuit Provincial Marcen and his colleagues, and how the Suprema was forced to submit.

While Philip thus was unable to dispute the papal right of intervention, he had as little scruple as his predecessors in disregarding papal letters. In 1571 he ordered the surrender of all briefs evoking cases to the Holy See. Some years later the Suprema instructed the tribunal of Lima that, if apostolic letters were presented, it was to "supplicate" against them--that is, to suspend and disregard them--and this was doubtless a circular sent to all tribunals.[350] They were practically treated as a nullity and it is a singular fact that, after so long an experience, the curia still found purchasers credulous enough to seek protection in them. In a Toledo auto de fe of 1591 there appeared twenty-four Judaizers of Alcázar, detected by Inquisitor Alava during a visitation. Among them was Francisco de Vega, a scrivener who, on hearing that the inquisitor was coming, had sent to Rome and procured absolutions for himself, his mother and his sister, thinking to find safety in them, but they were treated with contempt and all three culprits were reconciled with the same penalties as their companions.[351]

While thus the supreme jurisdiction of the Holy See was admitted and evaded, the Inquisition sought to create the belief that it had been abandoned. Zurita who, as secretary of the Suprema, unquestionably knew better, makes such an assertion and Páramo, whose experience as inquisitor in Sicily had taught him the truth, does not hesitate, in 1598, to say that, since Innocent VIII decreed that appeals should be heard by the inquisitor-general, no pope had permitted cases to be carried to the Apostolic see.[352] It is a fair example of the incurable habit of the Inquisition to assert its possession of whatever it desired to obtain.

***

Under Philip III, the papal supremacy continued to be exercised and was submitted to as reluctantly as ever. In 1602 a Doctor Cozas, under prosecution by the tribunal of Murcia, managed to escape to Rome and to have his case tried there. Philip labored strenuously and persistently to have him remanded, first through his ambassador the Duke of Sesa and then through the succeeding envoy, the Duke of Escalona, to whom, on April 1, 1604 he sent a special courier, urging him to renew his efforts, for every day the Roman Inquisition was intervening in what the popes had granted exclusively to the inquisitor-general, thus threatening the total destruction of the Spanish Inquisition.[353] In 1603 a Portuguese appealed to the Roman Inquisition, alleging that his wife was unjustly held in prison; he obtained an order on the inquisitor-general to transmit the papers and meanwhile to suspend the case; Acevedo demurred, eliciting from Clement VIII a still more peremptory command, whereupon the documents were sent and, while the case was under consideration in Rome, the woman was discharged.[354] It was preferable to let an assumed culprit go free than to allow the Roman Holy Office to exercise jurisdiction.

***

The subserviency of Philip IV to his inquisitors-general was even more marked, and we have seen how vigorously he supported the Inquisition in its extension of its jurisdiction over matters foreign to the faith, leading the clergy of Majorca to procure papal briefs exempting them from it in such cases. The chapter of Valencia was less fortunate and was exposed to the full force of the royal indignation in 1637. Inquisitor-general Sotomayor had obtained a pension of nine hundred ducats on the archdeaconry of Játiva and one of three hundred and forty ducats on a prebend vacated by the death of the canon Villarasa. The chapter refused payment; Sotomayor sued them in the tribunal and of course obtained a decision in his favor. The aggrieved chapter revenged itself by ceasing the customary courtesy of sending two canons to receive the inquisitors at the door of the cathedral on the occasion of publishing the edict; this continued for two years and, on the second, the door of the great chapel was locked and the inquisitors had to await its opening. For this disrespect they prosecuted the chapter, which then appealed to Rome on both suits and obtained briefs committing the cases to a special commission of the Roman Inquisition, granting a faculty to relieve them from any excommunication and citing Sotomayor to appear in Rome. The case was assuming a serious aspect and the Suprema, November 30, 1637, presented to Philip a consulta with letters for his signature, addressed to his ambassador, to the pope, to the viceroy, the archbishop, and the chapter. Philip was in the full ardor of a contest with the pope over the jurisdiction of the nuncio and the Roman condemnation of books supporting the royal prerogative; he was not content with the measures proposed and returned the consulta with the comment that much more vigorous methods were required, nor did it comport with the royal dignity to ask for what he could legally enforce. He had therefore ordered the Council of Aragon to write to the chapter, through the viceroy, expressing his displeasure and his determination to resort to the most extreme steps. Letters were also to be written to the viceroy and the archbishop commanding the prosecution of the chapter in the Banco Real unless the briefs were forthwith surrendered; the Inquisition was not to appear in the matter, but only the archbishop, and a minister of justice was to be at hand when the demand was made, so as to seize the briefs as soon as they were produced. This violent program was duly carried out; Canon Oñate, the custodian of the briefs, was forced to surrender them; through the hands of the Council of Aragon they were passed to Sotomayor and were carefully preserved as trophies in the archives of the Suprema.[355]

If this inspired in ecclesiastics the terror desired it did not influence defendants under trial, who continued to appeal to Rome, for a carta acordada of August 3, 1538, orders the tribunals, when such cases occur, to send reports not only to it but direct to the Roman agent of the Inquisition, in order that no time should be lost by him in working for their withdrawal.[356] A few years later there followed the most bitter and stubborn conflict that had yet occurred between Madrid and Rome on the subject of appeals--the case of Gerónimo de Villanueva, which is so illustrative in various ways that it merits a somewhat detailed examination.

APPEALS TO ROME

Gerónimo de Villanueva, Marquis of Villalba, belonged to an ancient family of Aragon, of which kingdom he was Prothonotary, or secretary of state; while his brother Agustin was Justicia. He won the favor of Olivares, as well as of Philip, and accumulated a plurality of offices, rendering him at last one of the most important personages of the state, for he became a member of the Councils of Aragon, War, Cruzada and Indies, of the Camara of the Council of Indies, Secretary of State and of the "Despacho universal de la Monarquia."[357]

VILLANUEVA'S CASE

In 1623 there was founded in Madrid, with the object of restoring the relaxed Benedictine discipline, a convent under the name of La Encarnacion bendita de San Placido, with funds furnished by Villanueva and by the family of Doña Teresa de Silva (also called Valle de la Cerda), who was elected abbess. She had for some years been under the direction of Fray Francisco Garcia Calderon, a Benedictine of high reputation, who was inclined to mysticism. Villanueva had an agreement with the superiors of the Order giving him the appointment of spiritual directors and he naturally placed Calderon in charge. Before the year was out, one of the nuns became demoniacally possessed; the contagiousness of the disorder is well known and soon twenty-two out of the thirty were similarly affected, including Teresa herself. Calderon was reckoned a skilful exorcist, but he was baffled, as was likewise the Abbot of Ripel, who was called in. At the suggestion of the latter, the wild utterances of the demoniacs were written down, and a mass accumulated of some six hundred pages, for it was a current belief that demons were often compelled by God to utter truths concealed from man. These largely took the shape of announcing that the convent would be the source of a reformation, not only of the Order but of the whole Church; eleven of the nuns were to be the apostles of a New Dispensation, one having the spirit of St. Peter, another that of St. Paul and so forth, while Calderon represented Christ. They would go forth to redeem the world; when Urban VIII should die he would be succeeded by Cardinal Borgia, who would bestow the cardinalate on Calderon; then Calderon would be pope for thirty-three years and Villanueva, who would be made a cardinal, would have a share in the great work.

For three years this went on, to the despair of the exorcists; people began to suspect some underlying evil and Fray Alonso de Leon, who had been associated with Calderon in the direction and had quarrelled with him, denounced the affair to the Inquisition in 1628. Calderon's prosecution was ordered; he endeavored to escape to France but was caught at Gerona and brought back to Toledo for trial. The nuns were all cast into the secret prison, where it was not difficult to extort from their fears such evidence as was wanted. Calderon endured without confession three rigorous tortures, but nevertheless he was condemned as an Alumbrado, guilty of teaching impeccability and the other heresies ascribed to Illuminism. April 27, 1630 he was sentenced to a living death in a cell of the convent designated to receive him. Doña Teresa was relegated to a convent for four years and the nuns were scattered in different houses.[358]

Apart from Illuminism, there were the consultation of demons and the prophecies of a renovation of the Church through a new apostolate. The latter was qualified as a heresy; the former was a debatable point. The six censors appointed by the Suprema held that belief in prophecies made by demons was superstitious divination, aggravated by the character of the prophecies and the practice of writing them out; it was no excuse to say that the demon acted as the minister of God, for this could be made to justify all heresies, and even to believe the demon to be the minister of God was superstitious divination.[359]

In all this Villanueva was compromised. His house adjoined the convent and he was much there, especially at night, after his official duties were over. The conventual discipline became inevitably relaxed and, in the subsequent proceedings, it was in evidence that he had been seen sitting in Teresa's lap while she cleaned his hair of insects. He took much interest in the demonic prophecies, especially those which foretold his importance in the Church, and he treasured a picture which was drawn of his guardian angel, in which he was represented as a pillar sustaining the Church. He took part in interrogating the demons and writing what they said and he kept these writings in his house. This appeared in the evidence taken in the trial of Teresa and the nuns and, according to inquisitorial practice, the portions relating to him were extracted and submitted to censors who reported, March 12, 1630, unfavorably; he was an accomplice or, if not, he was at least a fautor of the heresies. Then other censors were called in and a junta was held, March 20th, which reduced the finding to his being moderately suspect of having incurred the above censure.[360]

There was evidently no desire to attack so influential a personage who was supported by the favor of Olivares, and the Inquisition carried the matter no further, but doubtless Villanueva felt the danger of his position and possibly hints may have reached him of the evidence collected which might at any time be used for the furtherance of some court intrigue. He seems to have hesitated long but finally on January 7, 1632, he presented a self-denunciation to Fray Antonio de Sotomayor, confessor of the king, not as yet inquisitor-general, but a member of the Suprema. In this he naturally extenuated matters; he alleged his misplaced confidence in Calderon and Alonso de Leon and professed that, being unable to judge the import of it all, he made the statement in order that the proper remedy might be applied. Six months elapsed without action but, in July, five different groups of censors were consulted, whose opinions varied from holding him as an accomplice to declaring him guilty of no mortal sin. July 30th the Suprema considered the case and decided that there was no ground for prosecution--one member, however dissenting and voting for further consultation with competent theologians. The majority opinion governed and, on November 22nd, a certificate was duly given to Villanueva.[361]

***

He might well congratulate himself on his escape and turn his attention to rehabilitating the unfortunate nuns of San Placido. It was well-nigh unexampled that the Inquisition should confess fallibility by revoking a judgement and to accomplish it demanded time and perseverance. When all was ready, on February 5, 1638, Fray Gabriel de Bustamente, in the name of the Benedictine Order, petitioned the Suprema to revise the case and that the nuns be set free and restored to their honor. This was referred to nine censors, who reported, April 14th, that the nuns were innocent of anything rendering them amenable to the Inquisition; they had merely obeyed their spiritual director and what was guilty in him was innocent in them. To save appearances, however, they added that, if they had acted on the evidence laid before their predecessors, their conclusions would have been identical. The Suprema delayed action until October 2nd, when it decided that the imprisonment of the nuns and their sentences should not affect their good name and repute or that of their kindred, monastery, or Order. They were thus rehabilitated, the convent was reorganized and, to erase from human memory all that had occurred, in November an edict was published requiring, under severe penalties, the surrender of all relations and copies of the former sentence, many of which were fabulous.[362] As though to secure the future of San Placido, a new building was commenced for it by Villanueva, in 1641, the cornerstone of which was laid with much ceremony.

It was never safe to reckon upon the Inquisition. If it could reverse a condemnation, it could reverse an acquittal, especially as St. Pius V had decreed that no acquittal for heresy should be held to be res judicata and permanent, whether pronounced by inquisitors, bishops, popes or even the Council of Trent.[363] For awhile, matters were quiescent. Villanueva was receiving fresh proofs of the royal favor. October 27, 1639 Philip gave him a seat in the Council of War and, on January 16, 1640, granted him additional graces in reward of services performed in Aragon. Even the fall of his protector Olivares, in February, 1643, did not affect his position, for his membership in the Council of Indies was bestowed on April 23d of that year.[364] Yet the disgrace of the chief favorite opened the way to many intrigues and especially to those directed against his return to power, of which, at one time, there seemed much probability. It would be impossible now to assert with absolute certainty what was the direct object sought for in Villanueva's ruin, but we may feel confident that, in addition to the desire to divide his spoils, a powerful motive was the wish to get possession of his papers, in the hope of finding in them compromising material for use against Olivares.

The first attack was skilfully directed against San Placido and not against Villanueva. Sotomayor, the aged inquisitor-general, was forced, as we have seen, to resign on June 20, 1643, although he continued nominally in office until his successor, Arce y Reynoso, took possession, November 14th. Arce had already been designated for the post and, on July 13th, a royal letter informed him that Sotomayor had promised to subdelegate to him any cases that the king desired. Philip went on to say that the affair of San Placido had never ceased to give him concern; the truth had never been ascertained and, as it concerned so greatly the Catholic religion, it required a searching and impartial investigation, such as it would receive at Arce's hands, wherefore, as soon as he received power from Sotomayor, he must undertake it in such wise as would give public satisfaction. The commission from Sotomayor followed the same day and comprehended not only the nuns but all persons concerned, whether lay or clerical.[365]

The letter was evidently drawn up by Arce for the signature of Philip, who was but a tool in the hands of the intriguers. With the existence of the monarchy imperilled by three wars at once and the affairs of state disorganized by the sudden removal of the minister who had managed them for twenty years, it is absurd to suppose that he could spontaneously have given a thought to the concern of the little nunnery, the settlement of which had been acquiesced in for five years, or that he had the slightest inkling of what was to follow. That this action was but a pretext is shown by the fact that, although there were some proceedings taken against the nuns, which for several years gave them anxiety, they were allowed without protest to appeal to the pope who, in 1648, committed the case to the Bishop of Avila, after which it seems to have been dropped, for in 1651 we find them in full enjoyment of their honor.[366]

***

Arce had evidently been preparing in advance for the attack on Villanueva; on July 15, 1643, he acknowledged the royal commands which he was ready to obey; on July 24th the king sent him an order for all the papers in the case, expressing confidence that he would act as expected from his zeal, rectitude and prudence, and, only two days later, July 26th he wrote to the king that the case of one of the accomplices was ready for definite sentence but, as it involved confirming or setting aside a judgement of the Suprema, he hesitated to take the responsibility. He suggested various methods and invoked the angel of the kingdom to bring light from God to aid the king in solving so difficult a problem. To this Philip, in total ignorance of what was on foot, replied that he had placed the matter absolutely in Arce's hands, who then concluded to let it take the form of an ordinary trial. Matters were already so far advanced that although the papers amounted to the enormous bulk of 7,500 folios, by August 27th the fiscal already had his clamosa or indictment prepared and presented. This displays the animus of the matter in being directed, not against the nuns but exclusively against Villanueva and the proceedings of 1632 which had acquitted him. Then, on September 18th the fiscal asked for the examination of new witnesses and, on January 13, 1644, he demanded that the affair should be submitted to new censors. He recapitulated the charges which we have seen, that Villanueva wrote down the utterances of the demons and kept them in his own house, his enquiring into future events dependent upon human free-will, his belief in the demons after experiencing their mendacity, his treasuring the picture of the angel, etc.[367] There was nothing new in all this, but at a time when the Inquisition was daily trying and penancing old women for fortune-telling and divination and superstitious practices, which were held to imply what was called a pact with the demon, there was technical ground for Villanueva's prosecution, although not for the manner in which it was carried on.

The new censors were selected--learned men, we are told, and eminent theologians, many of them professors in Toledo and Alcalá de Henares. A formidable array of twenty-one articles was submitted to them, including not only Villanueva's dealings with the demons of San Placido but his subsequent dabbling in astrology, through which he used to predict the result of campaigns. The censors could not well hesitate in pronouncing him vehemently suspect in the faith and some even held that those who had signed the exculpation of 1632 should be prosecuted.[368] All this was conducted with the inviolable secrecy of the Inquisition, both the king and the intended victim being kept in profound ignorance of what was on foot.

***

The opinions of the censors were furnished at various times up to May 15, 1644 and then the Suprema took three and a half months to consider them, until Philip was conveniently absent, conducting the campaign in Catalonia. After much prayerful thought, we are told, and supplication to God, a sentence of arrest was adopted, August 31st, and executed the same day. Two inquisitors, Juan Ortiz and Calaya, went to Villanueva's house about 2 P.M., woke him from his siesta, placed him in a coach and hurried him off to Toledo, where he was thrust into a narrow cell with a little cot, and kept as usual, strictly incomunicado. Six keys were found on him, which he said covered papers belonging to the king. He declined to give orders as to his own papers and we are informed that large quantities were found concerning San Placido, but there is discreet silence about other matters. That same day and the next there came for him important despatches from the king, which had to be opened by his principal secretary. Arce at once wrote to Philip announcing the arrest and assuring him that the case would be prosecuted with the utmost desire for the greater service of God. Philip's reply is the most abject expression of weakness; the mere assumption that the faith is concerned seems to paralyze his intellect and deprive him of all power of self-assertion. He was completely taken by surprise and expressed his astonishment at such action without consulting him or the queen. Villanueva was a minister in two tribunals and also secretary of state, having in his hands papers of the utmost consequence to the kingdom; there was no risk of his flight, nor would Philip have interfered had it been his own son, wherefore it was a matter for prior consultation. As it is done, however, he can only order the Suprema to act with the sole object of the service of God and exaltation of the holy Catholic faith, which are his chief desire and the only purpose of its existence. Arce answered this, September 21st, in a tone almost contemptuous. The inviolable secrecy of the Inquisition required that no one but the king should be informed of the commencement of the trial of one of the accomplices in the case of the nuns of San Placido, which was revived by his command. As to the queen, the arrest was made between one and two o'clock, which was an hour inconvenient for intrusion on her. This would appear sufficient as to giving notice to the king and queen, besides the disadvantage of delay and the risks of correspondence. Promptitude was essential and the king's holy zeal always desires that there should be no delay in the affairs of God and the holy faith. When the king returns he can give orders about the papers, which are under lock and key.[369] These were all the reasons that Arce deigned to give his sovereign for increasing the confusion of that terrible time by suddenly imprisoning a principal minister of state, for the furtherance of a court intrigue.

The arrest of course created much excitement. The Council of State promptly presented a consulta, which Arce, in his letter to the king, characterized as very remarkable, and it was followed by similar appeals from the other councils of which Villanueva was a member--War, Indies, Aragon, and Cruzada. The kingdom of Aragon remonstrated with the king in a memorial setting forth the long and faithful services of Villanueva, his sudden imprisonment, without allowing time to settle official and personal affairs, and the infamy cast upon all his kindred; in view of the nature of the charges and his character it would have sufficed to assign as a prison his house or a convent, as was frequently done with those of much lower rank. The kingdom begged, for the sake of a family which had so long served it, that while his case was pending he might be restored to his home under sufficient guard and that he might have the benefit of the royal clemency and justice. Temperate as was this appeal, it aroused Arce's wrath and he expressed to Philip a doubt whether it could be genuine, it being so extraordinary and amounting to fautorship, for which the parties should be prosecuted, although the Inquisition had not yet done so. Appeals to Philip's humanity were in vain. Although he was speedily recalled to Madrid by the illness of the queen, who died October 9th, he made no remonstrance against the unnecessary cruelty shown to Villanueva, who was left in his cell, cut off from the world. In September he fell seriously ill and was allowed to have a servant, a youth of his chamber much attached to him, who was not allowed to leave the cell until the trial was concluded.[370]

The case followed the ordinary routine, the only new matter introduced being a little book found in his desk, setting forth fortunate and unfortunate days for him as deduced from the letters of his name. Over this the censors differed, two of them pronouncing it innocent, while five held it to be included in the prohibitions of the Ars Notoria as a tacit pact with the demon. Villanueva in his defence pleaded his former acquittal and there was a learned discussion, between his advocate and the fiscal, as to the applicability to the case of the bull Inter multiplices which defined that in heresy there could never be a final decision in favor of the accused. Philip urged despatch on the tribunal but it proceeded with the customary exasperating deliberation. After eighteen months had passed, when Philip was holding the Córtes of Saragossa, the deputies presented, January 18, 1646 an appeal in the name of the kingdom, expressing entire confidence in Villanueva's innocence and urging that a period be put to the cruel suspense by the early conclusion of the trial. This was as fruitless as all previous efforts had been; it was not until he had passed two dreary years in his cell that a vote was taken in the case, August 3, 1646. There was general agreement that his sentence, with full details of his offences, should be read in the audience-chamber and not in a public auto de fe, that he should be severely reprimanded and be forbidden to occupy the house which he had built alongside of the convent, but there was discordia as to the number of persons to be present, as to whether or not he should be required to abjure de levi--for light suspicion of heresy--and as to banishing him, and there were some who voted for fining and suspending him from office for two years. Evidently, at the worst, there was no serious culpability proven and there were probably few courtiers of Philip IV against whom superstitions as grave could not have been alleged.[371]

***

In the estilo of the Inquisition, when there was discordia in the consulta de fe, the case was referred to the Suprema, which thus became the judge. September 1st, Villanueva recused one of the members, Antonio de Aragon, and the recusation was admitted after a hearing. Finally, on February 7, 1647, the Suprema pronounced sentence; there were to be present in the audience-chamber four ecclesiastics, four frailes, and four laymen; Villanueva was to be severely reprimanded and warned, he was to abjure de levi, be prohibited from communicating with the nuns or living in the adjoining house and be banished for three years from Toledo and Madrid and from twenty leagues around them.[372]

This sentence may not appear severe but, to understand the rest of the story it must be borne in mind that to be penanced by the Inquisition and be required to abjure for even light suspicion of heresy inflicted an ineffaceable stigma, not only on the culprit but on his kindred and posterity. The whole race was involved in infamy and no temporal punishment, however severe, could be so disastrous in its effect upon the honor of a noble family as the blot on its limpieza, or purity of blood, resulting from such a sentence. The extreme length to which this was carried will be considered hereafter; at present it suffices to point out that, while Villanueva's worldly career was ruined already and his wanton incarceration in the secret prisons had been a severe infliction on him and his kindred, there had still been hope that this might yet be at least partially effaced by an acquittal. Penance and abjuration destroyed this hope and, to the Spanish noble, no effort was too great to avert so crushing a misfortune.

The nature of the sentence must have leaked out, for before its publication by the tribunal of Toledo, to which it was sent, the brother and sister of Villanueva, Agustin the Justicia and Ana, now abbess of San Placido, with Luis de Torres as proctor of Gerónimo, presented an appeal from it to the pope and a recusation of Arce y Reynoso and of others of the judges. The appeal was not admitted and they were told that the Inquisition did not listen to kindred in matters of faith. Then, on March 18th, Torres, in the name of Gerónimo, presented to the tribunal of Toledo a recusation of all the inquisitors and fiscals of Spain as being dependents of the inquisitor-general. It was all in vain. On March 23d Villanueva was brought into the audience-chamber to hear the sentence, but he acted in a manner so disorderly and made such outcries that the publication was suspended--a thing, we are told, unexampled in the history of the Inquisition--and the presiding inquisitor ordered the alcaide to take that man back to his cell. He recused every one who had acted as judge and appealed to the pope, to the king, and to any other competent judge.[373]

The tribunal consulted the Suprema and was ordered to execute the sentence. Another attempt was made on March 29th, but Villanueva refused to abjure and this was repeated on several subsequent occasions, in spite of warnings of the excommunication that would follow persistent obstinacy. At length, on June 7th, he offered to abjure under a protest, which he presented in writing, to the effect that he did so through fear of the censures and without prejudice to his appeal or other recourse that he might take and, on this protest being publicly read, he made the abjuration.[374] He was not set at liberty, but was transferred from the secret prison to the Franciscan convent, the tribunal giving as a reason his outcries and the disturbance that he made. This leniency the Suprema disapproved and, in a few days, he was remanded to the secret prison, where he was treated with much rigor. On June 18th he was notified that the fiscal accused him of contumacy for not complying simply with his sentence and, on July 18th, he made the abjuration and was released. There is an intimation that he withdrew the recusation and appeal, but the statement is not clear, though it is quite possible that means were found to effect it. John Huss was burnt for refusing to abjure; a bull of Martin V, quoted by the Inquisition, authorized the prosecution and relaxation of suspects who refuse to abjure and there is probably truth in a contemporary statement that the fiscal of the Suprema went to Toledo and threatened Villanueva that he would be publicly stripped of his habit as a knight of Calatrava and be relaxed to the secular arm for burning.[375] He was helpless in the hands of those who would shrink from nothing to accomplish their ends; they had gone too far to hesitate now and his power of endurance was exhausted.

***

Meanwhile his brother Agustin had not been idle. In several interviews with the king he had presented memorials which Philip forwarded to Arce, March 27th, exhorting him to observe justice but to take care that the severity and authority of the Inquisition do not suffer. He added that the memorials showed that the secrecy of the Inquisition had been violated; this must be investigated and exemplary punishment be administered.[376] There was no hope of justice in this quarter and Agustin turned to Rome as a last resort. Don Joseph Navarro, who is spoken of as secretary, a devoted follower of Villanueva, was despatched thither to procure a brief and was doubtless well provided with funds. His errand soon was known and, on June 7th, Philip wrote to his ambassador, the Count of Oñate, to use every means to prevent the granting of the brief and, if issued, to procure its revocation; a personal note to the pope, at the same time, pointed out the irreparable injury which the admission of the appeal would cause to the holy Catholic faith and the free exercise of the Inquisition. Communications were slow for, on July 26th, Oñate reported the arrival of Navarro and asked for instructions.[377]

Navarro found little difficulty in obtaining the desired brief, in spite of Oñate's efforts. Villanueva seems to have awaited it, while recuperating in retirement from his three years' incarceration and final struggles. When it arrived he went to Saragossa, which he reached August 31st. His coming aroused many fears, for people thought it might be the prelude to a bloody drama, like that of Antonio Pérez. On September 2nd he presented himself at the prison of Manifestacion, where bail was entered for him by the sons of his brother Agustin and of the Count of Fuentes, after which he applied for a firma, to protect him from molestation during the course of his appeal, which was duly granted. He was given the city--or as some said the kingdom--as a prison and, on September 4th the Bishop of Málaga, who was captain-general, reported to the Count of Haro, Philip's new minister, that the city was quiet and there was nothing to fear. The bishop enclosed a letter of September 1st from Villanueva to the king, announcing that, during his imprisonment, his representatives, without his knowledge, had appealed to the pope, who had granted a brief empowering either the Bishop of Cuenca, Segovia or Calahorra, to hear the case in appeal and to render a final decision. While anxious for this means of obtaining justice, he would desist from it if such were the royal pleasure; the brief had not been presented to either of the prelates, nor would it be without the royal licence.[378]

Arce had already been informed of the brief and had lost no time in taking steps to neutralize it. On September 3rd orders were sent to the Bishop of Calahorra--and doubtless to the others--ordering him not to receive it. He promptly replied that it had not been presented, but that if it should come he would refuse to accept or to execute it, trusting to the royal protection against all penalties that it might contain; he had been connected with the Inquisition and knew its justice with regard to Villanueva and, if these appeals to Rome were allowed, the consequences to the Catholic religion would be lamentable.[379] Apparently the Spanish episcopate had small reverence for the Vicegerent of God.

***

The leading statesmen of Spain took a different view. A junta had been assembled to consider the situation, of which five members out of six (including the President of Castile and the Commissioner-general of the Cruzada) united in a consulta of September 15th. This set forth that when the Toledo tribunal sentenced Villanueva he had a right of appeal to the Suprema; he presented reasons for recusing the inquisitor-general and some of the members and was denied a hearing; he was seized again for the protest and appeal and held until he accepted the sentence and renounced all defence. He was thus forced to have recourse to the pope, whose jurisdiction is supreme in matters of faith and is the source of that of all inquisitors. In ordinary cases three decisions in conformity [through appeals] are required to render a sentence conclusive, while here, in a case involving the honor of a whole family, the single sentence of an inferior tribunal is all that has been allowed. Villanueva did not violate his sentence in going to Saragossa, for it required him not to come within twenty leagues of the court, and he had gone away fifty leagues. He was justified in applying for the firma, for the right of appeal includes the means necessary to enjoy the appeal. The inquisitor-general should be instructed not to order his arrest for, besides that no man should be deprived of his defence, it might cause some disturbance in Saragossa, under pretext of a violation of the fueros, for it is notorious that he was discharged by the Inquisition. There are two courses open--one to solicit the pope to withdraw the brief; the other that the fiscal of the Suprema apply for it and then retain it; but these raise the scruple that a man struggling for his honor and that of his family is denied all defence, after he has been forced to seek it beyond the kingdom and moreover, in the disturbed condition of Naples [then in revolt under Masaniello], it is well not to offend the pope, who might cause the loss of the Italian possessions of Spain. The sixth member of the junta, the Licenciado Francisco Antonio de Alarcon, denounced Villanueva as guilty for going to another kingdom [Aragon]; he was impeding the Inquisition and inviting the papal interference which would destroy its usefulness; the fiscal should demand the papal brief and the Council should retain it.[380]

The opinion of the junta doubtless prevented the re-arrest and renewed prosecution of Villanueva, which was evidently contemplated, but otherwise all reasons of justice and reasons of state were wasted on Philip, who was completely under the domination of Arce y Reynoso and ready to rush blindly into a contest with Rome. Equally fruitless was an appeal, made September 23rd, by Agustin Villanueva, who furnished a list of cases in which appeals to the pope had been admitted.[381] A warning came from Oñate, who wrote, December 17th and again February 12, 1648, that Navarro was busily utilizing the impediments thrown in the way of the brief to procure another, that the curia attributed all the trouble to Arce, that the delay was producing a bad impression and that there was serious talk in the Congregation of the Inquisition of disciplining him for it. This brought from Philip, March 17th, a rambling and inconsequential letter, scolding Oñate for his lack of success and urging him to fresh efforts; the brief was invalid as being obreptitious and surreptitious; Navarro was ordered home and Oñate must see that he left Rome forthwith. Letters, moreover, to the pope and the cardinals in the Spanish interest, drawn up by the Suprema and signed by Philip, manifest how every influence that Spain possessed was employed to deprive Villanueva of his last resource.[382]

Innocent X, in fact, had grown indignant at the opposition to his brief and had transmitted through his nuncio another to Arce, forbidding all further resistance under pain of deprivation of the inquisitor-generalship, suspension of all functions and interdiction from entering a church, while other officials would be removed from office and excommunicated. To this Arce replied, March 12th, assuring the pope that the case had been suspended awaiting the papal decision, and representing, what he knew to be also false, that for a hundred and fifty years the popes had refused to entertain appeals or had revoked the briefs and remanded the cases to the inquisitor-general. The authority of the Inquisition, he argued, was now more necessary than ever, in consequence of the spread of Judaism and heresy. Villanueva had been treated with extreme kindness and benignity, as would be learned from a person about to be sent to inform the pope, wherefore he begged that the case be remitted to him and the Suprema.[383]

This was a typical specimen of inquisitorial methods of mis-representation and of evasion--of practical but not open disobedience. Innocent, however, was not to be thus juggled with. He had substituted the Bishop of Sigüenza for him of Cuenca. Then the Bishop of Segovia died and Calahorra was transferred to Pampeluna, whereupon further letters commissioned Sigüenza, Pampeluna and the Bishop-elect of Segovia, but Pampeluna died and was replaced by the Bishop of Avila, so finally a brief of April, 1648 ordered Avila, Sigüenza and Segovia to act, on their obedience and under penalty of suspension from all functions and of ingress to their churches. They all refused the dangerous office, under various excuses, but the nuncio brought great pressure to bear on Avila and he finally accepted. It is noteworthy, however, that Villanueva never presented himself before the bishop, either in person or by procurator, to have the case reopened.[384]

***

The matter was evidently growing serious and juntas were held, July 14th and August 27th, to consider the situation. As the latter was presided over by Arce, whom Philip had made President of Castile, so as to increase his powers of evil, it decided that the king should not submit to the abuses of the curia in a matter in which the Catholic religion was at stake.[385] Philip scarce needed urging, but it was not until November 5th that he took the offensive by sending Don Pedro de Minerbe, of the Royal Council, to seize the brief, in whomsoever's hands it might be, and any others that Villanueva might have procured, together with all papers relating to it. These were to be considered by a junta to be assembled for the purpose so that, if they did not contravene the privileges of the Inquisition, they might be executed and, if otherwise, that his Holiness should be advised of it and be supplicated to revoke them. Any notaries who had served the briefs were to be arrested and imprisoned with a view to their prosecution.[386]

Minerbe fulfilled his mission, but the time had passed when Ferdinand and Charles V had treated papal letters thus irreverently. Philip IV was a prince of very different caliber and his tottering monarchy inspired but little respect. Arce felt the danger of his position, for Innocent had threatened him with deposition if the execution of the brief was impeded and an explosion of papal wrath was inevitable. He sought shelter in playing a double game and, on January 19, 1649, he presented to Philip a report as to cases which had been evoked by the pope. In this, after citing a number, he added that there were many more recent ones in which the cases and papers had been demanded and the demands had been obeyed, notably in 1626 and 1627; these proved the subordination of the Spanish Inquisition to Rome and even without them the papal supremacy was incontestable; Villanueva's appeal was directly to the pope, whom all the faithful were bound to obey.[387] Having thus placed himself on the record, doubtless with the royal connivance, he felt free to repeat his assertions that papal interference was unprecedented and to urge his master to stand fast.

The Suprema had sent its fiscal Cabrera to Rome on this business and his efforts, added to those of Oñate, were inclining Innocent to yield, when the news came of the seizure of the briefs. The papal displeasure was extreme and there was no hesitation in taking up the gage of battle. It had become a struggle for independence on the one side and for supremacy on the other, which had to be fought out, for there was no ground for compromise. All the advantage was on the side of the curia in the contest thus rashly provoked; it knew this and its next move showed that it felt assured of victory. A brief of

March 1st recited the preliminaries of the case and then evoked it from the Inquisition and the bishops to the Apostolic See. Perpetual silence was imposed on the Inquisition, the inquisitor-general and other officials, any action by whom would bring upon them, ipso facto and without further sentence, perpetual and irrevocable suspension from divine service, the exercise of pontifical functions and ingress into churches, together with deprivation of their offices and ecclesiastical revenues. Moreover, within three months after notice of this, they were to transmit to Rome all papers and documents, public and private, concerning Villanueva, under the same penalties, and finally all bulls, from those of Alexander VI onward, concerning appeals were derogated.[388]

The Suprema might well characterize to Philip this document as containing extraordinary and unusual clauses and it could only suggest to him the favorite Spanish formula, obedecer y no cumplir-- to obey and not to execute. The first thing done was the customary supplication to the pope to withdraw it, based on the laws of the kingdom and the high deserts of the Holy Office. This was done in such haste that there was no time to make a clean copy and it was despatched by a courier, April 24th. This gave breathing time, and more was gained by representing that it was impossible to trust the originals of the documents to the risks of transportation and that the copying of them would consume much more than the three months allowed, as the secretaries were busy and the records so voluminous that they occupied more than eight thousand pages--a gross exaggeration for when copied they amounted only to forty-six hundred. This served for the present, however, and successive postponements were obtained.[389]

***

The supplication against the brief was of course useless and the papal anger increased on learning that Villanueva's salaries had all been stopped--a petty persecution most unwise under the circumstances. At this time a curious incident was a memorial from Villanueva, May 23rd, asking that his case be heard by the Council of Castile--although that body could not assume jurisdiction in such a matter. It was probably a despairing effort to find some exit from the complication, for Philip transmitted it to the Council, with some subsidiary papers, to be considered in the junta which he had ordered and a consults to be presented to him.[390] It of course had no result, but it indicates the perplexities with which the situation had become surrounded.

These perplexities were increased by a demand from Innocent for satisfaction for the treatment of his brief to the Bishop of Avila. A junta was assembled which could do nothing but refer it to the Suprema and the latter could only reply with a consulta of July 15th, exculpating itself for paying no regard to Villanueva's appeal. Nor did it succeed much better in a paper, drawn up July 17th, for the benefit of the Duke del Infantado, the new ambassador to Rome, for it could only recite the old briefs granting exclusive jurisdiction and endeavor to explain away as exceptional the cases in which the pope had insisted on his rights. All this, however, was felt to be useless and there was preparation for war in instructions sent to the sea-ports to keep close watch on all vessels arriving from Italy, when, if there appeared to be papal agents or notaries among the passengers, their baggage was to be minutely examined and any papal briefs addressed to bishops or judges were to be sent to the secretary of state and the bearers were to be held until further orders--this being done with the utmost secrecy and as if in the ordinary routine of business. The precaution proved superfluous, but in December the Duke del Infantado reported that his efforts and Cabrera's had been in vain; the pope insisted that the process should be brought to Rome.[391]

On the plea of the time required for copying, successive postponements had been obtained, the latest of which expired in April, 1650. The pope was becoming more and more impatient, especially as no satisfaction had been given for the seizure of the brief to the Bishop of Avila, nor had it been returned as he demanded. February 5th orders were sent to the nuncio that, if the papers were not forthcoming in April, the full penalties of the brief of evocation must be inflicted, and due notice of this was given to Arce. These penalties withdrew all functions from the inquisitor-general and Suprema-- abrogated their offices, in fact--and the friends of Villanueva were busy collecting evidence of their being at work so as to prove to Innocent the disregard of his withdrawal of faculties. The gravity of the situation is reflected in a consulta presented to Philip at this time, weighing the courses that might be followed and hinting at a possible schism as the result of the king's standing firm in defence of the Inquisition. To avert this it is hoped that a further delay may be obtained and the pope be placated by returning the Avila brief. The plan finally adopted of offering to send the papers and letting the king detain them was deprecated because the pope would see through it, and the blame of the perilous situation was thrown on the Spanish cardinals whose indifference was ascribed to their belief that the king favored Villanueva.[392] Arce's court intrigue had brought matters to such a pass that the sundering of Spain from Catholic unity was looming on the horizon.

On April 8th, the Archbishop of Tarsus, the papal nuncio, made a formal demand on the king for the papers; the latest term of delay had expired and the penalties for contumacy would operate of themselves. The policy of delay was still followed and, on May 2nd, Arce notified the nuncio that the copying was completed--two secretaries and five other officials had been working on them for twelve or fourteen hours a day--but in view of certain risks it was thought better to wait till the pope should indicate how they should be sent. The nuncio asked for a formal certificate that the papers were ready, on the strength of which he would ask the pope for instructions, and thus a month or two were gained.[393]

***

This was all mere playing for time. There was no intention of letting the papers go to Rome for, on April 24th, the king sent secret instructions to Infantado to avert it, but he replied June 27th and again July 26th, that Innocent refused all suggestions and there was little hope of an adjustment. Then another scene of the comedy was acted, September 14th, by issuing a formal order to forward the papers and, on the 16th they were delivered to Damian de Fonolleda, notary of the tribunal of Barcelona, in five volumes aggregating 4600 pages. There was no intention of sending them, however, and Fonolleda was detained in Madrid until November 5th. Meanwhile a junta, assembled for the purpose, presented a consulta, September 24th, setting forth that in no case should the papers be allowed to leave the kingdom and suggesting as a compromise that the matter be decided by three bishops sitting in the Suprema, without Arce and the members. Innocent of course rejected this and Fonolleda was allowed to depart on November 5th. In due time he reported his arrival at Valencia and was instructed to take passage by the first vessel and deliver the papers to the pope, but before he could obey this order it was countermanded and he was told to wait. Meanwhile the Suprema, to keep itself right on the record and avert the papal wrath, addressed to Philip on September 16th, October 3rd and 19th and January 23rd and February 4, 1651, repeated requests to allow the messenger to sail.[394]

This transparent by-play did not deceive Innocent. Cabrera had an audience, January 8, 1651, and told him that Fonolleda was only waiting for a vessel, to which the pope replied that he had been in Spain and knew how things were managed there--there was collusion between the king and inquisitor-general. He added that he bore ill-will to Villanueva, of whom he had had to complain, and would probably punish him more severely than the Inquisition had done, to which Cabrera replied that this was a matter of indifference, for all that the Inquisition wanted was to close the door on these appeals. The tension was becoming dangerous for, on February 18th, the nuncio notified Arce that he and the Suprema had incurred the penalties of the brief of evocation, that they could not be absolved until the papers reached Rome and that still stronger measures would be adopted. When Arce attempted to explain, the nuncio told him that the pope would abolish the Inquisition, to which Arce rejoined that God would not permit him to do so. In reporting this to Philip, Arce recapitulated the heavy penalties incurred ipso facto, adding that if the pope should publish such a sentence there would be scandal and discredit to the Inquisition, wherefore, in the name of the Suprema, he begged, as had frequently been asked before, that there should be no further delay in Fonolleda's departure. Of this a certificate was asked for transmission to the pope, as was likewise a supplication of much urgency from the Suprema on March 1st.[395]

This was all purely for papal consumption. Philip himself was beginning to hesitate and, on March 2nd, he ordered the Council of State to consider the tenacity with which the pope was insisting upon his encroachment on the regalías and the privileges of the Inquisition. Arce at once took the alarm and, in a memorial to the king, he sought earnestly to dissuade him from yielding. He repeated the falsehood that, for a hundred and fifty years, there had not been an instance of the pope disregarding the royal wishes, and reminded him that he had declared that he would rather lose his crown than allow the case to go to Rome. Now he learns that the king, in consultation with the Council, has resolved to let the papers go to Infantado with instructions not to deliver them or to ask the pope to return the package without opening it; it is folly to believe that he would do so and such precedent will be ruin to the Inquisition.[396]

In this memorial, Arce alludes to a papal command, received some time before, to retire to his see of Plasencia, from which he had been absent for eight years--a favorite method, as we have seen, of getting rid of a troublesome inquisitor-general. The command had been disregarded and now it was emphatically repeated. Philip complained to his ambassador that this was even more offensive than the evocation of Villanueva's case; it would result in irretrievable damage to religion and to the state; he had asked the nuncio to suspend the order and now he requests the pope to accept Arce's resignation of his bishopric and pass the bulls of presentation for his successor. Innocent was too shrewd to forfeit his hold on his antagonist; he played fast and loose with the resignation until he had carried his point and it was not until December 2, 1652, that it was accepted and Arce's successor, the Bishop of Zamora, was preconized. Arce lost his see, but he gratefully acknowledged that Philip's liberality was such that he could forego the revenues. It must have cost the king dear, for Plasencia was one of the wealthy sees, estimated, in 1612, as worth forty thousand ducats a year.[397]

***

In spite of Arce's remonstrance, Philip yielded to the advice of his counsellors. In a letter of April 11, 1651, he announced to Infantado that orders have been given to Fonolleda to sail and deliver to him the papers. Then, with an earnestness that betrays the cost of the sacrifice, the duke is told to refresh his memory with all the arguments advanced in previous despatches and, when thus fully prepared, he is to seek an audience and express the king's mortification at being forced to submit to an innovation so unexampled and so subversive of the rights of the Inquisition. If this fails to move the pope, he is to ask that the process be returned unopened, when the Inquisition will revise the case. If this is unsuccessful he is to request that the case be referred back to the three bishops. In the event of the rejection of these proposals, the process is to be laid at the pope's feet with an exhortation to consider, before opening it, the disfavor shown to the royal person and to the kingdom of Spain, in the sight of all Christendom.[398] Philip was fairly beaten. If his humiliation was extreme it was because he had attributed such absurd adventitious importance to the question and had staked everything on a struggle in which the papacy had unquestionable right on its side. There was nothing left for him but retreat and, with curious infelicity born of weakness and obstinacy, he contrived to render his defeat as undignified as possible.

Permission to sail was issued to Fonolleda, April 14th, but it was not until September 17th that Infantado reported that he had delivered the process to the pope with the hope that it would be speedily returned without being read by the ministers, or at least by more than one. It suited the Spaniards subsequently to assert that a promise had been given that the package should not be opened, but such a promise would have been grotesque and this letter shows that at most there was some assurance that a knowledge of the contents would be confined to a few. At the same time there can be no wonder that the Inquisition felt acutely the disgrace of having such a record exposed to unfriendly eyes, and the effort to get the papers back commenced at once. As early as October 31st, Infantado reports his efforts to accomplish this, but as yet without success.[399]

Infantado was replaced by the Count of Oropesa, whose letter of instructions, April 23, 1652, orders him to pay special attention to the matter. Innocent had committed it to Cardinals Lugo and Albizi, but in June he stated to Cardinal Trivulzio, then the representative of Spain, that he had given much labor to it and had recognized in it contradictions and variations, leading him to the conviction that it was a matter of vindictiveness. He refused to return the papers, but did not care to intervene personally in the case and thought he might delegate it to some bishops.[400] Now that he had vindicated his jurisdiction he evidently felt little interest in what he regarded as merely an intrigue.

Nothing further was done until, October 12th, Innocent addressed two briefs, one to the king and the other to Arce. It is evident that the acquittal in 1632 and the condemnation in 1647 had excited no little comment in Rome, for in these briefs great surprise is expressed at the mutability in the opinions of calificadores, consultors and judges, such as might be expected of the populace but not of learned and thoughtful men. To soften this reproof some expressions followed highly commending the Inquisition as the ornament and protection of Spain and, to the king, Innocent added that, owing to the importance and prolixity of the case, he had not been able to reach a conclusion. The nuncio, however, in handing his brief to Arce, told him that the pope had concluded to place the case at the disposition of the king and that the papers had been returned to Trivulzio in Rome. Arce was radiant with triumph; Cabrera had reported the same and petitioned to be allowed to return and nothing remained but to get the papers back. They did not come, however, nor any brief recommitting the case; Arce grew anxious and begged the king, January 4, 1653, to urge Trivulzio to obtain them.[401]

Innocent either was taking malicious pleasure in exciting hopes and then disappointing them or else he was using the position to obtain diplomatic advantage in the growing tension between the courts over the Barberino marriage of the grand-daughter of his brother--a transaction in which he complained that the Spanish ministers had almost threatened him and that no present had been sent on the occasion. Cabrera's letters of December, 1652 and the first half of 1653 report a series of tergiversations and of promises made and broken by Innocent which show that to him Villanueva was merely a pawn in the game between Rome and Madrid.[402]

***

Villanueva died in Saragossa, July 21, 1653. In his will, executed the day before, he made ample provision for the salvation of his soul, and San Placido was in his mind to the last, for he appointed as its patron his nephew Gerónimo and his descendants, or in their default his niece Margarita and her descendants, they being the principal heirs of his large estate. The only change which this brought into the affair was that the Inquisition proposed to take advantage of the opportunity to commence a new prosecution against his fame and memory--apparently with the double purpose of vindicating its jurisdiction and, by sequestrating his property, of restraining the family, who continued their efforts in Rome for a vindication. Fortunately for them, Alexander VII, who saw in such action an invasion of his jurisdiction, prohibited, in 1656, this cowardly profanation of the ashes of the dead and when, with quenchless malignity, Arce, in 1659, sought to get this prohibition removed, the attempt was unsuccessful.[403]

It is scarce worth while to follow in detail the further weary progress of this affair, in which Spanish tenacity was pitted against the wily diplomacy of Rome. Pertinacious efforts continued for years to get the case remitted back, or at least to have the papers returned, in order to create the belief that it had been remitted. Stimulated by energetic instructions of August 24, 1658 from Philip, his ambassador Gaspar de Sobremonte had a stormy interview with Alexander VII, in which the pope finally told him that the case had never been considered by the Congregation of the Inquisition and that the king must content himself with the brief of October 12, 1652. To this Sobremonte retorted that that brief settled nothing, when the pope said vaguely that he would see whether any satisfaction could be given to the Inquisition. So it continued until Alexander, grown weary of the urgency which promised to be interminable, cut it short, March 29, 1660, by a brief to the king in which he said that the case had been finally concluded by Innocent X, as appeared from his letters to Philip and Arce of March 12 (October 12, 1652). There was nothing more to be said about it, as would be fully explained by the Archbishop of Corinth, the nuncio, to whom full credit was to be given.[404]

This ended the case which, from its inception in 1628, had lasted for thirty-two years. Cabrera had spent nearly twelve years in Rome and had richly earned the bishopric of Salamanca which rewarded his labors, but his efforts while there had cost the Suprema nearly a hundred thousand ducats, at a time when it was representing itself as wholly impoverished. Arce had succeeded in removing Villanueva from the court and in blackening his memory, but the victory remained with the papacy, which had vindicated its appellate jurisdiction, for, although it never decided the case it retained possession of it and the papers which were the symbol of its rights.

With its customary unscrupulousness, the Suprema endeavored to evade the precedent when, in 1668, it was alleged in the quarrel with the Bishop of Majorca (Vol. I, p. 501). In a consulta of that year it gives a summary of the case up to the delivery of the papers to the pope, who then, it proceeds to state, sent a brief full of favors to Arce, approving of Villanueva's sentence and the method of procedure; there was, it is true, an irregularity in allowing the papers to remain in Rome, but the pope excused himself because the originals were in Spain; the evil example led several powerful men to seek appeals to the Holy See, but the pope refused to entertain them, recognizing that it was injurious to the faith. When, in the same quarrel, it boasted of the bulls which it held prohibiting appeals, the Council of Aragon pointed out that the popes always preserved their reserved rights by a clause excepting cases in which they should insert in their letters the text of the bulls thus derogated.[405]

BOURBON RESISTANCE

In the subsequent quarrel with the canons and clergy of Majorca, in 1671 (Vol. I, p. 503) the latter appealed to the Holy See, under the brief obtained in 1642, and procured letters declaring void the excommunications fulminated by the tribunal and valid those uttered by the executors of the brief. The nuncio exhibited these letters to the inquisitor-general with a paper arguing that these appeals should be allowed and asking, in case there was a privilege or regalía to the contrary, that it should be shown to him. This was a test which the Suprema could not meet and, after a long delay, it sent, June 11, 1676, to the king all the documents bearing on the subject and asked him to assemble a junta to consider them and advise him what to do. It must have been impossible to solve the question favorably for, in a consulta of July 28, 1693, on the occasion of a fresh disturbance, it expressed its profound regret that the junta had failed to reach any conclusion.[406]

***

Two centuries of bickering thus left the Holy See in possession of its imprescriptible jurisdiction, but the Bourbons were less reverential than the Hapsburgs. In 1705, the hostility of the papacy led Philip V to forbid the publication of papal briefs without the royal exequatur and to prohibit all appeals to Rome. He held his ground in spite of the furious manifestos of Monroy, Archbishop of Santiago, proving that obedience was due to the pope rather than to the king, and the more temperate argumentation of Cardinal Belluga, then Bishop of Cartagena.[407] We hear little after this of appeals of individuals and, indeed, the experience of Villanueva, while apparently a defeat for the Inquisition, was in reality a victory, for it showed how hopeless was the contest of a prisoner against the whole power of the Inquisition and of the crown. Even when the Holy See had the advantage of being in possession of the person in dispute it could only fight a drawn battle, as in the case of Manuel Aguirre who, in 1737, escaped from the prison of the Inquisition, made his way to Rome, and presented his appeal in person. When the curia demanded the papers necessary for his trial, the Inquisitor-general Orbe y Larrategui did not in terms deny the papal rights but argued that the Inquisition was privileged to conclude a case before forwarding the papers for review and offered that, if the Holy See would return the prisoner, his flight should not be held to aggravate his offence and in due time all the desired information would be furnished to Rome. The acceptance of such a proposition was impossible, but the papacy was in no position to contest the matter. After the death of Orbe, in 1740, the curia took the case up again for discussion, but the only course open seemed to be to instruct the nuncio to persuade the Inquisition to obedience and we may safely conclude that Aguirre escaped without a trial.[408]

The ecclesiastical organizations, as in the Majorca cases, were in better position to engage in such conflicts, but Philip V was as little disposed as his predecessors to permit them. The multitudinous quarrels over suppressed prebends and the benefices held by officials of the Inquisition had always been a fruitful source of such appeals and the curia was never loath to entertain them. A typical case was that of Francisco Vélez Frias, private secretary of Inquisitor-general Camargo, who obtained the dignity of precentor in the cathedral of Valladolid, much to the disgust of the chapter. It applied to the inquisitor-general for the papers in the case, alleging that it would reply, but returned them without comment and appealed to Rome, where it obtained a rescript from Benedict XIII, committing the case to an auditor of the Camera and inhibiting the inquisitor-general from its cognizance. When Philip was informed of this he intervened in the spirit of Ferdinand. By his order the Marquis de la Compuesta wrote to the dean and chapter, June 19, 1728, expressing in vigorous terms the royal displeasure at an act so offensive to the inquisitor-general, whose jurisdiction in such matters was exclusive, and so contrary to the will of the king and to his regalías. They were ordered, without making a reply, to abandon the appeal and to apply to the inquisitor-general and the Suprema who would render justice in the case. It is safe to assume that they did not venture to disobey.[409]

The papacy of the eighteenth century was in no position to contest the growing independence of the temporal powers, while the revival of Spain under the Bourbons rendered hopeless any struggle against the resolve of the monarchs to regulate the internal affairs of the kingdom. Yet in this the Holy See was deprived of its inviolable rights, for the latest authoritative utterance of the Church, in the year 1899, tells us that it is an article of faith that the Roman pontiff is the supreme judge of the faithful and that in all ecclesiastical cases recourse may be had to him. It is therefore forbidden, under pain of excommunication, to appeal from him to a future council or to impede in any way the exercise of ecclesiastical jurisdiction, whether in the internal or external forum. Moreover it is against right reason to exalt human power over spiritual power, which is supreme over all powers.[410]

BOOK IV - ORGANIZATION

CHAPTER I - THE INQUISITOR-GENERAL AND SUPREME COUNCIL

The superior efficiency of the Spanish Inquisition was largely due to its organization. The scattered subordinate tribunals, which dealt directly with the accused, were not independent, as in the old papal Inquisition, but were under the control of a central head, consisting of the inquisitor-general and a council which, for the sake of brevity, we have called the Suprema. It has been seen how Ferdinand and Isabella, after a few years' experience, obtained from the Holy See the appointment of Torquemada as inquisitor-in-chief with power of delegating his faculties and of removing his delegates--a power which gave him absolute control. At first the commission of the inquisitor-general was held to require renewal at the death of the pope who issued it, although, in the old Inquisition, after considerable discussion, it was decided, in 1290, by Nicholas IV, in the bull Ne aliqui, that the commissions of inquisitors were permanent.[411] This formality was subsequently abandoned and, towards the close of the sixteenth century, the commissions were granted ad beneplacitum--during the good pleasure of the Holy See--and this continued until the end.[412] Similarly there was a question whether the powers of the inquisitors lapsed on the death of the inquisitor-general. When Mercader of Aragon died, in 1516, the Suprema, in conveying the news to the tribunals, instructed them to go on with their work; in some places the secular authorities assumed that they were no longer in office, a royal letter had to be procured to prevent interference with them, and, when Cardinal Adrian was appointed, he confirmed their faculties.[413] It became customary for each new inquisitor-general to renew the commissions on his accession, but as there frequently was a considerable interval, the question arose whether, during that time, all the acts both of the Suprema and the tribunals were not invalid. In 1627 it was concluded that they held delegated power directly from the pope and not from the inquisitor-general, so that their faculties were continuous.[414] This was a forced construction, somewhat derogatory to the authority of the inquisitor-general, and was upset in 1639, when the Suprema decided that the inquisitor-general could confer powers only during his own life and therefore each one on his accession confirmed the appointments of all officials during his pleasure, which continued to be the formula employed.[415] This left open the question of the interregnum, which seems to have been somewhat forcibly settled by necessity, as when Giudice resigned in 1716 and his successor, Joseph de Molines, was serving as auditor of the Rota in Rome. The Suprema, in notifying the tribunals of his appointment, told them that, until his arrival in Madrid, they were to continue their functions.[416]

THE SUPREMA ACQUIRES POWER

As regards the Suprema, it would appear at first to have been merely a consultative body. I have already alluded to the case in which Torquemada ferociously overruled the acts of the tribunal of Medina del Campo, acting autocratically and without reference to the Council, as though it had no executive functions. Neither had it legislative powers. The earlier Instructions were issued in the name of the Inquisitor-general and, when he desired consultation and advice in the framing of general regulations, he did not confer with the Council, but assembled the inquisitors and assessors of the tribunals, who discussed the questions and formulated the rules of procedure, as in the Instructions of Valladolid, in 1488.[417] The crown, in fact, was the ultimate arbiter for, in the supplementary Instructions of 1485, inquisitors were directed, when doubtful matters were important, to report to the sovereigns for orders.[418] It was the inquisitor-general also who held the all-important power of the purse. The instructions of Avila in 1498, still issued in the name of Torquemada, fix the salaries of all the officials of the tribunals and add that, when the inquisitors-general see that there is necessity or especial labor, they can make such ayudas de costa, or gratuities, as they deem proper.[419]

It was inevitable, however, that the Council should acquire power. Torquemada was aging and, although at this period the tribunals acted independently, convicting culprits and holding autos de fe at their discretion, yet he held appellate jurisdiction, which doubtless brought a larger amount of business than he could attend to individually, in addition to his other functions. Cases also must have been frequent in which the consultas de fe, or juntas of experts called in to assist in pronouncing judgement, were not unanimous, or where there were doubts which the local judges felt incompetent to decide. Thus we are told that, in the gathering of inquisitors at Valladolid, in 1488, there was full discussion as to the difficulties arising from the incompetence or insufficient number of the consultors, and it was resolved that when there was doubt or discordia (the technical name for lack of unanimity) the fiscal of the tribunal should bring the papers to Torquemada, who would refer them to the Suprema or to such of its members as he might designate--thus indicating how completely its powers were derived from him and how subordinate was its position.[420] As Torquemada grew more infirm, even though four colleagues were adjoined to him, the importance of the Suprema increased, as is seen in the 1498 Instructions of Avila, where this provision wears the altered form that when difficult or doubtful questions arise in the tribunals, the inquisitors are to consult the Suprema and bring or send the papers when so ordered.[421]

INQUISITOR-GENERAL AND SUPREME COUNCIL

When Torquemada passed away, in the absence of his vigorous personality, the Council rapidly became a determining factor in the organization. In 1499 and in 1503, instructions of a general character, although signed by one inquisitor-general, also bear the signatures of two or three members of the Council and are countersigned by the secretary "por mandado de los señores del consejo." A decree of November 15, 1504, although signed by Deza alone, bears that it is with the concurrence, opinion and vote of the Council.[422] It was also assuming the appellate jurisdiction, for it announced to inquisitors, January 10, 1499, that, if any parties came before it with appeals, it would hear them and administer what it deemed to be justice.[423] If papal confirmation of this were lacking it was supplied by Leo X, in his bull of August 1, 1516, in which he conferred on members of the Council, in conjunction with the inquisitor-general, power to act in all appeals arising from cases of faith.[424]

The death of Ferdinand, January 23, 1516, the preoccupations of Ximenes who, till his death in November, 1517, was governor of Spain, and the youth and inexperience of Charles V, gave the Suprema an opportunity of enlarging its functions. We find it regulating details and giving instructions to the tribunals much after the fashion of Ferdinand himself.[425] This was facilitated by the fact that it had a president of its own who, during vacancies, acted as inquisitor-general, a practice apparently commenced in 1509 when Ximenes, on the eve of his departure with his expedition to Oran, was required by Ferdinand to appoint the Archbishop of Granada, Francisco de Rojas, president of the Council during his absence.[426]

THE SUPREMA HAS A PRESIDENT

The Suprema, with a permanent president of its own, was evidently well fitted to encroach on the functions of the inquisitor-general and, as policy varied with regard to this presidency, it is perhaps worth while to follow such indications as we can find with regard to it. In 1516 Martin Zurbano was president of the supreme Councils of both Castile and Aragon and, in the interval between the death of Mercader and the accession of Cardinal Adrian, he acted as inquisitor-general of Aragon.[427] In 1520, when Charles at Coruña was departing from Spain, he appointed Francisco de Sosa, Bishop of Almería, as president. In 1522, Cardinal Adrian on August 5th, the day of his departure from Tarragona for Rome, appointed Garcia de Loaysa, the future inquisitor-general, president of the Councils of both Castile and Aragon.[428] It was inevitable that questions should arise as to the comparative standing of such an official and the inquisitor-general. Sosa, as president, had a salary of 200,000 maravedís, while Adrian as inquisitor-general had only 150,000, the same as the other members of the Council.[429] This implied superiority and it was evidently necessary to enforce subordination as when, in 1539, Cardinal Tavera was made inquisitor-general and Fernando Valdés president, the latter was told that he was not in any way to modify the orders of the former. So when, in 1549, Valdés succeeded Tavera and Fernando Niño, Bishop of Sigüenza, became president, Charles V wrote to him from Brussels, March 26th, that he was to obey the instructions given to Valdés on his accession.[430] It was doubtless found that this duplicate headship led to trouble, and the position of president was allowed to lapse for, in 1598, Páramo tells us that the inquisitor-general was president.[431] In 1630 Philip IV proposed to revive it under the title of governor of the Suprema, but the Council protested, arguing that it had from the beginning functioned successfully without such a head; if the office had no special prerogatives, it would be superfluous; if it had, there would be collisions with the inquisitor-general; in either case, the innovation would be regarded by the public as evidence that the Council needed improvement.[432] This may have postponed but did not prevent the creation of the office for, in 1649, we find a president acting.[433] It was probably soon discontinued for, in some lists of members about 1670, none is designated as president and if, in 1815, there is one found occupying the seat of honor as dean, he was probably only the senior member.[434]

Irrespective of the influence which the office of president may have had, the relations between the inquisitor-general and Suprema were ill-defined and fluctuated. Under Cardinal Adrian we sometimes find the Councils acting as though independent and sometimes Adrian doing the same. In the Aragonese troubles over Juan Prat, the Suprema nowhere appears--everything is in the name of Adrian or of Charles. During the interval between Adrian's election as pope, January 9, 1522, and his leaving Spain, August 5th, he and the Suprema acted at times each independently of the other.[435] As the vacancy was not filled until September 1523, by the appointment of Manrique, there can be little doubt that this effacement of the inquisitor-generalship established precedents for a development of the activity and functions of the Suprema which, under Manrique, is found taking part in all business, the signatures of the members following his in the letters and decrees; it was rapidly becoming the direct executive and legislative head of the Holy Office.[436] His disgrace and relegation to his see, in 1529, could not but stimulate this tendency. During his absence there are many letters from it submitting questions for his decision, but there are also many to the tribunals, showing that it was acting in full independence.

THE SUPREMA BECOMES DOMINANT

The result of this is seen, in 1540, when Cardinal Tavera, in announcing to the tribunals his accession to office, tells them that he will act with the concurrence and opinion of the members of the Council and when, in the same year, he appointed Nicolao Montañánez inquisitor of Majorca, he refers him to what the Council writes to him with regard to his duties. The appointing power continued to give to the inquisitor-general a certain predominance, but otherwise he and the Suprema had coalesced into one body--a fact emphasized by a declaration, May 14, 1542, that they formed together but a single tribunal and that there was no appeal from the one to the other.[437] Still, there was a primacy of honor in the inquisitor-generalship. When the Instrucciones nuevas--the elaborate code of procedure embodied in the Instructions of 1561--were sent to the tribunals, it was in the name of Inquisitor-general Valdés but, in the prefatory note, he is made to state that they had been maturely discussed in the Council, where it was agreed that they should be observed by all inquisitors.[438]

Thus the Suprema had fairly established itself as the ruling power of the Inquisition, and its independent position is described by the Venetian envoy, Simone Contarini, in his Relation of 1605, where he says that it is absolute in everything concerning the faith, not being obliged, like the other Councils, to consult with the king. The inquisitor-general, he adds, fills all the offices except the membership of the Council, whose names are presented to the king.[439] Even in the matter of these appointments, as we have seen, the instructions of Philip II, III, and IV, from 1595 to 1626, require the inquisitor-general to consult with the Suprema in appointing inquisitors and fiscals.

Various documents, during the seventeenth century, show that the inquisitor-general by no means attended all the daily sessions of the Council and rarely voted on the cases brought before it.[440] In the letters of the Suprema, a decision reached when he was present records the fact--"visto en el consejo, presente el ex^{mo} señor inquisidor-general"--but by far the greater number have no such formula, indicating that it acted without him and that its acts were binding.[441] Another formula frequently employed is "consultado con el ex^{mo} señor inquisidor-general," which makes the Suprema act and the inquisitor-general merely consult.[442] Yet of course the power wielded by the inquisitor-general must have varied greatly with the character of the individual and the influence which he had with the king. A man like Arce y Reynoso, in such a case as Villanueva's or Nithard under the queen-regent, used the tremendous authority of the Holy Office at his pleasure.

In the deliberations of the Council, as early as 1551, we find decisions reached by a majority vote and when, about 1625, there chanced to be a tie and the imperious Pacheco endeavored to decide the matter, he was bluntly told that he could not do so--his vote counted no more than that of any other member.[443] An elaborate account of the procedure, dating between 1666 and 1669, tells us that, when a letter, petition or memorial is read, if it is a matter of routine, the inquisitor-general decides it without taking votes; if it is doubtful, he takes the vote, beginning with the youngest member. If it is a question of justice, the majority decides; if there is a tie, it is laid aside until other members can be called in; all sign the papers, irrespective of how they had voted. It is not necessary for the inquisitor-general to be present throughout the session; it suffices for him to be there for two hours in the morning, for what especially concerns his jurisdiction and he need not assist in the afternoons, when matters not of faith are discussed with the two adjunct members of the Council of Castile. Another writer tells us that it was forbidden to give reasons for the vote and that absent members could vote in writing.[444]

The relations between the inquisitor-general and the Suprema thus had grown up without any precise definition and consequently were open to diversity of opinion. A writer who, about 1675, drew up an exhaustive account of the working of the Inquisition, admits that it was a disputed question whether the inquisitor-general could act by himself and dispense with the Suprema, but he states that the prevailing opinion is that the members are independent and act by immediate delegated papal powers; in his absence their acts are final and it is the same when the office is vacant. This, he says, is the invariable custom, nor can there be found an instance of his acting without the Suprema, while the Suprema in his absence acts without him.[445]

As we have seen, this was a usurpation, grown strong by prescription. It was fairly put to the test, in 1700, by Inquisitor-general Mendoza, in the trial of Fray Froilan Díaz, which was, in some respects, one of the most noteworthy cases in the annals of the Inquisition.

CASE OF FROILAN DÍAZ

Carlos II, the last of the Hapsburgs who were the curse of Spain, was imbecile equally in mind and body. A being less fitted to rule has probably never encumbered a throne and it was his misfortune, no less than that of his people, that, reaching it in his fourth year, through thirty-five weary years, from 1665 to 1700, he staggered under the burden, while his kingdom plunged ever deeper in misery and humiliation. He was but a puppet in the hands of any intriguing man or woman or artful confessor who might obtain ascendancy; prematurely old, when he should have been in the prime of manhood, with mental and bodily sufferings continually on the increase, he was restlessly eager for whatever might promise relief. His first wife, Marie Louise of Orleans, had died childless, and the second, Maria Anna of Neuburg, whom he married in 1690, in the vain hope of an heir, was an ambitious woman who speedily dominated him and ruled Spain through her favorites. It soon became recognized that a successor would have to be selected from among the collateral branches and, after active intrigues, parties formed themselves in the court in support of the two most prominent aspirants--Philip Duke of Anjou, grandson of Louis XIV, who was preferred by the mass of the people, and the Archduke Charles, son of the Emperor Leopold I, whose claims were urged by the queen. It was the misfortune of Froilan Díaz that he became the sport of the contending factions.

In 1698 there was a court revolution. The kingdom was practically governed by the royal confessor, a Dominican named Pedro Matilla, who controlled the queen by enriching and advancing her favorites, prominent among whom was Don Juan Tomás, Admiral of Castile. He asked nothing for himself--as he told Count Oropesa, he preferred making bishops to being one. Carlos hated and feared him and at last secretly unbosomed himself to Cardinal Portocarrero, Archbishop of Toledo, one of the leaders of the French faction. No time was lost in utilizing the opportunity and Carlos welcomed the suggestion of replacing Matilla by another Dominican, Fray Froilan Díaz, a professor of theology in the University of Alcalá, a simple-minded and sincere man, whose life had been passed in convents and colleges and who knew nothing of intrigues and politics. Carlos asked to have him brought secretly to court and Matilla's first intimation of his disgrace was seeing Díaz conducted to the king through the royal antechamber. He retired to his cell in the convent del Rosario where, in a week, he died--it was said of mortification.

In April 1698 Froilan Díaz took possession of the seat in the Suprema reserved for the royal confessor. Plots for his overthrow commenced at once and he unconsciously aided them by fomenting strife in his own Dominican Order so injudiciously that, at the next chapter, his most bitter enemy, Nicolás de Torres-Padmota, was elected provincial. His inconsiderate zeal soon led him into still more dangerous paths, which inflamed hostility and afforded opportunity for its gratification. The king's health had been growing steadily worse, the convulsions and fainting-spells which afflicted him had constantly increased, and the opinion had spread that he was bewitched. Inquisitor-general Valladares had brought the matter before the Suprema, when it had been anxiously discussed without taking action. Valladares had died in 1795 and had been succeeded by the Dominican Juan Tomás de Rocaberti, Archbishop of Valencia, who, in January 1698, was secretly consulted by Carlos concerning the rumors attributing his sickness to sorcery, and was asked to investigate the matter and devise a remedy. It was again laid before the Suprema but, as before, the council deemed it too perilous a matter to be meddled with. When Díaz became a member, Rocaberti appealed to him and he eagerly promised to assist.

***

There were no indications to guide an investigation until Díaz chanced to learn that, in the nunnery of Cangas (Oviedo), there were several nuns demoniacally possessed who were being exorcised by Fray Antonio Alvarez de Argüelles, a former fellow-student of his. It had for ages been the belief that possessing demons, under the torture of exorcisms and abuse lavished on them by the priest, could be compelled to reveal facts beyond human capacity to ascertain. Much of the current medieval conceptions concerning the spiritual universe were derived from this source and the practice of thus seeking knowledge for laudable purposes was recognized as lawful, provided it was done imperatively and not solicited as a favor. Even the gratification of idle curiosity with demons was merely a venial sin.[446] Froilan Díaz was therefore merely adopting a legitimate method when he suggested that the demons of Cangas should be made to reveal the causes of the king's illness, which would be a step to its cure. Rocaberti eagerly assented and applied to the Dominican Bishop of Oviedo, but that wary prelate hesitated to embark in a matter so dangerous and discouraged the suggestion. Díaz then addressed Argüelles, who at first refused but finally consented, if he could have written commands from the inquisitor-general and confessor. Rocaberti accordingly wrote, June 18th, to inscribe the names of the king and queen on a piece of paper, place it in his breast and ask the demon if either of them were suffering from sorcery; Díaz enclosed this in a letter of his own and arranged a cipher for the correspondence. The obliging demon swore by God that the king had been bewitched at the age of fourteen to render him impotent and incapable of governing. With this Argüelles endeavored to withdraw, but Rocaberti and Díaz were insistent that he should ascertain further particulars and antidotes for the sorcery and, on September 9th, he wrote that the spell was administered April 3, 1675 in a cup of chocolate by the queen-mother, in order to retain power; the charm was made with the members of a dead man and the remedies were inunction with blessed oil, purging and separation from the queen.

Carlos was industriously stripped and anointed and purged and prayed over, but to no purpose save to terrify and exhaust him. For a year correspondence was vigorously kept up, obtaining from the demons answers curiously explicit and yet evasive and contradictory. At one time it was said that he had been bewitched on a second occasion, September 24, 1694; then the demons refused to say more except that their previous assertions had been false and that Carlos had not been bewitched. There were also contradictions as to the sorceresses employed, who were named and their addresses were given, but the efforts to find them were fruitless. The destinies of Spain were made to hang on the flippant utterances of hysterical girls, who unsaid one day what they had averred the day before. The affair reached such proportions that the Emperor Leopold officially communicated the revelations of a Viennese demoniac implicating a sorceress named Isabel, who was searched for in vain, and he also sent to Madrid a celebrated exorcist named Fray Mauro Tenda, who secretly exorcised the king for some months, which naturally aggravated his malady.

Meanwhile a storm was brewing. The queen's temper had been aroused by her political defeat; she was angered by the enforced separation from her husband and she was inflamed to fury when she secretly heard of the second bewitching of September, 1694, which was attributed to her. A month after her learning this Rocaberti died, with suspicious opportuneness, June 19, 1699. This failed to relieve her, for soon afterwards three endemoniadas in Madrid were found confirming the story and implicating both her and the former queen-regent. Her wrath was boundless and she vowed Fray Froilan's destruction, for which the Inquisition offered the readiest means. To this end she sought to induce Carlos to appoint in Rocaberti's place Fray Antonio Folch de Cardona, a friend of Don Juan Tomás, Admiral of Castile, who had fallen from power when Matilla was dismissed. The king, however, who was resolved on pushing the investigation, appointed Cardinal Alonso de Aguilar and sent for the papal commission. In announcing his choice to Aguilar he said it was for the purpose of probing the matter to the bottom. To this Aguilar pledged himself and promptly sent for the senior member of the Suprema, Lorenzo Folch de Cardona (a half-brother of Antonio), telling him that all indications pointed to the guilt of the Admiral who must at once be arrested and his papers seized. Cardona replied that this was impossible; semi-proof was requisite prior to arrest and here there was no evidence. The queen grew more anxious than ever; Aguilar was taken with a slight indisposition, he was bled secundum artem and in three days he was dead--on the very day that his commission arrived from Rome. Suspicion was rife but there was no proof.

***

Carlos by this time was so enfeebled that the queen obtained from him the appointment of Baltasar de Mendoza, Bishop of Segovia, with whom she had a satisfactory understanding, he pledging himself to gratify her vindictiveness and she promising him a cardinal's hat as the reward of success. The first move was against the Austrian exorciser Fray Tenda, who was arrested in January, 1700, on a different charge, but under examination he described the revelations of the Madrid demoniacs, made in Froilan's presence and he escaped with abjuration de levi and banishment. Froilan was then examined, but he refused to speak without the consent of the king, under whose orders he had acted and with strict injunctions of secrecy. Meanwhile the Dominican Provincial Torres-Padmota used his authority to obtain from Argüelles at Cangas the letters of Froilan, on the strength of which he promptly accused him to the Suprema in the name of the Order, to which Froilan answered that he had acted under Rocaberti's order at the pressing instance of the king, in what was sanctioned by Aquinas and other doctors.[447] Mendoza informed the king that Froilan was accused of a grave offence but could not be prosecuted without the royal permission; Charles resisted feebly and then yielded to the pressure of the queen and Mendoza by dismissing him and replacing him with Torres-Padmota. Stunned, dazed and helpless, Froilan obeyed Mendoza's order to betake himself to the Dominican convent at Valladolid, but on the road he turned his steps and sought refuge in Rome. A royal letter to the Duke of Uceda, then ambassador, was speedily obtained ordering the arrest of Froilan on his arrival, as he was under trial by the Inquisition which permitted no appeal to Rome, while the tribunals of Barcelona and Murcia were instructed to throw him on arrival into the secret prison. He was shipped back to Cartagena and duly immured by the Murcia tribunal.

Then followed a struggle for mastery in the Suprema. Mendoza procured the assent of the members to the appointment of special calificadores or censors to consider the charges and evidence. Five theologians were selected who reported unanimously, June 23, 1700 that there was no matter of faith involved, whereupon the Suprema, with the exception of Mendoza, voted to suspend the case, which was equivalent to acquittal. Then, on July 8th, Mendoza signed an order of arrest and sent it around for the signatures of the members, who unanimously refused, whereupon he summoned them to his room and with alternate wrath and entreaty vainly sought their co-operation. In a gust of passion he declared that he would have his way and in an hour he had ordered three of them to keep their houses as prisons and the Madrid tribunal to prosecute the secretary for refusing to counter-sign the warrant. Folch de Cardona was the only member left and this was because his half-brother Antonio, now Archbishop of Valencia, was a favorite of the queen. This violence caused no little excitement, which was increased when Miguélez, one of the members, who talked freely, was arrested one night in August and hurried off to the Jesuit college in Compostella, followed by the jubilating, or retiring on half-pay, of all three in terms of reprobation, as unfaithful to their duties, while the secretary was banished.

The Council of Castile intervened with a consulta pointing out to the king that the members had been punished without trial for upholding the laws, the canons and the practice of the Holy Office. The queen became alarmed and urged Mendoza to be cautious but he assured her that in no other way could her wishes be gratified. Meanwhile he had sent the papers to the tribunal of Murcia with orders to prosecute Froilan and send the sentence to him. It obeyed and twice submitted the case to its calificadores and other learned men, who reported in favor of the accused, whereupon it voted for his discharge. Then Mendoza evoked the case to himself and committed it to the Madrid tribunal; he brought Froilan there and confined him in a cell of the Dominican house of Nuestra Señora de Atocha where, in the power of Torres-Padmota, he lay for four years, cut off from all communication with the outside world, his very existence being in doubt, while the tribunal selected another group of calificadores who had no difficulty in finding him suspect of heresy.

***

Carlos had died, November 1, 1700, appointing in his will Philip of Anjou as his successor, until whose coming the queen-dowager was regent. For some months the members of the Suprema, jubilated by Mendoza's arbitrary assumption of authority, were kept in reclusion, but were finally liberated. Mendoza, who belonged to the Austrian faction, was relegated to his see of Segovia, but this brought no redress to Froilan. The Dominican General, Antonin Cloche, a Frenchman without bias to either party in the Inquisition, felt keenly the injustice committed against him and sent from Rome successively two agents who for three years labored in vain for his release. Mendoza was at bay and, in defiance of the traditions of the Spanish Inquisition, he appealed to the pope, to whom he sent an abstract of the proceedings. Clement XI was delighted with this surrender of Spanish independence and referred the case to the Congregation of the Inquisition which, after much deliberation, reported that it could not act without seeing all the papers. Mendoza replied that he was in exile through political reasons and could not furnish them, which was false, as he had carried them with him; he sent an agent with an argument drawn up by the new fiscal of the Suprema, Juan Fernando de Frias, at the instance of the nuncio at Madrid, in which the Suprema was denounced as the canonizer of a doctrine, heretical, erroneous, superstitious and leading to idolatry. This paper had been prepared in answer to one by Folch de Cardona, arguing that the members of the Suprema had not merely a consultative but a decisive vote and that the inquisitor-general had no more. Frias, however, had foolishly devoted himself to proving that the interrogations of the demoniacs were heretical; this did not suit the nuncio who openly declared that, in place of refuting Cardona, he had published a thousand scandals and was a fool of no account. The argument, which he had printed, was condemned and suppressed and he himself was suspended from office, in 1702, by the queen, Marie Louise Gabrielle of Savoy, who was regent during the absence of Philip in Naples. It was probably about this time that the Suprema notified the tribunals that any orders from Mendoza, contrary to its own, were suspended.[448]

The intervention of the nuncio shows that the struggle had widened far beyond the theological question as to the lawfulness of interrogating demons and the guilt of the luckless Froilan Díaz. Two important principles had become involved--the appellate jurisdiction of Rome and its original jurisdiction in determining disputed points in the internal organization of the Spanish Inquisition. Pope Clement had eagerly welcomed the opening afforded by Mendoza, not only to claim that Froilan's case should be submitted to him, but he had also assumed, in Mendoza's favor, that the Suprema was subordinate to the inquisitor-general, through whom its powers were derived from the Holy See, which alone could decide the question. All this was vigorously combated by Cardona, with the aid of the Council of Castile. In the name of the Suprema, which now had three new members, he rehearsed all of Ferdinand's decrees against appeals and argued that the Suprema had always been a royal council, subjected to the king, and that the only distinction between its members and the inquisitor-general lay in his prerogatives as to appointments. He earnestly supplicated the king to order the seizure of a letter of Cardinal Paolucci, papal secretary of state, committing Froilan's case to Mendoza or to the Archbishop of Seville. The nuncio, on the other hand, insisted that the papacy had never divested itself of its supreme authority to judge everything throughout the world, and that the pope was the only authority entitled to construe papal grants, including the functions of the Suprema. While the controversy thus raged, Froilan lay forgotten in his dungeon.

Practically the decision lay with the king and, in the vicissitudes of the War of Succession, Philip had more pressing matters to vex his new and untried royalty. He seems to have vacillated for, in July 1703, there was circulated a paper purporting to confirm the jubilation of the members of the Suprema and to commit Froilan's case to Mendoza. This drew from the Suprema two energetic consultas, pointing out Mendoza's arbitrary course and the injury to the regalías of his appeal to Rome. Philip was embarrassed and, by a royal order of December 24th, sought advice of the Council of Castile, which responded, January 8 and 29, 1704, by vigorous consultas denouncing Mendoza's actions as inexcusable violence. The case seemed to be drawing to a conclusion when it was delayed by a new complication. The succession to Mendoza was actively sought by two churchmen of the highest rank, but the king declared that he would not appoint any one of such lofty station, when both withdrew and one of them, or some one in his name, started what Cardona calls the diabolical proposition that the Inquisition had become superfluous; the few Judaizers and heretics remaining could be dealt with by the episcopal jurisdiction--the case of Froilan Díaz could be settled by his bishop--and thus the enormous expense of the Holy Office could be saved. This revolutionary suggestion was warmly supported by the Princesse des Ursins but Philip rejected it--wisely, no doubt, for even had he been inclined to it his throne was as yet too insecure to risk the results of such an innovation.

***

The Admiral of Castile was a refugee in Portugal, whence he was actively fomenting resistance to Philip. Mendoza notoriously belonged to the Austrian party and Philip could ultimately scarce fail to decide against him. On October 27th he sent for Cardona, with whom he had a secret interview, resulting in a paper drawn up for his signature the next day. On November 3rd a royal order was read in the Suprema restoring to their places the three jubilado members, who were to receive all the arrears of their salaries. This was followed November 7th by a decree addressed to Mendoza ordering him and his successors to respect the members of the Suprema as representing the royal person, as exercising the royal jurisdiction and as entitled to cast decisive votes. Moreover, he was, under pain of exile and deprivation of temporalities, within seventy-two hours, to deliver to the Suprema all the papers concerning Froilan Díaz and to make known whether he was alive and in what prison. The next day it was ordered that the Suprema should decide the case and, on November 17th, after hearing the proceedings, a sentence was unanimously rendered, absolving Froilan, restoring to him his seat in the Suprema, with all arrears of salary, and also the cell in the convent del Rosario assigned to the royal confessors, of which he had been unjustly deprived. A copy of this sentence was ordered to be transmitted to all the tribunals for preservation in their archives.[449]

Froilan Díaz was duly reinstated in the Suprema and we find his signature to its letters at least until 1712.[450] In reward of his sufferings, Philip nominated him to the see of Avila; he was not, however, a persona grata in Rome and Pope Clement refused his confirmation on the ground that he must first see the papers in the case and determine whether the acquittal was justified, thus asserting to the last his jurisdiction over the matter.[451] Philip held good and would make no other nomination until after Froilan's death, the see remaining vacant from 1705 until filled by Julian Cano y Tovar in 1714.

As for Mendoza, he was obliged to resign the inquisitor-generalship early in 1705. When, in 1706, Philip returned to Madrid, after his flight to Burgos, Mendoza and the Admiral, with many others, were arrested as traitors and the queen-dowager was escorted to Bayonne. Mendoza, of course, missed the coveted cardinalate, but he survived until 1727, in peaceful possession of his see. In replacing him as inquisitor-general, Philip was true to his maxim not to appoint a man of high rank and he nominated Vidal Marin, bishop of the insignificant see of Ceuta, who had distinguished himself, in 1704, by his gallant defence of that place against the English fleet that had just captured Gibraltar. In confirming him, after some delay, Clement took occasion, in a brief of August 8, 1705, to reassert the papal position and urgently to exhort him to maintain the subordination of the Suprema. He is to remember that he is supreme and in him resides the whole grant of apostolic power, while the members of the council derive their power from him; over them he has sole and arbitrary discretion by deputation from the Holy See, and the consultas of the Royal Council have caused great scandal and spiritual damage to souls by seeking with fallacious and deceitful arguments to prove that he, after receiving his deputation, is independent of the Holy See. If he will examine his commission he will see that his powers are derived from the Vicar of Christ and not from the secular authorities, who have no rights in the premises, and whatever is done contrary to the rights of the Holy See is invalid and is hereby declared to be null and void.[452]

This was doubtless consoling as an enunciation of papal claims and wishes, but the Bourbon conception of the royal prerogative was even more decided than that of the Hapsburgs. The exhortation to reassert the supremacy of the inquisitor-generalship fell upon deaf ears and the rule in the Suprema continued to be what Folch de Cardona described in 1703--that the majority ruled; if there was a tie, the matter was laid aside until some absent member attended, while, if the meeting was a full one, the fiscal was called in to cast the deciding vote.[453]

CONTROL OVER TRIBUNALS

In its relations with the tribunals the Suprema had even greater success. As it gradually absorbed the inquisitor-general, it exercised his power, which was virtually unlimited and irresponsible, over them, until it became a centralized oligarchy of the most absolute kind. To this, of course, the progressive improvement in communication largely contributed. In the earlier period, the delays and expenses of special messengers and couriers rendered it necessary for the local tribunals to be virtually independent in the routine business of arresting, trying, sentencing and punishing offenders. Only matters about which there could be dispute or which involved consequences of importance, would warrant the delay and expense of consulting the central head. Items in the accounts and allusions in the correspondence show that, when this was necessary, the outlay for a messenger was a subject to be carefully weighed. The matter was complicated by the fact that the central head was perambulating, moving with the court from one province to another, and its precise seat at any one moment might be unknown to those at a distance. The permanent choice of Madrid as a capital by Philip II--broken by a short transfer to Valladolid--was favorable to centralization, and still more so was the development of the post-office, establishing regular communication at a comparatively trivial cost, although at first the Inquisition was somewhat chary about confiding its secret documents to the postmen.

At first there was hesitation in intruding upon the functions of the tribunals. A letter of November 10, 1493, from the Suprema to the inquisitors of Toledo, asks as a favor for the information on which a certain arrest had been made, explaining that this was at the especial request of the queen.[454] Where there was not unanimity, however, a reference to some higher authority was essential, and we have seen that, in 1488, Torquemada ordered that all such cases should be sent to him to be decided in the Suprema and, in 1507, Ximenes went further and required all cases in which the accused did not confess to be sent to the Council.[455] This seems speedily to have become obsolete, but the rule as to discordia was permanent. In 1509 a letter of the Suprema extends it to arrests and all other acts on which votes were taken, when a report with all the opinions was to be forwarded for its decision.[456] The costs attendant on these references were not small, for we happen to meet with an order, May 23, 1501, to pay to Inquisitor Mercado a hundred ducats for his expenses and sickness while at the court examining the cases brought from his tribunal of Valencia. Possibly for this reason references to the Suprema were not encouraged for, about this time, it ordered that none should be brought to it except those in which there was discordia, and in these it expected that the parties should be represented by counsel.[457] The same motive may have led to an order, in 1528, limiting these references to cases of great importance, but this restriction was removed in another of July 11, 1532, when it was explained that, if an inquisitor dissented from the other two and from the Ordinary, the case must be sent up.[458]

Practically, the authority of the Suprema over the tribunals was limited only by its discretion, and inevitably it was making constant encroachments on their independence of action. Its correspondence, in 1539 and 1540, with the Valencia tribunal shows an increasing number of cases submitted to it and its supervision over minute details of current business.[459] In 1543 the case of a Morisca, named Mari Gomez la Sazeda, shows that a sentence of torture had to be submitted to it and its reply indicates conscientious scrutiny of the records, for it ordered the re-examination of certain witnesses, but, if they were absent or dead, then she might be tortured moderately.[460] A further extension of authority is seen during a witch-craze in Catalonia when, to restrain the cruelty of the Barcelona tribunal, in 1537, all cases of witchcraft, after being voted on, were ordered to be submitted to it for final decision and, in a recrudescence of the epidemic, between 1545 and 1550, it required all sentences of relaxation to be sent to it, even when unanimous.[461] On this last occasion, however, the Barcelona tribunal asserted its independence of action by disregarding the command and a phrase in the Instructions of 1561, requiring, in all cases of special importance, the sentences to be submitted before execution, was too vague to be of much practical effect.[462]

CONTROL OVER TRIBUNALS

The supervision which the Suprema was thus gradually developing was most salutary as a check upon the irresponsibility of the tribunals, whose acts were shrouded in impenetrable secrecy except when scrutinized with more or less conscientious investigation by visitors at intervals of five or ten years. The conditions in Barcelona as revealed by successive visitations, between 1540 and 1580, show how a tribunal might violate systematically the Instructions, and how fruitless were the exposures made by visitors when the inquisitors chose to disregard the orders elicited by reports of their misdoings. They were virtually a law unto themselves; no one dared to complain of them and the victims' mouths were closed by the oath of secrecy which bound them under severe penalties not to divulge their experiences. The whole system was so devised as to expose the inquisitor to the maximum of temptation with the minimum risk of detection, and it was the merest chance whether this power was exercised by a Lucero or by a conscientious judge. The consulta de fe and the concurrence of the Ordinary furnished but a feeble barrier, for the record could generally be so presented as to produce the desired impression and the consultors, proud of their position and its immunities, were indisposed to give trouble, especially as their adverse votes did not create a discordia. When Salazar, in 1566, took the unusual trouble of investigating the interminable records of the individual trials, the rebuke of the Suprema to the inquisitors of Barcelona speaks of the numbers of those sentenced to relaxation, reconciliation, the galleys, scourging, etc., after the grossest informalities in the conduct of the trials.[463] The world can never know the cruelties perpetrated under a system which relieved the tribunals from accountability, and consequently any supervision was a benefit, even that imperfectly exercised by the distant Suprema.

There seems to have come a dawning consciousness of this, possibly stimulated by the revelations of Salazar's investigations into the three tribunals of the crown of Aragon, which led to the Concordia of 1568. In the same year a carta acordada of June 22nd ordered that even when sentences of relaxation were voted unanimously, the process should be sent to the Suprema for its action.[464] From this time forward its intervention, on one score or another, gradually increased. From the records of the tribunal of Toledo, between 1575 and 1610, it appears that it intervened in 228 cases out of 1172, or substantially in one out of five, while in only 82 of these cases, or one out of fourteen, was there discordia--sometimes as to arrest and trial, sometimes as to torture, but mostly as to the final sentence.[465]

At this period it would seem to be the practice in the Suprema to refer cases to two members and act on their report. Thus in the matter of Mari Vaez, condemned in 1594 to relaxation in effigy, the two are Vigil de Quiñones and Mendoza, whose names are inscribed on the back of the sentence and under them the word "Just^a" on the strength of which the secretary writes the formal letter to the tribunal, ending with "hagais, señores justicia"--the customary formula of confirmation.[466] As might be expected the degree of scrutiny exercised in the performance of this duty was variable. In the case of Jacques Curtancion, in 1599, it was observed that the ratification of the confession of the accused had been made in the presence of only one interpreter, when the rules required two; the papers were therefore returned to the tribunal of Granada for the rectification of this irregularity, but this exactitude was of no benefit to the sufferer.[467] On the other hand, Pedro Flamenco was tortured in Toledo at 10 A.M., June 10, 1570, after which the consulta de fe was held which condemned him to relaxation for fictitious confession. At the earliest the papers could not have reached Madrid until late on the 11th, but on the 12th was despatched the formal reply confirming the sentence. There could scarce have been time to read the voluminous record and certainly none to give it more than perfunctory consideration.[468] Again, delays attributable only to negligence were not infrequent. Diego de Horozco was sentenced to relaxation by the tribunal of Cuenca, which sent the process to the Suprema, September 3, 1585 and, at the same time, asked for instructions about the cases of Alonso Sainz and Francisco Caquen which had been previously forwarded. No reply was received for more than a month, when the tribunal wrote again, October 14th, that it was anxious to hold an auto de fe. This brought the prompt answer to torture Horozco and execute justice in accordance with the result.[469]

***

Besides this direct intervention there grew up a watchfulness over the proceedings of the tribunals through their reports of autos de fe, which were closely scrutinized and returned with criticisms. These reports were required to give full details of all cases decided, whether for public autos or private ones in the audience-chamber, and their regular transmission was enforced by conditioning upon it the payment of the annual ayuda de costa or supplement to the salaries of the officials. There was also an opportunity, which was not neglected, of administering reproofs on the reports required from inquisitors of their annual visitations of portions of their districts. These were closely criticized and errors were pointed out without reserve, such as judging cases that ought to have been sent to the tribunal for its action, punishing too severely or too lightly, imperfect reports of cases, etc.[470] Thus in various ways a more or less minute supervision was exercised, and the inquisitors were made to feel the subordination of their position.

This was greatly increased when, in 1632, each tribunal was required to send in a monthly report of all its current business and the condition of each case, whether pending or decided, and this in addition to an annual report on which depended the allowance of the ayuda de costa. It was difficult to enforce the regular performance of this and the command had to be frequently repeated, but it was successful to some extent and afforded an opportunity of criticism which was not neglected. Thus, in 1695, in acknowledging receipt of such a report from Valencia, its slovenliness and imperfection are sharply rebuked as deserving of a heavier penalty, which is suspended through benignity. The character, it is said, of the witnesses should be noted, the number or letter of the prisoner's cell, the ration assigned to him, whether or not he has property and, if sequestrated, a copy of the sequestration should be added; the crime and the time of entering the prison and the property items should be repeated in all successive reports. After this, each individual case is considered and much fault is found with the details of procedure.[471] Even the requests for information, made by one tribunal of another, were required, by an order of 1635, to be the subject of regular reports by the fiscal every four months.[472] It was impossible, however, to enforce with regularity the rendering of monthly reports and, in 1800, the Suprema contented itself with requiring them thrice a year, a regulation which continued to the end, although it was irregularly observed.[473]

The same process of centralization was developed in the control over individual cases. It was not only when there was discordia or sentences of relaxation that confirmation was required. A carta acordada of August 2, 1625, ordered that no sentence of scourging, galleys, public penance, or vergüenza should be executed until the process was submitted to the Suprema.[474] The records of the tribunal of Valladolid, at this period, not only show that this was observed when corporal punishment was inflicted, but also indicate that a custom was springing up of submitting the sentence in all cases involving clerics, and further that the habit was becoming frequent of consulting the Suprema during the course of trials.[475] When, in 1647, the Suprema required all sentences to be submitted to it as soon as pronounced, it assumed full control over the disposition of cases.[476] It was concentrating in itself the management of the entire business of all the tribunals. The minuteness of detail in its supervision is illustrated when, in 1697, the daily ration of four maravedís for a prisoner in Valladolid was regulated by it and the vote of the tribunal whether a prisoner is to be confined in the carceles medias or secretas had to be confirmed by it.[477]

CENTRALIZATION

Simple arrest by the Inquisition was in itself an infliction of no common severity and, from an early period, the Suprema sought to exercise supervision over it. In 1500, the Instructions of Seville require the tribunals, whenever they make an arrest, to send to the inquisitor-general, by their messenger, the accusation, with the testimony in full, the number of the witnesses and the character of the accused.[478] This salutary check on the irresponsible power of the inquisitors was too cumbrous for enforcement and it soon became obsolete but, in 1509, when there was discordia as to sentences of arrest they were ordered, before execution, to be submitted to the Suprema with the opinions of the voters.[479] In 1521, to check the persecuting zeal of the tribunals towards the Moriscos, or newly baptized Moors, Cardinal Adrian ordered that they should not be arrested save on conclusive evidence which must first be submitted to the Suprema--a humane measure speedily forgotten.[480] The religious Orders were favored, in 1534, by requiring confirmation of all sentences of arrest pronounced against their members--a measure which required to be repeated in 1555 and, in 1616, it was extended to all ecclesiastics.[481] The Instructions of 1561 order consultation with the Suprema before arresting persons of quality or when the case is otherwise important[482] and, in 1628, it was ordered that no arrest be made on the testimony of a single witness, without first consulting the Suprema; if escape were feared, precautions might be taken, but in such wise as to inflict as little disgrace as possible.[483] Under these limitations the practice is summarized by a writer, about 1675, who tells us that there are cases in which the tribunals can vote arrest, but not execute it without the assent of the Suprema; these are where there is but one witness (but this is not observed with Judaizers), when the accused is a cleric, religious, knight of the Military Orders, notary or superior officer of justice--unless, indeed, flight be apprehended. In these cases the sumaria, or summary of evidence, must be well drawn up and submitted to the Suprema with the votes of the inquisitors.[484]

Thus gradually the independent action of the tribunals was curtailed until it finally disappeared and centralization in the Suprema was complete. The precise date of this I have been unable to determine, but a writer of the middle of the eighteenth century tersely describes the conditions, telling us that the inquisitors determine nothing without the orders of the Council, so that, when they draw up the sumarias in cases of faith they submit them and, on their return, do what they are told; they do not sentence but only append their opinions to the processes and the Council decides.[485]

This continued to the end. The book of votes of the Suprema, in the restored Inquisition, from 1814 to 1820, shows that the tribunals had become mere agencies for receiving denunciations, collecting evidence and executing the orders of the Council. Even these slender duties were sometimes denied to them. In the case of Juana de Lima of Xeres, tried for bigamy, the sumaria was made up by the commissioner of Xeres and on it the Suprema, without more ado, sentenced her to four years in a house of correction and sent the sentence to the commissioner to be read to her; the functions of the Seville inquisitors were reduced to transmitting the papers and keeping the records.[486] If a tribunal ventured on the slightest expression of dissent, it was roundly taken to task. Thus, December 23, 1816 that of Madrid was sternly rebuked because, in the case of Don Teodoro Bachiller, it had described as unjustified his imprisonment; that imprisonment had been approved by the Suprema and the tribunal was ordered to expunge from the records this improper expression and never to repeat such an offence, if it desired to escape serious action. So, when the fiscal of the same tribunal remonstrated against an order to remove Caietano Carcer, on the ground of ill health, from the secret prison, the Suprema replied, January 14, 1818, that its orders were dictated by justice and there was no fiscal or tribunal that could object to them. It expected that the tribunal and its fiscal would in future be more self-restrained and obedient to its superior decisions, thus escaping all responsibility, and that they would not oblige the Council to enforce its authority by measures necessary although unpleasant.[487] To this had shrunk the inquisitor before whom, in the old days, bishops and magnates trembled.

APPELLATE JURISDICTION

It is satisfactory to be able to say that, as a rule, the interference of the Suprema with the tribunals was on the side of mercy rather than of rigor. It is true that torture, then the universal solvent of doubt, was frequently ordered, but there seems to have been a fairly conscientious discharge of the responsibilities which it had grasped. In the Valladolid records of the seventeenth century, the modifications of sentences are almost uniformly mitigations, especially by the omission of scourging, which the tribunals were accustomed to administer liberally, and there would seem to be especial tenderness for the offences of the clergy.[488] A typical instance of this moderation is seen in the case of Margarita Altamira, sentenced by the Barcelona tribunal, in 1682, to appear in an auto de fe, to abjure de levi, to receive a hundred lashes through the streets and to seven years' exile from Barcelona and some other places, the first two of which were to be passed serving in a hospital without pay. All this the Suprema reduced to hearing her sentence read in the audience-chamber and to four years' exile from the same places.[489] This mitigating tendency is especially apparent in the restored Inquisition, from 1814 to 1820, where the sentences are almost uniformly revised with a reduction of penalties. Scourging is more rarely prescribed by the tribunals and, when it is ordered, it is invariably omitted by the Suprema, the power of dispensing with it being attributed to the inquisitor-general.[490]

***

As the functions of the tribunals thus gradually shrank to mere ministerial duties, the appellate jurisdiction lodged in the inquisitor-general and absorbed by the Suprema, of which we heard so much in earlier times, became less and less important. The bull of Leo X, in 1516, prescribes that appeals shall be heard by the inquisitor-general in conjunction with the Suprema and that, pending the decision, the case shall be suspended.[491] This indicates that appeals were suspensive, although subsequently the Inquisition eluded this by arguing, as in the matter of Villanueva, that they were merely devolutionary-- that is, that sentences, in spite of them, were to be promptly executed, thus practically rendering them useless.[492]

At this period the relations between the Council and the inquisitor-general as to appellate jurisdiction do not appear to be definitely settled. In 1520, Antonio de la Bastida appealed about his wife's dowry from the judge of confiscations of Calahorra, and the decision in his favor was rendered by the Suprema "in consultation with the very reverend father, the Cardinal of Tortosa (Adrian)," and, as the crown was concerned, it was confirmed by Charles V.[493] In two cases, however, in 1527 and 1528, in which, on appeal, Cardinal Manrique remitted or mitigated sentences, the letters were issued in his name and without signature by the members of the Council.[494] During Manrique's disgrace, the Suprema apparently acted independently for, in a letter of December 9, 1535, to the Valencia tribunal, alluding to the cases on appeal pending before it, it promises to adjudicate them as speedily as possible.[495] That, by this time, at least its concurrence had become essential would appear from the modification, on appeal by Juan Gómez from a sentence imposed by the Valencia tribunal, when the letter was signed both by Inquisitor-general Tavera and the members of the Council.[496] When, as we have seen, the secular courts endeavored to entertain appeals in cases of confiscation and matters not strictly of faith, Prince Philip's cédula of March 10, 1553 emphatically declared that appellate jurisdiction was vested solely in the Suprema, which held faculties for that purpose from the Holy See and from the crown.[497]

CONTROL OVER DETAILS

This would seem to dispose of any claim that appellate jurisdiction was a special attribute of the inquisitor-general, and this is confirmed by a case, in 1552, in which Angelica Vidama appealed from the sentence of the Valencia tribunal condemning the memory and fame of her deceased mother Beatriz Vidama. On March 8th, Inquisitor-general Valdés and the members of the Council with some assessors declared that, after examining the matter in several sessions their opinion was that the sentence should be revoked. Then, on March 12th, in the presence of Valdés, the Council adopted a sentence restoring her and her posterity to honor and good fame and releasing the confiscation of her estate. The sentence is not signed by Valdés but only by three members of the Council, which indicates that his signature was unnecessary.[498] When he was held simply to have a vote, like every other member, he could claim no special authority as to appeals and, with the gradual intervention of the Suprema in all the acts of the tribunals, appeals themselves became obsolete.

***

From a comparatively early period the control assumed by the Suprema over the provincial tribunals was absolute. Already, in 1533, it tersely informed them that what it ordered and what it forbade must be obeyed to the letter; this it repeated in 1556 and, in 1568, it took occasion to tell them that it was not to be answered, nor were inquisitors to offer excuses when they were rebuked.[499] This control was not confined to their judicial proceedings but extended to every detail of their affairs. Even Ferdinand, with his minute watchfulness over the management of the tribunals, gave to the inquisitors a certain latitude as to expenses and instructed his receivers that they were to honor the requisitions of the inquisitors for outlays on messengers, lodgings, work on houses, prisons, stagings, etc.[500] The Suprema permitted no such liberty of action; it required to be consulted in advance and roundly scolded tribunals which incurred expenses on their own responsibility.[501] In 1569 a general order specified in minute detail the trifling matters of daily necessity for which they could make disbursements; for everything else reference must first be made to the Suprema.[502] This continued to the end and its correspondence is filled with instructions as to petty outlays of all kinds, and largely with regard to repairs of the houses and other properties belonging to the Inquisition. If Valencia, in 1647, wanted a clock in the audience-chamber, it had to apply for permission to purchase one and, in 1650, the Suprema ordered its price to be allowed in the receiver's accounts. In 1665 it ordered the fiscal of Barcelona to be lodged in the palace of the Inquisition and gave minute instructions how the apartments were to be redistributed so as to accommodate him.[503] It is scarce necessary to add that the determination of salaries, which had originally been lodged in the hands of the inquisitor-general, had passed absolutely under the control of the Suprema.

Among the perquisites of the officials was that they were furnished with mourning on occasions of public mourning, and a carta acordada of January 20, 1578 ordered that, when this was to be given, a detailed statement must be made out in advance of the persons entitled to it, how much there would be required, what kind of cloth and at what price. On the death of Philip II, in 1598, two persons in Valencia complained that they had been omitted in the distribution, whereupon it wrote to the tribunal for information, on receipt of which it ordered that one of them should be gratified.[504] So, in 1665, on the death of Philip IV, Dr. Paladio Juncar, one of the physicians of the tribunal of Barcelona, asked for an allowance such as had been given to his colleague Dr. Maruch, whereupon the Suprema called for a report as to the cost of the mourning given to Dr. Maruch and whether it was customary to give it to two physicians. A similar petition from Juan Carbonell, one of the advocates for poor prisoners, led to another demand for information and the result was that the Suprema refused them both.[505]

This close watchfulness did not diminish with time. In 1816, when returning the papers of a case to the tribunal of Madrid, a reprimand was administered because in one place there was a blank of half a page which might have been utilized for a certain record. So, in 1817, Seville was rebuked for the number of blank pages in the processes sent, causing not only a useless waste of paper but an increase of postage; six months later Seville sent the sumaria of Miguel Villavicencio, in which the Suprema counted fourteen blank pages, whereupon it referred to its previous instructions and commanded the tribunal to tell the secretaries that they must obey orders, else they would be not only charged with the excess of postage but would be severely punished.[506]

***

CONTROL OVER FINANCES

The development of this absolute authority was largely aided by the complete control over the finances of the tribunals claimed and exercised by the inquisitor-general or the Suprema or concurrently by both. This, after the death of Ferdinand, practically passed into their hands, except when Charles, in his early years, made grants to his courtiers from the confiscations. All that was gathered in by the labors of the provincial inquisitors was treated as a common fund at the sole discretion of the central power. Most of the tribunals, as we shall see, held investments, partially adequate to their support, in addition to their current gains, but even these were held subject to the Suprema. In 1517, orders were sent to the farmers of the revenue to pay to the receiver-general of the Suprema, instead of to the tribunals, the juros, or assignments on the taxes, held by the latter. Of these the holdings of the Seville tribunal amounted to 500,000 maravedís per annum--100,000 on the tithe of oil, 200,000 on the alcavala of oil and 200,000 on the alcavala of the shambles. Córdova suffered less from this, for that tribunal held only 103,000 maravedís of income--63,000 on the alcavala of meal, 16,000 on that of wine and 24,000 on that of fruit.[507] But it was not only on the investments but also on the current earnings of the tribunals that the Suprema laid its hand. Its salary list was considerable, it had no settled source of income and the royal policy was that the Inquisition must pay its own way besides having a surplus for the treasury. In 1515, while the Suprema of Castile was yet separate from that of Aragon, its pay-roll aggregated 750,000 maravedís, with 340,000 additional for ayudas de costa, or in all 1,090,000, without counting Inquisitor-general Ximenes who seems to have disdained the emoluments of his office. This large sum, the receiver of Seville, Pedro de Villacis, was required to defray in 1515, while, in 1516, the demand fell upon Guillastegui, receiver of Toledo; in 1517 the salaries were paid by Seville and the ayuda de costa by Toledo and, in 1518, by Valencia.[508] The burden was apportioned among them according to their luck. In addition to this were the innumerable orders to pay the salaries and expenses of the tribunals, which were sometimes issued in the name of Cardinal Adrian and sometimes in that of the Suprema.

It would seem that the receivers of the tribunals, who were practically treasurers, occasionally hesitated in honoring these calls for, in 1520, Charles V issued cédulas to all the receivers of Castile and Aragon to pay whatever the inquisitor-general and Suprema should order.[509] The theory that the funds belonged to the crown in no way limited the control of the inquisitor-general and Suprema and this, during the disgrace of Manrique, naturally passed into the hands of the Council. Under his successor, Tavera, orders were sometimes drawn in his name and countersigned by the members of the Council and sometimes all reference to him was omitted. There seems not to have been any settled rule until, about 1704, the victory of the Council over Mendoza was emphasized by an instruction that no order for the payment of money, given by the inquisitor-general, was to be recognized unless countersigned by the members.[510]

The Suprema called without stint on the tribunals to meet its expenses and its fluctuating sources of supply are indicated in its varying demands for a few ducats for some special payment to large sums from some tribunal which had made a fortunate raid on wealthy heretics as when, being in Valladolid in 1549, it demanded 2000 ducats from that tribunal for its pay-roll.[511] It seems to have made an attempt to levy a settled contribution on Saragossa which, in 1539, it ordered to furnish the money for its salaries, but the enforcement of this seems to have been difficult for, from 1540 to 1546, we find it paying its receiver-general Loazes 15,000 maravedís a year for making the collection. After an interval of ten years, in 1557, it demanded of Saragossa 10,000 sueldos (400 ducats) a year toward its pay-roll, but again there was trouble, for although the order was issued in April, the inquisitors in October were reminded of it, with the significant hint that, unless the money were forthcoming, their salaries would be cut off.[512] In 1559 a papal grant of 100,000 ducats on the ecclesiastical revenues of Spain kept it in funds for awhile and when the tribunals of the colonies were fairly in operation they contributed largely but, in the eighteenth century, we still find it drawing upon the tribunals, although it had accumulated a considerable invested capital, yielding a handsome income.[513]

CONTROL OVER FINANCES

While thus caring for itself, it also looked after the tribunals which were less fortunate than their fellows, treating the profits of all as a common fund to be distributed at its discretion. These transfers were incessant; as examples of them may be cited an order, in 1562, to Valladolid to pay 1000 ducats to Barcelona which was deeply in debt and, in 1565, Murcia was called upon to give it 400,000 maravedís for its salaries. Murcia, at this time, seems to have struck a rich vein of confiscations for, in 1567, it was required to contribute 1500 ducats for the salaries of Valencia. Barcelona continued in trouble; there were few heretics there and its chief business was quarrelling with the people, which was not productive financially, so, in 1579, Llerena was required to give it 500 ducats towards its pay-roll and, in 1586, Seville, Murcia and Llerena were ordered to furnish 500 ducats each for the same purpose. The expulsion of the Moriscos, in 1609-10, brought Valencia to destitution and, in 1612, Granada and Seville were obliged to lend it 1000 ducats apiece.[514]

This system remained in force until the last. Under the Restoration the Holy Office was seriously cramped for funds, as we shall see, and its financial troubles were frequent. In 1816, Majorca was required to furnish over 40,000 reales to Logroño and Logroño was called upon to supply the same sum to the Suprema. It was not prompt in meeting this demand but paid 15,000; in March, 1817, the Suprema notified it that the balance would be drawn for; on this a partial payment seems to have been made, leaving 12,000, for which, in 1818, the receiver-general of the Suprema drew, but his draft came back dishonored. This aroused the wrath of the Council which wrote, July 3rd, expressing its surprise; if the tribunal had no funds in hand, it should have gone out and borrowed them; it must do so now and not let such a thing occur again.[515]

A necessary feature of this financial control was the centralization in the Suprema of the auditing of the accounts of all the tribunals. Their receivers or treasurers were supposed to send, at regular intervals, itemized statements with vouchers of all receipts and expenditures, which were audited by the contador general, or auditor, of the Council.[516] The efficiency of this system was marred by habitual vices of maladministration and the hesitation to punish offenders, of which a petition of the historian, Gerónimo Zurita, affords us a glimpse. In 1538 he was made secretary, or escribano de camera of the Suprema. In 1548 Inquisitor-general Valdés gave this place to Juan de Valdés, presumably a kinsman, and Zurita was transferred to the contaduría general for Aragon. In a petition presented May 2, 1560, he represents that he has served as contador for twelve years at a salary less than that of his predecessor and with more work; there were the accounts of the tribunal of Sicily, which had not been rendered for twenty years, and it was notorious that the accounts of the receivers had been very confused and embarrassing, all of which he had straightened out with the utmost care, rejecting, for the service of the Holy Office, opportunities offering him better prospects, and now the only reward he asks is that his son, Miguel Zurita, a youth of 18, may be adjoined to him as an assistant--a moderate prayer which was granted.[517] That Zurita was a laborious and conscientious auditor it would be impossible to doubt, but the frequency of defalcations, as we shall see hereafter, would indicate that such officials were not universal and that the precautions of the system were negligently enforced.

SALARIES AND PERQUISITES

That the Suprema should exact all that it could from the tribunals was a necessity, for its pay-roll grew, partly as the result of its increased functions in the centralizing process, and partly in accordance with the inevitable law of an office-holding class to multiply. As the business and profits of the Inquisition decreased its officials consequently grew more numerous and costly. After the death of Ferdinand in 1516, when Aguirre and Calcena were dismissed, there were for some years only three members, a fiscal, a secretary, an alguazil, a "relator" (to report on cases sent up on appeal), a contador and receiver-general, two physicians, a messenger and a portero--twelve in all--with a pay-roll, including the ayuda de costa, of 1,090,000 maravedís or a little less than 3000 ducats.[518] In the seventeenth century all this had changed. Various gratifications had become habitual additions to the salaries proper, in lieu of the old ayuda de costa. Thus there were three larger propinas or pourboires a year, on the days of San Isidro (May 15th), San Juan (June 24th) and Santa Ana (July 26th) and five smaller ones, called manuales on certain other feasts. There were also luminarias or reimbursement for the cost of the frequent illuminations publicly ordered, which seem to have been averaged into a fixed sum, and at times there was an allowance for the Autos of Corpus Christi, or plays represented before the Council on Corpus Christi day, while the toros or bull-fights which were celebrated on the days of the three chief propinas sometimes replace the latter. There were other smaller perquisites, such as wax and sugar--the latter a distribution, on each of the feasts of Corpus Christi and San Pedro Martir, of an arroba (25 pounds) of sugar to the inquisitor-general, half an arroba to the members and a quarter to the subordinates, making in all nine arrobas. In 1657 we learn that sugar was worth 161 reales per arroba, making an annual outlay for this purpose of 2900 reales.[519] A larger gratuity was that of houses. The Suprema owned a number and allowed them to be occupied by its officials, while those who were not thus housed received a cash equivalent. Thus in various ways the nominal salaries were largely supplemented and, whatever were the necessities of the State, the Council took care that its members and officials should be abundantly supplied.

When, in 1629, there was some talk of reforming the Suprema, Philip IV called upon Castañeda, the contador-general, for a detailed statement of the salaries, propinas, bull-fights and illuminations, with their aggregate for each person connected with it, from the inquisitor-general down to the lowest employee, and the same information was required as to the tribunals. As usual the Suprema equivocated and concealed. All that it saw fit to reply was that the salary of a member was 500,000 maravedís, of a consejero de la tarde 166,666, of the royal secretary and receiver-general 200,000 each.[520] We happen to have a detailed statement of the personnel and emoluments of the Suprema at this period which furnishes the information thus withheld from the king. It shows that the salary of the inquisitor-general was 1,100,000 maravedís and the extras 352,920, or in all, 1,452,920. Each of the full members received one half of this, while the consejeros de la tarde had one third of the salary of a full member, one half of his propina and no luminarias. The whole number on the pay-roll was thirty-six; the aggregate of their salaries was 7,152,539 maravedís and of the extras 2,891,088, or in all, 10,043,627, equivalent to 295,400 reales or 26,855 ducats, being about ten-fold the cost of a century earlier.[521] Of course, the purchasing power of money had fallen greatly during the interval, but this does not wholly explain the later extravagance. It is observable, moreover that, in the case of the minor subordinates, where the salaries were low, the extras amount to twice as much as the regular pay, and also that as yet there were but three propinas a year and these and the luminarias were the only extras.

A statement of a few years later, probably 1635, may be summarized thus:

Salaries	7,644,600 mrs.
Propinas	2,382,900
Luminarias	1,232,875
Allowances to officials for houses, estimated	800,000
Expenses, repairs to houses, estimated	890,00
postage, couriers, secret service, estimated	400,000
------------	13,350,275

***

In this for the first time appears the name of the king as a recipient of the propinas and luminarias, with an allowance double that of the inquisitor-general, but though he figured in the estimates he was not paid.[522] So carefully were these extras observed that when, in 1679 and 1680 the fiestas de toros or bull-fights, on the feasts of San Isidro and Santa Ana, were omitted and, in 1680 the Autos Sacramentales of Corpus Christi, the Suprema indemnified itself, in 1680, by distributing 687,276 maravedís, from which we learn that the perquisites of a bull-fight amounted to 137,275 and of an exhibition of autos to 144,976.[523]

The terrible condition of the debased currency, known as vellon, at a discount from plata or silver, ranging from 25 to 50 per cent., gave further opportunities for quietly increasing salaries. As a rule, public officials had to take their salaries in the depreciated vellon--the government was obliged to accept it for taxes and to pay it out at its face value.[524] The Suprema, however, computed its salaries in silver and paid in vellon with the discount added. In 1680 the members made a special grant to themselves, for they ordered the salaries to be paid one half in silver and the other half in vellon with a hundred per cent. added, thus in effect doubling their salaries. How often this liberality was repeated it would be impossible now to say; it was not a settled matter, for the receipts in 1681 show a return to the usual practice of payment in vellon with 50 per cent. added.[525] Another device by which the depreciation in vellon was made a pretext for augmenting salaries is shown by the receipts for 1670. Payments were made every three months in advance; the first tercio, on January 1st, and the second on May 1st, were made in vellon with the customary addition of 50 per cent.; then, on September 1st this augmented sum was taken as a basis and 66-2/3 per cent. added, bringing the payment to two and a half times the legitimate amount.[526] The Suprema was not particular as to other devices for increasing its emoluments. In 1659, the birth of the Infante Fernando Thomás served as an excuse for two extra propinas and for five luminarias.[527] In 1690, when it probably was in funds from the confiscations in Majorca, under the transparent pretext of replacing various articles of which it had availed itself, it voted to its members and chief officers 14,160 reales in silver and to the subordinates 8555 in vellon.[528] It was also profuse in gratuities to its employees, as when, in 1670, it voted to Doña Juana de Fita y Ribera--evidently the daughter or niece of its secretary Joseph de Ribera--the handsome pension of four hundred ducats, to enable her to marry.[529] In spite of its perpetual complaints of poverty, it evidently was not an inexpensive department of the government. The Suprema was none the less liberal in providing for the amusement and gratification of its members, in ghastly contrast with the sources from which the funds were drawn--the confiscations that ruined thousands of industrious and happy families. In fact, it gives us a new conception of the grim tribunal, which held in its hand the life and honor of every Spaniard and had as its motto "Exsurge Domine et vindica causam tuam," to note its careful provision for comfort and enjoyment on festal occasions.

BULL-FIGHTS

We happen to have the details of the cost of the autos sacramentales performed before the Council on the Corpus Christi feast of 1659, amounting to 2040 reales vellon and 1168 of silver.[530] The fiestas de toros, or bull-fights, cost nothing for the performers but were attended with elaborate and somewhat expensive preparations for the enjoyment and refreshment of the members and officials. As there were three or four of these a year, the amusement was costly, but the Suprema did not grudge expense when its own gratification was concerned. As affording an insight into this unexpected aspect of the Holy Office, I give below the items of expenditure for the "toros" of June 5, 1690, amounting to 2067 reales 7 mrs., to which is to be added, as the exhibition was given at the palace of Buen Retiro, the sum of 4400 reales paid to the treasurer of the palace for the use of the balconies occupied by the Council and its servants.[531] This is a single example of a constant outlay on occasions where the Suprema defrayed the expenses of its members and attendants. They were by no means confined to the toros and autos. In this same year 1690, the Suprema paid 3300 reales for balconies on the Calle Mayor from which to see the new queen, Maria Anna of Neuburg, when she entered Madrid.[532]

In addition to salaries and extra emoluments, the officials of the Suprema had a fertile source of income from the fees which they were entitled to charge. Every act or certificate or paper made out was paid for by the party applying for it, in the multitudinous business flowing in to the Council, from applicants for favors, examinations into limpieza or purity of blood, or in the perpetual litigation subject to its extensive jurisdiction. From the fiscal and his clerk, who levied upon all documents passing through his hands, down to the portero who had his recognized fee for serving a summons, every one was entitled to charge for the services pertaining to his office. According to the arancel, or fee bill, issued in 1642, the secretaries were entitled to twenty reales for every grace issued--licences to read prohibited books, commutations of penance, dispensations and the hundred other matters in which the Suprema alone could grant favors. The secretario de camera, or private secretary of the inquisitor-general, had a fee for every commission issued--on one for an inquisitor or fiscal, he collected a hundred reales, besides eight for his clerk, on those for minor offices a doubloon and eight reales for his clerk, and so on, and these, according to the arancel of Cardinal Giudice, were payable in silver.[533] Burdensome as were these legalized fees, the limitations of the arancel were not enforced and complaints of imposition were constant. The members of the Suprema had not this source of income, but, as a rule, they held lucrative benefices with dispensation for non-residence.

RESOURCES

The Suprema could not be thus lavish in its expenditures without an assured and steady source of income. It no longer was dependent on what it could call from one tribunal or another, for it had so persistently utilized its control over their funds as to accumulate for itself an amount of invested capital the interest on which went far to meet its regular requirements, the deficiency being made up by contributions from the tribunals, especially those of the colonies. These latter had become very productive. Besides accumulating large capital for themselves, they were able to make heavy remittances to Spain. Mexico and Lima were expected to furnish regularly 10,000 ducats a year and this was frequently exceeded. Even from Cartagena de las Indias the Suprema received, in 1653 and 1654, more than 100,000 pesos.[534] About 1675, we chance to hear of a remittance of 40,000 pesos (about 29,000 ducats) of which Lima furnished 10,000 and Mexico 30,000.[535]

An estimate of income and outlay, of about the year 1635, shows that the Suprema held securities of various kinds bringing in an annual return as follows:

Assignments on the public revenues	7,497,703 mrs.
In the hands of the Fuccares (Fuggers) awaiting investment	2,618,200
@ 5 pr. ct.	130,000
Censos	2,210,625
----------------	9,839,228

Against this its regular expenses were estimated at 13,350,275, which, with a sum of 1,353,625 that it had been ordered to pay to Cardinal Zapata, the late inquisitor-general, left a deficit of 4,864,672, or 12,966 ducats.[536] This it could have had no trouble in making up from the tribunals at home and in the colonies, besides such amounts as might still come in from confiscations.

In the period of storm and stress for some twelve years, commencing with 1640, the incessant demands of the king unquestionably caused the Suprema some trouble. Already, in 1640, we find it borrowing considerable sums, but its resources were large and, about 1657, a statement of its indebtedness amounts, reduced to silver, only to 14,500 ducats. Against this may be set a list of investments and sources of income, yielding a revenue of 18,500,000 maravedis or 50,000 ducats, showing what power of accumulation it had possessed, in spite of the troublous times through which it had passed.[537] All this was clear interest on investment securities except 10,000 ducats from the colonial tribunals, about 2000 ducats estimated to come in from confiscations, etc., and 200,000 maravedis from

A History of the Inquisition of Spain: Volume II

the Fabrica de Sevilla. This latter item merits a word of explanation. In 1626, the Castle of Triana, occupied by the Seville tribunal, was threatened with ruin by an inundation. In view of the heavy cost of repairs, in 1627, it was determined to meet this by imposing for three years, on every calificador appointed, a fee of 10 ducats, on every commissioner and familiar 5, and on every notary 4. The three years passed away but the charge was continued and, in 1640, it was extended to a number of other minor positions, both salaried and unsalaried. The repairs had long been finished but the Suprema coolly appropriated the income as part of its regular resources and kept it to the end. In 1790 the receipts from Valencia amounted to 27-1/2 libras, and an allusion to it in 1817 shows that the Fabrica de Sevilla was still collected.[538]

LABORS

In 1743, Philip V made an effort to reduce the excessive number of officials and expenses of the Inquisition and some other departments, but he was unable to withstand the conservative influences brought to bear. It was probably in connection with this that an elaborate statement of the resources and expenditures of the Suprema was prepared. The work of the Inquisition by this time had shrunk virtually to censorship of the press and punishing bigamists, soliciting confessors, blasphemers, diviners, wise-women and incautious utterers of suspicious propositions, but its machinery was as ponderous and costly as ever. The pay-roll of the Suprema counted forty names whose salaries and emoluments aggregated in round numbers 64,000 ducats, to which were added the expenses of the Madrid tribunal, dependent on the Suprema, and other estimated outlays amounting to 12,000, making a total of 76,000 ducats. Its annual revenue was stated at 51,000 ducats, leaving a deficit of 25,000.[539] How this was made good does not appear; possibly there was concealment in the statement of resources, for the Suprema does not seem to have curtailed its liberalities, and a salary list of 1764 shows that there had been no change in the pay and emoluments, except that the number of officials had increased to forty-one.[540]

The financial condition of the whole Inquisition, however, was seriously compromised by royal orders, from 1794 onward, requiring investments to be sold and the proceeds to be placed in government securities to aid in defraying the costs of the wars, in which Spain became involved, with France and then with Portugal and England.[541] The virtual bankruptcy of the monarchy and the destruction consequent on the Napoleonic wars naturally reduced it to the greatest straits, the results of which will be seen when we come to investigate its finances as a whole.

***

Considering the liberal salary and allowances which, in the eighteenth century, amounted to 4030 ducats for each full member, the labor was not heavy. The council held daily sessions of three hours in the morning and, on three days of the week--Tuesdays, Thursdays, and Saturdays--a two hours' session in the afternoon at which were present the two auxiliary members from the Council of Castile, who received 1400 ducats. The pay of the inquisitor-general was nearly 7000 ducats,[542] besides which he usually held a bishopric and the members some comfortable preferment. The meetings of the Council were originally held in the apartments of the inquisitor-general, until the accession of Philip IV, when the house of the condemned favorite, Rodrigo Calderon, was purchased for it and became its permanent office.[543]

CHAPTER II - THE TRIBUNAL

During the active career of the Inquisition, it was the local tribunal which represented it to the people. The inquisitor-general and Suprema were distant and held no direct relations with the community. It was otherwise with the inquisitors, at whose bidding any one, however high-placed, could be thrown into the secret prison, to emerge with an ineffaceable mark of infamy, while his property, to the minutest item, was sequestrated and tied up, perhaps for years, and, if not confiscated, was largely consumed in expenses. Men wielding such power, and virtually irresponsible, shed terror around them as they walked abroad and, as we have seen, their habitual use of their position was not such as to allay these apprehensions. They were the visible agents of the Holy Office, the embodiment of its mysterious and all-embracing authority, empowered to summon to their aid the whole resources of the State and answerable only to their chief. The tribunal, in which they sat in judgement on the lives and fortunes of all whom they might call before them, could only be regarded with universal dread, for no one knew at what moment an unguarded utterance, or the denunciation of some enemy, might bring him before it.

***

The delimitation of the land into districts, each subject to its own tribunal, was naturally a work of time. In the early period, when there were Converso suspects everywhere, it mattered little where an Inquisition was set up, for it could find abundant occupation in any place and, when the field was temporarily exhausted, it could transfer itself elsewhere in search of a fresh harvest. Ferdinand, in his instructions to the inquisitors of Saragossa, in 1485, tells them that wherever in Aragon they think that an Inquisition is necessary, they are to notify Torquemada, who will send inquisitors there.[544] Thus we hear of tribunals in Aragon at Teruel, Jaca, Tarazona, Barbastro and Calatayud; there was one, partly Aragonese and partly Catalan--Lérida and Huesca, which was not divided between Saragossa and Barcelona until 1532. In Catalonia there were tribunals at Perpignan and Balaguer, and, in Castile, others more or less permanent, at Medina del Campo, Avila, Guadalupe, Osuna, Jaen, Xeres, Alcaraz, Plasencia, Burgos, Durango, Leon and doubtless many other places.[545] Even as late as 1501, a royal cédula announces that Deza is about to send inquisitors with their officials to various bishoprics to provide them with tribunals and all receivers were instructed to pay them such sums as he might designate.[546] Under such conditions there could be no very precise boundaries of jurisdiction, for it mattered little who burnt a Judaizing New Christian, but it was otherwise with the confiscations which required to be garnered by those responsible and authorized by the king, and the first strict definitions of districts would seem to have arisen in commissioning receivers. Thus, in 1498, the receiver of Saragossa is qualified for the sees of Saragossa and Tarazona; he of Valencia for those of Valencia, Tortosa, Segorbe and Teruel, while we hear of one for Huesca, Gerona and Urgel, apparently distinct from Barcelona.[547]

EXPROPRIATION OF HOUSES

For a considerable time, moreover, the tribunals, to a certain extent, were ambulatory, travelling around with their whole corps of officials and empowered to take possession of such buildings as they might require, wherever they saw fit to establish themselves for a time, while the receivers were instructed not to require of them an account of their travelling expenses. The regulations for such an itinerant court may be gathered from a cédula of May 17, 1517, addressed to all the officials and inhabitants of Leon and the bishoprics of Plasencia, Coria, Badajoz and Ciudad Rodrigo, instructing them to give free lodgement, but not in inns, to the inquisitors and their officials and to charge them only current prices for food. Where they settle for a time and set up their court, they are to rent lodgings in houses where they can have the use of one door and the owner of another, while suitable provision must be had for an audience-chamber and a secret prison; the rent is to be determined by appraisers mutually selected but, if the stay is less than a year, rent will be payable only for the time of occupancy. There is to be no opposition or maltreatment, but they are to have all aid and favor under penalty of ten thousand maravedís.[548] The power thus conferred of temporary expropriation was not always exercised considerately. In 1514, Hernando Sánchez of Llerena complained to Ferdinand that, seven years before, the inquisitors had taken his house, compelling him to build another, and this they were now about to seize; Ferdinand compassionated him and prohibited them from doing so. It was otherwise when the tribunal, in 1516, was transferred to Plasencia. The corregidor reported that the most suitable house was that of the dean who was residing in Rome and had rented it; when he was told to turn out the tenant and install the tribunal, the rent, as usual, to be determined by two valuers.[549] Even the episcopal dignity had to give way to the exigencies of the Inquisition. The Bishop of Cuenca was president of the audiencia of Toro and, during his absence, his palace was occupied by the tribunal. In 1519 he was about to return and gave it notice to quit, when Charles V wrote to him that, if he was going to Cuenca, he could find other buildings for his residence; the Inquisition had spent much money on the prisons and must not be disturbed--nor was this the only similar case.[550] Yet existing rights were sometimes respected. When, in Seville, the castle of Triana was assigned to the tribunal, the Count-duke of San Lucar was its hereditary alcaide; he ceded his position in exchange for the hereditary office of alguazil mayor of the tribunal and, in 1706, this office was still enjoyed by his descendants, the Marquises of Leganes, to whom it was reckoned to be worth 150,000 maravedís a year. A similar bargain was made with the Marquis del Carpio, who was hereditary alcaide of the royal alcázar of Córdova, when it was occupied by the tribunal of that city and, in 1706, the marquis of the period was drawing an income of 100,000 maravedís from it. In both cases the incumbents provided deputies at their own expense.[551]

In the original economical simplicity of the institution, Torquemada, in 1485, ordered that all the officials should lodge in one house, but, as the personnel of the tribunals waxed larger and self-indulgence increased, this rule became obsolete and houses were furnished to the subordinates, the rents of which, under instructions from Cardinal Manrique, about 1525, were defrayed from the fines and penances levied on culprits.[552] This became the general rule, although there are some instances of its inobservance and of individual officials complaining of adverse discrimination in not being thus favored.[553] In thus providing houses for its employees the Inquisition claimed the right of eminent domain and vindicated it after the usual arbitrary fashion, when it encountered resistance, as occurred in Valladolid in 1612. The secretary of the tribunal wanted a house which was occupied by an official of the chancellery, or high court of justice for Old Castile and Leon. The tribunal incontinently ejected him and installed its secretary, who in turn was ousted by the offended court. The judges were promptly excommunicated and the court rejoined by fining the parish priests for publishing the censures; arrests were made on both sides; the court imposed fines on the inquisitors who replied by threats of further anathemas. The chronicler fails to inform us of the outcome but, under Philip III, there can be little doubt of the final triumph of the tribunal.[554]

The cédula of 1517 was repeated in another of February 8, 1543 and remained as a permanent regulation. In 1645 a formula shows that, whenever any official travelled on the business of a tribunal, he was furnished with a letter embodying the cédula of 1543 and commanding, in the customary imperious style, that he be furnished with free lodging, and beds and provisions at current rates, under pain of excommunication and a fine of a hundred thousand maravedís.[555]

NUMBER OF OFFICIALS

The organization of the tribunal at first was exceedingly simple. We have seen how, in 1481, in Seville, two Dominican friars, with a legal assessor to guide them, and a fiscal as prosecuting officer, did such active work that they speedily required two receivers of confiscations to gather in the products of their industry. There must doubtless have been subordinates to attend to the clerical duties, to serve citations and to take charge of prisoners, but the tribunal was manned on the most economical basis and there was no time wasted. After four years' experience, Torquemada defined a tribunal as consisting of two inquisitors, an assessor, an alguazil and a fiscal, with such notaries and other minor officials as might be necessary; they were to receive salaries and no fees were to be charged under pain of dismissal, and no inquisitor was to use an official as a household servant.[556] In this no account was taken of the force necessary to secure and handle the confiscations, for these were the concern of the sovereigns and as yet their management was distinct from the prosecution of heretics. It constituted an intricate business, involving innumerable questions arising from claims of every description, which at first were settled in the secular courts, not always to Ferdinand's satisfaction. He grew intensely anxious to bring them within the jurisdiction of the Inquisition, declaring that if they were decided according to the law of the land he would never get justice.[557] For awhile these duties were therefore thrown upon the inquisitors; in 1499, in the tribunal of Burgos and Palencia, Rodrigo de Cargüello is styled inquisitor and judge of confiscations at a salary of 75,000 while his colleague, Alonso de Torres, receives only 60,000.[558] Eventually, as we shall see, a subsidiary court for this purpose was established in each tribunal under a juez de bienes, or judge of confiscations.

Ferdinand was thriftily resolved that the profits of persecution should be protected against the growth of expenses and he struggled, though in vain, against the expansion of the pay-roll. Writing to Torquemada, July 22, 1486, he protests against the efforts of the inquisitors to multiply salaried positions--the torturer, the scriveners, the deputy alguaziles--the alguazil should supply the latter and also pay the portero; the pay-roll is already excessive and the inquisitors demand so many salaries that they must be carefully watched.[559]

Ferdinand might chafe under the increasing burdens, but he could not check them. In this same year we find him obliged to give orders for the payment, in the tribunal of Saragossa, of two inquisitors, an assessor, an episcopal vicar-general, an advocate fiscal, a procurator fiscal, an alguazil, two notaries, a receiver of witnesses, two messengers, a receiver and his scrivener, a physician, and a royal notary for the confiscations, whose salaries amounted to 37,700 sueldos (about 1800 ducats), to which were to be added ayudas de costa, not as yet an established custom, but prevalent in one form or another. At the same time the pay-roll of the tribunal of Medina del Campo was somewhat smaller, amounting to about 1550 ducats, although there were three inquisitors and an assessor, for there were fewer minor officials.[560] In 1493 the tribunal of Valencia, one of the most active, was run with only one inquisitor and no assessor, costing only about 1450 ducats.[561] At the same time it should be borne in mind that these sums include the prison expenses, defrayed by the alguazil out of his salary, which was usually the largest in the list--an arrangement more economical than conducive to the welfare of the captives.

***

The law of growth continued to operate. A list of ayudas de costa for Valladolid, in 1515, shows three inquisitors, a fiscal, an alguazil, three notaries of the secreto or trial-chamber, a receiver, a notary of sequestrations, a gaoler, a messenger and a portero.[562] In 1568, Philip II, in defining the salaried officials exempt from taxation enumerates, for this same tribunal, two or three inquisitors, a fiscal, an alguazil, an auditor, a judge of confiscations, four notaries of the secreto, a notary of sequestrations, a receiver, a messenger, a portero, an alcaide of the secret prison and one of the penitential prison, a notary of the juzgado or court of confiscations, an advocate of the fisc, a procurator of the fisc, two chaplains, a physician, a barber, a surgeon and a steward for the poor prisoners.[563] Besides these salaried officials, there was an indefinite number of unsalaried ones, consultors, who served in the consultas de fe, calificadores or censors, who pronounced on the charges prior to arrest and sat in judgement on books and writings, advocates of the accused, "personas honestas" who were present at the ratification of witnesses, in addition to the familiars and commissioners with their notaries. Then there came subsequently to be other officials, either salaried or living on fees--the notary de lo civil or secretary in civil cases, the notary of actos positivos in matters of limpieza, the depository with whom applicants to prove their limpieza had to deposit in advance the cost of investigation, the superintendent of sequestrations, the superintendent of property, the proveedor or purveyor of food for prisoners and, in some tribunals, the locksmith and bricklayer were reckoned as officials.[564] Even when the salaries were trifling, the pressure for place was incessant, in order to enjoy the privileges and exemptions of the Inquisition, and we shall see that when financial despair caused offices to be offered for sale they were eagerly purchased, irrespective of profit.

This overgrown personnel was admitted to be an abuse and repeated efforts were made for its reform. A decree of June 19, 1629, repeated in 1638, prescribed the number to be allowed in each tribunal but, as usual, these provisions were disregarded or eluded. In 1643 Philip IV animadverted on this disobedience; the excessive number of officials caused the greatest evils, both to the tribunals and the kingdom, and he ordered their reduction to the ancient standard in the briefest time possible. To this the inquisitor-general replied, fully admitting that this overplus of officials was the cause of the impaired character of the Inquisition and of the insufficiency of the revenues to meet the salaries; the Suprema, he said, had repeatedly attempted a reform, but the misfortunes of the times and the pressure of the king had rendered it powerless and the only remedy would be a papal brief defining numbers and invalidating all surplus commissions. The Suprema, on its side, presented a consulta suggesting a reissue of the decrees of 1629 and 1638, while the inquisitor-general should be deprived of power to exceed these limitations. It further stated that it had sent orders to each tribunal prescribing the numbers and requiring them to be reduced forthwith.[565]

The effect of all this was nugatory. In the Aragon Concordia, forced upon the king in 1646, the number allowed to a tribunal, in addition to the inquisitors and fiscal, commissioners and their notaries and familiars, was twenty-three, which shows how excessive had been the practice.[566] What this was elsewhere is indicated in a memorial from Majorca, about 1650, occasioned by the imprisonment in chains of a familiar, named Reginaldo Estado, because he desired to resign on being appointed Consul del Mar. The opportunity is taken of representing the evils arising from the multiplication of officials, as set forth in a previous petition of January 11, 1647, and protesting that the civil and criminal jurisdiction of the Inquisition was the total ruin of the people, so that they would welcome its limitation to matters of faith as a full recompense for all the services rendered to the crown. In each of the thirty-four villages, outside of the capital, there were three officials, besides familiars. In Palma they were multiplied without limit, by creating places that had no duties and appointing assistants and deputies ad libitum, while all the tradespeople and mechanics employed were reckoned as officials, bringing the number up to a hundred and fifty besides familiars. All these, with their wives and children and household servants, and the widows of the deceased, enjoyed the active and passive fuero in both civil and criminal cases, bringing in large revenues to the tribunal, through the excessive costs of litigation, and stimulating oppression of all kinds endured through dread of its censures. This memorial, with evidence sustaining its allegations, was submitted to the Council of Aragon which, after due examination, reported it to the king with a recommendation that the officials and familiars in Majorca should be reduced to what was necessary for the business of the tribunal, but there is no trace that attention was paid to this advice.[567]

SALE OF OFFICES

These Mallorquin grievances reveal not only the consequences but the causes of this inordinate multiplication of official positions. It had been stimulated, moreover, by the suicidal policy of selling offices and of creating them for the purpose of sale--one of the ruinous expedients resorted to by Philip IV in his desperate efforts to make an exhausted treasury supply the extravagance of the court and the drain of foreign wars. There is no positive evidence that this example was followed by inquisitors for their individual profit, but it would be surprising if this were not occasionally the case. Venality had crept in as early as 1595, when Philip II, in his instructions to Manrique de Lara, speaks of an innovation by which offices were transferred for money--sometimes for large sums--which was very prejudicial and caused much murmuring.[568] These apparently were transactions between individuals, but they could not take place without the connivance of the appointing power, and from this the step to creating offices for sale was easily taken, when the pressure or the temptation was sufficient. It came in 1629, though in justice to Philip IV it must be said that he hesitated before succumbing. In that year the Suprema assembled, December 23rd, a number of theologians and submitted for their opinion the proposition that, in every place where there were six familiars, one of them should be permitted to purchase the vara or wand of an alguazil, with the title and all the privileges and exemptions, being a valuable privilege that would bring in much money. The theologians pronounced the scheme lawful, with advantages far outweighing its disadvantages, and suggested that districts might be combined so as to furnish the six familiars. The proceeds were evidently intended for the exchequer of the Suprema for, when the plan was submitted to Philip, he said that it might greatly prejudice the public peace and referred it to the Council of Castile and the Suprema. Finally, on March 20, 1630, he returned it to the inquisitor-general saying that it had been approved by persons of learning and conscience and he asked for an estimate of its productiveness.[569]

After some further parleying the scheme was adopted and announced to the tribunals by the Suprema, August 7, 1631. The limitation of one familiar out of six was abandoned and the offer was thrown open to all who could prove limpieza; the sale was for three lives, the commissions were issued by the inquisitor-general himself, the vara of the alguazilship carried with it a familiarship and the only limitation was that, if the third life fell to one who could not prove limpieza, the tribunal could sell it again and report to the Suprema.[570] Thus the sale went on, the ostensible object being the payment of the troops; there was no limit to the alguazilships and finally other offices came into the market--the depositario de pretendientes, the notariat of civil causes, of the juzgado, of sequestrations, and receiverships, auditorships, etc. It goes without saying that simple familiarships were sold and, in 1642, we hear of a block of three hundred being offered.[571] Regulations issued between 1631 and 1643 show that, although public auctions were nominally forbidden, the positions were put up privately and sold to the highest bidder. Even women sought to obtain the privileges attached to the offices and, in 1641, it was found necessary to prohibit receiving bids from them, except when made in favor of men whom they were about to marry.[572] In 1639 Philip proposed even to put up for sale the office of alguazil mayor of the Suprema and of all the tribunals, by which he expected to defray the pay of 400 foot and 200 horse. This staggered the Suprema, which represented that papal authority would be necessary and the proceeds would be small, as the places were all filled and would fall in slowly, while only that of the Suprema and three or four others would fetch considerable sums, reasoning which put a quietus on the project.[573]

***

From various indications we may assume that the confidential posts in the secreto were not sold and that offices of active duty in the tribunals were sold only when vacated, although a decree of 1641 shows that they were vacated for the purpose. The prices realized were large. February 6, 1644, Valencia reported that the sale by auction of the unimportant office of depositario de pretendientes for 6000 reales of full-weight silver had been cancelled because the purchaser insisted that it conferred the exemptions of an office in the secreto.[574] A reply of the Suprema, February 11, 1643, to a request from

Philip for means to pay 400 foot and 200 horse for eight months, gives us the prices fetched by a number of positions and also shows that the terms varied from spot cash to instalments running through a year or two. In Murcia, it says, there were still due 3500 ducats vellon for the offices of auditor and notary of sequestrations; in Seville the receivership had been auctioned for 8500 ducats, of which 2000 were in silver, and there was still due 1000 ducats in silver for an auditorship; in Llerena the notariat of sequestrations had brought at auction 3000 ducats vellon; in Logroño the auditorship had fetched 1000 ducats vellon; in Toledo the receivership had been sold at auction for 6360 ducats vellon; in Córdova the receivership had brought 5000 ducats, one-fourth in silver; the aggregate, payable at various periods, was 4250 ducats silver and 24,110 ducats vellon--but the final remark of the Suprema shows the incurable prodigality of Philip, even in his deepest distress, for it quietly adds that none of this is available because it had all been granted by royal decree to Don Pedro Pacheco, a member of the Suprema.[575]

We are told that when, in 1643, Arce y Reynoso assumed the inquisitor-generalship, he recognized that there were too many supernumeraries and that he prohibited the sale of offices until further orders. If so, the intermission was but temporary, for a royal decree of 1648 shows that it was still going on, and, in 1710, we happen to hear of the sale in Valencia of a notariat del juzgado for four lives for 16,000 reales.[576] In 1715 the tribunal of Peru seems to have been doing a little business of the kind on its own account, which the Suprema promptly stopped, stigmatizing it as simoniacal.[577] This probably indicates that it had ceased in Spain, but the custom of selling for three or four lives seems to have been conducive to longevity, for many continued to be thus held until late in the eighteenth century. An investigation ordered, in 1783, into the records concerning them, indicates that there were still survivors, or at least claimants, whose titles were to be scrutinized.[578]

It was impossible to get rid of those who held offices under these grants for successive lives, but efforts were made to reduce the numbers of the class that had not been put up at auction. In 1677, Valladares represented to Carlos II that the income of the Inquisition did not meet more than half the expenses for salaries, prisons, etc., wherefore he recommended that, as vacancies occurred, the offices should be suppressed until, in the busiest tribunals, there should not be more than three inquisitors, a fiscal and four secretaries, while in the smaller ones two inquisitors, a fiscal and three secretaries would suffice. The king assented and the plan was enlarged by leaving unfilled other superfluous places. Like other reforms, this was not permanent. In 1695 Carlos caused Rocaberti to investigate the personnel of the tribunals and to enforce the regulations of 1677. About 1705, Philip V, in his attempted reform, instituted a searching examination into the increase in numbers and salaries since the time of Arce y Reynoso and of Rocaberti, and the Inquisitor-general Vidal Marin again put in force the schedule of 1677, which continued to be, nominally at least, the rule. At intervals, as in 1714, 1728 and 1733, inquiries were made and reports were ordered from the tribunals, doubtless with a view to see that the limitations were observed for, under the Bourbons, the Inquisition was held to an accountability much stricter than of old.[579]

NUMBER OF OFFICIALS

We have seen the futile effort of Philip V, in 1743, to reduce the overgrown numbers of officials in the Santa Cruzada and Inquisition. It was possibly in connection with this that Prado y Cuesta, on his accession in 1746, demanded from all tribunals detailed reports as to all officials and their salaries, stating any vacancies or supernumeraries, and whether there were more familiars than were allowed by the Concordias. The answers to this ought to give a complete census of the Holy office. In the Appendix will be found a table compiled from these returns and also the report from Murcia, at that time one of the most active of the tribunals, which give a tolerably clear inside view of existing conditions. These documents represent an institution which had outlived its purpose, rapidly falling into decadence, no longer commanding popular veneration and chiefly useful as a refuge for those who were content to live on a miserable pittance in virtual idleness. The diminished number of consultors indicates, as we shall see hereafter, that the consulta de fe was falling into desuetude, while the army of calificadores points to the fact that the chief business consisted in the censorship of the press and the prosecution of propositions requiring theologians to define them. The irregularity in the number of commissioners is explained by the Murcia report which shows that, for the most part, they were omitted from the statements, but it is not so easy to understand the absence of alguazils, of whom at least one would seem to be necessary to each tribunal. There are many honorary officials and others serving without pay, while still others are jubilado or retired, especially among the secretaries and, where there are two receivers, one is jubilado or absent.

The paucity of keepers of penitential prisons shows that that punishment had become practically obsolete. With the absence of confiscations the juez de bienes has disappeared, except in Majorca. The blanks in the returns of familiars, although information concerning them had specially demanded, may be due either to the tribunals keeping no registers of them, or to concealment of the fact that the numbers allowed by the Concordias were exceeded. That there were serious omissions, indeed is proved when we consider that the total aggregate reported is only 951, while the census of 1769 gives 2645 as the number of those admitted to exemption through connection with the Inquisition. During the interval between this and the next census in 1787, strenuous and successful efforts were made to diminish the number of exempts, in spite of which the employees of the Inquisition had increased to 2705.[580]

Surveying the table as a whole it will be perceived that the higher offices of inquisitors and secretaries had rather increased than diminished from the standard set by Valladares in 1667. Yet there was virtually no serious work for them to do. Their predecessors had successfully enforced unity of faith and little remained except to repress all freedom of thought and aspiration for improvement. How they earned their salaries by laborious trifling is exemplified, in 1808, when three inquisitors and an inquisitor-fiscal of the Valencia tribunal pottered for eighteen months over the case of a poor laboring woman accused of "supersticiones," because she had suggested certain charms to some of her neighbors, and finally concluded to suspend it and to order her parish priest to reprimand and threaten her.[581]

The tribunals were constantly complaining of their penury and of the inadequacy of the salaries, doubtless with reason, but the pressure for appointment precluded the wholesome reduction in numbers which would have afforded relief. It was probably with a view to some practical re-adjustment that the Suprema repeatedly, in 1776, 1783, 1793 and 1806 called upon the tribunals for full and exact reports of all employees.[582] If so, the only result was a trifling increase in the salaries of the lower officials, averaging about fourteen per cent., leading to a complaint, in 1798, repeated in 1802, that the pay of the secretaries and messenger--the hardest worked of all the officials--had remained unchanged for a hundred years, while the cost of living had quadrupled and they had been deprived of their old exemptions and emoluments. It took, as the Valencia tribunal declared, half of their salaries to rent a decent house, which would seem to show that they were no longer furnished with dwellings.[583]

The excess of officials is emphasized by the fact that the Inquisition was empowered to call upon every individual for gratuitous service. Its commissioners were told that, if there was no appointed notary available, he could make another one serve and, when he summoned any one to accompany him on duty, even to a distant place, if the party refused to go he was to report the fact to the tribunal that it might take the proper steps.[584] Temporary commissions were constantly sent to the parish priest or to a canon, even when their names were unknown, with instructions as to what they were required to do. As the real work of the tribunals diminished there was an increasing habit of deputing what remained to outsiders. Inquisitors, who did not decide more than five or six trivial cases in a year, were too indolent to investigate denunciations or examine witnesses and would issue a commission to some priest or friar to do the work for them.[585] They spared their subordinates in the same way. Thus, in 1791, at Barcelona, there was some reason for identifying a man described as Alexandre Valle, sergeant in the second battalion of the Walloon guards. In place of sending one of the underlings of the tribunal on so simple an errand, a formal commission was made out to Francisco Lluc, Augustinian prior, who in due time reported that he had found him in the sixth battalion.[586] If the salaries were trivial so was the work which earned them.

HEREDITARY TRANSMISSION

Offices were virtually held for life, although the commissions technically expired with the death or removal of the grantor, for we have seen that, with each change in the inquisitor-generalship, the new incumbent renewed them and the interregnum was bridged over by the action of the Suprema. This did not cover the financial officials, who held from the crown and the same process was required on a change of sovereigns. Thus, when Philip II died, in 1598, the Suprema made haste to inform the tribunals that Philip III confirmed all the judges of confiscations, receivers and auditors.[587] Thus the incumbents came to regard themselves as holding vested rights in their offices and in fact were technically called "proprietors" of them, a corollary to which was to consider them as property, subject to hereditary transmission or to transactions more or less disguised.

A tendency to nepotism seems to have manifested itself early, for the Instructions of 1498 forbid the appointment, in any tribunal, of a kinsman or servant of the inquisitors or of any other official.[588] The force of this was weakened, in 1531, by a decision of the Suprema that the deputy of the receiver of Valencia was not an official in the sense of the prohibition--a decision which opened the door to hereditary transmission by enabling fathers to introduce their sons as deputies in their offices, as we have seen in the case of Géronimo Zurita.[589] Still, the prohibition was held to be in force and, in the instructions to visitors, one of the points to be investigated was whether two members of a family were employed in a tribunal.[590] Like all other wholesome rules, however, there was no hesitation in violating it. When the tribunal of Lima was established in 1570, it was specifically called to the attention of the inquisitors, but they had scarce been installed when a letter from Secretary Vázquez ordered them to appoint Pedro de Bustamente, brother of one of them, to any office for which he was fitted, and he was duly made notary of sequestrations.[591]

Hereditary transmission seems to have been favored from an early period. In 1498, we find Ferdinand not only approving the resignation of Pedro Lazaro, alguazil of Barcelona, in favor of his son Dionisio, but increasing the salary of the latter because he is a person who cannot live upon the regular stipend. So, in 1502, when Juan Pérez, notary of the tribunal of Calatayud, was incapacitated by age, he executed a will leaving all the papers and documents to his son Juan, and Ferdinand confirmed the bequest and empowered Juan to act.[592]

So completely did this become the policy of the Inquisition that when an official died, leaving a minor son, the place was filled temporarily till the boy should reach adult age and he was provided for meanwhile. In 1542, Luis Bages, notary of sequestrations in Saragossa, died and Tavera appointed Bartolomé Malo to the vacancy, ordering the receiver to pay from the fines and penances five hundred sueldos a year to Juan Bages, the young son of Luis. Accompanying this was a private communication to the inquisitors, informing them that Malo was appointed only until Juan should have age and experience for the position and, as the arrangement does not appear in his commission, a notarial act must be taken so as to insure Juan's succession. Secret arrangements such as this, however were not usually considered necessary. The next year died Miguel de Oliban, notary of the secreto in the same tribunal, when a temporary appointee was inducted who divided the salary with Juan Pérez de Oliban, son of Miguel, till he should be old enough to take the place.[593] The requirements of age were waived in favor of such transmissions. About 1710, Carlos Albornoz, receiver of Valencia, asked to be allowed to transfer his office to his son, aged twelve; this was refused but when, two years later, he renewed the request, it was granted.[594] Of course the service suffered from the incompetence of those thrust into it, but when they were absolutely unfit they were allowed to employ substitutes who served for a portion of the salary. Thus when Juan Romeo, in 1548, resigned a notariat of the juzgado in favor of his brother Francisco, Valdés wrote to the inquisitors that he hoped that Francisco would soon learn his duties and be able to fill the office personally without employing a substitute as had previously been the case.[595]

***

It would be useless to multiply examples of what was of daily occurrence. Officials were constantly resigning or retiring on half-pay in favor of their sons or grandsons or nephews, who were accepted as a matter of course. So completely was office regarded as property that a bereaved widow sometimes held it as a dowry, with which to tempt a new husband, or was granted a pension on it to be paid by the successor. Or, a man with a marriageable daughter would secure the promise of the succession for whoever would marry her; or, if he died leaving a girl unprovided for, the tribunal would kindly look up a husband for her on the same conditions, as in the case of Juana de Treviño, daughter of Antonio Espanon in Valencia. Unluckily the first suitor failed to prove his limpieza and another one was found in the person of Antonio de Bolsa.[596]

The natural result of this was to found inquisitorial families who continued through generations to live on the Holy Office, rendering such service as might be expected from those who held their positions to be personal property, like purchasers for four or more lives. Many examples of this could be cited, but a single one will suffice. In 1586 we find Juan del Olmo officiating as notary or secretary of the Valencia tribunal--whether the first of the line or not does not appear. In 1590, his widow Magdalena asked the reversion for her son Joseph, to whom it was given, and during his minority it was served by the alcaide, Pedro Juan Vidal, who gave a third of the salary to the widow. In 1623 this Joseph secured the succession for his son Joseph, who seems to have been a somewhat turbulent gentleman for, in 1638, he and his son were accused of the murder of his fellow secretary, Julian de Palomares. Escaping punishment for this, he died in 1644 and was succeeded by his son Jusepe Vicente, who, in 1666, not without difficulty, obtained the reversion for his son Vicente. The latter was still functioning in 1690. Who followed him I have not been able to trace, but the male line seems to have failed and the office to have passed to a nephew for, in 1750, it is filled by a Vicente Salvador y del Olmo.[597]

Philip II was not blind to the evils of this abuse and, in his instructions of 1595 to Manrique de Lara, he ordered that offices should not be transferred to brothers or sons unless there were special cause and the recipients were capable of filling them without appointing deputies; but Philip III reversed this, in 1608, in his instructions to Sandoval y Rojas, and prescribed that, when an official died, his children should be borne in mind.[598] In the instructions of Carlos II, in 1695, there is exhibited the fatal Spanish tendency of recognizing evils while tolerating them. He prohibited the transfer of office, save from father to son or from brother to brother when there is a just cause and the appointee has capacity for the position, for it had often happened that sons and brothers so appointed were unfit, or were so young that the Inquisition had to wait long to its detriment and even more so when substitutes were taken temporarily, for they went out with a knowledge of the secrets of the Inquisition and imagined themselves no longer bound to secrecy. Yet, after this clear admission he proceeded to repeat the order of Philip III that, when an official died, care was to be taken of his children.[599] Of course the warning went for nothing and the abuse continued to the last. A certificate of limpieza issued, November 23, 1818, to Juan Josef Paris, describes him as secretary of the tribunal of Toledo, on half-salary, while his father, Juan Antonio Paris, jubilado, has the other half.[600]

LENIENCY TO OFFENDERS

When there was no lineal successor available, the custom arose of granting--doubtless for a consideration--coadjutorships with the right of reversion. In 1619 the tribunal of Valencia took exception to this and consulted the Suprema, resulting in a decision not to recognize such transactions for the future.[601] They still continued, however and, in September 1643, a papal brief was procured prohibiting them, in spite of which a well-informed writer tells us that the inquisitor-general still granted them.[602] Another frequent abuse was saddling an office with a pension in favor of some representative of the previous incumbent or even of a stranger, suggesting collusion of the appointing power. Even inquisitors themselves sometimes accepted office under these degrading conditions. In 1636, a commission issued to Don Alonso de Buelva, as inquisitor of Toledo, bore on its face the full salary, but it was secretly coupled with the condition that he was to draw only the half, while the other half was given to Don Francisco de Valdés. A man taking such an office on these terms would probably not be nice in his methods of recouping himself. Still more suggestive of this was the not infrequent custom of taking office "sin gages"--without pay. Thus, in 1637, the Licenciado Pedro Montalvo accepted such a commission as notary of the secreto in Toledo and, in 1638, a similar one was issued for Córdova to Pedro Gutiérrez Armentía. Even inquisitors did not disdain to stoop to this as when, in this same year 1638, Doctor Villaviciosa took the inquisitorship of Murcia without pay.[603]

It is easy to understand how a system such as this should encumber the tribunals with useless hangers-on whose only serious duty was the drawing of salaries. So well was this understood that when, in the confusion of the War of Succession, there often was not money enough to go around, an order was issued that those who were performing duties should be paid in preference to those who were not. So, one of the features of the reform of 1705, attempted by Philip V, was a royal decree declaring null and void all commissions issued without carrying the obligation to work in the office, that no jubilation with salary should be granted without consulting the king, and that no ayuda de costa or other gratification should exceed thirty ducats without the royal assent.[604]

***

Malfeasance was stimulated by the excessive tenderness which forbore to visit misconduct with punishment. Warnings and threats were freely uttered but rarely enforced and, even when the penalty of suspension was inflicted, the term was apt to be reduced before expiration. This patience under repeated and prolonged wrongdoing was partly owing to the paternalism which generally governed the relations between superiors and subordinates, but principally because dismissal was a public acknowledgement of fallibility, endangering the popular veneration which the Inquisition sought to inspire. It was so from the first. It is true that the reformatory instructions of 1498 declare that any notary, who does what he should not do, shall be condemned as a perjurer and forger and be perpetually deprived of office, besides such other penalty of fine or exile as the inquisitor-general may determine, but this carried few terrors for offenders.[605] The power of effective punishment lay exclusively with the central head, which was not readily moved to active indignation by offences committed at a distance. A letter of Ferdinand, May 17, 1511, to an inquisitor, who had complained bitterly of a subordinate and evidently had asked his discharge, embodies the principle to which the Inquisition remained faithful to the last. The complainant was told that, when any of his officials was in fault, he was to be admonished; if he persisted, he was to be rebuked in the presence of his fellows; if this did not suffice, consultation was to be had with those who had been present and every care be taken to avoid injustice before going further, for the dismissal of officials of the Inquisition is most odious; the utmost caution must be observed that it is founded on justice and the success of the work depends on all living in harmony.[606] This forbearance Ferdinand himself practised in cases which might well move him to inflict summary chastisement.[607] When the inquisitor himself proved incorrigible, he might be suspended for a year or two, but the usual course was to transfer him and inflict him on some other district. In extreme cases he might be jubilado or retired on half-pay as was done with officials who were superannuated or too infirm to work. Dismissal was almost unknown and I have met with but few cases of it.

Jubilation might be either a reward or a punishment. In the earlier time, when an official was obliged to retire on account of age or infirmity he was taken care of with either a pension or a substantial gift, of which various cases are to be found in the records. In time this became an established custom, known as jubilation, and the retiring pension was usually half the salary, sometimes, but not often, deducted from the salary of the successor. Applications for jubilation were common, as men grew old or incapacitated, and we have seen, in the enumeration of the tribunal of Murcia, how many wage-eaters of this kind weighed on the finances of the Inquisition.

RELAXATION OF DISCIPLINE

The use of jubilation as a punishment affords a striking illustration of the tenderness shown to offenders. Instead of the deserved dismissal, they were shielded as far as possible from disgrace and were retired with a pension, thus placing them on a par with aged officials worn out in service. So far was this sympathy carried that, in the instructions of Carlos II to Rocaberti, in 1695, he is warned that, as jubilation inflicts grave discredit, sometimes involving risk of life, it is only to be resorted to with ample cause, after taking a vote in the Suprema.[608] How superfluous was this caution could be instanced by a number of cases, of which it suffices to mention that of Melchor Zapata who, about 1640, succeeded his father-in-law as alcaide of the secret prison of Valencia. Then the correspondence of the tribunal becomes burdened with complaints of his disorderly conduct; he was constantly getting into scrapes and being tried on various charges, among others, that of hiring four soldiers to commit a crime of violence. At length, in place of dismissal, he was jubilated with a life-pension of 20,000 maravedís in silver and his office was given to his cousin, Crispin Pons. The titulo de jubilacion issued to him by Sotomayor describes his long and faithful service, for which he is thus rewarded and he was assured of the enjoyment of all the exemptions and prerogatives attached to his office--though his subsequent conduct was so disreputable that, in 1642, it was felt necessary to deprive him of them.[609] When this was the policy observed toward incapable and delinquent officials it is not difficult to understand the financial troubles of the Holy Office and the grievances endured by the people.

The natural effect of this misguided leniency was looseness of discipline and indifference to duty. Inquisitors could inflict fines on their subordinates, except the fiscal, but for serious offences they could only report to the Suprema and, as they had no power of appointment or dismissal, it was impossible for them to exert adequate authority.[610] How little control they possessed is indicated when, in 1546, it was necessary for the Suprema to issue a formal order to the janitor of the Granada tribunal to shut the inner gates of the castle, which was its residence, at such hours as the inquisitors might designate and, if he did not do so, he was to be reported for such action as the Council might see fit to take.[611] Under such a system it is not surprising that, in the suggestions for reform, in 1623, it was proposed to give the inquisitors power to punish and suspend, for the tying of their hands resulted in insubordination, causing grave troubles in the tribunals.[612]

That there was gross neglect of duty follows as a matter of course. The hours prescribed for work, during which all were required to be present, were only six--three in the morning and three in the afternoon--except on the numerous holidays, and visitors in their inspections were instructed to inquire especially into this.[613] From such reports of visitations as I have examined, it would appear that the enforcement of the rule was difficult; Cervantes, indeed, in his report on Barcelona in 1561, says that there is no hope of securing regular attendance unless the Suprema will impose a penalty for default of more than an hour.[614]

INSPECTORS

Absence from the post of duty was an abuse which also seemed incurable. Even under the vigilant rule of Ferdinand, a circular letter of the Suprema, September 7, 1509, calls attention to the absence of the officials on their private business; the inquisitors, in urgent cases, could grant leave of absence for twenty days in the year, but this was never to be exceeded; records were to be kept and salaries were to be proportionately docked.[615] This was perfectly ineffectual. In 1520 we find the Suprema writing to the officials of Barcelona to return to their posts within ten days, and rebuking the inquisitors for permitting this neglect of duty, but a repetition of the letter in 1521 shows how fruitless had been the first one. The trouble was by no means confined to Barcelona and, in 1521, Cardinal Adrian made an effort to check it by declaring vacant the office of any one absenting himself for two months.[616] It was not only the subordinates, for the inquisitors themselves had frequently to be taken to task for similar neglect of duty.[617] The trouble was endless and serves in part to explain the cruel delays which aggravated so greatly the sufferings of those under trial. In 1573 the rule of 1509 was repeated with the addition that, if the twenty days granted were exceeded by ten days, the absentee was not to be admitted to his office on his return and this again was reissued in 1597, together with an order that no inquisitor should absent himself without the permission of the Suprema.[618]

This was not the only matter in which inquisitors had to be kept in check. The frequent commands for them not to accept commissions to attend to outside business show how eager were people to secure the service of agents so powerful and how ready were the inquisitors thus to sell their influence. So, when Valdés, in 1560, ordered them not to ask for favors, for complaints were made by people that they were forced to grant what was asked, we recognize how infinite were the resources of petty tyranny afforded by the terror which they inspired. That they were not superior to the vices of the period may be inferred from an injunction of Valdés, in 1566, to exercise great moderation in gambling.[619]

***

Earnest efforts were not lacking to maintain a fair standard of efficiency and discipline in the tribunals, although they were largely neutralized by the restricted authority allowed to the inquisitors and the fatal clemency shown to delinquents. Isabella has the credit of reforming the administration of justice in Castile by periodically sending inspectors, incorruptible and inflexible, to scrutinize the operation of the courts, and it was not long after the organization of the Inquisition that a similar plan was found necessary for its tribunals. We happen to hear of a visitador or inspector at Medina del Campo, while Torquemada was still in the active exercise of his functions, probably before 1490.[620] From letters of 1497 we learn that the salaries of an inspector and his notary were the same as those of an inquisitor and notary--a hundred thousand maravedís for the one and forty thousand for the other. These were appointed by the inquisitor-general and carried royal letters ordering inquisitors to receive and treat them well and all officials to aid them, give them free passage and levy no tolls, dues, ferriages or fees of any kind.[621] The Instructions of 1498 create permanent inspectors-general, of whom there were to be one or two, to visit all tribunals and report their condition; they were not to lodge or eat with the inquisitors or to receive presents from them and were to exercise only the powers expressed in their commissions.[622] Under this Francisco de Simancas, Archdeacon of Córdova, was appointed inspector, with González Mesons as his notary; how long he served does not appear, but orders for the payment of his salary can be traced until 1503.[623]

When the Inquisitions of Castile and Aragon were separated, in 1507, each continued to employ inspectors. Alonso Rodríguez, of whom we hear in 1509, probably belonged to Castile; in 1514 Ximenes appointed Juan Moris as inspector, after which special inspectors ceased for a time to be employed for, in 1517, the Inquisitor of Córdova was sent to inspect Toledo, Seville and Jaen and the Inquisitor of Jaen to inspect Córdova, Cuenca and Valladolid.[624] In Aragon, Mercader in 1513 sent Juan de Ariola to inspect Majorca, Sardinia and Sicily and, about the same time, Hernando de Montemayor to inspect the tribunals of Aragon, Catalonia and Valencia.[625] After the reunion of the Inquisition, Cardinal Adrian introduced an innovation by appointing laymen to the office--the Licentiates Sisa and Peña--the former a judge in the high court of Valladolid. Their functions were enlarged, for Charles V describes them as persons of high authority, not connected with the Inquisition, sent to investigate all the tribunals and to reform whatever required amendment, for which he clothed them with ample powers.[626]

***

These regular routine inspections came to an end and, though the wholesome supervision was not abandoned, it became irregular, either employed occasionally or when complaints seemed to indicate its necessity. Barcelona was a troublesome tribunal, but it seems to have been visited only at intervals of from six to ten years. The inspections were not inexpensive and the cost had to be defrayed by the Suprema. When, in 1567, de Soto Salazar, a member of the Suprema, was sent to investigate Valencia, Barcelona and Saragossa, he was given at the outset four hundred ducats and his secretary, Pablo Garcia, two hundred.[627] The rule became established to employ only inquisitors and those in active service, not retired.[628] The work, when conscientiously performed, was not light. An inspection of the Canary tribunal, made by Claudio de la Cueva, lasted from 1595 to 1597 and his report forms a mass of 1124 folios.[629] This was unusually laborious, but reports covering three, four or five hundred pages are not uncommon.

The visitador was expected to make a thorough investigation of the condition and working of the tribunal, to discover all neglect of regulations, all abuses and malfeasance of the officials, all derelictions of duty, all maladministration of the property and revenues, all misuse of power, whether through oppression of the defenceless or remissness in vindicating the faith. He was to examine the records, not only to see that they were properly kept and indexed but also whether justice had been duly administered and the estilo of the Holy Office had been rigidly followed. He visited the prisons, listened to the complaints of the prisoners and investigated them. On arrival, he fixed a day on which he would appear in the audience-chamber; the inquisitors and all officials were assembled, his credentials were read and the inquisitors promised obedience in the name of all present. The next day the inquisitors were examined under oath, as to whether there was anything requiring amendment and whether the officials performed their full duty, the answers being taken down in writing. The inspector brought with him an elaborate series of interrogatories, usually forty-eight or fifty in number, covering all the points which experience had shown as likely to tempt to wrongdoing and on these he examined all the officials singly. He also listened to all who had complaints to make; if these appeared to be justified he investigated them thoroughly, summoning all witnesses, who were guaranteed that their names would be kept secret, and on this evidence he framed charges against those inculpated and heard them in defence. When his duties in the tribunal were accomplished he was expected to visit the district and investigate all complaints. The results were reduced to writing and, when his labors were completed, he sent or carried the whole to the Suprema for its action.[630] As a rule, he had no executive authority and could only make recommendations, but visitadores to the colonies were frequently invested with greater power, presumably in view of the long delays in communication. When, in 1654, Medina Rico came as inspector to Mexico, where maladministration was flagrant, he sat in judgement on the inquisitors, Estrada and Higuera, suspended them and occupied the tribunal for years.[631] It can readily be conceived that at times there was no little friction between inspector and inquisitors, and, in 1645, the Suprema presented to the king a consulta on the controversies thence arising.[632]

The necessity for these visitations diminished in proportion as the tribunals were subordinated to the Suprema. When they had to make monthly reports of all pending cases, so that their action was under constant supervision; when all sentences were submitted for confirmation or revision, with the papers showing the conduct of the cases; when no arrest could be made without presenting the sumaria and receiving authority; when, moreover, the business management of property was scrutinized through monthly reports of the junta de hacienda, there was no longer a justification for the expenses of visitations. The growing facilities of intercommunication encouraged centralization and enabled the Suprema to maintain a constant supervision. When, therefore, it concentrated in itself all the judicial faculties of the Inquisition, rendering the tribunals merely instruments for investigation, the functions of the visitador became superfluous, at least in the Peninsula.

THE SECRETO

The palace or building, which was the seat of the tribunal, was divided into the secreto and the outside rooms or apartments. It was expected to furnish lodgings for the inquisitors and, if spacious enough, for the other officials. The most important feature was the carceles secretas or secret prison for those on trial, for it was necessary that they could be brought at any moment to the audience-chamber without being seen by any one. There was, of course, a torture-chamber, which seems to have generally been underground. The secreto originally was merely a record-room in which the papers and documents were preserved. From the first these were guarded with jealous secrecy, not only on account of their importance in the trials but because their abstraction or destruction was so ardently desired by the kindred or accomplices of convicts. As early as 1485, Ferdinand, in his instructions to the tribunal of Saragossa, orders that no servant of any of the officials shall enter "lo secreto de la Inquisicion."[633] The Instructions of 1498 provide that the chest or chamber in which the papers are kept shall have three keys, two held by the notarios del secreto and one by the fiscal, so that no one can take out a document save in the presence of the others, and no one shall enter it except the inquisitors, the notaries and the fiscal, rules substantially repeated in the Sicilian instructions of 1516. Among the derelictions of the Barcelona tribunal, reported in 1561 by Cervantes, was the neglect of this rule, leading, he said, to grave abuses.[634] The functions and extent of the secreto were gradually enlarged. In Mercader's Instructions of 1514, the money-chest with three keys was ordered to be kept in the secreto, a provision which became permanent.[635] When the rule was established of conducting the trials in profound secrecy, and a veil of impenetrable mystery was thrown around all the operations of the Inquisition, the audience-chamber was included in the secreto, as well as the offices occupied by the fiscal and secretaries. The door to it was secured by three locks having different keys and entrance was forbidden save to those officially privileged or summoned.[636] In 1645, it was discovered that there was danger in the notaries or secretaries bringing in their swords, for a prisoner when led to an audience might in his desperation seize one and give trouble, and they were consequently ordered in future to be left outside.[637] In the Valencia tribunal there was considerable excitement, in 1679, when the pages of the inquisitors got possession of the keys and had false ones made, with which they gained at will access to the sacred precincts, but no harm seems to have arisen from the boyish prank.[638] One feature of the audience-chamber was significant--a celosía or lattice, behind which a witness could identify a prisoner, without being seen or recognized.[639]

THE INQUISITORS

In considering the personnel of the tribunal, we may dismiss the assessor with a few words. Such an official was unknown in the Old Inquisition, but we have seen that, when the first inquisitors were sent to Seville, they were accompanied by an assessor, and such a functionary continued for some time to be considered a necessary adjunct to a tribunal. At the beginning the inquisitors were Dominican friars, presumably good theologians but unversed in the intricacies of the law. It was therefore desirable to associate with them a lawyer as a guide, and his presence moreover might serve as an assurance to the people of the legality of the proceedings. In Torquemada's instructions of 1485 it is provided that they must always act in concert and that anything done by one without the other was invalid; even communications to the Suprema must be signed by both.[640] In the trials of this period we sometimes find the assessor sitting with the inquisitors and sometimes not, and the sentences are rendered by the latter with the concurrence of the former.[641] In the secular law of the period, the assessor had only a consultative and not a decisive vote, and this would appear to be his position in the tribunal, when the routine of the Inquisition had established its own precedents, when all doubtful questions were decided by the Suprema and the services of trained lawyers were no longer required.[642] In the early time their salaries were the same as those of the inquisitors--indeed, at Saragossa, in 1486, Martin Martínez, the assessor, receives five thousand sueldos while the inquisitors are rated at four thousand.[643] It was not long, however, before it apparently became indifferent whether there was an assessor or not. In 1499, the salary lists of Seville, of Burgos and of Palencia have no mention of such an official, while there is one at Saragossa and, in 1500, Ferdinand empowers the inquisitor of Sardinia to select for his assessor any doctor he pleases.[644] The office continued to exist for a time, as a kind of supernumerary, employed in hearing the civil cases of officials but, in the Aragonese Concordia of 1568, this duty was placed on the inquisitors and the assessorship was abolished. In Castile, the list of officials, promulgated in the same year by Philip II, as entitled to exemption from taxation, makes no mention of the assessor, who may be assumed by this time to disappear.[645]

The inquisitors, of course, were the superior officials of the tribunal. They were the judges, with practically unlimited power over the lives and fortunes and honor of all whom they summoned before them, until they were gradually restricted by the growing centralization in the Suprema. To the people they were the incarnation of the dreaded Holy Office, regarded with more fear and veneration than bishop or noble, for all the powers of State and Church were placed at their disposal. They could arrest and imprison at will; with their excommunication they could, at a word, paralyze the arm of all secular officials and, with their interdict, plunge whole communities into despair. Such a concentration of secular and spiritual authority, guarded by so little limitation and responsibility, has never, under any other system, been entrusted to fallible human nature. To exercise it wisely and temperately called for exceptional elevation of character, self-control and mature experience of men and things. That friars, suddenly called from the cloister or the schools and clothed with such limitless power over their fellow-beings, should sometimes grow intoxicated with their position and commit the awful slaughter which marked the early years of the Inquisition, gives no occasion for surprise, nor that their successors should have trampled with such arrogant audacity on all who ventured to raise a voice against their misuse of their prerogatives. It is therefore worth our while to examine what qualifications were required by popes and kings in those whom they selected as fitted for an office of such bewildering temptations and such vast opportunities for evil.

QUALIFICATIONS

Sixtus IV, in the bull of November 1, 1478, empowered Ferdinand and Isabella to appoint, as inquisitors, three bishops or other worthy men, priests either regular or secular, over forty years of age, God-fearing, of good character and record, masters or bachelors of theology or licentiates of canon law. The prescription as to the minimum age was as old as the Council of Vienne, in 1312, and had become a matter of course; the rest was as well-chosen a definition of the requisite qualities as perhaps could be expressed in general terms, considering the temper of the age and the work to be performed.[646] So, in 1483, when Sixtus, under the influence of Cardinal Borgia, desired to get rid of Inquisitor Gualbes, he asked Ferdinand to replace him with some master of theology who had the fear of God and was eminent for his virtues.[647] The only inquisitors that Spain had known were Dominicans and, although they were not specified, it seemed to be a matter of course that the Inquisition should remain in their hands, but Ferdinand, in his struggle with Sixtus for the control of the Aragonese Inquisition, had encountered the obstacle of the obedience due by the friars to their General, who of course was a creature of the curia. He was resolved to organize the Inquisition to suit himself, which explains why Torquemada, in his Instructions of December 6, 1484, simplified the formula of qualifications to letrados (either lawyers or men of university training) of good repute and conscience, the fittest that could be had.[648] This did not even require the inquisitor to be an ecclesiastic, except in so far as there were comparatively few letrados of the time who were not in orders. When Innocent VIII renewed the commission of

Torquemada, February 3, 1485, it empowered him to appoint as inquisitors fitting ecclesiastics, learned and God-fearing, provided they were masters of theology or doctors or licentiates of laws, or cathedral canons or holding other church dignities, but, while this was repeated in a subsequent bull of March 24, 1486, it was simplified, in another clause, into ecclesiastics of proper character and learning, not less than thirty years of age.[649] This reduction in the age limit was retained by Alexander VI, in the commissions issued to Deza, November 24, 1498 and September 1, 1499, when the requisite of being an ecclesiastic was omitted, for the qualification was reduced simply to suitable men of good and tender conscience, even if they have not reached forty years of age but are more than thirty.[650] This became virtually the accepted formula, as shown in the commissions issued, June 4 and 5, 1507 by Julius II, to Enguera for Aragon and to Ximenes for Castile, and in those of Leo X to Mercader and Poul in 1513 and to Cardinal Adrian in 1516 and 1518.[651]

The office of inquisitor was thus thrown open to the laity and there was no hesitation in employing them so long as they remained single but, if they married, they were obliged to resign--possibly because it was thought impossible for a married man to preserve the absolute secrecy regarded as essential in the Holy Office. The Licentiate Aguirre, Ferdinand's favorite member of the Suprema, was a layman. On June 28, 1515, Ferdinand writes to Ximenes that the Licentiate Nebreda, Inquisitor of Seville, desires to marry and, as he is a good servant, another office has been found for him, while the treasurer of the church of Pampeluna will make a suitable appointee for Seville.[652] Two other similar cases occur about the same time.[653] It was an anomaly to allow laymen to sit in judgement on matters of faith, but no action was taken to prevent it until Philip II, in his instructions of 1595 to Manrique de Lara, ordered that inquisitors and fiscals at least must be in holy orders--a clause omitted by Philip III in his instructions of 1608.[654] At length the Suprema met the question, November 10, 1632, by requiring all inquisitors to have themselves ordained and prohibiting them otherwise from exercising their functions, a provision which apparently met with slack obedience, for it had to be repeated January 12 and June 5, 1637, with the addition that inquisitors and fiscals who were not in orders should receive no salaries.[655] Even this does not seem to have been effective for, in 1643, a consulta called attention to the matter as a great evil and indecency, and suggested that a papal brief should be obtained, rendering priests' orders an essential qualification for inquisitors and fiscals.[656] This was not done, but we may presume that in time the functions were confined to ecclesiastics.

Legal training was prescribed as a requisite in 1608, by Philip III, who ordered that no one should be appointed inquisitor or fiscal who could not exhibit to the Suprema his diploma of graduation in law. Carlos II repeated this, in 1695, adding that inquisitors and secretaries must not be natives of the provinces to which they were assigned, so as to avert partisanship, and that the strictest investigation into character and limpieza must precede appointment.[657]

The papal requirements expressed in the successive commissions issued to inquisitors-general continued for a while to be simply that they should appoint prudent and suitable men of good repute and sound conscience who had attained the age of thirty years. Apparently this violation of the Clementine rule of forty years led to some animadversion and, in the commission of Valdés, in 1547, there is no allusion to age. This example was followed until, in 1596, Clement VIII, in the commission to Portocarrero, inserted a minimum age limit of forty years, as required by the canons, adding that if enough suitable men of that age could not be found, as to which he charged Portocarrero's conscience, then men of thirty-five could be appointed, but if this were done without necessity, the appointment would be invalid. To this Portocarrero objected, saying that it rendered it impossible for him to make appointments without scruples of conscience, as it was difficult to find suitable persons of the designated age to take the office, and he therefore begged that the limit should be reduced to thirty years, as had been done by all popes since Innocent VIII. Clement yielded, but was careful to insert a derogation of the apostolic constitutions and especially of the Clementine Nolentes.[658]

APPOINTING POWER

Thenceforth to the end all limitation of age was discreetly omitted, the formula being simply "prudent and suitable men of good repute and sound conscience and zealous for the Catholic faith."[659] Yet the minimum age was understood to be thirty and, when younger men were appointed, dispensations were required, as when, in 1782, Inquisitor-general Bertran gave the inquisitorship of Barcelona to Don Matias Bertran. Apparently objection was made to his youth and, in 1783, a papal dispensation was procured empowering him to exercise the office in spite of his not having attained the age of thirty.[660]

***

The patronage of the inquisitors was greatly limited by the gradual centralization of power in the Suprema. In the early period they had the appointment of porteros and nuncios--apparitors and messengers--and when, in 1500, Ferdinand reorganized the Sicilian tribunal, he sent inquisitors with power to fill all offices except that of receiver. In 1502 he even authorized the inquisitor of Lérida and Huesca to appoint a judge of confiscations and notary at each place.[661] Subsequently, as we have seen, the inquisitor-general absorbed all the patronage of salaried offices, even to the porteros and nuncios. If a vacancy occurred in a post of which the daily duties were essential, the inquisitors could fill it temporarily, while reporting it at once to the Suprema and awaiting its orders, but they had no other power.[662] As regards the numerous unsalaried officials, the inquisitor-general appointed the consultores and calificadores, or censors, and also the commissioners for cathedral towns, sea-ports and cities which were seats of tribunals. This left to the inquisitors only the appointment of familiars and of commissioners in other places, though at first in cathedral towns they might select a canon of the cathedral for commissioner.[663] It was the same with regard to expenditures, as to which originally they enjoyed a certain freedom of action. This, as has been shown above, was curtailed until ultimately the Suprema controlled even the smallest outlays.

It also kept watch over the morals of the inquisitors, recognizing the temptations to which they were exposed and the opportunities afforded by their position. Among the interrogatories which the inspector was instructed to make was whether the inquisitors lived decently, without publicly keeping concubines or corrupting the female prisoners or the wives and daughters of prisoners or of the dead whose fame and memory were prosecuted.[664] When attention was called to official misconduct it was promptly looked into, as in 1528, when the inquisitors of Barcelona were accused of receiving bribes and suborning witnesses, an inquisitor of Valencia with a notary of Tortosa was despatched thither, fully commissioned to investigate and report.[665]

DISTRICT VISITING

The most laborious work imposed on the inquisitors was the visitation of their districts. These were large, usually embracing several bishoprics, and, when the tribunals became sedentary, the necessity was apparent of a closer watch over aberrations than could be exercised from a fixed centre. Already, in the Instructions of 1498, a system of visitation, termed the General Inquisition, is seen at work and, in 1500, Deza ordered the inquisitors to visit all places where an inquest had not been held. Each inquisitor was to travel with a notary, receiving denunciations and taking testimony, so that on his return the colleagues could consult together and order such arrests as might be found necessary. In districts where such visitations had already been made, one of the inquisitors was ordered to travel every year, holding inquests in the towns and villages and publishing the Edict of Faith to attract denunciations; the other inquisitor remained in the tribunal to despatch routine business or, if there were none such, he too was ordered to take the road. Reports in detail of the work accomplished in the visitation were to be made to the inquisitor-general.[666] This remained the basis of the system and the Instructions of 1561 merely define more clearly the functions of the visiting inquisitor, who was told that he was not to make arrest unless there were danger of flight, but was only to gather testimony and carry it to the tribunal for action; if he made an arrest he was not to try the accused but to send him to the secret prison. Trifling cases, however, he could despatch on the spot, taking care that he bore delegated powers from the Ordinary for that purpose.[667] The importance attached to these visitations is apparent when, during the siege of Toledo in the Communidades, Cardinal Adrian and the Constable and Admiral of Castile joined in an order, November 3, 1521, to the commanders of the besieging forces, to allow the inquisitors to come out and perform their accustomed visits.[668]

In 1517 these visits were ordered to be made every four months, each inquisitor taking his turn under pain of forfeiting a year's salary. This indicates that the duty was distasteful and likely to be shirked and, in 1581, the obligation was reduced to once a year, starting at the end of January and taking such portions of the district as were deemed to require special attention. In 1607 the districts were ordered to be laid out in circuits, to be visited in turn until all were covered, when the process began anew.[669] In 1569 an elaborate code of instructions was framed by which it appears that the principal objects were the publication of the Edict of Faith with its consequent crop of denunciations, an investigation into the character and conduct of commissioners and familiars and the maintenance in the churches of the sanbenitos of those punished by the Inquisition, for which purpose the visitor carried lists for all the places to be visited.[670]

A certain amount of stateliness and ceremony attended the visit. Before reaching a town, word was sent forward of the hour of expected arrival, when the authorities, the church dignitaries and the principal gentlemen of the place were summoned to go forth to meet the inquisitor and escort him to his lodgings. The secretary was instructed to note the details of these receptions, whether honorable or otherwise, the character of the lodgings provided and utensils furnished.[671] Lack of respect on these occasions was punishable. In 1564, Dr. Zurita, visiting the sees of Gerona and Elne found the gates of

Castellon de Ampurias closed against him and one of the guards seized his horse's reins. He proceeded to prosecute the local authorities, when the consuls proved that they were not in fault, but two guards, Salbador Llop and Juan Maraña, were sent to Barcelona for trial.[672]

Although occasionally nests of Morisco and Jewish apostates were discovered in these visits, as a rule the practical results appear to have been rather the gratification of old grudges by neighbors in little towns and the gathering in of fines by the inquisitors. In 1582, Juan Aymar, Inquisitor of Barcelona, in reporting a visitation of the sees of Gerona and Elne and part of Barcelona and Vich, makes parade of having published the Edict of Faith in 263 places, but he brought in only seven trivial cases, of which four were of Frenchmen.[673]

These trips involved no little labor and even hardship; four months was the time prescribed for them, commencing early in February, and the vernal equinox was not likely to be agreeable, especially in mountainous districts. Naturally the duty was shirked whenever practicable, and the effort of the Suprema to compel its performance was endless. In 1557 it instructed the receiver at Saragossa that each inquisitor, on alternate years, must spend at least four months in visitations and that this performance is an absolute condition precedent to his receiving the customary ayuda de costa.[674] This was carried even further in a carta acordada of January 25, 1607, to all the tribunals; the inquisitor, in his turn, must start on the first Sunday in Lent, without attempting an excuse or a reply, and the report of his visit must be included in the annual statement of cases, for otherwise the ayuda de costa will be withheld from the whole tribunal, because these visits are the principal reason of its bestowal.[675] This solidarity enforced on all the officials was possibly owing to the recalcitrance of subordinates for, in 1598, we find a tribunal asking the Suprema to issue the necessary orders to them direct, which it obligingly did, while remonstrating that it should not be burdened with such details.[676] Throughout the seventeenth century, the correspondence of the Suprema with the tribunals of Valencia and Barcelona is filled with orders to the inquisitor whose turn it is to go and refusals to accept excuses and, in 1705, a letter to Valencia asks why the visit had been neglected.[677]

THE FISCAL

When there were three inquisitors, the absence of one did not interfere with current business, but where there were only two it was a serious impediment. From the beginning the rule was absolute that two must act conjointly in all important matters, such as sentencing to torture, ordering publication of evidence, or rendering final sentence, and this in both civil and criminal actions. Minor and trivial cases, however, could be despatched by one in the absence of his colleague and he could continue to hold audiences and gather testimony, while, in the habitual leisurely transaction of inquisitorial business, procrastination caused by the crippling of the tribunal for four months in every year was evidently not regarded as of any moment.[678] In the little tribunal of Majorca, however, which could support but a single inquisitor, he was deemed competent to act by himself and he probably was excused from visitations.[679]

***

Next in importance to the inquisitors stood the promoter fiscal, or prosecuting officer. In the original Inquisition of the thirteenth century there was no such officer; there was candor in the position of the inquisitor as both judge and prosecutor, infinitely preferable to the hypocrisy that the trial was an action between a prosecutor and an accused with the inquisitor as an impartial judge. How this came to pass will be considered hereafter.

We have seen that, even in the skeleton organization of the first tribunal in 1480, a fiscal was deemed essential. He ranked next to the inquisitors and, in 1484, it was ordered that he should assist in all public functions, after the inquisitors and Ordinary but before the judge of confiscations.[680] Yet he was a subordinate. In the regulation of salaries in 1498, the inquisitors received 60,000 maravedís, the receiver the same, while the fiscal was rated at 40,000, the same as the notaries, and even the messenger had 20,000.[681] So, in the Sicilian tribunal, in 1500, the inquisitors and receiver have 6000 sueldos, while the fiscal and notaries have only 2500.[682] It was the same with the ayuda de costa. In 1540 we find the fiscal allowed only the same as the notaries and alguazil, and when, in 1557, the scale was fixed for Saragossa, the fiscal was portioned with 1000 sueldos and the inquisitors with 3000.[683]

The fiscal was held to act wholly under orders from the inquisitors. In the Instructions of 1484, they are represented as ordering him to accuse the contumacy of fugitives and to denounce the dead against whom they find evidence. So, in a trial of 1528, we find the inquisitors ordering the fiscal to present his accusation against the defendant.[684] In 1561, among his duties was prescribed that of keeping the secreto clean and in good order; he opened and closed its door with his own hands and, in 1570, he was required to have all the multitudinous documents well arranged, sewed, covered and so marked that they could readily be had when wanted. The letters and instructions of the Suprema were placed in his hands and it was his duty to give in writing to each official such portion as applied to him. In 1632, there was added to his labors that of furnishing the Suprema a monthly report embracing every pending case with a summary of all that had been done in it since the beginning--a duty apparently not relished for the order had to be repeated in 1639.[685] With all these somewhat multifarious duties, we never hear of a fiscal having a clerk, assistant or deputy.

In 1582, it was prescribed that his seat in the audience-chamber was to be smaller than those of the inquisitors, placed to one side and without cushions. In public functions his chair was to be similar to theirs except that it had no cushion. The inquisitors were required to address him and the judge of confiscations as merced, and, when he entered, they were not obliged to rise but merely to raise their caps.[686]

NOTARIES OR SECRETARIES

The position of the fiscal gradually improved. In his instructions of 1595 to Manrique de Lara, Philip II couples him with the inquisitor, in requiring both to be in orders, and prescribes great care in the appointment for it is customary to promote fiscals to the inquisitorship. Similarly Philip III, in 1608, requires both offices to be filled by jurists and when, in 1632 and 1637, the Suprema made holy orders a condition it included fiscals with inquisitors.[687] The assimilation between the offices was rapid and, in 1647, in a payment of ayuda de costa in Valencia there occurs an item of thirty thousand maravedis to Inquisitor Antonio de Ayala y Verganza, "por la plaza de fiscal," showing that he was acting as fiscal.[688] The idea of coalescence was becoming familiar. When, in 1658, Gregorio Cid, after six years' service as inquisitor of Sardinia, was transferred to Cuenca, he suggested that there ought to be there two inquisitors and a fiscal, or at least that the junior inquisitor should serve also as fiscal.[689]

The identification of the offices was facilitated, in 1660, by a royal cédula prescribing that fiscals were to be held the equals of inquisitors in precedence and honors, canopies, cushions and the like, as well as in pay and emoluments.[690] Thenceforth the office of fiscal came to be filled by one of the inquisitors, though he took care to preserve his dignity by styling himself "inquisidor fiscal" or "the inquisitor who performs the office of fiscal." Thus at length the two offices coalesced and we have seen in the table of officials in 1746 that they were reckoned together. As a matter of course the inquisitor who acted as prosecutor did not enter the consulta de fe and vote on the fate of the accused whom he had prosecuted.[691] Sometimes, when there was no fiscal and no inquisitor willing to perform the duties, the senior secretary assumed the function. Such a case occurs as early as 1655, and it continued occasionally to the end.[692]

***

The notaries, or secretaries, formed an important part of the tribunal. They reduced to writing all the voluminous proceedings of the trials, all the audiences given to the accused with the interrogatories and answers, all the evidence of the witnesses and its ratification, the endless repetitions in the cumbrous and involved system of procedure which developed until the object seemed to be to protract business beyond the limits of human endurance. They kept the records which required an elaborate system of indexing, so that the name of any culprit and his genealogy could be found whenever wanted. In the later period, moreover, when the tribunals communicated to each other all their acts, the correspondence served to fill the gap arising from diminished business. At the beginning they were forbidden to employ clerks and were required to write everything with their own hands and this seems to have continued to the last.[693] In the earlier period they were styled notaries and sometimes escribanos or scriveners, possibly because as such their attestation authenticated all papers. Early in the seventeenth century the title gradually changed to secretaries, an innovation to which a writer in 1623 objects, as not distinguishing them from the secretaries of magnates and cities.[694] This objection did not prevail and a document of 1638 uses the terms as convertible, although an order of the Suprema, in the same year, forbids notaries to be called secretaries, while in 1648 we find the new appellation firmly established.[695] The importance of the office is shown by its fairly liberal salary. In the Instructions of 1498 it is placed at 30,000 maravedis, one-half of that of the inquisitors,[696] though the proportion diminished in time, for we have seen that, in 1746, the secretary received 2352 reales, while the inquisitor had 7352. There was compensation for this, however, in the heavy fees accruing to the secretaries from applicants for proofs of limpieza--a business shared with a new official known as "secretario de actos positivos." The number moreover had greatly increased for, while at the early period, with its heavy work, a tribunal was allowed but two notaries, in the later time there were often four or five salaried secretaries, to whom were sometimes added honorary secretaries with entrance to the secreto and honorary secretaries without entrance.[697]

THE ALGUAZIL

There was also a notary of sequestrations, whose duties were highly important in the early times of abundant confiscations. He was always present when arrests were made, so as to draw up on the spot an inventory of the property seized, but, as confiscations diminished, the office became superfluous and was suppressed by a carta acordada of December 1, 1634. After this we hear of a superintendent of sequestrations, in 1647, and subsequently its occasional duties were discharged by some other official for a moderate compensation as, in 1670, in Valencia, the procurator of the fisc received twenty-five libras a year for attending to them.[698]

***

The alguazil was the executive officer of the tribunal. In the early lists of salaries his pay is the same as, or even larger than, that of the inquisitors, but this was because the prison was at his charge.[699] From this he was relieved, in 1515, by Ferdinand, who empowered the inquisitors to appoint carceleros, at a salary of five hundred sueldos, after which the wages of the alguazil declined to those of the secretaries and even of the alcaide who succeeded him as gaoler.[700] His superior dignity, however, was recognized in a carta acordada of May 13, 1610, which provided that in public functions he should have precedence over the secretaries.[701] His long wand of office, which exceeded that of secular alguaziles, was also a distinction and when, in 1576, the alguaziles of the Santa Cruzada in Barcelona ventured to imitate him, the Suprema ordered the inquisitors to punish them.[702]

His functions were various. The inquisitors, the receiver and the judge of confiscations were forbidden to appoint any one else to execute their orders if he were at hand. If, in his absence, an arrest had to be made, the fact had to be attested at the foot of the warrant issued to another, without which the receiver was ordered not to pay the expenses incurred. He made all levies and seizures and was entitled to fees for the service.[703] By the instructions of 1488, if the duty was at a distance of more than three or four leagues, he was not to be sent, but a temporary substitute, whose commission expired with the performance of the errand. Perhaps this was because the thrifty Ferdinand had insisted that, if he was sent out of the city, he must pay his own expenses, but this was relaxed for, in 1502, we find the rule established that, if an alguazil is sent from one province to another, to a greater distance than four leagues, his expenses were to be paid. He had, however, to furnish at his own cost a satisfactory person to take charge of the prison during his absence and, if he required assistance in making arrests, the inquisitors selected the persons and determined their pay.[704]

The alguazil mayor seems to have been an ornamental personage, usually a man of distinction, who thereby proclaimed his purity of blood and devotion to the faith. We have seen that, in Seville and Córdova, the office was hereditary in noble houses whose ancestors had abandoned to the Inquisition royal castles of which they were alcaides, receiving in return this position with handsome emoluments. In 1655 the alguazil mayor of the tribunal of Córdova was Luis Méndez de Haro, Conde-Duque de Olivares and his deputy was Gonzalo de Cardenas y Córdova, a Knight of Calatrava. In Seville, Don Juan de Saavedra y Alvarado, Marquis of Moscoso, served as alguazil mayor at the auto de fe of March 11, 1691, and November 30, 1693. About 1750, the tribunal of Seville had the Marquis of Villafranca as alguazil mayor; that of Valladolid had the Marquis of Revilla; in Granada the incumbent was a minor, Don Nicolas Velázquez, and the office was served by Don Diego Ramírez de la Piscina.[705]

THE PORTERO--THE GAOLER

The humbler officials of the tribunal were the nuncio, the portero and the carcelero or alcaide de las carceles secretas. Strictly speaking the nuncio was a messenger or courier, bearing despatches to the Suprema or other tribunals and, before the post-office was organized, his life must have been an active one. In 1502 we hear of his salary being twelve hundred sueldos, out of which he defrayed his travelling expenses, but subsequently these were paid by the receiver and, in 1541, his stipend was five hundred sueldos.[706] His ayuda de costa, in 1567, was made dependent on his accompanying the inquisitors on their visitations.[707] At that period the tribunals seem to have been allowed two nuncios but, with the development of postal facilities, the functions of the position gradually shrank, the number was cut down to one and, in the eighteenth century we find him converted into a nuncio de camera, or interior attendant, called indifferently nuncio and portero, while a nuncio extraordinario makes the fires and attends to other servile work.[708]

The portero in the secular courts was a kind of apparitor, to serve summonses, authorized to take bail up to the sum of a hundred reales and forbidden to keep a shop or tavern.[709] In the Inquisition his function was to serve citations, notices of autos de fe, decrees and other similar work, and he was prohibited from engaging in trade of any kind; he was not allowed to enter the audience-chamber, but, in the eighteenth century we find him converted into a portero de camara, or usher and janitor, in which capacity he had entrance to the audience-chamber. When, in 1796, we find a Doctor Don Josef Fontana serving as portero in the Valencia tribunal, we may infer that the office was not servile, and it is observable that the portero and his wife are qualified as Don and Doña, a title withheld from the nuncio and his spouse. Their salaries, however, were the same, 1420 reales. When about 1710, porteros laid claim, in public functions, to seats on the banco de titulados--the bench of commissioned officials--their pretensions were rejected.[710]

The gaoler was necessary to a tribunal which had its special prison. At first, as we have seen, the alguazil had charge of this and his employees were not reckoned among the officials. The first allusion to a carcelero that I have met occurs in 1499, when Juan de Moya is spoken of as the carcerarius of the Barcelona tribunal; he must have been an exceptional official and a person of some consideration, for he was provided with a prebend.[711] In 1515 Ferdinand deemed it advisable to put the prisons under control of the tribunals, with which view he empowered the inquisitors to appoint carceleros with salaries of five hundred sueldos.[712] The gaoler thus became a salaried official, entitled to all the privileges and immunities of this position and gradually, toward the middle of the sixteenth century, the humble title of carcelero was exchanged for the more dignified one of alcaide de las carceles secretas.[713] He was necessarily a person of confidence, responsible for the safe-keeping of prisoners and for their proper maintenance, functions which will be more conveniently treated when we come to consider the prison system. From the report of the tribunal of Murcia, in 1746, it appears that the salary then was 2353 reales, in addition to which there was a jubilado alcaide with 330 reales. Possibly this habit of providing for supernumeraries explains why, in the table of officials, Toledo has four alcaides and Llerena and Valencia have three each.[714] In the early period the carcelero sometimes served as torturer, but subsequently it became customary to employ the public executioner.[715]

MINOR OFFICIALS

The prison, sometimes crowded with inmates and exposed to insanitary conditions, rendered necessary an official physician, whose services were also indispensable in examinations before and after torture and in the not infrequent cases of insanity, real or feigned. As his duties called him within the sacred limits of the secreto, he had to be a person of confidence, sworn like all the rest to secrecy. He was expected also to bestow gratuitous service on the officials, and the Suprema, in the eighteenth century, indulged itself in two, at the fairly liberal salary of 1258 reales apiece, though they did not share in the extra emoluments so freely bestowed on other officials.[716] At first the appointment of physicians was not universal, although the salary was inconsiderable--attributable, no doubt, to the fact that the physician was at liberty to continue his private practice. Thus, in 1486, Ferdinand designated ten libras as the pay of the physician of the Saragossa tribunal, while there was none provided for that of Medina del Campo.[717] The surgeon was rated at even less for, in 1510, one is furnished to Saragossa at a salary of five libras and the same is paid to an apothecary, who can scarce have furnished expensive drugs on such a stipend.[718] The surgeon, at this period, was also a barber and, in 1502, a grant, once for all, of fifteen libras was made to Joan de Aguaviva, "cirujano y barbero" of Calatayud, for fourteen years curing and barbering the poor prisoners, without salary or other advantage.[719] By 1618, apparently, the professions had become distinct, for there is an order to pay Narciso Valle, surgeon and Miguel Juan, barber, to the tribunal of Valencia.[720] A chaplain was also a necessity, not for the prisoners, who were denied the sacraments, but for the daily mass celebrated before commencing the work of the audience-chamber. In 1572, a stipend of 7500 maravedís is assigned for this but, in the eighteenth century, the Suprema paid the handsome salary of 5500 reales.[721] Confessors were also required for the penitential prison and were called in to the secret prison for the moribund.[722] There were also two personas honestas, or discreet persons, friars as a rule, whose duty it was to be present when witnesses ratified their testimony. In the earlier period these services were gratuitous but, in the later time, there was a small payment which, in the case of a friar, would enure to his convent. An alcaide of the casa de penitencia, or penitential prison, was also a necessity during the period of active work, although subsequently it was virtually a sinecure and in many tribunals was suppressed. We occasionally also meet with the office of proveedor, or purveyor of the secret prison, who seems to be identical with the dispensero or steward. In the sixteenth century this official had a salary of 2000 maravedís, besides two maravedís a day for each prisoner and five blancas for cooking and washing; he was required to have honest weights and not to charge more for food than it cost him; he kept an account with each prisoner and was paid out of the sequestrations.[723] Locksmiths, masons and other mechanics employed on the buildings were also sometimes reckoned as officials, but their duties in repairing the prisons were confidential. All tribunals moreover had from one to three abogados de presos or advocates of prisoners, whose duties will claim consideration hereafter; they were classed as salaried officials, though sometimes they received a small stipend and sometimes none, and they were allowed to serve other clients if they had any.

***

Besides these officials who were concerned in the primary business of the tribunal as a bulwark of the faith, there were others whose functions may be briefly dismissed here. The finances necessarily required a special organization, consisting of a receiver of confiscations, subsequently called the treasurer, whose duties in the active period were of the utmost importance, entitling him to a salary which sometimes was even larger than that of the inquisitors.[724] The fines and penances also amounted to large sums for which, in the earlier period, there was usually a special receiver, for they were kept as a separate fund, but finally they likewise passed through the hands of the treasurer. The receiver had to pay his own assistants and agents but, in the enormous amount of complicated business thrown upon him, he was aided by the abogado fiscal, a salaried official of legal training, while the notary of sequestrations had charge of sequestrated property until its confiscation was pronounced, and further served as a check upon the receiver. The intricate claims arising from these seizures were settled in a separate court of confiscations, known as the juzgado, presided over by the juez de bienes or judge of confiscations and furnished with its notary and nuncio. We sometimes also meet with a procurador del fisco and also with a superintendent of property. All this, which, especially at first, formed so large a part of the business of the Inquisition, will be more conveniently considered in detail hereafter.

We have seen how much of the activity of the tribunals was consumed in the civil and criminal business of their officials, and it necessarily formed a separate department, which had its notario de lo civil and secretario de las causas civiles, the latter office being suppressed in 1643.[725]

SALARIES

The qualifications for holding office in the tribunal were simple. From some of the cases of hereditary transmission it would appear that the minimum age was nineteen or twenty. Limpieza, or purity of blood from admixture of Jewish or Moorish or heretic strain, was the chief essential, as will be seen when we come to consider that important subject. Legitimacy was also a requisite in both the official and his wife, although dispensations could be had for its absence.[726] By a carta acordada of June 15, 1608, those who were unmarried could not marry without permission of the Suprema; they were obliged to furnish proof that the bride was limpia and, if a foreigner or the daughter or grand-daughter of foreigners, a dispensation was necessary, of all of which the appointee was solemnly notified when he took the oath of office.[727]

There was also a well-intended informacion de moribus concerning applicants for office. When the inquisitor-general proposed to make an appointment in a tribunal he notified it; it then issued a commission to some one at the residence of the nominee, with an interrogatory asking whether he was a person modest, quiet, peaceable, of correct life and habits and what was known as to his limpieza, which, when returned, was forwarded to the inquisitor-general. As the witnesses examined were, however, presented by the applicant, the whole was scarce more than a formality.[728]

**

In spite of the constant complaint of the meagreness of the salaries, they seem to have been fairly adequate, at least during the first century and a half of the existence of the Inquisition. The rapid fall in the purchasing power of the precious metals necessitated frequent advances and I have met with allusions to these in 1548, 1567, 1581, and 1606, after which they seem to have remained stationary until 1795, although the vellon coinage reduced still further the value of the currency.[729] The salary of an inquisitor, which, in 1541, was 100,000 maravedís, including ayuda de costa, by 1606 had become 300,000 or 800 ducats. This was not extravagant, but was fairly remunerative. In 1630, Arce y Reynoso, when occupying one of the highest professorships in Salamanca, as catedratico de prima de leyes, received only 300 ducats.[730] It must be borne in mind that most of the lower officials had a comfortable additional source of revenue from the fees which they were entitled to charge for nearly all their work outside of cases of faith and, when the arancel or fee-bill of 1642 sought to regulate these charges it was generally disregarded and the inspectors winked at its violation, charitably alleging the increased cost of living as an excuse.[731] The inquisitors and fiscal, on their side, usually held some canonry or other benefice which served to make good all deficiencies. In fact towards the middle of the eighteenth century, when the salaries had become really inadequate, a writer ascribes the inefficiency of the Inquisition to the fact that the inquisitors-general were obliged to appoint ignorant men who happened to possess prebends or other benefices.[732]

AYUDA DE COSTA

There were also the gratifications for house-rent, illuminations, bull-fights and mourning, which the officials of the tribunals enjoyed, like those of the Suprema, although not on so liberal a scale, while the ayudas de costa replaced the propinas.[733] There was also a kindly liberality in granting extra ayudas de costa to those in need and to their widows and children when they died. Applications of this kind were perpetual and innumerable; they were made to the Suprema, which naturally found little difficulty in being charitable at the expense of others.[734] It would be needless to enumerate examples of what was of such constant occurrence and these liberalities, together with the exemptions and the economies in the cost of the necessaries of life, rendered the financial position of the officials reasonably secure. Perhaps the resources of the tribunals might have justified larger salaries if they had not been drawn upon to supply the extravagance of the Suprema and been squandered on other objects with careless profusion characteristic of the age. Thus, in 1633, a Doctor Pastor de Costa, of the Royal Council of Catalonia, obtained from Inquisitor-general Zapata, on the plea of services rendered by his father, a grant of a hundred ducats a year, in silver, on the tribunal of Barcelona. Doubtless it was suspended during the Catalan revolt to be subsequently resumed and, in 1665, he applied to Arce y Reynoso to confirm it to him for life, but Arce only ordered it to be continued for four years. Not content with this, he asked for an ayuda de costa on the ground of his poverty.[735] It is not surprising that Philip V, as we have seen, in his attempted reform of 1705, forbade all grants of over thirty ducats without his confirmation.

***

The ayuda de costa, of which we hear so much, was either a more or less definite increase of salary, or a special gift for cause, or else a simple merced or benevolence. While the salary was a matter fixed and due, the ayuda was always to a certain extent arbitrary and was used as an incentive to compel the performance of duties regarded as onerous. We see the germ of it in Torquemada's instructions of 1485, prohibiting fees and bribes, for the king provides a reasonable support for all and in time will give them mercedes.[736] An advance is marked in the Instructions of 1498 where, after specifying salaries, it is added that the inquisitors-general, when they see that there is much labor or necessity, can grant such ayudas de costa as they deem proper.[737] Accordingly about this time, while we find no regular ayudas given, there are constant examples of special ones, sometimes of large amounts, granted for the most varied reasons, of which two or three instances will suffice. Thus Ferdinand, April 30, 1499, in ordering the payment of the salaries in Seville, includes 40,000 maravedís of ayudas de costa for one of the inquisitors, but none for any one else. August 10, 1502, Juan Royz, receiver of Saragossa, is given an ayuda de costa of 10,000 sueldos to meet expenses incurred in illness and, on September 27th, an official of Seville is gratified with 20,000 maravedís to help him in his marriage.[738]

It cannot have been long after this that the ayuda de costa was becoming a regular annual payment as an increment of the salary. December 3, 1509, an order for the payment of arrears to Diego de Robles, fiscal of the Suprema, speaks of there being due to him his ayuda de costa for 1506 and half of 1507, at the rate of 20,000 maravedís per annum. The first formal statement of it as a settled thing, that I have met, occurs in this same year 1509, in the list of salaries made out for the attempted Inquisition of Naples, where the ayuda de costa is designated for each official. It varies from a little over half the salary to considerably below that proportion and for two of the officials there is none. Yet it was not a universal custom for, in the salaries assigned to the Sardinia tribunal, September 10, 1514 there is no allusion to ayuda de costa.[739] That the custom, however, was gradually establishing itself as a substantial addition to the regular salaries is deducible from formal lists of the ayudas de costa of the Suprema and the Valladolid tribunal in 1515 and, by this time, it may be regarded as fairly established, although innumerable special grants continued, such as one of 75,000 maravedís, June 30, 1515, to Alonso de Montoya, notary of the Seville tribunal, to assist in his marriage.[740] Confiscations, at the time, were fruitful, and the laborers were not deprived of their share in the harvest, if only to stimulate their industry. Reimbursements of travelling and other expenses also frequently took the form of ayudas de costa although, as the grants were made in round sums, it is evident that no accounts were rendered and that the payments were arbitrary.[741]

However customary the annual payments had become, they still were regarded as a special grace to which the recipients had no claim of right. In 1540, the officials of Barcelona complained to Inquisitor-general Tavera that the receiver refused payment on the ground that the grant had expired with the death of Manrique, in 1538, and that it required confirmation, which Tavera hastened to give, February 12, 1540. In fact, a number of orders issued by Tavera, in 1540, would indicate that this was the accepted view of the matter.[742] Another marked distinction at this time is that the ayudas de costa are ordered to be paid out of the fines and penances inflicted for the "gastos extraordinarios" of the tribunals, while the salaries come from the funds arising out of the confiscations.

RECORDS

For awhile there was a regular scale of fifty ducats for the inquisitors, thirty for the fiscal, alguazil, notaries and receiver, fifteen for the nuncio and ten for the portero and alcaide but, in 1559, this was increased by twenty per cent. Care was taken to make it understood that it was a grace and not a right and the ordinary formula was that it was given in view of the labor in determining the cases of the auto de fe of the previous year and when, in 1561, Calahorra was exceptionally active and celebrated a second auto, it was rewarded with a supplementary ayuda of half the customary amount.[743] The grant was dependent on the receipt of detailed reports of all the cases in the previous auto, which were frequently accompanied with an humble petition for it, setting forth the insufficiency of the salaries and the cost of living, and begging the Suprema to obtain the grace from the king, who was technically the giver.[744] Subsequently, as we have seen, it was made conditional on rendering monthly reports and on the discharge of the duty of visiting the district and other matters apt to be neglected, such as rendering prompt statements of accounts and of properties. Finally, in the later period, when the tribunals were under close supervision of the Suprema, it sometimes took the form of a Christmas-gift.[745] Perhaps the most remarkable of all ayudas de costa was one granted by Carlos IV, in October 1807, in the midst of his troubles with his son Fernando, when the shadow of Napoleon was already darkening Spain and the treasury was empty. It was possibly with the object of securing the fidelity of the Inquisition that he ordered an ayuda de costa of 100 ducats to be given to every official of all the tribunals who did not enjoy an income of 7000 reales outside of his salary.[746] In the existing condition of Spanish finances the money could probably have been better employed.

***

The perfected system of records kept by the tribunals so greatly increased the effectiveness of the Inquisition and rendered it such an object of dread, that some reference to it is indispensable. Its development was slow. At the start, amid the enormous labors of the slenderly manned tribunals, there could be little thought bestowed on the preservation and arrangement of the records of their operations. In the Instructions of 1484 the only allusion to them merely prescribes that the notaries shall enter on their registers all orders issued by the inquisitors to the officials.[747] As the registers accumulated, the Instructions of 1488 require all writings and papers to be kept in chests, in the public place where the inquisitors transact business, so that they may be at hand when wanted; they are never to be removed and the keys are to pass through the hands of the inquisitors to the notaries, all this being under pain of deprivation of office.[748] Ten years later we hear of a chamber assigned to their safe keeping, with three keys, held by the fiscal and the two notaries, so that all must be present when they are consulted.[749] By this time indexes to facilitate references to the rapidly growing mass of papers had become necessary, and an article in Deza's instructions, in 1500, shows that this had become recognized.[750] The disabilities inflicted on descendants of culprits rendered it essential that genealogies should be traceable, but the incredible crudeness of these early lists shows how informal was the rapid work of that awful time. One kept at Toledo, about 1500, contains such entries of the individuals despatched as "un porquero del alguazil que tiene un ojo remellado," "un converso retajado," "un converso judyo," "un sastre," "un platero sobrino de lope de cuellar platero." In Valencia, from 1517 to 1527, the index to the fifth volume of persons denounced shows equal indifference to the identification of individuals catalogued as "le boges, mare y filles," "la condesa que lleve el habito penitential," "el bachiller que esta en companya del calonge Proxita," "uno que ha sido flayle," "un remendon sastre, esta delante la rexa de mosen Penaroja," etc.[751]

***

After some contradictory decisions as to furnishing papers or information from the records to competent courts applying for it, the Suprema, in 1556, forbade the tribunals, without its express order, from giving any information tending to prove that any one had not been condemned or reconciled, or penanced or arrested by the Holy Office--a most cruel regulation in view of the tremendous consequences to the posterity of those who had fallen under suspicion of heresy and had been tried or even arrested. An order by the Suprema, in 1576, to the Valencia tribunal to erase from its records the name of Maestro Jusepe Esteban, because he had not been arrested for a matter of faith, is suggestive of the fearful power which the Inquisition possessed of inflicting infamy on whole families and of the importance of the accuracy of its registers.[752] The abuse of its power in this respect is indicated, as we have seen above, by the instructions which sometimes followed visitations, to remove from the records the names of those who had been improperly prosecuted for offences not of faith.

It was not easy to preserve the completeness of the records. Officials were apt to regard them as personal property and to keep them, like the notary of Calatayud who thus secured for his son the reversion of his office. In 1512, Ferdinand desired from a tribunal complete statements concerning the finances; there arose delay, during which the notary of sequestrations died, whereupon he ordered that the receiver should have all the papers or copies of them and, if the heirs of the notary refused to surrender them, execution should be levied on his estate for the whole of his salary received during his incumbency.[753] It was not only the notaries, however, but other officials who took and kept documents. In 1517 Cardinal Adrian complained of this and ordered that papers should never be removed from their depository, except to the audience-chamber for the purpose of conducting a trial.[754] This was disregarded and, about the middle of the century, the instructions to inspectors require them to order inquisitors, under pain of excommunication, to return all papers that they had taken and to discontinue the practice.[755] Even inquisitors-general were guilty of this, for Philip II issued an order March 6, 1573, on the executors of Ponce de Leon, to allow his papers to be examined and everything pertaining to the Inquisition to be removed--an order which can only be regarded as revealing a general custom, for Ponce de Leon died, January 17, 1573, before entering upon his office.[756]

The looseness which had prevailed during the early period is strikingly manifested when, in 1547, the Suprema made an attempt to gather in and preserve its past records. A commission was issued to its secretary Zurita, reciting the importance of having an inventory of all the papal bulls, briefs, registers and other papers relating to the Inquisition, which had been in the custody of the secretaries and other officials. There is, it says, information that many of these are at Calatayud and others at Huesca, among the papers of Calcena and Urries, the secretaries of Ferdinand and Charles V, and Zurita is ordered to collect these and is armed with full powers to examine witnesses and inflict penalties. All holding such papers are required to surrender them, under pain of excommunication and a hundred ducats. The inquisitors of Saragossa are instructed to assist him with censures, while letters to various parties indicate that the task is expected to be arduous. The instructions are not clear as to whether he is expected to seize the papers or merely to make inventories of them, but there can be little doubt that whatever he laid his hands on was kept.[757] What success attended his mission we have no means of knowing, but we probably owe to it many of the important documents illustrating the early history of the Inquisition.

In addition to this source of incompleteness, it seemed impossible to compel the tribunals to keep their records in proper shape. In 1544, Dr. Alonso Pérez, in an inspection of Barcelona, found them in complete disorder. Another inspection, in 1550, showed still greater confusion. In 1561, Inspector Cervantes described them as being in such a state, without indexes and inventories, that it was impossible to find anything. After the visit of Salazar, the Suprema, in 1568, took the inquisitors sharply to task for not having yet provided indexes and registers; it ordered them to do so at once and to furnish a certificate to that effect within twenty days of receipt.[758] The certificate was doubtless supplied, but we may question whether the work was done. Possibly Barcelona was worse than other tribunals, but the memorial of 1623 to the Suprema states that in many of them there are processes, books, papers, informations of limpieza etc., requiring to be inventoried, sorted into bundles and reduced to order, causing great inconvenience.[759]

***

Meanwhile the masses of papers had been accumulating more rapidly than ever. In 1570 the Suprema had ordered nine books to be kept--one of the commissions of officials, their oaths and royal provisions, one of commissioners and familiars with full details, one of the votes in the consultas de fe, one of letters from the Suprema and another of letters to it, one recording the inspections made of the prisons, one of the orders issued on the receiver, one of the pecuniary penances inflicted and one of the autos de fe, with statements as to the culprits and their punishments. Besides these the alcaide of the prison was to keep lists of those relaxed and penanced with three indexes. All this was exclusive of the voluminous records of the trials which it was the duty of the fiscal to keep in order.[760] Then, in order to accommodate the increasing bulk, it was ordered, in 1566 and 1572, that there should be four apartments in the camara del secreto, one for pending cases, one for suspended ones, one for those finished, divided into the relaxed, the reconciled and the penanced, and the fourth for papers concerning commissioners and familiars and informaciones de limpieza.[761] In 1635, alphabetical lists of all persons tried were ordered to be kept, with dates and references to the papers of the case, commencing with 1620. The order had to be repeated in 1636 and 1638, with further instructions in 1644, and these lists furnished additional means for tracing the antecedents and kindred of those who were brought before the tribunals.[762] But more potent than the mandates of the Suprema to keep the archives in order and thoroughly indexed was the mania which arose for limpieza, or purity of blood, which, as we shall see hereafter, pervaded all classes and furnished a source of very profitable business to the officials, for the Inquisition was the ultimate arbiter and its records contained the evidence.

Gradually these records became an immense storehouse of minute and detailed information concerning all heretics and suspects and their kindred. Under the Instructions of 1561, the first thing in examining a prisoner was to require of him an account of parents and grandparents, brothers and sisters, uncles, aunts and cousins, with their wives and children and whether any of them had been arrested or penanced by the Inquisition.[763] Then, when the accused was brought to profess conversion and to beg mercy, his confession was not accepted unless he gave information, to the best of his ability, as to all other heretics, whether kindred or strangers, whom he had known or heard of, with details as to their culpability. All this was carefully entered and indexed, until the records became a fairly complete directory of the suspects of Spain. A Jew arrested in Granada might compromise twenty others, scattered from Compostella to Barcelona, each of whom when seized became a new source of information, and the intercommunication established between the tribunals placed the records of all at the service of each. This vastly increased the effectiveness of the Inquisition and rendered the chances of escape slender indeed. The trials of the seventeenth century, when the system became fairly perfected, show that, although the arrest of a few might scatter their accomplices, the Inquisition was ever on their track and change of name and habitation was unavailing. As soon as a suspect was arrested and his genealogy was obtained, the sister tribunals were called upon for reports, and testimony poured in, reaching back, perhaps, for twenty or thirty years, concerning himself and his kindred. The net of the Inquisition covered the land and its meshes were fine. Go where they would, hide themselves as they might, the Judaizers lived in the knowledge that it was ever remorselessly in pursuit and that its hand might fall upon them at any time.

***

In the eighteenth century the system was elaborated by what were known as the Libros Vocandorum. When any one was denounced to a tribunal or came forward spontaneously, his name, description and offence were transmitted to all the other tribunals, which entered them in alphabetical registers, arranged under the first baptismal names. These entries give the name, the date, a brief description of the person, and the nature of the charge, with a blank to be filled in with the result of the trial, which was also reported to all. Thus each tribunal possessed a digested record of the current business of the whole Inquisition, clearly arranged for ready reference, and, as the years passed, it afforded at a glance the means of ascertaining whether any culprit had been in the hands of the Holy Office before, and of facilitating researches into limpieza. The importance of the Libros Vocandorum was so fully recognized that the Suprema required the monthly reports of the fiscal always to specify that they were kept posted up to date. These registers were not arranged uniformly in all the tribunals, but the usual plan was that adopted in Valencia, where there was one general index in two volumes and a third for confessors accused of soliciting women ad turpia in the confessional.[764] Thus all the tribunals co-operated and, with their machinery of commissioners and familiars in almost every town and village, they formed one harmonious organization for the detection and punishment of culprits. Human ingenuity could scarce devise a more perfect system of promptly suppressing all deviations from the standards established by the Inquisition.

CHAPTER III - UNSALARIED OFFICIALS

We have seen, when treating of privileges and exemptions, the distinction drawn between salaried and unsalaried officials. The former, except in the case of physicians and advocates of the accused, were understood to devote all their time to the service of the tribunal. The latter were only called upon incidentally for special work. It is true that the Inquisition was empowered to summon every one for aid, but its service was confidential and its ministers, at least in the later period, had to be of unblemished lineage, so that it was requisite to have at hand those on whom it could rely and whom it could summon at any moment. There was no difficulty in finding men ready to serve without pay. The honor of connection with the Inquisition, the privilege of its fuero in greater or less degree and the assurance of limpieza which it carried with it, rendered applicants for appointment more numerous than positions to be filled. These unsalaried officials consisted of calificadores, consultores, commissioners with their notaries, and familiars.

The functions of the calificador or censor were important. When the sumaria, or preliminary array of evidence against the accused, was collected, the theological points involved were submitted to three or four calificadores, who pronounced whether the acts or words testified to amounted to heresy or suspicion of heresy. If there was doubt or disagreement, another group was called in, to whom the opinions of the first were given, along with the evidence. If the conclusion was that the matter did not concern the Inquisition, the case was dropped or suspended; if it held that there was heresy, expressed or implied, arrest and trial followed. We have seen the working of the system in the cases of Carranza and Villanueva, in both of which it played so momentous a part. In addition to this was the censorship of books. Any work against which suspicion was aroused was submitted to them and, according to their decision, it was approved, expurgated, or suppressed.

To perform these duties properly required learned theologians, and they seem to have enjoyed the opportunity of displaying their erudition in prolix and elaborate opinions, developing vast ingenuity in discovering traces of the beliefs of the Marcionites and Carpocratians and other forgotten heresies in the careless propositions submitted to their criticism. As a matter of course only ecclesiastics were eligible and, in 1627, the minimum age was fixed at forty-five.[765] The duties of this profitless office were not light, if we may believe the experienced Fray Maestro Alvarado. In 1811 he complains that, if a book is sent to a calificador, no matter what his other engagements may be, he must devote a month or two to reading it and forming a judgement, expressed in an elaborate opinion, such as would command for a lawyer two or three thousand reales. Or, some modern philosopher utters scandals and the calificador must investigate his words and acts and point out the errors as a guide for the inquisitor; if a trial follows, the calificador must wait on the tribunal and rack his brains to decide whether the culprit's explanations are valid; if he is contumacious, conferences must be held with him until he is converted or found incapable of conversion, and all this without recompense.[766]

The calificador was thus an important and laborious assistant in the current work of the tribunal, and it is somewhat remarkable that, although reckoned among the officials, with a recognised place in public functions, there should be doubt whether he was entitled to the fuero. Yet, in 1662, when Doctor Vicente Cortes, a cathedral canon and calificador of the Valencia tribunal, was involved in a suit, it declined to defend him. It reported to the Suprema that it was ignorant whether calificadores were entitled to the fuero and the Council replied, asking on what ground the privilege was claimed.[767]

CALIFICADORES

The need of calificadores was not likely to be felt in the early period, when almost the whole business of the Inquisition was with Judaizers and Moriscos, whose guilt was assumed from their adherence to well-known customs and rites. The first allusion I have met occurs in 1520, when the inquisitors were ordered to make no appointment without submitting to the Suprema the petition of the applicant.[768] There is no reference to them in the Instrucciones Antiguas, but in the Nuevas of 1561 their employment is fully developed.[769] As the appointment was in the hands of the inquisitors, there was a tendency to undue multiplication and, in 1606, there was an effort to check this by calling for reports as to the number existing and how many were necessary, pending which no applicants were to be admitted. This resulted, the following year, in an order limiting the number to eight in each tribunal; only the most eminent theologians were to be selected and appointments were to be made only to fill vacancies.

Again, in 1619, reports were called for and emphasis was laid on the importance of the position and the necessity of discrimination in the choice. This received scant attention, and the memorial of 1623 to the Suprema recommends the reduction of the number to three or four in each tribunal and the exercise of great care in appointments, for lack of which they had fallen so greatly in public estimation. Nothing was done and, in 1630, the fiscal of the Suprema called attention to the fact that but few tribunals had made the reports demanded in 1619; meanwhile the necessity for reform had increased and he asked that information be called for again so that, with full information, the Suprema might remedy the evils existing.[770] The futility of the effort to limit the tribunals in the exercise of their patronage is visible in the statistics of 1746, where Valencia has forty calificadores, Saragossa has twenty-nine and even the little tribunal of Majorca has twenty-four. If Llerena has none and Logroño only two, this is explicable, as we learn from another source, by the absence in those places of men competent for the position. Yet not much attention was paid to the selection of suitable material if we may believe an official report presented to Carlos IV, in 1798, which says that it is notorious that calificadores are mostly people of little learning, full of preconceptions and errors, who have had money enough to take out proofs of limpieza.[771]

***

In the medieval Inquisition all sentences were agreed upon in an assembly of experts summoned for the purpose by the inquisitors, prior to holding the auto de fe in which the sentences were executed. This custom was naturally followed in Spain, and these consultas de fe, as they were called, will be considered hereafter when treating of the conduct of trials. At present we have merely to consider the consultores who assisted the inquisitors in passing judgement.

At first they had no permanent connection with the Inquisition. The inquisitors had an unlimited power of summoning all persons in whatever capacity, but sometimes it was not easy to obtain the services of competent men, especially when migratory tribunals were sitting in places where jurists were few, and the Instructions of 1488, in response to complaints on this score, tell inquisitors in such cases to send the papers to the Suprema which will decide on them.[772] At this time the inquisitors were theologians and, to supplement their lack of legal knowledge, it was customary to call in lawyers; the incongruity of laymen sitting in judgement on matters of faith was waived, and they were freely employed, the inquisitors summoning such doctors and maestros and licenciados and bachilleres as they saw fit, who served without pay and might never be called in again.[773] In 1502 the Barcelona tribunal complained that it sometimes had difficulty in securing the services of the lawyers of the Audiencia, whereupon Ferdinand wrote to his lieutenant-general that, as it is a work of God and the service is required only two or three times a year, he must see that the inquisitors get them whenever they are wanted.[774] In 1515 the same trouble showed itself at Valladolid, where the inquisitors were in the habit of calling in the judges of the high court, who endeavored to evade the duty by alleging certain royal cédulas, prohibiting their engaging in other functions than those of their office. Ferdinand was appealed to and promptly ordered them to serve when called upon, but they were not to be obliged to absent themselves from court, during the hours of its sessions.[775] Apparently there was no eagerness to perform gratuitous service which brought with it no privileges.

CONSULTORES

When in time jurists were preferred in the tribunals, the inquisitors called in theologians, mostly from the regular Orders who, to a great degree, monopolized the learning of the Church. Even with these there was sometimes difficulty and, in 1544, the Suprema asked the Dominican vicar to rebuke the Prior of San Pedro Martir for forbidding his frailes to serve.[776] It had already been found that the chance selection made, when a consulta de fe was to be held, was unsatisfactory. The permanent office of consultor was created and was rendered attractive by attaching to it the privileges and immunities of the Holy Office; formal commissions were issued by the inquisitor-general and the appointee swore to the faithful discharge of his duties. The earliest commission that I have met is one issued, April 2, 1544, to Doctor Miguel de Nuedes, Archdeacon of Murviedro, as consultor in the tribunal of Valencia.[777] This continued for some twenty years when confusion and contradictions arose. January 16, 1565, the Suprema writes that neither it nor the inquisitor-general is accustomed to notify any one of his appointment as consultor; the inquisitors can appoint properly qualified persons whenever they are needed. In 1566 this was followed by admonitions as to the care necessary in examining into the fitness of aspirants and then, in 1567, inquisitors were scolded for making appointments without reporting them and awaiting orders. This was repeated in 1571 but, in 1572, Rojas asserts positively that consultors are not selected by inquisitors, but are appointed by the Suprema.[778]

The Suprema continued to retain control but ceased to issue regular commissions for, in 1645, a writer informs us that the consultor and calificador are received and sworn in on the strength of a letter from the Suprema.[779] Finally however, the matter was restored to the inquisitors. A Formulary of about 1700 contains the form of a commission issued to consultores. It is drawn in the name of the inquisitors who confer on the recipient the powers necessary for the discharge of his duties and order all secular officials to yield him all the honors, graces, franchises, exemptions, liberties and prerogatives inherent in his office. He was obliged to furnish proofs of his purity of blood and, if he was married, of that of his wife, thus giving another example of the capacity of laymen to act in judgements of faith.[780]

With the progressive centralization of business in the Suprema, the consulta de fe gradually diminished in importance and, as we shall see, in the eighteenth century it became virtually obsolete. The table of officials in 1746 shows that, at that time, there were only eighteen consultores in all the tribunals and, of these, eight were in the little Inquisition of Majorca.[781]

***

The office of commissioner was peculiar to the Spanish Inquisition and, although its powers were strictly limited, it was an important factor in keeping the authority of the Holy Office constantly before the people and in detecting offenders in obscure places where they might otherwise have enjoyed security. It was not part of the original organization and there is no reference to it in the Instructions. It is true that, in 1509, Ferdinand addresses a certain Beltran de la Sala, of Perpignan, as commissioner of the Inquisition, but he is also "hoste de correos" or in charge of couriers on the important line between Spain and Italy.[782] He was therefore not a commissioner in the later sense, but probably was employed to look after the sequestrations which had been extensive in Perpignan. As the tribunals became sedentary in their extensive districts, the need of representatives scattered everywhere made itself felt, and the first suggestion seems to have come from Valencia. The Suprema represented, December 4, 1537, to Cardinal Manrique, the size of the district of Valencia, where the difficulties of intercommunication were such that it never had been and never could be properly visited. It was therefore proposed that, in the cathedral towns, commissioners should be appointed with power to publish the edicts and to take testimony and ratifications with notaries. The cathedral clergy would probably furnish proper appointees, serving without pay, as the duties would be only occasional.[783] This corresponds so nearly with the plan adopted that it may safely be assumed to be its origin.

COMMISSIONERS

Authority was given to inquisitors to appoint commissioners, but apparently at first the limitation on their powers was ill defined. The visitation of Barcelona, in 1549, showed that they undertook to arrest and prosecute, in fact to make themselves inquisitors in their little districts and, in 1550, the Suprema instructed the tribunal to grant faculties only to receive denunciations, collect evidence and send it to the Inquisition for its action.[784] This remained the rule until the end. In the cartillas, or detailed printed instructions, they were forbidden to make arrests unless three conditions coexisted--that the case clearly pertained to the Holy Office, that the evidence was ample, and that there was apprehension of flight. Even then they were warned to act only on mature deliberation, and they were forbidden to sequestrate property, though they were to keep an eye on it. If an arrest took place, the prisoner and the evidence were to be transmitted to the tribunal under guard of familiars, without being allowed to communicate with any one. In addition the commissioner could hear the civil cases of familiars, up to the value of twenty libras and execute his decisions. All this was concisely expressed in the commission issued to him.[785]

As in everything else, it was impossible to enforce compliance with wholesome regulations. Cervantes, in the report of his Barcelona visitation of 1561, says that commissioners paid no attention to the limitations of their powers. They were thoroughly untrained and ignorant of their duties and had no hesitation in appointing other commissioners. As they had authority to appoint a notary and an alguazil, they set up little courts throughout the land, armed with the awful authority of the Holy Office, and it requires no stretch of the imagination to conceive the tyranny and extortion with which they afflicted the people.[786]

Not much was gained when, in 1561, the Suprema ordered that they should be appointed only in places where it was necessary and that they must be quiet and peaceable persons; or, in 1565, when it prescribed great care in issuing commissions, which must be so limited as to prevent them from appointing deputies.[787] Salazar's report of his inspection of Barcelona, in 1566, shows that the evil continued unchecked; commissioners were appointed in unnecessary numbers, often by a single inquisitor during a visitation, and sometimes they were ignorant laymen, although the office inferred that it should be reserved exclusively to those in holy orders.[788] It is not strange that this new infliction, which seemed to bring the terrors of the Inquisition to every man's door, should form the subject of vigorous remonstrances, and the Concordias of 1568, by their enumeration of what was forbidden, show the abuses under which the populations were suffering. That of Valencia provided that there should be such officials only in Tortosa, Segorbe, Teruel, Gandía, Castellon de la Plana, Denia and Játiva, with two in the city of Valencia, and that they should be called deputized commissioners and not, as heretofore, lieutenant inquisitors. That of Aragon limited them to Lérida, Huesca, Tarazona, Daroca, Calatayud, Jaca, Barbastro and towns on the French frontier. Both provided that in future they should not try cases, or make arrests save to prevent flight, nor should they grant licences for the importation or exportation of provisions and other matters. They might have an assessor and a notary, enjoying all privileges and exemptions, and, if an alguazil was needed, they could assign that post to a familiar without enlarging his exemptions.[789] All this is eloquent of the methods by which these would-be local inquisitors had magnified their office to the vexation of the people.

Catalonia rejected the Concordia of 1568 and, in the Córtes of 1599, it demanded that neither rectors of churches nor frailes should be appointed as commissioners. To this the Suprema, in its memorial to Clement VIII, replied that the object was to prevent the Inquisition from having proper commissioners, as Catalonia was too poor in the requisite material to exclude these classes in places where there were no cathedrals or collegiate churches.[790]

In 1572, the Suprema made an effort to check the multiplication of these officials by decreeing that they should be appointed only in the chief towns of archpriestly districts, but it promptly receded from this and, the next year, authorized them wherever it seemed necessary, which amounted to unlimited permission. An order, in 1576, that they were not to be defended in prosecutions for concubinage is suggestive as to the prevailing morality and, in 1584, they were instructed to keep in constant correspondence with the tribunals, reporting everything that occurred in their districts, which indicates how comprehensive a system of espionage was established.[791]

***

The Suprema, in a carta acordada of March 24, 1604, made a serious attempt to check existing evils. It called attention to the abuses in appointing commissioners, notaries and familiars, whose multitude and general unworthiness resulted in greatly impairing the authority of the Inquisition. In future, commissioners were to be appointed only in the chief towns of the partidos, or local judicial districts, or at least four leagues apart. Inquisitors should bear in mind that their duties embrace cases of the utmost importance, requiring men of intelligence, virtue and silence; they should have benefices or revenues sufficient to live with the dignity befitting their high office.[792] The prescription as to number and location received scant obedience. We chance to meet with them in obscure places like Cobeña and Fuentelsas, and a list of them in the little province of Guipúzcoa, which has but four partidos, amounts to seventeen. An experienced writer, in 1648, after reciting the limitations, states that there are places where there are three or four, disguised by appointments nominally to neighboring hamlets.[793]

Although without salary, the office had become attractive, not only on account of the importance and immunities which it conferred, but also because a large part of the attendant labor brought in satisfactory fees. In the eagerness to prove limpieza, investigations into genealogies were perpetual; nearly all these passed through the Inquisition and were confided to the commissioner nearest to the birth-place of the applicant. He was expected to pay roundly and the commissioner was entitled to sixteen reales a day for his time, or to two ducats if he had to leave his residence. Moreover the knowledge thus acquired of the genealogies of his neighbors gave him power to render them uncomfortable, as we may gather from a carta acordada of 1622, forbidding commissioners to make notes of the ancestry of those who were not officials of the Inquisition and threatening dismissal for stigmatizing any one as a Jew, Moor, Converso or descendant of such.[794] At sea-ports and frontier towns, also, the commissioners had a considerable source of revenue from fees for the examinations requisite to prevent the entrance of heretics and heretic books--fees which, as we shall see hereafter, were the abundant source of complaint. These positions the inquisitor-general reserved for his own appointment and finally also those in the cathedral towns and larger cities.[795]

In the effort at reform made by Philip V, investigation was made into the character of the commissioners, their notaries and the familiars and, soon after this, in 1706, the Suprema asserted that, in Castile, there was not one fourth of the number permitted by the Concordia of 1553, which it attributed partly to the War of Succession then raging and partly to the molestation to which they were exposed.[796] Unquestionably the number declined rapidly during the eighteenth century, as will be seen by the table in the Appendix where, although Saragossa still has thirty-eight and Barcelona twenty-eight, the other tribunals report only from two to seven, except the Canaries, where the scattered group of islands necessarily demanded a considerable number. This diminution may be explained by the growing habit of appointing temporary commissioners in any place where work was to be done. Moreover the increasing facilities of communication favored local centralization in the tribunal, even as general centralization was stimulated in the Suprema. Denunciations were readily sent by mail and temporary commissions were issued for their investigation. So, too, in the matter of limpieza, the tribunal could dispense its patronage more profitably by sending out from head-quarters special commissioners who earned a larger per diem at the expense of the applicant. To accommodate this new development, when in 1816 a new cartilla of instructions for commissioners was printed, it was provided at the end with a number of blank commissions which could be detached and filled in for use. A hundred copies were supplied to each tribunal, twenty of them bound to be used as a whole and eighty in sheets to be thus cut up. Within a month one tribunal applied for a further stock and fifty copies were sent.[797] Little as the inquisitors of the time had to do, they were evidently devolving their duties upon others more generally than ever.

FAMILIARS

In a previous chapter it has been seen that of all the officials of the Inquisition those who occasioned the most frequent trouble and who aroused the most strenuous animadversion were the familiars. They were the most numerous, they were largely drawn from the turbulent element, seeking the position for the protection afforded against secular justice, and they abused their privileges accordingly. For more than two centuries they were an object of dread to all peaceable folk, and no stronger evidence can be furnished of the subjection to which the Inquisition had reduced Spain than the tolerance of this dangerous class, whose services were overpaid by the immunities which relieved the Inquisition from paying salaries.

In the medieval Inquisition the inquisitor had the right to surround himself with armed guards, whether to protect his person or to execute his orders. They were reckoned as members of his family, thence obtaining the name of familiars, entitling them to immunity from justice. They were dreaded and hated, not without reason, for the position was attractive only to the ruffian and brawler, nor was anything gained when, in 1213, the Council of Vienne warned inquisitors to be moderate and discreet in their use of the privilege.[798]

Of course the old Aragonese Inquisition enjoyed this prerogative and when the new institution was organized it inherited the right. This, moreover, was developed in an entirely novel manner, for the familiar was not attached to the person of the inquisitor. Appointments were made all over the land, the Inquisition thus obtaining, without cost, a small army of servitors, scattered everywhere, sworn to obedience and ready, at any moment, to perform whatever duty they might be called upon to render. They served, moreover, as spies upon their neighbors and were eager to manifest their zeal by volunteer action, for it was a commonplace of the canon law that the heretic could be arrested by any one.

It was impossible that such a class as this, released from the restraints of law, should not prove troublesome and even dangerous. Inquisitors appointed them at discretion, furnished them with licences to bear arms and turned them loose on the community. It would have been some slight protection if registers of these appointments had been kept, and the names of the appointees furnished to the magistrates, so that it could be known whether those who claimed immunity were entitled to it. It was impossible, however, to induce the inquisitors to do this. Ximenes and the Suprema ordered the names to be entered in a book and a copy to be furnished to the corregidors and Ferdinand, in a general order of July 11, 1513 emphasized this, but to no purpose and it was repeated endlessly with the same result.[799] The inquisitors steadily refused obedience, for it would have imposed some check upon multitudinous and indiscriminate appointments which had a recognized money value. The result of all this appears in a letter of Ferdinand, in 1514, to the inquisitors of Toledo, informing them that the royal and municipal authorities complained of the number of turbulent fellows, carrying licences signed by only one inquisitor, who went around in bands disturbing the peace and, if the civil magistrate endeavored to restrain them, the tribunal at once interposed, leading to dissensions between it and the ministers of justice, to the great injury of the city and its vicinity. Ximenes had already endeavored to check these disorders without success, and Ferdinand now insists that his orders must be obeyed, that all such licences must be signed by the three inquisitors, a record of them must be kept and a copy be furnished to the corregidor.[800]

The same troubles existed in the Aragonese kingdoms where, it will be remembered, the Córtes of Monzon, in 1512, endeavored to remedy them in the Concordia, by providing that for Aragon there might be twenty armed familiars in Saragossa, while in other towns, where the tribunal was in actual session, there might be temporary appointments, not exceeding twenty for the whole kingdom. Notwithstanding the acceptance of this agreement by Ferdinand, its confirmation in 1516 by Leo X, and its solemn ratification in 1520, it never received the slightest respect from the Inquisition, and its only interest lies in its proof of the popular anxiety for relief and that a very moderate number of familiars sufficed at a period of great activity in the work of the Holy Office.

***

The complaint was renewed, about 1530, by the Córtes of Aragon, that familiars were appointed in every place in the three kingdoms, and that no lists were furnished, so that the Inquisition could set free any offender by declaring him to be a familiar, to which Cardinal Manrique merely replied that no more were appointed than were necessary, and that the instructions were observed.[801] Again, in 1547, the Córtes of Catalonia declared that the abuse had been carried to a point that seriously limited the royal and ecclesiastical jurisdictions, and it requested that Barcelona should be restricted to fifty, with five each for the Catalan districts subjected to Valencia and Saragossa, and also that lists be furnished, but Prince Philip only answered that he would consult the Suprema and do what was fitting.[802] Of course nothing was done.

While thus the Suprema defended the tribunals against the public, it was constantly scolding them for their excesses and issuing orders to diminish the evil. A carta acordada of 1543 alludes to the excessive numbers of familiars, their turbulence and evil lives; they must be persons of good repute and the rest must be dismissed. In 1546 moderation in appointments was enjoined. When the Castile Concordia of 1553 was framed, instructions were issued for its strict observance; all not registered and reported to the authorities were not to be held as familiars. In 1560 and again in 1573, they were ordered to be married men, quiet, peaceable, limpios and not ecclesiastics; all others were to be removed. In 1562 the inquisitor of Majorca was rebuked for unnecessary appointments of turbulent and unfit men and for not giving a list to the magistrates. In 1566 lists were ordered to be given to the civil authorities and none not borne on them were to enjoy exemption. In 1573 instructions were issued requiring them to be householders and heads of families, residents of the place for which the commission was given and none to be appointed for uninhabited places. In 1578 it was ordered that appointments should only be made to fill vacancies. In 1586 a carta acordada commanded the number to be reduced to the provisions of the Concordia; the surplus must surrender their commissions and support themselves honestly, new appointments were restricted to quiet and peaceful men of good life and habits, and evidence of compliance with the order must be furnished.[803]

This brief summary could be largely extended, but its only interest lies in its showing that the Suprema recognized the evil and sought to abate it, while the tribunals paid no attention to its commands, secure in the assurance that it would defend them through thick and thin, whenever a question arose between them and the people or the authorities. Sometimes, indeed, continued pressure might induce temporary compliance but it was abandoned as soon as it appeared safe to do so.

A single instance will illustrate the tenacity and successful evasions of the inquisitors. Valdés wrote to the Valencia tribunal, March 12, 1551, that the excessive number of familiars interfered with its proper functions in consequence of the time required for their cases. They were to be reduced to a hundred in the city of Valencia; in towns of three thousand inhabitants the maximum was to be eight; in smaller places, if any were needed, the number was not to exceed four without notifying the Suprema. To effect this, all commissions were to be revoked and, if necessary, he revoked them. Instructions were given as to reappointments; every commission was to be signed by both inquisitors and countersigned by one of the notaries; the commissions were to be limited to two or three years so as to stimulate good behavior and lists were to be furnished to the Suprema.

***

To this promising scheme of reform the inquisitors replied that they suspended its operation because the Governors of Valencia thought the number assigned to the city inadequate. July 9th the Suprema ordered them to learn from the governors their views as to numbers. This was left unanswered and, on November 5th, the Suprema ordered a report within thirty days of what had been agreed upon with the governors; otherwise the provisions of March 12th were to be put into execution and, if this was not done, a person armed with full powers would be sent to do it. This looked like business and brought from Inquisitor Artiaga the reply that, as soon as his colleague returned from visiting the district, it would be complied with. Valdés waited till December 23rd and then wrote that there must be no further delay; the king had repeatedly ordered a reduction of the familiars on account of the daily complaints received against them. He therefore commanded peremptorily that, without reply or further excuse, the instructions be executed and a notarial attestation of the fact be furnished during January; if both inquisitors were not in Valencia, the one in residence must do the work; if it was not accomplished within the time named, they must present themselves personally before him to give their reasons for disobedience. This would seem to leave no opening for evasion, but it received no attention and, on March 10, 1552, Valdés wrote again, repeating the injunctions of the previous March, but conceding that there might be two hundred familiars in the city. Public proclamation of the revocations was to be made and evidence of execution with lists of those retained was to be furnished during April. Again no attention was paid to this and it was repeated September 10th. This, in time, brought a statement that the number in the city had been reduced to two hundred, but there is no evidence as to reductions elsewhere or that the wholesome limitation of commissions to two or three years had been observed.[804] If it were, it was but for a brief time, and we have seen what were the familiars of Valencia early in the next century.

It was the same in Castile. When the Concordia of 1553 was agreed upon, a royal cédula of March 10th prescribed the number of familiars to be allowed in cities and towns and ordered that all in excess should be deprived of their commissions, while lists of those retained were to be given to the secular authorities. The Suprema seems to have honestly endeavored to enforce these provisions by letters issued under the same date, but the inquisitors were sullen and refractory and the Valencia experience was repeated. July 13, 1555, another royal cédula and circular letter of the Suprema repeated the command to reduce the number and furnish lists. Again, in 1565 these orders were renewed, which brought out the fact that the tribunals had not even kept registers of the appointments, for in 1566 they were ordered to call in all commissions and compile lists from them, with a warning that all who were not borne on such lists would not be allowed enjoyment of the fuero and, if the judges were inhibited in such cases, when the competencia reached the Councils it would be abandoned. Even this required to be supplemented with another order the next year.[805]

It would be a weariness of the flesh to follow in detail these fruitless efforts of the Suprema to force the tribunals to comply with the law, but a carta acordada of 1604 affords a glimpse into some of the tricks and evasions resorted to. It lays down salutary rules as to the observance of the Concordia and the character of appointees, and proceeds to forbid the granting of expectative appointments, the admission of applicants to prove limpieza unless there is a vacancy, and then he must be a resident of the place where it occurs and not one with a supposititious domicile. Appointments in derogation of these rules will not render the individual an official of the Inquisition and no competencias will be entertained for him. It shows how slack was the observance of this that it had to be repeated in 1620 and again in 1626.[806]

***

While thus the Suprema was vainly busied in repressing the exuberance of its subordinates, it fiercely resented any assistance offered by outsiders. The Concordia of 1553 was part of the law of the land, and as such it was printed in the official Nueva Recopilacion (Lib. IV, Tit. i, ley 20). In 1634 the Council of Castile, apparently wearied with the stubbornness of the tribunals, undertook to enforce it by printing the articles concerning the numbers and qualifications of familiars and sending them to the magistrates of the towns and villages with instructions that, if the number was in excess, they were to strike off the surplus; if a list had not been furnished, they were not to regard any one as a familiar and entitled to exemptions and privileges. When this practical method of enforcing obedience to law came to the knowledge of the Suprema, it was highly incensed. On December 22nd it addressed an indignant consulta to the king; the Council of Castile, it said, was meddling with concerns wholly beyond its competence; it had no authority in matters concerning the Inquisition; if inquisitors transgressed the law, specific complaints could be made and settled in a junta of the two bodies; the Council was leading the local magistrates to sit in judgement on inquisitors and get themselves into trouble. Besides the familiars are so molested when they seek to avail themselves of their privileges that they think it better to abandon them; they are fewer already than the Concordia permits, are diminishing daily and, in a few years, the Inquisition will not have ministers to attend to its business. The consulta concludes by asking the king to order the Council to erase the paper from its records and not to issue similar ones in future. For once this arrogance overshot the mark. There must have been a desperate contest waged over the matter for Philip kept the consulta until October 3, 1636, when he returned it with the endorsement that the Council of Castile can issue the provision embodying the articles of the Concordia and can order the local magistrates to observe and execute them.[807]

***

The reasons inducing inquisitors to the perpetual and illegal multiplication of these officials are not far to seek. The position was much coveted and the high value set upon it, notwithstanding the assertions of the Suprema as to diminishing numbers, is shown in one of the expedients for raising money resorted to in 1641, when an additional familiarship was created in each place, to be sold for fifteen hundred ducats. The offer was withdrawn in 1643, possibly because, as we have seen (p. 213), in 1642 a block of three hundred was thrown upon the market, thus breaking the price.[808] When such estimates were placed on the office, the opportunity for illicit gains was tempting to those who had power to issue commissions and, in addition to this, were the profits of litigation and the abundant fees for officials in the investigation into the limpieza of aspirants and their wives. The fines also arising from cases in which familiars were concerned were a not inconsiderable addition to the income of the tribunals. Thus, in 1564, Dr. Zurita, in a four months' visitation of the dioceses of Gerona and Elne, collected a hundred and six ducats for offences committed by or against familiars and, in addition, five culprits were sent to Barcelona on more serious charges which doubtless yielded still larger returns.[809] It is easy then to understand the temptation to enlarge so profitable a jurisdiction, and the steady opposition to revealing the number of appointees by furnishing lists.

It is true that the Suprema drew up an excellent list of qualifications as requisites for eligibility. No one was to be appointed who was not an Old Christian, at least twenty-five years of age, married or a widower, head of a household, virtuous, quiet, peaceable and fitted for the office, as well as of legitimate and not of foreign birth.[810] Yet there was no difficulty in obtaining dispensations for age, for celibacy, for illegitimacy and for foreign birth or parentage, the considerable fees for which went to the secretary of the inquisitor-general.[811] There was no formal dispensation for the moral qualities, but these were elusive and the general character ascribed to familiars, as we have seen in Valencia, shows how little care was frequently taken as to these. They are not even alluded to in the formalities required, in the middle of the seventeenth century, when we are told that the petition of the applicant must be accompanied with a certificate from the secretary of his place of residence setting forth the number of inhabitants, the number of familiars, evidence of baptism to show his age, that he did not follow any mechanic or low occupation, and that he had property sufficient for his decent support. He was also of course required to furnish the genealogies of himself and his wife for investigation into limpieza.[812]

To what extent precautions were taken to avoid improper appointments depended of course upon the temper of the tribunal and necessarily varied with time and place. In 1561, Inquisitor Cervantes says that in Córdova, Seville and Saragossa, where he had served, aspirants for appointment were taken on probation for two or three months, after which inquiry was made as to their limpieza and mode of life when, if they were married and peaceable men they were appointed, but that nothing of this was observed in Barcelona.[813] It is not likely that such scrutiny was frequent, for the appointments were treated as patronage by inquisitors, who took them in turn until, in 1638, this was forbidden by the Suprema, which ordered that they should be decided by voting; the fiscals were required to report whether this was observed, which it doubtless was, because it could be so easily eluded by a private understanding.[814]

***

There was some effort made, but without success, to maintain the dignity of the office by excluding those engaged in trade or in pursuits regarded as degrading, such as butchers, shoemakers, pastry-cooks and the like. On the other hand there was naturally welcome for personages of distinction and of these there was no lack. The bluest blood of Spain did not disdain to serve the Inquisition in the office of familiar. This excited apprehension in the Aragonese kingdoms and, in the Concordias of 1568, it was provided that familiars should be plain men and not powerful ones such as gentlemen and barons. At once the Valencia tribunal enquired of the Suprema whether this excluded gentlemen who were not barons and it was assured that barons only were excluded. The tribunal disregarded even this limitation and appointed barons and gentlemen holding vassals, turbulent men, rendered reckless by the exemptions, leading to quarrels with the Audiencia, in which Philip II interposed, in 1590, by ordering all such appointments made since the Concordia to be revoked. Loud were the complaints of the inquisitors; they denied that they had appointed barons; if the gentlemen with vassals were deprived of their commissions the Inquisition would be dishonored and, what made matters worse, the Audiencia had registered the decree where it could be read by every one, and had sent it to the governors of provinces, thus publishing it to the world.[815]

How long this exclusion lasted under the crown of Aragon it would be impossible to say, but probably it was not permanent. In Castile there was no such distinction. At the Madrid auto de fe of July 4, 1632, the standard of the Inquisition was borne by the Admiral of Castile, assisted by the Constable of Castile and the Duke of Medina de las Torres, all familiars.[816] Fernando VI, however, adopted the Aragonese precaution and required all familiars to be pecheros or taxpayers, when an indignant memorial, apparently from Inquisitor-general Prado y Cuesta, called his attention to the fact that there was not, in all Castile, Aragon, Valencia and Andalusia, a grandee or gentleman of illustrious birth who did not find ancestors on the rolls of the Holy Office, or count it among the glories of his house that they were enlisted in the militia of the faith.[817]

By this time the number of familiars had greatly fallen, though not to the extent that would be inferred from the table in the Appendix, for the tribunals had evidently not reported them--in fact, it is probable that few if any had kept registers enabling them to do so. The diminishing influence of the Inquisition, the curtailment in the privileges of the office, the new spirit vivifying Spain under the Bourbons, all combined to render the position less sought for, and thenceforth we hear comparatively little of the familiar as a disturbing element in the social order.

***

It was a matter of course that the officials of the tribunals should form organized bodies. They did so under the name of the Cofradia or Congregacion or Hermandad de San Pedro Martir, which assumed to be the same as the Cruce-signati, founded in Italy by Innocent IV, after the murder of St. Peter Martyr, in 1252. The bulk of the membership was naturally formed by the familiars, who were the most numerous class of officials, and there are occasional allusions to Colegios de Familiares, which may have been a subdivision of the general body. At what date the Cofradia was organized it would be impossible to assert, but, as early as 1519, it was a formidable body with chiefs known as mayordomos for when, in that year, there were rumors of an attempt in Saragossa to liberate Juan Prat by force, Charles V ordered the Zalmedina of Saragossa to assemble it and resist the movement, and he wrote to the mayordomos to obey the Zalmedina.[818]

The Hermandad became elaborately organized in the inquisitorial centres with a constitution which was printed in 1617. Each branch had as officers a padre mayor, a secretary, a mayordomo mayor, a mayordomo menor and a fiscal. The entrance-fees were considerable and the reception of new members was attended with a certain amount of ceremonial, in which the candidate took a solemn oath, in the hands of an inquisitor, to imperil his life in executing the commands of the Holy Office and to denounce all heretics, after which the inquisitor gave him a cross and imparted to him all the privileges and indulgences of the crucesignati.[819]

COFRADIA DE SAN PEDRO MARTIR

The extension of the Hermandad over Spain was by no means simultaneous. It was not established in Seville until 1604 and then only after considerable opposition. Even as late as 1700, in a Formulary, there is a formula of a grant by inquisitors to the commissioners and familiars of an arch-priest district to found a cofradia.[820] The functions of the body may be assumed as purely ornamental, giving lustre to the solemnities of the auto de fe and an occasion for the Inquisition to exhibit its strength. Marching in procession under the standard of the Holy Office in the Seville auto of November 7, 1604, they formed a body four hundred strong and at that of Córdova, in 1655, they were reckoned at over five hundred. At the last of the great autos, celebrated in Madrid, in 1680, the Suprema ordered all the familiars of the city to join the Congregation, under penalty of forfeiting the fuero, and each member was required to carry in the procession a wax candle of two pounds' weight, with the insignia of the Inquisition, whereupon it ordered three hundred candles. On this occasion it received a splendid standard which it continued to use in solemn celebrations.[821]

The organization was not always as faithful as it might have been to its oaths of obedience. In 1603, in 1675 and again in 1715 there was trouble over the right claimed by the members to wear habitually their crosses and habits as insignia of St. Dominic, though the Suprema restricted this to occasions of solemnity, and it finally required a threat of dismissal to enforce the rule.[822] There was still greater indiscipline in 1634 and 1635, at Valencia, where they excited a popular tumult and refused to obey the orders of the Suprema in the matter of the celebration of the feast of the Cruz nueva.[823]

When, under the Restoration, Fernando VII endeavored to revive the somewhat dilapidated glories of the Inquisition, it was suggested to him to elevate the Hermandad into a Royal Order of Knighthood. He welcomed the idea and, on March 17, 1815, he issued a decree in which he says that, at the request of the mayordomos of the Most Illustrious Congregation of San Pedro, composed of the Suprema, the inquisitors and the subordinates of all the tribunals, and in order that they may be distinguished and honored, he commands that they wear daily on their outer garments, like the other orders of knighthood, the habit and badge of the Inquisition. To set the example, on the feast of St. Peter Martyr (April 29th) he presided over the Congregation in person, accompanied by the infantes Don Carlos and Don Antonio, when he wore these insignia, which was imitated by the members, so that it became the fashion in the court. April 26th the Royal Council promulgated the decree, in accordance, it said, with concessions from the Holy See, and it ordered that no individual or court should impede the members in the enjoyment of this right. On May 10th the Suprema communicated the decree to the tribunals, with orders for its strict observance by all officials. It was disheartening to find that all this was not taken seriously by the people, for it was not long before the inquisitor of Valladolid had occasion to complain to the Suprema of the insults offered by the ecclesiastical authorities to the officials, on account of the decoration of the Royal Order of Knighthood of St. Peter Martyr.[824]

CHAPTER IV - LIMPIEZA

Repeated allusions have occurred above to the limpieza, or purity of blood, required in all officials of the Inquisition. This was so remarkable a development of the prevailing fanaticism and exercised so much influence on the social condition of Spain that it deserves a somewhat detailed investigation.

The first indication of this exclusiveness is seen in the Sentencia Estatuto of Toledo, in 1449, under which all Conversos were stripped of official positions as being suspect in the faith (Vol. I., p. 126). This, as we have seen, elicited the bull of Nicholas V, denouncing such legislation as unchristian, forbidding discrimination between Old and New Christians and confirming the laws to that effect of Alfonso X, Henry III and Juan II. This was evaded in the founding of a confraternity, under the title of Christian Love, in Córdova, in 1473, from which all Conversos were rigorously excluded, leading to the tumults and massacres described above.[825] It may have been this which induced Archbishop Carillo of Toledo, in a provincial synod held at Alcalá, to denounce the growing practice of brotherhoods, bound under oaths to exclude Conversos and alleging these oaths in justification. All such statutes were declared invalid and all who had taken such oaths were released from them.[826] In 1473, also, Juan II of Aragon abrogated the statutes of a similar association in Majorca and ordered that Conversos should have full enjoyment of all faculties in his dominions.[827] A somewhat ludicrous aspect was given to this prejudice by a guild of stone-masons in Toledo, composed principally of Mudéjares, which, in 1481, adopted a rule forbidding members from teaching their art to Conversos, and the next year a still more prescriptive statute was adopted in Guipúzcoa, prohibiting Conversos from settling or marrying in the province.[828]

The earliest official recognition of a distinction between Old and New Christians was the bull of Sixtus IV, in 1483 (supra, p. 11) ordering that episcopal inquisitors should be Old Christians. The next step was more portentous of the future. When, in 1485, the temporary Inquisition was established in the Geronimite monastery of Guadalupe, a Jew was found among the monks, who had been living as one of them for forty years and yet had never been baptized. His prompt burning in front of the convent gates did not allay the dread that other heretics might find similar refuge in the Order, leading the General Chapter to decree that no descendant of a Jew should be admitted; those already entered, if they had not professed, were expelled, and those who had professed were incapacitated for any honor or dignity. Much discussion ensued; the decree was held as contravening the bull of Nicholas V in 1449, and there was prospect of trouble, leading Ferdinand and Isabella to apply to Innocent VIII for a remedy. He evaded a decision in the brief Decet Romanam, September 25, 1486, by clothing the Archbishop of Seville and the Bishops of Córdova and Leon with authority to decide all questions under the decree and to revoke, modify and strengthen it at their discretion. This of course was held to be a practical confirmation of the new rule, and we are told that Our Lady of Guadalupe was so delighted that she coruscated in miracles, which Fray Francisco Sancho de la Fuente undertook to record, but they were so abundant that his zeal was exhausted and he abandoned the pious task.[829]

The next instance was a special and limited one. After Torquemada had founded at Avila his convent of St. Thomas Aquinas, he grew apprehensive that the hatred which he had earned from the Conversos might lead them to enter it with evil intent. In 1496 he therefore applied to Alexander VI for a decree forbidding the reception of any one descended, directly or indirectly from Jews, a request which the pontiff readily granted, subjecting to ipso facto excommunication any prior or other person contravening the rule.[830]

DEVELOPMENT OF PROSCRIPTION

The tendency to discriminate against Conversos was stimulated by the disabilities inflicted under the canon law on the children and grandchildren of impenitent heretics. This will be treated more fully hereafter and it suffices to say here that it was construed as applying to the children and grandchildren of all condemned or reconciled by the Inquisition. It was the subject of some debate, and the Instructions of 1488 required inquisitors to enforce by heavy penalties the incapacity of such descendants to hold any public office or to be admitted to holy orders.[831] These disabilities were extended still further by the sovereigns, in two pragmáticas of 1501, forbidding the children and grandchildren by the male line and the children by the female to hold any office of honor or to be notaries, scriveners, physicians, surgeons, or apothecaries. These pragmáticas were promptly sent by the Suprema to all tribunals, with orders for their strict enforcement, as the sovereigns did not permit exceptions to be made.[832]

In this rising tide of proscription it is pleasant to find an exception. There was no more uncompromising defender of the faith than Ximenes but, in organizing his University of Alcalá, he made no discrimination against Conversos. In his carefully elaborated details as to qualifications for professorships, fellowships, degrees and the other objects of academic ambition, there is not a word indicating that the taint of Jewish or Moorish blood was an obstacle.[833] It was doubtless this which excepted Alcalá from the ominous decree of the Suprema, November 20, 1522, prohibiting Salamanca, Valladolid and Toledo from conferring degrees upon any convert from Judaism, or on any son or grandson of one condemned by the Inquisition.[834] Where it found warrant for such assumption of authority it might be difficult to say, but the effect of such proscription can scarce be exaggerated, in thus barring the way to all the learned professions and consequently to public employment and ecclesiastical preferment.

The next step was taken by the Observantine Franciscans who, in 1525, procured from Clement VII a brief providing that in Spain no fraile descended from Jews, or from one convicted by the Inquisition, should be promoted to any office or dignity, and that thereafter no one laboring under such defect should be admitted into the Order.[835]

By this time the question of limpieza was ever present and every one was popularly classed as an Old Christian or a New, for genealogies seem to have been public property. When, in 1528, Diego de Uceda was tried for Lutheranism and claimed to be an Old Christian, the Toledo tribunal sought testimony in Córdova, where the witnesses unhesitatingly described his family, paternal and maternal, as perfectly pure from stain of Converso blood, which they said was notorious throughout the city.[836] The increasing importance of the matter led the Inquisition to amass evidence for itself and, in 1530, the tribunals were ordered to summon before them the descendants of all who had been relaxed or reconciled and ascertain whether they had changed their names. From this general inquest each tribunal compiled for its own district a register of genealogies, comprising all the infected families which, when duly kept up, preserved a mass of testimony infinitely disquieting to subsequent generations.[837] The growing importance of the questions involved, to society at large, is indicated by a petition of the Córtes of Segovia in 1532, that those should be held as Old Christians who could prove their descent from Christian parents, grand-parents and great-grand-parents--or, if necessary, from great-great-grand-parents--and that no imputation of lack of limpieza should be cast on them, unless there was evidence to prove their descent from Jews or Moors, or that an ancestor had been condemned by the Inquisition.[838]

**

The Dominicans were not as active as the Franciscans in obtaining papal protection of their limpieza. In a long list of briefs conceded to Spanish Dominican houses there is no allusion to the exclusion of Conversos between Torquemada's of 1496 and 1531 when the houses of Santa Maria Nieba and San Pedro Martir of Toledo were forbidden to receive any fraile suspected of Jewish or Moorish origin, while in the college of Santa Maria the professors and students of arts and theology were required to be free from all suspicion of such descent.[839] The sentiment of the Order was less proscriptive than that of the Franciscans. Its most conspicuous member of the period was Thomas de Vio, better known as Cardinal Caietano who, when consulted, in 1514, by the regent of Salamanca, as to the legality of excluding those of Jewish blood from the Order, replied that it was not a mortal sin but, seeing that the race had furnished Jesus Christ and the apostles and the salvation of man, it was irrational and ungrateful to discriminate against them, as well as an obstacle to their conversion.[840] Paul III agreed with him for, in a motu proprio of 1535 addressed to the Dominican Provincial, he forbade any impediment to the entrance in the Order of those of Jewish or Moorish blood and, on learning that this was disregarded in some houses, he repeated and confirmed it with censures by a brief of August 3, 1537.[841]

In this, as in so much else, any one seemed able to get from the Holy See whatever he wanted and Paul reversed himself, in 1538, when the convent of San Pablo of Córdova represented that, in most of the colleges of the Order, descendants of Conversos were not received or, if admitted in error, were ejected, and it desired the same concession to its college, as necessary for its preservation and the peace of the house. Paul promptly acceded to this request and ordered the inquisitors and the dean of Córdova to defend the convent in these privileges, even to calling in the aid of the secular arm.[842] This was followed by a more general measure, in 1542, when, by command of Paul, Cardinal Juan de Toledo, Bishop of Burgos, prohibited the Dominicans of Aragon from receiving into the Order descendants of Jews or of convicts of the Inquisition to the fourth generation. It is not likely that this was confined to Aragon and, in the next year, we find the Suprema addressing the provincial and the definitors urging that no Conversos be allowed to enter.[843]

Charles V was as inconsistent as Paul III. In 1537 he issued a decree reciting that as, in some colleges of the universities, admittance was refused to New Christians he ordered that the constitutions of the founders be observed.[844] Yet when the chapter of Córdova, in 1530, adopted a statute of limpieza applicable to all the ministrants of the cathedral, and was unable to obtain papal confirmation, he ordered its observance and contributed by his influence to induce Paul IV, in 1555, to confirm it.[845]

The movement was one which was constantly gaining momentum. In 1548, Archbishop Siliceo of Toledo enumerates, among the bodies refusing admission to all except Old Christians, the three great military Orders of Santiago, Calatrava and Alcántara, membership in which was the object of ambition to almost every Spanish layman of gentle birth. In all the Spanish colleges, including that of Bologna founded by Cardinal Albornoz, none but Old Christians were received and from these colleges were drawn the members of councils and chancelleries and other judicial officials. It was the same with the Minims, by express statute of the founder St. Francis de Paula, and in other Orders and monasteries of both men and women. Cathedral chapters were beginning to adopt it, such as those of Córdova and Jaen; numerous confraternities were based upon it, and many mayorazgos, or entailed estates were conditioned on it.[846] Thus the mania for absolute purity of blood was spreading irresistibly and, while it would be impossible now to enumerate accurately the bodies which made it a condition precedent of membership, it is safe to say that the avenues of distinction, and even of livelihood, in public life and in the Church, were rapidly closing to all who bore the fatal mancha or stain. In time even admission to holy orders required proof of limpieza.[847]

SILICEO'S TOLEDO STATUTE

The Conversos, however, were too able and energetic to yield without a struggle and how the losing battle was waged is seen in the decisive case of the primatial church of Toledo. The Cardinal Archbishop Tavera attempted, in 1539, to procure the adoption of a statute of limpieza in the cathedral, but the opposition was so strong that he was obliged to desist.[848] His successor was Juan Martínez Pedernales, who adopted the classic appellation of Siliceo--a Salamanca professor who had the luck to be appointed tutor to Prince Philip and was rewarded with the see of Murcia, in 1541, whence he was translated to Toledo, in 1546. He was roused to indignation when, in September of that year, papal letters were presented to the chapter granting a canonry to Doctor Hernan Ximenes, whose father had been reconciled by the Inquisition. Although the chapter had several Converso members it refused admission to Ximenes and wrote a rambling and inconsequential letter to Paul III justifying its disobedience. To prevent such contamination for the future, Siliceo drew up a statute forbidding that any but an Old Christian should hold a position in the cathedral, even down to the choir-boys; all aspirants were to present their genealogies and deposit a sum of money to defray the expense of an investigation. In July, 1547, he came to Toledo, with a large retinue of gentlemen, and secretly assured himself of the assent of a majority of the canons, who bound themselves with oaths to adopt it; a meeting of the chapter was called and the measure was sprung upon it, in violation of its rules of order-- as he frankly said, if notice had been given and discussion allowed it could not have been passed, for the Conversos would have intrigued successfully against it. The vote in its favor was twenty-five to ten, not including the dean, who opposed it but had no vote. The minority claimed that they were the wiser and better part of the chapter, and probably they were, for they included the archdeacons of Guadalajara and Talavera, both sons of the Duke del Infantado, and Juan de Vergara, one of the most illustrious men of letters of the day, who had had experience of the rigor of the Inquisition. This action aroused so much excitement in the city that the Royal Council sent an alcalde de corte, who reported that, for the sake of peace, the statute had better not be enforced, in consequence of which Prince Philip, then holding the Córtes of Monzon, sent orders to suspend it until the emperor's pleasure could be learned. The struggle was thus transferred to the imperial court and to Rome. The matter was argued publicly in the Rota, when the conclusion was against confirmation and the pope signed a brief to that effect, but the archbishop's envoy, Diego de Guzman, used such persuasive arguments that Paul secretly evoked the matter to himself and signed another brief, May 28, 1548, confirming the statute, so that each side could boast of his support. Charles referred the question back to the Royal Council, to which both sides presented memorials. Their temper may be judged by the argument of the chapter that, after so many religious bodies had adopted the exclusion, if the opponents contend it to be unscriptural, they are manifest heretics and should be burnt to ashes.

A memorial of Siliceo to Charles is in the same key. A strange medley of evils is attributed to Jews and Conversos--even the German Lutherans are descendants of Jews. On taking possession of his archbishopric he had found that nearly all the beneficed priests and those having cure of souls were of Jewish extraction, and there was danger of Conversos obtaining entire possession of the Church, owing to the sale of preferment in Rome, where there were at the time five or six thousand Spaniards, most of them Conversos, bargaining for benefices. It was the same in the other professions, where judges, lawyers, notaries, scriveners, farmers of the revenue, etc., were mostly of Jewish stock, and they alone were physicians, surgeons and apothecaries, in spite of all that the Inquisition had burnt and was daily burning; they adopted these callings solely for the purpose of killing Christians--it was but the other day that, in a Toledo auto, there was reconciled a surgeon who always placed a poisonous powder in the wounds of his Christian patients. If Charles did not confirm the statute, the outlook was that the Conversos would govern the church of Toledo. Wild as all this may seem to us, it gives us a valuable insight into the impulses which governed Spain in its dealings with the alien races within her borders. It was a humiliating admission that they were regarded as men of superior intelligence and ability, whose wrongs for generations had converted them into irreconcilable enemies, the object of mingled dread and detestation; as they could not be matched in intellect, the only policy was brute repression and extermination.[849]

Of course Siliceo carried the day. The confirmation of his statute by Paul III was conclusive and was regarded as establishing on irrefragable grounds the necessity of limpieza as a qualification for all who aspired to position in Church or State.[850] Toledo maintained it even against the pope. In 1573, the Venetian envoy, Leonardo Donato, reports that he had seen all the authority of the stern Pius V vainly exerted to secure the archidiaconate of Toledo for a servant of his who was not limpio and who finally had to content himself with transferring the dignity to another and retaining a heavy pension on the revenues.[851]

It was not only in Toledo that the capacity of the Conversos was filling the minds of the faithful with direful apprehensions of their ultimate triumph over their oppressors. While Siliceo was at work, the Inquisition was endeavoring to enforce the brief by which, in 1525, Clement VII had excluded them from the Observantine Franciscans. To the Suprema its fiscal represented that the unbridled licence of frailes of Jewish descent had prevailed to such an extent that they were elected as general and provincial ministers, guardians, vicars, procurators, visitors and other officials, to the oppression of the Old Christians of the Order, who were thus excluded from office, causing daily scandals and threatening worse. Valdés consequently ordered the brief to be published anew and observed everywhere under heavy penalties. Thereupon the General of the Order, Andreas de Insula, was incensed and, on the assumption that this had been instigated by Old Christian frailes, threatened to punish them severely. The Suprema therefore appealed to Julius III, reciting all this and pointing out the crafty and unscrupulous ways in which that unquiet race disturbed the peace of all bodies to which it found entrance, forming factions and aspiring to rule, with the object of ruining the Old Christians, thus opening the way to a return to Judaism and the destruction of Christianity. Julius responded favorably, in a brief of September 21, 1550, instructing Valdés to summon the General Andreas and all concerned to obey the decree of Clement, and granting him full powers to decide summarily the prosecutions proposed with a view to protect the Old Christians from molestation, using for the purpose whatever censures might be necessary.[852] It shows how indomitable were the Conversos that confirmatory briefs had to be procured from Gregory XIII and Sixtus V.[853] Yet again the Holy See manifested its inconsistency for, when the chapter of Seville, in 1565, petitioned Pius IV to confirm a statute of limpieza, he refused and condemned the Spanish practice as contrary to law and as upsetting the churches. Cardinal Pacheco defended it and described the evils wrought by the Jews, when Pius turned fiercely on him, saying that he would do as he thought best and that the Spaniards all tried to be popes.[854]

When those who had the slightest taint of Jewish or Moorish blood were thus regarded as not only implacable enemies of the Christian faith, but as gifted with pre-eminent intelligence and craft, it became impossible for the Inquisition to consider them as fitted for its service. One would have expected it to take the initiative and the only subject of surprise is that it should have been so late in adopting for itself the rule which it was enforcing on other bodies. Discrimination may have been exercised in special cases but, till the middle of the sixteenth century, there is no trace of any systematic adoption of limpieza as a test. A carta acordada of July 20, 1543 and a decree of Prince Philip in 1545, respecting the numbers and character of familiars, are silent as to this as a qualification.[855] The first allusion to it that I have met occurs in a commission issued to Francisco Romeo as scrivener of confiscations in Saragossa, signed April 16, 1546, by the inquisitor-general, but not countersigned by members of the Suprema until July 9th, "after the inquisitors of Aragon had ascertained the limpieza of the said Francisco Romeo."[856] A step forward is seen in the instructions issued by the Suprema, October 10th of this same year, in which it ordered that no familiar be received until it is ascertained that he is an Old Christian.[857] Still this was rejected as a general principle for, when the Córtes of Monzon, in 1547, complained that Moriscos were appointed as familiars, the answer of the Suprema was a formal declaration that the Inquisition regarded as capable of holding office all who had been baptized and who lived as Christians, except heretics or apostates or fautors of heretics.[858]

ADOPTED BY INQUISITION

This vacillation continued. A number of appointments subsequent to that of Romeo have no allusion to limpieza until 1549, when, on April 8th, Valdés enquires of the inquisitors of Barcelona whether Gerónimo de Torribos, candidate for the receivership, possesses the qualifications of limpieza and habits required in officials, and whether there is anything connected with his wife to prevent his appointment. So, on April 8th, when Moya de Contreras, inquisitor of Saragossa, proposed to employ commissioners of the Cruzada, Valdés emphatically negatived the suggestion, giving, among other reasons, the fact that the officials of the Cruzada were not "tan limpios de sangre." Yet, in an order of October 8th of the same year to the tribunal of Cuenca, remodelling its familiars, there is no allusion to the necessity of limpieza.[859]

This uncertainty continued yet for a while, of which further instances could be cited, but a decisive step seemed to be taken when Philip, in instructions of March 10, 1553, concerning the Concordia of Castile, prescribed that all familiars must be Old Christians and yet a carta acordada of March 20th on the same subject makes no allusion to such a condition.[860] The tribunals appear to have been somewhat slack in conforming their patronage to the new regulation. December 23, 1560, the Suprema felt it necessary to order that all familiars must be married men and limpios.[861] When the inquisitor-general made an appointment and required the inquisitors to certify to the limpieza of the nominee, they would do so, as appears from the commission of Bernaldo Mancipi, as assistant notary of sequestrations in Barcelona in 1561, but in this same year Inspector Cervantes reported that they paid no attention to it in their appointments of commissioners, consultores and familiars, a negligence which continued for, in 1568, the Suprema was obliged to rebuke them for it.[862] This is scarce surprising when Philip II himself, in 1565, had issued a series of conciliatory instructions regarding the Moriscos of Valencia, in which he ordered that their leading men should be made familiars.[863]

Thus far there does not seem to have been any definite system adopted as to verifying limpieza. The statute of Toledo required aspirants to furnish genealogies and deposit money for expenses and this was probably the common plan. In 1557 we are told of Beltran Ybañez de Arzamendi, appointed alguazil in the tribunal of Sardinia, that the examination of his paternal genealogy was made in Valencia and of his maternal in Calahorra, the birth-places of his respective parents,[864] but doubtless much of this was perfunctory. It was evidently felt that the highest authority must be invoked to prescribe a settled system and Philip II was called upon for this. In 1562 he accordingly issued a decree in which, according to custom, antiquity was claimed for innovation, for it recited that, since the Inquisition had been founded in Castile and Aragon, all inquisitors and officials appointed by the inquisitor-general had been required to furnish genealogies to prove that there was no trace of descent from Jews or Moors, or from those condemned or penanced by the Inquisition. The king therefore ordered that all appointees, in tribunals of the kingdoms of the crown of Aragon and of Navarre, and of Logroño, should furnish satisfactory proofs of limpieza, even though they might hold canonries or churches or be members of Orders which required limpieza. Moreover married men were obliged to furnish proofs of the limpieza of their wives and those already in office were to be dismissed if there was defect of limpieza in the wife. These rules were to be embodied in the Instructions and were to be inviolably observed.[865] Undoubtedly a similar order was issued for Castile and the utterance is important as embodying the first absolute demand for proofs of limpieza and as marking the extravagant extension of the rule to wives.

This royal cédula was interpreted as applicable to existing incumbents, and investigations as to their genealogies were set on foot, with the intention of weeding out at least the familiars who were not limpios. Several efforts had already been made to this effect after the Castile Concordia of 1553, without apparent result, and it was now undertaken again with instructions that, if any were found to be Conversos, they were to be dismissed without assigning a reason.[866] It was a work ungrateful both to the investigators and investigated and dragged along in the most perfunctory fashion. Cartas acordadas in 1567 and 1575 called for lists of those who had been investigated and those who had not and, when it came to taking action, the habitual tenderness manifested toward officials was displayed in orders issued in 1572 and again in 1582 that if any officials, commissioners or familiars, were found lacking in the requisite qualifications, they were to be reported to the Suprema without dismissing them.[867]

LIMITATIONS DISREGARDED

As a matter of course the test was applied to all new appointments and no one was admitted to office in any capacity in the Inquisition who was not free from the mancha of Jewish or Moorish blood or of ancestral punishment. Even for temporary employment, limpieza was essential. In his visitation of the Canaries, in 1574, the Inspector Bravo de Zayas brought an accusation, against the Inquisitor Ortiz de Funes, of appointing officials without preliminary investigation, the cases being two emergency appointments to fill temporary vacancies, and the appointees being montañeses, or highlanders from the northern provinces of Spain, where purity of blood was presumable--to say nothing of the fact that an investigation would probably have consumed a year or two.[868] Yet this was but the natural expression of the infatuation which had taken possession of Spain. In 1595, Philip II, in his instructions to Manrique de Lara, lays especial stress on the importance of limpieza. Investigation as to this and as to habits must be made with the utmost rigor and no dispensations must be granted. No examinations are to be made before the party is selected, because otherwise, if he is not appointed owing to other reasons, it may be ascribed to a mancha and thus undeserved infamy be cast upon an entire kindred.[869] Strangely enough, however, the inquisitor-general himself was never required to furnish proofs of purity of blood.[870]

Unfortunately, in the craze for absolute limpieza, no limit was set to the number of generations through which the taint could be carried. The canon law, as we have seen, limited disabilities to grandchildren and, in 1573, Leonardo Donato describes the rule as extending to what were called the four quarters, that is, the parents and the four grandparents, and in this moderate shape he says it was the cause of constant strife and of preserving the old Judaizing memories.[871] In this, however, he greatly understated Spanish craving for purity of blood. We have seen the Córtes of Castile, in 1532, petition that it should be satisfied with great-grandparents, indicating that it was carried beyond this, and Siliceo's Toledo statute affixed no limit. Each body, it is true, could prescribe its own rules, but the more important ones discarded all limitations and refused admission to those against whom a stain could be found, however remote. In 1633 Escobar informs us that among these were included the Inquisition, the Orders of Santiago, Alcántara, Calatrava and St. John, the church of Toledo and all the greater colleges and universities, including that of Alcalá; these all required the most rigorous investigation to trace out the slightest mancha in the remotest grade of parentage.[872]

IMPURITY ARISING FROM PENANCE

There were two sources of descent which caused impurity of blood--from an ancestor of either of the proscribed races, or from one who had ever been penanced by the Inquisition. As regards the former, the line was drawn at the massacres of 1391 for Jews and at the enforced baptisms of the early sixteenth century for Moors. Voluntary converts, prior to those periods, were accepted as Old Christians, the subsequent ones were considered as unwilling converts and were regarded as New Christians, together with their descendants, no matter how zealously they had embraced the Christian faith. The prevalence of intermarriage with Conversos throughout the fifteenth century had led to infinite ramifications throughout the land in the course of generations and, about 1560, Cardinal Mendoza y Bobadilla, apparently moved by some discussion on limpieza, drew up and presented to Philip II a memorial in which he showed that virtually the whole nobility of Castile and Aragon had a strain of Jewish blood.[873] There was no lack of material for tracing the dissemination of this blood through the land. In Aragon, Juan de Anchias, the zealous secretary of the first Saragossa tribunal, compiled what was known as the Libro Verde de Aragon, giving the affiliations of all the leading Conversos who had suffered, so as to serve as a beacon for all who desired to avoid contamination. In Castile there was no such authoritative publication, but the records of the tribunals had accumulated ample material, and the sanbenitos of the relaxed and reconciled, hung in the parish churches, kept the memory of the sufferers green, to the discomfiture of their descendants. Many individuals, moved by zeal or by malignity, from these and other sources, with greater or less exactness, and including much that was mere idle hearsay, compiled books which were circulated under the name of Libros verde or del Becerro. No one of the upper or middle class, except in the remote mountainous districts of the North and East, could feel secure that investigation might not reveal some unfortunate mésalliance of a distant ancestor. In fact, only those could feel safe whose obscurity precluded any prolonged research into their ancestry. As a writer remarks, in 1629, if it were not for limpieza the Inquisition could select the best men for familiars, in place of appointing the low-born whose ignorance enables them to pass the examinations successfully.[874]

The second source of impurity--descent from one penanced by the Inquisition--originally applied only to those who had incurred the heavier penalties of relaxation or reconciliation, but there was nothing to check the scrupulosity of the examiners, who worked in secret, and they came to regard any penance inflicted by the Holy Office as affixing an indelible stigma on the descendants. The results of this are forcibly described in a memorial presented, in 1631, to Philip IV by Doctor Diego de Sylva, a member of the Suprema. After alluding to the greatly increased rigor of investigation, dating from the later years of Philip II, he proceeds to state a further source of wrong only appreciable by one who has handled the records of the Inquisition, and not to be openly mentioned. In contrast to the exquisite justice and benignity which he ascribes to the existing tribunals, the proceedings in the earlier period were hurried and violent; many to save their lives made confessions which may have been groundless; whole districts were reconciled rather as a spiritual than a judicial process; in that dangerous period careless words and propositions created suspicion, and people were tried and dismissed with some trivial penance--a few masses, some almsgiving or a light fast--for offences belonging really to the exterior forum. Yet all these were sentences and, as there has since grown up the rule requiring immemorial limpieza, whole families are branded with infamy.[875] As, in fact, since the Reformation, the Inquisition had grown more and more exacting and had inflicted on Old Christians innumerable penances for careless words, it is easy to conceive how this rigorous definition of limpieza spread infection throughout the land, even outside of those who had a drop of Jewish or Moorish blood.

These evils were aggravated by the looseness with which adverse testimony was admitted in the investigations. Anonymous communications were received and acted upon, for, although this was prohibited by law and by papal briefs, these were commonly disregarded.[876] In a decree by Philip IV, in 1623, designed to curb some of the evils, it was ordered that no weight be attributed to idle talk, but the diffuseness with which Escobar, in his commentary on this section, dwells upon the worthless character of scandal and idle gossip and angry words uttered in quarrels, shows how largely such evidence entered into the conclusions reached. Common fame or reputation, he tells us, suffices, even if the grounds for it be unknown, and purity or impurity of blood is for the most part a matter of common fame and belief.[877] That this was so is seen in an elaborate series of instructions for the conduct of such investigations, where the fiscal is warned that great weight is to be given to such expressions of opinion, even though the witness can offer no proof except that he has heard it from his elders.[878] The avenue thus opened to the malignant to gratify hatred is dwelt upon by the writer with too much insistance for us to question the frequency with which it was utilized.

ROUTINE OF INVESTIGATION

This was facilitated by the secrecy which shrouded these investigations. The applicant put in his genealogy, named his witnesses and awaited the event. The process at best was a deliberate one and, if the result was unfavorable, the answer never came, though the failure to secure an appointment might arise from any other cause. As Doctor Sylva says, the silence and mysterious authority of the Inquisition will not give the slightest glimmer of light to the applicant, even through twenty years of suspense, though meanwhile the opinion gains ground that his family is impure, without his being able to rebut or investigate it, and thus a whole lineage suffers with all its kindred.[879] A glimpse into the anxieties thus caused is afforded by a consulta of February 26, 1634, from the inquisitor-general to the king, respecting a memorial from the Marquis of Navarrez asking for a speedy decision for his son, Don Francisco Gurrea y Borja, who had put in his proofs for an appointment as familiar, as the delay is damaging to his reputation. The inquisitor-general reports to the king that no conclusion had been reached; perhaps the king may please to decide it, for the marquis has been in court for a long time pressing the matter, and the delay has brought upon him suffering and stigma.[880] The suspense endured by all the kindred, when one of its members decided to undergo the ordeal, is visible in a letter of 1636, from Fernando Archbishop of Cuzco to his nephew, the Coronel Jacinto de Vera, on learning that he was about to apply for admission to one of the military Orders. He gives him advice and information, and so important did he consider it that he had seven copies made, to be forwarded by different routes and vessels, and another member of the family wrote to Jacinto earnestly cautioning him not to let any eye but his own to fall upon the archbishop's letter.[881]

In the routine adopted by the Inquisition for these investigations, the applicant handed in his genealogy and, if married, that of his wife, giving the names and residences of parents and grandparents. If thorough search through the registers, by names and districts, revealed a fatal blot, that of course was sufficient. If not, commissioners or secretaries with notaries were sent from the tribunal, or the nearest commissioners were ordered to go to the places of residence, where from eight to twelve of the most aged Old Christians of good repute were summoned as witnesses, with precautions to prevent the interested parties from knowing who was called upon. The witnesses were examined under oath, on a series of printed interrogatories, as to their knowledge of the parties, whether they were descended from Conversos or from penitents, what were the sources of information and whether it was public fame and report. The replies were duly taken down and attested. If salaried officials or familiars were concerned, the results of the information were transmitted to the Suprema, to which were also referred doubtful questions and votes in discordia.[882] In a more perfected form, known as the nueva orden, in use in the seventeenth century, stringent additional precautions were taken to prevent the insufficient secrecy observed by officials which was supposed to deter witnesses from giving adverse evidence. A carta acordada of January 22, 1628, threatened excommunication and deprivation of office for this and, under subsequent regulations, all concerned were forbidden, under rigorous penalties, to reveal to any one, even to a minister of the Inquisition, any evidence taken or papers, or records, or even the name of a witness, so that the applicant should be kept in perfect ignorance of the progress of his affair.[883]

The commissioners were invested with full power to cite witnesses, to examine into sanbenitos suspended in churches, and to demand any papers bearing upon questions that might arise, whether these were in private hands or public archives, and, at their discretion, to make copies or carry away the originals, the owners of which were told that if they wanted them back they might apply to the tribunal. If a witness absented himself, a summons to appear before the tribunal was left with the parish priest to be served on him when he should return.[884] Evidently no family records were too sacred to escape these searching investigations.

EXPENSES

All this, of course, involved expense and the fees earned in the work by the officials formed a welcome source of revenue. In 1625 the pay of notaries or secretaries was fixed at a per diem of sixteen reales.[885] This was subsequently raised for, in 1665, a statement of expenses in the case of Doctor Martin Roig, applicant for the position of consultor in Valencia, shows that the secretary was paid 30 sueldos a day and a local commissioner 20. This was only part of the cost, for every act and every blank filled in, every piece of writing bore its separate charge. The bill rolled up for him and his wife in Barcelona, for this unsalaried position, amounted to 955-2/3 sueldos and this was only the beginning. Similar researches were required in the tribunals of Valencia and Cuenca, which must have been still more costly, for the Barcelona report only occupied twenty-three folios, while that of Valencia was in ninety and one against his son Vicente was in a hundred and eight. Two years later, in 1667, the affair was still dragging on.[886] It was a large price for the honor of an unpaid position, even if he proved successful. These extortions were multiplied as often as possible. In 1661, Juan Temprado Múñoz made his proofs as receiver of the tribunal of Murcia and of course this included his wife, but when, in 1667, their son Juan Temprado de Cereña desired an office in the tribunal of Barcelona, he had to go through the same process afresh, when the examination of the Barcelona registers alone cost him 546 sueldos. In addition to this the registers of Cuenca and Valencia had to be examined and evidence had to be taken in the home of his ancestors. This chanced to be in Roussillon, which was now French territory; there was war between the nations and, even in peace, France refused entrance to officials of the Inquisition, so the ingenious formality was devised of sending a commissioner to the border and examining there the requisite number of old men as witnesses. The evidence of course was valueless, but it gathered in the per diem all the same.[887] In time this per diem for the secretary was increased to 50 reales and, from one or two cases in 1815, it appears that it was a perquisite which the secretaries took in turns, and, when the commissioner nearest to the place of examination was employed, it was without prejudice to the secretary--that is, the commissioner who did the work received 30 reales a day, while the secretary took the other 20.[888]

In order to secure the payment of these fees, the applicant was required, when he presented his genealogy, to make a deposit, originally of 300 reales. As the business increased it became evident that a separate fund and separate accounts of these moneys must be kept and, in 1600, it was ordered that a special chest be provided, with two keys, one entrusted to the fiscal and the other to a secretary. Abuses crept in, effectively described in the memorial of 1623 to the Suprema, as a remedy for which a new official was created, known as the Depositario de los Pretendientes, who received and accounted for the deposits, charging two per cent. on the sums passing through his hands. This he remitted to the Suprema, for his office was salaried and he was relieved of the temptation of perquisites. The office was one of those put up for sale, for three or four lives, under Sotomayor.[889]

The whole business was provocative of fraud and perjury and bribery. Despite the well-meant efforts of the Inquisition to preserve the profoundest secrecy, the writers of the period are too unanimous in deploring the success of enemies in casting infamy on those they hated, for us to doubt that means were found to ascertain what was on hand and to abuse the opportunity. To the applicants the stake was too great for them to shrink from any means that promised success. Cases become not infrequent in the records of prosecutions for false-witness in matters of limpieza, showing that aspirants were not remiss in furnishing testimony to prove fraudulent claims.

FRAUDULENT TESTIMONY

Although, in 1560, Valdés humanely ordered that descendants of penitents, who committed perjury in getting up statements of limpieza, should not be prosecuted, this policy changed in 1577, when they were subjected to prosecution and in 1582 the thrifty plan was adopted of inflicting pecuniary penance.[890] This proved profitable, for the culprits were many, not only among aspirants to office but because limpieza was requisite in many careers, and the Inquisition took cognizance of all cases of perjury in this matter, whether it was concerned or not in the investigation. Thus, in 1585, Bernardino de Torres, a prominent citizen of Toledo, had occasion, in a suit, to prove his nobility and purity of blood, which he did with a number of witnesses. The tribunal had evidence in its records that, on both father's and mother's side, he was descended from Conversos who had been penanced, and it promptly prosecuted both him and his witnesses. Among them was the Regidor of Toledo, Diego de Parades, who had likewise sworn to his own limpieza, although the records showed his descent from reconciliados in a time of grace. Altogether there were sixteen witnesses, the advanced age of most of them showing that old men found profitable occupation in testifying to their recollections. Bernardino himself was penanced in fifty thousand maravedís. Many of the witnesses were let off with perpetual disability to testify in such cases, but a hundred and thirty-six thousand maravedís were collected from the rest. A few other Toledo cases at the same time may be mentioned to show the various motives impelling men to these frauds. Gerónimo de Villareal desired to place his daughter in a convent where limpieza was required. The Licenciado Antonio de Olvera was about to emigrate to the colonies and wished to protect himself from insult. Hernando de Villareal had a son who proposed to take orders and another who aspired to an appointment as familiar. The records showed them to be descended from grandparents or great-grandparents who had been burnt or reconciled and they were duly punished.[891] The taint spread with every new generation and a large part of the population was heavily handicapped in life.

If there were frequent perjury and subornation of testimony it is not to be supposed that the seekers for limpieza hesitated to corrupt the officials who controlled their destinies, nor is it unreasonable to assume that many of the latter were accessible to bribery. The opportunities were tempting and they were freely exploited. An experienced writer, in 1648, describes this as the most troublesome business in the tribunals, leading to quarrels, which he hints arose between those honestly endeavoring to discharge their duty and those who had been bribed. The fiscal is reminded that he must set his face like flint against all efforts to pass a genealogy in which there is a flaw, for the aspirants tempt the officials, there is collusion between them and forged documents are to be expected. The chief reason, he says, why commissionerships are sought is because of the opportunities thus afforded and, writing in Toledo, he declares that all the commissioners and notaries attached to that tribunal are untrustworthy and venal.[892]

***

It was natural that the evils with which this absurd cult of limpieza afflicted the land should arouse opposition and call forth suggestions to mitigate its hardship. The earliest writer who ventured publicly to urge a reform seems to have been Fray Agustin Salucio, a distinguished Dominican theologian. In 1599 he issued a brief tract, pointing out that practically all Spaniards, in the course of ages, had contracted some more or less infinitesimal impurity of blood and that, unless investigations were limited to some moderate period, such as a hundred years, only the lower orders, whose genealogies were untraceable, could escape the consequences. He tells us that both Pius V and Gregory XIII drew up briefs prescribing narrow limits to these investigations but that, on communicating their designs to Philip II, discussions arose as to the term, which proved so protracted that the briefs were never published. Philip himself became convinced of the necessity of some limitation and, towards the close of his reign, he assembled a junta, including Inquisitor-general Portocarrero (1596-99) which unanimously agreed to a term of a hundred years, but Philip's death caused the project to be dropped. Salucio's tract was promptly suppressed by Philip III, but it was reprinted, in 1637, by Fray Gerónimo de la Cruz with a verbose confutation. Yet, while he indignantly denied the aspersion on the limpieza of the nation, he was fully alive to the misery caused by the current practice and he urged a limitation of time, placing it at 1492, the year of the expulsion of the Jews.[893]

ATTEMPTED REFORM

At length Philip IV was induced, in a pragmática of February 10, 1623, to attempt some amelioration of existing conditions. Anonymous communications were to receive no attention and precision as to dates and persons was required in alleging punishment inflicted by the Inquisition. Witnesses were prohibited to testify as to common rumor unless they could allege reasons and details. Some tribunals, especially colleges, were so rigorous that they required not only proof of limpieza but also that no doubts had been expressed, whereby many families had been unjustly defamed through the malice so frequent in these matters, all of which was forbidden for the future. A significant clause pointed out that, in the early days, persons sometimes confessed to matters about which there was no other evidence and such confessions, unsupported by external proofs, were not to be prejudicial to their descendants. The practice of many persons in compiling books called "Libros verdes ó del Becerro," fabricated with no greater authority than their own malignity, was condemned, because they caused irreparable injury and injustice and disturbance of the public peace, seeing that many persons gave evidence based only on having read such books. Any one possessing books or papers calling in question the limpieza or nobility of others was therefore commanded to burn them under pain of five hundred ducats and two years of exile. Then, to place some limit on the multiplication of investigations, it was decreed that when there had been "tres actos positivos"--three positive decisions affirming limpieza or nobility--it should be deemed a proved and settled matter for the party involved and his lineal descendants, not thereafter to be called in question, provided always that the decisions were made, with full knowledge of the case by proper tribunals, which were defined to be the Inquisition, the Council of Military Orders, the Order of St. John, the four principal colleges of Salamanca, the two principal ones of Valladolid and Alcalá and the Church of Toledo.[894]

Considering the acute perception of existing evils displayed in the preamble to the law, the slender restrictions imposed manifest the strength of the prejudices to be overcome. Slight as they were, the Inquisition and the Council of Military Orders, after nominally accepting the law, proceeded vigorously to nullify the provision of the tres actos positivos. A writer, in 1629, tells us that they had succeeded in requiring regular investigations, in spite of the production of the three acts; they also held that these only related to parents and grandparents and that they were conclusive only as to the articles covered by them and not as to new points that would require fresh examinations and thus the fees of the officials and the anxieties of the applicants remained undiminished.[895] As regards the character of the testimony received, the secrecy of the procedure renders credible the assertion of Escobar, in his commentary on the law, that there was little if any improvement. There was some mitigation of rigor in an order of the Suprema, about 1645, that when an applicant could prove the tres actos positivos it was not necessary to push investigations as to his great grandparents. Somewhat halting was another rule promulgated in 1639, requiring submission to the Suprema of matters more than a hundred years old, before rejecting the applicant, but this was withdrawn in 1654.[896]

***

The futility of the system and its unfortunate influence are forcibly set forth by the writer of 1629, who tells us that those who succeed best in their proofs are the poor peasants, whose grandparents have been forgotten, and the great nobles, against whom no one dares to testify. The chief sufferers are the lesser nobility and gentlemen--too conspicuous for their ancestry not to be known and too powerless to exclude adverse witnesses. Everybody knows that he who has friends succeeds and that he who has enemies fails, irrespective of the truth, and thus the statutes wholly fail of their object. This is facilitated by the secrecy enabling the enemy to produce false witnesses and the accomplice to bribe and bring forward perjured testimony, so that it is notorious that in no other class of cases are the results so fallacious. In this way there has been created a sort of factitious nobility--that of limpieza--the possessors of which look down with contempt on the old nobility of the land.

EVILS

Another evil of magnitude is the fearful waste of money. He who succeeds, after paying his agents for things too scandalous to be described, finds himself penniless, and he who fails has not money enough left to make another attempt; his proofs are destroyed and he hangs around the court, wasting his life and perhaps that of his father and sons, and all this under the ban of being infamous--he and his latest posterity.

The damage to men's honors is incredible and also to the kingdom, for strangers call us all Marranos. Moreover those whose talents would be of great service to State and Church are lost to us, for they have not confidence to seek to enter a college and, what a base cobbler can risk and gain, those who are noble and ambitious fail in, because there may be a single drop of tainted blood in their veins. It is also one of the causes of depopulation, for women enter nunneries and men remain celibates rather than inflict infamy on descendants, while large numbers emigrate. Besides all this are the hatreds arising from adverse testimony and the infinite bribery and collusions and perjury, so that Satan has no greater source of winning souls. It is not required for an Archbishop of Toledo, but it is insisted on for the beadle of his cathedral; it is not demanded for an inquisitor-general, but for the messenger of a tribunal; not for the President of Castile, but for a familiar or the purveyor of a college.[897]

This is not exaggeration, for it is merely an amplification in detail of the preamble of the pragmática of 1623 and is fully borne out by Escobar in his commentary on the law.[898] That in fact it was the conviction of all sober-minded and thinking men of the period may be gathered from the emphatic testimony of Fray Benito de Peñalosa, though he does not venture to suggest a remedy more radical than restricting the effect of impurity of blood to five generations.[899]

The effects of this proscription were manifold. As early as 1575, Lorenzo Priuli, the Venetian envoy, describes the descendants of the Conversos as living like other good Christians and being among the richest and noblest of the land, yet perpetually incapacitated from the honors and employments which were the ambition of every Spaniard--an evil which was increasing every day. Thus Spain, being full of discontented persons and divided in itself, some rising would be feared but for the severe execution of justice and the presence of the king. In 1598, Agostino Nani repeats the assertion--the descendants of all, who have at any time been punished by the Inquisition, live in a state of despair for, to the third and fourth generation they are regarded as infamous and incapable of any office in Church or State.[900] Navarrete does not hesitate to suggest that, but for the exclusion from public life of all but Old Christians of purest lineage, the fatal necessity of the expulsion of the Moriscos might have been averted: they might have been Christianized had they not been driven to desperation and hatred of religion by the indelible mark of infamy to which they were subjected.[901]

In fact, the statutes of limpieza created a caste of pariahs who infected all with whom they might form alliances, but the caste was not recognizable by exterior signs and no one could tell what corruption of blood he might entail upon his family by any marriage that he might contract. As Fray Salucio says, no one, entering into wedlock, could make the investigations required by the colleges and the Military Orders. Thus the infection was constantly spreading; every man stood upon a mine which might explode at any moment when some distant kinsman of his own or of his wife might provoke an investigation during which a taint might be discovered in the common line of ancestry. When we recall the history of the Conversos anterior to the sixteenth century and the enormous operations of the early Inquisition we can conceive how this indelible stain must have spread throughout society, to be revealed at any moment in the most unexpected places.[902] A writer in 1668 reflects the popular prejudice when he compares a marriage with a man whose father has been penanced by the Inquisition to sleeping in a bed full of lice or in sheets that have been used by one who has the itch.[903]

EFFECTS

Another result was greatly to increase the authority of the Inquisition and the terror which it shed around it, by the fact that at a word it could inflict this undying infamy upon a lineage. To be arrested and cast into the secret prison, even without cause, was sufficient. In 1601, Philip III, when instructing the Inquisition to furnish to the Council of Military Orders full information as to any one, when called upon, required the report to include, not only the imprisonment of an ancestor subsequently acquitted, but even the fact of an accusation never acted upon.[904] It can readily be understood that even a summons to appear, in a matter not of faith, was felt acutely through a whole kindred. In the long struggle at Bilbao over the visitas de navios, the corregidor Mendieta took an active part against the commissioner Leguina who, to silence him, caused him to be cited by the tribunal of Logroño. This caused intense excitement and the Señorio of Biscay had him accompanied by two caballeros. When he demanded to know the charges against him, there were none forthcoming and he was dismissed. The affair was regarded as so serious that the Council of State presented a consulta to the queen-regent in October, 1668, setting forth that the citation might lead to the disgrace of his family and posterity and suggesting that some relief should be found for him.[905]

All this is of supreme importance in estimating the benignity and mercy of which the Inquisition was constantly boasting. The sentences rendered may frequently appear to us trivial, but the penance was the smallest part of the penalty. Villanueva, as we have seen, was condemned merely to abjure for light suspicion of heresy and to a few years' absence from Madrid, but that cast disgrace upon his whole kindred; he and his descendants fell into the class of pariahs and could form no alliance outside of that caste; through generations they were branded with an ineffaceable stigma. To Spanish pundonor the scaffold were merciful in comparison. The mercy of the Inquisition was more to be dreaded than the severity of other tribunals and men might well beware of incurring the enmity of those who could at discretion consign them and their posterity to infamy.

***

The limpieza test survived the Revolution and purity of blood was as essential under the Restoration as under the old monarchy, but there was some relaxation of rigidity. Thus, if a man and wife proved their limpieza, it sufficed for their children, only a legal certificate of baptism being required, and in the same way the proofs presented by one brother answered for another on his furnishing evidence of their common paternity.[906] A couple of years was also allowed to appointees in which to put in their proofs, and there is even a case of secretaries admitted without proofs, but with a warning that it would not be allowed again.[907] In the extreme penury of the time the Suprema imposed a fee, for its own benefit, of 60 reales on every investigation, which the receivers were required to collect and to remit yearly.[908] It was also in receipt of the two per cent. levied by the depositarios de los pretendientes, and one of its last acts was the acknowledgement, February 10, 1820, of 360 reales remitted by the depositario of Seville, which would show that 18,000 reales had passed through his hands.[909] The part of the business which fell to the Suprema was not large. Its first certificate is dated January 3, 1816 and the last one January 4, 1820, the whole number being only one hundred and eight.[910] From these certificates it would appear that the investigation was scarce more than a formality.

The demand for limpieza survived the Inquisition, though with its closure it is not easy to conjecture where any serious proofs could be found. Up to 1859 it was still requisite for entrance into the corps of cadets but, in 1860, the Córtes unanimously abolished this survival of prejudice and intolerance.[911]

MAJORCA

Yet there is still a corner of Spain where that prejudice has proved superior to law. We shall have occasion hereafter to refer to the terrible persecution of the Judaizing New Christians of Majorca, in 1679 and 1691. Padre Francisco Garau, S. J., who promptly printed an exulting account of the four autos de fe celebrated in the latter year, tells us that the descendants of Conversos formed a community of some two hundred families, living huddled together in the calle and apart from the rest of the population, for there never was intermarriage between them and the Old Christians. The people called them Jews and, on their complaining of this, an offensive nick-name was speedily invented and they were termed chuetas in allusion to their avoidance of pork. They were not allowed to hold public office, although great efforts, supported by the government, were made by the wealthy and influential among them. The same proscription was exercised by the guilds and brotherhoods, especially by the surgeons, confectioners, candle-makers, grocers and silk-weavers, so that they were virtually all traders.[912] Thus there was a solid foundation of inveterate prejudice which was stimulated, in 1755, by the malicious reprint of Father Garau's book, followed by the circulation of lists, furnished by the secretary of the tribunal, of all Conversos punished by the Inquisition, comprising all the families of Jewish extraction. This caused a recrudescence of ill-feeling, and complaint was made to Carlos III, who responded in cédulas of December 10, 1782, October 9, 1785 and April 18, 1788, ordering that they should not be impeded from residing in any part of Palma or of the islands, that the entrance-gate of the calle should be destroyed, and that insults or calling them Jews or chuetas should be punished with four years of presidio. They were declared fit for service in army or navy or any other department, and free to exercise all arts and trades, and all this was extended to the descendants of Conversos throughout Spain.[913]

Yet even an autocratic monarch could not overcome prejudices so deep-rooted. Church and State in Majorca had bitterly opposed the appeal to the throne and had succeeded in postponing action for ten years. The University, in 1776, had revived its statute of limpieza and had closed its doors to the proscribed class. When the royal decrees came they provoked warm opposition on the part of the municipal authorities who resolved not to yield obedience. It was the force of events rather than the growth of tolerance that gradually brought relief. In 1808, when the nation rose against the French, they were admitted to military service, but when the local levies were ordered to the mainland, there was a mutiny in which the barrio del Segell was sacked.

After the reaction of the Restoration, under the revolution of 1820 they were enrolled in the National Guard, but when came the counter-revolution of 1823 they were disarmed and the rabble promptly sacked their houses and made bon-fires of what was too cumbrous to steal. After the death of Fernando VII the enforced constitutionalism of the Cristina government restored them practically to citizenship and military service and gradually their exclusion from civil office disappeared.

Popular aversion however was not to be overcome by statute. It was rekindled, in 1856, by a suit brought to establish their right to membership in the Circulo Balear, or Balearic Club, which led to republication of the essential portions of Father Garau's book. This was answered, in 1858, by Tomás Bertran Soler, from whom we learn that the New Christians were still excluded from Christian society and continued to dwell in the calle; they were refused all public offices and admission to guilds and brotherhoods so that they were confined to trading; they were compelled to marry among themselves, for no one would contract alliance with them, nor would the ecclesiastical authorities grant licences for mixed marriages. Since then there has been some abatement of popular prejudice, but the latest accessible view of the situation, in 1877, by Padre Taronji, a priest of the proscribed class, represents the clergy as still obstinately impervious to all ideas of extending fellowship to their fellow-believers and as busily fanning the dying embers of class hatred, based on events two centuries old.[914]

Wise statesmanship in Spain would have sought the unification of the races within its borders. In place of this, race hatred was stimulated in the name of religion, with the deplorable results recorded in Spanish history.

Henry Charles Lea, LL.D.

BOOK V - RESOURCES
CHAPTER I - CONFISCATION

When the Inquisition was established it was expected to be not only a self-sustaining institution but a source of profit. To what extent the anticipation of gain, by seizing the substance of their subjects, may have influenced Ferdinand and Isabella, in adopting this method of vindicating the faith, it would be useless now to enquire, but they refused to permit any division of the spoils as in the older papal Inquisition of Italy. These were reserved to the crown and, when the first inquisitors were sent to Seville, in 1480, they were accompanied by a receiver of confiscations--a royal official whose appointment shows what were the expectations entertained. Yet the support of the Inquisition had to come out of the product of its labors; the basis of its finances was confiscation and the use which it made of its powers in this respect, whether for its own benefit or for that of the sovereign, exercised so large an influence on the prosperity of Spain that it demands a somewhat careful examination. Spoliation on such a scale, continued unremittingly for nearly three centuries, was a tremendous burden on the productivity of the most industrious class of the population. At the commencement, a very large portion of the accessible wealth of Spain was in the hands of the Jews and Conversos. By the expulsion of the former and the prosecution of the latter they were stripped of it. The marvellous persistence of the New Christians, their tireless activity and business aptitude, kept them incessantly at work making acquisitions which continued to render persecution profitable and contributed to maintain the institution which was laboring, with equal persistence, for their destruction. It would not be wholly true to assert that the exhaustion of confiscations caused the inertia of the later decades of the Inquisition, but it unquestionably was a contributing factor.

The cruelty of confiscation was equal to its effectiveness. To strip a man, perhaps advanced in years, of the results of the labors of a life-time and to turn his wife and children penniless on the street was a severity of infliction which rendered the sparing of his life a doubtful mercy, and it was not without reason that the legists deemed it equivalent to capital punishment.[915] To the persecutor this was a recommendation, in addition to its financial advantages, and we can readily understand why it was enforced with such remorseless perseverance.

***

Confiscation as a punishment for crime was too settled a principle of the imperial jurisprudence for any jurist to call in question its propriety. As heresy was held to be treason to God, more detestable than treason to an earthly prince, the Church naturally adopted it as soon as, in the twelfth century, persecution became systematized. In 1163, Alexander III, at the Council of Tours, commanded all potentates to seize heretics and confiscate their possessions, and Lucius III, in his Verona decree of 1184, sought to divert this to the benefit of the Church.[916] Under the Roman law of treason, the property of a traitor was forfeited from the time when he first conceived his crime and this was applied to the heretic, whose earliest act of heresy was the date from which the fisc claimed his estate--a provision of much importance in the settlement of debts.

RESPONSIBILITY

In Aragon, the introduction of the Inquisition in the thirteenth century rendered confiscation for heresy a matter of course. In Castile a more tolerant spirit, as expressed in the laws of Alfonso X, forbade it, so long as there were Catholic heirs or kindred; if there were none, the king inherited, subject to the right of the Church, if the culprit were a cleric, to claim it within a year.[917] This code however was not confirmed until 1348, by which time scruple had diminished, for Alfonso XI, followed by Henry III, confiscated to the royal treasury one-half of the possessions of the convicted heretic.[918] It was reserved for Ferdinand and Isabella tacitly to accept the canon law in all its rigor, while diverting to the royal treasury all the proceeds. A contemporary asserts that they divided it into thirds--one for the war with the Moors, one for the support of the Inquisition and the third for pious uses,[919] but there is no trace of such allotment and we shall see that the crown made such use as it pleased of its acquisitions.

Strictly speaking, the Inquisition did not confiscate but merely pronounced the culprit guilty of that which implied confiscation, and it seems to have felt some hesitation as to assuming the responsibility. In the earliest trials that have reached us, there is no settled formula, either in the demand of the fiscal for punishment or in the sentences, confiscation being sometimes expressed and sometimes inferred and left for the alcalde to pronounce.[920] The Instructions of 1484 are silent as to confiscation in cases of the living but, in treating of prosecution of the dead, they order the heirs to be heard, so that the property may be confiscated and applied to the fisc of the sovereigns, and it is noteworthy that in sentences on the dead, immediately after this, the Instructions are referred to as though to shield the inquisitor from responsibility.[921]

There evidently was popular repugnance to this spoliation and no one wished to be responsible for it. Ferdinand, in a proclamation of October 29, 1485, declared that the confiscations were made by order of the pope, in discharge of his conscience and by virtue of his obedience to holy Mother Church.[922] It was probably owing to his instructions that the tribunals finally assumed the responsibility, as is seen in a sentence of July 8, 1491, in Saragossa, on the deceased Juan de la Caballería, where the king is ordered, in virtue of holy obedience, to take the property and hold it as his own.[923] Apparently all did not acquiesce promptly for we find him, in 1510, ordering the inquisitor of Majorca, when pronouncing any one to be a heretic, to add at the end of the sentence that he declares the property confiscated and applied to the royal fisc and orders the receiver to take it, when the receiver is to do so in virtue of the sentence.[924] In accordance with this the official formula adopted bore that the tribunal found the culprit guilty of heresy and as such to have incurred excommunication and the confiscation and loss of all his property, which it applied to the royal treasury and to the receiver in the name of the king, from the time when he commenced to commit the crime of heresy. Or, if the offender was an ecclesiastic, it was applied to whom it lawfully belonged. This rather evaded the question whether confiscation was self-acting, but the Fe de confiscacion, given by the notary to the judge of confiscations, formally asserts that the inquisitors and Ordinary had confiscated the property to the king's treasury and by the sentence had applied it to his receiver in his name.[925] If any uncertainty remained, it was removed by a carta acordada of 1626, which ordered that, in all cases of formal heresy, the sentence should include confiscation for, if there was to be any mitigation, the granting of such grace belonged to the inquisitor-general.[926] The anterior date to which the confiscation operated was determined, under the Instructions of 1561, by the consulta de fe when voting on the sentence.[927]

GRANTS TO FEUDAL LORDS

The phrase, in the case of ecclesiastics, of adjudging the property to whom it legally belonged, was a recognition of the claims of the Church. What these were seems to have been open to question. Under the Partidas the Church had the right, if it put forward the demand within a year, but Ferdinand, in a letter of March 11, 1498, says he is told that he has a right to a third in such cases. Whence this was derived we are not told, but he established the rule and it remained in force as late as 1559 when two-thirds of the estate of Dr. Agustin Cazalla passed to the Bishop of Palencia who, however, transferred it back to the Inquisition.[928] This was probably a compromise, for the Inquisition had asserted its right to the whole, and Bishop Simancas, in 1552, had said that many hold that the property of clerics goes to the bishop, but the truer opinion, which had always been followed in Spain, was that it belongs to the fisc, for the use of the Inquisition.[929] The question, however, was not definitely settled for, in 1568, the Suprema called upon all the tribunals to report without delay what was their practice and what was their formula of sentence.[930] It was inevitable that any doubts should eventually be construed in favor of the Holy Office and, in the seventeenth century, the authorities assume as a matter of course that the confiscations of clerics enure to the tribunals, although the sentence still attributed them to whom they lawfully pertained. Forfeited benefices of heretics, however, were a papal perquisite, by decree of Paul IV, June 18, 1556 and this is cited, about 1640, as still in force in Spain.[931]

For awhile the confiscations were subject to another diversion. The feudal lords, who saw the property of their vassals swept into the royal maelstrom, grew restless and, although they do not seem to have put forth any legal claim, Ferdinand, in many cases, deemed it wise to pacify them with a grant of one-third of the confiscations made in their estates. The earliest grant of the kind that I have happened to meet is to the Infante Enrique, Duke of Segorbe, April 20, 1491.[932] These grants were subject to a deduction for the expenses of the trials, which led to a good deal of friction, as none of the parties concerned were over-scrupulous. If the grantee quarrelled with the receiver over the question of expenses he had a fashion, when the customary auction of the property was held, of announcing that he desired to bid and that nobody should bid against him. By this device the Duke of Bejar enforced a settlement in 1514 and again in 1517.[933] The experience of the Duke del Infantado shows how skilful were the officials in neutralizing these grants. In 1515 he obtained a grant of one-half of confiscations up to that time and one-third for the future, subject to expenses. Disputes arose as a matter of course and, in 1519, he prevented auction sales till he should be paid and, in 1520, he compromised for two hundred ducats in settlement of claims up to that time and ten per cent. for the future, free of expenses.[934] It is safe to say that Ximenes was exposed to no such trouble in his settlements but, with his enormous revenues and his position as inquisitor-general, it would have better comported with his dignity to have abstained from procuring, in 1515, a grant of one-third of the confiscations made in his estates and in the Cazorla lands assigned for the expenses of his table.[935] With the gradual weeding out of the wealthier Conversos and the increasing expenses of the tribunals, the share of the feudal lords doubtless diminished until it was not worth contesting, for shortly after this period we cease to hear of this division of the proceeds.

VERIFICATION OF PROPERTY

Confiscation, as we have seen, was one of the invariable penalties of heresy under the canon law. The heretic was outside of the Church; if persistent he was relaxed and burnt; if he repented and professed conversion he was "reconciled" to the Church, but though he thus escaped death the forfeiture of his property remained. Reconciliation, as a rule, inferred confiscation. An exception to this was when a Term of Grace was published, usually of thirty or forty days, during which those who made full confession of their sins and gave full information about others were received to reconciliation, under promise of release from imprisonment and confiscation, but subject to public penance and giving as "alms" such portion of their property as the inquisitors should designate.[936] This was an abandonment by the king of the property which had become forfeit through heresy and was confirmed by a formal grant by him to them of what was lawfully his, empowering them to sell and convey a good title, which otherwise they could not do.[937] This did not apply to what the penitent suffered from the crimes of others, and thus children so reconciled could not claim estates forfeited by their parents. Outside of the Term of Grace there was no escape. Espontaneados--those coming forward spontaneously--after its expiration, had already forfeited all their possessions and, as it was explained, it was not the intention of the sovereigns to remit the penalty to them, save when, in special cases, they might exercise clemency.[938] This covetous policy, which discouraged the repentant sinner, was continued until, in 1597, the Suprema ordered that espontaneados should be reconciled without confiscation.[939] Yet, in spite of this, when, in 1677, Alvaro Núñez de Velasco, came forward voluntarily to denounce himself and was reconciled, his sentence included confiscation.[940]

Occasional instances are met in which confiscation was spared on account of the extreme youth of the penitent, but I have been unable to find any formal rule to that effect and it seems to have been discretional with the tribunal. In 1501, at Barcelona, when Florencia, daughter of Manuel de Puigmija, was condemned to perpetual prison, it is said that her property was spared in view of her tender age. In the reconciliation, at Toledo, April 20, 1659, of Ana Pereira, aged ten, confiscation was included; in that of Beatriz Jorje of the same age, December 8, 1659, there is no allusion to confiscation and, in that of Diego de Castro, aged ten, December 8, 1681, it is stated that confiscation is omitted in view of his age.[941]

***

The enforcement of confiscation was a business matter, reduced to a thorough and pitiless system. The sufferers naturally sought to elude it and every possible means that experience could suggest were adopted to prevent the loss of the minutest fragment. When the accused was arrested, all his visible possessions were simultaneously sequestrated and inventoried. His papers and books of account were examined to ascertain what debts were owing to him, and he was at once subjected to an audiencia de hacienda in which he was interrogated under oath, in the most searching manner, as to all his property, his debts and credits, his marriage settlement, dowries or gifts to his children, their estates if they were dead, whether he had secreted anything in apprehension of arrest, and every detail that the circumstances suggested. Any failure to answer fully and truly was perjury, for which he could be punished, as occurred in the case of Louis de Perlas, tried in Valencia for Lutheranism in 1552.[942] The most repulsive incident in this perquisition was the advantage taken of the terrors of approaching death, when the confessors of those who were to be executed in an auto de fe were employed during the preceding night in exhorting them to reveal any portion of property that might have escaped previous investigations. Thus, June 29, 1526, Fray Castell reported that Pedro Pomar, whom he had confessed during the night of the auto de fe "estando en el suplicio de la muerte" had revealed where certain account books could be found and also some debts due to him. So, December 21, 1529, Anton Ruiz, under the same circumstances, confessed to debts due to him which had eluded previous search.[943]

EMPLOYMENT OF INFORMERS

This prostitution of religion to the service of greed was exploited to the utmost. Excommunication was so habitually abused for temporal purposes that it was naturally resorted to, and all who concealed or held any property of a convicted heretic were subjected to it. In 1486 Ferdinand writes that certain notaries refuse to give copies of contracts passed before them, relative to obligations due to heretics, to which they must be constrained by censures and the invocation, if necessary, of the secular arm, and the same course must be taken with debtors refusing to pay what they owe.[944] October 17, 1500, he scolds some inquisitors for their negligence; those who know that they are suspected commonly hide their property or place it in the hands of third parties and "in this way those who hold such property become excommunicated to the great damage of their souls, for they continue under the censure and my fisc suffers, for the property escapes confiscation."[945] In 1645 a writer gives us the form adopted in such cases. If the fiscal thought that there was property of a confiscated estate concealed or debts due to it unrevealed, the tribunal issued an edict to be read from the pulpits, ordering under pain of excommunication every one holding such property, or cognizant of facts concerning it, to make it known to the commissinoner or to the parish priest within three days. On the expiration of this term the priests were required to denounce from their pulpits all such persons as excommunicated and to be avoided by all Christians. Then, after three days more, followed the anathema, in its awful solemnities of bell, book and candle, with the imprecatory psalm, and invoking the wrath of Almighty God and the glorious Virgin his Mother and of the Apostles Peter and Paul and all the saints of heaven and all the plagues of Egypt on the wicked ones who were withholding its own from the Holy Office.[946]

This spiritual punishment did not exclude temporal. In 1671, Manuel Fernández Chaves, tried in Toledo for the "occultation" of confiscated effects, was fined in five hundred ducats and was banished for two years from Toledo, Pastrana and Madrid. When the concealment was for the benefit of a culprit, there was the additional charge of fautorship, as in the case of Gabriel de la Sola and Joseph López de Sossa, who secreted property of the latter's sister Beatriz and whose trial, in 1697, in Valladolid, lasted for two years.[947]

More effective, at least in the earlier period, when the press of business rendered minute investigation difficult, was the offer of heavy commissions to those who would furnish information as to confiscated property that had escaped the search of the receivers. This resulted in creating a gang of professional detectives and informers of whom a certain Pedro de Madrid, "delator," may be taken as the type. Under a provision of 1490 he was entitled to one-third of all the hidden property that he might discover, whether alienated or conveyed under other names or otherwise concealed. In 1494 he complained that this was not enough, in view of his heavy expenses, travelling to France, sharing with other informers, etc., whereupon Ferdinand agreed to give him one-half, and moreover to those who should furnish information he pardoned the offence committed by their knowing without revealing; the inquisitors were to remove the excommunication and all receivers were to comply with these instructions under penalty of a thousand florins.[948] Ferdinand however did not always play fair with these gentry. Under the stimulus of his fifty per cent., Pedro worked hard and successfully but, when in 1499 the account of a receiver who had settled with him came in for audit, Ferdinand ordered the payments to be disallowed for the present; Pedro ought not to have such large sums; his success was attributable to the negligence of the receiver rather than to his own activity and, in fact, it was a voluntary gift to him. A year later we find Ferdinand agreeing to let him have one-half of thirty libras that he had discovered and promising to determine what share he should have when other properties unearthed by him should be settled.[949]

The frequent allusions to these transactions in Ferdinand's correspondence show what an active business it was, both with professionals and volunteers, and Ferdinand was sometimes liberal in rewarding the zeal of the latter as when, in 1501, he made a gift to Don Antonio Cortes, his sacristan mayor, of a house and an oil warehouse in Seville, which Cortes had discovered to be the property of Beatriz Fernández, condemned to perpetual imprisonment, which had escaped the receiver.[950] This indicates that men of standing did not disdain to engage in this disreputable business, and it would seem that Juan de Anchias, the secretary of the Saragossa tribunal, to whom we owe the Libro Verde, gave up his office to speculate in it for, in 1509, we find him complaining that the receiver refused to pay him the one-third which he had been promised on certain discoveries and Ferdinand ordering the bargain to be carried out. There was no settled rate of commissions. About this same time Clíment Roderes, of Barcelona, was only allowed one-seventh of the property recovered through his investigations, while the Majorca tribunal was authorized to offer twenty-five per cent. and, when the case seemed desperate, in 1514, Juan Martínez was encouraged by a promise of fifty per cent. to devote himself to looking up the concealments in Teruel and Albarracin, which were understood to be large.[951]

INVALIDATION OF CONTRACTS

While doubtless the fisc, by thus stimulating detectives, recovered property which might otherwise have escaped, the system was one which invited collusion between them and the officials. Frauds of this kind were probably not uncommon for, in 1525, the Suprema complained of the abuses that had sprung up through the disregard by the receivers of their instructions. These were to be strictly observed and, in future, commissions must be paid only on property of which nothing had been known to the officials, and the informer must not be an official whose knowledge had been acquired in the discharge of his duties. Moreover the compensation was strictly limited to twenty per cent. of the amount realized through the information furnished.[952] This is the latest allusion that I have met with to this phase of the business; it evidently diminished with the falling off in the confiscations, though doubtless special transactions continued to occur, for it was inevitable that the victims should exhaust their ingenuity in the effort to save for their children some fragments of their possessions.

***

Cruel as was confiscation in principle, its enforcement by the older papal Inquisition was iniquitous to a degree which multiplied to the utmost its cruelty and power of evil. The forfeiture of property from the time when the first act of heresy had been committed was construed to invalidate all subsequent acts of the heretic, for he had lost his dominion over all his possessions. All alienations thus were void, all debts contracted and all obligations given were invalid and the prescription of time against the Church had to be at least forty years' possession by undoubted Catholics, ignorant of the former owner's heresy. Prosecutions of the dead, moreover, for which there was no limit, carried back to previous generations the claim of the Inquisition to upset titles. Thus in practice, when a man was adjudged a heretic, all debts due to him were rigorously collected, while all due by him were cancelled, and all real estate that he had sold was reclaimed. The only mitigation of this was a declaration, by Innocent IV in 1247, giving to a Catholic wife, under certain conditions, a life-interest in her dowry, expiring at her death, for her children were incapable of inheritance.[953]

It is pleasant to be able to say that, in time, some of the worst features of this all-grasping rapacity were softened in the Spanish Inquisition. Its early operations were so extensive and the commerce of the land was so largely in the hands of the New Christians, that we can readily imagine the general consternation aroused by the strict enforcement of the canon laws which vitiated all alienations and stripped all creditors of their claims. It could lead only to wide-spread ruin and general paralysis of trade, and there doubtless arose a cry for relief which the sovereigns could not disregard. With a wise liberality, therefore, they consented to a partial abandonment of their claims, which is set forth in the Instructions of 1484, in a manner showing how fully they knew what were their rights. The clause recites that they could recover all alienations and refuse to pay all debts unless the proceeds could be identified among the effects of the confiscated estate, whether of those condemned or of those reconciled outside of the term of grace, but, out of clemency and to avoid oppression of vassals who had dealt with heretics, they ordered that all sales, donations, exchanges and contracts, prior to the year 1479, should be valid, if duly proved to be genuine. Attempts to take fraudulent advantage of this were declared punishable, in reconciled heretics, with a hundred lashes and branding in the face with a hot iron; in Christians, with confiscation, deprivation of office and penalties at the royal discretion.[954]

***

While there was substantial relief in this abandonment of the right to upset all transactions prior to the introduction of the Inquisition, yet it was retained with regard to all subsequent dealings and no man could know whether the banker or merchant or tradesman with whom he dealt might not soon fall into the hands of the Holy Office. It thus can readily be conceived how fatally credit was affected and what risks were encountered in the daily transactions of business. That there was difficulty in making the tribunals respect even this concession is visible in its promulgation anew by the Suprema in 1491 and again in 1502.[955] Cases, in fact, occur which show that the officials paid slender attention to it. Thus in 1499, Costanza Ramirez appealed to Ferdinand for property comprised in the dowry given to her mother, in 1475, by her grandfather Juan López Beltran, whose estate had been recently declared confiscated, and the king ordered its restoration if the statement was true. So, in 1509, the widow and wards of Johan Pérez de Oliva petitioned him for the release of certain houses which Oliva had bought in 1474 and which were now claimed as having been purchased from a condemned heretic.[956] Here was a perfectly legitimate transaction, thirty-five years old, which the Inquisition was endeavoring to set aside.

In the Instructions of 1484, prosecutions against the dead, including confiscation, were ordered, even if they had died forty or fifty years before. As it stands in the printed collections, this virtually postponed indefinitely the prescription against the Inquisition, as the transactions of the deceased might have extended anteriorly through forty or fifty years and, in fact, it was quoted, about 1640, as a proof that there was no prescription.[957] This however was a later additional severity for, in a MS. copy of the Instructions of 1484, there is a clause, omitted by the official compilers, to the effect that, if the heretic had died more than fifty years before the accusation was brought and, if the heirs or owners of the property had been good Catholics and had held it in good faith, they were not to be disturbed.[958] There is significance in this suppression and, under such a system, it is conceivable what a cloud hung over the titles of all property that had ever passed through the hands of a New Christian, and how poignant was the feeling of insecurity of its possessors.

In the struggle made by the kingdoms of Aragon against the oppression of the Inquisition the iniquities of confiscation were prominent. They were illustrated in the Córtes of Monzon, in 1512, by a special grievance which illustrates the working of the system. The local government had borrowed money and secured it by a censo or obligation given to Maestro Miro and Juan Bertran, who were condemned for heresy and the censo was demanded. The authorities showed that the censo had been paid off and the debt cancelled twenty-nine years before, but the receiver insisted on their paying it again because the heretical acts of Miro and Bertran were anterior and their release of the censo was therefore invalid. They petitioned Ferdinand for relief but he contented himself with ordering that they should not be unduly oppressed, which left the matter open.[959] Still, one of the concessions granted in 1512 was that prescription of time should be reduced to thirty years; this was confirmed in Mercader's Instructions of 1514 and when, in 1515, the Catalans complained of its inobservance, Ferdinand ordered it to be maintained. Leo X went even further in his bull of 1516, confirming the Concordia of 1512 and, in that of 1520 this was defined as protecting from confiscation all property acquired in good faith from those not publicly noted for heresy even though they should subsequently be condemned and the prescription of thirty years had not expired. This was declared applicable to all pending cases and, to render it more emphatic, Charles V made a formal grant of all such property to the holders.[960] We have seen, however, how completely the Inquisition ignored this settlement, denying its authority and even its existence. Castile was no more successful for, when the Córtes of 1534 petitioned that possession for three years in the hands of Catholics should confer immunity from confiscation and that dowries of Catholic wives should be exempt, Charles flatly refused both requests.[961] Finally the question settled itself in the canonical prescription of forty years' undisturbed possession by orthodox Catholics, for this is what Simancas informs us was the rule. The old Instructions requiring longer possession, he says, had been abrogated and, although some authorities argued that five years sufficed, or at most twenty, these were not recognized by the tribunals.[962] How business adjusted, itself to the risks attending all transactions with New Christians, we can only conjecture.

RECOGNITION OF CREDITORS

In one important respect the Inquisition mitigated the iniquitous harshness of the older institution by recognizing the claims of the creditors of the condemned heretic. This, however, was not the case at first and it would not be easy to exaggerate the general confusion and distress when it came to be understood that confiscation included the debits as well as the credits of the victims. The early extensive arrests were followed by the wholesale flight of those who felt themselves under suspicion; flight was regarded as confession and the fugitives were condemned in absentia as soon as the necessary formalities could be despatched. The losses of the consequent confiscation of debits fell not only on individuals connected with their extensive transactions but on the public bodies and ecclesiastical establishments, the collection of whose revenues was largely in their hands. The conditions thus created are impressively reflected in the records of Xeres de la Frontera, where the municipal taxes were largely farmed to Conversos who had fled; the public funds had been in their hands and they were naturally in debt to the town as well as to churches and private persons. It would appear that all these obligations were calmly ignored by the Inquisition and the municipality appealed to the sovereigns who replied, December 6, 1481, that the matter had been referred to the Licenciado Ferrand Yañez de Lobon--the very commissioner who, for about a year, had been busy in enforcing the collections of the confiscations. This boded ill for relief; the documents do not reveal the outcome but, as all the efforts of the authorities only brought them in contact with the officials engaged in gathering the spoils, it is evident that the sovereigns did not propose to abandon their rights.[963]

We have seen that the Instructions of 1484-5, when recognizing the validity of transactions anterior to 1479, asserted absolutely the right of the fisc to refuse payment of debts and made no concessions as to those contracted subsequently to that period. At the same time a clause concerning claims made by nobles, who had received fugitives in their lands, shows that the Inquisition felt the matter to be within its discretion.[964] The earliest positive admission that I have met of an obligation to pay debts due by a confiscated estate is an order by Ferdinand, May 12, 1486, to Alfonso de Mesa, receiver at Teruel, that wages due in good faith by heretics to their Moorish servants, are to be paid--but this may perhaps be attributable to the special preference allowed to servants' wages by the laws of Aragon.⁹⁶⁵ Various contradictory decisions illustrate the uncertainty hanging over the matter at this time, and it is clearly manifested by two letters of Ferdinand, evidently drawn up for him by his unscrupulous secretary Calcena. The first of these, March 6, 1498, relates to the Castillo de Calanya, which Calcena had obtained from the confiscated estate of Johan Benete and against which certain parties held censos (ground-rents) and other claims. The king is made to order the receiver to suspend action, because the debts had been contracted after Benete had committed acts of heresy. The other letter, March 11, 1498, reiterates an order of August 29, 1497, to a receiver to pay out of the sequestrated property of Antoni Cones a hundred ducats which Calcena had lent him and to pay him before any other creditors.⁹⁶⁶

By this time however the claims of creditors were beginning to be officially recognized. The Instructions of 1498 give detailed orders as to surrendering property belonging to others, and promptly paying debts clearly due out of sequestrated estates and, when confiscation was pronounced, a proclamation was to be made to all claimants to present their claims within a designated time, which in 1499 was fixed at thirty days, while no property was to be sold until the claims against it had been determined.⁹⁶⁷ Yet, in spite of this, the rights of creditors were admitted with difficulty by the receivers and numerous instances occur in which they were obliged to appeal to Ferdinand. As late as 1515, Margarita Dartes, wife of Doctor Francisco Dartes, assessor of the Valencia tribunal, complained that in 1499 she had bought a censo secured on a house of Aldonza Cocarredes; Aldonza had now been relaxed and Aliaga, the receiver, refused to recognize the censo because it had been created after she had committed heresy. Ferdinand admitted the validity of this argument and said that, in the rigor of justice, she had lost her claim but, in view of the fact that her husband had been in the service of the Inquisition since its foundation, he ordered it paid as a favor.⁹⁶⁸

OBSTACLES OFFERED TO CREDITORS

An examination of the records of the Valencia court of confiscations, in 1531 and 1532, evinces on the whole an evident desire to administer the law rigidly, whether in favor of or against the fisc. Among the claimants were a number of serving women for wages, which were always allowed, although the court exercised somewhat arbitrary discretion in cutting down the amounts.⁹⁶⁹ Gradually the honest policy prevailed and, in 1543, the Suprema instructed the tribunals that the first thing to be paid were the debts that were properly proved--a rule which apparently was difficult to enforce, for the order had to be repeated in 1546 and again in 1547.⁹⁷⁰ Yet it was no easy matter for creditors to obtain payment against the resistance offered by receivers and their advocates. In 1565, after Pierre and Gilles de Bonneville were burnt for Protestantism in Toledo, the fiscal reported to the inquisitors that numerous creditors had come forward whose claims were pending before the juez de los bienes, wherefore he asked for a certificate as to the date of the culprits' heresies, in order to use it before the court. The inquisitors duly certified that the date was about 1550, the object being to plead the obsolete canonical rule that subsequent obligations were invalid.⁹⁷¹ That chicanery of all kinds was employed to exhaust the patience of creditors and accumulate costs is plainly admitted in the memorial of 1623 to the Suprema, which states that, in the suits of creditors, there is much that brings discredit on the Inquisition, for confiscations are managed solely for the benefit of those who administer them, the appointees of the juez de los bienes and ordinarily his kinsmen or friends, for whose advantage the suits are prolonged until they become immortal.⁹⁷² Abuses such as these were inevitable in a system which confined everything within the circle of the Inquisition, permitting no outside interference or supervision, while dealing so tenderly with official malfeasance. It would be difficult to overestimate the wide-spread damage resulting when the accused were merchants with extensive and complicated transactions, as in the immense confiscations in Mexico and Peru from 1630 to 1650 and those of Majorca in 1678, when funds and merchandise of correspondents were tied up for an indefinite time to the destruction of their credit. The hazards to which business was thus exposed was a factor, and by no means the least important, in the decay of Spanish commerce, for no one could foresee at what moment the blow might fall. Sequestration accompanied arrest and, in 1635, it was ordered that, during the pending of a trial, no payments or delivery of property should be made to creditors, no matter what evidence they presented, without awaiting the decision of the Suprema, the only exception being claims of the king, which were to be paid without delay. In 1721 this prohibition to pay debts was made absolute, excepting a few trivial matters such as servants' wages and house-rent.⁹⁷³ That foreigners dealing with Spain had ample cause to dread the decisions of the juez de los bienes is shown by a remarkable clause in the English treaty of 1665 which provided that, in case of sequestration of property by any tribunal of either nation, the effects or debts belonging to a subject of the other should not suffer confiscation but should be restored to the owner.⁹⁷⁴ On the whole, however, the Spanish Inquisition is entitled to the credit of mitigating, in favor of creditors, the abhorrent harshness of the inquisitorial law of confiscation, although in practice its officials were guilty of minimising, as far as they could, the benefits of this moderation.

DOWRIES

In the matter of dowries there was also a partial mitigation of the old severity. The dowry was forfeited by the wife's heresy but not by that of the husband and, in the latter case, it descended to her children. There was one provision, however, which worked infinite hardship for, if the parents of the wife had been guilty of heresy at the time of her marriage, it was forfeited on the ground that all their property then belonged to the fisc and they had no power of alienation. The cases are numerous in which the parties, after prolonged married life, thus suddenly found themselves despoiled by the condemnation of parents who had enjoyed the reputation of faithful Christians and, in the inter-marriages, so frequent in the earlier period, the blow thus often fell upon Old Christians. We hear of these cases through despairing appeals to Ferdinand for mercy--appeals to which he not infrequently responded by abandoning his claims or surrendering a part. A typical case, illustrative of many others, is that Juan Quirat, of Elche, whose petition to the king, in 1513, represents that, twenty-five years before, he had married Violante Propinan, receiving ten thousand sueldos as her dowry from her parents, Luis and Blanca. Eight years ago they were condemned, and now the receiver claims the dowry; he is a poor escudero or squire and the enforcement of the claim would send him with his wife and children to the hospital, in view of all which Ferdinand charitably waived his right.[975] More peculiar was the case of Juan Castellon of Majorca who, when trading in Tunis, was enslaved by a brother of Barbarossa; after forty-two months of captivity he was ransomed for four hundred ducats and returned home in 1520 to find that his wife's mother, Isabel Luna, had been condemned and the dowry received from her was claimed by the receiver. He petitioned Cardinal Adrian; the matter was referred to Charles V, who humanely ordered that, if his story was true and he was unable to pay, the confiscation should be remitted.[976] The hardship was sometimes aggravated by an ostentatious custom of inserting in the marriage-contract a larger sum than was actually paid. Thus, in 1531, the magnifico Diego de Montemayor, Baile of the Grau of Valencia, swore that he received only three thousand sueldos of the six thousand specified in his marriage-contract with Beatriz Scrivana, in 1510, and that the larger sum had been inserted honoris causa.[977]

The dowries of nuns were subject to the same merciless absorption. In 1510, the convent of Santa Inez of Córdova appealed to Ferdinand, stating that, some twenty years previous, Pedro Syllero had placed his niece there as a nun, giving as her dowry certain houses which it had peacefully enjoyed until her grandfather had recently been condemned for heresy and the property was seized as part of his confiscated estate. This was strictly legal and it was a pure act of grace when the king ordered the houses to be released.[978]

Still, the dowry of an orthodox wife was exempt from the confiscation of a heretic husband's estate, but it was imperilled by the possibility that the estate might be exhausted in the maintenance of the husband in prison during a prolonged trial and by the sacrifice of values in the realization of assets at auction, which was imperative. In the proceedings of the juzgado de bienes of Valencia in 1531 there are numerous cases which show that this claim of the wife was fully recognized and a fair adjudication made in the complicated questions which frequently arose.[979]

Correlative to this was the liability of the husband to pay to the fisc the dowry of a wife condemned or reconciled for heresy. How pitilessly in time this was exacted is manifested in 1549 by a petition to Valdés from Don Pedro Gascon, who represents himself as an hidalgo whose ancestors had served the king faithfully. The judge of confiscations at Cuenca had condemned him in a hundred and fifty ducats for the dowry of his wife and the receiver had cast him in prison to enforce payment. While there he had sold a large part of his property and had paid fifty ducats, but the rest of his estate would not produce the remaining hundred. Ferdinand would have forgiven him the balance, but Valdés only looked to obtaining assurance of ultimate payment when he empowered the receiver to grant him six years' time on his furnishing good security.[980]

SYSTEMATIC ABSORPTION

Another feature, which frequently complicated these settlements, was the question of the conquests--the ganancias or creix--the gains made during married life, in which both spouses had an equal share. The laws of Toro, in 1505, provide that neither husband nor wife could forfeit claim to half the ganancias for the crime of the other, even if the crime were heresy, and the ganancia is defined to be the whole increase during wedlock until the decree of confiscation, no matter when the crime was committed--a rule which remained in force.[981] The complexity introduced by these various interests in the settlement of confiscations is illustrated in the case of Diego López, a merchant of Zamora, reconciled in the auto de fe of Valladolid, in June, 1520. He kept no books and the number of debits and credits rendered his affairs exceedingly complicated; moreover the paternal estate had never been divided between him and his brothers, while his wife put in claims for her dowry and share of the ganancias. In this perplexity the only solution was a compromise, which was reached by the wife and brothers agreeing to pay four hundred and fifty thousand maravedís in instalments, giving adequate security.[982] The Valencia court of confiscations, however, invented a method of evading the wifely claim to the accretions for, in 1532, when Angela Pérez, widow of Luis Gilabert, burnt for heresy, demanded her dowry of three thousand sueldos and the creix, the court ordered the receiver to pay the dowry but refused the creix on the ground that the date of his committing heresy showed that he could not lawfully make any gains.[983]

The exemption from confiscation of those who came in under Edicts of Grace, confessed and were reconciled, gave rise to an impressive illustration of the passionate greed aroused among all classes by the legalized spoliation of the New Christians and the corollary that they had no rights. Prelates and chapters of churches, abbots and priors of convents, rectors of hospitals and pious institutions and other ecclesiastics and laymen, who had mortgaged their properties to the heretics or had sold ground-rents to them or otherwise hypothecated them, repudiated their engagements and would render no satisfaction, whereby, we are told, many were deterred from seeking reconciliation. A more practical objection was that those who were thus despoiled were hindered in paying the heavy fines laid upon them by the inquisitors. Ferdinand and Isabella therefore applied to Innocent VIII for a remedy which he furnished, in 1486, by a brief in which, after reciting the above, he granted to those thus reconciled the mortgages and censos and other liens which they held on properties, forbidding the debtors from claiming release and pronouncing invalid any judgements which they might obtain.[984]

***

While thus the Spanish Inquisition, in some respects, dealt more liberally than its medieval predecessor with the unfortunates subjected to its operations, it was ruthlessly systematic in its absorption of everything that was not covered by the above exceptions. It was in vain that, in 1486, Innocent VIII--probably induced by the gold of the Conversos--represented to the sovereigns that, as the confiscations had been conceded to them, it would stimulate the penitents to be firm in the faith if their property was restored to those who were reconciled.[985] It was much more profitable for greed to disguise itself as zeal for religion, as when, in 1533, at the Córtes of Monzon, Valencia petitioned that an exemption from confiscation granted to the forcibly converted Moriscos should be extended to their children, and the Suprema replied that confiscation was the penalty most dreaded and that which most deterred from heresy; as for relying on the terror of burning as a preventive, the fact was that the Church received to reconciliation all who repented and, if they were not punished with confiscation, they would enjoy immunity.[986] In the same spirit, Bishop Simancas argued that it was for the public benefit that the children of heretics should be beggared and therefore the old laws which allowed Catholic children to inherit had justly been abrogated.[987]

This heartless remark indicates that, by the middle of the sixteenth century, there was no compassion for the helpless offspring, but at first there was some responsibility felt for them, possibly through a reminiscence of the old laws. The Instructions of 1484 provide that, when the children of those condemned to the stake or to perpetual prison are under age and unmarried, they were to be given to respectable Catholics or to religious, to be brought up in the faith, and a record of such cases was to be kept, for it was the intention of the sovereigns that, if they proved to be good Christians, they should have alms, especially the girls, to enable them to marry or to enter religion.[988] There is no trace of any systematic attempt to carry out this humane provision, but when cases of special hardship were called to Ferdinand's attention, he occasionally was moved to make liberal concessions. When, however, in 1486, the inquisitors of Saragossa asked for authority to grant relief to some poor culprits, not very guilty, who were encumbered with daughters likely to be forced to evil courses, the canny monarch evidently distrusted this sudden access of benevolence and, while approving the kindliness of the suggestion, he said that he was better acquainted than they with the people of Saragossa and less likely to be deceived, so they could send him the names of the parties, their properties and the number of their daughters, when he would determine what should be done.[989] It was evidently a question only of kindly impulses; there was no obligation, moral or legal and, as the wants of the Holy Office grew more urgent in the shrinkage of the stream of confiscations, inquisitors like Simancas argued that the service of God required the sacrifice of the innocents.

***

In practice, everything on which the officials could lay their hands under any pretext was swept remorselessly into the fisc. Even the bedding and clothes of those led out to execution at the autos de fe were seized, as appears from occasional donations of them to officials.[990] When, in 1495, Charles VIII occupied Naples, it became a place of refuge for fugitives from Spain, but the pious skippers of the vessels carrying them not infrequently served God by stripping their defenceless passengers and carrying home the spoils. This was an invasion of the rights of the crown which vindicated itself by sending to Biscay and Guipúzcoa Anton Sánchez de Aguirre to search for the jewels and merchandise thus taken from heretics and sell them for the benefit of the fisc.[991] In 1513, when Jayme de Marrana, scrivener of the court of Segorbe, was condemned, all his subordinates were called upon to surrender the fees which they had received during his term of office.[992] A dying man could not make even a pious bequest if his natural heir was a heretic, for when, in 1514, Nicholas de Medina, a merchant of Seville returning from France, died at Bayonne in the Hôpital du Saint-Esprit and bequeathed to it a bill of exchange for a hundred and twenty-six ducats, the procurator of the hospital came to Seville to collect it. Villacis, the receiver there, promptly sequestrated it on the ground that Medina's heir, Rodrigo de Córdova, had been condemned for heresy and, although the Suprema finally released it, this was done as an act of charity to the hospital.[993] The same rule applied when there was heresy in the ascendants. Juan Francisco Vitalis, a native of Majorca, was settled in Rome as a merchant. He desired to trade with Spain but feared to do so, for his father and grandfather had been condemned for heresy and any merchandise or funds that he might send would be liable to confiscation as constructively derived from them. He therefore, in 1511, applied for a safe-conduct for his goods which Ferdinand issued, exempting them from seizure by the Inquisition; it was good however, only during the royal pleasure and for six months after its withdrawal should be notified to Vitalis or be publicly proclaimed in Valencia.[994]

Heresy shed around it an infection which contaminated everything with which it came in contact. Not only was a ship carrying heretics forfeited but also its cargo. In 1501, Vicencio de Landera, a merchant of Gaeta, shipped some cotton by a Biscayan vessel for Alicante. On her arrival the receiver seized the cargo because she carried two persons condemned by the Inquisition, but the Bishop of Gaeta, head chaplain to Ferdinand's sister the Queen of Naples, brought influence to bear, and the king ordered Landera to be paid the proceeds of his cotton.[995] Apparently the other owners of the cargo had no redress. Ferdinand was more obdurate, in 1511, when a ship and its cargo were condemned in Seville for carrying heretics. This included a quantity of pepper belonging to a Portuguese merchant named Juan Francisco. King Manoel interposed to protect his subject, when Ferdinand replied that he had ordered justice done but that the Inquisition had represented that Francisco had bought the pepper from King Manoel and had paid for it with bills of exchange drawn by heretics, and thus with heretic money, which was held to forfeit the pepper.[996]

ALIENATIONS INVALIDATED

This policy was not merely transient. In 1634 the Inquisition seized the goods and credits of Portuguese merchants, residents of Holland, Hamburg and France, trading with Spain. Agents had been sent abroad to secure evidence of their Judaism; they naturally sought to defend their property and presented certificates of their orthodoxy; the affair dragged on and, in 1636, Doctor Juan de Gosa presented an elaborate opinion in justification of this, proving that the property must be confiscated, although the owners were not Spaniards, nor domiciled in Spain, nor had committed heresy in Spain. His argument was based on the principle of the canon law that the heretic had no rights and that any Catholic could seize and despoil him; heresy is a crime all-pervading and not limited to the spot where it is committed for it is an injury to the whole Christian Republic. No evidence was required, for it was notorious that the Portuguese absented themselves in order to indulge their heretical proclivities and that they frequented the synagogues in Amsterdam and elsewhere. The Inquisition was to hold the property and, for greater justification, to summon by edict the owners to appear and defend it within a fixed term, or it could appoint defenders to act for them, but in no case was it to raise the sequestration or surrender the property.[997] It is superfluous to point out the effect of all this on Spanish commerce.

***

As regards property alienated subsequently to the commission of heresy, the only limitation on its confiscation is found in the provision prohibiting interference with transactions anterior to 1479.[998] All later ones were subject to forfeiture, without compensation to the purchaser, unless, indeed, he had made improvements, the value of which was reimbursed to him. The frequency of these cases and the hardship to which they exposed innocent third parties are amply illustrated by the numerous appeals to Ferdinand for relief, which, be it said to his credit, he often granted. The cloud thus thrown on the title to all property that had passed through the hands of New Christians, at any time subsequent to 1479, continued to hang over it, and the Inquisition grew stricter in the interpretation of its rights. A letter of

May 6, 1539, from the Suprema to the inquisitor of Saragossa, says that he is reported to have decided that, when a person is condemned or reconciled with confiscation, and has alienated real property subsequently to the commission of heresy, if the purchaser is required to surrender it to the fisc, he is entitled to reimbursement of the purchase-money. The inquisitor is therefore summoned to state his authority for this decision, as law and custom are to the contrary and it is so practised.[999] This was peremptory and it is not likely that the question was raised again, although it took no count of the rule, which Simancas soon afterwards tells us was still in vigor, that if the purchase-money or what represents it is found in the confiscated estate, restitution should be made to the purchaser.[1000] The Spanish Inquisition preferred to both keep the money and take the property.

***

Ferdinand and Isabella manifested liberality in setting free the Christian slaves of confiscated estates, and this was extended by the Instructions of 1484, at the cost of those reconciled under Edicts of Grace, for, though they were not subject to confiscation, their Christian slaves were manumitted.[1001] It was, perhaps, a kindly care that kept these freedmen in a species of serfdom, for Instructions about 1500 direct the inquisitors to place them with proper persons under agreements as to wages and, if they are not reasonably treated, to transfer them to other masters.[1002] Embarrassing cases sometimes arose, such as that in which a slave was owned jointly by a good Catholic and a condemned heretic, but it would seem, from a decision in 1531, that the manumitted half carried with it into freedom the enslaved half, and the Catholic owner had no redress.[1003] The inquisitors did not always respond to the humane intentions of the Instructions; they seem to have sometimes kept slaves for themselves, in place of setting them free, for which, in 1516, they were rebuked and were also ordered that, during the trials of the owners, the slaves should be hired out and their wages be strictly accounted for--all of which points to current abuses. These did not cease for, in 1525, Dr. Mercader, in a visitation of Sicily, found similar ones flourishing.[1004]

While thus considerate of the slaves of culprits, confiscation seems sometimes to have extended to the persons of the culprits themselves. One of the few letters concerning the Inquisition, in which Isabella joins with Ferdinand, is of December 28, 1498, addressed to the Count of Cifuentes, Governor of Seville, ordering him, for the service of God and good execution of justice, to take all the Jews condemned for heresy, now held as prisoners by the Abbot of San Pedro, and sell them as slaves at such prices as he deems fit, the proceeds to be handed over to the receiver and be applied to the debts and necessities of the tribunal. An intimation of a similar kind is made, November 6, 1500, respecting Maestre Luis Carpano of Antequera and his wife, who are described as confiscated to the royal fisc, with all their property, real and personal.[1005]

ROUTINE OF BUSINESS

In the rigor of collection, debtors to the confiscated estates, who were unable to pay, were imprisoned without mercy. Thus, in 1490, the judge of confiscations at Segovia orders the alguazil to seize the lands and goods and money of Don Mosé de Cuellar, who was indebted in the sum of 393,000 maravedís to the late Gonzalo de Cuellar, regidor of Buitrago, burnt for heresy; if he cannot find property enough to satisfy the debt he is to seize the person of Don Mosé and confine him in the public prison of Segovia.[1006] It was the same with husbands who were liable for the dowries of their wives, as we have seen in the case of Don Pedro Gascon (p. 334). Forbearance, however, was sometimes found to be better policy. In 1509 Sancho Martínez of Hellin was sentenced to pay 50,000 maravedís for the dowry of his wife whose parents had been reconciled. He pleaded poverty to the Suprema, which ordered that, if his property was insufficient, he should not be imprisoned and that, at the auction of his effects he should be allowed to purchase to the amount of 10,000 or 12,000 maravedís on a year's credit. The event showed the wisdom of the arrangement. The auction realized 17,000; he was the purchaser and paid for it at the expiration of the year. He accumulated, as the years went by, 100,000 maravedís and the judge ordered execution on him for the 33,000 still due on the dowry. Again he appealed to the Suprema, some members of which doubted whether his subsequent acquisitions were liable and the matter was compromised, July 5, 1519, by ordering him to pay half the deficiency.[1007] These instances are not without interest as illustrations of the manner in which this gigantic spoliation was effected through more than a couple of centuries.

***

The elaborate system adopted is revealed to us in the records of the Valencia court of confiscations in 1530 and 1531. When an arrest was made with sequestration, the receiver opened an account in his Libro de Manifestaciones, in which the notary of sequestrations entered all the items of the inventory. Then followed the audiencia de hacienda and the summons to debtors, to declare their obligations, which were likewise entered. If the prisoner was engaged in trade, his books were examined and all debts were duly placed in the same record. Information of all kinds was diligently sought and, no matter how vague and worthless, was similarly recorded. Much of this was obtained from prisoners, who testified to gossip heard from cell-companions in the dreary hours of prolonged confinement. Thus, July 9, 1527, Violante Salvador testified that Leonor Benin told her that Angela Parda, when arrested, had entrusted certain small coins to Leonor Manresa. Angela Parda and Leonor Bonin were both burnt and Violante Salvador was reconciled. Leonor Manresa, when summoned to account for the deposit, denied it under oath and, as there was no other witness, the claim for a few pennies was abandoned.[1008]

The persistence with which these shadowy claims were pursued is illustrated in the case of Rafael Moncada, arrested in 1524. A certain Sor Catalina testified that she had heard say, by some one whose name she could not recall, that Moncada had said that, during the revolt of the Germanía (1520-1522), he had hidden a large amount of goods. His wife, or widow, Violante, when summoned, declared that during the troubles he had hidden some silks in the dye-house; when peace was restored, he had taken them out and when, two years later, he was arrested, they were among the effects sequestrated. She was brought forward again and again, always adhering to the same story, and it was not until 1531 that she was discharged.[1009]

This persistence is explained by the fact that the receiver was responsible for every item entered by the notary of sequestrations unless he could show that it was not collectable, to the satisfaction of the judge, who would then relieve him by a sentencia de diligencias, signifying that he had made due exertion. The care thus induced in following up the minutest fragments of property is manifested in a petition presented by the receiver, March 4, 1531, to the effect that he had made every effort to recover fourteen sueldos, the dowry given by Pere Barbera and Grabiel Barbera to their sister Leonor Barbera on her marriage to Grabiel Mas. More than twenty years ago Pere Barbera was burnt in effigy, Mas went to the Canaries covered with debts and died there poor. Leonor died eighteen years ago, leaving her property to Pere's son Anrich and he, too, had been reconciled with confiscation. Anrich was called and duly interrogated and then the judge allowed the entry to be cancelled.[1010]

POWERS OF RECEIVERS

Besides the excommunication incurred by all who did not voluntarily reveal their indebtedness to a confiscated estate, the receiver was clothed with ample powers enabling him to perform his duties thoroughly. When the first appointments were made for Aragon, in 1484, all officials, secular and ecclesiastic, were required to assist him when called upon, under pain of the royal wrath and three thousand gold florins.[1011] Apparently this was found insufficient, for the formula in a commission issued, September 5, 1519, to Alonso de Gumiel, receiver of Ciudad Rodrigo, sets forth that, if any one refused or delayed to deliver up confiscated property, the receiver could impose penalties at discretion and these penalties were confirmed in advance, while every one, of whatever station, was required to obey his orders under the same discretional penalties.[1012] It is easy to imagine the wrong and oppression which an unprincipled official could inflict, under powers so vague and arbitrary, and the terror which the office shed around it is exemplified in a Valencia case, decided in 1532. September 2, 1528, Noffre Calatayut mustered courage to present to the court of confiscations a petition setting forth that, in 1507, as heir to his father, he became liable for a violario--a sort of annuity--of fifty sueldos a year, redeemable at fifteen libras, due to Luis Alcanys, which he paid sometimes to Jayme Alcanys and sometimes to a daughter of Joan Alcanys. Jayme was condemned and the receiver seized the violario. Through fear of the consequences, Noffre continued to pay it up to the present time, although it did not belong to Jayme and the parties on whose lives it was based, Guillem Rancon de Belvis and Johan Voluda, had been dead for twenty years. The case must have been bitterly contested for it was not until April 17, 1532, that a decision was rendered in his favor, to the effect that the violario had not belonged to Jayme Alcanys and that the lives had ended a quarter of a century before, wherefore the receiver was ordered to refund all the payments that he had received.[1013] It was fortunate that a court was sometimes found to check the lawless rapacity of the receivers.

***

It would not be easy to exaggerate the confusion and the hardships caused by the enforcement of confiscation, especially in the early period. The New Christians had filled so many positions of public and private trust, and the trade of Spain was so largely in their hands, that the long procession of arrests, accompanied with sequestration and followed by confiscation, could not but be paralyzing and affect interests far wider than those of the victims and their kindred. Even after the first wild torrent of persecution, the industry of the tribunals was constantly involving men hitherto unsuspected, bringing ruin or inextricable perplexities on the innocent who had chanced to have dealings with them. The backward search, moreover, included into the heresies of those long since dead, vitiated old transactions and invalidated titles to property that had long been held by innocent owners. During Ferdinand's life we hear of many of these cases brought before him on appeal, and for the most part not in vain, for, when the injustice of his receivers was clear, he was prompt to revoke their action, and when there was doubt he would often kindly waive a portion or the whole of his claim. A few typical instances will illustrate some of the various aspects of the troubles which pervaded the land and crippled the development of Spanish prosperity.

HARDSHIPS ON THE INNOCENT

Early in 1498, Ferdinand was startled to learn that the Barcelona tribunal had arrested Jaime de Casafranca and had sequestrated his property. Casafranca was deputy of the royal treasurer-general of Catalonia; he had served long and faithfully, without suspicion of his orthodoxy, and possessed the king's fullest confidence. In his hands were the moneys of the crown and also sums sent thither for the repairs of the castles of Roussillon, and the embargo laid on these funds threatened serious complications. Had private interests only been concerned, the embarrassment would have been irremediable, but Ferdinand set aside the established routine by ordering all the sequestrations to be placed in the hands of his advocate-fiscal, who was directed to employ the moneys as instructions should be sent to him and to furnish an inventory so that public and private property could be separated. Then a messenger to Italy had just been despatched in hot haste with orders to Casafranca to provide immediate passage for him to Genoa and, as delay would be most injurious, this must be seen to at once. Besides this there were two chests of silk, in the name of Gabriel Sánchez, but belonging to the king, and two chests of paper for the royal secretary and some horse-covers and tools, the property of the treasurer-general, and some books belonging to the heirs of González Ruiz, all of which had to be looked after. Moreover Ferdinand recommended Casafranca to the kindly consideration of the tribunal, as the accusation might be malicious, and he charged the conscience of the inquisitors to observe justice. Casafranca, however, in the end was convicted and Ferdinand consoled his children with some fragments of the confiscation.[1014]

The arbitrary comprehensiveness of inquisitorial procedure and the difficulties thrown in the way of the New Christians are exemplified in the case of Gilabert de Santa Cruz the younger. When his father, of the same name, was penanced, the son made a compromise with the receiver, under which he received a portion of his father's property in settlement of his mother's dowry and some other claims. Then he married María Cid and pledged this property in the nuptial contract. In 1500 the father was again arrested, when the property was at once sequestrated again; he was living with the son, under which pretext all the latter's household effects, even to the clothes and trinkets of the wife, were included in the inventory. Moreover, the son was a member of a firm who employed the father as a factor, on which account all their goods and books were sequestrated, threatening the ruin of their business. In this emergency the only recourse was to Ferdinand, who responded with instructions to the tribunal that his will was that injustice should be done to no one; it was to examine the papers and at once to act according to the facts, without oppressing or injuring the parties in interest and without awaiting the result of the father's trial.[1015]

The insecurity which overshadowed all transactions is illustrated by the case of Diego de Salinas of Avila, who had received as a marriage portion with the daughter of González Gómez, since deceased, a rent of forty-five fanegas of wheat, which the latter, in 1499, had bought for the purpose from Rodrigo del Barco for 30,000 maravedís. In 1501 it was found that Rodrigo had inherited this rent from his grandfather, Pedro Alvárez, whose fame and memory were condemned, and it was legally claimed by the fisc. Luckily for Diego, he had rendered services to the sovereigns, in consideration of which they granted him 25,000 maravedís of the rent; it was to be valued and he was to pay whatever it was worth over and above that sum.[1016]

Ferdinand's kindly interposition was sought by Pascual de Vellido, who had sold to Pedro de Santa Cruz a house for 1000 sueldos, reserving the right of redemption at the same price. Pedro was reconciled with confiscation and Pascual applied to the receiver to allow him to redeem the house but, as he had mislaid his carta de gracia, he was denied, and the house was sold for 1600 sueldos. In 1502 he found the document and claimed the excess of 600 sueldos which the receiver refused to pay, until Ferdinand ordered him to do so, because Pascual was poor and had a daughter to marry.[1017]

It was by no means the Conversos only who suffered in this way, for Old Christians were constantly finding themselves embarrassed by the cloud thrown on titles. In 1514, Don Pero Nuñez de Guzman, Clavero, or treasurer of the Order of Calatrava and majordomo of the Infante Ferdinand, represented to the king that his uncle, Luis Osorio, Bishop of Jaen, had a majordomo named Rodríguez Jabalin who fell in debt to him and settled with certain properties renting for 4500 maravedís. The bishop died in 1496 and Guzman, who inherited the properties, gave them to the dean and chapter of Jaen to found a perpetual mass for his uncle's soul. The chapter sold them and, in 1514, the Inquisition seized them because Jabalin had inherited them from an ancestor whose fame and memory were condemned. Guzman represented that, if the present possessors were ejected, the chapter would have to make it good; the mass thus would be discontinued and, at his prayer, Ferdinand ordered the seizure to be withdrawn.[1018]

REVIVAL OF OLD CLAIMS

As an insurance against such losses, sellers and purchasers sometimes sought to procure, from the king or the tribunals, licences to convey property, real and personal. This was probably rare, as I have met with but a single case, that of Johan Garriga, his wife and children who, in 1510, from Majorca, petitioned Ferdinand for licence to sell his property and faculties for others to purchase. Ferdinand referred the matter to the Mallorquin inquisitor, saying that he did not know whether the property was in any way liable to the fisc, but if the inquisitor thought the licence ought to be granted he was empowered to issue it with the royal confirmation.[1019] If Garriga obtained his licence he probably had to pay roundly for it, for the officials were often by no means nice in the abuse of their unlimited power. In this same year, 1510, Antonio Mingot of Alicante complained to Ferdinand that he had been sentenced to pay 294 libras as a debt due to Gonzalo Roiz, condemned for heresy. He had appealed to the inquisitor-general, who referred the matter back to the inquisitors but, before they had decided the case, the receiver put up at auction property of his worth more than 4000 ducats, and then, for a payment of 100 ducats, postponed the sale to St. John's day. Mingot sought to appeal to the king, but could not get copies of the necessary papers, delays being interposed to carry the matter over the postponement. Ferdinand warmly expressed his displeasure, in a letter of May 21st, ordering copies of all papers to be furnished and proceedings to be suspended for seventy days thereafter--but the peccant officials were not punished.[1020]

Old claims, long since satisfied, were constantly turning up and prosecuted, from which the only recourse would seem to be the king. A few months later than the last case, he had a petition from the people of the hamlets of Scaviella and La Mata stating that on November 3, 1487, they had paid off a censo of 400 sueldos to Leonart de Santangel and now, after nearly a quarter of a century, the receiver demands it of them on the ground that Santangel at the time was in prison and incapable of receiving the money. Ferdinand ordered the receiver not to trouble them, as they were ignorant peasants and the payment was made with the assent of their lord, the Bishop of Huesca. Similarly, in 1511, Domingo Just of Saragossa represented that, in 1484, he had given an obligation for 3000 sueldos, as security for the issue to him of a bill of exchange on Rome. On his return he had been unable to secure the surrender of the paper, in consequence of the flight of the holder, but it had turned up and was now demanded of him. Ferdinand ordered him to be relieved on his taking an oath guaranteed by excommunication.[1021]

Old and forgotten heresies were exploited with equal rigor. In 1510, Pedro de Espinosa of Baza represented to Ferdinand that, when Baza was recovered from the Moors (December 4, 1489) he married Aldonza Rodríguez, niece and adopted daughter of the esquire Lazaro de Avila and Catalina Ximenes and, on Lazaro's death, they went to live with Catalina. Now Catalina has been condemned for an act of heresy committed when a child in her father's house (probably a fast, or eating unleavened bread) and her property, worth some 18,000 ducats, has been confiscated. In view of his services in the war with Granada, Espinosa begged that the confiscation be remitted and Ferdinand liberally assented, to the amount of 18,000 ducats.[1022]

With the death of Ferdinand these frequent appeals to the crown become fewer and are met with less kindliness, though the call for relief from the rigor of the law was undiminished, as will be seen from the case of the monastery of Bonifaza. In 1452, Pedro Roy, priest of Tortosa, sold to Dalvido Tolosa of Salcet for 400 libras a rent of 20 libras per annum secured on certain property, and this property Roy subsequently sold to the monastery. In 1475, Dalvido died, leaving the rent to his son, Luis Tolosa, from whom the monastery redeemed it, March 1, 1488. Luis, or his memory, was condemned and, about 1519, the receiver demanded of the monastery the 400 libras and all arrearages of rent, claiming that the redemption had been in fraud of the fisc, as Luis's heresy antedated it. The case was clear and judgement against the monastery was rendered, June 7, 1519. Pleading poverty, it applied for relief to Charles V, who instructed the receiver that, if it would pay 100 libras during July and 50 more within a year, he should release the claim.[1023]

JURISDICTION EXCLUSIVE

The avidity of the Inquisition did not diminish with time, nor its disastrous influence on all exposed to its claims. In 1615, a German Protestant, known as Juan Cote, was condemned by the Toledo tribunal to perpetual prison and confiscation. He was then twenty-four years old and had been taken, in early youth, by his uncle Juan Aventrot, to the Canaries, where the uncle married María Vandala, a widow with four children, who died in 1609, leaving one-fifth of her estate to Cote. In 1613 Aventrot sent him to Spain with a letter to the Duke of Lerma, which led to the discovery of his heresy. Proceedings for the confiscation of his share in the widow's estate dragged on interminably. September 7, 1634, the Suprema ordered the Toledo tribunal to furnish papers in the case, including a certificate of the date of Cote's heresy, which, in view of his having been brought up as a Protestant, it fixed at the age of fourteen, when he could be considered responsible. In this the Inquisition overreached itself, for in 1635 the Canary tribunal reported that the heirs alleged Cote to have been incapable of inheritance, seeing that he was brought up as a Protestant and both he and his uncle had pretended to be Catholics, and they called for a copy of the sentence to demonstrate this. The unabashed Suprema then shifted its ground and procured, September 10, 1640, from the Toledo tribunal, a certificate that Cote had commenced his heretical acts in 1613, when he brought the letter to Lerma and delivered it to Philip III, in August, 1614. How the affair terminated and how much longer it was protracted we have no means of knowing, but the Inquisition had at least succeeded in tying up the estate for twenty-five years.[1024]

The hardship of the system on innocent third parties was intensified by the fact that in this, as in all else, the Inquisition claimed and exercised exclusive jurisdiction. There was no appeal to a disinterested tribunal but only from the judge of confiscations to the Suprema, which was as much interested as its subordinates in obtaining as large returns as possible from all sources. As these fell off, the liberality, so often displayed by Ferdinand, was no longer in place and it became inexorable. Confiscations were specially assigned to the payment of salaries and the judges were thus directly interested in their productiveness. The danger and the humiliation of this were fully recognized. In his futile plan of reform, in 1518, Charles V proposed to assign to the officials definite salaries and relieve them from dependence on the sentences which they pronounced.[1025] In 1523, he received from his privy council a memorial in which, among other matters, he was urged to see that proper appointments were made in the Inquisition and that they had fitting salaries from other sources, so that they should live neither by beggary nor on the blood of their victims, and that their labors should tend to instruction rather than to destruction and to rendering Christianity odious to the infidel.[1026] The Córtes of Castile remonstrated repeatedly to the same effect. Those of 1537 complained of the salaries being thus defrayed; those of 1548 asked Charles to provide fixed salaries so as to put an end to the notorious evil of the judges paying themselves by fining and confiscating, and again, in 1555, they pointed out that, besides the danger of judges deriving their pay from the condemnations which they decree, it diminished the respect due to the Holy Office. To this the answer was merely that the matter has been considered and will be fittingly decided.[1027] Spanish finances, however, were never in a position to assure the Inquisition that, if it paid over its receipts to the crown, it would get them back in appropriations for salaries and expenses. As we have seen, it kept them under its own control and it jealously repelled all intrusion, even by the crown, on its exclusive jurisdiction over confiscations.

***

This position had not been won without a struggle. January 20, 1486, Ferdinand empowered the inquisitors of Saragossa to act as judges in the complicated litigation which was growing, and he commissioned them to decide all questions thence arising. On March 31 he reiterated the injunction; if the secular judges were allowed to intervene, everything would be lost; they were to be restrained by censures, as had already been done and, if royal letters or exequutorias were required, they would be promptly furnished. There evidently was active resistance to this for, on May 5th he wrote that all questions must be settled by ecclesiastical law for, if the fueros were admitted, he would never get justice. The inquisitors must therefore act, the receiver and fiscal must try the cases before them alone, and they must be speedy.[1028] When persecution was active, this threw upon the inquisitors too heavy a burden and one, moreover, for which they were unprepared, for they were theologians and not canon lawyers. The assessors, it is true, assisted them, but a special tribunal evidently was a necessity and this was furnished by the erection of courts of confiscation, presided over by the jueces de los bienes. In Castile, where the fueros were not an impediment, this had already been tried. As early as 1484, there is an allusion to such an official[1029] and a commission as such was issued, April 10, 1485, to the Bachiller Juan Antonio Serrano, of Córdova.[1030] For some time, however, such appointments continued to be unusual. In 1490, we hear of Juan Pérez de Nieva as juez de los bienes in Segovia,[1031] but for the most part the inquisitors and their assessors continued to perform the functions and, when a juez existed, his position was subordinate, as appears by a letter of Ferdinand, August 27, 1500, to an assessor, telling him that the juez was only to relieve him in ordinary cases and not to tie his hands in important ones.[1032]

Inquisitors also continued to act for, in 1509, we hear of Niño de Villalobos as inquisitor and juez in Cartagena and a certain Dembredo as filling both positions in Seville, while as late as 1514 Toribio de Saldaña is spoken of as inquisitor and juez.[1033] With the gradual disappearance of the assessors, however, the necessity of a separate functionary became apparent, and the courts of confiscations grew to be an established feature of the tribunals, so long as confiscations continued to be numerous and profitable. Towards the end, when they had become infrequent, the senior inquisitor performed the duties of the juez.[1034]

Ferdinand, meanwhile, persisted in asserting the exclusive jurisdiction of the Inquisition over all matters connected with confiscation, recognizing that his interests would suffer if the secular courts were allowed to intervene. The establishment of this as a rule of practice is attributable to the year 1508. The receiver of Jaen had sold a confiscated house to Diego García el rico for forty-two thousand maravedís on a year's credit. When the term expired, García, instead of paying, exhibited a grant made to him of the house by Philip of Austria. After Philip's brief career was over, his acts were not treated with much respect, and the juez de los bienes refused to recognize the grant, on the ground that it was not countersigned by the Suprema. García appealed to the chancellery of Granada which ordered the grant to be recognized, but Ferdinand interposed, January 18, 1508, commanding the judges to keep their hands off and not to interfere with the Inquisition, in any way, either in its civil or criminal jurisdiction.[1035] The chancellery did not take this kindly and invited, in 1510, another rebuke for meddling in suits concerning sequestrations and confiscations; if any cases of the kind were pending they must be forthwith remitted to the tribunals to which they belonged, and in future nothing of the kind was to be entertained.[1036]

It was impossible that this monstrous policy, of making it the judge in its own cases, should be submitted to without resistance, but it was stoutly maintained by the crown. The tribunal of Jaen invested some of its funds in a censo created by a cleric of Alcalá. He died in 1524, when his mother and brothers attacked the censo as being secured on a property in which they held undivided interests, and another party came forward with an incumbrance on the same property. The Inquisition seized it and also collected some debts due to the deceased, which reduced its claim to seven or eight thousand maravedís. The other parties appealed to the chancellery of Granada, which entertained the case, but the Inquisition invoked Charles V who, in letters of May 19 and July 7, 1525, repeated the commands of Ferdinand to abstain from all interference. The Inquisition was the sole judge and parties thinking themselves aggrieved must appeal to the Suprema.[1037] Still, those who smarted under injustice sought relief in the secular courts, which were nothing loath to aid them; complaints were loud on both sides and competencias were frequent until, as we have seen, they led to the settlement of 1553, in which Prince Philip emphatically forbade cognizance of such matters to all courts and ministers of justice, and confined appellate jurisdiction strictly to the Suprema.[1038]

As has been seen in other matters, the great high court of Granada was recalcitrant and persisted in asserting its jurisdiction. In 1571 and 1573 it entertained cases relating to confiscations, in both of which it was told by Philip II to hold its hand and not to meddle with such affairs. Despite this, in 1575, it intervened in a case which suggests the reasonable objection felt to rendering the Inquisition a judge in its own cause. The creditors of Don Diego de Castilla had embargoed his property and the court had placed it in the hands of an administrator for their benefit; but the tribunal of Murcia chanced to hold a censo of his for a thousand ducats; the juez de los bienes stepped in, seized the property, sold it and kept the money. The chancellery was seeking to obtain justice for the other creditors; it arrested the juez and threw him into prison, when Philip again intervened, ordering his liberation and the abandonment of the case.[1039]

COMPOSITIONS

It illustrates the independence of the kingdoms of the crown of Aragon that, when the tax-collectors of Valencia levied taxes and imposts on confiscated property and its sale, Charles V was obliged to appeal to the Holy See for its prevention. Clement VII obligingly granted a bull, July 7, 1525, forbidding this under pain of excommunication and a fine of a thousand ducats to the papal camera; the inquisitor-general was named as conservator and judge to enforce it by censures and interdict and invocation of the secular arm, which doubtless put an end to the practice.[1040]

**

As the operations of the Inquisition developed, an additional source of gain was found in speculating upon the terror pervading the New Christian communities. Whether the idea originated in their mercantile instincts, or in the desire of the sovereigns for prompt realization, cannot be determined, but it was in essence a kind of rude and imperfect insurance against certain contingencies of confiscation, for which those in danger were willing to pay a heavy premium. As early as September 6,

1482, in a letter of Ferdinand to Luis Cabanilles, Governor of Valencia, there occurs an allusion to an arrangement of this kind, made with the Conversos of that city, under which apparently they had agreed to pay a certain sum in lieu of the confiscations and had appointed assessors to apportion the share of each individual. Some of those thus assessed refused to pay, and Ferdinand ordered them to be coerced by imprisonment.[1041] What were the exact terms of this we have no means of knowing but, on June 6, 1488, he made another bargain with the Valencia Conversos, who were reconciled under an Edict of Grace, by which they paid him for exemption from confiscation--apparently rather a fresh impost, for this reconciliation substituted fines for confiscation. Then, April 6, 1491, he confirmed this and, for a further payment of five thousand ducats, he added exemption for heretical acts subsequently committed, if they did not amount to relapse, and for imperfect confessions made under the Edict of Grace--for, as we shall see hereafter, such confessions were frequently a source of danger arising from trifling omissions, construed by the inquisitors as rendering them fictitious and entailing relaxation. It is an indelible disgrace to Ferdinand that, in these compositions, he did not keep faith with those whose money he took. In 1499, the Suprema took exception to this arrangement, probably in consequence of complaints that it was violated by the seizure and sale of properties comprehended under it. Then Ferdinand declared that it had not been his intention to relieve from confiscation those whose confessions had been imperfect, whereupon the Suprema ordered the inquisitors and receiver to prosecute and confiscate the property of all such penitents in spite of the agreement. Even the hardened receiver Aliaga seems to have hesitated to obey these orders, for Ferdinand was obliged to write to him, September 27th, that they were to be executed notwithstanding the privilege and its confirmation.[1042]

The hardships inflicted on the innocent by this breach of faith are illustrated in a petition presented, in 1519, to Charles V by Juan and Beatriz Guimera, children of Bernat and Violante Guimera who, after the composition of 1488, had been condemned for imperfect confession and their property confiscated. Juan and Beatriz, with other children in the same position, appealed to Ferdinand who, under the provision of April 6, 1491, ordered the receiver to restore all such property. They received and enjoyed possession for twelve years, after which, under the orders of 1499 the inquisitors took it from them. From this they appealed, but were too poor to follow it up, and the Suprema declared the appeal abandoned. Now they prayed Charles for the restoration of their property and showed that, after the execution of their parents, they had paid all the instalments remaining of the composition. In view of this, Charles, as a special grace and in the exercise of the royal clemency, ordered--not that the property of which they had been robbed should be restored--but that the receiver should repay them what the inquisitors might find that they had paid of the composition after the death of their parents, without deducting therefrom the claim of the fisc for the income of the property during their twelve years' possession.[1043]

***

Even worse, if possible, was Ferdinand's course in a composition made, September 10, 1495, with the heirs and successors of all who in Aragon had died up to that time and whose memories had been or might in future be condemned. For the sum of five thousand ducats he abandoned, to those who contributed, all the confiscations of their inheritances and also the inheritances of those who refused to contribute, to be distributed among them in proportion to their contributions. Inferentially this was confirmed when, in 1499, in view of trouble with the receiver, at the prayer of the contributors, he appointed Vicent de Bordalva administrator of the property, to claim and hold it and distribute it to the owners. After seven years had passed, in 1502, he was seized with qualms of conscience at thus violating the canon law which incapacitated the children of heretics as inheritors. It is true that he might have assumed the property and then made a free gift of it, as was frequently done in special cases, but his scruples were too delicate for such a subterfuge. By letters of December 13, 1502, to the inquisitors and assessor, he ordered the seizure and confiscation of all the property thus devolved and the return to the contributors, in all cases where they were sufferers, of the moneys which they had paid--thus retaining the contributions of those who had not profited by the composition. This breach of faith made an immense sensation in Saragossa and even his son, the archbishop, ventured to remonstrate, when he replied sanctimoniously that he was acting by the advice of learned and God-fearing men, who had demonstrated to him that he could not, with a clear conscience and without peril to his soul, grant a privilege contrary to the canon law; the sufferers must have patience, for it was in accordance with the canons of holy Mother Church which were obligatory on him.[1044]

The inquisitors and receiver were not over-nice in utilizing their opportunity and complaints speedily came pouring in that, besides the inheritances, they seized all the property belonging to the heirs, including their acquisitions and the dowries of their wives, and that moreover they did not repay the contributions. Thus, before the month of December, 1502, was out, the brothers Buendia appealed to him; they had paid fifteen thousand sueldos to the composition and now the receiver had seized what they had inherited from their father; much of this they had sold; they had acquired other properties by their labor, they had inherited from their mother, who was an Old Christian, and had received dowries with their wives, all of which was included in the seizure. Ferdinand merely reported this to the inquisitor, with a vague order to do justice so as not to afford grounds for complaint. It is easy to conceive the confusion of titles, the multiplicity of suits and the amount of misery resulting from this arbitrary abrogation of a contract. Resistance was prolonged, but it was unavailing, for Ferdinand held good and repeated his peremptory orders, January 4 and March 8, 1503, July 8 and November 7, 1504 and October 7, 1508.[1045] It would appear, moreover, that many of the contributors who suffered never obtained a return of their money, for this formed the subject of one of the articles of the Aragonese Concordia of 1512, confirmed in the 1516 bull of Leo X, providing that whoever had joined in a composition for the property of the dead and had paid his money, if the deceased was subsequently convicted and the fisc seized his inheritance, he should recover from the estate what he had paid, provided the payment had not been made out of the effects of the deceased.[1046] It was thus admitted that the contracts were no bar to the Inquisition.

There were various forms of these compositions, insuring against the different risks and disabilities to which the property of the Conversos was exposed, but they all had this in common that the contributor threw his money into a pool from which his chance of deriving advantage was in the highest degree problematical. It is therefore a striking evidence of the desperation to which the New Christians were reduced that they were eager to grasp at these forlorn chances and to pour their money into the ever-gaping royal treasury, while Ferdinand, in spite of his conscientious scruples, was always ready to speculate on their despair. It is impossible now to say how many compositions were made, from first to last, but they probably covered nearly the whole of Spain, at one time or another. We have seen that there was one in Córdova, prior to 1500, which was highly profitable to the inquisitor who managed it and another of uncertain date in Andalusia (Vol. I, pp. 190, 220); there was one in Orihuela in 1492 and a second in Valencia in 1498 and, in 1515, there were others in the Biscayan provinces and in Cuenca. Occasionally, moreover, inquisitors were authorized to enter into such bargains with individuals, as in Majorca in 1498 and in Catalonia in 1512.[1047]

***

A specimen of these individual compositions is revealed to us in an investigation made in 1487, by Doctor Alfonso Ramírez, juez de los bienes de Toledo, into the accounts of Juan de Urría, the late receiver, who was reported to have defrauded the fisc of more than a million and a half maravedís. Pedro de Toledo had fled to Portugal, to escape trial, and his wife, Isabel Díaz, arranged with Urría for a royal letter of security and pardon for him, his property and his paternal inheritance, for which the price agreed upon was half a million maravedís, in addition to which Urría was promised a hundred florins for his services. Pedro returned and paid for the letter, when Isabel gave Urría thirteen gold cruzados and fourteen pieces of cloth, which he sold and claimed that he was five hundred maravedís short.[1048] This was productive but still more so was one, in 1514, by which Francisco Sánchez of Talavera ransomed the estate of his deceased father for a million maravedís.[1049]

These transactions justify the conclusion that persecution was largely a matter of finance as well as of faith. Such conviction is strengthened by the history of the greatest of the general compositions, a most prolonged and involved transaction, of which space will permit only the barest outline. It commenced with a composition, signed December 7, 1508, with Seville and Cádiz, by which, in consideration of twenty thousand ducats, there was made over to the penanced and condemned, or to their heirs, all confiscated property in suit, or that had not been discovered and seized, from the commencement of the Inquisition up to November 30th, except what was included in the auto de fe of October 29th. The property of those who did not join in the agreement and pay their assessments was liable to seizure and all amounts thus realized were to be deducted from the payment. There was also granted the valued privilege of going to and trading with the Indies, forbidden to all reconciliados. This was extended, October 10, 1509, in the name of Queen Juana, covering the archbishopric of Seville, the bishopric of Cádiz and the towns of Lepe, Ayamonte and la Redondilla, and providing for the payment of forty thousand ducats, for which the queen made to the contributors a donation of all real and personal property forfeit to her from persons reconciled and guilty of imperfect confessions or other offences prior to reconciliation; also all the property of those who had died reconciled or to be reconciled and forfeitable by reason of prior offences, together with all property confiscated on those who refused to contribute. All alienations made by contributors were confirmed to the purchasers and contributors were relieved from all penalties incurred for disregarding the disabilities inflicted on those reconciled and their descendants. On the other hand, it was expressly stated that the grant did not exempt the property of those who relapsed or committed offences subsequent to reconciliation, nor did it relieve them from prosecution in person or fame. After this, for some cause, the total payment was increased to eighty thousand ducats, of which sixty thousand were for the composition and twenty thousand for rehabilitation or removal of disabilities.

The first obstacle lay in the assembling of the enormous mass of papers relating to the old confiscations. The tribunal of Leon, which held some of them, refused to deliver them, and the same occurred with papers concerning Ecija, requiring repeated peremptory orders from Ferdinand to procure their deposit in the Castle of Triana for inspection. At last the unwieldy business was got under way. Assessors were appointed to make the assessments on contributors, but troubles arose and the whole affair was put in the hands of Pedro de Villacis, the experienced receiver of Seville, who had been instrumental in getting up the agreement of 1508. The work went on and large collections were made, although delays in payment incurred penalties which, by 1515, amounted to seven hundred and fifty thousand maravedís, to be paid to the tribunal of Seville--but it never got the money.[1050]

***

Encouraged by this initial success the scheme was extended over the kingdom of Granada, the bishoprics of Córdova, Jaen, Badajoz, Coria, and Plasencia and the province of Leon, the sum agreed upon for them being fifty-five thousand ducats. Complaints however arose about injustice in the assessments; payments were not forthcoming in time; difficulties apparently insuperable accumulated and Ferdinand, after consultation with Ximenes and the Suprema, revoked the composition. Then it was revived and Ferdinand, January 18, 1515, placed it in the hands of Villacis, whose instructions justify the assumption that, under the guise of an act of mercy, the whole scheme was merely the pretext for fresh exactions on the defenceless. He was ordered to proclaim the composition in all places within the districts concerned; to order all persons obligated to pay their contributions; those proposing to join were to appear before him by their procurators at a specified time and arrange the assessments to be paid by each place or person, such assessments being binding on the absent. As for those who refused to join, Villacis was empowered to levy on their property as being jointly liable and to sell it at auction, giving to the purchasers good and sufficient title, guaranteed by the crown, while all secular officials were required to give him whatever aid he required. Inquisitors were to do the same and were to commission as alguazils such persons as he might name. Letters were sent to the corregidors of the towns, telling them that some contributors refused to pay, and they were empowered to decide all such questions summarily and finally.[1051]

That the matter was really an unauthorized impost, enforced by the authority of the Inquisition, would appear not only from this admittance of secular jurisdiction but also from what we know as to the methods pursued in the original composition of Seville. Each town was assessed at a certain sum which it divided at discretion among the contributors. When Alcázar was assessed at a thousand ducats it remonstrated to Ferdinand, who kindly ordered execution suspended. Other places were not so fortunate and the pitiless exaction of the assessment provoked resistance. Thus in March, 1514, when, by order of the tribunal and as representative of Villacis, Fernando Royz went to San Lucar de Barrameda, he seized some slaves and other property and placed them in the prison for safe-keeping. The Duchess of Medina Sidonia ordered the alcalde to return them to their masters and would allow no further levies to be made. Ferdinand forthwith rebuked her, ordering her to assist the officials and never again to interfere in matters concerning the Inquisition. He also wrote to the inquisitors to inflict due punishment on the person and property of the alcalde and all connected with the affair; the levies and executions must proceed and the money be collected, for the last instalment of the composition was to be paid by the end of May.[1052]

This indicates that the Seville composition had been fairly productive, but the other had continued to drag. With the death of Ferdinand, in January, 1516, pressure was removed and resistance became general. A cédula issued in the name of Queen Juana, February 24th, states that those who were assessed were refusing to pay and were supported by nobles and magnates, wherefore the inquisitors of Seville, Córdova, Jaen and Leon were instructed to enforce the payments by levy and execution and to prosecute with all rigor those who impeded the collection, irrespective of their rank and dignity. This was ineffective. In Córdova, the Count of Cabra and the Marquis of Priego forced the agents of Villacis to abandon work among their vassals, and the latter compelled them to deposit sixty thousand maravedís which they had collected. It was in vain that the Governors of Castile ordered them to desist and when, in September, the Count of Cabra justified his persistence by stating that his people had paid their composition to Rodrigo of Madrid--who had organized the scheme--and he would not allow them to be coerced into duplicate payments, he and the marquis were told that Rodrigo had no authority and that his receipts were worthless, which suggests the impositions practised on the victims. In the lands of the Duke of Medina Sidonia the same opposition was offered and the high court of Granada took advantage of the opportunity by issuing mandates restraining the collection, nor is it likely that it respected a royal cédula of July 4th commanding it to abstain from interference.[1053]

***

This resistance was fully justified. Even before Ferdinand's death, the proceedings of Villacis and his underlings had aroused general indignation. At the Córtes of Burgos, in 1515, the procurators of Seville had called the attention of the nation to their extortions in a petition which set forth their misdeeds, doubtless with exaggeration, but which, coming from those not personally interested, must have had substantial foundation in fact. Villacis was accused of arbitrary assessments and of making up deficiencies by assessing again those who had already paid, of cruelty, extortion and fraud, of selling at auction property taken in execution, at unusual places and times, so that he and his friends could buy it in, of using the machinery of the composition to collect his private debts, of defrauding the fisc by false returns, of charging to the contributors the exorbitant fees and expenses of his collectors, although the agreement provided that the fisc should bear them, of rendering to the contributors only a partial account of his collections and refusing to complete it, and in this charging himself with only forty ducats as collected in the Canaries, when there was evidence that the amount was more than a thousand. In short, he was accused of abusing his arbitrary powers in almost every conceivable way to oppress the people and enrich himself, and numerous specific cases were cited in support of the allegations. The magistrates of Seville had endeavored to restrain him but he scorned their jurisdiction and therefore, in the name of the whole community, the king was supplicated to send to Seville some one empowered to investigate and punish and make restitution to those wrongfully despoiled.

It was impossible to ignore such an appeal made in the face of the nation, and the Licenciado Giron, one of the judges of the high court of Granada, was despatched to Seville, but only with power to investigate and report to the Suprema within sixty days. The time proved too short and, after exceeding it, he begged to be relieved on making a partial report. In December, 1516, the Licenciado Mateo Vázquez, a resident of Seville, was commissioned, with the same powers, to complete the investigation and also to enquire into many complaints coming from various places that, prior to the appointment of Villacis, Pedro del Alcázar and Francisco de Santa Cruz and their employees had made large collections, of which they had rendered no account; that they had retained more than a million of maravedís, while those who had paid them were subjected to levy and execution to enforce duplicate payments. Altogether the whole business would seem to have been a Saturnalia of spoliation and embezzlement. Vázquez undertook the task and, on September 17, 1517, he was ordered to furnish to Villacis a copy of the evidence to enable him to put in a defence, after which all the papers were to be submitted to the Suprema for its action.

If anything resulted from this it has left no trace in the documents. The influence of Villacis carried him through, for he was continued in office and went on with the work. August 13, 1518, Charles V ordered an audit of his accounts and payment of balances due, which he skilfully parried. A new assessment was ordered to make good any part of the eighty thousand ducats that might still be uncollected and this was given to him to enforce. The old methods were still pursued for, in March, 1519, Charles was obliged to write vigorously to the Count of Cabra, the Marquis of Priego and the alcalde mayor of the Marquis of Comares, who had again interfered with his collectors and stopped all proceedings in their lands.

DILAPIDATION

Charles's Flemish favorites were growing impatient to share in the elusive spoils. He had granted to his chamberlain, M. de Beaurains, the rest of the composition, but it was not forthcoming, nor were the accounts of Villacis. In January, 1519, he wrote to Torquemada, one of the Seville inquisitors, to enforce on Villacis, with the utmost rigor of the law, the payment to Beaurains of any amounts collected and not paid over, while, if there was a balance uncollected, Villacis was to assess it afresh and account for it to Beaurains. This produced nothing and, on March 24th Charles emphatically repeated the order, granting full power to enforce it with penalties at discretion. Villacis, however, had experience in eluding such demands and Ferdinand had not left much to glean. In 1515 he had divided up the Córdova composition, giving twenty thousand to the Inquisition and reserving thirty thousand for himself. Of this he had received twenty thousand and the remaining ten he granted to the Marquis of Denia, but when the latter presented this order to Villacis, he was told that eight thousand was covered by previous grants and he could only have two thousand. Denia complained to Ferdinand, by that time mortally sick, who, on December 4th, assented to the transfer to him of the previous grants, but Ximenes, in transmitting this order to Villacis, made a condition that the twenty thousand for the Inquisition must first be paid and he subsequently suspended Denia's grant altogether. The marquis complained of this to Charles, who from Ghent, May 22, 1517, ordered Ximenes to lift the suspension, but again Ximenes insisted with Villacis that the Inquisition must first be paid. The funds seemed to evaporate and vanish into thin air. It is probable that Denia got little or nothing and that Beaurains fared no better, for Charles's prime favorite, Adrien de Croy, received as his share of the spoils only the seven hundred and fifty thousand maravedís, the penalties for delay, which had been assigned to the tribunal of Seville. The insatiable

Calcena and Aguirre, however, secured a thousand ducats which, in 1515, Ferdinand granted them in recompense for their labors on the composition.[1054] Thus for ten years the New Christians of a large part of Spain had been harried and impoverished under delusive promises of exemption and, of the moneys thus extorted, but little reached either the crown or the Inquisition. The tribunal of Seville, indeed, can have received virtually nothing for, as we have seen, in 1556, its Archbishop Valdés asserted that, since the beginning of the century, it was so impoverished that it could support but a single inquisitor and pay only one-third of the ordinary salaries.[1055]

***

It would be impossible now to conjecture what was the amount of which the industrious and producing classes of Spain were thus despoiled, or what was the sum of misery thus inflicted, although we may estimate the retribution which followed in the disorganization of Spanish industries and the retardation of economic development. What reached the royal treasury and the money-chests of the Inquisition was but a portion of the values of which the owners were deprived. The assets taken melted in the hands of the spoilers. The expenses of the trials, which became inordinately prolonged, and the maintenance of the prisoners consumed a considerable part. Dilapidation and peculation, which even Ferdinand's incessant vigilance could not prevent, were the source of constant loss. Even without these, the necessity for immediate realization, to supply the peremptory demands of the treasury and the tribunals, threw an enormous amount of property and goods of all kinds on the market, in forced sales which were inevitably sacrifices. It was the established rule, perpetually enunciated, that every thing, except money and securities, was to be sold at auction, the real estate on the thirtieth day after condemnation, in presence of the receiver and notary of sequestrations.[1056] Notwithstanding all precautions, collusion and fraud were perpetual. It was doubtless as an effort to check them that Valdés, in 1547, ordered that real estate or censos, or government securities should not be sold without consulting the Suprema, together with an attested statement of past income and probable proceeds, and this was followed, in 1553, with an order that property in litigation was not to be sold.[1057] Precautions however were unavailing. The memorial of 1623 to the Suprema remarks that there are many opportunities for human wickedness in the sequestration, valuation and sale of sequestrated property; the valuations are habitually too low and the sales are made at the lowest prices. Whenever possible, property should be brought to the city of the tribunal, be properly valued and the receiver be forbidden to sell it for less. When sales have to be made at the place of arrest, they should be by public auction, in the presence of the commissioner and of a familiar, to see that just prices are obtained.[1058] The Suprema seems to have mooned over this until 1635, when it called for reports as to the manner in which the auctions were held and whether just prices were obtained; if the property was in some small place it must be brought to a larger town to prevent fraud.[1059]

During the period of active confiscation, moreover, when the moneyed classes were either ruined or anticipating ruin, it was sometimes impossible to effect sales and, in the pressure and confusion, property was allowed to go to waste. A letter of March 20, 1512, to the receiver of Huesca and Lérida, speaks of the uninhabited houses and lands which had not been sold, because fair prices could not be had, and which were perishing in consequence, and he was told to see whether he could not sell them on ground-rent, redeemable or irredeemable.[1060] It is impossible not to see in this the commencement of the despoblados which were the despair of Spanish statesmen for more than two centuries. So, in 1531, the dwelling in Játiva of Juan Sanz, on whom it was confiscated, was allowed to fall into such disrepair that no one would take it subject to the incumbrances, and the rentals did not meet the ground-rents, so it was abandoned to the incumbrancers.[1061]

***

The manner in which property melted away is seen in the settlement, made in 1519, of the estate of Mayor de Monzon, burnt for heresy. It was appraised at 110,197 maravedís, but against this were the expenses of the woman and her children while in prison, amounting to 41,100, and the widower, Diego de Adrade, finally agreed to take the estate for 17,000 maravedís, subject to whatever claims there might be against it.[1062] Everybody concerned grasped at what he could. In 1532, the Valencia tribunal sent Rafael Diego to Majorca to arrest and fetch Leonor Juan, wife of Ramon Martin who was blind. She was reconciled with confiscation and Charles V made a grant to the husband of a hundred libras from the estate, but when the account was made up the expenses did not leave enough to pay him. One item against which he protested was twenty-five ducats to Diego for twenty days' work, when his salary was only eighty ducats a year; the Suprema consequently suspended the item but, in 1545, Inquisitor-general Tavera ordered it to be paid.[1063] * * * * *

It is perhaps superfluous to insist upon what was inevitable in an age when integrity was exceptional in public affairs, and in a business affording peculiar temptations to malversation, through the fluctuating uncertainty of receipts and the difficulty of effecting competent supervision. Ferdinand did his best to establish accountability, and his incessant activity exhibits itself in his minute criticisms on his auditor's reports of the accounts of receivers, but even his vigilance could not prevent frauds and peculation, nor was it possible for him to penetrate the mysteries lurking behind statements of receipts and expenditures, when the receivers were apt to use the funds as their own. When Juan Denbin, the receiver of Saragossa, died and his accounts were balanced, after all possible allowances were made, he was found, in 1500, to owe 9367 sueldos, which Ferdinand vainly endeavored to collect from his heir, the Abbot of Veruela. Denbin's deputy at Calatayud improved on his example and was found, in 1499, to be short 24,000 sueldos, of which he paid 8000 and promised the rest at the rate of 4000 a year; the installment of 1500 was obtained after some delay and, when we last hear of him, Ferdinand was endeavoring to secure that of 1501.[1064]

It is easy to understand the chronic reluctance of such officials to render statements, and Ferdinand's correspondence shows how difficult it was to force them to do so. There is much suggestiveness in a letter of October 15, 1498, to the Maestre Racional or Auditor-general of Catalonia, telling him that, as Jayme de la Ram, the former receiver, and Pedro de Badia, the present one, refuse under various pretexts to hand over their books so that their accounts can be settled, he is to take legal steps to compel it; they can have until March 1, 1499, to obey and, if they still refuse, their salaries are to be stopped. When the books are obtained no time is to be lost in striking a balance, and especial care is to be taken that they do not give themselves fraudulent credits. Juan de Montaña, receiver of Huesca and Lérida was another whose accounts were chronically in arrear.[1065] This continued to the end of Ferdinand's reign. In 1515 we find him writing to a receiver, who had flatly refused to obey an order of Ximenes to go to Valencia with his books and papers and render an account of his collections, for persistence in which the king threatened him with prosecution.[1066] After his death Ximenes labored energetically to evoke order out of disorder. He appointed a receiver-general, with power to collect by levy, execution and sale, all moneys due by the receivers, and all fines, penances, commutations and rehabilitations; moreover, to a new auditor-general Hernando de Villa, he addressed a cédula, February 21, 1517, reciting that the receivers had collected from the confiscations and other sources large sums of which for a long time they had rendered no account, wherefore he was instructed to visit every tribunal, to demand an accounting from the receiver, to examine all papers and vouchers and ascertain the balances due, while all notaries were instructed to furnish whatever documents he might call for, and he was empowered to enforce his orders with punishment at discretion.[1067]

PRODUCTIVENESS

Possibly this may have produced improvement, but if so it was but temporary. We have just seen how recalcitrant about his accounts was Pedro de Badia, the receiver of Barcelona; he did not improve and when he died, in 1513, he left his office in bad condition. He was replaced by Martin de Marrano, transferred from Majorca, who proved to be no better. In 1520 Cardinal Adrian, to punish him, reduced his salary to 2880 sueldos and then, April 16, 1521, wrote a long and indignant letter to the inquisitors, principally devoted to Marrano's misdeeds, among which was refusal to settle his accounts and alleging claims for which he had no vouchers. Yet, to all appearances, with the inexplicable tenderness shown to official culprits, he was retained in office.[1068] The tribunal of Sicily, where the confiscations were large, was in even worse hands. Diego de Obregon, who served as receiver from 1500 to 1514, left its affairs in lamentable confusion. He was succeeded by Garcí Cid, who was sent to reduce it to order. How he accomplished this is seen in a report of Benito Mercader, sent as inspector, describing the financial management as characterized by every vice, while peculation was rife among all the officials. Garcí Cid returned to Spain in 1520 and it was not until 1542 that the Suprema ordered him to pay the 1420 ducats, which he was found to owe, as well as what he had collected of 9300 more which were charged against him.[1069] Things did not mend for, as we have seen, Zurita, who became Auditor-general for Aragon in 1548, describes his untangling of the Sicilian accounts, which had not been received for twenty years and were in the utmost disorder.[1070]

***

It is evident that the receipts of the royal treasury formed but a portion of the amount wrung from the victims. What those receipts were, we have no means of knowing but, in 1524, the Licenciado Tristan de Leon, in an elaborate memorial addressed to Charles V, asserted that Ferdinand and Isabella obtained from this source the enormous amount of 10,000,000 ducats, which greatly assisted them in their war with the Moors.[1071] Occasionally we have scattering indications of the productiveness of inquisitorial labors. Thus in the little temporary Geronimite Inquisition of Guadalupe, in 1485, the sovereigns appropriated the proceeds to the erection of a royal residence for their frequent devotional visits to the shrine. It was a magnificent palace, the cost of which, 2,732,333 maravedís, was almost wholly defrayed from this source.[1072] In 1486, the Valencia tribunal must have been productive, for Ferdinand wrote from Galicia to the receiver Joan Ram, to supply all that was needful for a fleet, as he had not the money in hand at the court.[1073] The impression produced on contemporaries is conveyed in Hernando de Pulgar's grim remark, when, describing the violent expulsion from Toledo of the Count of Fuensalida, he adds that the populace, like rigid inquisitors of the faith, found heresies in the properties of the count's peasants, which they plundered and burnt.[1074]

The large sums which were raised in the various compositions, in return for the very slender exemptions offered, are an index of the magnitude of the confiscations and so is a proposition, made to Ferdinand and declined, of a loan of 600,000 ducats if he would transfer the adjudication of such matters to the secular courts.[1075] Although receipts were perhaps diminished, with the weeding out of the Judaizing New Christians, we have seen (Vol. I, p. 220) the offer made, in 1519, to Charles V, to provide an endowment which would meet all the salaries and expenses of the Inquisition and, in addition, to pay him 400,000 ducats in compensation for the abandonment of the confiscations. Soon after this another offer was made of 700,000 ducats, which seems to have been held under consideration for a year or two.[1076]

***

During the remainder of the sixteenth century, the constant drafts by the Suprema on the several tribunals shows that they were, as a rule, supporting themselves, with a surplus for the central organization, although occasionally a tribunal in bad luck had to be helped by some more fortunate brother. The grant, in 1559, of a prebend in each cathedral and collegiate church, supplied the growing deficiency of confiscations, but the latter received a notable augmentation after the annexation of Portugal, in 1580. This was followed by a large influx of New Christians from the poorer to the richer kingdom, where their business ability speedily led to the acquisition of wealth, while their attachment to the ancient faith gave to the Inquisition a new and lucrative field of operations. We shall see hereafter the curious transaction by which, in 1604, they purchased a brief immunity, and this led soon afterwards to an offer, by the New Christians of Seville and the western provinces, of 1,600,000 ducats for a forty years' suspension of confiscation, coupled with the release of descendants from disabilities and infamy, the rating of testimony at its true worth, and papal intervention with the king in the rendering of sentences. The offer was seriously considered, but an investigation of the treasury accounts showed that, in its financial aspect, it would be a losing bargain for the crown, which would have to support the Inquisition, and it was rejected.[1077]

The persecutions in Peru and Mexico furnished evidence against wealthy merchants at home which was profitably utilized. In 1635, the Pereiras, who were large contractors in Madrid, were implicated and also "the Pasariños and all the rich merchants of Seville." Then too, Francisco Illan of Madrid, rated at 300,000 ducats, was accused and we hear of the arrest of Juan Rodríguez Musa, described as a wealthy merchant of Seville.[1078] It is true that when, in 1633, Juan Nuñez Sarabia was arrested, and his books showed a fortune of 600,000 ducats, hope was dashed by Gabriel Ortiz de Sotomayor, a member of the Suprema, who claimed the major part of it as a deposit by him as curador of Doña María Ortiz and as executor of Don Bernabé de Vivanco.[1079] Still, a class of culprits such as these, composed of rich bankers and merchants, gave ample opportunity of swelling the assets of the Holy Office. In 1654, in an auto de fe at Cuenca, there were fifty-five Judaizers, many of them evidently in easy circumstances, one of whom said, on the way to the brasero, that his chances of heaven were costing him 200,000 ducats.[1080] Yet these were uncertain resources and we have seen that the Suprema, in its budget for 1657, only reckoned on receiving from the tribunals 755,520 maravedís, or about 2000 ducats, but, on the other hand, in a consulta of May 11, 1676, it boasted that, within a few years, it had contributed to the royal treasury confiscations amounting to 772,748 ducats vellon and 884,979 pesos in silver.[1081] In addition to this the confiscations were not only defraying any deficiencies in its income, but it was gradually becoming richer, for, in the years 1661-1668, the surplus of the Suprema and tribunals invested in government securities amounted to 21,064 ducats.[1082]

Towards the end of the seventeenth century, the persecution of the Judaizing New Christians became sharper and we have seen the large results obtained, in 1679, by the Majorca tribunal from its wholesale prosecution of the Conversos of Palma. This persecution lasted till near the middle of the eighteenth century, with a large number of victims and, as they belonged in great part to the commercial class, the receipts must have been substantial. In sixty-six autos de fe, celebrated between 1721 and 1727, there were 776 sentences of confiscation. Many of these were unproductive, for confiscation was included in the sentence, whether the culprit had property or not, and the formula "confiscacion de los bienes que no tiene"--of the property which he has not got--is one of frequent occurrence, but there were doubtless enough possessed of wealth to make a fair average.[1083] Then there were occasional windfalls from others than Judaizers, as in the case of Melchor Macanaz, in 1716. The financial management seems not to have improved since the days of Ferdinand. No account of the estate was rendered until

December 31, 1723. This shows that his real estate brought in a revenue of 1269 libras, indicating a value of about 25,000 libras. There had been collected 9320ll. 7s. 10d. and expended 5838ll. 1s., leaving a balance of 3482ll. 6s. 10d. If the results were not greater it was not owing to any scruples. Melchor's brother Luis had an interest of 770 doubloons on the books of the glass-factory of Tortosa. It was guessed that he had not sufficient capital to justify such an investment, so the Madrid tribunal, October 21, 1716, ordered Valencia to sequestrate it.[1084] Another piece of good fortune was the discovery, in 1727, of an organization of Moriscos, who had preserved their faith and whose confiscations were so profitable that the principal informer, Diego Díaz, received as reward a perpetual pension of 100 ducats a year.[1085]

USE MADE OF RECEIPTS

As the eighteenth century advanced, confiscation gradually grew obsolete. Heresy had been so successfully extirpated that relaxation and reconciliation grew rarer and rarer. In the records of the Toledo tribunal, extending to 1794, there is no sentence of confiscation later than 1738.[1086] In the census of all the tribunals, about the year 1745, there is but a single juez de los bienes, though occasionally we find that office tacked on to an inquisitorship, as in Valencia in 1795, where an addition of 52ll. 10s. is made to the salary in consequence, but that it was a sinecure is apparent from the fact that, in a record of the sentences of that tribunal from 1780 to 1820, there is not a case of confiscation.[1087]

***

It is not without interest to examine what was the use made of the large receipts during the early period, when they were controlled by Ferdinand and Charles V, and before the Suprema monopolized them for the support of the tribunals, save an occasional concession extorted by the crown. Pulgar and Zurita loyally assure us that, large as they were, the sovereigns employed them solely for the advancement of the faith--the war with Granada, the maintenance of the Inquisition and other pious uses.[1088] Supported by these authorities, modern writers assume that no covetousness can be attributed to the sovereigns in the employment of these means for the public weal.[1089]

Unfortunately, the records do not bear out these flattering assurances. The Inquisition, of course, had the first claim on the product of its labors and its expenses were defrayed from this source. I have met with but two cases, one in 1500 and one in 1501, where a salary was paid from the royal treasury and in both of these the recipient was Diego López, member of the Suprema and royal secretary--a duplicate position which might justify calling upon either source of supply.[1090] During the war with Granada, ending with 1491, undoubtedly the funds derived from the industry of the Holy Office were largely employed in its prosecution which, according to the standards of the age, was not only a patriotic but an eminently pious use. While this drain continued it is not likely that much of the confiscations was otherwise employed, and I have met with but one or two pious gifts--in 1486 a thousand sueldos to aid in the construction of an infirmary for the Franciscan convent of Santa Maria de Jesus and, in 1491 a rent of five hundred sueldos a year to the church of San Juan of Calatayud.[1091] After the conquest of Granada we find occasional grants to convents and churches, but they are not frequent and, as a rule, are meagre in comparison with the profusion lavished on courtiers and servants. The only large recipient of bounty seems to have been Ferdinand's favorite Geronimite convent of Santa Engracia of Saragossa to which, in 1495, he gave thirteen thousand sueldos for the purchase of certain lands and gardens and, in 1498, ten thousand more. There was, in addition, a yearly allowance of six thousand sueldos for the maintenance of the frailes; the payment of this was suspended, in 1498, on account of lack of funds, but Ferdinand, after some hesitation, made this good by transferring to the convent certain censos that had been appropriated to the Inquisition.[1092] In his correspondence of this period, up to 1515, there occur a few more pious expenditures, but all are of moderate amount and in no way justify the assertion that the confiscations were largely expended in this manner.

GRANTS TO FAVORITES

The acquisitive secretary Calcena was a much more frequent beneficiary. His position gave him exceptional facilities for watching the confiscations and of profiting by his knowledge. His name continually recurs as the recipient of gifts of censos, houses and money, and he had indirect means of participating, as we have seen when he shared in the ruin of the Archdeacon of Castro. Some light is thrown on the methods in vogue when, in 1500, the estate of Francisco López of Calatayud was confiscated. In this certain houses, valued at ten thousand sueldos, were included, which the son of López hoped to save, as belonging to his mother's dowry, but the father's papers had been seized and the marriage settlement was inaccessible. The son thereupon promised Calcena a third of the valuation for a copy of the document; the effort failed, the houses were confiscated and Ferdinand, compassionating Calcena's loss, not only gave him the promised third but pledged himself to defend the title in case it should be attacked.[1093] This suggests a possible source of profit in favoring the sufferers by confiscation. Many instances have been cited above of Ferdinand's kindly consideration in mitigating exceptional cases of hardship, and we shall have occasion to refer to others; it would be pleasant to attribute them wholly to a side of his character that has not hitherto revealed itself in history, but one cannot escape an uneasy suspicion that, as Calcena was the channel through which these bounties flowed, in some cases, at least, the successful petitioners were those who had made it worth his while to aid them.

The abuse of making to favorites grants out of confiscations antedated the establishment of the Inquisition. The Córtes of 1447 petitioned against it and Juan II assented in a fashion too equivocal to hold out much prospect of improvement.[1094] It continued and, when the property of the New Christians came pouring in, Ferdinand yielded to the greed of his courtiers and nobles with a profuseness which explains where much of the products of confiscation disappeared. His recklessness in this matter is illustrated by a complaint, in 1500, of the Admiral of Castile, representing that he had been given a censo on his vizcondado of Cabrera, confiscated in the estate of Juan Beltran, but that certain parties to whom it had also been granted were suing him for it. Ferdinand evidently kept no record of these heedless gifts, for he could remember nothing as to this duplication, and he applied to the tribunal for a list of the provisions respecting the estate so that he could decide between the claimants.[1095]

His only serious collision with the Inquisition arose from this source and he found its censures more effective than his own. His lavishness kept the tribunals drained to the point that frequently there was no money to pay the salaries. As early as 1488 the inquisitors assembled at Valladolid complained of this and supplicated the sovereigns to order receivers to provide for salaries before honoring royal drafts; if they failed to keep sufficient funds on hand for salaries they should be subject to removal by inquisitors.[1096] This was ineffective; the royal treasury was chronically bankrupt, endurance ceased to be a virtue and the question came to a head at the close of 1497. On November 15th, Ferdinand wrote to receiver Juan Royz of Saragossa to pay some small amounts, less than a hundred ducats in all, chiefly needed for an inspection and reform of Franciscan convents then on foot. He knew, he said, that the Saragossa tribunal was in great straits, but he could not furnish the money himself and means must be found to raise it, without compelling him to write again. Royz however refused to make the payments, stating that the inquisitors-general had placed him under excommunication if he should pay any royal grants. Ferdinand shifted the order to the receiver of fines and penances, but the inquisitors-general had been beforehand with him by removing that official. Thus baffled, he wrote to them, January 28, 1498, telling them that these payments were absolutely necessary and he had nothing wherewith to meet them; besides, there were other pressing demands. The Córtes were about to meet at Saragossa and he had ordered certain alterations in the Aljafería to accommodate him during his residence, the cost of which Royz refused to pay and the work was stopped. There was also the tomb of his father and mother, with alabaster statues, which he was building at the abbey of Poblet (the burial-place of the kings of Aragon) at a cost of fifteen hundred ducats; five thousand sueldos were due to the architect, Maestre Gil Morlan, and when Royz refused to pay this from the confiscations, Ferdinand ordered the amount to be collected from the ground-rent of Parascuellos, but it chanced that Royz himself owed that ground-rent and was in no haste to pay it. Meanwhile the salaries were paid, but the excommunication still hung over Royz and he refused obstinately to furnish money for these needs and for some more that were crowding in. February 28th, Ferdinand vainly endeavored to induce the inquisitor to make Royz yield by excommunicating him, and he then appealed to Suárez de Fuentelsaz, one of the inquisitors-general, but equally without success. Finally, on March 30th, he wrote to Torquemada by a special messenger, with orders to bring an answer, telling him that, as the salaries were paid, the excommunication must be lifted, for he would not permit it. This was successful and, on April 10th, he wrote again, promising that in future he would not make grants from the confiscations and penances. On April 20th he communicated to Royz the removal of the excommunication and urged the speedy completion of the alterations of the Aljafería and the payment to Santa Engracia of what was due.[1097] Thus ended this episode, which sheds a curious light on the relations of Ferdinand with the Inquisition and on the precarious nature of public finance at the time.

***

The excommunication had not been confined to Saragossa, nor was it removed elsewhere when Saragossa paid its salaries. In July, 1500, we find Ferdinand arguing with the obdurate Juan de Montaña, receiver of Huesca and Lérida, that it did not apply to the completion of an old donation to the church of Lérida, which had never been fully paid. We hear nothing subsequently of the censure, though complaints continued of salaries in arrears, and the Archdeacon of Almazan, who was inquisitor at Calatayud, was consequently unable to pay his debts when, in 1500, he was transferred to Barcelona. The tribunal of Valencia was hopelessly bankrupt when, in 1501, there came a lucky composition with the heirs of Juan Macip, for sixty thousand sueldos, which Ferdinand ordered to be applied to its liabilities so that, for once, it might be out of debt.[1098] It is scarce necessary to add that Ferdinand's promise to make no more grants was violated almost as soon as made.

In the profusion which kept the tribunals exhausted it by no means followed that those who had no influence profited by the royal favor. In 1493, Ferdinand granted to Leonor Hernández two thousand sueldos as a marriage-portion. Under various pretexts, payment was evaded. Leonor married and died, leaving the claim to her husband and brother who, in 1502, procured from Ferdinand an order for its immediate settlement, but whether this was honored is problematical.[1099] Even more delayed was a concession, in 1491, to Martin Marin of Calatayud, of three thousand sueldos on the confiscations of his father and mother-in-law; in 1512 Marin represented that he had never been able to obtain it and Ferdinand ordered its payment forthwith. These postponements were not always due to poverty. In 1491, a grant was made to Anton del Mur, royal alguazil, of a vineyard, forming part of the confiscated estate of Pascual de Santa Cruz. Receiver Royz of Saragossa made answer that the vineyard had been sold, but when the king ordered him to make over the proceeds to del Mur, the latter got nothing and Royz managed fraudulently to keep the vineyard in the hands of a third party. After nineteen years, del Mur, in 1510, revived the matter, when Ferdinand ordered the inquisitor and receiver to find out who held the vineyard and by what title and, if it was not found that Royz had sold it for a just price, del Mur was to be placed in possession.[1100]

The eagerness for these spoils was such that claims for them were put in without waiting for confiscation to be decreed, and it is evident that, when a man of wealth was arrested, there were agencies to convey the news to the expectants and the prey was divided before the quarry was killed. After Isabella's death, in 1504 these grants were an economical way to secure the fluctuating allegiance of the Castilian nobles, which Philip of Austria was ready to exploit and the nobles eager to profit by. When the Licenciado de Medina, of Valladolid, was arrested, the Admiral of Castile, Fadrique Enríquez, petitioned him at once for the confiscation and Philip from Brussels, May 5, 1505, granted the request, repeating it six months later. While awaiting Juana's confinement, before sailing for Spain, the two spouses, on September 12th, sent orders to all the cities, the nobles and officials not to obey Ferdinand or to pay taxes to him, and the receivers of the tribunals were specially told to withhold from him the confiscations.[1101] Philip's orders from Flanders, however, received scant respect and his reign in Castile was too transitory for him to exercise any notable influence on the disposition of the confiscations.

***

As for Ferdinand, what he granted with one hand he withheld with the other. February 23, 1510, he issued a cédula to all receivers saying that, in consequence of the falling off in confiscations, if all the grants which he had made and was making were paid, the officials would not receive their salaries and would abandon the work, to the great disservice of God, wherefore in future, no matter what orders he or the inquisitor-general might issue, no grants were to be paid until all officials had received their salaries and ayudas de costa and, when such grants were presented, he or the inquisitor-general was to be consulted. The rule was to be that debts must be paid first, then salaries and grants not until the last.[1102] Yet, on the day previous, he had given to Fernando de Mazueco, a member of the Suprema, certain olive orchards and censos confiscated on Gonzalo Ximenes of Seville; the same day he ordered the receiver of Jaen to deduct twenty thousand maravedís from the appraised value of some confiscated houses wanted by Dr. Juan de Santoyo, former judge of confiscations of Jaen, and he continued making gifts with reckless prodigality as though the royal treasury were overflowing and the Inquisition were richly endowed. In January, the Admiral of Castile had had a grant of houses valued at eight or nine thousand sueldos and, on April 2nd, he ordered the receivers of Toledo, Seville, Córdova and Jaen each to pay 375,000 maravedís, or 1,500,000 in all to his servant Juan Rodríguez de Portocarrero.[1103] Apparently it was exceptional for the Inquisition to enjoy the product of its exertions for, in May, we find him assuring the Suprema that no one had asked him for a confiscation of 100,000 maravedís just made in Valladolid, and that he will reserve it for the known necessities of that tribunal and, in July, that, although he has been much importuned for another confiscation, he will make no grant of it, so that the officials shall not suffer want.[1104] It is needless to point out what a stimulus this state of things gave to the condemnation of those whose estates promised relief.

Ferdinand went on precisely as before and it would be superfluous to multiply instances of his reckless profusion, save that we may mention a gift to his wife Queen Germaine, in 1515, of 10,000 florins from the confiscations of Sicily and we may recall his attempted grant of 10,000 ducats to the Marquis of Denia from the composition of Córdova.[1105] In this general scramble for fragments of the spoils, there is one point that may be noted--the demand for attractive slave-girls. How their existence came to be known to those who asked for them we can only guess, and it would be indiscreet to enquire why reverend members of the Suprema seem to be especially desirous of such acquisitions. April 7, 1510, Ferdinand writes to the receiver of Cartagena that he is told that, in the confiscated property of Ramado Martin de Santa Cruz, there is a Moorish female slave named Alia; if this is so she is to be delivered to Doctor Pérez Gonzalo Manso, of the Suprema, to be his property as a gift. March 18, 1514, the Licenciado Ferrando de Mazuecos, of the Suprema, petitions for a Moorish slave-girl, confiscated among the property of Juan de Tena de Ciudad Real, and Ferdinand orders her to be given to him, to do what he pleases with her. There was some contest over Fatima, a white Moorish slave-girl confiscated in the estate of Alonso Sánchez del Castillo. The Marquis of Villena asked for her and Ferdinand granted his request, June 15, 1514, but when the order was sent to Toledo, the deputy receiver refused to obey it, alleging that it was obtained by false representations, as the Suprema had already given her to the fiscal, Martin Ximenes. This was promptly answered, in a letter signed not only by Calcena but by the members of the Suprema, reiterating the grant to Villena and ordering the receiver to compensate Ximenes for her value.[1106] It is suggestive that no such eagerness is shown to obtain male slaves.

Ferdinand himself was not above appropriating articles found among the spoils of his subjects. In 1502 we find him taking fifty-five pearls from Sardinia, a part of the confiscation of Micer Rejadel, burnt for heresy. Sometimes he did not even wait for the conviction of the owner, as in the case of a horse which, in 1501, he gave to the inquisitor of Córdova, and then, on learning that the animal would be serviceable to him in the chase, he had it sent to him and ordered four thousand maravedís to be paid to the inquisitor wherewith to buy a horse or mule.[1107] He was even more unscrupulous, in 1501, when in Granada, on hearing of the death of Bernaldalla, a prisoner not yet convicted, he ordered that the garden belonging to him in the Rambla should be seized and given to the Princess Juana for her pastime, although he did not know whether it had been sequestrated.[1108] It manifests the abiding confidence felt in the conviction of all who fell into the hands of the Inquisition.

***

Yet it would be unjust to Ferdinand not to allude again to the numerous cases in which he softened the hardships of confiscation by concessions to the sufferers or their representatives--and this when, as we have seen, his own treasury was empty. No doubt in many instances the influence of Calcena was purchased but, as a whole, they are too numerous not to find their origin in a kindliness which has been deemed foreign to the stern consolidator of the Spanish monarchy, nor could Calcena have ventured to presume too far, during a long series of years, in making his master an unconscious almoner. Two or three examples of this must suffice to show the spirit actuating him. In 1509, Juan de Peralta of Segovia betrothed himself to Francisca Nuñez, daughter of Lope de Molina and his wife, who were prisoners of the tribunal of Jaen. They were condemned and burnt, their estate was confiscated and Peralta petitioned the king, saying that he could not marry without a dowry and begging an allowance out of the estate, whereupon Ferdinand ordered the receiver to give them two hundred thousand maravedís. The Inquisition was not to be balked; Francisca in turn was tried and reconciled with confiscation. Peralta made another appeal and this time Ferdinand granted twenty thousand maravedís.[1109] October 21, 1500, he writes to the receiver of Leon to release to Leonor González, reconciled, a vineyard confiscated on her, of the value of two thousand maravedís, because she is poor and has a daughter to marry.[1110] In 1510, he instructs receiver Badia of Barcelona to collect from the Bishop of Urgel ninety libras due to the confiscated estate of Guillen Dala, and, in view of the poverty and misery of Beatriz, Violante, Isabel and Aldonza his daughters, the money is to be paid to them. There was also an old debt due to Dala by Ferdinand's father, Juan II; this he orders to be collected from the rents of property set aside for the benefit of Juan's soul and to be also paid to the daughters.[1111] These are only examples of numerous similar acts, which afford a welcome sense of relief as mitigations in some small degree of the miseries inflicted on thousands of the helpless through the pitiless enforcement of the cruel laws of the Church.

It would be wrong not to bear testimony also to the spirit of justice which is apparent in many of Ferdinand's decisions of questions brought before him. Thus on January 8, 1502, in instructing a receiver about a censo in dispute with Galceran de Santangel, he concludes by telling him to act without legal delays, so that justice may be administered with rectitude and promptitude, and that nothing may be taken but what belongs to the fisc, without wronging any one. September 12, 1502, he wrote that Garcí Corts complains that he had granted him certain censos and then, by a second letter, had stopped the transfer, whereupon he now orders the matter to be settled according to justice, without reference to what he may have written to the contrary, for it is not his will to inflict wrong on any one.[1112] It would be easy to multiply these examples, from his confidential correspondence with officials, when there could have been no possible object in a hypocritical affectation of fairness. If he not infrequently rebuked inquisitors and receivers for negligence in gathering in confiscations, it may be truly said that he more often scolded them for undue harshness and delay in settling honest claims.

The pressure on Ferdinand for grants from the confiscations continued to the last and was yielded to more often than prudence would dictate. The courtiers maintained intelligence with the tribunals to obtain advices in advance of the arrest or condemnation of wealthy Conversos, in order to make early application, and occasional letters from the king to receivers asking information as to such estates and forbidding their sale without further orders, indicate a growing sense on his part of the necessity of caution. One of his latest utterances, as mortal sickness was stealing over him, is a letter of September 23, 1515, to the receiver of Toledo, in reply apparently to a statement thus furnished. He had received, he says, the information as to the confiscated property of Pero Díaz and his wife, and also the representation as to the pressing needs of the tribunal, in consideration of which he will change his mind and make no grants from it except of a hundred thousand maravedís to his treasurer Vargas to reimburse him for certain outlays.[1113] Thus to the end was maintained the struggle between those who labored for the harvest and those who sought to reap its fruits.

RESISTANCE OF RECEIVERS

When, after his death, Ximenes sought to bring order into the finances of the Inquisition, he seems to have felt that his conjoined power as inquisitor-general and governor was insufficient to remedy these abuses, and he procured from the young King Charles a pragmática dated at Ghent, June 14, 1517, which was assuredly drafted by him. This recites that the salaries and ordinary expenses of the Inquisition are defrayed by the confiscations, but experience shows that often they cannot be paid, in consequence of the grants made by the crown; this must be remedied, or the Inquisition cannot be sustained, to the great damage of the royal conscience, and therefore, during the good pleasure of the king and until the salaries and ordinary expenses are provided for, no graces, donations or reliefs are to be complied with, under pain of a thousand gold ducats. Copies of this are to be sent to every tribunal and all officials are exhorted to see to its enforcement.[1114] The gloss put on this by Cardinal Adrian, when sending it to the tribunal of Sicily, shows that there was no scruple in construing its provisions most liberally. He says that he has heard that many are obtaining grants on the Sicilian confiscations; what was collected under Ferdinand must be used as he had ordered, which was to buy rents for the support of the tribunal. The new pragmática postpones all grants to the salaries and charges of the Inquisition and, as Sicily must provide for the support of the Suprema and of some of the home tribunals, it can be alleged in refusing to pay all grants that are presented, wherefore none must be paid without consulting him.[1115]

Having issued this pragmática, Charles proceeded to nullify it with all convenient speed, but it served as a justification to the receivers in withstanding him. Three months later, on September 19th, he landed in Spain, surrounded by a crowd of hungry and greedy Flemish favorites, eager to enrich themselves at the expense of their master and his subjects. This reinforcement of the importunate native beggars made the profusion of Ferdinand seem niggardly by comparison. Peter Martyr tells us that the Flemings, in less than ten months after their arrival, had already sent home eleven hundred thousand ducats, drawn partly from the indulgence of the Santa Cruzada and partly from the Inquisition, for they obtained grants not only of estates confiscated but also of those of prisoners still under trial--showing how promptly they established relations which gave them secret information of the operations of the tribunals, and how little chance of escape had the unlucky prisoners whose estates would have to be refunded if they were not convicted. This was one of the abuses of which the cure was sought in the project of reform in 1518, which failed through the death of Jean le Sauvage.[1116]

The booty thus secured by the Flemings shows how the confiscations had increased under this pressure, especially as the Spaniards were no less eager, if not quite so fortunate. This thoughtless prodigality of Charles is emphasized by the fact that he was impoverished in the midst of his profuseness. July 5, 1519, we find him ordering the receiver of Cartagena to pay the paltry sum of thirty ducats to Fernando de Salmeron, receiver-general of the Suprema, to reimburse him for a loan of that amount.[1117] The receivers did all that they could to check these extravagant liberalities for, large as were the receipts, the tribunals were threatened with bankruptcy. Saragossa, in reporting, March 18, 1519, to the Suprema, some impending convictions, endeavored to avert the dissipation of the results by representing its poverty; the salaries of most of the officials were more than a year in arrears and, if the king did not exercise more restraint, the tribunal could no longer be maintained.[1118]

One or two instances of the struggles between the receivers and the recipients of the royal bounty will illustrate the existing conditions, and incidentally show how Adrian and the Suprema were forced to bow to the tempest and to connive at the pillage of the resources of the Holy Office. A letter of Charles, January 19, 1519, to Juan del Pozo, receiver of Toledo, relates how he had granted to M. de Cetebrun, of his body-guard, the confiscation of Alonso de Baena and had ordered Pozo to convert it into money and pay it to him; how Pozo had subsequently been notified that Cetebrun had sold it to Iñigo de Baena, son of Alonso, and had been ordered to deliver it to the latter; how neither of them had been able to make him surrender it; how another royal order had been served on him and then one from

Adrian and the Suprema, with no result save an assertion that he had no funds; how Baena had made four journeys to Madrid, to his great loss and expense, the whole winding up with a peremptory command to obey the repeated mandates without further delay or excuse. It is probable that still more energetic measures were requisite to get the property, for Pozo was an obstinate man. A letter from Charles to him, September 5, 1519, refers to an order on him for six hundred ducats, in favor of M. Baudré which remained unpaid, in spite of repeated commands from the king and Cardinal Adrian, whereat Baudré is much aggrieved, especially as he has been keeping a man in Toledo, at his expense, to collect it. Charles now orders it to be paid within sixty days, in default of which Pozo must, within twenty days thereafter, present himself at the court, wherever it may chance to be, with all his books and papers for examination. This was a most formidable threat and perhaps brought Pozo to terms for, on December 2nd we find him ordered to pay on sight four hundred ducats to La Chaulx, as procurator of the Toison d'Or and, the next day, five hundred more to Jean Vignacourt, a gentleman of the royal chamber.[1119]

***

Cristóval de Prado, receiver of Cuenca, was another troublesome subject. Charles granted to Cortavila and Armastorff, two of his chamberlains, the confiscated estate of Francisco Martínez and his wife. It must have been a large one, for a suggestion was made of giving the courtiers four thousand ducats and reserving two thousand to pay the salaries, but they demanded the whole and Charles, April 10, 1518, ordered it to be turned over to them and, if any part had been converted to the use of the Inquisition, it was to be made good out of other confiscations. Prado staved it off for nearly eighteen months, pretending to hesitate about including the dowries and marriage portions of the children, until Charles, September 5, 1519, ordered all these to be swept into the grant. Soon after this, on November 9th, there was another crop of confiscations at an auto de fe at Cuenca when, in preparation for fresh bounties, Salmeron, the receiver-general, was ordered to report as to their value and also as to the condition of the salaries and other indebtedness. This probably deprived Prado of excuses for awhile, and we hear of no more refusals to pay until April 16, 1520. The Duke of Escalona had asked for the confiscations of three of his vassals at Alarcon, amounting to three hundred and fifty ducats, but Prado alleged that only two of the parties named had been condemned and that the order therefore must be surreptitious. He wrote in this sense to Charles and to the Suprema but, on September 7th he was commanded to pay it, and the letter was signed by Doctor Manso of the Suprema and countersigned by Cardinal Adrian. Cuenca, at this time, must have been a mine of wealth. Just before sailing from Coruña, Charles, on May 8, 1520, ordered Prado to pay a thousand ducats to Antoine de Croy, two hundred to Henri d'Espinel, four hundred to Simon Fisnal, mayordomo to Charles de Croy, Prince of Chimay, and five hundred to Adolf Duke of Cleves. On October 23rd Charles writes that his secretary Gui Morillon, who had been charged with these collections, reported that Prado refused to pay them, but he adds that, as there are now funds sufficient, after paying salaries and expenses, and the thousand ducats to Cardinal Adrian, they must be paid in preference to subsequent grants. As Adrian had been given an interest in this heavy raid on Cuenca, it is probable that Prado was coerced into obedience.[1120]

Our old friend Villacis of Seville was wary and experienced and accustomed to hard blows. He gave the courtiers infinite trouble, but the cases in which he was involved were too numerous to be detailed here and space can only be found for one of five hundred ducats to Francisco Guzman and Antonio Tovar, gentlemen of the king's chamber. This had originally been drawn on Cuenca, but Prado had been found too impervious and it was transferred to Seville. Villacis evaded it until Charles, on May 6, 1519 threatened him with merced--being placed at the king's mercy--if it was not paid at once. This was serious, but Villacis was unmoved and merely replied that he had no money to pay the overdue salaries, besides large sums owing for services and for judgements rendered against the confiscations. The affair dragged on until, on August 23, 1520, Adrian and the Suprema ordered immediate settlement, in default of which an agent would be sent, at his expense, to do it personally. This was probably effective, as we hear no more of it.[1121]

DANGER OF WEALTH

Aliaga of Valencia was one of Ferdinand's oldest and most trusted receivers and had given evidence of similar powers of resistance, if we may judge from the anticipatory measures taken when the interests of the powerful favorite, the Prince of Chimay, were involved. When news was brought to the court of the reconciliation and confiscation of the wealthy Alonso de Abella of Valencia, a speedy partition was made among the vultures. Eight hundred ducats were assigned to Jean de Baudré and Philibert de la Baulme, gentlemen of the chamber, three hundred to another gentleman, Jayme de la Trullera, and the rest of the estate to the Prince of Chimay, after paying salaries, if they could not be met out of other confiscations. Orders to this effect were despatched to Aliaga, July 5, 1519, with a pressing letter from Charles to the inquisitors. Apparently the beneficiaries felt that more active measures were necessary; Simon Tisnot, the prince's majordomo, was empowered to receive the property and, as his agent, Gui Morillon was sent to Valencia, July 9th, with letters to the inquisitors, to the Governor of Valencia and to Aliaga. The inquisitors were told that, as the clause concerning salaries might be so construed as to consume the whole, they must order Aliaga, under pain of excommunication, to deliver to Chimay's agent, within three days, all the property, goods, debts and money of the confiscation, except the eleven hundred ducats to the other courtiers; if the necessities of the tribunal required any portion, it must be very moderate so that Chimay, if possible, might get the whole. The governor was ordered to help Tisnot and to urge the inquisitors to compel Aliaga to obey. Aliaga was told that, under pain of deprivation of office, he must deliver the estate to Morillon within three days and must strain every nerve to meet the needs of the tribunal from other sources, so that Chimay may suffer no deduction. If the salvation of the monarchy had depended on the realization of the grants, the letters could scarce have been more vehement. Yet it was all in vain; Aliaga was imperturbable and, on December 8th, Charles expressed his displeasure that the eleven hundred ducats had not yet been paid though he had postponed to them the grant to Chimay, but it is not likely that his vague threats, in case of further delay, proved effective.[1122]

 In this carnival of plunder, there is small risk in assuming that the pressure on the tribunals gave a stimulus to the prosecution of the richer class of the Conversos and that wealth became more than ever a source of danger. In fact, the number of large estates referred to in these transactions would seem to indicate that few escaped whose sacrifice would supply needful funds to the Inquisition, while ministering to the greed of the courtiers. It need occasion no surprise, therefore, if the threatened New Christians, in their despair, appealed to Leo X and rendered it worth his while to remonstrate with Charles. Yet the latter, while scattering ducats by the thousand among his sycophants, had the effrontery to instruct his envoy, Lope Hurtado de Mendoza, September 24, 1519, to disabuse the pope as to the accusation that the Inquisition was prosecuting the rich for the confiscations, the truth being that all, or nearly all, of those prosecuted were poor, and that the fisc had to support them while in prison and to pay their advocates and procurators.[1123]

 After Charles's departure, in May, 1520, to assume the imperial dignity, we hear of few new grants. He was rapidly ripening under the weight of the tremendous responsibilities accumulated upon him and was recognizing that his position implied other duties than the gratification of his courtiers' greed. It would seem that he willingly shifted upon the inquisitor-general and Suprema the burden of such trivial matters, and left it to them to assent to or dissent from such graces as he might bestow. A grant from a confiscation at Saragossa, dated at Brussels, October 1, 1520, bears the formula that it is with the assent and advice of the inquisitor-general and Council of Aragon, and, though it is signed by Ugo de Urries by order of the emperor, it has the vidimus of Cardinal Adrian.[1124] Practically thus the control was lodged with the Suprema, whose needs, as we have seen, prevented any accumulations in the tribunals and we hear little or nothing subsequently of this dissipation of the confiscations.

RESULTS

 If I have entered thus minutely into the details of this branch of inquisitorial activity, it is because its importance has scarce been recognized by those who have treated of the Inquisition. It not only supplied the means of support to the institution during its period of greatest activity, but it was recognized by the inquisitors themselves as their most potent weapon and the one most dreaded by the industrious classes which formed their chief field of labor. Its potency is the measure of the misery which it inflicted, through long generations, on the innocent and helpless, far transcending the agonies of those who perished at the stake. To it was largely owing the ultimate extinction of Judaism in Spain, for the exalted heroism which might dare the horrors of the brasero might well give way before the prospect of poverty to be endured by disinherited offspring. To it also is greatly attributable the stagnation of Spanish commerce and industry, for trade could not flourish when credit was impaired, and confidence could not exist when merchants and manufacturers of the highest standing might, at any moment, fall into the hands of the tribunal and all their assets be impounded. Even the liberality of the Spanish Inquisition, in not confiscating the debts due by the heretic, was but a slender mitigation of this, for the creditor was liable to ruin through the difficulties and delays interposed on the realization of his credits, and past transactions were not secure until protected by a proscription of forty years. The Inquisition came at a time when geographical discovery was revolutionizing the world's commerce, when the era of industrialism was dawning, and the future belonged to the nations which should have fewest trammels in adapting themselves to the new developments. The position of Spain was such as to give it control of the illimitable possibilities of the future, but it blindly threw away all its advantages into the laps of heretic Holland and England. Many causes, too intricate to be discussed here, contributed to this, but not the least among them was the bleeding to anæmia, through centuries, of the productive classes and the insecurity which the enforcement of confiscation cast over all the operations of commerce and industry.

CHAPTER II - FINES AND PENANCES

Although, at least in the earlier period, confiscation was the main financial reliance of the Inquisition, it had other resources. Of these a productive one was the pecuniary penance which the tribunals had discretionary power of imposing on those whose offences amounted only to suspicion of heresy and not to the formal heresy which entailed reconciliation or relaxation with confiscation.

Almsgiving in satisfaction of sin formed a feature of ecclesiastical practice and, in the middle ages, the schoolmen had no difficulty in proving that pecuniary penance was more efficacious than any other[1125]--and it certainly was more efficacious in the sense that the enormous possessions of the Church were largely gathered from this source. Moreover, the inquisitor inherited from his medieval predecessors an undefined duplicate function of confessor and judge--his culprits were penitents and the punishments he inflicted were penances.[1126] Even when the canon law required the hardened or relapsed heretics to be relaxed to the secular arm for burning, they are sometimes alluded to as penitenciados[1127] When, under the early Edicts of Grace, penitents by the thousand flocked to confess their sins and escape corporal penalties and confiscation, the inquisitor was instructed to make them give as "alms" a portion of their property, according to the quality of the person and the character and duration of his offences, and these penitencias pecuniarias were to be applied to the war with Granada as to the most pious of causes.[1128] Thus, at the start, pecuniary penance and almsgiving were regarded as convertible terms, both equally applicable to the discretionary fines which the inquisitor could impose on his penitent. There was a technical, though not a practical, distinction between these and the mulcts inflicted on offenders for other than spiritual offences, in the exercise of the royal jurisdiction conferred on the Holy Office. They formed together a common fund which was known as that of the penas y penitencias--the fines and penances--of which the former were drawn from the secular and the latter from the spiritual jurisdiction. This distinction at best was shadowy and though it was observed at first, in time the tribunals grew indifferent and recognized that penance was punishment.

The earliest formality is seen in the case of Brianda de Bardaxí, where the consulta de fe, March 18, 1492, pronounces her guilty of vehement suspicion, to be penanced at the discretion of the inquisitors. Accordingly, on March 20th, the inquisitors deliberated on the "penance" and pronounced an Impositio penitentie, consisting of five years' imprisonment, with certain spiritual observances, "and moreover we penance her in the third part of all her property, which we apply to the coffer of penances of this tribunal and to the costs of her trial, which third part, or its true value, we order to be paid within ten days to Martin de Cota, receiver of penances."[1129] By the middle of the sixteenth century this scruple was overcome. In the case of Mari Serrana, at Toledo in 1545, the consulta de fe, it is true, votes that she be "penanced" in a third of her property, but the public sentence, which customarily did not specify the amount, after enumerating certain spiritual observances, adds "also the pecuniary punishment imposed on her, for a certain reason is reserved for the present." So, in the case of Mari Gómez, in 1551, it is stated that she is "condemned" in twenty ducats for the expenses of the tribunal, which she is to pay within nine days to the receiver. When the sentence was read to her in the audience-chamber, she asked how she was to pay the twenty ducats and was told it would come out of the property sequestrated at her arrest.[1130] Sequestration, we may observe, enabled the tribunal to help itself at discretion from the culprit's property and to proportion the penalty to his ability.

DISTINCT FROM CONFISCATION

There was an advantage to the Inquisition in considering these fines as penitential, for penance was part of the sacrament of absolution which was an ecclesiastical function, the proceeds of which were controlled by the Church, and it differed thus wholly from confiscation. It is true that practically this was merely a verbal juggle, for the inquisitor did not absolve and, as he was not necessarily a priest, his office did not comprise the administration of the sacraments, but the verbal juggle sufficed and serves to explain the rigid separation of the funds arising from penance and from confiscation, even after both were controlled by the Inquisition. We have seen (Vol. I, p. 338) the prolonged struggle made by Ferdinand to obtain possession of the penances, which finally terminated in favor of the Inquisition. This was rather beneficial to the accused, as the tribunal would be inclined to find him guilty only of suspicion of heresy, enabling it to inflict a pecuniary penance for its own benefit, rather than of formal heresy which inferred confiscation. Of course this passed away when financial control practically lapsed to the Suprema, but the distinction between the funds was still maintained.

In the earlier period the distinction was emphasized by the office of special receiver for the penances, who seems to have been subject to the inquisitor-general, while the receiver of confiscations held from the king. Thus the sentence of Brianda de Bardaxí shows us Martin de Cota as receiver of penances in Saragossa in 1492 and we still hear of him in that position in 1497, while Ferdinand had, as his own receiver, Juan Denbin, succeeded by Juan Royz. As early as 1486, Esteve Costa was "receptor de las penitencias" in Valencia, whose salary of fifty libras shows the office to be of much less importance than that of the receiver of confiscations.[1131] Still, there came to be no settled rule about this. In 1498, Juan Royz was receiver of both penances and confiscations in Saragossa and, in Valencia, Juan de Monasterio was inquisitor and at the same time receiver of penances, while, in 1512, in Barcelona the fiscal also filled the latter office, as we learn from his salary being suspended until he should render an account of his receipts.[1132] As late as 1515 there was still a special receiver of penances in Huesca, the Canon Pero Pérez, whose death revealed him to be a defaulter to the extent of four thousand sueldos, when the office was consolidated with that of the receivership.[1133] In 1516, among his other reforms, Ximenes abolished this special office and put the fines and penances in the hands of the receivers of confiscations, with instructions, however, to keep the funds separate and not to disburse the fines and penances except on orders from the inquisitor-general. There had previously been, in the Suprema, a receiver-general of fines and penances, an office which was likewise suppressed and all the revenues were placed in charge of a single official, a regulation which was confirmed by Manrique in 1524.[1134]

***

There was difficulty in preventing the unauthorized collection of these funds, by other officials, with the consequent absence of responsibility and risk of embezzlement. In instructions for the prevention of abuses, October 10, 1546, it is prescribed that all fines be paid to the receiver; again, August 20, 1547, it is ordered that neither the inquisitors nor other officials save the receiver shall collect the penances or other moneys. Inspection of the Barcelona tribunal, in 1549, showed that this was not obeyed; other officials made the collections and they were not reported to the receiver, all of which was forbidden for the future, but the order of 1547 had to be repeated December 4, 1551, May 9, 1553, and December 20, 1555.[1135] Evidently there were leaks which the Suprema was vainly seeking to stop. A special commission was issued, January 12, 1549, to Gerónimo Zurita, as contador for the kingdoms of Aragon, to audit the accounts of all receivers, past, present and to come, concerning the fines and penances and other parties casuelles, with full powers to send for persons and papers under such penalties as he might designate, which is highly significant.[1136] Possibly his investigations led to a carta acordada of September 23, 1551, which states that, in some tribunals, some of the pecuniary penalties are not entered in the Book of Punishments; the notaries of sequestrations are therefore impressively ordered, under holy obedience and major excommunication latæ sententiæ, to make such entries when sentence is rendered, stating whether they are applicable to the Inquisition or to some pious work, so that the contador may know whether they are collected, and all fines thus omitted are to be deducted from the salaries of the notaries.[1137] As, by this time, the fines and penalties were invariably applied to the Inquisition, the pretence of appropriating to pious uses was presumably a mere device for embezzling them. The Suprema evidently had no doubts as to this, when the inquisitors of Barcelona, in the case of Pirro de Gonzaga, imposed a penance of three hundred ducats and appropriated twenty-five to the convent of N. Señora de los Angeles, twenty-five to the nuns of San Gerónimo and the remainder to beds and garments for the poor. It told them, in 1568, that all fines were for the expenses of the Inquisition and required them, within thirty days, to furnish authentic evidence of the disposition made of the two hundred and fifty ducats, under pain of rigorous proceedings against them.[1138] As for holding the notaries responsible, there was manifest injustice in this, for they were powerless to prevent fraud by the inquisitors. In 1525, some instructions to the tribunal of Sicily mention that the notary had repeatedly and vainly requested that notice be given to him of all penances, in order that he might charge them to the receiver.[1139] How reckless sometimes were the inquisitors appears in the case of the murder of Juan Antonio Managat, deputy receiver at Puycerda. In 1565 the three Barcelona inquisitors inflicted on the accused certain heavy fines which were duly collected and placed in the coffer with three keys, after which they coolly helped themselves to a thousand reales apiece, under pretext that it was for fees in trying the case. On this being discovered, in the inspection by de Soto Salazar, the Suprema ordered the money to be returned to the coffer and satisfactory evidence of the restitution to be furnished within thirty days.[1140]

***

The distinction between the confiscations and the fines and penances was rigidly maintained when both were concentrated in the hands of the receiver. A special commission was issued to authorize him to receive the latter[1141] and he was straitly instructed to keep the accounts separate. The confiscations were devoted to salaries and, if there was an overplus, to investments of a more or less permanent character, while the fines and penances were levied, as the formula of the sentences habitually expressed it, for the gastos extraordinarios--the other and extraordinary expenses of the tribunals. Still, when the confiscations ran short, there was no hesitation in drawing upon the other fund, although a special order of the Suprema was necessary for its authorization. Ayudas de costa were generally drawn from the fines and penances, though frequently the receiver is told to pay them out of any funds in hand.[1142] In 1525, Manrique directed the house-rents of the officials to be paid from the fines and penances; in 1540 Tavera granted, from the same fund in Valencia, three thousand sueldos to the nunnery of Santa Julia as the dowry of a reconciled Morisca, placed there to save her soul; in 1543 he calls upon the receiver of Granada to furnish, from the same source, two hundred ducats to Juan Martínez Lassao, secretary of the Suprema, on the occasion of his marriage; in 1557 the inquisitors of Saragossa were allowed, in the same manner, to defray the cost of alterations in the Aljafería.[1143] In short, this fund was expected to meet the innumerable miscellaneous expenses of the tribunals and to supply all deficiencies, rendering the inquisitors watchful to keep it abundantly supplied.

There were occasions when penances replaced confiscations, to the manifest advantage of the tribunals. Thus, in 1519, when the estate of Fernando de Villareal was subject to confiscation, Charles V authorized the inquisitors to impose on him such penance as they deemed fit and released to him the surplus. It is not likely that this surplus was allowed to be large for, when in 1535, the tribunal of Valencia was trying the Bachiller Molina and learned that the viceroy had promised Molina's wife that, in case of confiscation, he would ask the emperor to forego it, the inquisitors wrote to the Suprema that they proposed not to confiscate his property but to impose a penance of something less than its value.[1144] This indicates that the penances were not subject to the crown and thus it exposes the disingenuousness of the Suprema, in replying to a petition of Valencia, in the Córtes of Monzon in 1537, that the Inquisition should be restrained from penancing the Moriscos. It argued that these pecuniary penances were applied to the royal treasury and that his majesty should not be asked to remit them, or be required to supplicate the pope to revoke what the canons prescribe.[1145]

REPLACE CONFISCATION

The canons prescribed confiscation, but there was no hesitation, as we have just seen, in substituting penance. The largest scale on which this was tried was in the kingdoms of Aragon, where the Moriscos were mostly vassals of the gentry and nobles, who suffered when they were impoverished and their lands were taken. The fueros of Valencia provided that feudal lands confiscated, whether for heresy or other cause, should revert to the lord, and this was repeatedly sworn to by Ferdinand and Charles, but the Inquisition calmly disregarded all laws and insisted on confiscating for its own benefit. Even a brief of Paul III, August 2, 1546, decreeing that for ten years and subsequently, at the pleasure of the Holy See, there should be no confiscations or pecuniary penances inflicted on the Moriscos, received no attention and the practical answer to the remonstrances of the Córtes of 1564 was a specific instruction from the Suprema to the Valencia tribunal to go on confiscating, no matter what the people might say about their privileges.[1146] Aragon, meanwhile, had obtained, in 1534, a pragmática by which Charles renounced his right to the Morisco confiscations, which were to revert to the heirs or be distributed as intestate, and to this the assent of the Suprema was secured. This was, however, practically nullified for, in 1547, the Córtes complained that confiscations were replaced by penances greater than the wealth of the culprits, who were obliged to sell all their property and, in addition, to impoverish their kindred, to which the Suprema loftily replied that, if any one was aggrieved, he could appeal to it or to the inquisitors.[1147] A lucrative bargain was finally made with Valencia, which had the largest Morisco population. In 1537 the Córtes proposed that, for a payment of 400 ducats a year, the Inquisition should abstain from penancing the Moriscos, but the Suprema refused, on the ground that it would be a disservice to God. It was shrewd in this for, in 1571, it secured an agreement under which, for an annual payment of 50,000 sueldos (2500 ducats) it abandoned confiscation and limited penance to 10 ducats, the payment of which was rendered secure by levying it on the aljamas of the culprits.[1148] Favorable as was this, the inquisitors did not restrain themselves to its observance. In the auto de fe of January 7, 1607, there was a penance of 50 ducats, one of 30 and one of 20 and, while there were only eight reconciliations, there were twenty penances of 10 ducats. The Suprema took exception to this, saying that, without reconciliation, the fines were uncalled for, in the absence of some special offence.[1149] The agreement, in fact, was one under which the gains of the tribunal were limited only by its industry, for there was no lack of Morisco apostates. The little village of Mislata, near the city, must have been well-nigh bankrupted, for it was liable for the penances of its inhabitants, of whom there were eighty-three penanced in 1591 and seventeen in 1592.[1150]

***

As confiscations diminished throughout Spain, the unrestricted power to impose fines and penances came in opportunely to fill deficiencies. They could be levied in a vast variety of cases--not only for suspicion of heresy and for fautorship, but for bigamy, blasphemy, ill-sounding expressions and all offences against the tribunal and its officials, as well as for those of the officials themselves and the familiars. The temporal jurisdiction especially afforded large opportunities, for the defendant, whether he was a familiar or an outsider, could always be fined for the benefit of the tribunal and this was rarely omitted. It was no secret within the Holy Office that this discretional power was to be exercised, not in accordance with the merits of the case, but with the needs of the Inquisition. As early as 1538, this was intimated in the instructions to Inquisitor Valdeolite of Navarre, when sent on a visitation to investigate witchcraft. He was forbidden to inflict confiscations but was told that he could impose fines and penances, in proportion to the offences and wealth of the culprits, in order to meet expenses and enable the receiver to pay salaries.[1151] In time the Suprema grew more outspoken. A carta acordada of October 22, 1575 told inquisitors that they could impose pecuniary penalties while on visitations, as well as when sitting in the tribunal, and must bear in mind the poverty of the Suprema as well as the wealth of the culprits and the character of the offence. This was repeated in 1580, and in 1595 attention was called to the necessity of relieving the wants of the Inquisition in this manner, an exhortation repeated in 1624.[1152]

PRODUCTIVENESS

This stimulation was apparently superfluous, for the inquisitors exploited their powers in this respect to a degree that sometimes moved even the Suprema to reproof. In a visitation of Gerona and Elne by Doctor Zurita of Barcelona, in 1564, we find him inflicting fines and penances continually, of 4, 6, 10, 20, 30 or 100 ducats, apparently limited only by the means of the victim. His colleague, Dr. Mexia, on a visitation penanced Damian Cortes in 100 ducats because, thirty years before, when some one told him to trust in God, he had exclaimed "Trust in God! By trusting in God last year I lost 50 ducats" and, when Juan Barbero made a comment on this sentence, he was fined 20 ducats and costs. When this last exploit was reported by de Soto Salazar, the Suprema ordered the fines to be refunded, as it also did with those inflicted by Mexia, of 60, 40 and 15 ducats, on the Bayle of Vindoli and two jurados for an offence so trifling that their names were ordered to be stricken from the records. When sitting as a tribunal these inquisitors were even more liberal to themselves, for they fined the Abbot of Ripoll 400 ducats for keeping a nun as a mistress--an offence wholly outside of their jurisdiction.[1153] As late as 1687, the tribunal of Logroño furnished a flagrant instance of this abuse of arbitrary power, when it excommunicated and fined in 200 ducats D. Miguel Urban de Espinosa, a Knight of Santiago and familiar, because, when summoned to attend at the publication of the Edict of Faith, he sought to enter the church while wearing a sword. The inquisitor-general promptly ordered his absolution and suspended the fine until further information.[1154]

The receipts from penances, although fluctuating, were a substantial addition to income. In the Seville auto de fe of May 13, 1585, a penitent accused of Lutheranism was penanced in 100 ducats, a bigamist in 200, provided it did not exceed half his property; for asserting fornication to be no sin one man was penanced in 200 ducats or less, according to his wealth, another in 200 and two in 1000 maravedís apiece, while, for concealing heretics, there was a penance of 50 ducats. In all, the auto yielded 850 ducats and 2000 maravedís.[1155] Even more productive was the auto of June 14, 1579, at Llerena, where the tribunal harvested 626,000 maravedís and 2700 ducats, or about 4375 ducats in all--owing to some of the penitents being well-to-do ecclesiastics, given to Illuminism.[1156] Toledo, in 1604, imposed a penance of 3000 ducats on Giraldo Paris, a German of Madrid, guilty of sundry heretical propositions, including the assertion that St. Job was an alchemist.[1157] The same tribunal, in 1649 and 1650, penanced four persons engaged in endeavoring to shield a Judaizer, two of them 500 and the other two 300 ducats apiece. In 1654, again, in two autos, November 8th and December 27th, it realized a total of 4000 ducats. After this it had occasional good fortune and, in 1669, it was supremely lucky in a rich penitent, Don Alonso Sanchez, priest and physician to the Cuenca tribunal, whom it convicted of fautorship and penanced in the large sum of 13,000 ducats.[1158] In 1654, Cuenca realized 2250 ducats, besides thirteen confiscations, from its auto of June 29th.[1159] Córdova was more fortunate, in an auto of May 3, 1655, when a group of wealthy Judaizers and their friends yielded an aggregate of 7000 ducats.[1160]

In addition to this source of revenue from penance imposed on penitents there were the fines inflicted in the exercise of the secular jurisdiction of the Inquisition. How liberally this power was exercised, even when the delinquents were officials, is seen in the defence offered by the Suprema, in 1632, when strenuous complaints were made about the familiars of Valencia. It instanced the case of Jaime Blau, who was fined 600 libras, half to the complainant and half to the fisc; Vicente de San German fined 300 libras; Hierónimo Llodra, 500 ducats; Pedro Carbonel, 500 ducats; Tomás Real, 300 ducats; Miguel Rubio, 400 libras, and Hierónimo Pilart, 500 libras.[1161] Doubtless through these inflictions the culprits escaped corporal punishments much less endurable, and they serve to explain the persistent multiplication of familiars, coupled with disregard of the character of the appointees. It was the same with outsiders who were prosecuted for offences against officials, as when, in 1565, Don Tristan de Urria of Saragossa was fined 60 ducats for insulting a notary.[1162]

LUCRATIVE RESULTS

In the seventeenth century the Suprema claimed these fines as its special perquisite. When Jaime Blau, for instance, was mulcted in 300 ducats for the fisc, no sooner was the Suprema apprised of it than it ordered the amount to be remitted at once, and the length of correspondence which ensued indicates that this was a novelty submitted to unwillingly.[1163] Even a fine of 100 libras, imposed on Ignacio Navarro, in 1636, was called for immediately and remitted, as was also soon afterwards 100 ducats with which he purchased his pardon; as he was forthwith arrested again for murdering Don Juan Augustin Saluco, he probably yielded another series of fines.[1164] In the extreme exigencies of the royal treasury, the king claimed a portion of these receipts and, by a decree of September 30, 1639, he ordered one-fourth of all fines for secular offences to be paid to the official designated to receive the fines of the royal courts.[1165]

In the unscrupulous exercise of discretional power, fines and penances were frequently imposed beyond the culprit's ability to pay, and inquisitors had a habit of adding in the sentence the alternative of some corporal punishment, such as the galleys, scourging or vergüenza, with the object of inducing the kindred to contribute, in order to avert from the family the shame of the public infliction. The Instructions of 1561 strictly forbid this cruelty; the sentences are to be without conditional or alternative and inability to pay is not to be thus visited.[1166] This received scant obedience. In 1568 it was the ordinary practice of the Barcelona tribunal to enforce payment of its arbitrary impositions by the alternative of such punishment.[1167] About 1640, however, we are told by an inquisitor that the question was evaded by the prudent custom of sending poor men to the galleys and reserving pecuniary penance for the wealthy.[1168]

In fact, after the middle of the seventeenth century, the number of such penances diminished and they are usually for larger amounts. In a record of the autos de fe of Toledo, from 1648 to 1794, there is but one that is less than 100 ducats and that one is for 50. In all there are but sixty-four penances imposed up to 1742 and none subsequently. The aggregate is 30,600 ducats, besides fourteen of half the property of the culprit.[1169] Whether from a growing sense of their indecency or from a lack of material, the custom of imposing pecuniary penances rapidly declined in the eighteenth century. In a collection of sixty-six autos de fe, between 1721 and 1745, comprising in all 962 cases, there is not a single pecuniary penance.[1170] Fines, however, continued to be imposed to the last. March 27, 1816, Pasqual Franchini of Madrid, for possessing two indecent pictures, was fined 100 ducats and, as these are defined as applicable to the royal treasury, it would appear that the crown had absorbed this trifling source of revenue.[1171]

In this matter the Roman Inquisition offered a creditable contrast to the Spanish. Except in Milan, Cremona and other places under Spanish rule, pecuniary punishments were rarely to be inflicted; the assent of the Congregation of cardinals was required, and they were at once to be distributed in pious uses, of which a strict account was required. Thus in 1595, one of 4000 crowns was given to the poor of Genoa and, in the same year at Naples, one of 400 crowns was parcelled out among the charitable establishments. Even this was felt to derogate from the character of the Holy Office and, in 1632, Urban VIII decreed that papal confirmation must be had in each case and, at the same time, he withdrew the special privileges of the Milanese tribunals.[1172] So strong was the disgust felt in Rome for this commercialized zeal for the faith that, when the Fiscal Cabrera was there representing the Inquisition, in the case of Villanueva, and Arce y Reynoso sent to him, for presentation to the pope, a report of an auto celebrated by the tribunal of Santiago, with the expectation of arousing his sympathy for an institution that was doing so much for religion, Cabrera replied, January 6, 1656, that he would not present it without special orders. Alexander VII, he said, disliked pecuniary penalties in matters of faith, and there were some of these in the report; his Holiness had already spoken to him on the subject and it was wiser not to call his attention to it afresh.[1173]

CHAPTER III - DISPENSATIONS

The Roman curia had so long accustomed Christendom to the idea that pardon for the consequences of sin was purchasable, that we cannot be surprised if relief from the penalties imposed by the Inquisition was a marketable commodity to be regarded as a source of revenue. We have already seen this exemplified in the compositions for confiscation, and it was carried out with regard to the more personal inflictions prescribed by canon and municipal law--the disabilities of culprits and their descendants alluded to above (p. 287). The Instructions of 1484 and 1488 adopted these and extended the sumptuary regulations by including the carrying of arms and riding on horseback; they enlarged the list of prohibited callings and applied them all to the descendants of those who were burnt in person or effigy. Then Ferdinand and Isabella, by pragmáticas in 1501, made the prohibition of office-holding and the following of numerous trades and professions a matter of municipal law, reserving the right to grant relief by royal licences. Thus these disabilities, which weighed cruelly upon penitents and their descendants, drew their origin from different sources. The sumptuary restrictions, which came to be known as cosas arbitrarias, were considered to be the act of the tribunal, which could remove them. Permission to hold office, or to follow the inhibited callings, was a royal prerogative, while the Holy See, as the guardian of the faith and of the canon law, and as the supreme source of inquisitorial jurisdiction, claimed a general control, which was grudgingly conceded.

In addition to these disabilities were the personal punishments, relief from which was claimed by the Inquisition. Those which concern us here were the galleys, exile, imprisonment and the wearing of the sanbenito or "habito"--a kind of yellow tunic with a red St. Andrew's cross--a mark of infamy and a severe infliction, as it largely impeded the efforts of the penitent to gain a livelihood.

The curia was not long in recognizing the abundant market opened for its dispensations by the large numbers of those subjected to disabilities. In the Taxes of the Penitentiary there was inserted a clause offering the fullest possible dispensation for "Marrania." To a cleric the price was 60 gros tournois, or 15 ducats; to a layman 40 gros, or 10 ducats, besides a fee to the datary of 20 gros. When the dispensation was partial, allowing a layman to follow his accustomed calling, or a priest to celebrate mass, the charge was 12 gros, or 3 ducats, but, if the profession was that of a physician or advocate, the charge was double.[1174]

We have seen the extreme jealousy which existed as to any papal interference with the Inquisition and Ferdinand's repeated efforts to suppress papal letters, but the power to issue these dispensations could not be questioned. Cardinal Mendoza, Archbishop of Toledo, held from Innocent VIII a faculty to grant rehabilitations, and one of these, issued to Pero Díaz of Cifuentes, whose mother had been burnt, was recognized and confirmed, in 1520, by the Suprema and Charles V.[1175] At the same time, the Inquisition claimed the right to control relief from the punishments which it inflicted, and it held these favors at a far higher price than the cheap papal dispensations. Anchias, the secretary of the Saragossa tribunal, tells us how Juan Gerónimo was sentenced to wear the sanbenito and carried it for a long time, until his father paid for him to the tribunal a thousand florins for permission to abandon it. Some of the gold proved to be of light weight and eighteen or twenty florins were demanded of him to make good the deficiency, when he handed them to the messenger saying "How is this? Are not the señores well paid for the merchandise they sold me? But take it and welcome."[1176] When exactions on this scale were possible, we can readily believe that Dr. Guiral, the embezzling inquisitor of Córdova, could easily secrete a hundred and fifty thousand maravedís from the dispensations sold to the wearers of the sanbenito (Vol. I, p. 190), nor can we wonder that the Holy Office was resolved to maintain a hold on so prolific a source of gain.

CONTEST WITH THE CROWN

The situation was complicated by the pretensions of the sovereigns to intervene and claim their share, and this they sought to establish by procuring from Alexander VI a brief of February 18, 1495, which recites that the inquisitors collect various sums from those who had obtained papal rehabilitations and retained them; all such moneys theretofore and thereafter received for commutations and rehabilitations were to be placed at the disposal of the sovereigns, under pain of ipso facto excommunication.[1177] It is obvious from this that the papal dispensations were not admitted without the exaction of further payments; that the pope was content with this, so long as the taxes of the

Penitentiary were paid in Rome, and that Ferdinand was concerned only with the destination of the proceeds and was quite willing to acknowledge the papal authority when it was exercised for his benefit. He lost no time in availing himself of the papal grant on a large scale and, before the year was out, we find him selling relief in mass to all those disabled by the tribunal of Toledo, a transaction which brought in large returns for, in 1497, Alonso de Morales, the royal treasurer, acknowledges the receipt of 6,499,028 maravedís from Toledo commutations and rehabilitations, and this was doubtless only one of numerous similar compositions.[1178]

The Inquisition was not disposed to abandon its profitable commerce. The Suprema continued to assert its control, in instructions, June 3, 1497, ordering inquisitors to take no fees for rehabilitations without consulting it; May 25, 1498, it declared that if there were no inquisitors-general there would be no one able to grant rehabilitation or to relieve from sanbenitos, and it forbade the tribunals to commute for imprisonment except by spiritual penances.[1179] There was evidently a contest on foot between the Inquisition and Ferdinand, of which the details are lost, for we have a letter from him, February 24, 1498, to a tribunal in which he says "You know that we have granted a privilege through which the children of condemned heretics are rehabilitated as to the cosas arbitrarias imposed by you. As it is our will that this privilege be maintained, we charge you not to levy or take anything from them for the enjoyment of it and if, perchance, the inquisitors-general have written or shall write anything contrary to this, consult us before acting on it and we will write to them and to you what most comports with our service."[1180]

The sovereigns, however, yielded the point when, by a cédula of January 12, 1499, they formally made over to the inquisitors-general all the moneys accruing from penances, commutations and rehabilitations in the kingdoms of Castile and Aragon, in order to provide for the salaries, but this grant as usual was practically subject to the exigencies of the royal treasury and the promise was irregularly kept.[1181] The inquisitors seem to have speedily arrogated to themselves this profitable privilege, for the Instructions of 1500 forbid them to grant dispensations and commutations, the right to which is reserved to the inquisitors-general.[1182] It was greatly impaired, however, by the next move in the game, the pragmáticas of 1501, which made disability to hold office or to follow numerous callings a matter of municipal law and reserved to the crown the right to issue licences in derogation of it, thus depriving the Inquisition of control over this important section of the penalties.

PAPAL COMPETITION

While Ferdinand thus secured a share in the business, he fully admitted the necessity of papal rehabilitation as a condition precedent. In 1510, writing to a member of the Suprema about the rehabilitation of the Jurado Alonso de Medina, issued at the request of Queen Juana, he says that it was granted under the belief that Medina held a papal brief; if he did not, it was invalid as there must first be papal rehabilitation. Yet papal action amounted to nothing in these matters without the royal licence. About this time the Licenciado Portillo applied to him stating that, as the memory of his grandfather had been condemned, he was incapacitated from holding office; he had been rehabilitated by the pope and now he asked for a licence in view of certain services rendered, and Ferdinand granted the prayer. The strictness with which these licences were construed is illustrated by a petition, in 1515, from Dr. Jaime de Lis, a physician of Logroño, representing that, by the condemnation of his parents, he had been incapacitated; he had procured a papal brief authorizing him to practice everywhere, and a royal licence to practice in Logroño. Unable to resist importunities, he had exceeded his bounds, for which he craved pardon and also permission to attend the Duke of Najera, who joined in the supplication. This was granted, with a warning not to transgress again, and the tribunal of Calahorra and the magistrates of all the towns were charged to make him observe the limits.[1183]

When the papal dispensation was issued to ecclesiastics, the king did not intervene, but there can be no doubt that the vidimus, or confirmation of the Suprema, was required and had to be paid for, for it had, on January 8 and February 12, 1498, summoned all reconciled penitents to present the absolutions and dispensations which they had procured from Rome, a significant indication that otherwise they would not be respected.[1184] Such dispensations were issued as readily as those to laymen, though, as we have seen, the price was fifty per cent. higher. Thus, April 8, 1514, Leo X dispensed Cristóbal Rodrigo, priest of Luduena, from the disabilities incurred by the condemnation of his parents and authorized him to retain his benefices, acquire others and perform all his functions. So also, November 3, 1514, he dispensed Bartolomé Eruelo, beneficed in the convent of Santa Cruz of Saragossa, from all the disabilities resulting from the heresy of his paternal grandfather.[1185]

Yet there frequently occur cases of rehabilitation in which there is no mention of papal intervention, under circumstances where it could scarce fail to be alluded to had it existed.[1186] There would seem to have been no thought of invoking the co-operation of the Holy See in the great composition of Seville, under which twenty thousand ducats were obtained by Ferdinand for the rehabilitations alone and, when it was extended to Córdova and other places, they formed part of the inducements offered.[1187] So, when Cardinal Manrique issued by wholesale licences to hold office, to the large districts of Seville, Córdova, Granada and Leon, there is no allusion to papal dispensations. For some reason, probably financial, these licences were issued for short terms and required renewal; in one case, a document, issued in February, 1528, prolonged the time to April 15th and then, on April 6th, it was extended to the end of June.[1188]

This disregard of papal participation seems to have provoked the curia to retaliatory action, and it issued rehabilitations with clauses of censures and penalties for all who might impede them, thus rendering unnecessary the concurrence of the king and the Inquisition. Charles thereupon reissued the pragmáticas of 1501 and empowered the Inquisition to enforce them, while the Suprema explained to the tribunals that there was a disability under the canons and another under the pragmáticas, so that the papal rehabilitation was insufficient without the royal and vice versa, wherefore inquisitors were instructed to look closely into this and prosecute those who did not possess both. It withdrew however from this position and issued cartas acordadas May 15, 1530 and May 16, 1531, complaining of this new form of papal dispensations. If these were allowed to continue, it said, all the disabled would be rehabilitated and the laws of the kingdom would be annulled, wherefore, when such letters were presented, the fiscal was ordered to draw up a supplication to the pope setting forth that the disabilities were enacted by the laws of the land and that it had been found by experience that these children of heretics, if they obtain judicial positions, condemn Christians to death unjustly, or, if they become physicians, surgeons or apothecaries, give their patients poisons in place of remedies. All these supplications were to be sent to the Suprema, which would forward them to the Roman agent of the Inquisition--and meanwhile, we may assume, the papal letters were suspended. In another document of the period, opposition to the papal rehabilitations is enumerated as one of the regular duties of the fiscal. It is somewhat remarkable that this seems to have been confined to Castile for, in 1535, the Suprema learned that the Valencia tribunal accepted and respected papal rehabilitations and hastened to instruct it to follow the Castilian method. The struggle continued and the instructions of 1531 were repeated July 19 and October 26, 1543 and May 14, 1546.[1189]

PAPAL COMPETITION

The strenuous days of Ferdinand were past and resistance was vain. The curia continued imperturbably to sell dispensations of the most liberal character which completely annulled Spanish legislation. One bearing the name of Paul III, February 1, 1545, issued to Juan de Haro of Jaen, whose grandparents had been burnt in effigy, gives assurance of his high deserts and concedes that, even if his progenitors had been condemned and burnt, he can ascend to the degrees of bachelor, licentiate and doctor; he can assume the office of judge, corregidor, advocate, procurator and notary, legate, nuncio, physician, surgeon, apothecary, farmer of revenue, collector and receiver of taxes and all honors and dignities, including professorial chairs; he can wear garments of any color and material, ornaments of gold and silver and jewels; he can bear arms and ride on horses and mules, inherit from any kindred, acquire property of all kinds, enter the priesthood and obtain any dignity or preferment, and all inquisitors and secular powers are forbidden to interfere with him in the enjoyment of these privileges.[1190] This is evidently the customary formula of these dispensations, and it was galling to have the laws of the land and the jurisdiction of the Inquisition thus calmly set at naught, but there was no help for it. Sometimes, however, the recipients of these papal rehabilitations deemed it wise to show humility, in which case they were fairly assured of a benignant reception. In 1548, the Saragossa tribunal penanced for fautorship five hidalgos, vassals of the Count of Ribagorza, in a way disabling them from holding office. They procured letters from Rome, but submitted them to the Suprema and declined to use them, whereupon Valdés told the inquisitors to follow the letters and dispense the penitents from their disabilities.[1191]

Roman competition, however, by no means destroyed the home traffic in dispensations. Whatever was imposed by the inquisitors could be removed by the inquisitors-general, as when Valdés, May 27, 1551, granted licence to Leandro de Loriz to accept the position of assessor to the bayle of Valencia after he had been disabled by the tribunal from holding any office of justice.[1192] When, however, disabilities were the result of the pragmáticas, it was recognized that their removal was a function of the crown. Thus, in 1549, the Suprema expresses pleasure that those reconciled under an Edict of Grace should procure rehabilitations from the king and, in 1564, it explains that the dispensations granted by the inquisitor-general only relate to the sumptuary cosas arbitrarias, so that those obtaining them who exceed in this are to be prosecuted.[1193] The functions of the Inquisition thus were restricted to enabling the disabled to wear costly apparel and jewels, to bear arms and ride. These, which were known as dispensations "en lo arbitrario" were in great demand and a brisk business was done in them. In the records of course there is nothing said about their being sold, or the prices paid for them, which were doubtless proportioned to the station or wealth of the penitent or of his kindred, but that they were articles of traffic is shown by their being frequently given as gratifications to the lower officials, issued in blank, to be disposed of at the best price that could be had.[1194] So customary, indeed, became the issue of these dispensations that, towards the close of the sixteenth century, Peña closes his remarks on disabilities by saying that, after a time, it is usual to dispense for them.[1195]

The rehabilitation for holding office and trading was likewise a source of profit to the crown and its officials. The sale of these became so general that, in 1552, it formed a subject of complaint by the Córtes of Madrid, which represented that the children and grandchildren of condemned heretics were rich and obtained rehabilitations from the king, in contravention of the pragmáticas, to the great detriment of the Republic. To the petition that this should cease the reply was that the supplication would be borne in mind and the pragmáticas be observed.[1196] That this promise was kept may well be doubted, especially as, in time, the curia abandoned its claim to issue dispensations of this nature. When, in 1603 and 1604, several applications for such a grace were made to it, the Congregation of the Inquisition refused to interfere.[1197]

COMMUTATIONS

The curia had never assumed to interfere with the commutation or redemption of the punishments inflicted by the Inquisition. In these it therefore had a free hand, and the resultant revenue must have been important, for it was always ready to show mercy for a reasonable consideration. The speculative value of such commutations were recognized, at least as early as 1498, when they were already regarded as a regular source of income, for Juan de Monasterio was then characterized as inquisitor of Valencia and receiver of penances and commutations.[1198] In 1524 we find Manrique commissioning Francisco de Salmeron to collect from the receivers of the tribunals all "penas y penitencias, conmutaciones y habilidades" and a similar grouping in 1540 and 1544 shows that they all continued to be sources contributing to a common fund.[1199]

Of these punishments the one most productive and most commonly commuted was the sanbenito or penitential habit, release from which in the early period, as we have seen, was reckoned, in one case at least, at a thousand gold florins. The severity of the infliction is well set forth in the petition, about 1560, of "lo povero Notar Jacobo Damiano" to the Sicilian tribunal. He says that he has tried in every way to earn a living without success, and his only resource is a return to his birth-place, Racalmuto, where his family will aid in his support and he can end the few days that remain to his age and infirmities, but, as his kindred are persons of honor, if he comes with the sanbenito they will drive him away and leave him to die of starvation. He therefore begs to have the habit commuted to a money payment for the redemption of captives and some other penance, and he will raise the amount from his family; otherwise he is in peril of death from want, as he is abandoned by all.[1200] What between the degradation and the impediment to winning a livelihood, those subjected to the penalty and their kindred were likely to pay whatever sum they could afford for release. It was commonly coupled with imprisonment--the "carcel y abito" usually went together and commutation covered both.

As a rule, inquisitors were prohibited from granting these commutations--the temptation to retain the proceeds was doubtless too great. In 1513 Ximenes, on learning that some inquisitors were doing so, forbade it for the future and reserved the right to the inquisitor-general.[1201] There were some exceptions however, especially in the case of distant tribunals, as in a commission granted to Sicily in 1519, to Navarre in 1520, and a limited one to Majorca in 1523.[1202] As a rule all applications were submitted to the Suprema, which gave the necessary instructions and directed the money to be remitted to it, or to be held subject to its order for pious uses.[1203] Its full realization of the financial possibilities of the matter is seen in instructions, in 1519, to Barcelona--and doubtless to the other tribunals--to report how many penitents were wearing sanbenitos and how much could be obtained from them for commutations.[1204] When conviction would bring not only confiscation but the prospect of another contribution from the kindred, it will be realized how great was the temptation to severity.

The "pious uses" for which the payments were ostensibly received were various. Doctor Arganda, Inquisitor of Cuenca, in rendering, May 9, 1585, a statement revealing a deficit in revenue, renewed a request of the month previous, that the Suprema would grant to the tribunal the commutations of Francisco Abist and Juan Joaibet, Moriscos; they were very old, had been sentenced ten years before, and would die Moors; therefore it would be well that the tribunal should have the benefit of the four thousand reales which they offered. The Suprema replied with an inquiry whether this was the utmost that could be obtained from them. Then on August 9th the inquisitor urged the acceptance of the offer, so that the money could be used for a much needed prison for familiars and other purposes, and reminded the Suprema that, in 1583, it had made a similar grant of commutations for a building.[1205] Another pious use was giving to Dr. Ortiz, when sent to Sicily as inquisitor, in 1541, certain commutations as part of his salary. They must have been considerable, for the fees accruing on them to Secretary Zurita amounted to fifty-five ducats.[1206] Still another pious use is indicated in an order from the Suprema, in 1549, to the tribunal of Granada, to commute the sanbenito of Catalina Ramirez into spiritual works and such pecuniary penance as she could pay for pious uses. The latter are explained, in an accompanying private note of instruction, to hold the money until the apparitor Cuebas marries his daughter, when he is to be aided with it. He evidently had petitioned for a "comutacion de abito" and it was accorded in this form.[1207]

***

These commutations, in fact, became a sort of currency in which favors were asked and granted, replacing, to some extent, the confiscations of an earlier period. Thus, in 1589, the Valencia convent of the new Discalced Carmelites of Santa Teresa petitioned for the grant of the commutations of certain sanbenitos and soon afterwards the Dominican convent made a similar request.[1208] The most usual pious work, however, for which they were ostensibly employed, was in assisting the redemption of captives. Yet this formula frequently covered other destinations, as in the case of Martin de Burguera of Calatayud, who was relieved of prison and sanbenito for fifteen ducats "para reducion de cautivos" and the ducats were simultaneously granted to Pedro Salvan, apparitor of the Saragossa tribunal.[1209] When the proceeds were really to be employed for the redemption of captives, precautions were taken to see that they were so applied. These are expressed, January 18, 1559, by Valdés to Horozco de Arce, Inquisitor of Sicily, when empowering him to grant commutations to four penitents, provided their sentences are not irremissible and they have completed three years of imprisonment, when, besides the money payment, there are to be simple penances of fasting, prayer and pilgrimage. The penitents are to be designated by Nicolas Calderon or his agent, who will bargain as to the amounts of payment, and the money is to be given to him for the ransom of his mother, sister and two nieces, on his furnishing good security that, within a term to be designated by the inquisitor, he will present them to the tribunal or refund the money.[1210] The condition in this, that the penalty commuted must not be irremissible, was not always observed. Such sentences, as we shall see, were reserved for cases of special guilt, but they yielded to the powerful solvent of money, a larger price presumably being demanded. Thus March 7, 1560, the Sicilian inquisitor was ordered to select some one who had served not less than nine years under such a sentence and commute it for the ransom of the wife of ---- of Cibdadella.[1211]

Even the galleys, which were regarded as a much severer punishment than the "carcel y abito," were commutable, though, as the prisoner was an incumbrance, while the galley-slave was useful and the supply was always deficient, we may infer that his commutation was held at a higher price. Condemnation to the galleys was also much less frequent than to the sanbenito, and of course was only inflicted on able-bodied men, so that cases of its commutation do not occur in such abundance. Yet they were sufficiently numerous to lead to complaint by the Suprema to Charles V, in 1528, that when it sent messengers to liberate those whose sentences were thus commuted, the commanders of the galleys refused to surrender them, whereupon Charles issued a cédula ordering their liberation under pain of two thousand florins.[1212]

***

Commutations for the galleys had various shapes. In 1543, Don Luis Muñoz, Lord of Ayodan, offered two slaves as substitutes for two of his Morisco vassals, Juan Maymon and Juan Muñoz, condemned to serve, the one for ten and the other for twelve years, of which three had elapsed and, after investigation to see that the substitutes were able-bodied, the bargain was closed. In 1547, Miguel Mercado obtained the remainder of his sentence to the galleys commuted to service on the French border, when presumably there was some money consideration.[1213] It is probable that commutations for money became too frequent for the good of the naval service, for in 1556 the Suprema strictly forbade them for the future, doubtless under royal command.[1214] This prohibition seems to have lasted for a considerable time, as the Spanish armada was greatly in need of men and we happen not to meet with cases until near the close of the century, when they reappear in the Valencia records. In 1590, Jusepe Gacet, a familiar condemned for the murder of his wife, obtained a commutation of his sentence. In 1596, a New Christian, Gaspar Moix, negotiated for release from the three years which he still had to serve and, after investigation into his means, it was fixed at seven hundred libras and a slave. Moix, however, on his liberation, found that his sanbenito was not included in the bargain and he had to pay a hundred libras more for its removal. In 1597, Onufre Quintana offered two thousand reales and a slave which were accepted. In the same year Miguel Saucer applied for a commutation, when the Suprema instructed the tribunal to ascertain what he would pay for it and the same answer was given, in 1600, to a similar petition from Jaime Cornexo.[1215] It is apparent from the high value set on these mercies that comparatively few convicts could afford their purchase.

Evidently the Suprema paid little heed to the instructions of Philip II to Manrique de Lara, in 1595, to be very cautious in granting dispensations for galleys, exile, reclusion and sanbenitos; there must be ample cause and no attention should be paid to prayers, and favors, for it was essential that sentences should be completely executed. This was repeated, with some amplification, by Carlos II, in

1695, showing that there was still occasion to restrain the Holy Office from bartering pardons for money.[1216]

CHAPTER IV - BENEFICES

When the Inquisition was established, it was apparent that if its officials, or a portion of them, could be quartered on the Church there might be less diversion of the confiscations from the royal treasury. At the very commencement, in 1480, Ferdinand and Isabella obtained, from Sixtus IV, an indult authorizing them to present the four earliest inquisitors to benefices, of course without obligation to reside. As yet, however, the Inquisition had not inspired general terror, and the people refused to admit the intruders, whereupon the sovereigns provided them with four chaplaincies in the royal chapel.[1217] The attempt was not abandoned and, in the supplementary Instructions of December, 1484, Torquemada announced that it was the intention of the sovereigns to procure a papal indult authorizing them to bestow benefices, not only on the inquisitors but on all the clerics employed in the holy work.[1218] Something of the kind was evidently obtained for, when the Holy Office was organized, in 1485, under Torquemada, the brief confirming his appointment dispensed from residence all officials in its service who held or might thereafter obtain preferment; new appointees were released from the customary temporary residence, and all were assured of their full revenues without deduction, all apostolical and conciliar decrees to the contrary notwithstanding.[1219] There was nothing in this to shock public opinion, for the canon law permitted canons to be absent for study in any recognized university, and the enjoyment of benefices everywhere by the creatures of the curia was legalized by assuming service to the pope to be equivalent to service in a chapter.[1220] Yet the Spanish Church, apparently, was not disposed to submit quietly to this and its resistance may be assumed as the cause of another brief of Innocent VIII, February 8, 1486, which limited the grant to five years and required the beneficiary to supply a vicar to fill his place. At the same time it specified all officials, down to messengers and gaolers, as entitled to its benefits and provided for opposition by appointing the Bishops of Córdova and Leon and the Abbot of San Emiliano of Burgos as executors with full powers to suppress recalcitrants.[1221] When the five years expired, the indult was renewed for another five years and so it continued until the end of the Inquisition--the popes steadily refusing to prolong the term, as it gave them an important advantage, in their frequent collisions with the Spanish Holy Office, to say nothing of the fees consequent upon the issue of briefs so voluminous and so valuable.

The next step was to procure the power of presenting to benefices, and this was secured by another brief from Innocent VIII, in 1488, granting to the sovereigns the patronage of a prebend in each metropolitan, cathedral and collegiate church, excepting, in prudent deference to the Sacred College, those of which the bishops were also cardinals. Of this brief, Alonso de Burgos was made executor, enabling him to fulminate censures and take all necessary steps, until the appointee enjoyed pacific possession of his prebend. Under it Ferdinand and Isabella, on October 30th of the same year, made the first presentations, amounting to ten, six being inquisitors, two fiscals, one an apparitor and one designated merely as an official.[1222]

OPPOSITION OF CHAPTERS

This brief probably was good only for five years for, in 1494, the sovereigns obtained from Alexander VI another, with enlarged powers, of which Martin Ponce, Bishop of Avila, was executor. Under this, on April 11, 1495, they made twenty-four appointments, mostly inquisitors, but comprising seven fiscals, two members of the Suprema and two Roman agents of the Inquisition. Among the inquisitors we recognize the notorious Lucero and his predecessor in Córdova, the embezzling Dr. Guiral.[1223] It is probable that these briefs encountered resistance, for, in this latter case, we chance to hear of a prolonged struggle required to install Doctor Manuel Fernández Angulo of the Suprema in the Seville canonry given to him.[1224] Haughty canons of noble blood might well resent the intrusion of low-born officials such as Ferdinand sometimes thrust upon them. Thus, in 1499, on the death of Inquisitor Cevallos of Barcelona, his first appointee to a prebend in the church of Santa Ana, in the same city, he replaced him with Juan Moya, a simple tonsured clerk and gaoler of the tribunal, nor was this the only instance of such abuse of patronage.[1225] He also availed himself largely of the privilege of non-residence by appointing canons and other beneficed clerks to positions in the tribunals, and his letters of the period are numerous in which he notifies the chapters that their members have been thus drafted to the service of God, during which they are, under the papal letters, to be reckoned as present and are not to be deprived of any of the fruits of their preferment. So, when he drew the Licentiate Pero González

Manso from the professorship of law in Valladolid, he told the college that the chair would be filled by a substitute at half-price during Manso's absence.[1226] Everything was subservient to the Inquisition and all other institutions were expected to minister to its needs.

When Julius II, November 16, 1505, renewed the quinquennial indult, he no longer appointed executors but empowered the inquisitor-general to coerce with censures the chapters to account for and pay over to the appointees the revenues of their benefices. It appears that they sometimes compelled the appointees to agree under oath that they would take only a portion of the fruits, for Julius pronounced such agreements to be void and released the incumbents from their oaths. This brief he repeated, September 8, 1508, with some additions, of which more hereafter.[1227] The opposition of the chapters, in fact, had in no way diminished and defeat only seemed to intensify their obstinacy. When, in 1501, Diego de Robles, fiscal of the Suprema, was granted a canonry in the church of Zamora, the persistence of the chapter carried the matter to Rome, where Gracian de Valdés, nephew of the bishop, boasted that he would get the pope to reserve the benefice to himself. It gave infinite vexation to Ferdinand, who wrote to the canons, July 24th that, if they did not admit Robles within three days, they must leave the city and present themselves before him within thirty days, under pain of forfeiture of citizenship and temporalities. Similar orders were sent to the provisor; the corregidor was commanded to see to their execution, while urgent letters were addressed to Rome to counteract the labors of Valdés. These vigorous measures brought the chapter to terms and Ferdinand, on September 2nd, accepted their submission, revoking their banishment to take effect after their giving possession to Robles.[1228] Simultaneously a similar quarrel was on foot with the chapter of Barcelona, over the grant of a canonry to the Inquisitor of Saragossa, who was already Archdeacon of Almazan, and this was likewise carried to Rome.[1229] So resolutely did the chapters resist the invasion of their rights that Enguera, Inquisitor-general of Aragon and Bishop of Lérida, in 1512, had to invoke both royal and papal authority to secure the revenues of benefices held by him in the churches of Tarragona and Lérida and, with regard to the latter, the pope was obliged to appoint executors to enforce his briefs.[1230]

If Ferdinand had expected, by this abuse of patronage, to lighten the burden of supporting the Inquisition, he was doomed to disappointment. He probably found that those, who thus obtained positions for life, could not be depended upon to perform gratuitous service in the tribunals. Their full salaries had to be paid and their benefices were only an extra gratification, so that his anxiety to secure these for them must be attributed to his desire to obtain able and vigorous men for the moderate remuneration provided by the pay-roll. When Pedro de Belorado was sent to Sicily, in 1501, as Archbishop of Messina and also as inquisitor, the receiver was ordered to continue to him the salary paid to his predecessor Sgalambro.[1231] So it continued. When, in 1540, Blas Ortiz was commissioned as inquisitor of Valencia, the orders were to pay him the regular salary of six thousand sueldos, although, as canon of Toledo, he possessed a handsome income.[1232]

***

By this time these matters were in the hands of the Suprema, and its members and officials were too eager seekers after pluralities not to enforce the papal indults with vigor, giving rise to incessant struggles with recalcitrant churches. Thus, in 1546, when Pedro Ponce de Leon was made a member, he was maestre escuela in the church of Alcalá de Henares. There was trouble about his revenues for, on February 27, 1547, Valdés summoned the abbot and chapter to keep on paying him and expressed the hope that they would not compel him to resort to censures. Similar letters, about the same time, were issued in behalf of the private secretary of Valdés, Fortuno de Ibarquen, who was an insatiable pluralist, being Archdeacon of Sigüenza and canon in the churches of both Leon and Oviedo. Simultaneous were letters to the chapter of Segovia about the revenues of its dean and canon Miguel de Arena, who was Inquisitor of Seville, and to that of Sigüenza for its treasurer and canon, Menendo de Valdés, who was Inquisitor of Valladolid. A couple of months later there were letters to the chapter of Badajoz, about its canon Baltodano, who was Inquisitor of Toledo, and in August to the chapter of Majorca, about Joan García, who had been appointed consultor to the tribunal of Saragossa. In October prosecutions were commenced against the recalcitrant chapter of Leon, which had refused to pay the fruits of the canonries of Ibarguen and of Cervantes, the Inquisitor of Córdova.[1233]

It would be useless to multiply examples of this incessant strife, in which the chapters persistently, but unavailingly, sought to prevent the absorption of their revenues by the Holy Office. The resistance was hopeless for, even with the most resolute, it was only a question of time when opposition was broken down by excommunication and the summons to appear before the Suprema, while appeal to Rome was fruitless when it was the duty of the Spanish ambassador to watch for such cases and oppose them.[1234] Of course the greater number yielded without remonstrance and we hear only of those who dared to offer futile opposition.

It is observable that all the cases which thus come before us involve benefices without cure of souls. The papal indults comprised both those with and without such cure, and it is not to be supposed that the former were not extensively exploited, though we do not hear of them because, in such cases, there was no organized body to feel aggrieved and raise a contest. When came the Counter-reformation, the Council of Trent pronounced strongly against non-residence by beneficiaries holding cure of souls; special episcopal licence was required for absence which, save in exceptional cases, could not exceed two months and no privilege could be pleaded.[1235] Accordingly when, in 1567, Pius V was called upon to renew the quinquennial indult, he expressly excepted parochial churches and benefices with cure of souls. This was somewhat tardily obeyed and it was not until June 8, 1571, that the Suprema announced the limitation.[1236]

There was another provision of the Council of Trent which met with less observance. It required all obtaining preferment of any kind to make, within two months, profession of faith in the hands of the Ordinary or chapter. No attention was paid to this and the chapters, waking up to the advantage that it gave them, refused to pay the fruits, giving rise to multitudinous suits. At length, in 1612, a brief was procured from Paul V, declaring that the work of the inquisitors was most necessary to the Church and could not be interrupted to travel to the distant seats of their benefices. He therefore evoked all pending cases, imposing perpetual silence on the chapters and validating all payments made to incumbents, who were allowed in Spain six months, and in the colonies two years, to perform the duty; in future it should suffice to do it in the place of their residence and furnish a public instrument attesting the fact within six months or two years.[1237] The Council of Trent was of small importance when brought into collision with the Inquisition.

DOCTORAL AND MAGISTRAL CANONRIES

At length Philip III listened to the complaints of the chapters and, in a decree of December 24, 1599, addressed to the Suprema, he called attention to the injury inflicted on the cathedral services by withdrawing canons from their duties, and he ordered that in future much caution be exercised, especially as regarded the deans, the doctoral and magistral canons and the penitentiaries.[1238] If this produced an effect it was but temporary. In 1655 we chance to learn that, in the tribunal of Córdova, of the three inquisitors, Bernardino de Leon de la Rocha was a prebendary of Córdova and collegial of the cathedral of Cuenca; Bartolomé Bujan de Somoza was a canon of Cuenca and Fernando de Villegas was collegial of San Bartolomé. In addition, the fiscal, Juan María de Rodesno was collegial of Cuenca and the secretary, Pedro de Armenta was prebendary of Córdova.[1239] This single tribunal thus deprived Cuenca of three of its dignitaries and Córdova of two.

The doctoral and magistral canonries alluded to by Philip afforded a special grievance. These were stalls in each chapter to be occupied respectively by a doctor of laws and a master of theology, for the purpose apparently of furnishing to the church what it might need as to law and faith. They had been instituted by Sixtus IV, who decreed that the holders should not absent themselves for more than two months without express licence of the chapter under pain of forfeiture. The Inquisition was restive under this limitation on its acquisitiveness and, at its special request, Julius II, in his second brief of September 8, 1508, revoked the decree of Sixtus and included them among the benefices that could be held by officials without residence.[1240] At length, in 1599, the chapter of Córdova, in a contest over the matter, procured a papal brief requiring the residence of the doctoral canon, who was not to be excused under pretext of serving the Inquisition.[1241] Apparently this was disregarded, for Philip III, in his instructions of 1608 to Sandoval y Rojas, called special attention to the matter.[1242] Even this failed until there was a sharp conflict with the chapter of Toledo, over the case of Doctor Bernardo de Rojas, in which the chapter won and he was forced to resign an appointment as inquisitor. Then again the question came up, in 1640, when Philip IV appointed Doctor Andrés de Rueda Rico as supernumerary member of the Suprema; it resented the intrusion and addressed to the king a very free-spoken consulta, in which it laid particular emphasis on his being doctoral canon of Córdova and therefore obligated to residence. Yet, in spite of this, when the Córdova chapter refused to pay him his fruits, the Suprema decided against it. Then the chapter carried the case to Rome where, as the agent of the Inquisition reported, September 12, 1640, Urban VIII, to evade a direct decision, revived the brief of Sixtus IV forbidding the use of the doctoral and magistral canonries in this manner. Córdova followed up its victory and, in 1641, obtained another brief forbidding Rueda from receiving the fruits and appointing the nuncio and the Ordinary of Córdova executors to enforce it and to relieve the chapter from any censures fulminated in consequence. The Suprema was flushed with its recent victory, over the chapter of Valencia, in the matter of Sotomayor's prebend and pension and, in 1642, it addressed to the king an urgent appeal to suppress all such briefs, as Ferdinand had done, and representing the eagerness of the curia to destroy the independence of the Inquisition and the prerogatives of the crown. Philip, however, was now embarrassed with the Catalan and Portuguese revolts and for once was moderate, merely ordering the chapter to desist from the appeal and to surrender the briefs, while the inquisitor-general must require Rueda to abandon the canonry, seeing that he had enough to live on, with his salary in the Suprema and the wealthy archidiaconate of Castro which he also held. Incidentally the Suprema declared that the magistral canonries were out of reach, but the doctoral ones were not, probably presuming on the royal ignorance.[1243]

Trouble continued to the end. In 1684, the chapter of Santiago contested vigorously the right of the receiver-general of the Suprema to hold a canonry and, in spite of the prohibition to appeal to Rome, it carried the matter there, arguing that the officials of the Suprema were not included in the papal briefs. In this it had the support of the churches in general, which united in a memorial to the Holy See, but the effort was fruitless.[1244] Close watch seems to have been kept on the expiration of the quinquennial periods for, in 1728, the chapter of Valencia refused the daily distributions to non-resident members on the ground that the indult had run out; the tribunal appealed to the Suprema which replied, April 22nd, with a copy of the renewal of the grant by Benedict XIII, carrying it to 1733.[1245] Apparently there had nearly been a lapse.

SPOLIATION OF THE CHURCH

Commissioners were frequently selected from the chapters of their places of residence, and it was a long-debated question whether they were entitled to constant non-residence, seeing that their duties were occasional and mostly local. It was finally settled that they should enjoy the fruits when absent on duty for the Inquisition, but even this was disputed, in 1780, by the collegiate church of San Ildefonso of Llerena, in the case of the prebendary, Pedro Enríquez Verones, a commissioner of the Valladolid tribunal, who was refused his share of the distributions during absence by order of the inquisitors. Inquisitor-general Bertran complained to Carlos III, who peremptorily ordered payment whenever absent on business of the faith. A similar question apparently arose in 1818, for the Suprema sent, July 18th, to the tribunal of Llerena, a statement of the case with a copy of the letter of Carlos.[1246]

The Napoleonic wars caused a slight lapse in the quinquennial indults. One expired, February 6, 1813, a few days before the publication of the edict of suppression by the Córtes of Cádiz. When the Inquisition was re-established, it promptly applied for a renewal of the privilege and, on November 19, 1814, the Suprema announced that Pius VII had not only granted it but had ratified the receipt of revenues by non-residents during the interval. This renewal expired, February 6, 1818, when there was delay and the new brief was not issued until March 15th, but it does not appear that any chapter took advantage of the interval.[1247] When this expired, there was no longer an acting Inquisition.

***

The overgrown church establishment of Spain, with its accumulation of wealth, afforded a fair mark for acquisitiveness, and several efforts were made to obtain from it a permanent foundation for the Inquisition. We have seen how waste and prodigality, to say nothing of peculation, notwithstanding the active business of confiscation, rendered it difficult, in 1497 and 1498, to pay the salaries of officials. A remedy for this was sought in the spoliation of the Church, and Ferdinand and Isabella turned to Alexander VI, representing the constant increase of heresy, the additional efforts required for its extirpation and the insufficiency of confiscation to meet expenses. If the holy work were not to end, aid was needed and those engaged in it were performing a service to God equivalent to that of canons in the recitation of the daily offices. If a canonry with its prebend, in each metropolitan, cathedral and collegiate church, were devoted to the support of the officials, so long as the Inquisition should last, it would be a great safeguard to the faith and aid in the destruction of heresy. Alexander granted the request and, by a brief of November 25, 1501, he incorporated in the Inquisition a canonry and prebend in every church, authorizing the inquisitor-general to take possession of the first vacancies and appointing the Bishops of Burgos, Córdova and Tortosa as executors with power to suppress all resistance without appeal.[1248]

GRANT OF CANONRIES

It is remarkable that we hear nothing more of this portentous grant. No evidence has reached us of any attempt to enforce it or of any resistance. Probably even Ferdinand recognized an opposition too dangerous to be provoked and contented himself with using it as a threat against unruly chapters, which objected to his using canonries to pay his inquisitors. In the project of reform drawn up in 1518, it was proposed that, in place of living on the confiscations and penances, the inquisitors should have one or two canonries for their support. After this scheme fell through, Charles adhered to the idea and, on October 29th, he instructed his ambassador at Rome to procure from Leo X a brief similar to that of Alexander VI; without some such support, he said, it would be impossible to procure the services of men of proper character and learning.[1249] Leo was not as complaisant as Alexander, although Charles repeated the request in a personal letter to him, September 3, 1520.[1250] Then, on August 14, 1521,

Cardinal Adrian wrote to Charles, reminding him that, long before, the pope had conceded a prebend in every church where there was a tribunal, in order to remove the infamy, ascribed by some persons to inquisitors, of desiring the condemnation of the accused in order to assure their support. That concession had not been enforced, principally because the revocation was awaited of the bull against the Inquisition. Now the Bishop of Alguer, the Roman agent of the Inquisition, has announced the revocation of the bull and, in order to remove the infamy and perpetuate the Inquisition, he urges Charles to write to Don Juan Manuel in Rome to procure the grant of the prebends in accordance with a list prepared by the Bishop of Alguer.[1251] Charles was probably too much engrossed in the attempt to suppress Luther to devote much attention to the matter and Adrian, when he succeeded to the papacy, did not use his power to make the grant, although he was involved in a quarrel with the stubborn chapter of Almeria, which refused to admit his transfer, to Inquisitor Churruca of Valencia, of a precentorship which he held in that church--a quarrel which lasted until 1524 and required the united efforts of the Suprema, the tribunal of Murcia and of the emperor to bring to a termination.[1252]

We hear nothing more of the effort at this time, but Charles bore it so strongly in mind that, in his will, executed in Brussels, June 6, 1554, he dwelt upon the advantages of the measure and ordered Philip, in case of his own death without obtaining it, to labor with the Holy Father to procure what would be of such advantage to the Inquisition and service to God.[1253] The occasion came in a few years with the panic caused by the discovery of Protestantism among a few people of quality--a panic skilfully stimulated and exploited. Philip urged his ambassador Vargas to obtain from Paul IV a grant of one per cent. of ecclesiastical revenues, to relieve immediate necessities, and the suppression of a canonry and prebend in each cathedral and collegiate church. The Suprema aided, in a report to the pope, September 9, 1558, on the alarming progress of Lutheranism. After exaggerating the danger and the labors of the Inquisition, which could only have been carried on through the gift of ten thousand ducats by the king and contributions from Valdés, for it was penniless, the report went on to state that, when the Inquisition was established, there was a tribunal in almost every bishopric but, as the confiscations fell off, they were diminished to the few that remained, so that there was one which had fifteen sees in its district and it had not funds enough to pay the slender salaries of its officials. Although this had been repeatedly represented to the popes, no remedy had been granted, but now, in these perilous times of heresy, it seemed necessary that the tribunals should be multiplied, as at the beginning, and rendered permanent. All this could very readily be accomplished if the pope would apply some ecclesiastical revenues, which were of little service to God and could be better employed in sustaining the Holy Office, now so enfeebled through lack of funds. Although its work was pushed with all possible diligence, its future was uncertain if it could not be sustained and the remedy for this lay with his Holiness.[1254]

This lying plea aided the pressure brought to bear by the king and, on December 10th, Vargas was able to report that he and Cardinal Pacheco had had an audience of the pope, who manifested great goodwill and offered to grant a concession of a hundred thousand ducats to be levied on the clergy, in place of one per cent. on their revenues. After considering the question of the prebends, including the doctoral and magistral ones, he was content to apply to the Inquisition the first vacancy in each cathedral and collegiate church in Spain. This, Vargas adds, should receive special consideration, as it might be refused by another pope and, when this was gained, if the expenses of the Inquisition increased, there would be little trouble in getting it duplicated.[1255] The spread of heresy in France and the dread of its infecting Spain had brought the curia to a complying mood.

The Suprema needed no urging to secure so great a prize without loss of time. There could have been little opportunity for discussing details between Rome and Madrid, for the brief was signed January 7, 1559. It recited the reasons set forth in the report of September 9th and argued that, as the churches could not subsist without faith, it was better for them to sacrifice a portion of their substance than to risk the whole. Wherefore, motu proprio, with certain knowledge and in the plenitude of apostolic power, the pope suppressed one canonry and prebend in all cathedral and collegiate churches in Spain and the Canaries, the first falling vacant, no matter who might have the collation of it, and applied its revenues in perpetuity to the Inquisition. As each fell vacant, the inquisitor-general should appropriate it and collect the fruits, the consent of the diocesan or of any one else being in no way requisite, notwithstanding all conciliar decrees and papal constitutions to the contrary, or the claims of holders of expectatives or reversions, or of a long list of possible claimants, which shows how these benefices had been made matters of trade in every possible way.[1256]

***

It can only have been the haste in which this long and elaborate document was prepared that explains the omission of executors empowered to break down the opposition to be expected from the whole Spanish hierarchy. Valdés, however, boldly assumed that he had the power. On April 29th, he sent the papal letter to all prelates and chapters, with a missive exhorting bishops, under pain of interdict of entrance to their churches, and requiring all deans, chapters, etc., under penalty of excommunication and two thousand gold ducats, to hold as suppressed, extinct and perpetually united to the Inquisition the first vacant canonry and prebend. In the name of the Inquisition he accepted them and declared them incorporated in it, and ordered the revocation of all nominations and collations that might have been made since the date of the letters or might be made thereafter. The chapters were commanded to pay over all emoluments as completely as though the canonry were served by an incumbent at all services, and inquisitors were empowered to prosecute all who resisted and to inflict censures and penalties, as well as to appoint procurators to take possession and collect the revenues--and all this he audaciously said that he did "by virtue of the said apostolic faculty conceded to us."[1257]

Pius IV died, December 9, 1565, and Valdés was shelved in 1566. The brief had conferred the power on his successors as well as on himself and there was no necessity for its confirmation, but one was procured from Pius V, July 15, 1566. The object evidently was to cure the defect as to executors, who were now appointed with full and arbitrary powers, those named being the Bishops of Sigüenza and Palencia and the auditor-general of the papal camera. Some details were added, an unusual feature being a prohibition to assail the letters as surreptitious and obreptitious, showing that this argument had been freely used in the endeavor to escape from their operation. A further confirmation was obtained from Gregory XIII, July 8, 1574, but none seems to have been subsequently thought requisite.[1258]

No time had been lost in gathering the fruits of the papal grant. April 16, 1559, a provision was despatched to take possession of a prebend, which had fallen vacant in the church of Palencia; April 27th another for one in Leon and soon afterwards for others in Calahorra and Saragossa. Frequently they were found to be burdened with pensions that had to be recognized, but the process went on and, in comparatively a few years, it would seem that vacancies had occurred in most of the chapters.[1259] Possession, however, was not had without sturdy resistance, during which, at one time or another, nearly all the chapters were under excommunication. Legal proceedings were frequently resorted to in the desperate hope of averting the absorption, but it was futile. The Suprema was the court of appeal, the cases practically were prejudged before they were commenced and there was no escape.

***

In the end, of course, it made little difference, but a more shameless mockery of justice can scarce be conceived than that which made the tribunal, which was to profit by the suppression, the judge in its own case. The process may be followed in the voluminous proceedings attending the seizure of a prebend in the collegiate church of Belmonte--a town of some importance in the diocese of Cuenca. In 1559 it fell vacant by the death of Gregorio Osorio and was filled by the appointment of Francisco García del Espinar, at the instance of the Duke of Escalona, who seems to have had the collation. Valdés ordered its seizure and the matter took the form of a suit between the fiscal of the tribunal of Cuenca on the one side and, on the other, the duke, Espinar and the prior and chapter of Belmonte, with the Cuenca tribunal as judge, by virtue of a commission from Valdés. The judicial farce ended, October 8, 1560, by the inquisitors gravely reciting that they had heard the case and duly considered it with the assistance of persons of conscience and learning, and had found judgement in favor of the fiscal, suppressing the prebend and ordering all the income to be turned over to the receiver of the tribunal, including what had accrued since the death of Osorio. It is a striking illustration of the perversion of the sense of justice, induced by the inquisitorial process, that they were unconscious of the grotesqueness of such a performance, which was rounded out with a long and detailed enumeration of the penalties of disobedience--first a fine of two thousand ducats and then all the steps of excommunication, anathema and cursing with bell, book and candle and interdict on the town of Belmonte. This formidable sentence was served, October 15th, on each member of the chapter, and a notarial act was taken of the service. Resistance was felt to be useless. On the 16th the chapter met and adopted a formal act of obedience, stating that it was through fear of the penalties threatened; the suppression of the prebend was ordered to be entered on the capitular records, with the addition that, as the sentence gave no instructions as to the services or masses dependent upon it, or as to the payment of the accrued revenues received by Espinar, the necessary action would be taken subsequently.[1260]

While thus summarily enforcing the papal grant, the Inquisition prudently respected papal infractions of it. Advantage was taken of the papal claim to all benefices falling vacant while their possessors were in Rome--doubtless a costly proceeding, but better than forfeiture. Thus Gaspar Escudero promptly went to Rome and resigned his canonry of Calahorra in the hands of the pope, and his brother Rafael obtained bulls for it--probably subject to a pension. Similarly Diego de Ortega went through the same form and Francisco de Vellasañe secured the bulls. The inquisitors claimed them as vacancies, but there was risk in contesting the papal prerogative; Valdés decided, July 6 and 8, 1559, in both cases, that the vacancies had occurred in Rome and that the bulls were good. We meet, in 1560, with several similar cases, in Córdova, Alcalá de Henares and Tudela, where, after proceedings more or less vigorous, the papal action was respected.[1261] Another device to save something from the wreck was to obtain papal grants of pensions. Thus January 29, 1560, Andrés Martin presented bulls entitling him to a pension of thirty ducats on a canonry of Calahorra vacated by the death of his brother and it was ordered to be paid. It was the same with a pension of fifty ducats, on a suppressed canonry of Cuenca, for which bulls were obtained by Juan Rodríguez and Pedro Vara.[1262]

Respect at first was also shown to canonries under royal patronage. In Logroño the inquisitors seized one in the church of S. María la Redonda, but it proved to be a patrimonial one and was released.[1263] In time, however, this respect for the crown was surmounted, as we have seen in the century-long contention over the canonries of Antequera, Malaga and the Canaries.[1264]

It was necessary to systematize the new business thus thrown upon the tribunals and, in August 1560, agents were appointed in the inquisitorial districts to keep watch over vacancies occurring and to take the necessary action. They also made the collections and rendered accounts; but, as the income was largely payable in kind, the disposal of which was a matter of judgement, they were to make no sales without consulting the Suprema nor payments without its orders.[1265] This arrangement was soon found unsatisfactory. The variable character of the revenues, chiefly based on tithes and dependent on harvests and markets, afforded abundant opportunity for malversation; it seemed best to come to some understanding with the chapters and, after much investigation into details, the policy was adopted of farming out the prebends to them. In 1565 and 1566 we find numerous arrangements made of this kind. This too proved short-lived and, in 1567, it was determined to farm them out to the best bidders. Finally, in 1570, regulations were adopted for putting them up at auction, thus insuring full competition and preventing collusion and, in 1586, the returns were required to be placed in the coffers with three keys-- a system which seems to have continued to the end.[1266]

INCOME FROM CANONRIES

There were many intricate questions affording prolific causes of quarrel to keep alive the hostility between the chapters and the Inquisition, engendered by the seizure; there were frequent appeals to Rome, which appear rarely to have benefited the appellant, and the Inquisition eventually was left in assured possession of its acquisitions. Yet the friction was constant, as was inevitable when the relations were so close between parties who disliked and distrusted each other. Thus, in 1665, we find the Suprema rebuking the Barcelona tribunal for requiring a chapter to exhibit its books to show what were the allotments made to the resident canons; the information, it said, could be obtained in a less offensive way. Again, about the same time, when the tribunal ordered the farmer of the revenues of the prebend of Guisana to investigate whether the chapter was defrauding it, the Suprema wrote that, as no increase of revenue could be thus obtained, it would be more prudent to keep quiet, especially if the farmer was a beneficed member of the church; it would be better to order the commissioner at Agramont to examine the books of the chapter, because the fifty libras paid by the farmer, when compared with the two hundred distributed to the canons, was too small. To this the tribunal replied that it had long been exposed to frauds and suppression of the value of fruits by some of the chapters; as for that of Guisana, it would be useless to examine the books, as the contador would be the first of the conspirators.[1267]

Petty quarrels such as these are significant of much that was going on everywhere and of the chronic condition of enmity between the tribunals and the chapters. The former doubtless received considerably less than their dues and the latter, regarding themselves as despoiled, felt justified in withholding from the spoiler whatever they could, per fas et nefas. Yet, however much the revenues may have suffered in this way, the prebends constituted, as we shall see hereafter, three-eighths of the resources of the tribunals, reaching, in 1731, to nearly six hundred thousand reales a year and enabling them to prolong their existence during the later period, when the confiscations and fines and rehabilitations had ceased to furnish available means of support. But for the brilliant stroke by which Valdés secured them, in 1559, it may be doubted whether the Inquisition would not have proved so heavy a burden that Carlos III would have allowed it to perish of inanition.

CHAPTER V - FINANCES

Indications are not lacking that, when the Inquisition was established, it was not regarded as a permanent institution but as one to last only until it had purified the land of Jewish apostates. Had its prolonged existence been expected, doubtless provision would have been made, during the early period of large confiscations, to lay aside a fund sufficient for its support after the tide of spoliation should have ebbed. Ferdinand occasionally manifested a desire to establish a foundation for its maintenance, but his own necessities and the greedy pressure for grants rendered nugatory whatever intentions of the kind he may have entertained from time to time. In the proposition made to Charles V, in 1519, there is allusion to such a plan, proposed by Ferdinand, of securing censos which should place the institution on a firm financial basis and which had been partially carried out in some places.[1268] There is slender trace, however, of any results of such policy. When there were large confiscations in Sicily, he ordered, June 27, 1513, that none of the censos so obtained should be sold, but that they should be kept for the support of the tribunal. Apparently this was not done by the receiver, Diego de Obregon who, on quitting Sicily in 1514, left behind him the considerable sum of twelve hundred ounces, which Ferdinand ordered his successor, Garcí Cid, to invest in censos,[1269] but the subsequent condition of the tribunal shows that peculation and extravagance rendered impossible any accumulation. We have seen that, in 1517, Seville and Córdova had reserved funds in public securities, but they were absorbed by the Suprema.[1270] Possibly these were derived from the great composition described above; a cédula bearing the name of Queen Juana, February 24, 1516, states that it was devoted to the purchase of censos for the Inquisition, but we have had occasion to see how it was frittered away so that only a moderate portion can have reached its destination.[1271] The Toledo tribunal, in 1515, received from Ferdinand the absolute ownership of the building occupied by it and some other properties.[1272] Doubtless there were other donations of greater or less amount, but these are the only appropriations for the permanent support of the tribunals of Castile that I have met with.

As for those of Aragon, a letter of Cardinal Adrian, January 30, 1520, allowing Saragossa to draw upon the fines and penances for its expenses, until it could get some confiscations, shows that it had no other source of support.[1273] Barcelona was somewhat better off, for the local government, in consideration of the Concordia of 1520, granted it twelve thousand libras and, though the Inquisition subsequently saw fit to deny this, a letter of the Suprema in 1521, directing the diputados to invest in censos the sum, which they had already deposited, shows that on their side, at least, the bargain was honestly carried out.[1274] What between this and the results of the somewhat irregular industry of the inquisitors, the tribunal must have been fairly well supplied for, in 1550, we chance to hear of an ayuda de costa of twenty-four ducats granted to its notary Bartolomé García for his labor in copying the books of censos which it held in Perpignan and the accounts of the receiver.[1275] As for Valencia, at this period, I have met with no data.

IMPROVIDENCE

These indications are fragmentary but they suffice to justify the conclusion that the proceeds of the great confiscations in the early period were dissipated without laying up any permanent provision for the future. As the Suprema, throughout the first half of the sixteenth century, was constantly drawing upon the tribunals, it proves that, as a rule, they were making more than their expenses and that when one chanced to run short its deficiency was supplied from some more fortunate one. The grant, in 1559, of a hundred thousand ducats, levied upon the Spanish ecclesiastics, was probably, for the most part, invested by the Suprema for its own benefit, though ten thousand ducats were placed in the hands of its alguazil mayor Ibarra, to be drawn upon for special purposes.[1276] Then came the suppression of the prebends, which was expected to relieve all necessities, but it seems to have led to improvidence for, in 1573, the Suprema complained that moneys received from redemption of censos had not been reinvested but had been spent, and it called for reports as to amounts received and expended. Apparently the explanations were not satisfactory for, in 1579, peremptory orders were issued that, when a censo was paid off, the money must be reinvested in another, no matter how imperative might be other calls.[1277] Thus, in 1586, the tribunals were called upon for reports of their revenues, as it was understood that these had increased, together with statements as to the product of the prebends and censos.[1278] It is not likely that these were fully and frankly rendered. Under the rules, as we shall see, monthly statements were required, which should have made demands for special reports superfluous, but the tribunals were apt to observe towards the Suprema the same reticence which it showed to the king. We happen to have the report of Valencia, made in 1587, in response to this order, and find that it is quite imperfect. No mention is made of the confiscations and penances, and various items are omitted, while the 2500 ducats levied on the Moriscos shrink to 1500 libras, and the total amounts to about 5000 libras for the year.[1279] Yet Valencia must have been abundantly supplied for, when in 1601, the Suprema gave it permission to have a canopy, for occasions of extraordinary sentences, made at a cost not exceeding 500 ducats, when it was finished the bill amounted to over 900. The Suprema grumbled at this extravagance, but finally ordered it to be paid.[1280] The tribunal of Logroño must also have been in funds, for we chance to learn that, in 1587, it lent to the Countess of Osorno the sum of 155,535 reales 17 mrs. for which it received the annual interest of 4552 reales 5 mrs., or about three per cent.[1281]

At this period the Inquisition ought to have been financially comfortable, with its prebends and ordinary sources of income, besides having nearly all its higher officials quartered on the churches, but the fall in the purchasing power of money had necessitated a rise in salaries and it was not backward in making complaint. In 1595, a memorial of the Suprema to Philip II refers to frequent previous appeals representing the diminution of its property and income, together with the multiplication of officials, and declares that, if some remedy is not found, the king will be obliged to make up the deficiency.[1282] Soon after this the tribunals of the kingdoms of Aragon suffered considerably from the expulsion of the Moriscos in 1609-10, to which they had so largely contributed. The blow fell with special severity on Valencia, where the Moorish population was largest, and the tribunal lost its 2500 ducats a year and unlimited power of inflicting ten-ducat fines. In 1615 we find the Suprema ordering the salaries prorated in conformity with the collections--though, at the same time, the alcaide Gil Noguerol was jubilated with a salary of 40,000 maravedís and Nicolas Claver, the steward of the prison, was told to look for something from which a grant could be made to him.[1283]

COMPLAINTS OF POVERTY

Ample use was made of the distress in Aragon to stimulate royal liberality. January 30, 1617 the Suprema represented it to Philip III, but his extravagance had kept him penniless and the appeal was unanswered. It returned to the charge, October 22, 1618, perhaps thinking that the fall of the Duke of Lerma might lead to a more favorable hearing. The condition of the tribunal of Majorca was represented as deplorable; it could no longer be helped, as formerly, by Valencia, for that tribunal had a yearly deficit of 400 ducats. Barcelona was in like evil plight, and the tribunals of Castile could no longer afford it the aid they used to give. As for Saragossa, its distress had already been represented to the king, who was prayed to order the Vice-chancellor of Aragon to make provision for its relief.[1284] Then, in another consulta of 1619, the Suprema asserted that, taking the Inquisition as a whole, its expenses exceeded its income and that the deficiency must be supplied by the king; as a convincing argument it added that, when vacancies occurred, it proposed to suppress three inquisitorships, sixteen secretaryships and its own three supernumerary members--an intention that failed of realization.[1285] We may reasonably hesitate to accept these clamorous complaints of poverty, when the Suprema so carefully kept the sovereign in the dark as to its real resources, nor is it easy to reconcile with them the assertion of Fray Bleda, in 1618, that the Spanish Inquisition was so richly endowed that it had a hundred places in receipt of incomes larger than those of many Italian bishoprics.[1286]

No doubt, during the ensuing period of war, misgovernment and elaborate financial blundering, the Inquisition, in some degree, shared the distress which was universal throughout Spain, but it had resources more available and more jealously husbanded than the other departments of the State; it was exposed to less pressure and it managed to meet the incessant demands of Philip IV with no very severe sacrifice of its invested capital. Of course the customary complaints continued. In a consulta of March 28, 1681 the Suprema bewailed the poverty of the organization, the lack of means among the tribunals to pay the salaries and maintenance of prisoners, which it had repeatedly represented, with statements of the contador-general showing the income of each tribunal with its deficit.[1287] This may have been true as regards some of them, owing to special causes. Thus a consulta of November 6, 1677, asserts that the Concordia of 1646 had reduced Saragossa to such penury that the last statement of its very moderate salaries showed an amount of 111,246 silver sueldos due to the officials, forcing the Suprema this year to assist it with 1750 pieces of eight, a grant that it cannot repeat owing to its own very narrow means.[1288] In other cases, distress may be attributed to incurable laxity of management, as in Toledo, where a statement of 1647 shows a payment by the receiver of 105,984 mrs. to the Inquisitor Santos de San Pedro, accompanied with the remark that lack of means prevents his paying the balance still due. But it also shows that the receiver held 801,724 mrs. of obligations so worthless that the auditor did not consider advisable any attempt to collect them, and that there were arrearages due on censos and other sources of revenue amounting to 1,353,452 mrs.[1289]

POWER OF RECUPERATION

This justifies what is asserted in the plain-spoken memorial of 1623 to the Suprema--that through negligence there have been such losses that, if they had been avoided, the tribunals would be abundantly provided. This is attributed to the beggarly salaries of the financial officials; not having enough to support them, they engage in other occupations and, being sure of their salaries, they pay no attention to their duties. Another effect is that it is necessary to appoint natives who, through kinship or fear of offending their neighbors, do not execute orders, or who grant such delays that the chances of collecting are lost. Moreover, as they get no fees for looking up evidence and documents, suits miscarry.[1290] Incompetent, slovenly and often corrupt administration such as this affords ample explanation of whatever distress may have existed. Nor was malversation confined to the local tribunals. In November, 1642, Madrid was startled when, by order of the inquisitor-general, the presiding member of the Suprema, Pedro Pachecho, was suddenly arrested for malversation in office and was hurried off to Leon, without allowing him to communicate with the king or with Olivares, and every one said that it was a judgement of God on him for his extortions[1291]--the same Pacheco to whom Philip had just granted some 30,000 ducats accruing from the sale of offices (p. 215). There is significance in the cautious remark of Pellicer, August 15, 1643, comparing the death of Don Lope de Morales, of the Council of Castile, who died very poor, and of Inquisitor Alcedo, of the Suprema, who died very rich, leaving 40,000 ducats in gold and silver.[1292]

The financial elasticity of the tribunals was remarkable, especially when stimulated by the pressure of poverty, for they held the means of recuperation in their own hands. Valencia undoubtedly suffered for awhile from the Morisco expulsion, yet in 1630 we chance to learn that it had 45,500 ducats invested in municipal bonds at five per cent., yielding an income of 2275 ducats. In 1633 the Suprema is scolding it for its extravagance in illuminations and bull-fights and, in the same year, it is seeking investments for its spare funds. This prosperity continued for, in 1660, a statement of its income shows 4600 libras from interest on bonds and 530 from the rents of some houses, in addition to the four canonries and the fines and confiscations.[1293] After the suppression of the Catalan rebellion, in 1652, the restored Barcelona tribunal had to reconstruct itself from the foundations, but it speedily became opulent for, in 1662-4, it spent more than 4200 libras in damask hangings, repairs and extraordinary ayudas de costa and, in 1666, it was investing 1000 libras in a censo.[1294]

As in duty bound, a portion of the savings of the Inquisition was invested in government securities. Between 1661 and 1667 there were placed in this manner, from the proceeds of confiscations, sums amounting to 691,272 mrs. and, in 1668, this was increased by 202,771, the whole aggregate at this date being 7,877,999. With customary favoritism, its holdings were exempted from the deductions, amounting to partial repudiation, in which the necessities of Spanish finance sought relief.[1295]

Taking it as a whole I think we may assume that, during the vicissitudes of the seventeenth century, the Inquisition had abundant means for its support and that, despite its incessant complaints of poverty, it suffered less from the exigencies of the times than any other department of the government. Internal mismanagement or external causes may have brought temporary distress on individual tribunals, but persecution was still a lucrative business and such troubles were speedily overcome. As for the Suprema, we have seen that it was always in funds, not only for its necessities but for its luxuries and for the liberalities showered upon its members and subordinates, while the examination of a large series of receipts for salaries and perquisites shows that payments were made with a punctuality rare in the Spanish administration of the period. Certain it is that the Count of Frigiliana, in his addition to the Consulta Magna of 1696, assumes that the Inquisition was richly endowed with the prebends, the real estate acquired through confiscation and the censos and other investments which it had accumulated.[1296]

***

The opening of the eighteenth century was ominous of troubles to come. The War of Succession threw everything into disorder. Not only were the inquisitorial finances affected, but the exigencies of the Bourbon government caused it to levy exactions which Philip IV in his deepest distress had not ventured upon. About 1704 a tax of five per cent. was laid on the salaries of all officials, and this soon afterwards was increased to ten. Then, in 1707, the Inquisition had to bear its part in a general donation, the collection of which was entrusted to the bishops, as though the Suprema was distrusted and, in 1709, this was followed by an "honesto subsidio."[1297] To obtain some return for this, the Suprema ordered lists to be made up of all benefices not requiring residence throughout Spain, under royal patronage, and asked the king to incorporate them in the Inquisition, but this somewhat audacious request was refused.[1298]

CONDITION IN 1731

Complaints of poverty continued and, if we may trust a tabular statement of the receipts and expenditures of each tribunal, drawn up in 1731, they were fully justified, for the finances must have undergone a most notable deterioration under Philip V. Indeed, it is a mystery how the institution continued to exist under such conditions, with a yearly deficit of over half a million reales and nearly a million and a half of overdue wages to its employees.[1299] The expenses of the Suprema are represented as about double its receipts. Only two tribunals, those of Santiago and Seville, show a small excess of income, while Valencia prudently squares its accounts to a maravedí. The rest all show a greater or less deficit. The Suprema no longer draws at will on the tribunals, but some of them have to make to it definite subventions; thus Santiago is obliged to contribute 18,000 reales, Córdova 10,000, Seville 20,000, Murcia 45,000 and Majorca 10,000, the rest nothing, but on what principle these payments were based does not appear. Each tribunal, although subordinate to the Suprema in financial matters, has its own budget, its own independent resources, and is left to manage its deficit as best it can. The result, as might be expected, is various. Córdova, Murcia and Majorca would be solvent but for the subventions to the Suprema. The little Majorca tribunal, formerly so necessitous, has now the largest salary list of all, amounting to 104,694 reales, but it likewise enjoys the largest revenue from investments, 96,829 drawn naturally from its lucky confiscations in 1678 and 1691, from which it doubtless secured an endowment. Toledo, with but a moderate deficit of 27,000, owes over 250,000 reales to its officials. Saragossa continues unfortunate; it was ejected from the Aljafería, probably as an incident of the War of Succession, but Philip V, in 1708, granted it 5200 ducats a year out of the confiscations to rent buildings. This was withdrawn in 1725 and, in 1727, the Suprema appealed to the king with a deplorable account of its condition, dependent on its prebends and with an income less than half of its pay-roll.[1300] Its position had not improved in 1731. It had undertaken to put up new buildings, on which 20,000 ducats had been spent and more than 20,000 additional were required for their completion. It was very expensively managed, with a salary list of nearly 93,000 reales and total expenses of 118,000, on an income of about 80,000, while Barcelona paid in salaries only 50,000 and its whole expenditure was less than 60,000 on an income of 48,000. Santiago was fortunate in its prebends, which brought in nearly 88,000 a year; outside of this it had only 5000 from investments, but it was able to pay its subvention and had a surplus of nearly 4000. In only four tribunals--Santiago, Seville, Murcia and Valencia--were the salaries fully paid up.

The whole statement illustrates the curious lack of system under which the Inquisition had continued since its foundation. Under Ferdinand, he handled its finances as his own, using them according to his necessities, with improvident disregard of the future, and without formulating an arrangement by which its affairs could be placed on a stable basis, although its gains were aleatory and subject inevitably to diminution as it accomplished the object of its creation. Then, under Charles V, the Suprema assumed control, supplying its own wants from any surplus presumably existing in any tribunal, and transferring sums from one to another as exigencies presented themselves in the fluctuating stream of confiscations. The absorption of the prebends afforded for the first time a more stable revenue, although these too were variable. Each tribunal acquired those which fell within its district, thus obtaining an unequal basis of support, and becoming in a certain sense financially independent, although subject to the scrutiny and control of the Suprema. Thus one might be wealthy and another poverty-stricken. There was no solidarity, no common treasury into which the receipts of each were poured and from which their necessities were supplied. The Suprema had a general auditor's office, to which the accounts of all the receivers or treasurers were rendered, enabling it to exercise supervision and a more or less fitful and efficient direction, but it was more intent on providing for its own wants than on enforcing responsibility upon the local financial officials. It wasted its energies on the pettiest details, while distance and difficult communication forced it practically to leave important questions to the discretion of the tribunals. The anomalous financial organization, which thus developed, combined the vices of centralization and local self-government, with divided responsibility and inefficient supervision. A tribunal which chanced to have large confiscations or numerous and lucrative prebends, with honest and capable administration, prospered, while others not so fortunate were reduced to penury.

PROJECTS FOR RELIEF

Towards the middle of the century the condition seems to have slightly improved. A writer, evidently well-informed, who complains bitterly that the usefulness of the Inquisition was crippled by inadequate means, states its revenues at 948,000 reales derived from invested property and 637,000 from a hundred prebends and some pensions, while its salaries and expenses amount to 1,900,000, leaving a deficit of 400,000. He proposes that the property derived from confiscations, representing a capital of 36,000,000, should be abandoned to the king and that the Church be levied upon to raise the total income to 2,700,000 which he assumes to be absolutely essential. It is scarce necessary to enter into the details of this proposed levy, except to mention that he says that there were a hundred and thirteen collegiate churches, in which no prebend had been suppressed and these, averaging them at 2500 reales, would yield 282,500 a year; also that there were forty-nine inquisitors enjoying prebends and benefices, averaging 11,000 a year which should be incorporated, yielding 539,000.[1301]

Another writer of the same period seeks relief by suppressing unnecessary officials and absorbing some more prebends, after which the king should assume the whole responsibility, appointing the salaried officials, collecting the revenues and paying the expenses, when, if he had to make good a deficiency, he could not devote public money to a cause more useful and just. This writer also makes a most earnest appeal for increased salaries for the inferior officials, who, he says, were objects of popular derision in consequence of the meanness of their appearance. When one died, the expenses of his sickness and burial had to be defrayed by the tribunal in the shape of an ayuda de costs and, while living, they were overwhelmed with debts which they had no means of paying, as shown by the number of claims filed by creditors. In the provinces they often had to supplement their wages by beggary, and their integrity suffered, for the starving are easy subjects for temptations.[1302]

I have not met with statistics as to the subsequent condition of each tribunal, but there are indications that some, at least, were comfortably endowed. Thus Valencia which, in 1731, showed a carefully balanced statement of receipts and expenditures, is found, in 1773 and 1774, purchasing real estate as an investment for surplus funds.[1303] In 1792, the Suprema, in response to a demand for increase of salaries, ordered from all the tribunals a statement of income and expenses for the seven years, 1784-90. The return of Valencia shows, for 1790, an income of 12,207 libras and an expenditure of 7777, or a surplus of 4430, though its pay-roll comprised twenty-five officials, receiving in all 5616. Its coffer contained at the time an accumulation of 32,707 libras, although, for the five previous years, it had spent an average of 5000 libras a year in permanent improvements and investments. Perhaps this can scarce be taken as an example of all the tribunals, but it would indicate that some, at least, were not oppressed with poverty, while the absurdly small item of 39 libras 4 sueldos expended on maintenance of prisoners, in 1790, indicates how little real work was performed by its overgrown staff.[1304]

This flourishing condition was not destined to continue. The necessities of the Government, in its foolish wars with France, England and Portugal, caused it to call upon the Inquisition to convert its investments into public funds. The Valencia tribunal reported to the Suprema, February 23, 1802, that, in obedience to its order of January 22nd, there had been realized from the sale of farms the sum of 62,584 libras, which had been duly paid over to the "Caja de consolidacion de vales," and of course all such patriotic contributions disappeared in the years of trouble which ensued. Equally unfortunate was an investment made in 1795, likewise by order of the Suprema, of 6640 libras in an obligation of the Real Compañia Maritima, on which, as it reported in 1805, it had never received any interest. In the same year it presented a dolorous account of the misery of its officials who, from their inadequate salaries, had been forced to make a voluntary donation of four per cent. to the Government and, under pressure from the captain-general, to contribute 175 reales to the support of the silk-weavers thrown out of employment, which, it suggested, should be paid for them by the tribunal as, for two years and a half, it had had no fiscal and thus had saved his salary.[1305] The tribunal of Logroño must have husbanded its resources, for it was able, July 23, 1808, to lend to the authorities 30,000 reales towards a fund demanded by the French General Verdier for abstaining from sacking the town. Under the Restoration a return of the loan was vainly claimed.[1306]

THE RECEIVER

Worse was to come in the revolutionary times which followed. Napoleon, on his arrival at Madrid, December 4, 1808, issued a decree abolishing the Inquisition and confiscating its property to the crown and this, of course, was enforced wherever the French armies penetrated. On the other hand, the Córtes of Cádiz had learned, from the example of the Inquisition, that useless benefices were a financial resource, and one of their earliest acts was a decree of December 1, 1810, forbidding the nomination of incumbents to all prebends, raciones and benefices, vacant or falling vacant, except magistral, doctoral, lectoral and penitentiary prebends, or benefices having cure of souls, under which the suppressed canonries were made to contribute to the War of Independence.[1307] The Holy Office was virtually extinct when it was suppressed by the Córtes in 1813, and we shall see hereafter how painful was the resuscitation of its finances under the Restoration.

***

The financial organization of the Inquisition at first was simple and even crude. The receiver of confiscations, or treasurer, was a royal official. Ferdinand always speaks of him as mi receptor and it was the king who issued commissions to all the officials on the financial side of the tribunals--the receiver, the auditor and the judge of confiscations--although, after the incorporation of the prebends, the inquisitor-general added powers to administer the revenues from ecclesiastical sources, as this was his exclusive province under the papal briefs.[1308] When Ferdinand died, January 23, 1516, it is not surprising that difficulties were thrown in the way of the receivers, on the ground that their commissions expired with him. To meet this, letters were issued to them, in the name of Queen Juana, February 28th and March 4th, instructing them that they were still in office, with full authority to make collections and to pay salaries and expenses.[1309] By the time of the resignation of Charles V, the system had become so firmly established that no questions seem to have arisen, although probably with each new monarch commissions were renewed.

The office was rightly considered to be one of much importance, especially in the early period of large confiscations. In 1486, the receiver figures, in the Saragossa pay-roll, for a salary of 3000 sueldos to 4000 for the inquisitors, while, in those of Medina del Campo and Jaen, he has 80,000 mrs. to 60,000 for the inquisitors. In 1515, the receiver and the inquisitor in Sicily both receive 300 ducats.[1310] The receiver necessarily required assistants and agents, as the properties under his charge were scattered throughout his district. At first these were paid by the fisc, but Ximenes, in his reform of 1516, required receivers to pay for them out of their salary of 60,000 mrs.--an economy of doubtful wisdom.[1311] In time the comparative importance of the receiver diminished and, in the middle of the eighteenth century, we find him--or treasurer as he was then called--rated at 400 ducats, while the inquisitors and fiscal have 800.[1312] At times there were distinct receivers for the confiscations and for the fines, penances and rehabilitations, but usually one sufficed, though the accounts were kept separate. The receiver was required, by the Instructions of 1498, to give satisfactory bonds to the amount of 300,000 mrs.[1313] A regulation of 1579 prescribed that these bonds were to be renewed every three years and that, when one of the bondsmen died, he was to be replaced at once, under pain of major excommunication, latæ sententiæ, but the frequency with which this rule was enunciated indicates how difficult was its enforcement.[1314]

ITEMIZED ACCOUNTS REQUIRED

While the power of the receiver in making collections was almost boundless, in disbursements he was prudently limited. An instruction of Deza, in 1504, requires the auditors not to pass in the accounts any item for which the receiver could not exhibit an order from the king, the inquisitor-general, the Suprema, or the judge of confiscations in matters adjudicated by him.[1315] In Aragon, the accounts were audited by the maestre racional or auditor-general of the kingdom and, in Castile, by the auditor of the Suprema, after which they were submitted to Ferdinand, who examined them minutely and decided as to the items disallowed by the auditors.[1316] All this, as we have seen, passed into the hands of the Suprema, which exercised the most careful watchfulness over all gastos extraordinarios, or expenditures other than the regular payment of salaries and the like. Thus, in 1645, Martin Pretel, the treasurer of Toledo, paid out, on orders of the inquisitors, 190-1/2 reales for repairs to a house occupied by one of them and 116 reales for repairs to the prison. The auditor refused to pass these trivial outlays, and it was not until 1654 that the Suprema allowed them, with a caution that in future the cartas acordadas must be observed.[1317]

The utmost precision and minuteness were exacted, with elaborate vouchers containing the order authorizing payment and the receipt of the payee. In the accounts for 1524, of Cristóval de Medina, receiver of Valencia, he recites an order issued by the inquisitors to Pere Sorell, who was repairing the palace of the Inquisition, granting him an old chain which hung under some of the windows and he includes Sorell's receipt for it.[1318] Similarly in the Valencia accounts for 1759 we find the inquisitors issuing orders and receipts taken in the case of the charwoman Josefa Serra, who was paid 3 libras for sweeping out the rooms from January 1st to St. John's day and 5 libras for carrying the seat of honor twice to the church of Santa Ana and once to San Salvador. So with Juan García, paid 1 libra 10s. for taking up and putting down the mats and 1 libra 4s. for two cords for the well.[1319]

There was perhaps some excuse for dilatoriness in rendering accounts so elaborately minute, accompanied with the requisite orders and vouchers, but a more efficient reason was that the receiver was apt to be in arrears, using the funds for his own profit, in defiance of stringent regulations, and his account rendered was sure to be followed with a demand to pay a balance due. Ferdinand, as we have seen, and after him the Suprema, labored vainly to secure promptitude and regularity. In 1560 it devised an elaborate plan of appointing an auditor for every two tribunals, with a salary of 40,000 mrs., for which he was to spend alternate years in examining their several accounts. Collusion between him and the receivers was guarded against by severe penalties for paying his salary except on orders from the Suprema and threats of prosecuting him for neglect of duty. When a balance was struck, the receiver was to deposit it within nine days in the coffer of the tribunal and furnish the Suprema with evidence of the fact within nine days more; if he failed in this, the inquisitors were to imprison him under pain of forfeiting their salaries from that time forth. As each account was completed, the auditor was to forward a copy to the Suprema, and he was further to supervise the accounts of the collectors of the suppressed prebends and to see that all receipts were duly deposited in the coffer.[1320] The scheme has interest from the insight which it gives into the disorder and dilapidation characteristic of inquisitorial finance, rather than from any improvement which it caused, for it seems to have proved impracticable. It is true that, in 1570, there were some additional instructions as to details, which look as if, after ten years, there was an effort to make it work, but it was soon afterwards abandoned and, in 1572, there was a return to the old system by ordering from each tribunal an annual statement.[1321] This was followed by requiring a monthly report as to the management of property and the returns collected, but this seems to have received as little obedience as previous instructions.[1322]

The memorial of 1623 to the Suprema urges strongly the enforcement of the instructions of 1560--that an auditor should, every year, audit the accounts of the treasurer, in the presence of an inquisitor, under penalty of forfeiture of a year's salary by both. The statements thus rendered should then be examined by the fiscal of the Suprema, with the aid of an expert accountant for, through the lack of this, in the previous accounts there have been great errors, and if they were reviewed by a shrewd examiner it would be discovered how large have been the losses.[1323] The writer evidently had little faith in the receivers-general and auditors-general on whom the Suprema depended, but his suggestions were not acted upon, and the Suprema contented itself with calling upon the dilatory treasurers for annual reports and occasionally getting their statements. The secret of the delay is indicated in instructions to the Valencia tribunal, in 1633, that, when Melchor de Mendoza, the treasurer, has finished the accounts which he has commenced, pressure must be brought to bear to make him pay the balance against him.[1324]

NEGLIGENCE IN RENDERING ACCOUNTS

The Depositarios de los Pretendientes, who had charge of the deposits of those seeking proofs of limpieza, emulated the treasurers. A letter of March 28, 1665, to the Barcelona tribunal calls attention to a carta acordada of January 16, 1620, ordering the accounts of the depositario to be included in the annual statements required for the auditor-general. The latter, however, reports that he has received none for many years, wherefore it is ordered that an itemized statement in detail, including everything since the last account rendered, shall be made out, showing what is due to all parties concerned. It may reasonably be doubted whether the command was obeyed. In 1713, orders were sent to Valencia that, if the depositario did not pay the balance in four months, pressure was to be brought to bear upon him, and the secretaries were to be forced to pay him what they owed him. The pressure was unavailing, for a prolonged correspondence ensued on the subject, throughout 1714. Towards the close of the century, however, we find the depositario of Valencia rendering statements with some degree of regularity every two years.[1325]

If the accounts of the tribunals were thus carelessly kept, those of the Suprema would appear to be equally disordered. At least such conclusion is justified when, in 1685, we find it asking the tribunal of Valencia for a statement of the remittances which it had made to the treasurer-general. In 1695 the request is repeated for the years 1693 and 1694 and again in 1714, 1715 and 1726--all of which would argue most slovenly bookkeeping.[1326]

Towards the close of its career, apparently, the Inquisition had succeeded in establishing a more methodical system. In 1803, Barcelona is rendering monthly statements of receipts and expenditures with commendable regularity and we may attribute to the political perturbations the fact that the accounts of Valencia for the years 1807, 1809 and 1810 were not audited by the Suprema until 1816.[1327]

Confidence in the integrity of the average receiver was evidently neither felt nor deserved, and, at an early period, the device was adopted of the arca de tres llaves--a coffer placed in the secreto with three locks of which the keys were held by the receiver, by an inquisitor and by the scrivener of sequestrations, so that it could be opened only in presence of all three. In this repository the receiver was required to place all moneys coming into his hands and so it remained until the last, as a fine example of archaic simplicity. To this there were occasional variations, such as requiring two arcas, one for confiscations and one for fines and penances, or, when the tribunals were living on their incomes, one for capital and the other for revenue. As a rule, however, one sufficed and it was customarily divided into two compartments, for confiscations and fines and penances respectively.

The rules prescribed, in 1514, by Inquisitor-general Mercader, indicate the precautions regarded as necessary to reduce to a minimum the temptations of the receiver. He was to receive no money save in presence of the scrivener of sequestrations or of the secreto. All collections were to be placed in the coffer within three days of their receipt, in the presence of an inquisitor and of a scrivener. When subordinates brought funds from other places, they were to be delivered to him within two days in presence of a scrivener and he was required to deposit them within twenty-four hours. Fraud and deceit, Mercader says, must cease in the collection and sales of confiscations and in depositing and taking out moneys from the coffer. All expenses, ordinary and extraordinary, were to be paid with money taken from the coffer. The scrivener must, with his own hands, keep duplicate books, with dated entries, of all deposits and withdrawals, one copy to be kept in his possession and the other in the coffer. No moneys must be taken out for loans or other purpose, save the expenses of the tribunals, without the express licence of the king and inquisitor-general. Every two months the receiver and scrivener, in presence of an inquisitor, must verify the accounts and the money on hand, and must send a written statement of the latter to the inquisitor-general. Any omission or deviation from this by receiver, inquisitor or scrivener was punishable with excommunication and a fine of five hundred ducats. All the officials concerned were to be furnished with copies of these instructions and one was to be placed in the coffer.[1328]

THE COFFER WITH THREE KEYS

It was one thing to frame precise regulations and another to secure their observance. These instructions were sent to Sicily in 1515, but evasions were speedily invented for already, in 1516, a letter of the Suprema asserts that experience had shown that the custodians of the three keys, by lending them to each other, committed frauds on the moneys in the coffer. To prevent this it devised wholly inefficient regulations as to the parties to whom the keys should be confided, in the absence of the regular custodians, so that, as it naïvely remarked, no frauds may be committed in the future.[1329]

It argues a singularly hopeful spirit in the Suprema if it expected that such precautions would preclude embezzlement, when the standard of official morality was so low that malversation was prevalent everywhere and was rarely if ever punished by dismissal from office. How tenderly such indiscretions were treated is manifested in a case occurring in Barcelona, in 1514. Francisco de San Climent owed 186 libras to the confiscated estate of Bernardo and Dionis Venet; his father paid 150 on account, but this was not credited, being evidently embezzled, and, on June 13th, Ferdinand ordered the receiver, Mateo de Morrano, not to press the suit against San Climent on account of the damage that it would inflict on the honor of the officials--the matter was to be hushed up in order to spare the reputation of the tribunal.[1330] When theft was thus condoned we need not wonder at the condition of the receptoria of Saragossa, characterized by fraud, disorder and neglect, as described by the auditor Anton Navarro in a letter which Ferdinand gave, in 1515, to the Archdeacon of Almazan when sending him thither as inspector.[1331]

Allusion has been made above to the remedy sought by Ximenes in 1517, by sending an auditor-general to inspect all the tribunals and ascertain the balances due. It was probably in consequence of this that Juan Martínez de Guilestegui, the former receiver of Toledo, was found indebted in the sum of 51,500 mrs., but there was no thought of punishing him and, with customary tenderness, Charles V forgave him half of the debt and promised that on payment of this he should be free of all further claim.[1332] Apparently it was a matter of course that receivers should be in debt to the fisc, although, if the rules as to the three-keyed coffer were observed, there was no opportunity for them to be in arrears. The rules in fact were disregarded with impunity. Inquisitor-general Manrique, writing to Sicily in 1525, says that they had not been observed for several years and orders them to be enforced under the prescribed penalties, but as he did not inflict those penalties for past disobedience, his threats were a mere brutum fulmen.[1333]

The consequence of this condonation of malpractice appears whenever there is opportunity of investigation. One of Ferdinand's most trusted receivers was Amador de Aliaga of Valencia. On his death, about 1529, when concealment was no longer possible, he was found to be a defaulter and, as one of the inquisitors was his heir, the Suprema ordered him to make good the deficit out of the estate. Then Pedro Sorell, a notary of the secreto, was in the enjoyment of certain confiscated houses, granted to him by Ferdinand, subject to a censo of 2975 sueldos; this had clandestinely been paid off out of the funds of the tribunal; Sorell refused restitution, and the Suprema merely told the inquisitors to persuade him to refund the amount without a suit. This same Sorell had covertly, through a third party, purchased a censo of 8000 sueldos, particularly well secured, sold by the fisc in order to pay salaries. The Suprema rebuked the tribunal for parting with so choice an investment, but there was no talk of dismissing or punishing the guilty notary.[1334] When the officials enriched themselves with impunity it is not difficult to understand the incessant complaints of the poverty of the tribunals.

THE JUNTA DE HACIENDA

That a receiver was expected to use the money in his hands and to be in arrears is indicated by a letter of the Suprema, in 1542, on learning the death of Ramon de Esparza, receiver of Majorca. He had not sent in his accounts and the inquisitor was empowered to compel his heirs to render a statement and to pay whatever balance might be found due.[1335] The device of the coffer had fallen evidently into complete neglect and the Suprema endeavored to resuscitate it by a carta acordada of December 9, 1545, which prescribed that all collections were to be deposited within three days of receipt, if made in the city, or within four days if made in the country, and salaries and other expenses were to be paid only from the money in the coffer, under pain of excommunication latæ sententiæ and of ten ducats for each infracion. This was the commencement of an endless series of legislation reiterating or modifying the regulations in a manner to indicate how impossible it was to enforce observance. The delay allowed for deposit was increased from three days to ten; receivers were required to take an oath to obey; reports of all deposits and withdrawals were ordered to be rendered every four months. These constant repetitions are the measure of their inefficiency, and the hardened indifference of the receivers is evidenced by a complaint of Reynoso, Inquisitor of Toledo, in 1556, that since the accounts of the receiver had been balanced he had received large sums which he refused to deposit in the coffer, saying that his accounts had been settled. Then, in 1560, the order of 1545 was reissued with instructions that, in case of infraction, the receiver was to be prosecuted and punished, evidence of which was to be furnished to the Suprema.[1336] It was all in vain and the receivers continued to hold their collections at their convenience.

In 1569, with the object of reducing to some kind of order the finances of the tribunals, a junta de hacienda, or finance committee, was constituted in each, consisting of the inquisitors, the judge of confiscations, the receiver and the notary of sequestrations, which was to meet on the last day of each month and consider all questions of property and income, deciding them by a majority vote. This, with occasional modifications, remained a standing feature of the tribunals, although the repeated exhortations and commands that the sessions be held regularly show how difficult it was to secure business-like action and management.[1337] The attempt was made to utilize this organization in compelling the receivers to deposit their collections in the coffers. In 1576 and again in 1579, orders were issued that, at the monthly meetings, the receiver should declare, under oath and under excommunication, the amount of money in his hands, what he had collected and what placed in the coffer. This was ineffectual and then it was tried to compel the notary of sequestrations to make a declaration that the receiver had deposited all that he admitted to have received. Then, in 1584, a concession was made allowing the receiver to make his deposits monthly, which of course only increased the risk of defalcations. This was followed, in 1586, by orders that he must be compelled to collect and deposit promptly the revenues of the prebends and that, at the monthly meetings, the schedule of income was to be examined in order to see what had been collected and deposited.[1338] It would be wearisome to pursue further these details, which continued indefinitely, with perpetual and ineffectual iteration, to compel the receivers to hand over their collections without delay. It hardly needs the assertion of the memorial of 1623 that the coffer was used in but very few places as a depository for the funds of the tribunals. The writer adds that the receivers thus incur excommunication and commit perjury monthly; the finances suffer great losses and the receivers are ruined by squandering the money, but the only remedy that he can suggest is that the penalties be increased and strict orders be issued that, under no pretext, should funds be left outside of the coffers. These expedients had been abundantly tried but, in the absence of rigid discipline and of punishment of offenders, they had been and continued to be fruitless. Another and most serious omission pointed out was that in many tribunals there was no Libro Becerro or register of property, with descriptions and titles, the lack of which led to great losses and much difficulty in making collections.[1339] The cause of the poverty complained of is not far to seek.

DEFALCATIONS

Under the flagrant disregard of the prescribed safeguards, it is not surprising that defalcations were by no means infrequent. The general negligence and the tenderness manifested to official malfeasance facilitated and encouraged embezzlement. It could be concealed by skilfully falsified statements but, when a receiver died, his estate was not uncommonly found to be indebted to the fisc. Thus, in the account of Lazaro del Mar of Valencia, in 1647, there is an item of 372ll. 14s. 2d. still due by the heirs of the late receiver Minuarte, although 2400ll. had already been collected of them during the previous five or six years.[1340] So when, in 1664, Joan Matheu, receiver of Barcelona, was murdered and his accounts were finally reduced to order, in 1666, they were found to be short in the large sum of 47,359ll. 1s. The widow petitioned to be released, or at least to have an abatement, which was refused, but she was given two years in which to settle.[1341]

A somewhat typical ante-mortem case was that of Carlos Albornoz, receiver of Valencia, who, it may be remembered, endeavored, in 1713, to secure the reversion of his office for his son aged twelve, and a few years later succeeded in so doing. There was trouble in getting him to render his accounts for 1723 and three or four subsequent years, and making him pay over the tolerably large confiscations of Alarcon and Macanaz. In 1727 he was allowed to resign in favor of his son and, in 1728, active measures were taken to compel him to furnish his accounts and make payments, which resulted in obtaining 6000 reales and a statement. On this, in December, 1728, the auditor-general found a balance against him of 6248ll. 10s. 1d. besides sums paid by the towns of Villanueva de Castellon and Denia which were not entered in his books. Then commenced the attempt to effect a settlement, which continued, until 1734, with more or less success, his son being meanwhile continued in office, while in the whole voluminous correspondence there is no intimation of any thought of punishing him for his inveterate disobedience and dishonesty.[1342] The confiscations, in fact, seemed to carry with them an infection. The Licentiate Vicente Vidal was administrator of the Valencia portion of the estate of Macanaz and, on settlement of his accounts, he was found to be in debt some 1800ll. The administration was transferred to Manuel Molner, to whom he gave a deed for a property renting for 100ll.; in 1729 he paid his debt and then, in 1732, he had the effrontery to ask the Suprema to refund to him the rents received from his property while in Molner's hands.[1343] While thus much of the chronic complaint of indigence may reasonably be attributed to mismanagement and peculation, it would be unjust to the Inquisition to ascribe to it a specially bad eminence in this respect. It was probably neither better nor worse than the other departments of the Government. Neglect of duty and misappropriation of funds, common enough to this day in public affairs, were in past times rather the rule than the exception and flourished in Spain, perhaps, to a greater extent than elsewhere. Multiplication of offices and inadequate salaries are direct incentives to irregular gains, and the practical immunity of offenders, caused by the unwise effort to preserve the external reputation of the Holy Office, was an encouragement which could not fail to induce slovenly service, disobedience of rules and frequent embezzlement.

BOOK VI – PRACTICE

CHAPTER I - THE EDICT OF GRACE

Allusion has occurred above to the Edicts of Grace which, in the earlier period, played an important part in the machinery of the Inquisition. It was a custom inherited from the thirteenth century of which the conditions, as adopted in Spain, are expressed in the Instructions of 1484. When, at any place, a tribunal was opened, at the close of the initial sermon the inquisitors were to publish a Term of Grace, lasting for thirty or forty days, during which those conscious of heresy could come forward, making complete confession of all errors remembered, including those of others. They were to be assured that all who did so, with contrition and desire to abjure, would be charitably received, would be given salutary penance and would not be condemned to death, to perpetual prison or to confiscation, but the inquisitors were empowered to reconcile them and, at their discretion, to require them to give as alms a certain portion of their property in aid of the holy war with the Moors. Spontaneous confession after the Term of Grace, provided the parties had not been testified against, secured reconciliation with confiscation; where adverse testimony had been received, heavier penalties, even to perpetual prison, could be inflicted.[1344] In the supplementary Instructions of December 6, 1484, Torquemada added that the sovereigns granted to those thus reconciled the right to collect debts and confirmed all alienations made prior to the reconciliation, but that no subsequent alienations or encumbrances on real estate would be valid without special royal licence.[1345] This still left questions unsettled and, in Torquemada's further Instructions of January 5, 1485, it was provided that, if the reconciled held public office, they were to be temporarily disabled, until their steadfastness in the faith was proved; those who had been prevented by sickness, or other just impediment, from availing themselves of the Term of Grace were to be admitted but, if there was proof against them, they were subject to confiscation and their cases would be submitted for the royal decision. Those who did not confess fully as to themselves and others were to be regarded as fictitious converts and, if evidence was received against them, were to be prosecuted with the utmost rigor. Fugitives coming forward within the term were to be admitted.[1346]

A case occurring in 1483 shows that this was a mitigation of the pitiless strictness with which the limits of the Term of Grace had been observed. When, in December of that year, Juan Chinchilla was on trial at Ciudad Real, one of the articles of accusation was that he had not come forward during the term. In reply he stated that the Comendador del Carral had sent him away during that time; that he had gone to the Inquisition to confess, but Padre Caetano had retired after hearing mass and he had been told to return at another time; then he went to the receiver and begged him for God's sake to get him admitted; the receiver had promised to do so and came to summon him; he thought that he was being taken to the inquisitors, but found himself thrown in prison. His explanation availed him nothing, nor did his free confession of his errors, and he was duly burnt.[1347] In the awful confusion and haste of those opening years, such cases must have been frequent. There were few formalities observed, for there had not been time to develop an elaborate course of procedure, and each inquisitor, to a large extent, followed his own devices.

CONFESSIONS UNDER THE EDICT

I have nowhere met with the full text of an Edict of Grace, but the substantial formula is given in the sentence pronounced, January 30, 1484, in Ciudad Real, against the fugitives Sancho de Ciudad and his wife. This recites that, as there was public report that in Ciudad Real many nominal Christians followed the Law of Moses, the inquisitors had verified it by testimony; that, desiring to treat them with clemency, they had issued their Edict that all thus guilty should come forward and abjure within thirty days, when they would be treated with all possible mercy; that they had extended this for thirty days more and had received all who desired to present themselves, after which they had issued their summons and edict against all who had fled and had been testified against as suspect and defamed for heresy.[1348]

We have seen what was this mercy, in penitential processions and heavy amercements, and we shall see how illusory, in many cases, was the promised immunity, owing to the diminucion or imperfection of the confession. It was required to be full about themselves and others; the assumption necessarily was that they were genuine converts at heart and as such must be eager, not only to discharge their consciences as to all past errors, but to aid in the punishment of all heretics and apostates, including those nearest and dearest to them. Anything short of this showed that their confession was fictitious and thus it only added to their guilt. Ample evidence against them was obtainable, not only from informers who were numerous and active, but from the confessions of others, whether coming in under the edict or on trial. The tribunals were watchful in utilizing all this material, and reconciliation under the edict was apt to be supplemented by arrest and condemnation.

The confessions under the Edicts of Grace are pitiful reading. The poor creatures naturally admit as little as possible, in the hope of diminishing the pecuniary penance. They strive to extenuate their errors and throw the blame on those who misled them; they grovel before the inquisitors, profess the deepest contrition and promise strenuous perseverance in the faith. They rarely go out of their way to compromise others, but they frankly state who it was that perverted them and have no hesitation in implicating parents and kindred and benefactors. Unlike the priest in the confessional, the inquisitors abstained from interrogating them or seeking information about themselves or others. It was not their policy to stimulate confession and the penitent was allowed to state as much or as little as he chose. The results are evidently the unassisted work of the penitents, inconsistent, rambling, frequently almost unintelligible, whether written by themselves or taken down verbatim by the notaries, for it was essential that they should be of record, to be brought up against them, in the probable case of backsliding or of testimony to omitted facts. The confession of Maria Gonsales de la Panpana, Ciudad Real, October 9, 1483, may be taken as a specimen. In it she throws all the blame upon her husband and recites the thrashings received at his hands to force her to follow Jewish observances. She was duly admitted to reconciliation but, in about three months, she was arrested and tried and was burnt in the great auto de fe of February 23, 1484.[1349] The unsubstantial character of the mercy promised in the Edict of Grace is illustrated in the typical case of Andres González, parish priest of Talavera. Soon after the tribunal of Toledo had been organized and before there had been any proclamation in the archidiaconate of Talavera, he sought to protect himself by appearing before the tribunal, making confession and obtaining reconciliation. Doubtless prisoners on trial testified against him, for he was soon afterwards arrested. November 5, 1484 he made a fuller confession, covering all the points of Judaism and disbelief in the sacraments which he had been administering. In spite of his professions of repentance, the fiscal claimed that this was extorted by fear, and presented the evidence of ten witnesses, whose testimony as a whole was but a confirmation of his confession. He gained nothing by his self-denunciation; he was degraded from the priesthood and burnt in the auto de fe of August 17, 1486.[1350]

THE TIME OF MERCY

If thus the Edict of Grace was of little benefit to the New Christians, it was of the utmost service to the Inquisition. The multitudes who came forward contributed large sums in their "alms;" they gave the tribunals wide knowledge of suspects and a means of subsequently convicting them on the score of their imperfect confessions--for their confessions could not fail to be technically imperfect. Moreover, the necessity of denouncing all accomplices furnished an invaluable mass of testimony for further prosecutions. Thus, by this simple and apparently merciful expedient, the inquisitor was provided with funds and had his work laid out for him, enabling him to gather in his harvest with small labor of investigation and with full certainty of results. The fisc also had a further advantage in the opportunity afforded by the imperfect confessions of the reconciled. Besides the general compositions for confiscation described above, there were special ones exempting the Conversos from this particular peril. Thus a royal cédula of April 6, 1491, grants to those of Valencia, for five thousand ducats, release of confiscation for all imperfect confessions and for heresies committed up to that date, except in cases of relapse.[1351] Their fears were speculated upon in every way conceivable.

This probably explains some obscure allusions to a Time of Mercy, as distinguished from the Time of Grace, of which the clearest account we have refers to Majorca. A contemporary relates that "Some years after the Time of Grace, perhaps two, when many heretics had confessed some errors but not all, and had suppressed the names of many accomplices, a rigorous inquisition was made against them. Then, at the persuasion of a certain great Rabbi, nearly all the apostates, seeing the afflictions visited upon them, came to the palace of the inquisitors with loud cries and tears (I wish they were sincere) begging for pardon. Then new confessions were made and, by command of the inquisitor-general, with the consent of King Ferdinand, they were admitted to mercy with a moderate pecuniary fine to redeem their lawfully confiscated property. And that time was called the Time of Mercy. And this occurred in our city of the kingdom of Majorca, viz., the Time of Grace in 1488 and the Time of Mercy in 1490, when I was ten years old. Yet the grace and mercy were of little avail for, from then until the current year 1524, the inquisition against them has never ceased; many were delivered to the secular court and very many exposed to shame and imprisoned for life and their property confiscated, yet never would they amend."[1352]

However successful was the device of the Edict of Grace, from the point of view of inquisitor and king, it evidently won over but few to the faith and, after a comparatively brief experience, the Conversos recognized that those who availed themselves of it were in a distinctly worse position than before, as their confessions were on record against them in case of relapse, and they were exposed to the added danger that any imperfections in those confessions were legally construed as impenitence, which was mortal. We shall see, when considering the subject of confession that this question of imperfection was treated so rigidly as to render its avoidance practically impossible, and of this the Inquisition took full advantage, for we find the Suprema instructing the tribunals to scrutinize carefully all confessions made by those under trial and compare them with those presented in the Time of Grace, to see whether anything had been concealed and whether the so-called penitents counselled with each other to shield their friends and kindred.[1353] This latter clause points to another serious bar to the success of Edicts of Grace, in the obligation to denounce accomplices, which involved the exposure to prosecution of all the friends and kindred of the penitent. This was especially felt when the enforced conversion of the Moriscos subjected them to the Inquisition, for one of their evil qualities, we are told, was that, while they could be forced to confess freely about themselves, they could not be induced to betray their neighbors, wherefore they were burnt for impenitence.[1354]

The Moriscos offered the largest field for the exploitation of Terms of Grace during nearly a century. There was an earnest desire, for reasons of state, to secure their conversion, and special concessions were made to them with little result. The details of these will be more conveniently considered hereafter, and it will suffice here to mention that Philip II, towards the close of his reign, proposed to issue an edict of a comprehensive character which should determine the question of expulsion. Convinced of the futility of such measures involving the denunciation of accomplices, he applied to Clement VIII for permission to omit it, but the pontiff was more rigid than the king and, in his brief authorizing the edict, he insisted on the denunciation of apostates.[1355] Philip's death, in 1598, postponed the issue of the edict until August 22, 1599. Every effort was made to render it successful and the twelve months conceded in it were extended to eighteen, expiring February 28, 1601. The result was awaited with anxiety and, on August 22, 1601, the inquisitors reported that during the whole term only thirteen persons had taken advantage of it, and these had made such imperfect confessions and had so shielded their accomplices that they deserved condemnation rather than absolution.[1356]

UNDER THE RESTORATION

For two centuries after the expulsion of the Moriscos we hear nothing more of Edicts of Grace. There were no longer in Spain bodies of heretics or suspects to whom such expedients were applicable, and the desired unity of faith was secured so far as practicable but, with the Napoleonic wars, there came new sources of infection. Spain was traversed from end to end by armies composed of heretics like the English or largely of free-thinkers like the French. Jews had taken advantage of the troublous times to pollute the sacred soil and liberal ideas, abhorred alike by Church and State, had ample opportunity of dissemination. With the re-establishment of the Inquisition, in 1814, it seemed opportune to meet the flood of heresy and libertinism by the old methods. On January 2, February 10 and April 5, 1815, therefore, the inquisitor-general issued Edicts of Grace, promising that all who, during the current year, should come forward and denounce themselves for heresy or other crimes justiciable by the Inquisition, should be absolved without punishment and without obligation to denounce accomplices. This was followed, April 12th, with orders to collect all information possible, but not to prosecute until after the expiration of the term, when all who should not have spontaneously presented themselves were to be put on trial. This comprehensive plan can scarce be pronounced a success. The records show that a few espontaneados availed themselves of the promised grace, but the number was lamentably insignificant. This did not encourage prolongation of the term and, on January 12, 1816, another edict announced its expiration and the revival of the old obligation to denounce all offences known to the penitent.[1357] There does not seem to have followed any outburst of prosecutions. The tribunals, doubtless, had been too much occupied in repairing their shattered fortunes to waste much thought on accumulating information as to heretics.

CHAPTER II - THE INQUISITORIAL PROCESS

In considering the judicial functions of the Inquisition, we shall meet with much that is abhorrent to our conceptions of justice. We shall see that the accused was assumed to be guilty and that the object of the tribunal was to induce or coerce him to confess his guilt; that, for this purpose, he was substantially deprived of facilities for defence and that the result, for the most part, depended on his powers of endurance which the judges, at discretion, could test to the utmost. It would not be easy to construct a system more repugnant to rational methods for the ascertainment of truth.

At the same time, the vices of the inquisitorial process, at the period under consideration, were not wholly confined to the Inquisition. It is true that it was responsible for their origin, in the thirteenth century, when the jurisprudence of Europe was undergoing reconstruction, and the methods which it framed for the conviction of heresy offered such advantages to the prosecution that they were adopted in the secular courts of nearly all the lands where the Holy Office found a foothold, and became an essential part of criminal codes. The judge, in place of an impartial dispenser of justice, grew to be virtually a prosecutor, with unlimited power of wringing confession from the accused; the latter was practically compelled to prove his innocence, and the trained and subtle intellects of the bench were engaged in conflict with the cunning or stupidity of the miserable wretches brought before them. On the one side was the pride, resolved not to be baffled, on the other the desperate effort at self-preservation and, in the unequal struggle, innocence was much more apt to suffer than guilt to escape. So completely did this identification of judge and prosecutor dominate the criminal jurisprudence of Latin Europe, that in France, until the law of December 8, 1897, after the jury system had been in use for a century, the judge, armed with the sumaria or dossier of incriminating evidence, opened the trial by interrogating the accused and assuming his guilt--an interrogation which was liable speedily to degenerate into a duel between them, in which the judge endeavored to break down the line of defence which the accused was obliged unskilfully to reveal.[1358]

In this the kingdoms of Aragon were strikingly exceptional, for the inquisitorial process, as we have seen, was prohibited. In Aragon itself the interests of the accused were carefully guarded. There were elaborate provisions against arbitrary arrest, although admission to bail was limited. Accusers had to give security and were liable to double costs and damages in case of failure to prove charges. Witnesses were diligently cross-examined and, in cases involving serious punishment, five disinterested jurists were associated with the judge in passing sentence, against which there was right of appeal. There was no public prosecutor, before the revision of procedure by the Córtes of Monzon in 1510, and then it took many years to bring the office into general use. The abuse existed of prosecutions in absentia though, if the accused subsequently appeared, he had the right to appeal, and still worse was the custom of keeping the prisoner chained until his trial was concluded.[1359] In Valencia, and probably elsewhere, there was a peculiarly valuable privilege that no one, whether defendant or witness, was compelled to answer questions that would criminate him.[1360] In Biscay, the fueros, as revised in 1526 and in force until the Revolution, were very emphatic in providing the accused with all information necessary to his defence.[1361]

SECULAR PROCEDURE

In Castile the processes by accusation and by inquisition were both employed. An accuser, however, was obliged to give security and was subject to fines if it appeared that he acted through malice. If there was no accuser, the judge, or alcalde, made inquisition and proceeded summarily to try the case. When, under the impulse of Isabella and the guidance of Alfonso Díaz de Montalvo, the Córtes of Toledo, in 1480, revised the criminal jurisprudence of the land, their action served as a basis for all subsequent legislation. It breathes the spirit of justice--the rigorous punishment of guilt and avoidance of punishment of innocence. The courts were enjoined to quick despatch, the accused was to have all necessary opportunities for defence; if poor, counsel was supplied at the public expense; he could recuse any judge for cause and appeal from any decision, and he was always entitled to give bail. Prosecution in absentia, however, was allowed; after three summonses of nine days each, the accused could be prosecuted in rebeldia, as contumacious and be condemned.[1362]

While thus in Castile legislation was dictated by a sincere desire for justice, in practice the accused was subjected to unnecessary disadvantages and hardships. We chance to have the proceedings in the case of Francisco Fernández de Montemayor, of Seville, tried in Ciudad Real in 1499, on a charge of petty thefts on fellow-lodgers in an inn, in which the general course of procedure bears sufficient resemblance to that of the Inquisition to show that the latter borrowed its forms from the secular courts with modifications to facilitate conviction. When Montemayor was arrested in his inn, September 10th, his effects were sequestrated, locked in his chest and left in charge of the innkeeper. When money was needed for his prison expenses, the judges, on his application, sent the prison scrivener to take out a prescribed sum in the presence of witnesses. The witnesses on both sides were examined on a series of written interrogatories, a most imperfect method, and were not cross-examined. Their names were not concealed, but the accused was kept in gaol and was not present. His own examination was made by the judges in an audiencia de cárcel. He was allowed to retain an advocate, who presented a written defence. The charges were frivolous and, on October 28th, the judges pronounced that the fiscal had not proved his case, which acquitted the prisoner. His treatment in gaol had been harsh; he was an hidalgo and, a few days after arrest, he asked to be treated as a man of good lineage and not to be herded with criminals, whereupon he was placed in a cell, with a heavy chain, under close guard. On acquittal he begged to be released from his fetters, which was done on his swearing not to leave the prison--for he was not discharged. Unluckily, the testimony contained some heretical speeches, though the witnesses believed them to have been uttered in jest, as he was always striving to be jocular. The secular court could take no cognizance of them but the Inquisition claimed him and he was delivered to it in chains, November 9th. His trial had occupied six weeks; the Inquisition kept him for two years and, on November 10, 1501, it penanced him and made him abjure de vehementi. Doubtless the poor wretch was ruined.[1363]

THE SPIRITUAL COURTS

If we find reason to believe that the tribunals of the Inquisition were largely actuated by passion or greed, they were in this no worse than the secular courts. The constantly reiterated complaints of the Córtes, during the sixteenth century, assume that the whole judicial system of Castile, from the highest to the lowest, was not so much an instrumentality of justice as a venal organization to extort the largest possible sums from pleaders and to oppress the poor for the benefit of the rich.[1364] We might, perhaps, regard this as rhetorical exaggeration if we had not the opportunity of seeing how a court of the highest rank--the royal Audiencia of Seville--in 1598, disregarded all law and justice when it sought to gratify its spite on the magistracy of that city. We have seen (Vol. I, p. 362) the absurd quarrel raised with the judges by the inquisitors on the occasion of the obsequies of Philip II. The judges, unable to avenge themselves on the tribunal, discharged their wrath upon the civic authorities, who had sought to mediate and keep the peace. They arrested on the spot several of the highest officials, including two members of the great house of Ponce de Leon and, in spite of the indecency of sitting as judges in their own case, they prosecuted their prisoners. They took the testimony of thirty-seven witnesses on written interrogatories, containing leading questions, and accepted hearsay evidence of the veriest gossip. The accused were allowed to see the accusation framed by the fiscal, but not the evidence, and no opportunity of making defence was permitted. Thereupon their advocates recused the judges, but the recusation was not only rejected on the day of its presentation, but the accused and their advocates were all heavily fined for offering it and, the next day, sentence was pronounced condemning the prisoners to various terms of suspension from office, exile, fines and costs. Both they and the fiscal appealed, and a second hearing was held, in which the defendants at last were allowed to see the evidence. Both parties meanwhile had been applying to the Council of Castile, which ordered that the sentence should not be confirmed without being first submitted to it, but the judges anticipated this and, the day before the order was received, hastily assembled with closed doors and, in the absence of the accused and their counsel, affirmed the decision and ordered its immediate execution, with the exception of Ponce de Leon Almansa, who was of kin to one of them. The sentences were carried out with cruel vindictiveness. There was pestilence in the district to which the exiles were sent and they were brought back sick to Seville, where the Alcalde mayor, Juan Ponce de Leon, died and the others were treated with the utmost harshness.[1365] When the royal courts permitted themselves such arbitrary perversions of justice, we need not be surprised that the Inquisition was reckless, shielded as it was from responsibility by impenetrable secrecy. Between them, the Spanish people were sorely vexed.

To this the spiritual courts offered a contrast in their customary benignity towards clerical offenders, amounting almost to immunity. The course of procedure was that, when a denunciation was made to the provisor or vicar-general, he took testimony or sent an official to make inquisition; the accused was summoned and was admitted to bail; the trial took the shape of an action between him and the fiscal, who presented an accusation to which the defence made reply. Witnesses for the defence were examined, publication of evidence was made and, when both parties had concluded, the judge named a day for pronouncing sentence. From two cases of the sixteenth century, of which the papers are before me, it would appear that there was little delay, that formalities were loosely observed and that the proverbial leniency shown to the cloth rendered the whole a matter of comparative indifference. One of these illustrates the expiring episcopal jurisdiction over heresy and its supplantation by the Inquisition. In 1551, Diego de Carcano, a priest of Ciudad Real, was tried for heretical acts and speeches, which he freely admitted, saying that they had been in jest and that he ought not to have trifled with the things of God. The trial was concluded within three weeks and Diego was confined for a few days in a parish church with spiritual exercises, besides paying costs, amounting to about thirty-two reales. Two years later, Inquisitor Valtodano, on a visitation, chanced to hear of the affair; he treated the episcopal trial as invalid and vindicated together the faith and the inquisitorial jurisdiction by a second prosecution of the unlucky priest.[1366]

The laxity of the Church towards its erring members was still further illustrated by the reforms adopted in the provincial synod of Toledo, held in 1565 to receive the Council of Trent. The fiscal was ordered not to denounce any one to the judge; no inquisition was to be made, unless there was a legitimate general report against a culprit, and then the judge was required to investigate carefully whether it arose from malevolence or from reputable persons. If the fiscal desired to accuse any one he was subjected to the laws concerning accusers and, if he failed to prove the charges, he was liable for the costs and to punishment at the discretion of the judge. All pecuniary penalties were to be expended in pious uses, and not for the advantage of the bishop or his vicar-general, and an official was to be deputed to receive them and render a strict account.[1367]

***

The most marked distinction between the procedure of the Inquisition and that of the other jurisdictions was the inviolable secrecy in which all its operations were shrouded. There were, indeed, other evil peculiarities, but this it was which inflicted the greatest wrong on its victims and exposed the inquisitor to the strongest temptation to abuse his power. It was an inheritance from the thirteenth century, when the Inquisition early discovered the greater freedom of action and the increased popular dread resulting from the mystery which emancipated it from public opinion and veiled all its actions, until their outcome was revealed in the solemnities of the auto de fe. The Roman Inquisition retained it, but in a somewhat modified degree. All its officials were sworn to silence as to everything that occurred in the Congregation but, in 1629, this was explained as restricted only to matters that might prejudice cases.[1368] Very different was the awful silence so enforced in Spain that it formed an important factor in the power of the Holy Office.

SECRECY

It is not a little remarkable that, when the institution was introduced in Castile, so little was known of its practical working that its procedure was public, like that of the secular and spiritual courts. Thus, in 1483, the record of a trial in Ciudad Real speaks of the inquisitors sitting in public audience; the notaries specify as present at the hearing certain persons by name "and many others who were there present;" the inquisitors were listening to all who came before them, while the fiscal and notary were making reports.[1369] It was deemed necessary that there should be spectators to bear witness to the proceedings; sometimes these were connected with the tribunal, sometimes they were citizens called in for the purpose, whose names were regularly entered upon the record.[1370] Even the prison, subsequently guarded so jealously, was not as yet known as the cárceles secretas, but as a cárcel publica.[1371] In 1488, the Instructions order the records to be kept "in a public place, where the inquisitors customarily perform the duties of the Inquisition."[1372] The earliest indication of a change in this respect occurs in the Instructions of 1498, where the oath prescribed for inquisitors and other officials contains a pledge of secrecy.[1373] This did not, as yet however, extend to a complete exclusion of publicity, for some Toledo trials of 1501 describe the fiscal as presenting his clamosa, or demand for prosecution, where the inquisitors were sitting as customary in their public audience, but, during the trial itself, they sat in the "audiencia de cárcel."[1374] From the expressions used we may assume that as yet the inquisition building and the prison were separate; that public audiences were held in the former, and that the latter contained a room to which the accused could be brought from his cell when on trial. The secreto, which subsequently embraced the prison and everything beyond the ante-chambers, as yet only designated a chest or a room in which the records and registers were kept in safety.[1375]

Yet even during this early period there had commenced, in certain portions of procedure, a practice of secrecy which markedly differentiated the Inquisition from the ecclesiastical and secular courts. The suppression of the names and identity of witnesses and the strict seclusion of prisoners from the outside world are matters which will be more fully discussed hereafter, but already they had become distinctive features of the inquisitorial process, inflicting great hardship on the accused, which was keenly felt. The tendency of all such abuses to development, the facility with which the reasons alleged in justification could be extended over all the acts of the Inquisition, and the attraction of the arbitrary and irresponsible power thus gained, readily explain the rapid evolutionary process which enveloped, with an impenetrable veil of secrecy, everything connected with the tribunals, from the preliminary inquest and the arrest of the accused, to his discharge or appearance in an auto de fe.

***

The obligation of the oath of secrecy was rigidly construed when, in 1523, the vicar-general of Saragossa seems to have babbled about what he had heard when called in to vote at a consulta de fe, and the Suprema ordered the inquisitors to summon him and warn him not to reveal the secrets of the Holy Office.[1376] In 1544, Mari Serrana, on trial at Toledo, was charged with impeding the Inquisition, because she had endeavored to ascertain whether a certain person had testified in another case and what he had said--the mere attempt to learn what went on within those mysterious walls was treated as a crime.[1377] In 1547, when the tribunal of Granada was moved into new quarters, it found its secrecy imperilled by the fact that it was overlooked by some windows in the house of Francisco de Santa Cruz, and, on its complaint to Prince Philip, he ordered the corregidor to have those windows closed up--apparently without compensation to the owner.[1378] So impenetrable was the shroud enveloping all that took place within the tribunal that, when Philip II deemed it imperative to consult a distinguished surgeon who had been arrested, Inquisitor-general Quiroga left two applications unanswered and to a third replied that, if the person was there, he could not be taken out, nor could it even be told whether he was or was not a prisoner, whereupon the king desisted from his request. On this the comment of an inquisitor is that to all inquiries the answer must be that nothing is known.[1379] So when, in 1643, the Suprema argued against the claim of the Justicia of Aragon to grant his manifestacion or habeas corpus in secular cases, the chief reason alleged was that, if a tribunal could be required to differentiate cases of faith from others and to admit that it had a certain person in its prison, and the cause, its secrecy would be violated.[1380] This was emphasized, in 1678, by a declaration of the Suprema that an inquisitor admitting that any individual was in the secret prison would incur excommunication removable only by the pope.[1381] It is easy to understand why the prison was habitually designated as the cárceles secretas and why, when a person was arrested, he disappeared as utterly as though the earth had swallowed him.

At every step in the progress of a case minute precautions were taken to insure absolute secrecy. It was not only all officials who were thus sworn, but accuser and accused and their witnesses were subjected to the same obligation. As early as 1531, a witness when dismissed was ordered to observe silence as to all that he had said or heard, under pain of excommunication and a thousand ducats, and of the other penalties of those who violate the secrecy of the Holy Office.[1382] As late as 1817, in a trifling case which was suspended, the informer was fined for not having preserved secrecy.[1383] It was the same with the accused. At the very first audience, the oath administered to tell the truth contained a clause pledging him to silence, not only as to his own case but as to all that he might see or hear. When he was dismissed, whether to punishment or to freedom, he was required to sign a pledge under oath to the same effect, to which was added a threat of punishment, occasionally taking the shape of one or two hundred lashes.[1384] In the later years of the Inquisition this was frequently reinforced by including in the sentence a clause prohibiting the culprit from talking in any manner about his case.[1385] The tribunal thus was relieved from responsibility and could commit injustice without fear of unpleasant revelations, and the Holy Office could boast, as it customarily did, of the exquisite equity of its judgements, without danger of contradiction. To what extent this was justified may be guessed from a remark of Peña, that no inspection was allowed of the acts of the tribunals because they were often in conflict with the common law and the universal opinion of the doctors.[1386]

Nothing connected with the proceedings of the Inquisition was allowed to remain outside of its walls. Every letter, or mandate, or instruction, or warrant, sent out was invariably required to be returned with the answer or endorsement of its execution. Even the Edicts of Faith and Anathemas given out for publication in the churches were returned with statements of the day on which they were publicly read.[1387] This applied to the counsel entrusted with the defence of the accused. Not only was he sworn to secrecy and to communicate with no one concerning the cases, but the scanty papers entrusted to him were to be kept under lock and key and be scrupulously returned to the tribunal, so that there should be no trace or memory of them. The formal defence which he prepared had to be written by his own hand and no rough draft of it be preserved; no printer was allowed to print such a document nor, indeed, any other paper relating to the Inquisition, without special licence from the inquisitor-general or Suprema, under pain of excommunication and a hundred ducats.[1388] This jealous reserve explains the form in which the records of the Inquisition reach us--those of each process rudely but firmly sewed together and never bound, for they could not be given out to a binder nor could one be admitted into the sacred precincts of the secreto. These injunctions of secrecy were not allowed to be a dead letter. In the Edicts of Faith special clauses called for the denunciation of all cases of violation, or of papers concerning its acts being in the possession of any one.[1389]

Its procedure was guarded with the same anxious care from public knowledge. In 1573, Leonardo Donato, the Venetian envoy, who regarded the Inquisition as necessary to Spain, describes its action as so secret that nothing was known of its victims and their cases until their sentences were published in the autos de fe, but the fear entertained of it was so universal that little was said concerning it through dread of arousing suspicion. He had been able to learn nothing of its methods, but was told that they were good and that the sentences were always just.[1390] No one, in fact, was allowed to know what was its form of procedure. The Instructions, it is true, were necessarily printed. There was an edition of the Antiguas in Seville, in 1536, reprinted in Madrid in 1576. The Nuevas of 1561 were printed in 1612 and the whole were re-edited by Arguello, an official of the Suprema, in 1627 and 1630, but these were strictly reserved for use in the tribunals and their details were constantly subject to modification by the cartas acordadas of the Suprema, which never saw the light. Experienced inquisitors drew up manuals of practice, many of which are still preserved in the MSS. of the archives and libraries, but this knowledge of the estilo or methods of procedure was strictly confined to officials sworn to secrecy. It was apparently soon after the preparation of the Instructions of 1561 that a Doctor Blasco de Alagona had the audacity to ask for a copy of them, when the fiscal, to whom the petition was referred, declared that the granting of such a request would be unexampled, and he had no difficulty in proving that parties before the tribunal had no business to inquire into its methods; the Instructions were solely for its guidance and were to be known to others only by their results in the administration of justice. If they came to public knowledge, evil-intentioned men could debate whether the estilo of the Inquisition was good or bad.[1391]

***

The extreme importance of the "seal" was fully recognized in assuring freedom of irresponsible action and in creating the popular impression of mysterious impeccability. Philip II, in his instructions to Manrique de Lara, in 1595, dwelt on this and pointed out that "without it the Holy Office could not preserve the untrammelled exercise of its functions" wherefore any official violating it must be punished with the utmost rigor.[1392] Apparently cases of infraction occurred, drawing from the Suprema a carta acordada pointing out that all the power and authority and reputation of those serving in the Holy Office rested upon secrecy. The more secret its affairs were kept, the more they were venerated by those from whom they were concealed. The neglect of this had aroused in the Suprema the greatest resentment, as it was a matter of so great moment to the estimation and respect in which the affairs and the members of the Inquisition had always been held. Therefore it had been resolved that the oath of secrecy, taken on admission to office, should be so construed that its infraction should constitute perjury and infidelity. Single witnesses should suffice for conviction; on a first offence the culprit should be suspended irremissibly for a year and pay fifty ducats, and on a repetition be perpetually dismissed. Even if not convicted he should realize that, in the forum of conscience, he could not draw his salary. This secrecy covered not only matters of faith and depending thereon, but all votes, orders, determinations, letters of the Suprema, informations of limpieza and all other matters, no information concerning which was to be given to the parties concerned or to any outside person, while even the public utterances of the tribunals were not to be spoken of. Moreover, the above penalties and major excommunication were incurred by all who, knowing of infractions of secrecy, did not report them to the Suprema. Finally, this carta was ordered to be filed with the Instructions, to be read annually to the assembled officials.[1393]

The instructions to commissioners warned them that the existence and preservation of the Inquisition depended chiefly on the absolute secrecy to be observed as to all its affairs.[1394] This continued to the end. A decree of the Suprema, December 7, 1814, speaks of the seal which is the soul of the Inquisition.[1395] In fact, there was no hesitation in assimilating it to the seal of confession and in employing the casuistry which justified a confessor in denying under oath what he had learned in the confessional. Similarly the official was told that no oath was binding when the affairs of the Inquisition were concerned--he could depose as to what he knew as an individual, but not what he knew as an official entrusted with its secrets.[1396] We can understand the significance of the popular saying con el rey y la inquisicion, chiton!--keep silence as to the king and the Inquisition.

Even within the tribunals the same mystery was observed in investigating cases of infraction. When an intimation was received that secrecy had been violated, the junior inquisitor examined into it and wrote out the "information" with his own hand, and without allowing any one to know of it. This was then deposited in a separate chest, of which the senior inquisitor held the key; the Suprema was advised of the matter and its instructions were awaited.[1397]

Not the least important result of this secrecy was the fact that it enabled the Inquisition to combine legislative and judicial functions in a manner known to no other tribunal. It framed its own code and administered it in darkness. It is true, as we shall have occasion to see, that many of the regulations and limitations of the Instructions were inspired by a sense of justice, but this mattered little when the secrecy, so jealously preserved, practically left everything to the discretion of the tribunal, until the Suprema absorbed and centralized everything into itself. Shielded from responsibility--save to the more or less perfunctory occasional visitation of an inspector--there was scarce any injustice that could not be safely perpetrated, or any enmity that a perjured witness could not gratify. The secrets of those dark prison-houses will never be known, even by the records, for these were framed by those whose acts they recount and they may be true or falsified. What was the real administration of so-called justice can only be guessed by occasional revelations such as we chance to have in the trials of Archbishop Carranza, of the Nuns of San Placido, of Gerónimo de Villanueva, of Fray Froilan Díaz and, when the principles of justice were set at naught by the chiefs of the Inquisition in the cases of those so prominent, it is not likely that the obscure were treated with greater consideration by the tribunals. At its best, the inquisitorial process left much to the temper and disposition of the judge; as modified by the Inquisition, the fate of the accused was virtually at the discretion of the tribunal, and that discretion was relieved of the wholesome restraint of publicity. At a time when, as we have seen, the secular courts, although open to the public, were little better than instruments of oppression and extortion, it is not to be imagined that the inquisitorial tribunals, shrouded in impenetrable secrecy, and largely dependent for support on fines and confiscations, were scrupulous in the administration of the cruel laws against heresy.

USE OF THE FISCAL

In the original medieval Inquisition the procedure was a pure inquisitio, the inquisitor frankly acting as both prosecutor and judge, collecting testimony, examining witnesses, seeking to make the accused confess or convict himself, and passing sentence. As the institution, in the fifteenth century, declined and became disorganized, its duties were to some extent resumed by the bishops, in whose courts the pressure of multifarious business had long rendered necessary a prosecuting officer, known as the promotor fiscal, duly trained in the civil and canon law. Cases of heresy inevitably followed the routine of the court and consequently assumed the form of actions between the fiscal and the accused, as plaintiff and defendant, with the bishop or his Official as judge.[1398]

This, at least in appearance, removed one of the most repulsive features of the pure inquisitorial process, as the judge was no longer a party to the case and could affect a semblance of impartiality, even though he were, in reality, the instigator of the prosecution. When the Holy Office was established in Castile, it assumed to be merely the continuance of the Old Inquisition; in its collections of privileges it included papal thirteenth century bulls, along with the modern ones, and the ferocious laws of Frederic II with the cédulas of the Catholic kings.[1399] Yet it knew so little of the older formulas and procedure that it adopted those of the secular and spiritual tribunals of the period, and thus its practice assumed the external form of accusatio rather than of inquisitio, with a fiscal, or public prosecutor, as an accuser. While, on the surface, this was a step towards fairness and justice, care was taken that the interests of the faith should not suffer. It gave to the inquisitors the assistance of a trained lawyer, whose business it was to prove his charges, who lost no opportunity of exaggerating the offences imputed to the accused, who assumed that they had been proved, who resisted all the efforts of the defence to disprove them, and who was free from all the penalties and responsibilities of an accuser. The form of sentence, adopted at the beginning and steadfastly adhered to, asserts that the judges have been listening to a case pending between the fiscal and the defendant, and they find that the fiscal either has proved his charges completely or partially, or that he has failed to do so.[1400] This was an assumption perfectly false and intended to deceive the people when read in an auto de fe.

It was the inquisitors who gathered testimony. The Instructions of 1484 expressly order the examination of witnesses to be made personally by an inquisitor and not to be committed to a notary, unless the witness is too sick to appear and it should be indecent for the inquisitor to go to him, when he could empower the ecclesiastical judge to perform the duty with a notary.[1401] Business was too pressing, however, for the inquisitors always to examine witnesses and they frequently deputized persons to act for them, but those deputies were never the fiscal, and the apologetic tone of the commission shows that it was irregular and demanded an excuse.[1402] As time went on, the tendency to shirk the labor increased; the notaries were allowed to examine, by the Instructions of 1498, provided it was in presence of the inquisitor; then this condition was neglected, in spite of vehement remonstrance by the Suprema, and finally, in the later period, when there was little serious work to be done, special commissions, as we have seen, were common, apparently with no greater excuse than the indolence of the inquisitors.[1403]

***

Still, the fiction was preserved that the witnesses were presented by the fiscals, although the Suprema, in 1534, informed them that it was no part of their duty to collect evidence, although if they obtained any, they were to communicate it to the inquisitors.[1404] Their duties, in fact, in addition to seeking the condemnation of the accused, were those of a superior clerk of the court--to draw up accusations, to conduct correspondence, to advise the inquisitors, to marshal the evidence, to keep the records in order or to see that the secretaries did so, to attend to the execution of sentences, and to exercise a general supervision over the officials, besides attending the meetings of the junta de hacienda and looking after the financial interests of the tribunal.[1405] The fiscal, moreover, served a useful purpose as a bogey to frighten the accused, who were constantly threatened with what would happen if they did not confess before he was admitted to present a formal accusation, in which he customarily demanded torture and relaxation for them--but, after all, his chief use was to preserve the fiction that the prosecution was an action between parties. As Simancas says, even when the culprit confesses, the fiscal must present an accusation, in order that a judgement may be based on accuser, accused and judge.[1406] In short, he was simply one of the officers of the court who, as a trained lawyer, gave to the inquisitors, who were apt to be theologians, the benefit of his legal knowledge. His only real position as a party to an action was a distinct disadvantage to the accused for, in case of acquittal or of a sentence which he deemed too light, he had the right, not infrequently exercised, of appealing to the Suprema, and consequently his assent to the decision was necessary. As his dignity gradually increased, he was classed among the judges by the Córtes of Aragon in 1646;[1407] we have seen how he finally came to be known as "inquisitor-fiscal" and how his place was generally filled by one of the inquisitors, who, however, abstained from the final vote on the case. The fiscal, indeed, from an early period was admitted to the consulta de fe, where he could state facts and advance arguments--a most indecent privilege--though he was required to depart before the vote was taken. In 1660 this was discontinued, not in consequence of its shocking incongruity, but because there was a troublesome question of precedence between him and the episcopal Ordinary, whose duty it was to be present.[1408]

There was nothing in the function of the fiscal to prevent the inquisitor from initiating proceedings on the strength of any rumors that might reach him, or of compromising evidence gathered from the confessions of others. He had not to wait for the fiscal's action, but could order an inquest to be made and testimony to be taken and, when this was done, it was given to the fiscal to be put into shape for the formal prosecution. No matter how upright might be the inquisitor, the mere fact that he had ordered an arrest and trial necessarily committed him to belief in the guilt of the accused; he was unconsciously prejudiced from the start and to acquit cost a greater effort than to convict. Thus although externally the form of procedure was accusatio, in reality it was inquisitio, and the injection of the fiscal as accuser only diminished the chances of the defence, by giving the inquisitors a skilled legal assistant in the conduct of a prosecution, in which they were all prosecutors.

Yet, whatever we may think of the morality of the inquisitorial process, there can be no doubt as to its efficacy. In studying the long and minute records of the trials, where every detail is set forth in writing, it is instructive to see how often the accused, who commences by boldly asserting his orthodoxy, comes in successive audiences to make some admission of which advantage is skilfully taken and gradually the denial breaks down, or perhaps yields to the terrors of the accusation and the publication of evidence, ending in complete confession and eager implication of kindred and friends. The situation of the accused, in fact, was helpless. Standing up alone before the stern admonitions of the trained and pitiless judge; brooding in his cell, cut off from all external communication, during weeks or months of interval between his audiences; apparently forgotten, but living in the constant uncertainty of being at any moment summoned to appear; torturing his mind as to the impression which his utterances might have made, or the deductions drawn from his admissions or denials; balancing between the chances of escape, by persistent assertions of innocence, and those of condemnation as an impenitente negativo, and urged by his so-called advocate to confess and throw himself on the mercy of the tribunal--it required an exceptionally resolute temperament to endure the prolonged strain, with the knowledge that the opponent in the deadly game always had in reserve the terrible resource of the torture-chamber. The whole course of the procedure was based on the assumption that the accused was guilty; that it was the province of the tribunal to induce or compel him to confess his guilt and, in the great majority of instances the assumption was correct. To those who regarded aberrations from the faith as the greatest of crimes before God and man, and their punishment as the most acceptable service that man could render to God, this presumption of guilt served to justify the cruelty of the procedure and the denial of all facilities for defence which, to those trained in the principles of English justice, seem the imprescriptible right of the accused, whether innocent or not.

THE INQUISITORIAL IDEAL

There can, indeed, be no doubt that, amid much greed and callous indifference to justice, there were men engaged in the service who deemed themselves to be doing the work of God and that their methods were merciful. The Inquisition was not as other tribunals which only punished the body; it asserted its high and holy mission to be the saving of souls. As the inquisitors of Valencia said, in 1536, to Miguel Mesquita, on his trial for Lutheranism, they required of him nothing but the truth and, if he had fallen into error, they sought to disabuse him and to cure his conscience so that his soul might not be lost.[1409]

The Instructions of 1561, which remained to the last the basis of procedure, are emphatic in cautioning inquisitors not to be led astray, either by the witnesses or by the confessions of the accused, but to determine all cases according to truth and justice; they must preserve strict impartiality for, if they lean to one side or to the other, they can readily be deceived.[1410] If we may believe the veteran inquisitor Páramo, the Holy Office was so conducted on this lofty plane as to be an unmixed blessing to the land. Its holiness, he says, is so conspicuous that there is no opening for hatred, favor, subornation, love, intercession, or other human motive. Every act is performed with such conscientiousness and regard for equity and justice; the inquisitors so investigate everything, undisturbed by the multitude, that they inspire all men with dread of the crimes which are brought before them and, in the all-pervading silence, they act with incredible conscientiousness. The evidence of witnesses is scrutinized in the light of their character and quality and those who are found to bear false-witness are most severely punished. The accused, while detained in the prisons, are treated kindly and liberally, according to their condition; the poor and the sick are abundantly furnished with food and medicines, at the expense of the fisc, and are favored in every way. Not only are the utterances of witnesses investigated with distrust but, as Time is the revealer of truth, cases are not hurriedly finished but are prudently prolonged, as is requisite when there is such peril of the life, fame and property, not only of the accused but of his kindred. If his innocence appears probable, every effort is made to prove it and, if it is proved, to avert from him any loss of reputation, for which reason he is carried on horseback, adorned with laurels and palms like a victor in a triumph--a spectacle inspiring to the souls of the timid, depressed by the severity with which the guilty are punished. Those who are restored from such peril to their former condition never cease to thank God for placing on earth a tribunal of which the chief care is to uphold the honor of the innocent. When inquisitors punish heretics it is not with the desire to destroy them, but that they shall be converted and live. In judging and chastising, the Holy Office labors to amend him whom it punishes, or to benefit others by his punishment, so that they may live in security when the wicked are removed.[1411]

To what extent this idealization of inquisitorial methods was justified, we have had some opportunity to see, and we shall have more.

Henry Charles Lea, LL.D.

CHAPTER III - ARREST AND SEQUESTRATION

Although the power to arrest arbitrarily was inherent in the inquisitorial functions, and all secular officials were bound to lend assistance if necessary, still, in practice, it required justification by sufficient evidence in hand. This was obtained in various ways. The inquisitor might learn that public rumor designated a person as guilty of heretical acts and might cause secret inquest to be made in verification. In the prevalent forms of heresy, such as that of Jewish and Moorish apostates, the most frequent source of incrimination was the confessions of accomplices on trial or under Edicts of Grace. In other matters, the initiative came largely from denunciations, which were stimulated and favored in every way, especially by the secrecy which relieved the informer from responsibility.

No duty was more strenuously inculcated on the people than that of denouncing any utterance or act partaking of calidad de oficio--that is, which came within the cognizance of the Holy Office. Divine law required this under penalty of mortal sin, and ecclesiastical law under that of excommunication.[1412] From this no ties of blood furnished release. It is true that, under the imperial jurisprudence, accusations of near relatives were forbidden; a mother could not accuse a son except of offences against herself and even a man brought up in another's house could not accuse his benefactor.[1413] But Simancas, while highly approving of this, says that there are two cases in which a son must accuse his father--one, when under examination by the Inquisition, the other, when the father is a persistent heretic and, as the obligation of the son to the father is of the highest, this includes all other cases.[1414] The Instructions of 1484 offer mitigation of punishment to minor children who spontaneously denounce their parents, and Alfonso de Castro relates that he denied absolution to a young man, perfectly orthodox in faith, who in confession, in response to interrogatories, admitted that his father was a Judaizer, but refused to denounce him in view of the consequences to himself of poverty and infamy.[1415]

The annual publication of the Edict of Faith, with its accompanying anathemas, proclaimed this imperative obligation in the most solemn manner and, at the same time, furnished a list of the offences to be denounced, thus rendering every one a spy upon his neighbor. The denunciation might be either verbal or written and, if written, either anonymous or signed; it could be made to a tribunal or to any commissioner, and it was expected to contain the names of witnesses to be summoned in its support. These denunciations came in more frequently after the publication of the Edict of Faith, and also about Easter, when the faithful confessed in preparation for the indispensable paschal communion, and the confessors enquired whether they had denounced whatever they had heard, seen or understood that was, or appeared to be, contrary to the faith or to the rights of the Inquisition, and absolution was withheld from those refusing to do so. This denunciation and the evidence of the witnesses summoned in its support, or the testimony acquired by inquest, or by the confessions of those on trial, constituted the sumaria--the instruction préparatoire of French practice.

The tribunal, however, was held not to act summarily in so grave a matter as an arrest casting infamy on an entire lineage. After the first tumultuous period, when no one was safe from arbitrary imprisonment, the portions of the evidence which conveyed the nature of the charge, without the name of the accused, underwent the process of calificacion, or censorship, to determine whether they presented calidad de oficio. We have seen, in the cases of Carranza, of Villanueva and of Froilan Díaz, how important was the function of the calificadores, or censors, and how much sometimes depended on the manner in which the evidence was submitted to them. In the rehabilitation of the Nuns of San Placido, they were careful to declare that, if they had had to act upon the testimony laid before their predecessors, they would have reached the same conclusion. Against such garbling there could be no guarantee, in the profound secrecy enveloping every act of the tribunals.

CALIFICACION

The calificadores were learned theologians, whose duties we have already referred to (p. 263). Some were regular appointees, but any one could be called upon, nor could he refuse to serve without pay. When there was not unanimity, the inquisitors decided or submitted the case to others. There seems to have been no settled or absolute rule. In 1634, in the case of Jacques Garrigues, a wandering French beggar, professing sanctity and curative powers and claiming to be a messenger of God, not without indications of insanity, the two inquisitors joined with four calificadores in considering the evidence before arrest, but this seems to be exceptional.[1416] The resource of calling in successive calificadores in obscure cases frequently led only to a hopeless divergence of opinion, bewildering rather than assisting the inquisitors. When, in 1640, the Bernardine Fray Tomas de Nieba defended some subtle conclusions in scholastic theology, there were eleven calificadores called into service, of whom some found nothing to censure, others that the doctrine was a condemned one, others again that it merely approached to error. In the same year, in the similar case of the Franciscan Fray Juan Lazaro, one calificador pronounced his doctrine to be obscure and perilous, if not formally, at least virtually, heretical; another that to defend it was a most grave error, while two others could find in it nothing objectionable. Yet Lazaro was put on trial and, after the case had traversed its various stages for months, it was suspended, though Lazaro was ordered in future to teach the opposite opinion.[1417]

At length a carta acordada of October 8, 1708 sought to regulate the system. In all cases requiring calificacion, a correct extract was to be made from the evidence as to the acts and speeches charged, with all circumstances contributory to a clear understanding. This was to be sent to one of the calificadores, who was to keep it at least three days, and return it with his opinion, not only as to the requisite censure but also as to the defence that could be made. It was thus to pass from one to another, after which the tribunal was to call them together to frame a common opinion. Books and papers were to be treated in the same way and there was no obligation of secrecy between the parties called in.[1418]

All classes of charges were not subjected to calificacion, for there were numerous and important groups of offenders who were deprived of this safeguard, slender as it was at the best. Judaizers and Moriscos, renegades, bigamists, those administering sacraments without being in priestly orders and solicitors of women in the confessional were not entitled to it.[1419] Thus taken as a whole, up to the middle of the eighteenth century, the major portion of the business of the tribunals was exempt from calificacion and practically it was limited to the refinements of venturesome theologians, to the degree of heresy involved in more or less picturesque blasphemy, the culpability of careless or reckless talkers, and the implied pact with the demon in the conjurations of wise-women and treasure-seekers. Like much else in the Inquisition, designed for the protection of innocence, its working effect was reduced to a minimum.

THE CLAMOSA AND THE CONSULTA

At what period calificacion was introduced it would be difficult to say with precision. Llorente assures us that in 1550 it was not as yet in use.[1420] This is incorrect for, in 1520, we find the Suprema ordering that calificadores shall not be appointed without its consent and on the simple petition of aspirants.[1421] By that time the custom was evidently established and, in 1556, the Suprema explained it, not as a protection of innocence but as a means of placating the Ordinaries and showing them that inquisitors were not seeking to extend their jurisdiction beyond heresy.[1422] The Instructions of 1561 merely provide that, when there is sufficient testimony in a case pertaining to the Inquisition, if it requires calificacion, theologians of approved learning and character shall be consulted, thus inferring that this is unnecessary when ceremonies known to be Jewish or Moorish are concerned, or manifest heresy or fautorship.[1423] The Suprema felt it necessary, in a carta acordada of July 11, 1569, to warn calificadores to confine themselves to defining the nature of propositions submitted and not to say whether or not there was calidad de oficio--a limitation which they outgrew. Another carta of November 22, 1577, shows that it had become by this time a recognized preliminary to arrest, by ordering that, if an arrest should be necessary without it, there should at least be calificacion before the formal accusation is presented, which occurred in a later stage of the proceedings.[1424]

In the gradual absorption of all initiative by the Suprema, so that eventually no arrest could be made without its order, the importance of calificacion declined. Calificadores continued to be appointed, but they seem to have been rather ornamental than useful members of the official family, if we may judge from the variation in the number attached to the different tribunals. The table in the appendix shows that, in 1746, Madrid and Llerena had none, while Valencia rejoiced in forty. They still had a function, however, in the censorship of the press, and tribunals that were insufficiently supplied could always summon theologians to their aid when necessity demanded their services.

***

As the sumaria was careful to recite that there was sufficient proof, that all formalities had been observed, and that further investigation was unnecessary, the calificacion completed the preliminaries. The next step was the presentation by the fiscal of his clamosa or demand for the arrest of the accused. In the fully developed formula of this, he presented and swore to the sumaria, and embodied the calificacion as showing that the culprit merited the severest punishment, to which end he asked for arrest and imprisonment, with sequestration or embargo of property, promising in due time to present a formal accusation and asking that meanwhile the registers of the other tribunals be examined with the view of securing further evidence. Forms of this were provided suited to the various classes of offences and to the cases of the absent or dead.[1425]

It manifests a praiseworthy desire to avoid precipitate action that a consulta de fe, or consultation of the inquisitors with the consultores and Ordinary, was still technically required before issuing the warrant of arrest. The existence of something of the kind is indicated, as early as 1509, by an order of the Suprema that when there is not unanimity it must be consulted before arrest is made.[1426] Yet, in 1521, a special order requiring such a consulta de fe in the case of Moriscos would infer that the rule was otherwise obsolete.[1427] That it was so is shown by subsequent cases and, even as regards Moriscos, in a number of prosecutions at Daimiel, between 1540 and 1550, the warrants are issued immediately on presentation of the clamosas.[1428] The Instructions of 1561 revived the practice, but did not enjoin it as essential, leaving it virtually to the discretion of the inquisitors.[1429] After this we find it frequently observed and, in the case of Elvira del Campo, accused of Jewish practices, in 1567, there is a consulta prior to the clamosa and a second one afterwards before the warrant of arrest is issued.[1430] When solicitation in the confessional was subjected to the Inquisition, the desire to shroud the offence in obscurity led to a regulation, in 1564, that only the vicar-general should be called into consultation and, in 1600, even he was excluded; the inquisitors were to consult only with each other and then await the orders of the Suprema.[1431] As the rule became established that the Suprema was to be consulted before arrest, these formal preliminaries became of less importance and, in the eighteenth century, we are told that the consulta was no longer held, the reason alleged being that the inquisitors then were jurists.[1432]

ARBITRARY ARREST

Apart from these formalities, there was an evident desire on the part of the chiefs of the Inquisition to prevent injustice arising from hasty and inconsiderate action. In the reformatory Instructions of 1498, inquisitors are ordered to be careful and to arrest no one on insufficient evidence--an order the frequent repetition of which proves how little it was regarded.[1433] It was thoroughly understood that the mere fact of imprisonment inflicted indelible infamy and all the authorities urge the utmost caution in the exercise of this tremendous power.[1434] In theory, at least, stronger proof was therefore required by inquisitors than by the judges of other courts; it ought to be as strong as that which justified torture--what was known as semiplena--but this merely consisted in the evidence of a single unexceptionable witness; when there was apprehension of flight, less was required and Sousa, a Portuguese authority, tells us that in heresy flight is always to be apprehended.[1435] It is true that, in 1630, the Suprema ordered that arrest on the testimony of a single witness should not be made without its permission, but this exercised little restraint. Such an arrest was made, in 1638, of Domingo de Mezquita, with a sort of apologetic explanation that he was a Portuguese and had already been tried on the same charge of Judaism.[1436]

One or two cases will show how little real benefit in practice the accused derived from all this elaborate parade of preliminary precautions. In Toledo, June 5, 1501, the fiscal informed the tribunal that Isabel, daughter of Alvaro Ortolano, was defamed for heresy and asked for her arrest. The inquisitors replied that they would order it if sufficient evidence was presented, whereupon he offered the testimony of a prisoner that she had heard Isabel say that she observed the Jewish fasts and on this a warrant of arrest was promptly issued. Considering that the accused was a child ten years of age her summary arrest on evidence so flimsy shows how little impression the Instructions of 1498 had produced.[1437] The Toledan inquisitors did not grow more cautious with time. September 16, 1541, two workmen on the cathedral appeared before them and accused Juan García, a fellow-workman, of having revelations from God in his dreams. A warrant was at once made out; the portero was ordered to have him present that afternoon and, if he demurred, to take him to the prison. He accordingly had his first audience the same day.[1438]

In these arbitrary proceedings the function of the fiscal was purely fictitious and he and the inquisitor, if they had any sense of humor, must have smiled as they acted their parts in the tragi-comedy. In 1532, before Fernando Loazes, the distinguished inquisitor of Barcelona, the fiscal appears and states verbally that it has come to his knowledge that, when the impenitent and relapsed heretic Joana, wife of Gil Tacis, was to be arrested, her husband had sought to conceal her, wherefore he should be arrested as a fautor of heresy and impeder of the Inquisition and, in due time, the proper "information" would be presented. The only evidence was that of Joana, taken by Loazes himself, but he gravely demanded to be informed and he ordered the summoning of all the witnesses whom the fiscal desired to produce. Then the fiscal, to enlighten him, presents the evidence from the record; Loazes orders it to be inserted in the acts of the case, pronounces it sufficient and issues the warrant of arrest.[1439]

In the secrecy of the tribunals there was thus nothing to prevent the exercise of discretional power to oppress the innocent as well as to punish the guilty. That it was so abused appears from the remonstrance of the Córtes of the kingdoms of Aragon, about 1530, complaining that the inquisitors arrested people for the slightest causes and on mere report, and then sometimes dismissed their prisoners without penance or with very slight sentences, thus inflicting infamy on the parties, their kindred and descendants, which was not effaced by the release. Arrests, they urged, ought to be made only for grave offences and on sufficient proof. To this the inquisitor-general disdainfully replied that the laws had been observed; if the complainants thought otherwise, let them produce instances.[1440] This spirit did not promise amendment and, although the Instructions of 1561 prescribed caution and restraint, matters must have grown worse through subordinates aping their masters, for the Concordia of 1568 provides that familiars must not be allowed to make arrests without orders from the inquisitors.[1441]

SEGREGATION OF ACCUSED

Even after the Suprema had required to be consulted prior to ordering arrest, small respect was paid to formalities. In criticizing, August 25, 1695, the report of cases pending in Valencia, the Suprema expresses astonishment that an arrest should have been made previous to the calificacion of the charges. In this case the accused was thrown into prison October 22, 1694, and the calificacion followed, February 9, 1695, but the Suprema contented itself with this rebuke and merely ordered the prosecution to be pushed and not be allowed to become immortal.[1442] The Suprema need not have been surprised at this trifling informality in view of the atrocity of a group of cases comprised in a Valladolid report of July, 1699. Francisco Hernández Castañeda had been imprisoned August 30, 1697; his case is reported in the same state as before, there being no testimony against him. Baltazar González Cardozo, aged 14, was arrested August 15, 1698, and there is no evidence against him. Ana Gutiérrez, aged 9, was arrested August 14, 1697, and there is nothing against her as yet. Leona de Paz was arrested September 15, 1698, and there is no proof against her.[1443] Thus these poor creatures had lain in gaol for one or two years without a scintilla of evidence to justify their arrest, and the fact that the tribunal coolly makes this report indicates that there was in it nothing unusual or regarded as scandalous.

Among the reforms which Carlos III attempted to introduce towards the close of the eighteenth century was that of requiring manifest proofs of heresy as a necessary preliminary to arrest, but Llorente informs us that his decrees were not obeyed.[1444] Still, in time there was an improvement in this as in so many other directions, perhaps partially influenced by the poverty of the Holy Office and its desire to avoid the maintenance of poor prisoners. Thus, in the case, at Cuenca, of Juan Francisco de la Landera, a jubilado notary of confiscations, prosecuted in 1816 on suspicion of being the author of a memorial to the king and of other offences, he was allowed to be at large during nearly the whole course of the trial and it was not until after the presentation of the accusation and his reply that it was voted to imprison him and embargo his property.[1445]

***

The reason commonly alleged, in deprecation of reckless arrest, was the infamy cast on the accused and his kindred, but this was by no means the only infliction peculiar to the Inquisition. There was special hardship in the segregation at once imposed on the prisoner. From the moment of his arrest, the utmost care was taken to prevent his exchanging a word with any one. When it took place at a distance, the commissioner was instructed to observe this with the utmost rigor, both in confining the prisoner on the spot and in sending him to the tribunal. If two or more were arrested simultaneously, they were strictly kept apart, both in prison and on the road. Thus, in 1678, when several Judaizers were to be seized at Pastrana, the instructions from Toledo were that they were at once to be shut up, incomunicado, in houses of officials, and to be sent to Toledo one by one, observing rigid precautions that they should speak with no one. Each was to be under charge of a familiar and, if there were not enough in Pastrana, those of the neighboring towns were to be called upon.[1446] The misery caused to the prisoner and his family by the arrest was intensified by this sudden inhibition of all exchange of affection and all instruction and advice as to what they were to do in their affliction.

IMPORTANCE OF SEQUESTRATION

Another feature, falling with especial severity on the poorer classes, arose from the rule of the Inquisition to cast all expenses on its prisoners. The officer who made the arrest was instructed to bring with him a specified sum to be deposited with the alcaide of the prison for the maintenance of the prisoner; also a bed for him to sleep on and clothes for him to wear. If, as usually was the case, the required amount was not found in cash among the effects of the culprit, enough of his household goods was sold at auction to meet the demand. The working of this is seen in the case of Benito Peñas, a poor ploughmaker of Cobeña, near Alcalá de Henares--a half-crazed devotee, who created scandal by denying that Christ had died on the cross. The order for his arrest by the Toledo tribunal, January 25, 1641, required the familiar to bring with him 30 ducats for expenses and a bed. The only coins found in Benito's possession amounted to 19 cuartos vellon, equivalent to about 2-1/2 reales: so on Sunday, February 10th, all his little possessions of tools, furniture and clothing, except the garments on him and two old shirts, were sold at auction. Even the rosary in his hands was included, but the total proceeds, after deducting charges, amounted to only 20 ducats. Of this about a half was absorbed by the expenses of guards and conveyance to Toledo, and only 105-1/2 reales were delivered with him at the carceles secretas, out of which the tribunal refused to pay anything to the familiar for his time and labor. Benito's mental unsoundness developed rapidly in his incarceration and, in August, he was discharged as irresponsible. The authorities of Cobeña were obliged to take him home at their own expense, and doubtless to support him afterwards, as he had been deprived of all means of earning his livelihood, while, with customary inquisitorial logic, in spite of his insanity, he was condemned to wear a particolored garment of gray and green, in penance for his heresy.[1447] In the case of a religious, if his peculium was insufficient to furnish the desired amount, the superior of his convent was required to complete it.[1448]

***

Another feature of extreme severity which, however, was common to secular and episcopal as well as to inquisitorial practice, was the sequestration which accompanied arrest in all cases involving confiscation. The losses and hardships incident to this were fully recognized in secular proceedings and, in 1646, the Córtes of Aragon endeavored to mitigate them and also to prevent the frauds which were admitted to be frequent.[1449] On the other hand, to have the property of the accused in the power of his family was to risk its dissipation before the conclusion of the trial; it had to be preserved at all hazards and the only way to do this was to make sure of it by seizure at the moment of arrest. The importance attributed to this by the Holy Office is seen in the details which form so prominent a portion of the Instructions. It is true that the canon law strictly prohibited the seizure of property, before a sentence of condemnation had been duly rendered, but this had been framed at a time when the temporal lords enjoyed the confiscations, and was disregarded when they enured to the benefit of those who decreed them.[1450]

The alguazil executing a warrant of arrest was accompanied by the notario de secrestos, or notary of sequestrations, who at once seized all visible property and compiled a minute inventory. It was then placed in the hands of a sequestrador or depositario, who held it until the case was decided, when, if confiscation was decreed, he handed it over to the receiver; if not, it was returned, or what was left of it, to the owner.

In the earliest instructions, the receiver and his scrivener accompanied the notary of sequestrations, and two copies of the inventory were made. Much conflicting legislation followed, directed to finding means for preventing the receiver from appropriating portions of the sequestrations, but the trouble was perennial and, in interrogatories drawn up for inspectors on their visitations, there was one which required all officials to declare whether the receiver had taken any sequestrated property before the case of the owner was determined.[1451]

THE INVENTORY

Irregularities continued and, in 1633, some respect was paid to the interest of the accused by a rule that a representative appointed by him should be present, with the receiver and notary, when seizing the property and making the inventory. In 1635, this was followed by requiring the senior inquisitor to report promptly to the Suprema all details as to kind and amount of property sequestrated, and whether any collusion or secreting of goods had occurred--a mandate of which the frequent repetition shows the difficulty of its enforcement.[1452] Finally, in 1654, Philip IV assembled a junta to formulate regulations by which, when farmers of the revenue were arrested, the interests of the royal fisc, of all creditors, and of the owner if acquitted, might be protected. These provided that the first duty, on making an arrest, was to search the prisoner for papers and keys. He was then told to name a representative to be present at the sequestration and inventory. If the hour suited, this followed at once, otherwise it was postponed to the next day, padlocks being meanwhile placed on everything, and one or two guards being stationed. The inventory was made in the minutest detail, room by room, specifying the contents of all desks, trunks, chests and other receptacles. The keys were then delivered to the depository selected, who receipted for the property and became responsible for it. Then followed immediately the audiencia de hacienda, in which the prisoner was made to give an account of all of his possessions. If among the effects seized were some of a nature requiring them to be sold, or if it was necessary to provide for the food of the prisoner, they were disposed of at auction, after appraisement made in the presence of his representative.[1453]

As the inventory was the basis of all further proceedings, from a very early period rigid instructions were issued that it should be complete to the minutest detail. Every paper found in the prisoner's possession was to be enumerated; in 1607 the Suprema complained of negligence in this respect and ordered that in future not only must every paper be set down but also its nature and contents.[1454] Such inventories as I have had an opportunity of examining show the laborious trifling entailed by these instructions. In the case, for instance, of Margarita Altamira, in 1681, the list covers four closely written pages, consisting of entries such as "an old pair of scissors," "a worn tow towel," "an old broom," "an old earthen pot," etc. She was the wife of an agricultural laborer, apparently separated from her husband and owning nothing save her little household plenishing and clothes.[1455] Official zeal sometimes outran discretion, gravely affecting the interests of others, as when, in 1597, the Suprema was obliged to issue instructions that, when heretic ship-masters were arrested in the sea-ports, only their own effects were to be seized and not the ships and cargoes.[1456] It was unavoidable that the property of third parties, in the hands of the accused, should be included in the sequestration and, as we have seen, from an early period the orders were that such goods should be surrendered as soon as owners should prove their rights. Such cases were of perpetual occurrence, causing much damage or inconvenience, and were attended with exasperating delays. The daughters of Brianda Royz, reconciled with confiscation, presented, March 19, 1530, a claim for some seventy articles of household furnishing, which were not adjudged to them until July 7, 1531. The list included a pair of chickens which had doubtless long before disappeared in the olla.[1457] The case of Margarita Altamira affords some quaint illustrations of the annoyances inflicted on those who chanced to have had dealings with the accused. She was arrested in November, 1681 and, on April 8, 1682, the priest Francisco Juan Sans presented a petition representing that, among the effects sequestrated, was a lot of shirts and undergarments of which he furnished a list--Margarita apparently having been his washer-woman. The paper was endorsed to be filed away and its proof to be received in proper time. The proper time was slow in coming for, in August, the good padre again petitioned for his shirts, but whether he eventually recovered them the documents fail to show. A year later, August 3, 1683, Margarita Batlle made application for a cradle which she said that she had lent to Altamira. The case was referred to the receiver who reported that there was in the sequestration an old cradle, which if sold might fetch two or three reales. Then, on August 25th, the inquisitors resolved that, as it was of so little value, it might be surrendered to her on her proving ownership under oath and, on October 6th, she was duly sworn and examined; she described the cradle, told from whom it was bought at the price of two reales, explained why she had lent it and why she had not reclaimed it prior to Altamira's arrest, whereupon it was ordered to be restored to her.[1458] Evidently there was no haste in relieving the necessities of those who were caught in the sweep of sequestration.

PROVISION FOR FAMILIES

It was very properly a cardinal principle, frequently reiterated, that sequestrated property was sacred and was not to be diverted, however great might be the necessity.[1459] It was easier, however, to enunciate such a self-denying ordinance than to observe it, in an institution practically secure from supervision. Ferdinand set the example by selling or granting as favors numerous houses in Perpignan, abandoned by fugitives before the Inquisition was in operation in Roussillon, and he had no scruple in assuming the condemnation of the owners before their prosecution had commenced.[1460] We have seen how, in 1644, the Suprema admitted to Philip IV that, to satisfy his exigencies, it had sold sequestrated property, for which the owners, who had been acquitted, were clamoring.[1461] In fact, the use of such property became habitual for, towards the end of the century, we find an official depositario of the Suprema in charge of the sequestrations, who was accustomed to meet, from the funds in his hands, the expenses of the Madrid tribunal, subject of course to repayment. In one transaction of the kind, the advance made July 3, 1680, was not refunded until November 17, 1681.[1462] The tribunal was thus exposed to the risk that its decisions might be influenced by the condition of its account with the depositario.

At first there would seem to have been no provision for the family of a prisoner whose property was thus suddenly seized. They were cast adrift and deprived of subsistence, regardless of the fact that confiscation might not be decreed. In the early Instructions there is no arrangement for their support during the trial, and any exceptions to this were matters of favor, as when Ferdinand, July 11, 1486, wrote to the receiver of Saragossa that, as the lands and personalty of Juan Navarro had been sequestrated, as his children had no other support, and as one of them had rendered him good service, all the rents and profits of the estate should be paid to them during the pendency of the case.[1463] Common humanity demanded that some attention be paid to the necessities of the innocent and helpless, while confiscation was as yet uncertain, and in time this severity was relaxed, though it cannot be positively stated when this commenced. The earliest allusion to it, that I have met, occurs in the memorial of Llerena, in 1506, which, while denouncing the cruelty of turning the family into the streets at night, admits that some allowance was made to them from the sequestrations. It complains, however, that this was miserably insufficient and so irregularly paid that sometimes months elapsed without anything being received. In one case two little daughters of a rich prisoner perished of hunger, and their elder sisters subsisted by beggary at night. A woman thus left with ten souls dependent upon her was allowed twenty-five maravedís a day, when two hundred and fifty were requisite, and even of this pittance she had received nothing for three months.[1464]

The matter was one which called for regulation, and various experimental instructions were issued from time to time. Absolute arrangements were not easy to provide and, between 1538 and 1558, a number of utterances show the difficulty of reaching a satisfactory result. The general features of these are that the inquisitors are to consult with the receiver and notary of sequestrations and assign an allowance proportioned to the amount of the property and station of the recipients, while consideration is to be given to the ability of individuals to earn a living, provided it is not derogatory to their rank.[1465] A definite policy was finally reached in the Instructions of 1561, which remained the standard. These provide that, if the wife or children of a prisoner apply for support, he is to be consulted and, if he so wishes, an allowance out of the sequestration is to be made to them, proportioned to their station, but if there are some of an age to work they must provide for themselves. This was a matter of grace and not of right, for a subsequent regulation restricts the grant to a limited time because the trial may be prolonged and it may be advisable to discontinue the payments. In 1567 it was added that common clothes and bedding could be given, but every article must be specified, as the depositaries were apt to be too liberal unless restricted.[1466] It thus became a settled principle that the family of a prisoner was to be cared for out of the sequestration of its head, if he had property and, in the printed form of a warrant of arrest, in 1696, this is specified as the object of placing it in the hands of a depositary selected by the prisoner.[1467]

THE SECRESTADOR

While recognizing the humanity of these provisions it may be questioned how far they relieved the hardships of dependents, especially in the later period, when the dilatory methods of the Inquisition prolonged the trials inordinately. Unless an estate was unusually large, it was apt to be speedily consumed by wasteful methods and the accumulation of expenses. As we shall see hereafter, unless the accused was penniless, the cost of his maintenance in prison was a first lien on his sequestrated property and, if there was not ready money, his effects were auctioned off to supply it. The strictness of the rule to pay all expenses out of the sequestration is illustrated in the case of two children of Antonio Enríquez Barrios, confined with their father in the prison of the tribunal of Madrid. When they were discharged, 1423 reales, the cost of their clothing and food, were collected from the sequestrated estate of their father, whose trial was unfinished.[1468] It may be assumed, under such a system that, when the accused escaped without confiscation, only a remnant of his property was restored to him, especially as he had to accept on account from the depositario whatever the tribunal had ordered to be paid out of the sequestration and be content with the balance, while whatever he might owe for his prison maintenance had to be paid before an order was issued to lift the embargo. In this respect, a suspension of the case was equivalent to an acquittal and entitled him to resume possession of what remained of his property.[1469]

Of course nothing could compensate a man engaged in trade for thus locking up during years all his business concerns. To such a one, arrest with sequestration meant ruin, however clearly his innocence might be demonstrated after the prolonged proceedings of the tribunal. A curious inventory of a printing office thus seized shows the breaking up of a business and the destruction of the means of livelihood. One item is "a hundred and twenty reams of the third volume of Rodríguez, the book at present in hand," which is highly suggestive of the loss inflicted, without redress, on other parties concerned, as author or publisher, as also of the sacrifice incurred by peremptory auction sales of such material.[1470]

***

The office of secrestador or depositary would seem, in the earlier period, to have been regarded as desirable, and it certainly offered opportunities for the dishonest. That these were sometimes improved is apparent from the case, in 1510, of Fernando de Mesa, a jurado of Córdova, who was secrestador of the estate of a certain Celamin. By the time the latter was condemned, Mesa had died and the sequestrated property was not forthcoming. He had placed four daughters as nuns in the convent of

Santa Ines and their share of the defalcation was thirty thousand maravedís, but the convent pleaded inability to pay through poverty and Ferdinand kindly forgave it the debt.[1471]

To the honest, however, the office was in every way undesirable. It involved labor, anxiety and responsibility without payment but, when selected and approved, the appointee was obliged to serve, under penalty of excommunication and a fine of ten or twenty thousand maravedis. It was recommended that, if possible, he should not be a kinsman of the prisoner or a Converso, and he was always to be of good repute and standing.[1472] If the accused was a householder, the house was locked and the keys were given to the depositary; otherwise he was put to the expense of storage; he was obliged to sign a paper subjecting himself to the penalties imposed on him by the alguazil and pledging his person and property to make good any deficiencies occurring through error or negligence, for which he renounced his fuero and submitted himself wholly to the Inquisition.[1473] The perplexities and tribulations to which he was exposed are illustrated by those of Jaume Taxes, who served as depositario in the case of Margarita Altamira. He appealed, April 26, 1682, to the inquisitors, representing that, when the sequestration was made, he was given the key of the house, but he is now required to surrender it to the owner and to have the goods stored safely; he has no room for them in his own house and petitions to have them delivered to some one else. No attention was paid to this and, on May 14th, the owner of the house, a priest named Francisco Canudes, came forward with a complaint; on March 26th he had obtained an order for the key, but Taxes refuses to surrender it, wherefore he desires that he be forced to do so and to pay him six months' rent.[1474] The documents fail to inform us what was the solution of the complication which the tribunal had thus created, but the affair illustrates the manner in which the Inquisition was wont to call for gratuitous services and to pay little regard to the convenience or interest of those on whom it imposed onerous duties.

LIMITATIONS

There were some limitations on the power of sequestration. It was confined to property found in possession of the accused; whatever he owned that was in the hands of third parties could not be sequestrated and had to await sentence of confiscation before it could be seized.[1475] An application of this principle led to the somewhat remarkable rule that there could be no sequestration in prosecutions of the dead, however convincing the proofs of guilt, because the possessions of the offender had passed into the hands of third parties. As early as 1537 this was prescribed by the Suprema, in a letter to the tribunal of Barcelona, and it was embodied in the Instructions of 1561.[1476]

A more important limitation confined sequestration to arrest on charges of formal heresy, and the fiscal was required in his clamosa to specify whether or not he asked for it, though as late as 1575 the Suprema was obliged to notify the tribunal of Valencia that heresy was a prerequisite of sequestration.[1477] The definition of heresy, however, was somewhat elastic and when, in 1573, a determined effort was made to eradicate the general popular belief that fornication between the unmarried was not a mortal sin, it was ordered to be prosecuted as heresy with sequestration.[1478] When formal heresy was involved, sequestration was to be decreed, whether the accused had property or not and, in 1665, the Suprema rebuked the tribunal of Barcelona for omitting it in the case of a galley-slave.[1479]

The Inquisition at length grew restive under the limitation of sequestration to formal heresy, for, as heretics grew fewer, it exempted a vast proportion of the cases which formed the current business of the tribunals, consisting of blasphemy, sorcery, bigamy, solicitation, marriage of clerics, propositions scandalous, audacious or ill-sounding, the possession of prohibited books, and, in fact, as we are told, all offences which did not in law import confiscation.[1480] In these cases the warrant of arrest, during the sixteenth century, instructed the alguazil to arrange so that the prisoner could leave his property in the hands of any one whom he should select, to be used for the maintenance of himself and his family, and an inventory was to be made to prevent misappropriation.[1481] In time the Inquisition outgrew this consideration for the innocent sufferers, which reduced it to sharing with them in the use of what was apt to disappear in the course of the protracted trials. To remedy this and without, so far as appears, any warrant of law, the expedient was devised of substituting for the word sequestration the euphemistic term of embargo, and ordering the property of all prisoners not liable to confiscation to be embargoed. The words had the same meaning and, in the earlier time, were used as identical, often copulatively as "embargo y secresto"--a mere pleonasm of legal phraseology, the context showing that sequestration was meant.[1482] The slight shade of difference was that in embargo the prisoner selected the depositary who was to hold the property and pay from it the expenses of his maintenance in prison during his trial.[1483] Thus sequestration, under the flimsy veil of calling it embargo, became a matter of course in all arrests and the fiscal was instructed, when the calificacion was of formal heresy, to ask for sequestration, in other cases for embargo and, when frailes were the culprits, for embargo of their peculium and papers. So universal was this that, in 1665, the Suprema required the Barcelona tribunal to furnish reasons for not embargoing the property in any case of arrest for minor offences.[1484] So it continued to the end. In 1815 we find numerous cases of embargo in arrests on charges of bigamy, solicitation, irreverence, propositions and the like, while the Dominican Fray Tomas García, for celebrating mass without priests' orders, had his peculium embargoed.[1485]

ILLUSTRATIVE CASE

In this illegal extension of sequestration there is something peculiarly heartless. When the offence charged inferred confiscation, there was some excuse for making sure that the property would not be secreted or dissipated, but in minor cases to subject the offender and his family to the hardship, and perhaps ruin, caused by seizing his property and holding it during the leisurely progress of his trial, merely in order to secure to the tribunal the reimbursement of his maintenance in prison, shows how thoroughly hardened the Holy Office had become to human suffering and how its selfish greed stifled all the promptings of humanity.

***

A practical illustration of the process of arrest and sequestration is furnished by the case of Ana de Torres, a woman of twenty-two, recently married to Gaspar Agustin, a confectioner of Ciudad Real. Testimony of Judaism had been gathered against her and, on May 9, 1680, the Toledo tribunal ordered its familiar, Don Alvaro Muñoz de Figueroa, a Knight of Santiago, to arrest her, sequestrate her property and send her to Toledo with bed and clothing and 100 ducats. On May 17th Muñoz reported that, after ascertaining her address, he had gone to her house at nine o'clock that night, with a notary, familiar and servants, had carried her off to his own, turning out the husband and placing two guards, so that the sequestration could be made the next day. From what he could see, all the contents of the house was not worth 100 ducats and he was told that they belonged to the husband, for she had come to Ciudad Real in September with nothing but her person. Moreover she was five or six months gone with child. He asked for instructions, which were given in apparent disregard of the husband's rights, for he was told to make the sequestration and send her with her bed and clothes and whatever he could get for her things. On May 24th he reported that he had started her on her journey with 400 reales (about 36 ducats) which was all that he had realized on the sale of the effects. Successive relays of familiars carried her gratuitously and the next day the receiver of Toledo acknowledged the receipt of the 400 reales to pay for her food. Then, on July 6th, the alcaide reported that she was suffering from an inflammation of the throat which, in her condition, threatened serious complications. The medico was called in, who prescribed bleeding and gargles and removal from the confined air of the prison. She was taken to the house of the alcaide, where she was duly bled and, on July 18th, was sufficiently recovered to ask for an audience. In due time, on September 13th, the alcaide reported her confinement and that he had provided a midwife, when he was ordered to take care that she had everything necessary for her recovery and comfort. On September 29th the child was baptized and the mother brought back to the prison, when she was placed in a cell with two other women and, in October, orders were drawn for 146 reales to pay for the clothes and swaddling-bands of the infant and for 14 reales to the chapel of the cathedral for its baptism.[1486]

The redeeming features of these latter details afford a welcome relief to the sordid eagerness of the Inquisition in grasping everything within its reach in order to escape the costs of persecution, regardless of the misery which it inflicted. In the present case we learn nothing as to the husband, presumably innocent, thus turned out of his house and stripped of his furniture. This was no concern of the Holy Office.

CHAPTER IV - THE SECRET PRISON

The cárceles secretas, or secret prison, was the official designation of the place of confinement during trial of those accused of heresy. It formed part of the building of the Inquisition, so that the prisoner could at any moment be brought into the audience-chamber without being exposed to public view--such a case as Carranza's, where confinement was in a different place and the inquisitors went there, being wholly exceptional. The secret prison was exclusively one of detention, the casa de penitencia, or punitive prison, being wholly different, and the contrast between the two--the laxity of the imprisonment as a punishment of the guilty and its rigor towards those whose guilt was yet uncertain--is not the least of the anomalies of the Holy Office.

As a general rule it may be said that imprisonment followed arrest and that admission to bail was an exceptional favor in the early time, virtually withdrawn afterwards. In 1530 we have an example in the case of Antonio de Parejo, a priest whose offences did not amount to formal heresy, who was released by the Toledo tribunal from the secret prison and given the city as a prison on bail in 100,000 maravedís, furnished by his brother Vizcaino, who renounced his fuero; Parejo moreover took a solemn oath not to leave Toledo on his own feet or on those of others, and that a certain Matheo Pérez could always tell where he was to be found.[1487] Various regulations, in 1535 and 1537, allow bail in cases where arrests had been made on slender evidence but, in 1560, Valdés ordered that no exceptions should be made when the charge was of heresy.[1488]

For those held on less serious charges there was less rigorous treatment. The inquisitorial jurisdiction extended over a wide range of offences, more or less trivial, and the tribunals did not care to be burdened with the expense of prisoners who were not likely to seek safety in flight or to warn their accomplices. For these there were various grades of confinement, under the practice known as aplacería, of assigning the city as a prison, or the offender's house, or the less rigorous prison for officials under trial, known as the cárcel de familiares. Thus, about 1640, a writer says that, in cases of blasphemy, the accused can be assigned the city as a prison or, if the offence has been especially shameless and scandalous and reiterated, it may be proper to confine him in the cárcel de familiares or, if flight is anticipated, even in the secret prison, although this is a rigor not now practised. He adds that, when astrologers spontaneously denounce themselves, they are not thrown into the secret prison but into the cárcel de familiares or are given their own houses or the city as a prison.[1489] Friars often, unless the charges were particularly grave, were assigned for detention to the convent of their Order, in accordance with the general policy of guarding the honor of the Church. When the prisons of the tribunals were crowded, convents were also sometimes used as subsidiary prisons, as they were provided with cells for detention.

LESS HARSH THAN OTHER GAOLS

In some tribunals we also hear of cárceles medias, cárceles comunes and cárceles públicas, for offences not of faith. These appear to be similar to the cárcel de familiares and, in all of them, confinement was held not to inflict the indelible stain of the secret prison. As a rule, the prisoner in these was not debarred from communication with his friends, although he might be confined sin comunicacion. In fact, the whole matter lay at the discretion of the tribunal. We have seen how, in the passionate conflicts of jurisdiction, inquisitors sometimes wreaked vengeance on their opponents by inflicting on them the infamy of confinement in the secret prison. So, on the other hand, culprits charged with heresy, when the proofs seemed slender, were sometimes placed in the cárceles medias and then, as the trial advanced and the evidence grew more compromising, were transferred to the secret prison. Thus, in 1678, Angela Pérez, on trial for Judaism by the tribunal of Toledo, was moved, June 22nd from the medias to the secretas; the same occurred at Valladolid, in 1697, in several cases of Judaism, and, as late as 1818 there is an example at Seville, where Ana María Barbero, tried for superstitions and blasphemies, was similarly shifted when the case reached the stage of formal accusation.[1490]

***

In compassionating the hardships of the secret prison, the horrors of the gaols of the period must not be lost to sight and, in the comparison, we shall see that those of the Inquisition were less vile than those of other jurisdictions. It is true that the ancient laws of Castile proclaimed that prisons were meant not for punishment but for detention while awaiting trial, and that Ferdinand and Isabella, in 1489, ordered a weekly inspection by the judges, who should listen to all complaints made by prisoners, a provision repeated by Charles V, in 1525.[1491] Yet the petition of the Córtes of Madrid, in 1534, shows how little attention these enlightened enactments received and the condition of the gaols can be conjectured from that of Valencia, where, about 1630, Pedro Bonet, secretary of the Inquisition, was confined, while a competencia was fought over him, and when he was surrendered to the tribunal he was in such a state that he died within three days.[1492] It is certain that the Inquisition regarded its secret prison as more humane than the royal gaol, even in modern times, for in 1816, when Don Agustin Pirala was tried by both jurisdictions, for certain irreligious and "anti-political" propositions, the tribunal of Madrid, in procuring his transfer to its cells, asserted that this was to relieve him from the inevitable hardships of the royal gaol in which he was confined.[1493]

This may well be true, for the secret prison had the reputation of being less harsh than those of the spiritual jurisdictions. In 1629, Fray Diego de Medina, when brought before the tribunal of Valladolid for uttering some radical heresies, explained that, in his convent de la Victoria, he was kept in the stocks in the convent prison, and he had made the heretical assertions in order to be transferred to the milder treatment of the Inquisition, whereupon he was dismissed with a reprimand. We might regard this as an isolated case were it not for a similar one, about 1675, where a cleric, confined in the episcopal prison, pretended Judaism with the object of being removed to the Inquisition. In this instance the tribunal rebuked him and remanded him to the tender mercies of his bishop.[1494]

Whether the secret prisons were better or worse than the royal and ecclesiastical gaols, they were dismal and unwholesome places of confinement. Of course as structures they varied greatly. Few, if any, of the buildings of the Inquisition were constructed for its use. In Saragossa the royal castle of the Aljaferia, in Barcelona the royal palace, in Valencia the archiepiscopal palace, in Seville the castle of Triana, in Córdova the Alcázar were occupied and utilized, and elsewhere such buildings as seemed suitable were taken. Those which had served as castles had dungeons already provided; in the others, cells were constructed. Under the circumstances there could be no common plan and no general standard of convenience or healthfulness. It is to be hoped that not many were like that of Palermo, where there were great subterranean caverns in which the inquisitors constructed cells for their prisoners, but probably not much better was part of the secret prison of Toledo, of which we get a glimpse in 1592. Mari Rodríguez, after lying there for nine months, with a year-old baby, asked an audience and begged to be removed from her cell, for it was entirely dark and she and her companions suffered greatly and they were sick, to which the inquisitor coldly replied that what she needed was to discharge her conscience and save her soul and, for the rest, she should have justice.[1495]

That the prisons should be unsanitary was a matter of course at the period and the death-rate must have been large, especially during the pestilences, which are of constant recurrence in the annals of the time. Statistics are of course unattainable, but the records frequently refer to the death of prisoners during trial. In Valladolid, the report of 1630 to the Suprema includes the names of twelve deceased prisoners, with the existing state of their cases and, in the great Madrid auto de fe of 1680, all the dead who were burnt in effigy, to the number of eight, had died in the prisons.[1496]

TERROR INSPIRED

Confinement in the secret prison was regarded as one of the gravest misfortunes that could befall a man, in consequence of the indelible stain that it inflicted on him and his descendants. The Consults Magna of 1696 dwells eloquently on the horror inspired by such imprisonment and the injustice of subjecting to it, at the whim of an inquisitor, those whose offences had no relation to the faith. In support of this it adduces the case of a woman of Seville, in 1682, who had some words with the wife of a secretary of the tribunal; the alguazil was sent to arrest her and, in her frenzied desire to avoid imprisonment, she threw herself from an upper window and broke both her legs. The Consulta adds that those who were guilty only of an insult to a familiar were not infrequently thrust into the deepest dungeons of the secret prisons.[1497] The terror thus caused was rated as one of the most efficient powers possessed by the Inquisition. When, in 1622, Gregory XV granted to the bishops concurrent jurisdiction over the crime of solicitation, the remonstrances addressed to him from Spain represented this dread as a deterrent much more powerful than anything that the bishops could bring to bear. In the royal instructions to the Duke of Alburquerque, then ambassador at Rome, it is argued that the fear of the infamy wrought by the prisons of the Inquisition restrains the hardiest culprits.[1498] Power such as this was liable to constant abuse, even after the Suprema had deprived the tribunals of initiative and, when the attention of Carlos IV was called to it, in 1798, by the case of Ramon de Salas, a professor at Salamanca, he proposed to require special royal permission before consignment to the secret prison, but

Llorente tells us that court intrigues prevented the enactment of this wholesome reform.[1499]

***

The cruelty which kept all prisoners in chains was not peculiar to the Inquisition, for we have seen that it was a common practice in the secular gaols. An Italian visiting Madrid, in 1592, describes three prisons there; that of the court, of the city and of the priests, and says that all prisoners, no matter how slight their offences, were fettered. It was evidently a novelty to him which he sought to explain by the insecurity of the buildings.[1500] None of the Instructions refer to chains, but a chance allusion of Pablo García shows that their use was assumed as a matter of course, and this occasionally presents itself in the trials as when, in 1565, Pierre de Bonneville asks their removal to enable him to change his drawers and, in 1647, Alonso Velázquez, who had escaped and was recaptured, describes how he rid himself of them.[1501]

While thus the Inquisition is not to be taxed with special cruelty in following the universal custom, it had its own methods of inflicting intolerable hardship in special cases. When a heretic proved to be impenitent, a mordaza, or gag, was applied to him. What was the exact form of this instrument of torture it would be impossible to say, but the allusions to it show that it was regarded as a severe infliction. When thus worn in prison it was not a mere precaution against the prisoner spreading his heresies, for an order of the Suprema prescribes that no one be allowed to speak with him except the confessor sent to him in the night before his execution, while even then the mordaza was not to be removed.[1502] There was another device of pure cruelty--the pié de amigo--an iron fork or crotch, fitted to the chin and secured by a band around the neck or the waist, to keep the head up and rigidly fixed. The customary use of this was on culprits scourged through the streets or paraded in vergüenza, but it was sometimes employed to heighten the sufferings of prisoners, either through mere malignity or to induce confession. When the celebrated Doctor Agustin Cazalla was burnt in Valladolid, in 1559, envoys from the tribunal sent to him the afternoon before the auto de fe found him in a dark cell, loaded with chains and wearing a pié de amigo, although he had freely confessed, recanted and begged for mercy.[1503] In 1599, in the case of Jacques Pinzon, a French Calvinist, in Toledo, who made a disturbance in the prison, fifty lashes were administered and a pié de amigo was ordered, April 20th. At an audience granted him six months later, October 19th, he is described as still wearing it, as well as two pairs of fetters and, in this case, the pié de amigo extended from the neck to the right hand.[1504]

ESCAPE

In spite of fetters, escape from the secret prison was by no means rare, but it was not often finally successful, for the organization of the Inquisition generally enabled it to recapture the fugitive. A description of the culprit was at once distributed, with a mandate ordering the civil authorities to summon every one to assist and the familiars and commissioners to scour the roads, under pain of excommunication and five hundred ducats.[1505] Thus an army was promptly on foot, every suspicious stranger was scrutinized, and the fugitive was usually soon arrested and returned. In the jurisprudence of the period, breaking gaol was held to be a confession of guilt and some authorities held that this applied to the prisoners of the Inquisition, but Simancas and Rojas agree in regarding this as excessive severity. If the fugitive was recaptured, the ordinary practice was to give him one or two hundred lashes; his trial was resumed and carried forward to the end. If he was not recaptured he was prosecuted for contumacy in absentia.[1506] Numerous cases attest the accuracy of this although, when the culprit was a person of condition, the scourging was replaced by stricter imprisonment and increased severity in the sentence.[1507] For those who eluded recapture, the prosecution for contumacy had but one ending--the absentee was held to be a self-confessed and impenitent heretic, fit only for the stake. Thus, in 1586, Jean de Salines, a Frenchman, on trial for Lutheranism in Valencia, succeeded in escaping with a number of fellow-prisoners. He was not recaptured; the necessary edicts of summons were issued in due order and, as a contumacious heretic, he was burnt in effigy, January 23, 1590 although, at the time of his evasion his case had already been voted on, with the insignificant sentence of abjuration de levi and six months' seclusion.[1508]

***

The cruellest feature of inquisitorial prison discipline was the rigid denial of all intercourse with the outer world. In the secular gaols, the state always had the right of imprisoning sin comunicacion, where there were special reasons for such rigor, but in the secret prisons of the Holy Office this was the universal rule, enforced with the utmost solicitude as an essential part of its highly prized secrecy. We have seen that, from the moment of arrest until delivery to the gaoler, the prisoner was not allowed to exchange a word with any one but the officials, and this was continued with the same strictness when he was within the walls, so far as concerned the outer world, to which he was as one already in the tomb. He could learn nothing of those whom he held dear, nor could they conjecture his fate until, after perhaps the lapse of years, he appeared in an auto de fe as one destined to the stake or to the galleys or to perpetual prison. It would be impossible to compute the sum of human misery thus wantonly inflicted by the Inquisition during its centuries of existence--misery for which the only excuse was that communication with friends might aid in his defence. According to inquisitorial theory, the presumption of guilt was so absolute that all measures were justified which would hinder fraudulent defence.

SEGREGATION

This strictness was not observed at first. The Instructions of 1488 call attention to the evils arising from communication with prisoners and order inquisitors to see in future that it is not permitted, except by the admittance of religious persons for their spiritual benefit.[1509] This received scant attention, for the Instructions of 1498 order alguazils and gaolers not to permit the entrance of wives or kindred, and whatever is sent to prisoners must be examined to ensure that no letters or messages reach them. Even inquisitors and other officials were forbidden to speak with prisoners except in the presence of another official.[1510] This rigor was relaxed, for an order of the Suprema, in 1514, provided that no one from the outside should speak with a prisoner, except by special licence of the inquisitor, and then only in his presence or that of a notary, and a further concession, in 1536, was that, if a prisoner desired an interview with his wife, the inquisitor, if he saw fit, could grant permission.[1511] These slender concessions, however, were soon withdrawn and, in 1546, officials were reminded that only those permitted by the Instructions could be admitted and any contraventions would be severely punished.[1512] Surreptitious communications were difficult to prevent, and so little were the officials trusted that two locks were required on each cell-door, so that the alcaide or gaoler could not enter without his assistant.[1513] The success with which all this was enforced is boastingly alluded to in a report of the Valladolid auto de fe of May 21, 1559, where it is declared that the inquisitorial process was so secret that no one knew what was the offence of any prisoner till he appeared on the scaffold.[1514]

The increasing importance attached to this is revealed in the Instructions of 1561, which take for granted that all access from outside is forbidden and which regulate the interior life of the prison with the same object. Everything brought to a prisoner, whether provisions or other matters, was reported to the inquisitors who decided as to its delivery; if allowed, it was minutely examined to see that it transmitted no message. If it were found that prisoners had communicated with each other, no pains were spared to find how it was done and what had passed between them. When prisoners were confined together, if their cell was changed, they were kept together and not scattered among others. The segregation from the world was maintained to the end; at the auto de fe no one was allowed to speak with penitents, except the confessors assigned to them, and those who were burnt were sent to their last reckoning without being allowed to learn what was the fate of those whom they held dear. When penitents left the prison, after the auto, they were subjected to the avisos de cárceles, in which they were examined under oath as to all that they had seen or heard while confined, and were ordered, under heavy penalties, to reveal nothing of their own experiences.[1515] All this was not wanton and cold-blooded cruelty; it was merely the pitiless enforcement of a rule which was superior to all the promptings of humanity.

In the fulfilment of the rule the most minute regulations were multiplied and reiterated. The alcaide was warned to be especially careful about his wife and children, who were never to be allowed to see the prisoners; no one was to be admitted to the cells, except the sworn attendant who served the food, and when, as in some tribunals, it was served uncooked for the prisoners to cook, it was not to be wrapped in paper but was to be brought in earthen pots. In serving food and in cleaning cells, the door of one was always to be securely locked before opening another; no windows which looked upon those of the cells were allowed to be opened; in Murcia, the water-carrier who served the Inquisition was not allowed to enter the court-yard to fill the jars, but to do so from a window opening upon the court, or to have the water in a room where the jars could be filled.[1516] No precaution was too minute, no watchfulness too careful, when the supreme object was concerned of isolating the prisoners from their friends and from each other.

WRITING MATERIALS

Yet there were ways of eluding the vigilance of the tribunals, of which bribery of the underlings was the most frequent. Even the alcaides were not insensible to such seductions and a writer advises them to take warning by the example of those who enter office in honor and leave it in ignominy.[1517] The kindred and friends of prisoners were frequently people of means and there could be no hesitation in outlays to circumvent the cruel rules which forbade to them and to the captives all knowledge of each other's fate. The Inquisition was by no means consistent in its treatment of those who thus violated its regulations. In 1635, Miguel de Maradillo, a bricklayer working on the roof of the prison of Valladolid, carried a message from one prisoner to another informing him that his wife and son had been arrested. On another occasion he told the same prisoner that his daughter had been relieved of the sanbenito and he conveyed a paper from him to them. In this he seems to have been actuated merely by compassion and his punishment was light--a reprimand, six months' exile from Valladolid and prohibition of future employment on the building of the Inquisition. In 1655, Francisco López Capadocia, on trial by the tribunal of Valladolid, was subjected to a second prosecution, for communicating with other prisoners and was sentenced only to reprimand and exile.[1518] Greater severity seems to have been shown when employees of the tribunals were the guilty parties. In 1591, when Don Alonzo de Mendoza was confined in Toledo on a charge of heresy, his friends outside established correspondence by means of the cook, Francisca de Saavedra, who conveyed the letters in the dishes. She admitted having received bribes to the amount of 8160 maravedís and was punished with a fine of 6000, besides a hundred lashes and four years' exile.[1519] Still harsher was the treatment, about 1650, in Mexico, of Esteban Domingo, a negro slave employed as an assistant in the crowded inquisitorial prison. He was detected in carrying for money communications between the prisoners and their friends, for which he was condemned to two hundred lashes and six years in the galleys.[1520]

Towards the close of its career the Inquisition seems to manifest a disposition to relax somewhat in its rigidity. In 1815 the Madrid tribunal referred to the Suprema a petition from Doña Manuela Osorno to be permitted to see her husband, Don Vicente Lema, then in its prison. The answer was that, after he had completed his declarations, she might be allowed to see him once or twice a week, in the presence of an inquisitor, but only to confer on their domestic affairs. To this tendency may also be attributed the leniency shown to Alfonso González, barber of the tribunal of Murcia, who made use of his position to convey letters and paper to Francisco Villaescusa, a prisoner, and who was benignantly treated with a reprimand and disability to hold office under the Inquisition.[1521]

A necessary feature of the prohibition of communication was that prisoners were debarred from the use of writing materials, except under the strictest supervision. Some use of them was unavoidable, when drawing up a defence or a petition to the tribunal, opportunity for which was never refused, but they were required to apply to the inquisitors for paper, stating the number of sheets wanted, when these were carefully numbered and rubricated by the secretary, at the upper right-hand corner, and were required to be scrupulously returned, so that there could be no withholding of any for another purpose. This device was prescribed by the Suprema in 1534 and remained the invariable rule.[1522] Thus when Fray Vicente Selles, in Valencia, at an audience of June 27, 1692, asked for two sheets of paper and, on June 30th, returned one and a half in blank, saying that what he had written on the other half-sheet was false and he had thrown it into the filth, he was made to fetch it, filthy as it was.[1523] Whatever quantity a prisoner asked was given to him, and some consumed paper by the quire--indeed, Fray Luis de Leon relieved the tedium and anxiety of his four years' imprisonment at Valladolid by writing his classical devotional work, the "Nombres de Cristo."

***

While, as we have seen, great care was taken to prevent prisoners from communicating with each other, it by no means follows that confinement was solitary. As a general rule it was regarded as preferable that male prisoners should be alone, and that women should have companionship, but there could be no hard and fast line of policy followed, except that accomplices and negativos (those who denied the accusation) should not be placed together. Husband and wife were thus always separated but, when occasion required, there was no hesitation in crowding four or five persons together and, in the careless confidence of common misfortune, this often opened a valuable source of information, for there never seems to have been any scruple in betraying that confidence in the hope of winning favor by reporting to the tribunal the compromising utterances of cell-companions. The object in keeping apart those who were accomplices was to prevent their encouraging each other in denial and agreeing on a common line of defence. Men who were confined by themselves sometimes asked for a companion and women more frequently did so.[1524]

REGULATIONS

It was impossible that discipline should be uniform at all times and places and we sometimes find it exceedingly lax. It infers great looseness when, in 1546, the Suprema felt it necessary to enjoin care in permitting prisoners freely to visit each other and, in the trial of Isabel Reyner at Toledo, in 1570, we find her stating, in an audience, that in passing through the prison she saw a fellow-prisoner who informed her that her husband and Estevan Carrier were also prisoners, and who asked her why she was imprisoned.[1525] In fact, as we gather from chance allusions in the trials, there must have been a certain freedom of movement. In the case of Benito Ferrer, in 1621, at Toledo, there was an investigation as to his sanity, in which the alcaide spoke of his going regularly to the cistern for water and cooking his food like the rest, while the assistant described taking him to the latrines when desired. From the trial of Jacques Pinzon, in Granada, in 1599, we learn that, in the morning, the alcaide brought the prisoners water and returned after mass with their food; the mention of a pan to hold ashes shows that they had fire, and we hear of pots, spoons and other utensils.[1526] There was evidently a diversity of routine in the different tribunals and when Valdés, in 1562, was obliged to order that prisoners were not to go for their rations, because they met the servants of the purveyor, and that the alcaide must receive the food and carry it to the cells, it argues that, in some tribunals at least, a considerable freedom of movement had existed.[1527]

In 1662, a minute code of instructions for the alcaide shows us what at that time were the regulations. On rising in the morning, he is to visit all the cells and see how the prisoners are; he is to examine carefully for openings through which they may communicate with each other; doors are to be carefully closed and he is not to leave with the prisoners knives, cords or scissors--if scissors are needed, he is to stay while they are used and take them away. He is not to give them books to read without permission of the inquisitors. Rations are served twice a week--on Sundays and Thursdays-- and, on the afternoon previous, he is to see each prisoner, ascertain what he wants, and set it down in a book so that the purveyor may provide it. Every nightfall he is to examine the cells to guard against attempts to escape, searching under the pillows for articles that would assist flight, or for writing materials. Prisoners able to cook their food will do so in a brasero; for those who cannot, the cooking is done by an appointee of the tribunal.[1528] All this shows a commendable desire to avoid unnecessary harshness, yet the regulations enforce one hardship which appears to have been universal at all periods after the earliest--the prohibition of lights, a severe infliction for, in the obscurity of their cells, the hours of darkness must have seemed interminable. It is probable that at first this was not the rule for, in 1497, in Valencia, there is an item of 7s. 4d. for lights, in the account of the expenses of Alonso de Roman, who had lain in the secret prison for nine months and nine days.[1529]

Of course, in the general venality of the period, prison officials were not always inaccessible to bribery, and money could procure relaxation of the rules but, when detected, it was visited with a severity not often shown to delinquent officials. This is illustrated by a case in Toledo, in 1591, when judicious liberality procured unlawful privileges, such as having cell doors open, allowing communications and other similar indulgences. Francisco Méndez de Lema, the alcaide, attempted flight, but was caught and sentenced to a hundred lashes, galley-service, exile and deprivation of office. His cousin and assistant, Miguel de Xea, confessed partially and was tortured without extracting more; he escaped with dismissal, disability for office and four years of exile.[1530]

There was one regulation which bore with especial severity on the innocent, while it was a matter of indifference to the heretic. This was the deprivation of all religious consolation during the period, often prolonged for years, of incarceration. It is difficult to understand this in the professors of a theology which teaches the infinite importance of the sacraments as aids to spiritual development as well as to salvation, especially when so large a portion of the prisoners were good Catholics tried on charges which did not infer formal heresy. Possibly it may be explained by the customary assumption of the guilt of the accused, who had thus incurred ipso facto excommunication, and the Spanish Inquisition had the example of the Roman, whose prisoners were similarly not allowed to receive the sacraments or to hear mass.[1531] Yet the great canonist Azpilcueta, whose attention was probably drawn to the matter by the case of his client Carranza, thus deprived of the sacraments for eighteen years, tells us that there is no law justifying the Spanish Inquisition in this, though perhaps it may have special authority and also good reasons. To him, however, it appeared that the sacraments would soften the hearts of prisoners and lead them to confess, while it was cruel to leave them exposed without defence to the assaults of the demon during the many years of their captivity.[1532] Yet the refusal was absolute. Fray Luis de Leon, after three years of imprisonment, pleaded earnestly for the sacraments, but the only reply of the Suprema to his petition was to tell the Valladolid tribunal to finish the case as soon as convenient.[1533]

SACRAMENTAL CONFESSION

While the sacraments were denied, sacramental confession was allowed, though of course the priest could not grant absolution. The earliest allusion I have met to this is an order by Cardinal Manrique in 1529, and, in 1540, formal instructions were issued that, when a prisoner asks for a confessor, if the case admits of it, a proper person should be given to him.[1534] This privilege was somewhat abridged by the elaborate provisions of the Instructions of 1561, which are framed to turn it to advantage. If a prisoner in good health asks for a confessor, it is safer not to grant the request, unless he has confessed judicially and has satisfied the evidence. But, as he cannot be absolved for heresy until reconciled to the Church, such confession is not of full effect unless he is in the article of death or a woman in the peril of child-birth, in which case the canon laws are to be observed. If a sick man asks for a confessor he shall have one, who shall be sworn to secrecy and to reveal to the tribunal any commission entrusted to him, if it is outside of confession, and to refuse it if within confession; the inquisitors shall instruct him to tell the prisoner that he cannot be absolved, if guilty, unless he confesses judicially. If his judicial confession satisfies the evidence, he is to be formally reconciled before he dies and, when judicially absolved, the confessor shall absolve him sacramentally when, if there is nothing to prevent it, he may receive Christian burial, as secretly as possible. If a sick man does not ask for a confessor and the physician is apprehensive of the result, he must urge him in every way to confess.[1535] The advantage thus afforded by the confessional is illustrated in the trial for Judaism of Ana López, at Valladolid, in 1637. She had denied, but was taken sick and declared by the physician to be in danger. To the confessor she admitted that, at the age of seventeen, she was taught Judaism, that she subsequently returned to the true faith until, on coming to Valladolid, a woman perverted her. The confessor warned her that she must confess judicially; she authorized him to report her confession and he absolved her sacramentally. An inquisitor with a notary went to her cell, when she repeated her confession and gave the name of the woman who had perverted her, and, on her recovery, her trial was resumed when she confirmed her confession.[1536]

It is the kindly rule of the Church that absolution is never to be refused to the dying; he is to be saved from hell and can settle the account of his sins in purgatory, or by an indulgence or a mass on a privileged altar. With this the Inquisition did not interfere, as its professed object was the saving of souls and it even, by a carta acordada of 1632, permitted communion to dying heretics who had confessed judicially and satisfied the evidence. It required, however, the wafer to be consecrated in the tribunal, if there was time; if the haste was extreme, it could be brought from the parish church, but without pomp or procession.[1537] Even the veneration due to the Godhead had to yield to the secrecy which forbade it to be known that a prisoner was dying in the Holy Office. In the same spirit, when a prisoner died without reconciliation, the alcaide reported it to the inquisitors, who ordered the secretary to identify the body and bury it secretly.[1538] It was thrust into a hole, without his family knowing his fate until, if his trial was unfinished, his heirs would be summoned to defend his fame and memory or, if it had reached a point where sentence could be pronounced, they saw his effigy reconciled or burnt in an auto de fe. Even when he had confessed and been reconciled on the death-bed, we have just seen that his Christian burial was to be as secret as possible. When the trial ended in acquittal or suspension, if he had property sequestrated, the lifting of the sequestration would announce it to the heirs; otherwise, it does not seem that there was any provision for their notification. Suicide in prison, which was not infrequent, was regarded as conclusive proof of impenitence, even if the prisoner had confessed and professed repentance, but his heirs were allowed to defend him on the score of insanity, failing which he was burnt in effigy.[1539]

FEMALE PRISONERS

Sickness was of frequent occurrence and was treated with creditable humanity. The Instructions of 1561 require that the sick shall have every care and that whatever the physician deems necessary for them shall be provided.[1540] Of course the fulfilment of this command must have varied with the temper of the tribunals, but nevertheless the spirit dictating it is in marked contrast with the conduct of the gaols of the period. When cases transcended the resources of the Inquisition, the ordinary course was to transfer the patient to a hospital, in disregard of the cherished secrecy of the prison. Instances of this are common enough in the records and a single case will suffice for its illustration. November 6, 1641, Juan de Valdés, on trial for bigamy in Valladolid, asked an audience to beg for despatch as he was very sick. This was confirmed by the alcaide and by the physician, who said that for nineteen days he had had a tercian and was too weak to be bled, and moreover he was suffering from stone and strangury; that he could not be cured in the prison and should be removed to a hospital. This was done, the hospital authorities being notified not to allow him to escape and to keep the tribunal advised of his condition. In January, 1642, he was reported as being still in mortal danger, but he recovered, was returned to the secret prison, and was sentenced on August 21st.[1541]

***

The care of female prisoners was naturally a subject of some perplexity, especially as the refinement of matrons and women assistants was unknown to the Inquisition. When the Instructions of 1498 order that the prison for men and for women shall be separate,[1542] it does not infer that previously they had been herded promiscuously together, but that in future distinct quarters should be provided for the sexes--a provision which was not observed, as it was deemed sufficient that women should be confined separately so that there could not be communication between them and the men. The condition of helpless women, virtually at the mercy of their male attendants, in the secrecy which shrouded everything within the prison walls, can readily be imagined, and there must have been outrages coming to the knowledge of Ximenes, in 1512, that aroused him to a sense of the dangerous opportunities existing, for in that year an order was issued threatening death to any attendant who should have intercourse with a female prisoner.[1543] The severity of the penalty measured the gravity of the necessity calling for it, but, like so many other salutary provisions, the tribunals were too merciful to enforce it on their subordinates. In 1590, Andrés de Castro, alcaide of the Valencia prison, was tried for seducing a female prisoner, kissing and soliciting others, allowing communications between prisoners and accepting bribes from their kindred. There were twenty-nine accusing witnesses; he denied the charges but virtually admitted their truth by breaking gaol. On his recapture, for this complicated series of offences he escaped with a hundred lashes, three years in the galleys, perpetual exile from Valencia, and disability for office in the Inquisition--a sentence which, when compared with the habitual severity of the tribunals, shows how lightly his sexual crime was regarded by his judges.[1544] It was not that the death-penalty had been abrogated, for we find it repeated, in 1652, in the Logroño instructions to alcaides.[1545] Doubtless the rule mentioned above, that women should be gathered together in their cells, was designed to afford them protection against their gaolers.

In the not unusual case of the arrest of pregnant women, due consideration was given to their condition, and suitable temporary accommodation was found for them, during confinement, outside of the prison. Thus, in the case of María Rodríguez, in the tribunal of Valladolid, who was arrested June 3, 1641, the delay in presenting the accusation, until September 16th, is explained on the record by her being pregnant and removed from the prison until she recovered.[1546] This was an improvement on the earlier practice, if we may believe the Llerena memorial of 1506, which states that women in the throes of child-birth were denied all assistance, even that of a midwife; they were abandoned to nature and many had perished in consequence.[1547]

HUMANE REGULATIONS

It was not only in the general prescriptions of the Instructions that regard for the welfare of the prisoners is manifested. Special orders issued from time to time as to details are animated by the same spirit. Thus, in 1517, Cardinal Adrian told the Sicilian inquisitors (in a letter probably addressed to all the tribunals) that they must pay particular attention to the qualities requisite in the gaoler; they must sedulously bear in mind that the prison is for detention and not for punishment; the prisoners are to be well treated and not be defrauded in their food, for which ample provision must be made; the prison must be inspected every Saturday, by one of the inquisitors, and not fortnightly as provided in the Instructions; those of the prisoners who have trades are to work and thus contribute to their support and, if the officials give the women sewing to do, they must be paid.[1548] An extract made, in 1645, from a book of instructions which was read annually in the tribunals, shows that this praiseworthy care for the welfare of the prisoners was the permanent policy of the Inquisition. It prescribes the utmost punctuality in inspecting the cells every fortnight and learning what the inmates desire, reporting this to the tribunal, which decided what each one should have and, if there was a surplus in the allowance for rations from which it could be procured, the alcaide was at once to be ordered to see that the purveyor bought it; if he neglected anything he was to be reproved for the wrong committed in his lack of punctuality. Special attention was called to serving the rations in the morning, so that the prisoners could prepare their midday meal. Meat was to be given daily, and only one day's rations at a time in hot weather, lest it should spoil; in cool weather, two days' supply; and this was so important for the health of the prisoners that it should be the special charge of some one, while an inquisitor ought occasionally to look to it.[1549]

All this is admirable in tone and spirit; unfortunately its execution depended on its enforcement by the inquisitors, on their regular performance of inspection, and on holding the gaolers responsible by rigorous punishment for derelictions. The duty of inspection by inquisitors had been prescribed as indispensable by the Instructions of 1488, but it was impossible to make them obey and complaints of their negligence are frequent. In 1632 it was found necessary to reissue the Instructions of 1488; in 1644 we have the testimony of a contemporary that, in some places at least, it was regularly, if perfunctorily, performed and the Logroño instructions of 1652 make it the duty of the alcaide to remind the inquisitors of it every fortnight, because it is customarily forgotten.[1550] The other requisite, severity of punishment for derelictions, was also lacking, through the customary tenderness shown to delinquent officials.

It would be manifestly unjust to condemn as a whole the management of the prisons: it would be equally unwarranted to praise them indiscriminately. Everything depended on the conscientious discharge of duty by the inquisitors and no general judgement can be formed as to the condition of so many prisons, during three centuries, except that their average standard was considerably higher than that in other jurisdictions and that, if there were abodes of horror, such as have been described by imaginative writers, they were wholly exceptional. There were good and there were bad. The memorials of Llerena and Jaen, in 1506 describe them as horrible dens, overrun with rats, snakes and other vermin, where the wretched captives sickened in despair and were starved by the embezzlement of a large portion of the moneys allowed for their support, while no physician was permitted to attend the sick and the attendants maltreated them like dogs.[1551] Making allowance for rhetorical exaggeration we can imagine that this description was applicable to Córdova under Lucero. Matters seem to have been not much better at Seville in 1560, where the oppression of the alcaide, Gaspar de Benavides, provoked a despairing revolt in which his assistant was mortally wounded. Vengeance was wreaked on the participators in the fray, of whom one was burnt alive and another, a boy of fourteen, had four hundred lashes and was sent to the galleys for life, while Gaspar, who had provoked it, was let off with appearing in an auto de fe, forfeiture of wages and perpetual banishment from Seville.[1552]

VARIABLE TREATMENT

When malfeasance in office escaped with such ill-judged leniency, it was impossible to maintain discipline and the prisoners suffered accordingly. As the result of an inspection of Barcelona by Doctor Alonso Perez, the alcaide Monserrat Pastor is scolded, in 1544, for keeping a mistress in his house, for placing a kinsman in charge of the prison and absenting himself, for receiving presents from discharged prisoners, for frequent absence, leaving the prison unguarded, for combining the incompatible positions of gaoler and dispensero, and of making the women prisoners work and taking their earnings, but Pastor was only reprimanded and ordered to restore the presents and the women's earnings. Virtual immunity invited continuance of abuses and, in 1550, after another inspection, we find the Suprema again adverting to the evil results of combining the functions of gaoler and dispensero and ordering the inquisitors to fill the latter position.[1553]

The prison of the Canary tribunal at times seems to have been equally mismanaged. An Englishman named John Hill was brought there from Ferro, June 23, 1574, with nothing but his clothes and no money. For nine months his complaints were loud and frequent; a day's ration was insufficient for a single meal; he begged for more bread and water, also for a mat to lie on, as he had to sleep on the ground and he could not rest for the lice and fleas; for more than two months he prayed for a shirt to cover his nakedness and, though an order was issued, January 22nd to give him one, it had to be repeated February 18th. Even as late as 1792, Don Juan Perdomo complained that for fourteen months the alcaide had kept him on a diet of salt fish, that he would allow him to change his linen but once a fortnight, and that he caused him to suffer such torment from thirst that he would go into the court-yard and cry aloud, hoping that some passer-by would summon the alcaide.[1554]

Yet other passages in the Canary record show a praiseworthy desire to alleviate the rigors of confinement and in general it may be said that the condition of the prisoners depended wholly on the temper and character of the officials in charge. When these were kindly, the prisoners were spared unnecessary hardships. Francisco Ortiz, in 1529, at Toledo, bore willing testimony to good treatment which he had not anticipated.[1555] In 1563, Fernando Díaz, a peasant, after a month's detention in Toledo, speaks of improved health; here, he says, he has mutton to eat, while at home he had only sardines.[1556] In 1567, a member of the Suprema, visiting the prison of Valladolid, was told by Leonor de Cisneros that she had nothing to complain of; she had mutton and bread and wine and fruit and was well treated.[1557] As she was a relapsed, whose husband had been burnt eight years before, she probably had no property and the expense was defrayed by the tribunal.

These are by no means isolated instances. In 1541, at Toledo, Juan García, a day-laborer on trial, after six weeks in prison, asked that night-clothes be given to him as to the other prisoners, as he was obliged to sleep in the garments worn during the day, when the inquisitor at once ordered him to be supplied.[1558] In 1657, the accounts of the tribunal of Madrid show 447-1/2 reales spent on clothing for a poor prisoner and those of the Suprema, in 1690, have an item of 688 reales devoted to the same purpose.[1559] We have seen that warrants for arrest ordered beds to be brought with the prisoner, as the Inquisition did not furnish them, in accordance with an order of 1525, which assumes that this was to relieve the hardships of those brought from a distance.[1560] Yet, even in the financial pressure of the seventeenth century, we find in the accounts of the Madrid tribunal, in 1659, an order, July 11th, to the receiver to pay 230 reales for the hire of beds for poor prisoners up to July 15th.[1561] Even more noteworthy are some entries arising from the trial in Madrid of Francisco de Matos, in 1680-81. He seems to have had five children for whose support was spent, in about a year from September, 1680, 3519 reales, of which 1284 were paid to the Hospicio Real de Pobres for its care of three of them during sickness.[1562] The tribunal evidently felt itself obliged to take care of the helpless children, and such incidents serve to show that, when the inquisitors had humanitarian instincts there was nothing in the policy of the Holy Office to prevent their full manifestation.

EXPENSES

It is remarkable that, during the period of most active work, there seems to have been no general settled system of defraying the maintenance of prisoners. There is no provision for it in the instructions of 1484, but in Torquemada's supplementary orders of December, the receivers were required to pay the expenses.[1563] Yet we have seen that immediately after this the alguazil was in receipt of a salary equal to, or more than, that of the inquisitors because, as Ferdinand said, he had to meet the great charge of the prisoners--"tiene tan gran costo con los presos"--and, as we find this in the salary lists of Saragossa, Burgos, Medina del Campo and Seville, it would seem to be a general rule, while the Instructions of 1498 appear to show it still in force.[1564] Yet the accounts of the Valencia tribunal, in 1497-8, indicate that the maintenance of those who had property was drawn from the sequestrations while the "pobres miserables presos en las carceles" were supported by outside friends or kindred, who were subsequently reimbursed by the receiver. The per diem was 9 dineros for men and 8 for women, while Ali Divit, a Moor and presumably abstemious, was reckoned at 5.[1565]

A letter of Ferdinand, in 1501, authorizing the receiver of Sardinia to include among his disbursements the cost of maintaining prisoners, would indicate that this was becoming the rule, but another letter of the same date calling for reimbursement to Anton López, a yeoman of his guard, who had been ordered by an inquisitor to support certain prisoners, shows that no definite system was as yet established.[1566] These irregular methods afforded opportunity for embezzlement and extortion, resulting doubtless in much suffering among the captives. The memorials of Llerena and Jaen, in 1506 complain of conspiracy among the officials to cut down the rations, and that only 10 maravedís a day were allowed, from which 2 were deducted for shaving, linen and cooking, when 25 or 30 were required, at current prices, for bread alone.[1567]

At length the alcaide or gaoler appears as the official handling the funds when, in 1510, Ferdinand ordered Villacis, the receiver of Seville, to pay him 5000 maravedís because he had fed the prisoners during a time of pestilence.[1568] This was evidently an exceptional case, arising from an emergency, but it was adopted, in 1516 and 1517, in some instructions of the Suprema to the tribunal of Sicily; where there were sequestrations, the amount was to be drawn from them; in cases of extreme poverty the cost of a moderate diet could be defrayed by the receiver from the confiscations.[1569]

Nearly forty years had passed since the founding of the Inquisition--years of intense activity--and as yet no regular system had been adopted in a matter so important. The necessity was felt and, in 1518, an order was issued in the name of Charles V, which shows that the kindred or friends of the prisoner had been expected to bring his food to the prison. The order recites that, as they come from all parts of the district and are far from their families and property, they suffer greatly. Therefore, in the case of non-residents of the city, the receiver is to pay for food and necessaries, under instructions from the inquisitor. An account is to be kept with each prisoner and, if he is discharged, he shall repay the receiver before his sequestration is lifted; if he is poor, he shall not be asked for it and the auditor shall pass the item in the receiver's accounts.[1570] The liberality of this clause seems to have been a novelty, and it took some time to establish the duty of the Inquisition to prevent its poor prisoners from starving, for we find the queen-regent, in 1531, authorizing their maintenance, at Barcelona, at the expense of the fisc.[1571]

RATIONS

Yet this was not held as relieving the family from supporting, as far as possible, an imprisoned member. The account of the dispensero or steward, of the Valencia prison, from October 8, 1540 to May 5, 1541, shows that during that period there were twenty-five prisoners thus supported, at least partially, husbands paying for wives, wives for husbands, sons for fathers, etc. The sums received were small and suggest the struggle endured by families to contribute to the necessities of those in gaol; they were paid in trifling amounts of from 5s. 5d. to 8s. 8d., representing probably a monthly assessment, and this was by no means continuous for, in eight cases, only one payment is recorded and in only one case is there more than two payments. For the whole period the aggregate is only 15 libras 19s. 4d., while during this time the steward obtained from the receiver 120 libras 2s., which probably included what the fisc had to pay and what was drawn from the sequestrations of the wealthier prisoners.[1572] With regard to the latter, the rule was to sell the personal property first and then the real estate, and inquisitors were urged, in 1547, to be prompt in collecting from the proceeds, as the sequestrations were apt to be consumed in supporting the family, leaving nothing to repay the fisc for its advances.[1573]

It was the duty of the inquisitor, when a prisoner was brought in, to ascertain, from the receiver and notary of sequestrations, his station in life and his wealth, and to fix the amount of his allowance in accordance with the current prices of provisions, but a wealthy man could spend more if he chose and, if a person of quality wished to have one or two servants incarcerated with him, as in the case of Carranza, this was permitted; what might be left over from their table was to be given to the poor and not to be made a source of profit to the alcaide and dispensero.[1574] There was liberality in this as, in case of confiscation, the estate was diminished by the extra expenditure. Even the ordinary allowance was at the disposition of the prisoner, who could economize on it and spend it in any manner that he chose.[1575]

Thus there never was at any time a fixed and absolute ration, although of course there was a general minimum standard for the poor who had to be supported. Whatever it was, it was liable to alteration as circumstances might dictate. After Jacques Pinzon was imprisoned in Granada, February 25, 1599, on March 9th the alcaide reported that he consumed in one day the ration of two and was dying of hunger, whereupon the inquisitors kindly increased his allowance to a real per day; this kept him quiet for three months, when there was a fresh complaint and 5 maravedís were added.[1576] In 1616, Padre Hieronimo de la Madre de Dios, tried for mysticism, sought his first audience to complain that his ration was insufficient; he wished it increased by a real a day, which could be charged to his sequestrated property.[1577] Evidently prisoners did not hesitate to make their wants known and there was readiness to listen to them.

With the gradual concentration of power in the Suprema it came to regulate this in all the tribunals. In 1635 Valencia reported that, in consequence of the dearness of bread, the prisoners were suffering from hunger, and it asked authority to increase the ration. The Suprema deliberated for five weeks and then ordered an increase to be made "with great compassion." The close supervision exercised is indicated, in 1695, in a criticism on a monthly report from the same tribunal, in which one of the omissions noted is that the ration assigned to each prisoner is not stated.[1578]

The fall in the purchasing power of money, and especially of the debased vellon coinage, necessitated an increase in the ration. In 1641, at Toledo, the ordinary daily allowance was 1-1/2 reales which, by 1677, had doubled to 3 reales.[1579] In Valencia, the ordinary ration had increased to 22 dineros in 1688 and, in 1756, to 2 sueldos.[1580]

COLLECTION OF COSTS

When the prisons were full and the trials, after the first hurried rush, grew more and more protracted, the expense of maintenance was not small, as can be gathered from occasional indications. Thus, in 1566, we find the Suprema ordering its alguazil mayor to remit to the tribunal of Calahorra 400 ducats to defray the food of prisoners.[1581] In 1586, Benito Sanguino, the receiver of Valencia, in settling his accounts, claimed credit for 19,856s. 11d. paid to the dispensero for the maintenance of poor prisoners, in addition to what he had disbursed for the purpose on the orders of inquisitors, an irregularity for which the Suprema demanded an explanation.[1582] Some light is thrown on the way in which these costs accumulated by the case of Fray Lucas de Allende, guardian of the Franciscan convent of Madrid and one of the dupes of Lucrecia de Leon, a beata revelandera. When arrested in 1590, his brother, Alonso de Allende, asked permission to give him an allowance of a real a day--a request which proved costly, as the trial lasted for six years and two months.[1583] In 1659, the orders given by the tribunal of Madrid, for the food and incidentals of its poor prisoners, who seem to have averaged about ten in number, reached an aggregate of 12,874 reales and, in 1681, the amount was 25,748.[1584] As the activity of the Inquisition diminished, and perhaps also as its resources fell short, this drain on its finances was greatly reduced. In a statement of the expenses of the Valencia tribunal, from 1784 to 1790 inclusive, the charge for maintenance of poor prisoners becomes trifling. The total expenditure during these seven years was 501 libras 18s., of which 300 libras 8s. were recovered from the parties, leaving a net outlay of 201 libras 10s., or less than 30 libras per annum.[1585]

The tribunals were unrelenting in the collection of these expenses from all who could be held responsible. In the case of frailes, who could own no property, their communities were liable. Thus, in 1649, the tribunal of Valencia issues an order to collect, from the Provincial of the Augustinians, 600 reales for certain members of his Order who were in its prison. When the trial of Fray Estevan Ramoneda was concluded, September 12, 1696, the Barcelona tribunal rendered to his Order of Merced a bill of 730 reales for his expenses. The Provincial assessed it on all the Mercenarian convents of Catalonia and, on November 15th, the inquisitors scolded the prior of the Barcelona convent for delay, when he replied that his convent had paid its share but that others were dilatory. In 1709, the Suprema issued an order that there must be no exceptions, even to the Barefooted Franciscans, showing that they had been endeavoring to procure exemption.[1586]

The Inquisition was not likely to be more lenient with the laity. Its determination to secure reimbursement is seen in an order of the Valencia tribunal, in 1636, that when Francisco Morales completes the term of galley service to which he has been condemned, he is to be sold to his neighbors to repay what he has cost to the fisc.[1587] These costs were not simply for maintenance in prison, but for expenses attending arrest and trial, including the fees of advocate and procurator and all postage incurred. The whole of this was a first lien on the property of the prisoner and, if he was a filiusfamilias, his father was liable and could be forced to pay.[1588] Before an auto de fe, the dispensero and notary of sequestrations carefully made up the account of every penitent who escaped confiscation, and it was the duty of the fiscal to see that, if he had property, he settled or gave an obligation to settle and, if he was poor, that he took an oath to pay whenever he should be able.[1589] How these accounts were swelled is visible in that rendered by the Barcelona tribunal, in 1756, to Don Antonio Adorno, a soldier of gentle blood in the regiment of Asturias. He was only fifty-eight days in prison which, at 2 sueldos a day, amounted to a little less than 6 libras, but the aggregate of the bill was 26. He subscribed his name to this as accurate, stating that he had no property with which to meet it, but that, if God should grant him better fortune, he obligated himself to pay it to the receiver or his duly authorized representative. As his sentence was banishment from the Spanish dominions, this was a pure formality, but it could not be omitted.[1590] A few months later we have a piteous letter from Dr. Agustin Tamarit, a physician of the town of Salas, whose enemies had involved him with the Inquisition, resulting in a charge against him of 5 libras 16s. In reply to a demand for payment he protests that he is miserably poor. During his enforced absence, his colleague, Dr. Rubert, had collected from the town the conducta, or stated salary due to both, and refuses to pay over his share; if the tribunal will compel Rubert to settle he will endeavor to sell some wheat and satisfy the account.[1591]

***

On the whole we may conclude that the secret prisons of the Inquisition were less intolerable places of abode than the episcopal and public gaols. The general policy respecting them was more humane and enlightened than that of other jurisdictions, whether in Spain or elsewhere, although negligent supervision allowed of abuses and there were ample resources of rigor in reserve, when the obstinacy of the impenitent was to be broken down. The one unpardonable feature was the seclusion which kept the unhappy captive ignorant of all that occurred outside of his prison walls and deprived him of facilities for defence and of communication with family and friends. This rendered doubly bitter the prolonged detention which often held him for years in suspense as to their fate and deprived them of all knowledge as to him.

CHAPTER V - EVIDENCE

In criminal procedure, the character of admissible evidence and the methods employed to test its veracity are of such determining importance that an investigation of the system followed by the Inquisition is necessary if we are to estimate correctly its administration of justice. In this, the fact must be borne in mind that the complicated rules of evidence, peculiar to English law, have grown out of trial by jury, where those who have to pass upon the facts are presumably untrained to estimate testimony, so that it has to be carefully sifted before it is allowed to reach them, while that which is admitted is subjected to the searching process of cross-examination. All this had no place in the systems which Continental Europe inherited from the civil law. The judge was assumed to be a trained jurist, equipped to distinguish truth from falsehood, so that the flimsiest evidence might be brought before him, secure that its worthlessness would not affect his judgement, while it might afford some clue leading to the truth. The defects of this were greatly exaggerated in the Inquisition, where unlimited discretion was allowed to judges, who were mostly theologians eager to prove and to punish the slightest aberration from the faith, and where the secrecy preserved as to the names and identity of the accusing witnesses precluded all thought of cross-examination, although the story of Susannah and the Elders might well have conveyed a warning as to the danger of unjust judgement by an unassisted bench.

In the ancient Castilian law, both parties to an action saw the witnesses sworn, but the judges examined them in secret, apparently as a precaution against their being tampered with. Great care was taken as to their character, and those were excluded who were of ill-repute or had been imprisoned, or perjured, or were Jews, Moors, heretics, apostates, or who were interested in the case, or dependents on one of the parties, or were less than fourteen years of age, or very poor, unless proved to be of good fame, while, in criminal cases, no witness was received who was under twenty and no member of a religious Order.[1592] In Aragon, the utmost care was prescribed as to the character of witnesses; if not personally known to the judge, the fact was to be entered upon the record and the judge was required to cross-examine them personally as to all minute details that might lead to the exposure of fraudulent testimony.[1593] Under the civil law, parents and children were not admitted to testify against each other nor could a freedman be a witness against his patron.[1594]

WITNESSES FOR PROSECUTION

All these precautions which the experience of ages had shown to be necessary as guards against injustice under systems of procedure where the judge was also in some sort a prosecutor, were cast aside by the Inquisition in its zeal to preserve the purity of the faith. The grossest partiality was shown in the distinction drawn as to eligibility between witnesses for the prosecution and those for the defence. For the former there was no disability save mortal enmity towards the accused. From the earliest times the Church had prescribed fourteen as the minimum age for witnesses[1595] and, in Spain, where majority was not attained until the age of twenty-five, minors younger than that were not admitted in criminal cases. Accordingly, in the records of the Inquisition, witnesses are customarily described as mayores or menores, but no difference was made in accepting their testimony, and Rojas tells us that formerly he thought that heresy could not be proved by two witnesses under twenty-five, but the rule is that the fiscal is not bound to prove that his witnesses are legal; everyone is presumed to be so and his evidence must be received until objection is made, which, considering that their identity was most carefully concealed from the defence, is tantamount to saying that none could be rejected on that score.[1596] Witnesses of the tenderest years were therefore admitted without scruple. In the case of Juan Vazquez, tried in Toledo for sorcery in 1605, one of the witnesses was a girl of twelve. In the same tribunal, in 1579, a witness only eleven or twelve was heard against Francisco del Espinar, for maltreating a cross, and the culprit, who was only thirteen, was held to be responsible.[1597] Witnesses under twelve were not sworn, because they were deemed incapable of understanding the nature of the oath, but their evidence was received and recorded without it, as appears in the report of a Valencia auto de fe in 1607.[1598] In the Roman Inquisition the canon law was treated with more respect, and the fiscal was not allowed to present a witness below the age of fourteen.[1599]

There would seem to have been at first some discussion as to the admissibility of the evidence of slaves against their masters, but it was settled, in 1509, by a provision of the Suprema, declaring it to be legal but as, in cases of heresy, they were working for their liberty in convicting their masters, their testimony should be carefully scrutinized and, if it appeared doubtful, it should be validated by torturing them.[1600] There was also a question as to Jews, for laws of the Fuero Juzgo (Lib. XII, Tit. ii, n. 9, 10) forbade them from testifying against Christians, but they were received in the Old Inquisition and the New was not more rigid.[1601] As regards kindred, Simancas tells us that, although not allowed to testify for the prosecution in other crimes, in heresy they are the best witnesses, as being beyond suspicion of enmity and they must be compelled to give evidence because religion is to be preferred to kinship.[1602] In fact, a large portion of evidence was derived from them, for no confession was accepted as complete that did not include denunciation of accomplices, and those who confessed to save their lives were perforce obliged to betray their families. The agonizing struggle, thus induced between natural affection and self-preservation, is illustrated in the case of María López, in 1646, at Valladolid. For nearly four months she resolutely denied everything, but her endurance was at last exhausted and, on April 25th and 27th, she confessed as to herself and others and ratified it on May 7th. In her cell she brooded over this until June 25th, when the alcaide reported that she had attempted to strangle herself with a strip of her chemise. The inquisitor hastened to her cell and found the poor creature hiding under the bed. Interrogated as to her motives, she said that a woman who had falsely accused her husband and only daughter, as also her mother and an aunt, did not deserve to live, whereupon she revoked her whole confession, both as to herself and others. As a revocante, the pitiless rules of the Inquisition doomed her to the stake; her fears triumphed and, on July 28th, she confirmed her confession of April, except as regards her husband. On November 29th she was condemned to reconciliation, confiscation and prison with the sanbenito, and she appeared in the auto of June 23, 1647.[1603] The Roman Inquisition was somewhat less inhuman and did not require husband and wife to testify against each other.[1604]

It naturally followed from all this that, in the Spanish Inquisition, the rule was observed that, where heresy was concerned, all witnesses were admissible, no matter how infamous. Excommunicates were not rejected and it would appear that even the insane were regarded as competent for, in 1680, Thomas Castellanos, on trial in Toledo, confessed to being a Lutheran, an atheist and to other heresies, for which he was charitably sent, not to the stake, but to an asylum, yet he was received as a witness against Angela Pérez, as to her utterances to him while in prison. He was duly sworn by God and on the holy cross although, if sane and an atheist, there could be no force in such an oath.[1605] In short, the only incapacity of an accusing witness, was mortal enmity. All other exceptions known to the secular law-- minority, heresy, perjury, infamy, complicity, conviction for crime--were disregarded, although they might affect his credibility. Mortal enmity was difficult of definition, but the doctors were liberal enough in admitting to the benefit of the term any quarrel of a serious character, but proof was rendered difficult by refusing to receive evidence concerning it from any one within four degrees of kinship or affinity with the accused.[1606]

WITNESSES FOR DEFENCE

It is true that some precautions were prescribed to guard against the admission of worthless testimony, but their very enunciation proves how unscrupulous was the current practice.

In 1516, the Suprema cautioned the tribunals that, when the veracity of a witness was doubtful, his testimony must be verified and, in 1543, it was ordered that the character of witnesses must be recorded so as to serve as a gauge of the weight of their utterances.[1607] There was also the formality used with all witnesses in commencing their examination by interrogating them on what were called the generales de la ley, as to their knowledge of the parties to the case and any enmity or other matter that might prejudice their testimony, the answers to which were always of course satisfactory. In the long run, however, all this, like most other matters, was left to the discretion of the tribunals which, in practice, admitted every body and used their evidence without discrimination.

This applies solely to the witnesses for the prosecution. When we turn to the defence, the contrast between the scandalous laxity of the rules prescribed for the former, and the equally scandalous rigidity of those applied to the latter, is the clearest proof that the object of the Inquisition was not justice but punishment. Throughout the whole judicial system the vital principle was that it were better that a hundred innocent should suffer than that a single guilty one should escape. Even the formula of the oaths administered to the two classes, in 1484, shows how early the distinction was drawn between them. The witnesses for the prosecution only received a solemn warning from the inquisitor, while those for the defence were sworn under the most terrible adjurations to God to visit, on their bodies in this world and on their souls in the next, any deviation from the truth.[1608]

The rules as to witnesses admissible for the defence were carefully drawn so as to exclude all who were likely to be serviceable to him, on the ground that their evidence would be untrustworthy, the inquisitor thus being sedulously guarded against misleading in favor of the prisoner, while he was trusted to discriminate as to the adverse testimony. Thus no kinsman to the fourth degree was allowed to testify for the defence, even when the accused was blindly striving to prove enmity on the part of those whom he conjectured to be the opposing witnesses. No Jew or Morisco or New Christian could appear for him, although they were welcomed for the prosecution, and the same distinction applied to servants. As formulated in the Instructions of 1561, the accused was told that he must not name as his witnesses kinsmen or servants, and that they must all be Old Christians, unless his interrogatories be such as cannot otherwise be answered, and Pablo García adds that, under such circumstances, he must name a number from among whom the inquisitor may select those whom he deems most fit. It became, indeed, a commonplace among the authorities that witnesses for the defence must be zealots for the faith-- zelatores fidei.[1609] Yet, in fact, all this is of interest rather as a manifestation of the pervading spirit of the Inquisition than from any practical influence which it exercised on the outcome of the trials for, as we shall see, the simulacrum of defence permitted to the accused was so limited that in but very few cases did it matter whether he had or had not any witnesses.

***

Prosecutions of course were not to be impeded by reluctant or recalcitrant witnesses. The tribunals had full power to summon them and to punish them for refusal. When they resided at a distance, it was discretional either to have them examined by a commissioner, appointed ad hoc, or to make them appear in person. In 1524 Cardinal Manrique even decided that they could be brought from Aragon to Castile although, as we have seen, this violated the fueros of Aragon, which forbade that any one should be forced to leave the kingdom.[1610] The official summons requires the witness to present himself before the tribunal, within a specified number of days, under pain of ten thousand maravedís and excommunication latæ sententiæ, this censure being pronounced in advance with notice that, in case of disobedience, it would be published and he would be proceeded against according to law. The summons was to be served with the utmost secrecy and, like all other documents, was to be returned to the tribunal with an endorsement of the date of service.[1611]

EXAMINATION OF WITNESSES

Witnesses were compelled to give evidence and were liable to punishment if suspected of withholding it. In Doctor Zurita's report of his visitation of Gerona and Elne, in 1564, it appears that he arrested Maestre Juan Fregola, canon of San Martin of Gerona, because he said that he did not remember a matter at issue; his memory was thus refreshed and he was released on giving the desired evidence.[1612] This continued to the end. In 1816, the Suprema, in confirming the vote of the tribunal of Cuenca to continue the case of Antonio Garcés, adds that it must take the necessary steps against the witnesses who refuse to testify.[1613]

***

The examination of witnesses for the prosecution was a duty of the inquisitors. It was one, however, that they threw upon the notaries, who were ordered by the Suprema, in 1498, not to take testimony except in presence of the inquisitors, while Cardinal Adrian, in 1522, said that, if the latter were too busy to be present, they must at least read the testimony before the departure of the witness and make the necessary re-examination.[1614] All this argues a very loose and slovenly system, in a matter of such primary importance, inherited doubtless from the early time, when the rush of prosecutions precluded all but the most superficial conduct of business. In that period there had been devices for the division of labor, for we hear of an official, in 1485, known as the receiver of witnesses, and of payments made to clerics whose presence was essential in the taking of testimony--devices which were abandoned about the close of the century.[1615] As business declined, the inquisitors seem to have taken a more active part in the examination of accusing witnesses, except towards the end, when indolence led them to issue commissions to conduct interrogations.

It was the rule that all examinations should take place in the audience-chamber, except in extreme urgency, when the inquisitors might hold them in their apartments or houses--a rule of which the Suprema had to remind them, in 1538, and again in 1580.[1616] Witnesses were sometimes sworn in groups, but were examined separately as a prudent precaution against collusion.[1617] When the estilo had been perfected, there was a prescribed form for commencing the interrogatory, by first asking the witness whether he knew or presumed the cause of his summons; this was usually answered in the negative, when the next question was whether he knew or had heard that any person had said or done anything which was or appeared to be contrary to the faith, or to the free exercise of the Inquisition. This had the appearance of careful abstention from guiding him but, if he persisted in the negative, the interrogatory rapidly assumed the aspect of letting him know for what he was wanted and what was expected of him. Thus in the trial at Barcelona, in 1698, of a woman named Ignacia, for sorcery, Jaime Guardiola asserted that he knew little except that he had forbidden her his house, when Inquisitor Valladares told him that the Inquisition had information of his having employed her on several occasions which he described, wherefore he adjured him, in the name of God and his Blessed Mother, to examine his memory and tell the truth.[1618] Sometimes the inquisitor went further and openly threatened a witness, warning him, by the reverence due to God, to tell the truth and not to make the prisoner's case his own.[1619] The Suprema might well restrain the excessive zeal of its subordinates by instructing them not to intimidate witnesses or to treat them as if they were the accused parties.[1620]

***

While thus with unwilling witnesses the inquisitor acted as counsel for the prosecution, with those who were willing he made no attempt to ascertain the truth of their stories. He asked leading questions without reserve and abstained from any cross-examination that might confuse the story and expose mendacity. When, in the trial of Juan de la Caballería, at Saragossa, in 1489, his procurator asked that certain interrogatories which he presented should be put to the witnesses, the inquisitors roughly refused, saying that it was their official duty to find out the truth for the discharge of their consciences.[1621] So long as witnesses incriminated the accused, as a rule there was no effort to test their accuracy or to obtain details of place and time or other points which would facilitate defence against false charges. In the case of Simon Nocheau, at Valladolid, in 1642, he succeeded in getting a series of interrogatories put to the witnesses which exposed discrepancies that it was the duty of the inquisitors to have discovered.[1622] Even the Suprema recognized the injustice of this, in the case of a priest whom the tribunal of Barcelona, in 1665, sentenced to imprisonment for "propositions," and ordered it to recall the witnesses and cross-examine them so as to verify their testimony and also to investigate whether they were actuated by enmity.[1623]

To estimate the conscious unfairness of this it is only necessary to contrast it with the treatment of evidence presented by the defence. The handling of this was likewise wholly with the inquisitor. All that was allowed to the accused was to offer a list of witnesses and a series of interrogatories to be put to them. It was the duty of the inquisitor to summon the witnesses and put the questions, or to forward the interrogatories to commissioners for the same purpose, but he had full discretional power to omit what he pleased, both as to witnesses and questions. In fact, he received the interrogatories only salvo jure impertinentium et non admittendorum, and he exercised this power without supervision and without informing the accused or his advocate as to what he threw out. In 1572, Luis de Leon on his trial presented six series of interrogatories to be put to his witnesses of which three were calmly thrown out as "impertinent."[1624] Not only was all knowledge of this concealed from the accused but also the answers of the witnesses to such questions as were permitted. It is true that, in 1531, even the Suprema revolted at this and ordered the evidence in favor of the accused to be submitted to him and to his advocate, so that it might not be said that he was deprived of defence, but injustice prevailed and the Instructions of 1561, in prescribing the suppression to the accused, gave as a reason for it that the accused might thus be prevented from identifying the adverse witnesses—thus showing how one denial of justice led to another.[1625] The witnesses for the defence were further subject to cross-examination which, at least in the earlier period, could be conducted by the fiscal—an indecency almost incredible in view of the crippling restrictions placed on the defence.[1626] In fact the distinction recognized in the treatment of evidence for the prosecution and for the defence is epitomized in the instructions sent by Toledo, in 1550, to its commissioner at Daimiel, about taking testimony in the cases of some Moriscos of that place. He is not told to investigate the credibility of the mass of idle gossip and hearsay evidence gathered for the prosecution but, when examining witnesses for the defence, he is to cross-examine them strictly to ascertain what are the grounds for their assertions.[1627]

***

There was one formality, not peculiar to the Spanish Inquisition, designed to protect the accused from random or false accusations—the ratification which was required of witnesses after an interval had elapsed since their original depositions. This was occasionally of service and, if preserved in its original form, would have been a considerable safeguard in detecting perjury. It was conducted in presence of two frailes, known as honestas personas, and the fiscal was not allowed to be present, a prohibition which Manrique was obliged to repeat in 1529.[1628] In the earliest period, ratification was frequently omitted, doubtless owing to the haste with which the Inquisition worked,[1629] but subsequently it was regarded as absolutely essential. Its importance was shown by making it an imperative duty of the inquisitor himself to take the ratification, either summoning the witnesses or going to them, but this was difficult of enforcement. Cardinal Adrian, in 1517, declared that ratification before a commissioner nullified the whole proceedings, yet orders were required in 1527 and again in 1532 to make inquisitors perform the duty, and finally the attempt was abandoned and commissioners were everywhere employed.[1630]

RATIFICATION

As a rule, no evidence could be used that was not ratified, and I have met with not a few cases--one as late as 1628--which were suspended and the accused were discharged because the witnesses were not to be found when wanted for that purpose.[1631] This arose from the fact that in strictness ratification was not to be made till immediately before the so-called "publication of evidence" which was the concluding step of the prosecution, involving a considerable interval during which the witnesses might die or disappear.[1632] To avert this, relaxations of the requirement of ratification were gradually introduced. In 1533, 1543 and 1554 the Suprema inferentially admitted that when witnesses were absent or dead their testimony could be used if the fact was noted on the record.[1633] There were authorities who held this to be the case in Aragon and it was so practised, but elsewhere opinions varied.[1634]

Finally a successful device was invented of two forms of ratification, one "ad perpetuam rei memoriam" and the other "en juicio plenario." They were virtually the same except that in the former the witness was told that the fiscal would use his evidence in a prosecution to be brought hereafter, and in the latter that it was for a case on trial. It became customary always to obtain the ratification when the testimony was given and then, if a witness was accessible during the trial, the ratification en juicio plenario was superadded. At what time this expedient was adopted it would be difficult to say, but it was probably about the middle of the seventeenth century; the earliest use of it that I have met occurs in 1650, in Mexico, where it seems already to be customary.[1635]

While this ostensibly retained for the accused the protection of ratification, it destroyed whatever value there was in a prolonged interval between the original deposition and its confirmation. At first a delay of four days was ordered for the form ad perpetuam, which seems to have been considered sufficient to excite the conscientious scruples of a possible perjurer.[1636] Even this was subject to the exigencies of the prosecution. An elaborate series of instructions to commissioners, about 1770, informs them that there should be four days' interval if possible, but if a witness is dying or about to absent himself, ratification may be immediate.[1637] In a case in 1758 ratification is ordered to be taken after waiting three hours; in others, in 1781 and 1795, after twenty-four hours; in another, in 1783, it is recorded that twenty-eight hours were allowed to elapse, all of which shows how purely formal was the whole business.[1638]

***

In truth it was the baldest formality, for the process habitually followed deprived ratification of whatever value it might have had originally. In place of testing the memory and veracity of the witness by making him repeat his testimony, it was merely read over to him. In 1519 and again in 1546, the Suprema sought to set some limit to this abuse by ordering that, after preliminary inquiries, the witness should be made substantially to repeat his testimony and, only after this, was the record to be read to him, but even this was soon afterwards abandoned and the Instructions of 1561 merely provide that the witness is to be told to repeat his testimony; if his memory fails, questions are to be put leading him to recall it and, if he asks to have the record read, it is to be read to him. Of course the witness always availed himself of the privilege and Pablo García says nothing about his repeating his evidence and directs the reading of the record as a matter of course.[1639] So perfectly was the whole business a matter of routine that tribunals kept printed blanks, to be filled in with names and dates, of the customary attestation that the witness declared it to be his testimony, that it was properly set forth, that he had no change to make in it, for it was the truth which he ratified and if necessary he repeated it, not through hatred but for the discharge of his conscience.[1640] In fact, although the witness was free to make what additions, alterations or omissions that he pleased, it was dangerous for him to diminish the record substantially, for any revocation exposed him to punishment for false-witness and both depositions were duly set forth in the publication.[1641]

Bishop Simancas tells us that, when there was suspicion of perjury, it was customary to examine the witness again, but that this was not done in other cases, so as not to lead him to commit perjury[1642]--a tenderness to the witness which had better have been displayed to his victim; but Simancas wrote before the Instructions of 1561 were issued and Rojas, whose work was subsequent, is very free-spoken in his denunciation of the customary practice. Some doctors, he says, argue that ratification supplies the place of letting the accused know the names of the witnesses, but this is a hallucination, for experience shows that this ceremony, with its two religious persons, is of no value, for it is a trait of humanity to persist in an assertion, whether true or false, especially where there is risk of perjury, and he urges that the witness should not be allowed to see his testimony, but should be examined anew and the two statements be compared so that, from their variations, his credibility could be determined and lying witnesses be detected.[1643] Few inquisitors could be expected to perform this conscientious duty, but one who wrote about 1640 indicates how fruitful it might prove. He tells us that, in suspicious cases, he had found the advantage of this plan and had brought to light perjuries which could have been proved in no other way; when witnesses betrayed their falsity by varying in important details, he confined them in solitary cells, where conscience did its work, and they confessed their frauds. He had also seen many ancient processes in which commissioners and notaries were convicted, deprived of office and punished in public autos de fe, which suggests unpleasantly how little reliance was to be placed on the officials who took down evidence.[1644]

Before the invention of the formula ad perpetuam, there was a hardship inflicted by ratification, in the excessive delays which it frequently caused. Thus Francisco Alonso, a Portuguese of Zamora, accused of bigamy, was thrown into the secret prison of Valladolid, July 10, 1627. As the alleged marriages had taken place in Coimbra, the evidence of their celebration had to be obtained from there, and it was a year before he had his first audience. When the time came for ratification, the depositions were sent for that purpose to Coimbra, September 28, 1628 but, in spite of repeated urgency, they were not received back until December 18, 1629. Then the case dragged on until the poor wretch died, June 10, 1630, after three years of incarceration, when it was perforce suspended.[1645]

SUPPRESSION OF WITNESSES' NAMES

Of all the devices for encouraging informers and crippling the defence of the accused, the most effective was the suppression of the names of the witnesses for the prosecution. This infamy was an inheritance from the Old Inquisition. In 1298, under the pretext that those who gave evidence in cases of heresy were liable to vengeance from other heretics, Boniface VIII provided that, where such danger was threatened, inquisitors were at liberty to conceal the names of the witnesses, but he expressly ordered that, in the absence of such danger, the names were to be published as in other tribunals. That he construed this literally is evident, for, when the Jews of Rome complained that in their case the names were habitually concealed, he decided that, as they were few and powerless, there was no danger and the names must be revealed.[1646] Permission to commit injustice is apt practically to assume the aspect of a counsel and then of a command and, in spite of Boniface's reservation, concealment became the universal practice of the Inquisition. So it was in Spain. At first it was a discretionary power for the inquisitor to use in exceptional cases, as when the inquisitor of Ciudad Real, in the trials of Sancho de Ciudad and his wife, ordered, January 7, 1484, that the witnesses' names be suppressed, it was an exception which he explained by the fact that Sancho was regidor of the city, with powerful friends, and that the witnesses had been threatened.[1647] Similarly, in the Instructions of November, 1484, the suppression of witnesses' names was permissive, not mandatory. Allusion was made to the danger of testifying against heretics; it was asserted that some witnesses had been murdered or wounded for that cause, wherefore inquisitors could suppress their names and all circumstances that would lead to their identification.[1648] All that was needed was permission, and suppression speedily became the rule.

Of course there was occasional danger and of course there were efforts, by threats or otherwise, to deter informers and witnesses, but this is common in all criminal justice, though there was no thought of applying concealment to the secular courts. It was a privilege exclusively in favor of the faith. Considering the provocation and the number of the victims, attacks on witnesses would appear to be singularly few and wholly inadequate to justify their protection by such means, although the Inquisition never ceased to proclaim it as an ever-present danger. In August, 1500, Ferdinand and Isabella asked of Manoel of Portugal the extradition of Juan de Zafra and his son-in-law for seeking to kill Juan López of Badajoz, who had testified against Zafra and, not finding him, had beaten to death his pregnant wife and stabbed his young son and had escaped to Portugal. They were surrendered, but there seem to have been no precedents for their prosecution and, in January, 1501, we find Ferdinand writing to the tribunal of Seville to hold a consultation as to the procedure in the case. Again, in January 1502, when a witness in Calatayud was threatened, Ferdinand ordered the inquisitor, if the report was true, to take such action as comported with the honor of the Holy Office and the protection of witnesses.[1649] Evidently cases had been so rare that no method of dealing with them had been formulated. Still, apprehension was lively and when, in 1507, at Llerena, some Conversos living near the Inquisition were suspected of watching to see what witnesses went there, Ferdinand empowered the inquisitors to remove six of them summarily and replace them with persons beyond suspicion.[1650]

The suppression of the names of witnesses was necessarily felt as an extreme hardship by the Conversos, not only as impeding defence but as stimulating false accusations, which there was no opportunity of disproving. The Jaen memorial of 1506 does not hesitate to accuse the officials of the tribunal of thus piling up fictitious charges, and Lucero's career at Córdova shows how successfully this could be done when witnesses need not be either named or produced. That efforts should be made to purchase relief was natural. When, in 1512, Ferdinand was lacking in funds for the conquest of Navarre, an offer of 600,000 ducats was made to him, if he would remove the seal of secrecy from the names of informers and witnesses, but we are told that he preferred his God and his faith and the preservation of religion. Soon after his death an attempt was made to tempt the young Charles V with a bribe of 800,000 crowns. His greedy advisers favored the petition, but Ximenes interposed with a strong remonstrance, reciting Ferdinand's refusal and predicting the ruin of the Holy Office. Recently he added at Talavera la Reina, a Judaizing Converso, punished by it, obtained knowledge of the informer, lay in wait for him and slew him, and such is the infamy inflicted by the Inquisition and such the hatred engendered by it that, if the names of the witnesses were published, they would be slain, not only in solitudes but in the streets and even in the churches; no one would be able to denounce heretics, save at the peril of his life, so that the Inquisition would be ruined and God would have no defender. Charles was convinced and the dazzling bribe was rejected.[1651]

***

Thus the policy of the Inquisition was settled, and so completely was it embodied in the estilo that it was frequently enforced in cases where its ostensible reason was inapplicable. When Juan Franco was burnt for Protestantism at Toledo, in 1570, the only witness against him was another Frenchman, Jean de Provins, who had confessed to being a Protestant dogmatizer and as such was undoubtedly burnt. His only evidence had been some idle talk between them, eight years previously; he was eminently safe from vengeance and yet his name was carefully suppressed in the publication of evidence.[1652] For all this, when the rule was applied to the inquisitors, as it was in the visitations, when the inspector was interrogating the officials about each other, they fully recognized its injustice. Thus, in 1574, during an inspection of the Canary tribunal, when the inquisitor Ortiz de Funes was inculpated, he complained bitterly that it rendered it impossible for him to verify or invalidate the testimony of the witnesses--a scruple which he had never felt when administrating justice in this fashion.[1653]

The fiction was persistently maintained that the usefulness of the Inquisition depended wholly on the suppression of the names of witnesses. In the struggle over the evocation to Rome of the case of Villanueva, the main argument, repeatedly advanced by the Suprema, was that if appeals to Rome were permitted they would destroy its efficiency in the suppression of heresy, for no one would denounce heretics or testify against them, if there was risk that their names would become known in Rome by the papers being carried thither.[1654]

The idleness of this talk is indicated by the rarity of cases of injury or threats to witnesses and the moderation with which they were customarily punished. The most serious case that I have met was that which followed the condemnation to lifelong reclusion in a monastery of Luis Pallas, Lord of Cortes, by the tribunal of Valencia, in 1571, for protecting his Morisco vassals from the Inquisition. Suspicion of having informed on him fell upon Francisco González and the Pallas family ordered his murder, for which, in 1577, four of the Pallas retainers were relaxed to the captain-general for execution. So unusual was the case that the latter had scruples as to his duty, which Philip II told him were superfluous and had unnecessarily delayed the punishment.[1655] Like any other murder, this involved the death-penalty, but as a rule offences of minor degree were leniently treated. In 1631, Francisca Muñoz of Segovia wounded Juan Martínez in the face, after asking why he had put her mother-in-law in the Inquisition, for which she was only reprimanded in the audience-chamber and banished for two years from Segovia.[1656] In various other cases of threatening witnesses, the severest punishment I have met is a hundred lashes, coupled with more or less exile and this, considering the liberality with which scourging was administered, implies that the offence was not regarded as requiring severe repression.[1657] Although thus the penalties were not greatly deterrent, the cases would appear to be singularly few. In the Toledo record, from 1648 to 1794, the only one occurred in 1650, when Pedro de Vega, alcalde of Mombeltran, after trial for a proposition without conviction, had threatened and insulted the witnesses; for this he was prosecuted and escaped with a severe reprimand and warning.[1658]

CONFRONTATION

To appreciate fully the hardship which the suppression of witnesses' names inflicted on the accused, it must be borne in mind that his only opportunity of knowing what was the evidence against him was in the so-called publication. This will be considered more in detail hereafter, and it suffices here to point out how the effort to mislead the prisoner as to the identity of his accusers led to the garbling of the evidence in a manner necessarily adding impediments to the exceedingly limited opportunities allowed him for defence. Yet we occasionally meet with cases which suggest that inquisitors were less solicitous about the safety of their witnesses than to create the belief in safety that would encourage denunciation. Thus, in the trial of Hans of Antwerp in Toledo for Lutheranism, in 1561, there was no scruple in setting forth the evidence in such wise that he could not fail to identify the witness.[1659] This could scarce be avoided in the very fruitful source of evidence volunteered by cell-companions. Thus in the Toledo case of Pedro Flamenco, in 1570, the testimony of two fellow-prisoners as to his talk and conduct in prison is so set forth as to render their identification inevitable and, as it included their opinions that he was a scoundrel and villain, there must have been lively times in that cell on his return from his audience.[1660] In cases of solicitation, the attempt to prevent identification was futile, for the confessor could not fail, from the incidents freely detailed, to recognize the women whom he had seduced or attempted to seduce.

In secular procedure there was occasional recourse to "confrontation"--bringing the accused face to face with the accuser or the witnesses and letting them debate the questions that had puzzled the judges, but it was regarded as a doubtful expedient, to be resorted to only when all else had failed.[1661] In 1491, in the case of the Santo Niño de la Guardia, where the accused were witnesses against each other and their confessions under torture were irreconcilable, confrontation was tried with dubious success.[1662] This indicates that under supreme pressure the veil of secrecy might be withdrawn, and probably the example was occasionally followed, for Valdés, in the Instructions of 1561, felt it necessary to say that, although confrontation was practised in other jurisdictions, it was not customary in the Inquisition for, besides the violation of secrecy, experience had shown that when tried it was disadvantageous.[1663] This did not wholly put an end to it for, in 1568, the Suprema sharply rebuked the tribunal of Barcelona for various irregularities, among which was the frequent recourse to confrontation.[1664] The latest allusion to the practice that I have met with in Spain occurs in the Valladolid case, in 1620, of the priest Juan de Gabana and his accomplice Gerónima González, when the consulta de fe proposed to confront them, but referred the matter to the Suprema. Its decision would doubtless have been in the negative, but was never rendered as Gabana died before it replied.[1665] In the Roman Inquisition confrontation was sparingly admitted, and only when both parties were of low estate--never between those of higher station or of different classes.[1666]

While sedulous care was taken to prevent the accused from identifying the witnesses, it often was necessary for the witnesses to identify the accused, to prevent mistakes liable to occur in the arbitrary methods of the Inquisition. This was so managed as to accomplish both objects. The somewhat crude plan adopted, in 1528, in the trial at Toledo of Diego de Uceda, was to conceal the witnesses in the torture chamber, while he was walked up and down for a quarter of an hour, until they fully identified him.[1667] Subsequently it was found expedient to furnish the audience-chamber with a celosia--a jalousy or lattice-work, through which the witness could peer without being discovered. Its utility was strikingly demonstrated in 1649, in a Valladolid case of alleged bigamy, when one of the wives, Ana Roman, was brought to inspect the accused through the lattice and declared that he was not the Juan González whom she had married, as he differed in age, in size, and in features, whereupon he was discharged.[1668]

***

In view of the temptation offered for the gratification of malice by shielding informers and witnesses, special care was advisable for the detection and punishment of false-witness. This was the more necessary as perjury was a popular failing and the sanction of an oath was lightly esteemed. In 1555 the Córtes of Valladolid asked that, in cases involving death or mutilation, oaths should be abolished, as they merely led to perjury and, in 1560, the Córtes of Toledo complained of the prevalence of false-witness as a matter so customary that there were provinces in which it was as abundant as any other merchandise, and it was openly said that for money a man could get as many witnesses as he desired.[1669]

FALSE-WITNESS

We have seen how, in 1488, at Toledo, eight Jews were torn with hot pincers and lapidated for bearing false-witness against good Christians with the object of rendering the Inquisition odious.[1670] This savage penalty compares strangely with the leniency shown to exculpatory perjury in the case of Mossen Pedro de Santangel, Prior of Daroca, who had sought, by the employment of several false-witnesses, to save his brother Luis de Santangel, burnt for complicity in the murder of San Pedro Arbués. He escaped with the simple penance of holding a lighted candle before the high altar and they were treated as benignantly.[1671] It was probably to secure greater uniformity that, in the Instructions of 1498, inquisitors were told to inflict public punishment, according to law, on those whom they detected in testifying falsely.[1672] The matter was one which might well excite solicitude for it is evident that perjury on both sides was rife and the tribunals might reasonably hesitate to believe any witness.

In 1500 and 1501 we find Ferdinand repeatedly interposing to shield those whom he favored and whom he declared to be persecuted by perjurers,[1673] and the career of Lucero shows how readily and unscrupulously they could be employed in the secrecy of the tribunals. The Jaen memorial of 1506 speaks of a certain Diego de Algecira, whom Lucero kept for five years to testify against all whom he desired to destroy and whom the inquisitors of Jaen borrowed for the same purpose, besides other adepts of the kind whom they employed and rewarded. When a raid was made on Arjona, the notary Barzena brought with him Luis de Vilches who, by changing his name and garments, testified repeatedly in different characters.[1674] One of the petitions of the Córtes of Monzon, in 1512, bears eloquent testimony to the same state of affairs in Catalonia, for it asks that, when a man was burnt through fraudulent testimony, the inquisitors should not prevent the king from punishing the false witnesses.[1675] Such a system necessarily produced professional perjurers who did for gain what others might do through malice. That the accused should resort to the same means was inevitable. In Segovia, in 1504, there appears to have been a perfect carnival of false-witness. On July 10th and 11th there were punished two accusing perjurers and twenty-two who had sworn falsely on the side of the defence; there were others who had died before sentence and still more who had confessed and were awaiting punishment, which consisted mostly in scourging and exile.[1676]

Thus far there seems to have been uncertainty as to jurisdiction. In the Catalan efforts for relief, the bull Pastoralis officii was procured from Leo X, August 1, 1576, which rendered perjury committed in the Inquisition justiciable by the inquisitors and ecclesiastical judges in conjunction but not severally.[1677] The result was naturally discouraging and papal intervention was again sought. In a brief of December 14, 1518, addressed to Cardinal Adrian, Leo deplored the condition under which, through false-witness, the guilty escaped and the innocent suffered, but the only remedy provided was in conferring full jurisdiction on inquisitors with faculties to punish, even by relaxation to the secular arm, without incurring "irregularity."[1678]

The crime was thus placed wholly in the hands of the Inquisition, which was no more likely than before to exert itself in checking perjured accusations. This proved to be the case and, in 1523, the Córtes of Valladolid asked that it should inflict on false witnesses the penalties provided by the Laws of Toro in 1502, which decreed the talio for perjury committed in criminal cases.[1679] Charles contented himself with replying that he had asked the pope to appoint as inquisitor-general Archbishop Manrique, whom he would charge to see justice done. That this remedy proved futile may be gathered from the memorial of Granada, in 1526, in which one of the arguments against the suppression of the names of witnesses is the number of souls condemned to hell for perjury, through the facilities offered by the secret system tempting them to destroy their enemies or to swear falsely through bribery, a thing which happens every day.[1680]

***

In fact the procedure of the Inquisition was such as to encourage the crime and to render its detection exceedingly difficult, at least when committed for the benefit of the prosecution. When every precaution was taken to prevent the accused from identifying his accusers, it was expecting too much of the average inquisitor that he should depart from the routine work of his office to discover, without assistance from those interested, whether the witnesses, mechanically examined by him or his commissioner, were telling the truth or not. Had there been any zeal in this direction, the Suprema would not have felt obliged, in 1531, to instruct the tribunals that perjurers should be punished as a warning to others, giving due consideration as to whether they were actuated by malice or ignorance. Possibly this may have stimulated some tribunal to inconvenient activity for, in 1536, it saw occasion to moderate zeal by ordering that the rigor of the brief of Leo X should not be observed, unless some one had been condemned through false evidence, and even in such case the Suprema was to be consulted before action.[1681] The infallibility of the Inquisition was too important to be rashly compromised.

Moderation thus remained the rule. Simancas tells us that, under Leo's brief, perjurers should be burnt, with confiscation, but this should only be done when the accused has suffered severely; in most cases the injury is but slight, for which such penalties suffice as appearing in an auto with a defamatory mitre and scourging, galleys or exile; even when burnt there are no disabilities on descendants; the talio has become virtually obsolete and should be used only in extreme cases; subornation of perjury is even worse than false-witness and incurs the same punishment.[1682]

Theoretically this reflects the ordinary practice. I have met with but one case in which a perjurer was burnt and this was in Sardinia, in 1562, but about 1640 an experienced inquisitor states that he has seen records of such cases in Logroño and it is possible that they occurred occasionally.[1683] So also we sometimes find scourging and the galleys in aggravated cases, while priests were let off with fines and exile. Still, the tendency was to extreme moderation. In Valladolid, Juan Gomez Rubio suffered imprisonment for nearly two years, from 1636 to 1638, on a charge of blasphemous propositions, when his case was suspended and he was dismissed with a reprimand and the corresponding infamy. His accuser was Pedro de la Cruz who had testified twice against him under fictitious names and had suborned others to appear against him, for which he escaped with parading in vergüenza and exile.[1684]

A still more significant case was that of Jean de la Barre, a Fleming, long settled in Madrid, where he was deputy alcalde of the royal palace of the Pardo. He was a man of somewhat excessive devoutness. He had a mass celebrated daily in the royal chapel by a chaplain of his own, until the regular chaplain, a Dr. Robles, who was also commissioner of the Inquisition, forbade it and forced him to the church of the Trinitarians. He endeavoured to form a cofradia for celebrating masses, but Robles demanded to be the head of it and to handle the funds without accountability, when la Barre abandoned the project, although he had spent five hundred ducats on a silver lamp for the chapel. They naturally quarrelled and, when Robles sought a reconciliation, his overtures were rejected. He revenged himself, in January, 1656, by denouncing la Barre for various heretical speeches, for neglecting mass and confession and, what was perhaps more serious than all, for saying that inquisitors were robbers who seized rich men to strip them of their property. La Barre had discharged several workmen for theft and idleness, and they were readily induced to appear as corroborating witnesses. He easily identified his accusers and in defence presented twenty-five witnesses in his favor, among them five Trinitarian fraiies and some officials of high rank, who testified emphatically to his unusual devotion; his rosary was never out of his hands, he heard mass daily and spent three reales a day for it. They also told of the mortal enmity and threats of Robles and the discharged workmen and showed the reasons. There could be no clearer case of a foul conspiracy to ruin an innocent man, but he was sentenced to reprimand and exile and was threatened with a hundred lashes if he dared to speak of his treatment. That his case was suspended and he was not required to abjure even de levi show that there was no suspicion of heresy proved and that the sentence, with its consequences of infamy on him and his posterity, was a mere wanton exercise of arbitrary power, while the false witnesses were not troubled, for there are no marginal notes on the record showing that extracts were taken from the evidence for their prosecution.[1685]

***

It was still admitted that the legal punishment was the talio, but that it should only be inflicted when the perjurer had encompassed the conviction of his victim, thus weighing the crime, not by its criminality but by its result.[1686] How lightly, indeed, false swearing was regarded per se is indicated by a curious case occurring in Valladolid, in 1630. A student named Luis Sánchez denounced certain Portuguese of Zamora of endeavoring to convert him. The receiver and an alguazil were sent thither, but could find no trace of the accused nor even of the street in which they were described as residing. Sánchez was sent for, was made to ratify his deposition, and was then accused of the fraud and mockery of the tribunal. He admitted it and explained that he had been thrown into gaol in a suit over a mare and had devised this expedient for getting out, in hopes of escaping to the asylum of a church. His trial went through all the regular stages; the vote of the consulta de fe was sent to the Suprema, which contented itself with sentencing him to a reprimand, six years' exile from Valladolid and a fine of two hundred ducats, with the charitable alternative that, if he was too poor, he should swear to pay it if he should ever be able.[1687] While thus the Inquisition was benignantly disposed towards perjury, the secular law did not relax its severity. In Aragon the Córtes of Monzon, in 1564, decreed the talio in criminal cases for accusing false witnesses and for those produced by the defence, in addition to the penalties prescribed by the fueros—scourging and perpetual banishment—besides making good all expenses incurred by the other party. In Castile, a pragmática of Philip II, in 1566, confirmed by Philip III, in 1603, when the case was not capital, substituted, for the talio, scourging and the galleys for life.[1688] The tenderness of the Inquisition for such offences was not derived from any softening of the law of the land.

With the development of limpieza there sprang up a new and fruitful source of perjury. Those who were endeavoring to prove immaculate descent had no scruple in filling any genealogical gaps by purchasing witnesses to supply deficiencies, and those who, through envy or malice, desired the defeat of an aspirant, found ready means of putting forward witnesses to swear as to public repute, or that they had seen sanbenitos of ancestors. As early as 1560, and again in 1574, the Suprema found it necessary to issue instructions to meet these cases.[1689] Bigamy trials also brought to light a contingent of perjurers, mostly employed by the guilty party desiring remarriage, to swear that he or she was single.[1690]

Notwithstanding these accessions and of the fact that in most cases there were several accomplices, the number in the records is surprisingly few. Partly this is explicable by the extreme difficulty of detection, owing to the suppression of witnesses' names and the impediments thrown in the way of the defence, and partly by the indifference of the tribunals, which do not seem to have regarded it as their duty to prosecute perjurers—at least those for the prosecution. When, in 1640, Agustin Gómez de la Peña, cura of Perdigon, was tried in Valladolid for carrying unconsecrated forms in the procession of Corpus Christi, and the case was suspended on the ground that the testimony was perjured, the Suprema, in approving the vote, felt it necessary to order that the fiscal should prosecute the accuser and his witnesses, showing that this was by no means a matter of course.[1691] Be this as it may, in Toledo a record, extending from 1575 to 1610, and embracing 1172 trials, only contains eight cases of false-witness, and a further record of the same tribunal, from 1648 to 1794, has not a single one in its aggregate of 1205 cases.[1692] In Valladolid, out of 667 trials occurring between 1622 and 1662, there are but seven cases of false witness.[1693] In Madrid, the records, from 1703 to 1751, present but a single trial for false-witness, and this arose out of a marriage case.[1694]

Unfortunately these slender returns do not prove that perjury was uncommon. Philip V, among his other attempted reforms, in a decree of July 26, 1705, called attention to the facility afforded to the execrable wickedness of false denunciations and false-witness, imposing on many innocent persons the difficult task of protecting honor, property and life, to the perversion and scandal of justice. These enormous and pernicious abuses he attributed to the non-enforcement of the penalties prescribed by the laws, because the moderate punishments, so rarely inflicted, encouraged rather than repressed the audacity of the evil-minded. He therefore ordered the Suprema to see that the legal penalties were rigorously imposed, and the Suprema obediently transmitted this to the tribunals with instructions to conform to it strictly.[1695]

***

This seems to have had some effect, but not much. In a collection of all the autos held in Spain, from 1721 to 1727, out of 962 sentences, there are but seventeen for false-witness and these represent only about half that number of cases, for in one there were five accomplices and, in two others, three each. The punishments remain as of old, scourging, galleys and exile, and there is no difference made between offenders in marriage-cases and those involving the death-penalty by accusations of Judaism. One of these latter excited considerable interest at the time. Three penitents from Cadiz, undergoing punishments for Judaism, accused fourteen persons of practising Jewish rites, but they had not studied their parts well, their stories did not accord and, on being arrested, they confessed. Their intended victims were honored with a special auto de fe in Seville, November 30, 1722, to which they were conveyed by familiars in the handsomest coaches of the city; in the church of San Pablo they were seated near to the inquisitors, the evidence was publicly read, their innocence was proclaimed, and they were carried home in the coaches. This was followed, June 6, 1723, by the auto in which the perjurers were sentenced to two hundred lashes apiece and the two of them, who were men, to seven years in the galleys. Somewhat similar was a case in Santiago, in 1724, when five culprits were concerned, of whom the leader, Pedro García Rodríguez, was punished with two hundred lashes and five years of galleys, while his accomplices had the lashes and eight years of exile.[1696]

The moderation shown towards perjury increased in the latest period. In 1817, the deacon Manuel González Ribadeneyra was prosecuted for it by the tribunal of Santiago but, when the sumaria was submitted to the Suprema, it sent a commission to the Benedictine Abbot of Monforte to warn the offender that in future he must conform his depositions to the truth, as becomes a minister in holy Orders, for otherwise he would not be treated with the benignity which now imposed on him only eight days of spiritual exercises in the monastery. Apparently even this was expected to excite resistance, for a further provision threatened him, in case of refusal, with prosecution according to law.[1697]

***

Theoretically there was laudable care as to the sufficiency of evidence for condemnation. The ancient Glossator on the Decretum says that two witnesses are sufficient to convict a pope, but the authorities, both of the Old and the New Inquisition, hold that, although this is good in ordinary law, yet, in a crime entailing such consequences as heresy, especially as the defence is crippled by the suppression of the witnesses' names, there should be much hesitation in convicting a man on the evidence of only two witnesses.[1698] Still, two were reckoned sufficient, unless they were accomplices, when three were required and these supported by other indications.[1699] Yet as one witness was sufficient to justify torture, these scruples did not save the accused but only exposed him to the risk of convicting himself if his endurance did not exhaust the resources of the torture-chamber. In fact, in the secrecy of the tribunal, the discretion of the judges was the only rule, and they could construe the laws of evidence as they saw fit, as when a visitation of Barcelona led the Suprema, in 1568, to rebuke the inquisitors because, on the evidence of a single witness they prosecuted Guillen Contada, tortured him twice and, without convicting him, abandoned him to the secular arm for burning; nor was he the only victim of the kind, for they did the same with Juan del Payen.[1700] How much of this occurred elsewhere the world will never know.

The theory that it required two witnesses to prove a fact was developed into the rule that they must be contestes--that is, witnesses to the same individual act of heresy--before it could be accepted as proved. It is often found urged in the arguments for the defence that the witnesses are singulares and not contestes, but in practice such a defence was usually disregarded or, at most, only led to the unfailing resource of torture. Thus, in a case referred to the Suprema for decision, the tribunal reported that there were many witnesses to prove that the accused was a Jewess, but they were not contestes, for none of them cited the others, but each one named somebody else who could attest the fact: they deposed to the same time and place, but varied as to the years. In the consulta de fe some members voted for relaxation and others for torture; the matter was sent up to the Suprema and, whatever its decision may have been, the accused suffered.[1701]

CHARACTER OF EVIDENCE

Even in the seventeenth century, Escobar affirms the rule absolutely; if one witness swears that he heard Pedro say in the market-place that God is not a Trinity and another that he heard him say so in a house, it does not convict him for neither fact is legally proved.[1702] Such a definition, however, threw too many obstacles in the way of the prosecution not to be eluded and, in fact, there were classes of cases, such as solicitation in the confessional, in which it was impossible to have more than one witness to each individual act. So, in prosecutions for Judaism, in which the evidence frequently covered a long series of years and turned on infinitesimal incidents in daily life, concurrent witnesses to any single one could scarce be had. Yet the claims of the Inquisition to extreme benignity required this to be understood as Escobar expresses it, while in practice it was disregarded. It was discovered that witnesses could be contestes in genere when they testified to different acts of heresy, and thus make full proof. It is true that Rojas, after citing authorities on both sides, concludes that the rule requiring two concurrent witnesses to a fact must be observed, but one of his authorities asserts that the contrary is the rule in practice, and the Suprema affirmed this, July 27, 1590, by ordering that, where formal heresy is concerned, depositions as to different ceremonies and points of faith are to be held as contestes.[1703] This was inevitable and it was only sanctioning what had long been the custom in the tribunals.

***

There was much laxity in the character of the evidence accepted. In the secular courts, hearsay testimony was not admitted as proof unless a witness had heard a matter from so many persons as to constitute public fame, in which case it was allowed a certain weight.[1704] In the Inquisition the same rule was nominally followed, but in practice hearsay evidence was welcomed and was utilized. All the gossip and tattle of a village was eagerly accepted and recorded, to be reproduced in the publication of evidence furnished to the accused, and it unquestionably had its weight when laid before the consulta de fe which voted the sentence. Witnesses were often brought in to swear that they had heard the direct witness assert that the accused was guilty of the heresy charged, and this was regarded as cumulative evidence. Sometimes it happened that these secondary witnesses made a much stronger statement than their principal and, in such case, the fiscal was directed to insert both in the accusation, with the reserve that the direct testimony would be considered when sentencing, the object being to terrify and mislead the prisoner.[1705] The kind of evidence that was gravely accepted and recorded is seen in the trial of the Licentiate Luis de Guevara, who was reconciled in the Toledo auto de fe of 1594. In an abstract of the more important testimony it is stated that the fourth witness had heard a man say that a certain Morisca was a great bitch, for she coupled with other dogs, meaning the said Luis de Guevara.[1706] Such hearsay gossip was laboriously accumulated to an incredible degree, and it is easy to appreciate its effect on the defendant, when cunningly mingled with the direct evidence in the publication of witnesses, which he was required to answer on the spot, item by item, tending to confuse him and leading him to entrap himself. In the trial at Valladolid, in 1641, of Sebastian de los Rios, cura of Tombrio, there were fourteen witnesses de visu, or direct, and twenty de oidas, or hearsay, and, in 1659, Guiomar Antunes was thrown into the secret prison, with sequestration on the testimony of one witness de visu and eleven de oidas. Latitudinarianism as to evidence could scarce go further than in the case of Fray Alonso Capera, tried in 1643, as a curandero for treating disease by conjurations, against whom there testified twenty witnesses, "men and women, minors and adults, some direct, others hearsay and others on suspicion."[1707] When it is remembered that no witness, however infamous or unfit, was rejected, we can conceive the quality of the evidence on which depended the fate of the accused.

***

While the Inquisition claimed jurisdiction over all heresy, internal and mental, as well as external and formal, it could only prosecute when heresy was manifested or inferable by external acts or words, and these had to be investigated with the utmost minuteness. The land was filled with those whose external conformity might be but the cloak for secret dissidence. The New Christian was regarded with suspicion, as a possible or even a probable apostate, whose baptism only served to render him guilty and to subject him to the jurisdiction of the Inquisition. He might be regular in religious observance, be liberal to church and friar, be a constant purchaser of the Cruzada indulgences, and yet be secretly a believer in the Law of Moses or of Mahomet. It was the business of the Inquisition to detect and punish these apostates; it was rarely that they betrayed their infidelity by imprudent avowals or hasty speeches, except to so-called accomplices or to cell-companions, and, in the absence of such witnesses, for the most part, the only proof against them arose from their adherence, in the privacy of their homes, to the rites and usages which, through long succession of generations, had become a second nature. It was on this, then, that prosecutions largely depended, and the simplest acts that savored of Judaism or of Islam were regarded as incontrovertible proofs of apostasy, requiring reconciliation to the Church, with all that it implied and, if subsequently persisted in, proving relapse with its penalty of the stake.

Familiarity with the practices of the condemned religions was therefore part of the necessary training of the inquisitor, and long descriptive catalogues were compiled for their information. In order also that the people might be duly instructed, and be on the watch to denounce their neighbors, these were incorporated in the Edicts of Faith annually published in all the churches. Much of the evidence recorded in the trials and, for the most part, accepted as conclusive, consists of acts in themselves perfectly innocent and appearing to us wholly indifferent and unworthy of consideration. Observing the Ramadan or the fast of Queen Esther of course would admit of no extenuation, but there were a host of trivial observances which seem to the modern mind altogether inadequate to the prominence accorded to them in the trials. This extreme minuteness with which such observances were held to prove apostasy was an innovation. Of old, the Church recognized the impossibility of changing abruptly customs so imbedded in the routine of daily life, and, while such practices were to be repressed, they were not treated as heresy. The great council of Lateran, in 1215, alludes to their frequency, but contents itself with ordering prelates to force converts to abandon all remnants of their old faith.[1708] It was otherwise in Spain and the evidence on which prosecutions were based and punishments inflicted would often appear to us to be of the flimsiest character.

Changing the body-linen or table-linen on Saturday, lighting candles on Friday and similar observances were proofs of a most damaging character; even eating amin--a broth liked by Jews--is enumerated among the offences entailing appearance in an auto de fe.[1709] When Brianda de Bardaxí was on trial at Saragossa, in 1491, she admitted that, when a child, she had eaten a few mouthfuls of Passover bread given to her by a playmate, and this was gravely detailed in her sentence as one of the proofs of "vehement suspicion" for which she was severely punished.[1710] Circumcision, in the later period, was an evidence almost decisive and, with male defendants, an inspection by the surgeon of the tribunal was customary but, in the earlier time, before the expulsion and forced conversion of the Jews, it was merely an indication that a man was a New and not an Old Christian, yet in an auto de fe at Saragossa, in 1486, Pedro and Luis de Almazan, on this evidence alone, were sentenced to perform penance with lighted candles and to ten years of exile.[1711] Among the Moriscos, staining the nails with henna was held to justify suspicion; refusing to eat the flesh of animals that had died of natural causes was highly damaging; a propensity to cleanliness by washing one's self was an indication of apostasy and, in the trial of Mari Gómez at Toledo, in 1550, as a relapsed impenitent, one of the charges was that, in her former trial, she had not confessed that, some fifteen years before, a kid had been killed in her house by cutting its throat.[1712]

***

How slender was the evidence requisite for prosecution is manifested in the trials of a whole family, in Valladolid, from 1622 to 1624. When Dr. Jorje Enrriquez, physician to the Duke of Alva, died, the body was soiled, requiring washing, followed by a clean shirt. A number of witnesses thereupon deposed that it was prepared for sepulture according to Jewish rites. The consulta de fe on the arrest was not unanimous, and it was referred to the Suprema, which ordered the arrest of all concerned, with sequestration. The whole family, widow, children and servants, with some cousins, were thrown into the secret prison and the eldest son, a youth of twenty, died from the effects of torture. After nearly two years of this, the evidence was so weak that the consulta de fe voted in discordia and the Suprema ordered the prisoners to be acquitted. So, in 1625, Manuel de Azevedo, a shoemaker of Salamanca, was denounced because he had removed the lump of fat from a leg of mutton which he took to a baker to be roasted. The consulta voted to dismiss the case but the fiscal appealed to the Suprema, which ordered arrest with sequestration. The trial went on through all the forms and when at length Azevedo learned from the accusation what was the charge, he said that he was ignorant of this being a Jewish custom, but had been told that a leg of mutton roasted better when the fat was cut out. When the defence was reached he proved that he was an Old Christian on all sides; he was not acquitted but the case was suspended. Had he been a New Christian he would have been tortured and penanced, whether he overcame the torture or not. In another case, in 1646, one of the charges was that the accused, in slicing bread, held the knife with the edge turned away and not towards his breast, as was customary with Christians. Trivial as all this may seem, one occasionally meets a case showing that the Inquisition did not always spend its energies in vain in following up the slenderest evidence, however great were the sufferings frequently inflicted on the innocent. In several Jewish cases in Valladolid, in 1642, the chief evidence was that the meat before cooking was soaked in water to remove the blood and grease. This led to the discovery and punishment as Judaizers of a group of some fifteen or twenty in Benavente, who appeared in the auto de fe of 1644. As soon as one was brought to confess, he implicated others, and the net was spread which captured them all. The fact, however, that torture was freely used casts an unpleasant doubt over the justice of the result.[1713]

Suspicion might be aroused by negative as well as by positive indications and, in the Spain of the

Inquisition, it behooved every man to be scrupulously exact in the performance of what were regarded as evidences of orthodoxy, as well as in the avoidance of what created doubt, for everywhere around him were zealous spies, eager to serve the faith. In 1635, Manuel Mardes, travelling with his wife and two other women, passed two men laboring in a field without saluting them. One of them asked him why he did not say "Praised be Jesus Christ" or "Praised be the most Blessed Sacrament," to which he imprudently replied that God was not known in his own land. The laborers promptly denounced him to the nearest commissioner of the Inquisition, who arrested him. The calificadores voted that this was manifest Judaism and he was thrown into the secret prison of Valladolid, with sequestration. Then there came additional evidence from a cell-companion that he washed his hands on rising and before eating. He denied all intention until he was smartly tortured, when he confessed all that was desired.[1714]

Naturally this negative evidence was habitually sought by the tribunals. In the trials for Judaism and Mahometanism, the accused was always interrogated as to his training in Christian formulas. He was asked to recite the credo and the customary prayers of the Paternoster, the Ave Maria and the Salve Regina, and was made to cross himself, to see whether or not he did it in a manner to show that it was habitual. In Spain there were two forms of this--santiguarse and signarse--the former consisting in making the sign of the cross, with the thumb and forefinger joined, passing them from forehead to cheek and from the left to the right shoulder; the latter in touching the forehead, mouth and chest with the thumb and forefinger of the right hand, or with the thumb alone. This was often a crucial test. Of Mari Gómez it is recorded, July 15, 1550, "She repeated the Ave Maria; she was imperfect in the Paternoster and the creed and said she did not know the Salve Regina. She performed the signo ill but the santiguada well."[1715]

***

It has seemed worth while to enter thus minutely into the details of inquisitorial treatment of evidence, as it was so largely a determining factor in the fate of the accused. From this examination it is impossible to resist the conclusion that the system of procedure was framed rather to secure conviction than to ascertain the truth. Guilt was presumed in the fact of arrest and the business of the tribunal was to prove it.

CHAPTER VI - CONFESSION

The heretic was not only a criminal but a sinner. This imposed on the Inquisition a two-fold function--to discover and punish crime and to save the soul of the sinner. Its position was anomalous. It could scarce be called a spiritual tribunal, for inquisitors and members of the Suprema, as we have seen, might be laymen. The jurisdiction over heresy was a special delegation from the Holy See but, although the inquisitor might excommunicate, when the censure was to be removed he did not do it himself but empowered any priest to perform the ceremony.[1716] He never received sacramental confessions or administered the sacrament of penitence; even when a Protestant applied to him to be admitted to the bosom of the Church, a priest was called in to hear the confession and grant absolution.

Thus, while exercising spiritual jurisdiction, the inquisitor, even if in holy orders, abstained from exercising spiritual functions. Yet, as a judge, his duties were not purely secular. In theory the object of the Inquisition was the saving of souls; the detection and punishment of heresy were merely a necessary means to that end. The burning of the obstinate impenitent, besides avenging the offence to God, was the removal of a gangrened member to preserve the body from infection. The penalties inflicted on the repentant were not punishment but penance and he was not a convict but a penitent; whatever statement he made during his trial, even in obstinately denying the charges, was a confession, and the penal prison to which he was consigned was a casa de penitencia or de misericordia. Even denunciations and the evidence of witnesses for the defence were sometimes called confessions.

While the distinction was fully recognized between judicial and sacramental confession, and the inquisitor was in no sense a confessor, there was a curious assumption that in the tribunal confession was of a mixed character, partaking of both classes.[1717] The whole procedure was directed to induce the accused to confess his errors, to profess repentance and to beg for mercy. He was adjured by the love of God and his Blessed Mother to discharge his conscience and save his soul by a full confession, as to himself and others, without uttering false testimony as to himself or to them. The so-called advocate who was furnished to defend him was instructed to urge him to this, and to explain that the Holy Office was not like the other tribunals whose business it was to punish the body, for here the only object was to cure the soul and to reunite to the Church those who, by their sins, had left the holy congregation of Christians, in violation of their baptismal promises; he should therefore cast aside all thought of that which concerns the body and think only of his soul, confessing his crimes so that the Holy Office could cure his infirmity, which was beyond the power of any other judge or confessor.[1718]

No doubt there were many inquisitors who conscientiously believed that this was the lofty duty to which they were devoted. There was another motive, however, which was not without weight in prompting the earnest and sometimes cruel means resorted to, for it was held that confession, however it might be obtained, cured all defects and irregularities in the trial.[1719] An inquisitor conscious of having overstepped the limits was therefore doubly anxious to extort from the accused admissions which should exonerate him.

Thus, from the first audience to the final reading of the sentence at the auto de fe, the effort of the tribunal was to bring the sinner to repentance, or at least to confession, by adjurations, by misleading promises of mercy, by threats and, if necessary, by torture. On his way to the stake, the man who had persistently denied his guilt was accompanied by confessors urging him to admit it and to repent. Similar advantage was taken of the death-bed fears of those who died in prison, when, as we have seen, confessors sent to them were instructed to listen to them only in case they confessed sufficiently to "satisfy" the adverse testimony.

SPONTANEOUS CONFESSION

This urgency to induce confession produced the natural result that the unfortunates subjected to it were led, not infrequently, to gratify their judges by admitting whatever they thought necessary to win the favor of the tribunal. This was recognized in a warning issued by the Suprema, in 1541, that much caution was required in weighing the truth of confessions, because the accused, through malice, were wont to confess against themselves and others in order to obscure the truth.[1720] This warning was doubtless needed, but there is little evidence that it was heeded. As a rule, the confession was accepted, provided it was sufficiently criminatory and, as far as regarded its implication of accomplices, it was used for their conviction.

Henry Charles Lea, LL.D.

***

An unexpected feature of the inquisitorial records is the number of espontaneados--of those who from various motives voluntarily accused themselves. In 1172 cases occurring in Toledo between 1575 and 1610 there are 170 of these or about one in seven. This of course is attributable to the assumption that self-denunciation was an evidence of contrition which merited benignity. It is true that, in the earlier period, when Edicts of Grace were published, those who came forward within the term were subjected to reconciliation and heavy mulcts; their confessions were taken down by notaries to be used against the friends whom they incriminated and against themselves in case of relapse. It is further true that, after the expiration of the term, spontaneous confession did not avert confiscation and such other penance as the inquisitor might impose--in fact it was virtually no better than if rendered under prosecution. But, after the first fury of persecution, when spontaneous self-denunciation might be considered as arising from conviction and not from fear of accusation by others, it was regarded more mercifully. In 1568 we find the Suprema sharply rebuking the tribunal of Barcelona for having condemned to reconciliation and confiscation a French girl of eighteen and Antoine Codrie, a Frenchman, who had spontaneously confessed to Protestantism and against whom there was no other evidence; the confiscated property was to be returned to them within nine days, whether or not it was still in the hands of the receiver. The tribunal was also told that it had erred deplorably in the case of Alonso de Montoya, who had spontaneously confessed to having been a renegade when captive in the hands of the Moors, and whom it had thrown into the secret prison and condemned to confiscation, reconciliation and appearance in an auto de fe with a mitre.[1721]

***

Not long after this the reports of the tribunal of Toledo present numerous cases of spontaneous self-denunciation which show that its influence on the sentence varied with the character of the confession and the motives to which the inquisitors attributed it. There was a curious case of twelve Judaizers of Alcazar de Consuegra who came forward to accuse themselves and implicate twelve others; all twenty-four figured in the great auto de fe of 1591 and all had the full penalty of reconciliation, confiscation and perpetual prison with the sanbenito. On the other hand, Andrés de Palacios, in 1586, presented himself and confessed that, when sailing in the galleys, he had made the acquaintance of an English captain who converted him to all the Lutheran heresies; for six years, and until within a few weeks, he had believed them, but now with tears he begged for mercy and for readmission to the Church. He was duly put on trial and was privately reconciled with only some spiritual penances. In the same year occurred the more complicated case of Ursule de la Croix, a French nun in the convent of Santa Margarita at Alcalá de Henares. She confessed to a commissioner there that she had imbibed some of the errors current in her native land; she had deliberately struck a crucifix and had eaten meat on Fridays. The Suprema examined the confession and ordered the commissioner to absolve her. Subsequently she returned to confess that she still held the errors which she had abjured. The Suprema ordered her to be confined in the secret prison and her trial to proceed, during which she repeated her confession, begged for mercy and professed her desire to live and die in the Catholic faith. The consulta de fe was puzzled and, on reference to the Suprema, it ordered her to be secretly reconciled, the sanbenito to be at once removed, and her reclusion for a year in a convent cell. As she was a relapsed and as Lutheranism was the object of special severity, this mercy shows ample consideration for spontaneous confession, but the event proved that the patience of the Inquisition might be tried too far. The unstable mind of the poor creature continued to torment itself and, in 1594, she again accused herself of the same errors. The tribunal reported this to the Suprema, with the statement that she had already been thrice reconciled, and the order came to relax her to the secular arm, when she was duly burnt.[1722]

Thus far there appears to have been no formal modification of the Instructions of 1484 which made no concessions to espontaneados, except during a Term of Grace, but evidently each case was treated on its merits. It was not until 1605 that the Suprema decreed that foreigners confessing their errors voluntarily were to be reconciled without confiscation. This did not apply to natives, especially Judaizers and Moriscos, in whose cases the Suprema was consulted which usually remitted the confiscation. The matter remained in this uncertain condition, with an increasing tendency towards leniency in practice. In trivial cases, such as heretical blasphemy or thoughtless propositions, the offender was reprimanded, warned and told to confess sacramentally, even though there might have been previous denunciation insufficient to justify arrest. In more serious matters we are told that the espontaneado was treated with great benignity, even when it appeared that he had come forward through fear of denunciation by accomplices who had been arrested. He was given his house or the city for a prison, unless it was necessary to seclude him from those who would pervert him. If he confessed to formal heresy, with belief and intention, it was customary to vote secret reconciliation with the immediate removal of the sanbenito and with confiscation, but the Suprema usually remitted the latter or agreed to a composition. In some cases at Santiago, in the seventeenth century, the parties offered a payment nearly equivalent to the value of their property, but the Suprema told them that they could retain it on paying what the tribunal thought proper.[1723]

IMPERFECT CONFESSION

Confession, whether spontaneous or after arrest, to be valid in the Inquisition, implied repentance, renunciation of error and prayer for readmission to Catholic unity. Although judicial, it had this in common with sacramental confession that it must be full and complete; every separate heretical act was a sin and, like sins in a confessional, it had to be enumerated. There must be no omission, else the confession was nugatory, ficta and diminuta, and an aggravated guilt, for the truly penitent sinner was held to be eager to expose all his sins, in order to gain absolution for them, and to betray all his accomplices in order to satisfy his new-born hatred of heresy. Thus the diminuto was as bad as the negative, for he was still a heretic at heart. The Instructions of 1484 treat diminutos as impenitents, to be prosecuted if subsequent testimony shows that they have concealed anything as to themselves or to others.[1724] Tried by this standard the confessions in the early Terms of Grace were apt to be imperfect and, in the endeavor to avert the awful consequences of this, it became customary to add to them a protest that, if through lapse of memory facts had been forgotten, the penitent on remembering them would come and confess them or, if testimony was received of matters omitted, he now accepted it as true and asked penance for them. These protests availed little. In the case of Mencia, wife of Diego González, before the tribunal of Guadalupe in 1485, she added this to her confession, but additional incriminating evidence was given by other penitents; she was duly prosecuted and the tribunal apologized for not sending her to the stake, in view of her youth, her tearful contrition and her heartfelt desire to return to the bosom of the Church, wherefore she escaped with perpetual prison.[1725] Beatriz Núñez was less fortunate. She was reconciled, January 13, 1485, in the Time of Grace, after presenting a long confession including all the recognized Jewish practices. July 1st she was arrested on the strength of evidence relating to acts running back for twenty years, embracing details that happened not to be contained in her confession, although it had included a protest admitting all that she did not remember. The tribunal held that her confession had been diminuta, that consequently it was feigned and she was an impenitent heretic, so she was burnt alive, July 31st.[1726] Similar was the fate of Andrés González, parish priest of San Martin de Talavera, who was reconciled in the Time of Grace but, when imprisoned November 12, 1485, made a fuller confession, imploring mercy in terms betraying the utmost despair. There were but two adverse witnesses--evidently prisoners on trial--whose evidence was simply confirmatory of the confessions, but it sufficed. There seems to have been some delay in getting a bishop and an abbot to degrade him, for he was not burnt until August 17, 1486.[1727] Now in all these cases the confessions had amply admitted Judaism and the subsequent testimony was but surplusage in detail. This cruel practice goes far to explain the great number of burnings, in the early period, and it long continued to furnish victims. In 1531 the tribunal of Toledo condemned to reconciliation, confiscation and prison an old woman named Teresa de Lucena; for nearly fifty years she had been living a Catholic life, but in 1484 she had been reconciled on a confession which subsequent testimony showed had omitted some Jewish observances and had not named every one whom she had seen practice them.[1728]

This demand for an absolutely perfect confession exceeded that of the confessional, where forgotten sins are charitably held to be included. It explains why inquisitors labored so strenuously and often so cruelly to make the penitent remember and declare everything testified against him--what they termed satisfying the evidence. It is true that Simancas argues that defective memory may render confession imperfect, that he who admits himself to have been a heretic includes all heretical customs, and that the rigor of the law should not be visited on those who return to the Catholic faith, while Rojas condemns the severity of those who hold that a penitent not stating the full term of his heresy should be burnt.[1729] Yet the old sternness was held to be in vigor throughout the eighteenth century, and the only concession of the authorities seems to be that, if the penitent omits in his confession anything worthy of relaxation or any accomplices, when these have been proved by witnesses, he may have the chance of purging himself by torture.[1730]

Yet this ferocity had become rather academic than practical. As early as 1570 the Suprema ordered that, in all cases of diminucion, the matters suppressed or omitted were to be recorded in the process, submitted to the consulta de fe, and then, without taking action, to be sent to it for its decision.[1731] This can only have been for the purpose of mitigating the execution of the law without modifying it in principle. It remained nominally in force but I have met, in the later periods, with no case in which its extreme rigor was enforced. It was not an infrequent occurrence that reconciled penitents were found, by testimony in later trials, to have made imperfect confessions. Apparently a careful watch for this was maintained and, when it was discovered, they were tried again, but in the second half of the seventeenth century the sentences were remarkably mild--a few years of prison and sanbenito and exile or possibly a parading in vergüenza.[1732] With the recrudescence of persecution in the first half of the eighteenth century, there was greater severity--irremissible prison and sanbenito for life and, in a Barcelona case of 1723, a woman had two hundred lashes in addition.[1733]

INTENTION

Closely connected with diminucio was the confession of acts accompanied by a denial of intention. As we have seen, the Inquisition relied for proof on acts or words from which heretical belief was inferred, it being assumed that, after baptism, any one practising Judaic or Moslem rites or customs was an apostate. Many of these were wholly indifferent in themselves and their significance depended on the intention with which they were performed, so that it was not unusual for the accused to admit the acts while disclaiming knowledge of their religious character. He might confess avoidance of pork but allege that it disagreed with him; he might acknowledge to washing hands or changing linen but assert that it was for the sake of cleanliness; he might not deny uttering an heretical proposition but say that it was thoughtless or jocular. As human intentions are inscrutable, in such cases resort was inevitable to the universal solvent of judicial doubt--torture--at least in the later period. In the earlier time it was more in consonance with the swift justice then habitual to condemn him; such acts, it was argued, did not admit of doubt, they were in themselves sufficient proof and the accused was not to be allowed the privilege of torture.[1734] In the later period the authorities are not wholly unanimous, for the shades of guilt and the collateral circumstances varied so infinitely that a definite rule was difficult to frame. In general it may be summed up as admitted that for heretical acts, under the law, no plea of non-intention could be entertained, and that the offender must be relaxed, but in practice he had the benefit of torture; if he succumbed in it he was reconciled with confiscation, the galleys and perpetual prison; if he endured it without confession, according to the judicial logic of the age, he was not acquitted but was punished, less severely, for the suspicion. For words and opinions and heretical propositions, if serious, he was to be tortured on intention, but not for lesser offences, in which the appropriate penalty would be less grievous than the infliction of torture--yet one writer admits the use of torture when intention is denied in the widely current proposition that simple fornication is no sin. When, in these minor cases, torture was used, if, according to the legal phrase, it was endured sufficiently to purge the testimony, it became customary to suspend the case or to acquit the accused.[1735]

In the previous chapter (pp. 566, 567) there are one or two instructive cases as to the danger of construing Judaic observances as implying heretical intention. In the wider sphere of propositions, an illustrative instance is that of the Augustinian Pedro Retorni, tried in 1601, at Toledo, for denying the papal power to release souls from purgatory. He admitted it, but denied intention, asserting that he had only used the phrase in the course of an argument. The consulta de fe voted for abjuration de levi and a sharp reprimand, but the Suprema ordered that he should be threatened with torture up to the point of stripping him in the torture-chamber. He endured this without confessing, and the sentence of the consulta de fe was executed.[1736]

***

One of the most essential requisites to completeness of confession was the denunciation of all accomplices--that is, of all whom the penitent knew to be heretics or addicted to heretical practices. This, as we have seen, was required of all who came in under Edicts of Grace, and, in the Instructions of 1500, the inquisitor was ordered, when any one confessed, to examine him exhaustively as to what he knew of his parents, brothers, kindred and all other persons, and this evidence to be used against them was to be entered in registers apart from the personal confession.[1737] There was usually little hesitation on the part of the penitent to incriminate his family and friends, for they might, for all he knew, be themselves under trial and informing on him, so that any reticence on his part would convict him of being a diminuto with all its fateful consequences. The information thus obtained was registered with alphabetical indexes, so that the tribunals obtained a mass of evidence, against those who were Jews or Moors at heart, which largely explains the rapid extension of its activity. The value attached by the Inquisition to this source of information is expressed by the Suprema in its remonstrance, February 23, 1595, to Clement VIII against a jubilee indulgence. One of its chief arguments was that, as heretics were all allied and known to each other, the principal means of detecting them was through the confessions of those who were converted, while the absolution obtainable through the indulgence would release them from pressure and this mode of extirpating heresy would be lost.[1738]

In the formulas compiled for interrogating the accused, we find special stress laid on making those who confess enumerate all who had joined with them in belief and worship, or whom they knew to be heretics. These were recorded, one by one, the penitent being required to state all details concerning them, including personal descriptions, so that they could be tracked or, if there were several individuals of the same name, error could be avoided in identifying them.[1739] Any omissions in this exposed the penitent to severe punishment. In the Seville auto de fe of July 5, 1722, there appeared Melchor de Molina, who had been reconciled for Judaism in 1720. From evidence gathered in subsequent trials it appeared that he had not denounced all whom he knew; he was prosecuted anew and for this, as a fautor and protector of accomplices, his temporary prison was now made perpetual and irremissible.[1740]

DENUNCIATIONS OF ACCOMPLICES

Perhaps the most striking illustration of the effectiveness of the rule requiring denunciation of others is furnished by a Morisco of Valencia named Francisco Zafar y Ribera. He had been a Christian only in outward show, when a miraculous change of heart sent him on a pilgrimage to Monserrat, where he confessed his heresy to a priest. The good padre, unable to absolve him, referred him to the Barcelona tribunal, where, as a condition precedent, he was required to denounce all whom he knew to be Moors. The inquisitors, finding these to be Valencians, despatched him to Valencia, where he gave the names of no less than four thousand. He had been a wandering tailor and his acquaintance was extensive.[1741]

Few of those who fell into the hands of the Inquisition had the heroic courage of Manuel Díaz, a victim in the great Mexican auto de fe of December 8, 1596. Although ten of his fellow-sufferers had testified against him, he steadily denied his guilt and was proof against both the threats and the blandishments of the inquisitors. There was nothing to do but to burn him as a negativo impenitente, except that he might be used to inculpate others, and for this he was sentenced to torture in caput alienum. When this sentence was read to him he simply said that he was ready for them to do with him as they pleased. He was in his thirty-eighth year and a vigorous man, for he endured torture of unusual severity and, although he shrieked and begged to be put to death and called upon his tormentors to have mercy on his five children, he denied all knowledge of the Law of Moses and went to the stake without bearing witness against his fellows. This was held to aggravate his guilt and, in his sentence, he was stigmatized as a fautor and protector of Judaizing heretics.[1742]

If the inquisitorial records occasionally ennoble human nature with such examples of self-sacrifice, they more frequently exhibit it in its most despicable aspect, through the eagerness with which unfortunates, enfeebled and despairing in their protracted incarceration, seek to gain the favor of pitiless judges, or to render their confessions complete, by hastening to betray the confidences of their cell-companions, who incautiously relieve their hearts in careless talk with comrades in misery. The instances are innumerable in which the recipient of such avowals at once asks an audience and proves the sincerity of his own conversion by detailing what he had heard. There is a certain grim satisfaction, however, in noting that these revelations, however damaging to the victim, seem never to benefit the informer, for I have nowhere observed that they are accepted as attenuating circumstances to diminish his own punishment.

***

The time at which a confession was made was an important factor in determining the grade of punishment. At first these distinctions were crudely drawn, and there was hesitation in accepting confession as an infallible sign of repentance and conversion. The Instructions of 1484 merely say that, if it is made early and before publication of evidence, the regular penalty can be commuted to those who manifest contrition; if after publication and before definite sentence, the culprit is entitled to reconciliation with perpetual prison, but the inquisitors must determine whether he is sincerely converted, for if they have no hope of this they should relax him as an impenitent heretic. It seems to have been thought that, under these rules, too many fictitious converts escaped for, in 1498, the tribunals were warned to be cautious about admitting to reconciliation those who confessed after arrest, in view of the length of time since the establishment of the Inquisition.[1743] Thus, after arrest, confession and profession of conversion by no means saved the victim from the stake, but it depended upon the inquisitor's belief in his sincerity.

TIME OF CONFESSION

This excessive severity was moderated in time and there came to be established a kind of sliding scale which gauged sincerity by the period in the trial at which confession was made. An elementary form of this is displayed in a report of an auto de fe at Saragossa, June 5, 1585, where many Moriscos suffered. There is a group of ten of whom it is said that, as they confessed at the beginning of their trials, they were imprisoned for two, three or four years according to the gravity of their offences. Then there are others sent to the galleys for terms of from three to eight years, because their confessions were tardy or delayed to the end of their trials. As women were exempt from galley-service, this classification was impossible for them, but their terms of prison were regulated in the same way, and two of them had their sanbenitos removed at the close of the proceedings, because they had come forward and confessed before arrest, though after they had been testified against.[1744] This system was gradually perfected and, as presented by a writer of the middle of the seventeenth century, it appears that, if confession was made before the fiscal presented his formal accusation, the prison and sanbenito were inflicted for a very short time; if after accusation, they were for one or two years; if not till after publication of evidence, for the three years styled perpetual; if after torture, irremissible prison and, if able-bodied, the first three or five years to be spent in the galleys. This might be modified according to the manifestation of repentance and whether the culprit was a good confessor, both as to himself and others and, in the case of slaves, to avoid wronging the owner, scourging was substituted for prison and galleys.[1745] Subsequently this resource of scourging was freely employed for those who were not slaves, and, in the frequent autos of 1721 and the following years, the cases are numerous in which men and women are sentenced to two hundred lashes and irremissible prison and sanbenito as a special punishment for tardy confession.[1746]

Confession under torture was originally not regarded as voluntary and did not relieve from relaxation, showing that its use on a culprit who denied was either merely to gratify curiosity or to obtain information as to accomplices.[1747] Subsequent casuists, however, argued that the ratification of the confession, which was necessary after twenty-four hours, rendered it voluntary, and the more usual practice was to admit such cases to reconciliation. The Instructions of 1561 accept this, but warn inquisitors that they must observe much caution as to such cases and consider the quality of the heresies and whether the offender had simply been taught or had taught others.[1748] Still, this distinction was disregarded and Simancas tells us that the universal practice was to receive to reconciliation those who confessed under torture.[1749]

It can readily be conceived that those who confessed under the awe-inspiring formalities of the trial, with the pressure of prolonged imprisonment, the threat of torture and the fear of the stake, and whose admissions came gradually with greater or less fullness, as they vacillated between opposing influences, were not infrequently inconsistent and variable in their utterances. This was naturally provoking to the inquisitor and the vario who thus wavered cast doubt upon the sincerity of his repentance. He was admitted to reconciliation, indeed, but he paid the penalty of his vacillation in extra punishment. Thus, in the Murcia auto de fe of October 18, 1722, Francisco Henríquez de Medina y Melo, besides the regular penance, was sentenced to a hundred lashes "por vario en sus confesiones."[1750]

Even more provoking was the revocante, who withdrew or revoked a confession--an occurrence by no means rare, as might be expected from the methods employed to obtain it. The writers all treat this as impenitence, requiring relaxation in cases of formal heresy.[1751] In practice it was so regarded, as a general rule, but we find occasional exceptional cases, in which, however, care was usually taken to inflict heavier punishment than if the confession had been adhered to. In a Toledo auto of 1603, a Morisco, Andrés Muñoz, who had revoked his confession and consequently had been sentenced to relaxation, was saved by the Suprema, which ordered torture and, on his overcoming it, gave him five years of galleys and a heavy fine. Another case occurred in Granada, in 1593, where Jusuarte López, a Portuguese, confessed to Judaism and then, on finding that there was little evidence against him, revoked his confession and was condemned to five years of galleys, followed by irremissible prison and sanbenito.[1752]

REVOCATION

This apparent inconsistency arose from the infinite perplexities caused to the conscientious inquisitor by the arbitrary methods employed to induce or to extort confession. We obtain a glimpse into this from the remarks of an old inquisitor, about 1640, who, after laying down the rule of relaxation, proceeds to warn the judge that he should proceed with caution and consider the circumstances under which the confession had been made. I have known, he adds, the mere fear excited by the fiscal's formal demand for torture at the end of the accusation, bring a confession which necessitated torture to ascertain its truth. In 1628, I had a case in Saragossa, where a Frenchman voluntarily confessed that he had been a Lutheran and that, as such, he had been reconciled in Toledo. On being arrested he stated that his father had taught him Lutheranism and that he was reconciled in Toledo. After several audiences, he revoked this, and asserted that what he had confessed in Toledo was false; that there were no heretics where he came from and that his father had not taught him, and then in his defence he proved this and that both he and his father were Catholics. I voted for relaxation but the Suprema ordered torture; he overcame the torture and was finally sentenced to abjure de vehementi, to undergo public vergüenza and to perpetual banishment from Spain. If the revocation, the writer concludes, is of things of which there is semiplena proof [as of one witness] and it appears that it is made to protect accomplices and friends, then in rigor he is to be relaxed, but in these times relaxation is rare if he confesses enough to justify reconciliation.[1753]

That the terrors of the situation frequently reduced the prisoner to a mental condition that was practically irresponsible is illustrated in a trivial case concerning the popular assertion that simple fornication was no sin. In 1579 at Toledo, Diego Redondo of Prado, on trial for this, denied at first; then, when the accusation was read, with its customary demand for torture, he confessed; then, when the testimony of five witnesses was read in the publication, he revoked his confession, saying that it was made through fear; he did not know whether he had made it or not, but if he did so he was out of his senses; he remembered that he had said he knew not what, and had retracted it, and he did not remember, and this was what he said. This crazed incoherence puzzled the tribunal; it referred the case to the Suprema which charitably sentenced him to hear high mass at Prado, while his sentence was publicly read, and then to spend two years in exile.[1754]

There was another form of revocation which greatly scandalized the Inquisition in consequence of the reflection cast upon its methods. This was the assertion by penitents, subsequent to trial, that they were innocent and had only confessed through fear of the consequences of denial. It was sufficiently frequent to be included, in the Edicts of Faith, among the offences to be denounced by all cognizant of it. In the earliest Instructions of 1484 it is ordered that such offenders are to be held as impenitent and as fictitious converts and are to be prosecuted as such--which of course meant relaxation.[1755] This severity was moderated in time, but the offence was still punished in a manner to discourage it. In 1578, Niccolò Salari, who had been reconciled by the tribunal of Sardinia, had the imprudence to present to the Suprema a petition revoking his confession; he was tried for this in Toledo and escaped with two years' exile from Sardinia and the royal court.[1756]

DENIAL OF GUILT

A wholesale case of this kind, in Valencia, in 1540, aroused much excitement. A large number of prominent Conversos had been punished--some with relaxation--on the charge of holding conventicles in which Jewish fasts were observed and a crucifix was scourged. Subsequently they asserted that their confessions had been extorted by fear; popular feeling was excited and there was danger that the Inquisition would be seriously discredited, for ecclesiastics of high repute had recommended them to revoke their confessions and had joined in a letter on the subject to Inquisitor-general Tavera. The honor of the Inquisition was to be preserved at all hazards. Doctor Azeve was sent as a special commissioner to investigate, and his report increased the disquietude. To reinforce the Valencia tribunal, in May, 1541, Tavera urged Loazes of Barcelona to hasten thither and take charge of the matter, promising him support for his advancement. Then, in October, two members of the Suprema were sent there to assist and two additional inquisitors were put to work. The crisis was evidently alarming and there was ample for them all to do. Prosecutions were instituted against all who had revoked their confessions. They were kept segregated to prevent collusion and, as the secret prison of the tribunal was inadequate, the inquisitors and officials were turned out of their quarters and seven adjoining houses were hired and converted into gaols. What was the number involved does not appear, but a letter of November 26, 1543, mentions that twenty-two cases had been voted on, twenty more were in progress, on which they were working night and day and on feast days, and the remainder it was hoped to conclude so that all might be included in a single auto. The prisoners had no chance. A letter of the Suprema suggests that publication of evidence be omitted, because many of the witnesses had retracted their evidence and a knowledge of this would encourage the accused in their defence; the consultas de fe were to be packed, taking care to admit none who were favorable to them, and, under such conditions, the result was inevitable. Full details are lacking; we only know that autos de fe were held in which the culprits appeared for the second time, the sentences appear not to have been severe, but the honor of the Inquisition was vindicated.[1757]

***

The negativo, who persistently denied his guilt, in the face of competent testimony, was universally held to be a pertinacious impenitent heretic, for whom there was no alternative save burning alive, although, as Simancas says, he might protest a thousand times that he was a Catholic and wished to live and die in the faith.[1758] This was the inevitable logic of the situation, for otherwise the guilty could escape, at the mere cost of asserting innocence, and the effort to purify the land might as well be abandoned. There were, indeed, comparatively few who did not at first assert their orthodoxy, nor many who did not ultimately yield to the effective methods to obtain confession. Those who resisted to the end and went to the stake, asserting their Catholicism, were unquestionably good Christians who preferred the most frightful of deaths rather than admit that they had been heretics and confess and abjure heresies that they had never entertained, for if they were really guilty there was nothing more to be gained by denial than by the defiant avowal of their beliefs. Cases of this kind were by no means rare. There were five in Toledo between 1575 and 1606; there were three in a single auto in Granada in 1593; there was one in the great Madrid auto of 1680, and two in those of Majorca in 1691.[1759] The inquisitors themselves admitted the danger of burning the good Catholic, whose conscience would not permit him of accusing himself of heresy, and Peña considers at some length the question whether, under the pressure of approaching death by fire, it is licit to make a false confession. He concludes that this is in no sense permissible and he comforts the victim by assuring him that his constancy will win him the palm of martyrdom.[1760] The Church will never know how many martyrs of this kind the Inquisition furnished to its roll of uncanonized saints.

It required indeed persistent constancy for the true believer to persevere to the end in denial, for the Inquisition held open the door to repentance to the latest moment possible. If, at the auto de fe, a negativo asked for an audience, it was at once granted. He was removed from the staging, he had an opportunity to confess and profess conversion, his case was gone over, and such penance was imposed as was demanded by the gravity of the charges and the delay in the confession.[1761] Such cases were by no means rare and bear witness to the awful strain on the weakness of average human nature.

***

When all other means failed to obtain a satisfactory confession, including the denunciation of accomplices, there was always in reserve the potent persuasive of torture.

APPENDIX OF DOCUMENTS

I. EDICT OF FAITH.

As Published in Mexico, November 3, 1571.
(MS. penes me, from General Vicente Riva Palacio).

Nos, el Doctor Don Pedro Moya de Contreras, Inquisidor Apostolico etc. A todos los vecinos y moradores estantes y residentes en toda las ciudades, villas y lugares de los dichos arzobispados, obispados y distrito de cualquier estado, condicion, preeminencia ó dignidad que sean, exentos y non exentos, y á cada uno y cualesquier de vos á cuya noticia viniere lo contenido en esta nuestra carta en cualquier manera, Salud en Jesu Cristo que es verdadera salud y á los nuestros mandamientos que mas verdaderamente son dichos Apostolicos, firmemente obedecer, guardar y cumplir. Sabed que ... por parte del promotor fiscal de este Santo Oficio nos ha sido hecha relacion diciendo que por no se haber publicado carta de Edicto ni hecho visita general por el Santo Oficio de la Inquisicion en esta ciudad y arzobispado y distrito no habria venido á nuestra noticia muchos delitos que se habran cometido y perpetrado contra nuestra Santa Fé catolica y ley evangelica y estaban por punir y castigar y que de ello se seguia deservicio á nuestro Señor y gran daño y perjuicio á la religion cristiana. Por ende que nos pedia mandasemos hacer y hiciesemos la dicha Inquisicion y visita general leyendo para ello edictos publicos y castigando á los que se hallaren culpados, de manera que nuestra Santa Fé catolica siempre fuese ensalzada y aumentada, y por nos visto ser justo su pedimento y quisiendo proveer y remediar acerca de ello lo que conviene al servicio de nuestro Señor mandamos dar y dimos la presente para vos en la dicha razon. Por lo qual vos exortamos y requirimos que si alguno de vos supieredes ó hubieredes visto ú oido decir que alguna ó algunas personas, vivas, presentes ó ausentes ó difuntas ayan hecho ó dicho alguna cosa contra nuestra Santa Fé catolica y contra lo que está ordenado y establecido por la sagrada escritura y ley evangelica y por los sacros concilios y doctrina comun de los Santos y contra lo que tiene y enseña la Santa Iglesia catolica Romana, usos y ceremonias de ella, especialmente los que hubieren hecho ó dicho alguna cosa que sea contra los articulos de la fé, mandamientos de la ley y de la Iglesia, y de los santos sacramentos, ó si alguno hubiere hecho ó dicho alguna cosa en favor de la ley muerta de Moisen de los Judios ó hecho ceremonias de ella ó de la malvada secta de Mahoma ó de la secta de Martin Lutero y sus secuaces y de los otros hereges condenados por la Iglesia, y si saben que alguna ó algunas personas hayan tenido y tengan libros de la secta y opiniones del dicho Martin Lutero y sus secuaces, ó el Alcoran y otros libros de la secta de Mahoma, ó biblias en romance ó otros cualesquier libros de los reprobados por las censuras y catalogos dados y publicados por el santo oficio de la Inquisicion. Los cuales mandamos se traigan ante nos dentro del termino que de juso ira declarado. Y si saben que algunas personas no cumpliendo lo que son obligadas han dejado de decir y manifestar lo que saben, ó que hayan dicho y persuadido á otras personas que no vinieren á decir y manifestar lo que sabian tocante al Santo Oficio, ó que hayan sobornado testigos para tachar falsamente lo que han depuesto en el Santo Oficio, ó si algunas personas hubiesen depuesto falsamente contra otras por hacerles mal y daño y macular su honra, ó que hayan encubierto, receptado ó favorecido algunos hereges dandoles favor y ayuda ú ocultando ó encubriendo sus personas ó sus bienes, ó que hayan impedido ó puesto impedimiento por si ó por otros á la libre administracion del Santo Oficio de la Inquisicion para efecto que los tales hereges no pudiesen ser acusados ni castigados, ó hayan dicho palabras en desacato del Santo Oficio, oficiales y ministros, ó de lo que hayan quitado ó hecho quitar algunos Sambenitos de donde estaban puestos por el Santo Oficio, ó los que han sido reconciliados ó penitenciados por el Santo Oficio no han guardado ni cumplido las carcelerias y penitencias que les fueron impuestas, ó si han dejado de traer publicamente el habito de reconciliacion sobre sus vestiduras, ó si saben que alguno de los reconciliados ó penitenciados haya dicho publica ó secretamente que lo que confesó en el Santo Oficio ansi de si como de otras personas no fuere verdad, ni lo habia hecho ni cometido y que lo dijo por temor ó por otros respetos, ó que hayan descubierto el secreto que les fué encomendado, ó si saben que alguno haya dicho que los relajados por el Santo Oficio fueron condenados sin culpa y que murieron martires, ó si saben que algunos que hayan sido reconciliados ó hijos ó nietos de condenados por el crimen de la heregia hayan usado de las cosas que les son prohibidas por derecho comun, leyes y pregmaticas de los Reinos é instrucciones del Santo Oficio, asi como si han sido corregidores, alcaldes, jueces, notarios, regidores, jurados, mayordomos, alcaides, maestre salas, fieles publicos, mercaderes, escribanos, abogados, procuradores, secretarios, contadores, concilleres, tesoreros, medicos, cirujanos, sangradores, boticarios, corredores, cambiadores, cogedores, arrendadores de rentas, alguaciles, ó hayan usado de otros oficios publicos ó de honra por si ó por interpositas personas, ó que se hayan hecho clerigos ó que tengan algun dignidad eclesiastica ó seglar ó insignias de ella, ó hayan traido armas, seda, oro, plata, corales, perlas, chamelotes, paño fino ó cabalgado á caballo, ó si alguno tubiere habilitacion para poder usar de los dichos oficios ó de las cosas prohividas, lo traiga y presente ante nos en el termino aqui contenido. Ansi mismo mandamos á cualesquier escribanos ó notarios ante quien hayan pasado ó esten cualesquier provanzas, dichos de testigos, autos y procesos de algunos de los dichos crimenes y delitos en esta nuestra carta referidos ó de otro alguno tocante á heregia, lo traigan exhiben y presenten ante nos originalmente, y á las personas que supieren ó hubieren oido decir en cuyo poder estan los tales procesos y denunciaciones lo vengan á decir y manifestar ante nos, y por la presente prohibimos y mandamos á todos los confesores y clerigos, presbiteros y religiosos y seglares no absuelvan á las personas que algunas cosas de lo en esta carte contenido supieren sino antes los remitan ante nos por cuanto la absolucion de los que ansi hubieren incurrido nos es reservada, y ansi la reservamos. Lo cual los unos y los otros ansi hagan y cumplan so pena de excomunion, y mandamos que para que mejor se sepa la verdad y se guarde el secreto, los que alguna cosa supieredes y entendieredes ó hayais visto ó entendido ú oido en cualquiera manera sabido de lo que en esta carta contenido, no lo comuniqueis con persona alguna eclesiastica ni seglar, sino solamente lo vengais diciendo y manifestando ante nos con todo el secreto que ser pueda, y por el mejor modo que os pareciere por que quando lo dijeredes y manifestaredes se vera y acordara si es caso que el Santo Oficio deba conocer. Por ende, por el tenor de la presente vos mandamos en virtud de Santa obediencia y so pena de excomunion mayor, trina canonica monitione premissa, que dentro de seis dias primeros siguientes despues que esta nuestra carta fuere leida y publicada y de ella supieredes en cualquier manera, los quales os damos y asignamos por tres plazos y termino, cada dos dias por un termino y todos seis dias por tres terminos y el ultimo perentorio, vengais y parezcais ante nos personalmente en la sala de nuestra audiencia á decir y manifestar lo que supieredes, hubieredes hecho, visto hacer ó decir cerca de las cosas arriba dichas y declaradas ó otras cualesquier cosas de cualquier calidad que sean tocantes á nuestra Santa Fé catolica y al Santo Oficio, ansi de vivos, presentes, ausentes como de difuntos, por manera que la verdad se sepa y los malos sean castigados y los buenos y fieles cristianos conocidos y honrados y nuestra Santa Fé catolica aumentada y ensalzada. Y por que lo susodicho venga á noticia de todos y ninguno de ello pueda pretender ignorancia se manda publicar. Dado en Mexico, tres dias del mes de Noviembre de 1571 años. El Doctor Moya de Contreras. Por mandado del S. Inquisidor, Pedro de los Rios.

II. CONFESSIONAL LETTER OF ABSOLUTION ISSUED BY THE PAPAL PENITENTIARY, DECEMBER 4, 1481.

(Archivo General de Simancas, Patronato Real; Inquisicion, Legajo unico, fol. 19).

Julianus miseratione divina Episcopus Sabinensis dilectis in Christo Francisco Ferdinandi de Sevilla et Blancæ Ferdinandi ejus uxori ac Floræ Martin ejusdem Francisci matri, civibus Ispalensibus, Salutem in Domino. Sedes Apostolica pia mater de vestro et aliorum Christifidelium salute sollicita, libenter vobis illa concedit per quæ conscientiæ pacem et animæ salutem Deo propitio consequi valeatis. Nos igitur auctoritate domini Papæ cujus poenitentiariæ curam gerimus, et de ejus speciali mandato super hoc vivæ vocis oraculo nobis facto, devotioni vestræ concedimus quatenus liceat vobis ydoneum et discretum presbyterum sæcularem vel cujusvis ordinis regularem in confessorem eligere qui vos et quemlibet vestrum, detestatis prius in ejus manibus secrete apostasiæ secta, superstitionibus et hæresis reatibus ac omnibus hæreticis reatibus, etiam si de præmissis diffamati, suspecti, convicti, probationibus superati, aut per hæreticæ pravitatis inquisitores seu loci ordinarium vocati et apprehensi ac post eorum monitiones deliqueritis, aut etiam quod alios hujusmodi criminum complices non manifestaveritis censuris ecclesiasticis illaqueati et ut tales publicati, ac in eisdem censuris per annum et ultra permanseritis, vel ut hæretici diffamati perseveraveritis, aut alias contra vos, præmissorum occasione, quomodolibet sit processum, a dictis sectæ superstitionibus reatibus et censuris ac excessibus hujusmodi, etiam si ritus et ceremonias judaicas observando et illos vel illas alios docendo, et ab orthodoxæ fidei credulitate recadendo alterius hæresis et apostasiæ notam incurreritis etiam a suis errorum [sic] anathematizationis et maledictionis æternæ censuris et poenis in tales tam per processus apostolicos quam alias a jure etiam per inquisitores prædictos et suos assessores et ordinarios vel alias quomodolibet latis et promulgatis præter præmissa incursis, absolvat in forma ecclesiæ consueta et injungat vobis pro modo culpæ poenam salutarem et secretam, ac a vobis omnem infamiæ maculam omnesque alias juris poenas etiam corporis afflictivas absolvat et totaliter remittat, et vos ad coetum christifidelium et sanctæ matris ecclesiæ necnon unitatem catholicæ ecclesiæ, ac in pristinum et purum statum in quo eratis antequam in prædictos excessus prolapsi fuissetis auctoritate et mandato prædictis reponat, reintegrat, restituat et reducat, contradictores per censuras ecclesiasticas auctoritate et mandato prædictis compescat, et omnibus juris remediis opportunis vobis assistat. Datum Romæ apud Sanctum Petrum sub sigillo officii poenitentiariæ, II. Non. Decembris, Pontificatus domini Sixti papa IIII. Anno duodecimo.

III. REVOCATION OF LETTERS OF ABSOLUTION AND OF EXEMPTIONS, MAY 17, 1488.

(Archivio Vaticano, Reg. 686 (Innoc. VIII) fol. 103.--Bulario de la Orden de Santiago, Tom. I. fol. 94).

Innocentius Episcopus Servus Servorum Dei dilectis filiis universis et singulis locorum ordinariis et inquisitoribus hæreticæ pravitatis in regnis et dominiis charissimi in Christo filii Ferdinandi Regis et charissimæ in Christo filiæ Helisabeth Reginæ Castiliæ et Legionis illustrium salutem et apostolicam benedictionem. Quia secut accepimus quamplurimi hæresis et fidei apostasiæ crimine polluti infra limites vestræ jurisdictionis degentes ut criminum hujusmodi publicam juxta sanctorum patrum decreta abjurationem vestramque jurisdictionem evitent, tam a fel. record. Sixto Papa iiii. quam a nobis super eorum exemptione a potestate et jurisdictione vestra necnon abjurationibus errorum suorum aliter quam in forma juris faciendis, ac alias diversimode literas obtinuerunt, quibus obstantibus quæ vestro incumbunt officio quo ad eos exequi hactenus non potuistis nec potestis non sine animarum eorundem periculo, orthodoxæ fidei detrimento, mali exempli pernicie et scandalo plurimorum. Ne igitur hac via tantæ pietatis officio tam grande impedimentum præstetur et ut commissi vobis officii debitum liberius et plenius exercere possitis felicis recordationis Clementis Papæ iiii. et aliorum prædecessorum nostrorum vestigiis inhærentes, motu proprio et ex certa scientia et mera deliberatione vobis committimus et mandamus ut quoscunque de hæresis et apostasiæ criminibus hujusmodi culpabiles suspectos vel diffamatos ac fautores receptatores et defensores eorum in Regnis et dominiis prædictis qui hactenus hujusmodi exemptionis privilegia et inquisitionis de eorum excessibus commissionem et super admittendis eorum abjurationibus aliter quam in forma juris literas hujusmodi a nobis seu Sixto prædecessore præfato obtinuerunt ad abjurandos errores eorum publice servata forma juris etiam si quovismodo relapsi dici possent infra mensem postquam presentes literæ fuerint in cathedrali et parrochiali ecclesia eorum publicatæ ita ut de illis nequeant ignorantiam allegare, recipiatis et admittatis perinde acsi relapsi non forent. Mense vero prædicto elapso, Deum præ oculis habentes contra eos et quoscunque alios ejusdem criminis reos, juxta sacrorum canonum instituta procedatis, commissionibus hujusmodi ac literis ad alios judices directis et quas dirigi contingat, necnon privilegiis quibuscunque personis cujusvis dignitatis, gradus, ordinis vel conditionis existant, etiam si Cistercientium Prædicatorum et Minorum aut alterius cujusvis ordinis et religionis fuerint, sub quacunque verborum expressione et cum quibusvis etiam motus proprii et certæ scientiæ ac plenitudinis potestatis aliisve fortioribus et efficacioribus clausulis etiam derogatoriorum derogatoriis concessis et concedendis, que omnia cum inde secutis pro infectis haberi volumus, necnon constitutionibus et ordinationibus apostolicis cæterisque contrariis nonobstantibus quibuscunque. Datum Romæ apud Sanctum Petrum, anno incarnationis Dominicæ millesimo quadringentesimo octuagesimo octavo, sexto decimo Kalendis Junii, pontificatus nostri anno quarto.

Gratis de mandato S. D. n. papæ. F. de VALENTIA.

IV. PETITION OF GERONIMO ZURITA

(Archivo de Simancas, Inquisicion, Sala 40, Libro 4, fol. 239).
Illmo y Rr^{mo} Señor:

El contador Geronimo Zurita dice que va en veinte y quatro años que serbe en el sancto officio de la Inquisicion: los doce serbio en Consejo de la general Inquisicion de secretario y va en doce que tiene a su cargo la contaduria general de los Inquisiciones de la corona de Aragon y en este tiempo a rrecibido las quentas de la Inquisicion de Sicilia que avia veinte años que no se rrecibian y se fenecieron, harto beneficio de aquella Inquisicion por estar las quentas de los receptores passados muy ofuscados y en muy mala orden, como es notorio en aquella Inquisicion, y assimismo ha recibido y fenecido las otras quentas questan a su cargo con toda la justicia y cuidado posible y con menos salario que se dio al contador mosen Granada que no entendio en las quentas de la Inquisicion de Cecilia, y en todo esto se a ocupado con grande trabajo y fatiga de su persona y con gastar su patrimonio sin recibir merced ni remuneracion ninguna de sus servicios. Suplico a vuestra señoria Illma que considerando que a enbejecido en este oficio y no espera por ello otras mercedes y que a dejado otros caminos adonde se le ofrecian mayores esperanças y mas ciertos de poder medrar y todo lo pospuesto por acabar en servicio del sancto oficio se le haga merced de dalle por aljunto en el dicho oficio de contador á miguel çurita su hijo al qual aunques mozo de diez y ocho años es bien abil y muy bien dotrinado y inclinado con admitirle en el con mayor aficion se dispondra a exercitarse e yndustrarse en todo lo que concierne al dicho oficio y el dicho contador empleara lo que le queda de la vida en su cargo.

***

En la ciudad de toledo a dos de mayo de quinientos y sesenta años vista esta piticion presentado por geronimo çorita contador general por el rr^{mo} señor don fernando de baldes arçobispo de sebilla enquisidor general y por los señores don diego de los cobos obispo de avila y licenciado valtodano y doctores andres peres y simancas y hernan peres del consejo de la santa general Inquisicion dixeron que teniendo el dicho miguel çurita su hijo hedad y la abilidad que se rrequiere para serbir el dicho oficio de contador se terna consideracion a lo mucho y con el cuidado y fidelidad quel dicho geronimo çurita y juan garcia su suegro an serbido en el sancto oficio para le hazer la merced que suplica. Lo que paso ante mi pedro de tapia secretario del dicho consejo.--Pedro de Tapia.

V. DETAILS OF THE ORGANIZATION OF THE INQUISITION OF MURCIA, AS REPORTED TO THE SUPREMA IN 1746.

(Archivo de Simancas, Inquisicion de Corte, Legajo 359, vol. 3).

VI. COMMISSION OF AN INQUISITOR

(Archivo de Simancas, Inquisicion, Libro 8, fol. 108)

Nos, Don Juan Tabera, por la miseracion divina Cardenal en la Sancta Iglesia de Roma, titulo de Sant Juan ante Portam Latinam, Arzobispo de Toledo, primado de las Españas, Chanceller mayor de Castilla, gobernador de estos Reinos e inquisidor apostolico general contra la heretica pravedad y apostasia en todos los Reinos y señorios de sus magestades etcetera.

Confiando de las letras y recta consciencia de vos el Doctor Blas Ortiz, canonigo de la sancta Iglesia de Toledo, y que sois tal persona que bien y fielmente y diligentemente hareis lo que por nos vos fuere cometido y encomendado, por el tenor de la presente, por la auctoridad apostolica á nos concedida de que en esta presente usamos, vos facemos, constituimos, creamos e deputamos inquisidor apostolico contra la dicha heretica pravedad y apostasia en el Reino de Valencia y su distrito y jurisdiccion y os damos poder y facultad simul et in solidum con el venerable Doctor Juan Gonzalez, inquisidor del dicho partido para que podades inquirir e inquirades contra todas y qualesquiera personas ansi hombres como mugeres, vivos y defunctos, absentes e presentes de qualquier estado, condicion, prerrogativa, preeminencia y dignidad que sean, exentos y no sean exentos, vecinos y moradores que son ó han sido en las ciudades, villas y lugares del dicho Reino de Valencia y su distrito que se hallaren culpantes sospechosos e infamados en el dicho delito y crimen de heregia y apostasia y contra todos los fautores, defensores y receptatores de ellos y para que podais facer y fagais contra ellos y contra cada uno de ellos vuestros procesos en forma debida de derecho segun los sacros canones lo disponen y para que podais tomar y rescibir qualesquiera procesos y causas pendientes sobre los dichos crimenes ó qualquiera de ellos ante qualquiera inquisidor que haya sido en el dicho partido en el punto e estado en que estan y continuarlos y facer y determinar en ellos lo que fuere justicia y para que podades á los dichos culpantes encarcelar, penitenciar, punir y castigar y si de justicia fuere relaxarlos al brazo seglar y facer todos los otros casos al dicho oficio de inquisidor tocantes y pertenecientes, para lo qual todo lo que dicho es y cada una cosa y parte della con todas sus incidencias y dependencias, anexidades y conexidades vos damos poder cumplido y cometemos nuestras veces fasta que nos especial y expresamente las revoquemos. En testimonio de lo qual mandamos dar y dimos la presente firmada de nuestro nombre y refrendada del secretario infrascripto.

Dada en la villa de Madrid á cinco dias del mes de Abril de mil quinientos quarenta años.
J. CARDINALIS.
Por mandado de su ilustrisima y reverendisima señoria.
JERONIMO ZURITA, secretario.
Con señales de loe señores Licenciado Aguirre y Obispo de Badajoz y Prior de Roncesvalles.

VII. PERSONNEL OF THE INQUISITION IN 1746

VIII. CERTIFICATE OF LIMPIEZA.
(Archivo de Simancas, Regístro de Genealogias, No. 916, fol. 12).

  D. Cristóval de Cos y Vivero, Secretario etc. Certifico: Que por el Exmo Señor Obispo Inquisidor General se hizo gracia de pruebas para Ministro Oficial del Santo Oficio al Exmo Señor Don Carlos Miguel Fizt James Stuart, Silva, Stolberg y Palafox, Duque de Vervich y Alba, y la de que se le reciviesen en esta Corte por Patria comun con dispensa de la extrangería de su Padre y Abuela Paterna y teniendose por bastantes las partidas que acompaña legalizadas, en su consecuencia por mandado de los señores del expresado consejo se reciviéron dichas ynformaciones al tenor de las Memorias de sus Padres y Abuelos que presentó y es del modo siguiente.--Arbol genealogico del Exmo Señor Duque de Vervich y Alba D. Carlos Miguel. El Exmo Senor Don Carlos Miguel Fizt James Stuart, Silva, Stolberg, Palafox, Duque de Vervich y Alba, Marques del Carpio, Alguacil mayor de la Santa Inquisicion de Córdova, nació en Madrid el año de 1794.--PADRES. El Exmo Señor Don Jacobo Felipe Carlos María Fizt James Stuart y Stolberg, Duque de Vervich y Liria, Grande de España de primera clase, nació en Paris el año de 1773, Difunto. La Exma Señora Doña María Teresa de Silva y Palafox nació en Madrid, año de 1772.--ABUELOS PATERNOS. El Exmo Señor Don Carlos Fernández Fizt James Stuart, Duque de Vervich y Liria, Grande de España de primera clase, nació en Liria año de 1752, Difunto. La Exma Señora Doña Carolina Augusta de Stolberg, Princesa de Stolberg nació en la Aldea de Geudem de Alemania año de 1755.--ABUELOS MATERNOS. El Exmo Señor Don Pedro de Alcántara Fadrique Fernández de Hijar, Silva, Duque de Hijar, Grande de España de primera clase, Presidente del Real Consejo de las Ordenes, Difunto, nació en Villaruvia de los Ojos de Guadiana año de 1741. La Exma Señora Doña Rafaela de Palafox Croy de Habre nació en Ariza año de 1744, Difunta.--Como agente de la casa de su Exmo presento testimoniadas las partidas de bautismo de los Señores comprehendidos en el arbol genealogico que antecede, cuya procedencia de Cristianos viejos, limpios de toda mala raza por notoriedad certifico y juro en Madrid á 26 de Junio de 1815.--Miguel Antonio Forrent.

  Y executadas las referidas ynformaciones en esta Corte por patria comun con arreglo á las referidas gracias y segun practica del Santo Oficio; vistas por los Señores del mencionado Consejo, por su auto que proveyeron con fecha de este dia los aprovaron y dieron por bastantes para que el nominado Exmo Señor Don Carlos Miguel Fizt James Stuart puede ser y sea Ministro oficial del Santo Oficio segun mas por menor resulta de dichas ynformaciones que por ahora quedan originales en la Secretaria de mi cargo á que me remito. Y para que conste donde convenga, en virtud de orden del propio consejo doy la presente al susodicho Exmo Señor Don Carlos Miguel Fizt James Stuart, sellada con el sello de la General Inquisicion en Madrid á veinte y quatro dias del mes de Mayo de mil ochocientos diez y seis.--D. Cristóval de Cos y Vivero.[1762]

IX. RECEIPT, MARCH 30, 1524, BY THE WIFE OF A RECONCILED HERETIC FOR HER DOWER, FROM THE CONFISCATED ESTATE.
(Archivo Histórico Nacional, Inquisicion de Valencia, Legajo 371.)

  Sea a todos manifiesto que yo Dona Beatrix Despuch y de Sant Boy, muger que soy de Pere Alcañiz y presente aquel y de voluntad de aquel de grado y de mi cierta ciencia otorgo haber habido y en poder mio recevido en la forma infrascrita de vos el magnifico Cristoval de Medina receptor de los bienes confiscados por el crimen de la heregia y apostasia en el Sancto Oficio de la Inq^{n} de Valencia que soys presente, es a saber treynta y dos libras siete sueldos moneda reales de Valencia, los quales me aveys dado y pagado á toda mi voluntad en paga rata de las cantidades que yo tengo de haber y cobrar por razon de mi dote in virtud de una sentencia dada por el muy R^{do} Doctor Micer Melchior Esteve teniente de Inquisidor y Juez subdelegado de bienes confiscados en dicho Sancto Oficio, que dada fue en veynte y dos dias del mes de Decembre proximo pasado de mil quinientos veinte y tres que pasó ante el discreto Francisco Mudarra Notario Escribano de la Audiencia y Judicatura de dichos bienes confiscados y por las causas y razones en la dicha Sentencia contenidas.

  El modo de la paga de las dichas treinta y dos libras siete sueldos de la dicha moneda es este, que de mi voluntad os las reteneys por consemblante cantidad que yo os debia de los precios y bienes muebles por mi comprados del inventario y secresto de dicho Pero Alcañiz mi marido como parece por acto recebido por el Notario infrascrito á treinta dias del mes de Junio del presente año (sic) la cual confesion y apoca otorgo y hago sin su perjuicio de mis derechos por quanto yo pretendo que los dichos bienes o parte de ellos que yo compré son mios propios y de los contenidos en el pagamiento que el dicho Pere Alcañiz mi marido me fizo, e porque es verdad por tanto renunciando toda excepcion de frao ó de engaño otorgo y fago vos la presente apoca en poder del Notario infrascrito que fecha fué en la Ciudad de Valencia á treinta dias del mes de Marzo del año del nacimiento de nuestro Salvador Jesu Cristo de mil quinientos veinte y quatro. + (se) ñal de mi la dicha Doña Beatriz Despuch y de Sant Boy que las dichas cosas otorgo y firmo.

Testimonio que fueron presentes á las dichas cosas los honrados Fran^{co} Mudarra Not^{o}, y Martin de Durango Scribiente y Visitadores de Valencia.

X. ABSTRACT OF PARTIAL STATEMENT OF RECEIPTS CHARGED AGAINST THE CANON JOAN DE ASTORGA, RECEIVER OF CONFISCATIONS IN VALENCIA FOR THE YEAR 1493.[1763]

(Archivo Historico Nacional, Inquisicion de Valencia, Legajo 383)

February 6. From Violant Domenega, for a loan made by her stepmother Violant Domenega, relaxed, to--Jordi on a pair of gold bracelets, in which loan she had an interest of 3 ducats 200s.

From the Mallorquin sempstress due to the said Domenega 8.8d.

February 6. From Violant Domenega twenty gold coins hidden by her stepmother in a saddle, amounting in all to 319.--

April 19. Confiscation of Isabel Amorosa, relaxed. Sale by auction of her effects, as per inventory 2.10

May 2. Confiscation of Master Anthony Tristan. Sale by auction of his effects as per inventory 137.--

Confiscation of Master Johan Aragones and his wife. Sale by auction of his effects as per inventory. (Sum not stated.)

Sept. 10. Sale by auction to Gaspar Ferroll of a house of said Juan Aragones1100.-- Sale by auction to Simon Sanchez of adjoining house1200.-- Valuation under commands of the king of three fields and two vineyards of Juan Aragones, after deducting incumbrances, the fields at 37 libras and the vineyards at 53, in all equivalent to 1800.--July 23 Confiscation of Luis Sarinyana. A house valued by experts at 45 libras. As the king had made a grant to Joanot and Francisco Sarinyana of 50l. out of the estate, the house was made over to them. Confiscation of Galceran Nadal, of Xativa. Sale to Luis Costa of a house in Xativa, subject to a censo of 100 sueldos per annum 3.-- Confiscation of Francisca Costa, of Xativa. Sale to Guillen Murta of a mulberry plantation, Subject to a censo of 32 sueldos10.--Aug. 9. Confiscation of Daniel Zapata. In virtue of a royal provision, composition made with his wife, Leonor Zapata of his whole property for the sum of 5000 sueldos, of which 1500 are paid down, 1500 to be paid in six months, and 2000 in one year, the said Leonor having brought suit for her dower and other large sums, all of which she renounced1500.-- Confiscation of Manuel Zapata. Received from the heirs of Blay de Comes andMaria Vizcaina a balance due to said Manuel 80.--February 13. Confiscation of Bernat Mancip relaxed. Sold by auction to Juan Guillen Catalan a censal on the corporation of Valencia of 6000s. principal and 400 interest, payable Sept. 14 in each year. With accrued interest for 5 months and one day 6205.7-- Sold to the heirs of Mosen Juan de Peñarosa a censal on the towns of Xerica, las Barraguas and Pina, of 15000 sueldos principal and 1000 interest, payable May 27. With accrued interest 15211.1 Sold by auction to Violant Catalá, a censal on the corporation of Valencia, of 7500 sueldos principal and 500 interest, payable Oct. 2. With accrued interest for 4 months and 12 days 7733.4February 18. Sold to Cristobal de Basurto two censales on the town of Xativa, one of 6000 s. principal and 375 interest, payable October 29, the other of 5000s. principal and 312s. 6d. interest payable Nov. 8. with accrued interest 11251.10February 23. Sold by auction to the Caballero Johan Luis de Vilarasa three censales of the said Bernat Mancip, one on the city of Valencia, of 13,000 s. principal and 1056 s. 8d. interest, payable July 14. One on the kingdom of Valencia of 13,200 s. principal and 880 interest, payable March 30. Another on the same of 11,250 s. principal and 650 interest, payable Sept. 7. Proceeds of all three, with accrued interest.700 libras, 5s.[1764]

February 21. Confiscation of Brigida, wife of BernatCortelles. Received of said Bernat on account of the 1200 sueldos which he has to pay for the dower of said Brigida 400s.February 8.

Confiscation of Miguel de Prochita. Rented to Franchet Quach a house of said Miguel de Prochita for twelve years at 12 libras per annum and received 6 libras 120s. February 11. Confiscation of Miguel Andreu Rosell relaxed. Received of Francisco Berdum a debt due to Rosell 32.--September 5. House sold to Gabriel Andreu Rosell, subject to a censal of 7000 sueldos, also to 500 and 400s. chargeable on it and to all other charges 10.--

XI. KING FERDINAND TO TORQUEMADA, MARCH 30, 1498.

(Archivo General de Simancas, Consejo de la Inquisicion, Libro I)

Venerable y devoto padre Prior. A causa de mi yda que en breves dias ha de ser para Zaragoza, Dios mediante, embie á mandar á mi Receptor Royz que diesse mucha priessa en acabar una escalera e las cavallerizas e otras cosas muy necesarias para mi aposentamiento en el palacio Real de la Aljaferia, y andando ya la obra quasi en acabamiento á causa de las excomunicaciones que le haveys embiado me escrive que ha parado la obra. E tambien diz que no pagare á los prior e frayles de Santa Engracia aquellos quatro mil sueldos que en cada un año les he yo mandado pagar en aquella receptoria fasta que yo les haya provehido en otra parte, lo qual fize por no les traspasar luego los censales de la Inquisicion, porque despues de remediado de otra parte los censales quedassen al Oficio. Cierto tengo desto algun enojo. E fuera razon que se mirara mejor en poner mas limitadas las excomunicaciones para que se salvara á lo menos lo que sea á mi servicio, ha respeto specialmente que en aquella receptoria, á Dios gracias, todos los oficiales stan bien pagados e á nadie se deve salario ni otra cosa alguna, y desto es razon que vos y estos perlados que con vos residen vos contenteys. E que no se ponga excomunicacion pues no hay necesidad para las poner porque seria forzado de otra manera proverlo. E aunque sobre ello he aquí fablado con el Obispo de Lugo[1765] para que lo remediase no lo ha querido fazer. Por ende he acordado de vos escrevir la presente por la qual vos ruego y encargo que sin dilacion alguna alceys y fagays alçar qualquiera excomunicacion con que se haya puesto a aquel receptor, pues todos los oficiales como dicho es, stan bien pagados en aquella Inquisicion, á Dios gracias, no deve nada á nadie. Y en esto no se ponga dilacion o dificultad alguna, porque havria enojo della, allende que no lo permitiera. Luego me respondet con este mensajero que por sola esta causa vos le embio. Dada en Alcalá de Henares á xxx dias de Marzo de xcviii.-- Yo el Rey.

XII. CEDULA OF KING FERDINAND, FEBRUARY 23, 1510, ON THE DIMINISHED RECEIPTS FROM CONFISCATIONS.

(Archivo General de Simancas, Inquisicion, Libro III, fol. 61).

EL REY.

A todos los receptores que soys o fueredes de los bienes confiscados e aplicados a la camara e fisco por el delito de la heregia en todas las ynquisiciones destos reynos e señorios e a cada uno de vos a quien esta mi cedula fuese mostrada o su traslado señado de escrivano publico, por quanto yo soy informado que en las dichas inquisiciones tiene alguna necesidad a causa de los pocos bienes que se confiscan e si se cumpliesen primero las mercedes que yo he hecho e fago en los dichos bienes los oficiales e menistros de las dichas ynquisiciones no serian pagados de sus salarios e ahuiran dexar el oficio de lo qual seria dios muy deservido, por ende yo vos mando que agora ni de aqui adelante no cumplays ningunas mercedes que yo aya echo e hago de los dichos bienes confiscados hasta que primeramente sean pagados los ynquisidores e oficiales e menistros de las dichas ynquisiciones de sus salarios e ayudas de costa que yo les mandare dar, no embargante qualesquier cartas o mandamientos que yo o les ynquisidores generales ayamos hecho e hicieremos en contrario e sy algunas cedulas o provisiones de merced se vos presentasen las obedeced e quanto al cumplimiento consultareys conmigo e con los dichos generales ynquisidores que asi cumple al servicio de dios e mio e los unos ni los otros non fagades ende al por alguna manera so pena de la mi merced. Fecha en la villa de Madrid a 23 dias del mes de hebrero de quinientos e diez años. Y esto se entiende con tanto que primeramente se paguen las deudas que deva el oficio antes que salarios ni otra cosa alguna. Yo el Rey. Por mandado de su alteza Juan Roiz de Calcena. Ya señalada por los del consejo de la ynquisicion.

XIII. RECITAL OF EDICT OF GRACE IN CIUDAD REAL, 1483.

(Archivo histórico nacional, Inquisicion de Toledo, Legajo 139, n. 145).

Como sobre la fama publica e notoria que en este Ciudad Real avia que muchos de los que estavan con nombre de Cristianos e en posesion de tales hereticavan e guardavan la ley de Moyses, ovimos nuestra informacion de algunas personas, por do nos constó la dicha fama ser verdad y que muchos de los vezinos e moradores de la dicha ciudad seguian y solemnizaban e guardavan en quanto en ellos era e pudia la ley de Moyses, haciendo sus ceremonias, siguiendo sus antiquos ritos Judaycos, e queriendo usar con ellos e cada uno dellos de clemencia e piedad dimos e descernimos nuestra carta de cita e hedicto para que todas las personas desta dicha Ciudad e su tierra que en la dicha eregia de seguir la ley de Moyses ubiesen caido e incurrido, que dentro de, treynta dias primeras siguientes veniesen ante nos confesando sus herrores e abjurando e renunciando e partiendo de si la dicha eregia e abrasandose con nuestra santa madre la Iglesia e ayuntamiento de los fieles Cristianos, e que los recibiriamos usando con ellos de toda piedad e misericordia que pudieremos, e non solamente en el dicho termino de los treynte dias mas por otros treynta despues los esperamos e rescibimos todos los que quisieran venir a confesar y dezir sus pecados cerca de la dicha heregia, e pasado el dicho termino de los dichos sesenta dias e mas tiempo, contra los que non venieran ni parescieran, en especial contra los que huyeron por themor de la dicha nuestra Inquisicion, de los quales teniamos informacion e eran testiguados cerca de nos, e siendo requeridos por nuestro promotor fiscal, avida nuestra informacion sumaria de la fuga e ausentamiento dellos e de la dicha heregia que avian cometido, mandamos dar nuestra carta de llamamiento e hedicto contra las personas sospechosas e infamadas e que si se ausentaron. E porque entre ellas nos consta ser muy publico e notorio Sancho de Ciudad e Mari Dias su muger etc.

XIV. CONFESSION UNDER EDICT OF GRACE, OCTOBER 9, 1483, OF MARIA GONSALES, SUBSEQUENTLY BURNT IN AUTO DE FE OF FEBRUARY 23, 1484.

(Archivo histórico nacional, Inquisicion de Toledo, Legajo 154, n. 375).

Maria Gonsales, muger de Juan Panpano, vecino de la collacion de Santiago, con mi omill reverencia, paresco ante vos e mi encomiendo a vuestra merced, ante lo qual paresco con gran arrepentimiento e contricion de mis pecados, e digo que puede aver vjx o cinco (sic) años que yo case con el e al tiempo que con el case era buen xpristiano, e en este tiempo puede aver dies e seys años, poco mas o menos, quel tomo otra opinion de se mudar de bevir en la santa fe catolica e faser cerimonias judaicas, e de esta cabsa porque yo non queria seguir su ayuno malo quel levava me dio muchas feridas e muchas contra mi voluntad que non filase el sabado e guysase de comer el viernes para el sabado e algunas veces comia dello e otras non queria comerlo, porque mi padre syempre vivio e murio conmo buen xpristiano, loqual me duro faser seis o syete años, e porque yo sabia que non traya carne de la carniceria non la queria comer, e de esta cabsa por muchas feridas que me dio algunas ves me la fasia comer e yo ha dies años que bivo syn el porquel se fue desta cibdad e yo nunca quise yr con el, teniendo que me faria bevir en el error quel tenia, y vino aqui una noche, puede aver seys años, a me rogar que fuese con el e non le quise acoger en mi casa e se fue luego, e puede aver dos años, poco mas o menos, quel me fizo coser pan cenceno dos o tres veses e contra mi voltad me lo fiso comer, por non pasar mala vida que continuamente me dava, e despues quel se fue yo non filava algunos sabados e confeselo con el cura de Santiago e me mando que filase e yo despues aca syempre he filado e fago mis faciendas conmo buena xpristiana, e despues quel se fue la segunda ves me ha embiado a rogar que me fuese con el e vendiese esta facienda que aqui tenia, lo qual nunca quise faser ni fise por non bevir con el de cabsa de su mal bevir, el qual me vendio dos pares de casas que me dio mi padre e una posada de colmenas, e quisiera vender estas casas en que yo moro e una viña por me dexar pobre e yo nunca lo consenti. Desto mi arepiento de buen coraçon e de buena voluntad e pido a Dios misericordia e a vosotros señores me deys penetencia lo qual yo con buen coraçon esto para la recebir, e dixo que su marido se degollava los abes quel avia de comer.

XV. REFUSAL OF A REQUEST FOR A COPY OF THE INSTRUCTIONS.

(Ms. of Royal Library of Copenhagen, 214 fol. Cédulas en favor).[1766]

Muy Ill^{res} R^{mos} Señores:
El Licen^{do} Alonso de la Peña, promotor y abogado fiscal del S^{to} Off^{io} como de derecho mejor puedo, con protestacion que antes todas cosas hago de no consentir en contestacion de causa por este acto ó por otros que por escripto ó por palabra hago á la respuesta de cierta nulla peticion por parte del Doctor Blasco de Alagona ante VV. SS. presentada, cuyo thenor havido aqui por repetido, so la misma protestacion la digo nulla, de ningun valor y effecto, y como tal debe no ser por VV. SS. decretada ó justamente no admittida. Por lo siguiente. Lo uno por las razones generales. Lo otro por no ser presentada por parte ni contra parte, ni en tiempo ni forma. Lo otro por tratarse de dar copia de los statutes y instruciones y nuevas refformas deste S^{to} Off^{io} y su archivo secreto de donde xamas se acostumbra ni es cosa conveniente darse por los daños que se siguirian. Y, caso negado, que lo fuera de derecho esta cada uno obligado, para fundar la yntencion de su demanda, buscar cerca de si las cosas que le son nezesarias. Lo otro por no ser las dhas ynstruciones, statutos y nuevas refformas hechas ni dadas en juycio contencioso, ni en contradicion de partes, ni daño de ellas, sino solo para ynstrucion, orden y buen gobierno tanto de la una audiencia como de la otra. Lo otro porque si los dhos officiales y ministros de este S^{to} Off^{io} ubiessen de dar sus deposiciones sobre este particular como el dho Blasco de Alagona pretende se siguería el mismo y mayor ynconveniente de que los estatutos ynstruciones y nuevas refformas dadas al S^{to} Off^{io}, las quales solo se han de conocer y saver por los effectos de la Justicia que en el se administra, se supiessen patentamente por todos y alguno de mala yntencion quisiesse de redarguir de bueno ó malo stilo el que en el S^{to} Off^{io} ay.

Otrosi. Respondiendo á los méritos de su injusta demanda y peticion nulla, digo que quando en este S^{to} Tribunal no ubiera la obligacion que ay de tener en buena custodia y secreto sus ordenaciones, statutos y refformas, no se le debia dar tal copia por la yncertitud, confusion y daño que se seguiría a las demas personas cuyas causas en el mismo tiempo fueron por los dhos jueces ordinarios determinadas. Las quales todas fueron juridicas y dadas por personas que tenian entera juriadiction para ello, que quando no la tubieran, la buena fe y comun opinion en que estaban de derecho se la daba. Lo otro y mas principal que ciera la puerta á que no se le ay de dar á lo dho Blasco de Alagona las dhas copias que pretende es que caso que la dha refforma fuesse como el dize que quitase los jueces ordinarios, aquella se debe y ha de intender seria quanto al conocimiento y difinicion de las causas que despues de ella se comenzasen y no de aquellas que ya estaban comenzadas y su jurisdiction perpetuada y las dhas causas quasi conclusas para diffinitiva.

Por las quales razones y otras muchas y mas eficaces que al savio parecer de VV. SS. reservo, cuyo auxilio para este efecto ynvoco, parece claro no debe se le dar al dho Blasco de Alagona las dhas copias de las ynstruciones de los officiales y ministros del S^{to} Off^{io}, antes ponerlos de nuevo perpetuo silencio para que cumplan y guarden el secreto de las cosas que en este S^{to} Off^{io} tienen jurado y prometido. Sobre que demando justicia y el officio de VV. SS. imploro.

XVI. CARTA ACORDADA OF FEBRUARY 26, 1607, ENFORCING SECRECY.

(Archivo de Simancas, Inquisicion, Libro 942, fol. 62).

Como en el secreto del Sancto Oficio consista todo su poder y autoridad y la rreputacion de las personas que en el sirven, assi la falta que de el ha havido y hay generalmente en todas las Inquisiciones y su publicidad nos ha causado grandisimo sentimiento y obligado a proveer del remedio necesario para que cesen los grandes daños y quiebras que se han seguido del rompimiento que ha habido en cossas tan importantes á la estimacion y respeto que siempre se ha tenido á las cosas de la Sancta Inquisicion y á sus ministros, pues quanto mas secretas son las materias que se tratan tanto mas son tenidas por sagradas y estimadas de los que no tienen noticia de ellas, y habiendo platicado sobre el remedio de este abuso introducido en estos tiempos en los tribunales, y considerando con el Ilustri^{mo} Señor Patriarca Inquisidor general, ha parecido estender y aumentar por via de declaracion el juramento que todos hacen antes de ser admitidos á sus oficios con todas las fuerzas, vinculos y estrechezas que el derecho requiere y dispone para que sea avido y caiga en pena de perjuro y de infidelidad quien fuere contra el tal juramento, y siendo convencido por indicios ó testigos aunque sean singulares por la primera bez sea suspendido de su officio por un año yrremisiblemente y pague cincuenta ducados de pena, y por la segunda privado perpetuamente y que lo contrario haciendo aunque no sea deducido en juicio el exceso no pueda en el fuero de la conciencia hacer suyo ni recibir los salarios de su plaza, declarando que la observancia del dicho secreto, demas de las cosas de la fee ó en qualquiera manera dependientes de ella sea y se entienda asi mismo de los votos, ordenes, determinaciones, cartas del Consejo en todas partes y materias sin dar noticia de ellas á las partes ni á personas fuera del secreto como se ha entendido que algunos indebidamente lo han hecho, y de las informaciones de la limpieza que se hubieren hecho ó hicieren para Inquisidores, Oficiales, Comisarios, Notarios y familiares, y de todas las cosas tocantes á ellas y de todos los votos y determinaciones de los Inquisidores de qualesquiera cosas y causas aunque sean publicas, pues en todas hay precisa obligacion de guardar el secreto de lo que cada uno vota. Y assimismo mandamos so pena de excomunion mayor y de la dicha pena de suspension y privacion de su officio á todos los que supieren ó entendieren que qualquiera persona que sirve en el Sancto Officio de la Inquisicion quebrantare en qualquiera manera el dicho secreto directa ó indirectamente lo manifieste secretamente al Ilustrisimo Señor Inquisidor General ó al Consejo por que asi conviene para que no quede sin castigo tan grande delito. Y para que en todo tiempo todos tengan noticia de esto y nadie se excuse con su ignorancia, queremos que esta nuestra carta acordada y provision se ponga con las instruciones y cartas acordadas que se acostumbran á leer en el principio de cada año en la sala del secreto á todos los Ministros del Sancto Officio de la Inquisicion quando se presentaren ó se les de su titulo en el ingreso de sus Officios, y en recibiendo esta mandareis juntar á todos los Officiales en la sala del secreto donde se les leera.--En Madrid, 26 de hebrero de 1607 años.

***

El ylustrisimo Señor Patriarca Inquisidor General estando en el Consejo de su Magestad en la Sancta General Inquisicion, haviendose leido en presencia de su Señoria Ilustrisima y de los Señores de el la carta acordada de arriva tocante al secreto del Sancto Officio de la Inquisicion, dixo que su intencion y voluntad y de los dichos Señores era que obligue y se entendienda desde la persona de su Ilustrisima y señores del dicho Consejo hasta los officiales de el, y mando que asi se pusiese por auto y que se notificase á todos y a los dichos Officiales de los dichos secretos y al nuncio y porteros, lo qual yo el presente secretario cumpli, de que doy fee.--Hernando de Villegas, Secretario del Consejo.

XVII. FINANCES OF THE INQUISITION IN 1731.

(From Archivo de Alcalá de Henares, Hacienda, Legajo 544^{2} (Libro 8).)
ESTADO DE LAS RENTAS, SALARIOS Y GASTOS DE EL CONSEXO Y TRIBUNALES DE INQUISICION DE ESTOS REYNOS.

Por manera que importan las rentas del Consejo y Tribunales, 1,603,782 rs. y 31 mrs de vellon, y necesitando para los salarios de sus Ministros y cargas precisas 2,149,973 rs. y 10 mrs. faltan en cada año 546,190 rs. y 13 mrs. segun ba demostrado. Previniendose que aunque el resumen se allan 554,064 rs. 25 mrs. consiste la diferencia en el corto sobrante de las Inquisiciones de Santiago y Sevilla, lo que se hace presente; y tambien que el mas cargo de 100,000 rs. que resulta al Consexo de consignaciones de los Tribunales es por la que se considera en el de Mexico. Asimismo se advierte que por haver quedado la de Zaragoza sin el palacio de la Aljaferia que ocupaba y buscando casa de alquiler la concedió el Señor Don Phelipe 5, el año de 1708, 5.200 ducados de plata sobre bienes confiscados y habiendo cesado por la paz de Viena; haviendo sido preciso fabricar casa se ha empeñado en 24,000 libras y necesita para acabarla mas de otras 20,000. Madrid 8 de Noviembre de 1731.
Felix Garcia del Pulgar.

FOOTNOTES:

1. Hæreticus animal pestilentissimum est: quamobrem punire debet antequam virus impietatis evomat, forasque projiciat.--Simancæ de Cathol. Institt., Tit. II, n. 17.
2. Archivo hist. nacional, Inquisicion de Toledo, Leg. 153, n. 331.--Burriel, Vidas de los Arzobispos de Toledo (Bibl. nacional, MSS. Ff, 194, fol. 8).
3. Las Quinquagenas, I, 342 (Madrid, 1880).
4. Revista crítica de Historia y Literatura, V, 148.
5. Archivo de Simancas, Inquisicion, Leg. 522, fol. 2.
6. MSS. of Library of Univ. of Halle, Yc, 20, T. VIII.
7. Instrucciones de 1484, § 12 (Arguello, fol. 4).
8. Archivo hist. nacional, Inquisicion de Toledo, Leg. 158, n. 431, 435.
9. Archivo de Simancas, Inquisicion, Leg. 552, fol. 44.
10. Ibidem, fol. 23.
11. Still, Protestant sailors arriving in Spanish ports, when not protected by treaty, and even prisoners of war in the American colonies, as we shall see hereafter, were claimed by the Inquisition.
12. Ferraris, Prompta Bibliotheca, s. v. Hæresis, n. 1-10.--Avila de Censuris ecclesiasticis, P. I, Dub. 10 (Lugduni, 1609).--Páramo, p. 570.
13. Cap. 1, § 1, Clement. v, iii.
14. Bibl. nacional, MSS., X, 157, fol. 244.
15. Boletin, XV, 579, 594.
16. Mich. Alberti Repert. Inquisit. s. v. Episcopus.--Arn. Albertini de agnoscendis Assertionibus Catholicis, Q. XI, n. 1 (Valentiæ, 1534).--Simancæ de Cath. Institt. Tit. XXV, n. 2, 3, 4.--Pegnæ Comment. LIV in Eymerici Direct. P. III.--Páramo, p. 536.

Rojas (De Hæret. P. I, n. 442-3) appears to be the only writer who assumes that the Clementines render episcopal jurisdiction merely consultative.

17. Archivo de Simancas, Inquisicion, Libro 1.
18. Simancæ de Cath. Institt., Tit. XXV, n. 5.
19. Llorente, Añales, II, 335.
20. Archivo de Simancas, Inquisicion, Lib. 926, fol. 139.
21. Archivo de Simancas, Inquisicion, Libro 688, fol. 228, 517; Libro 939, fol. 69.
22. Concil. Tarraconens. ann. 1591, Lib. v, Tit. vi, Cap. 2 (Aguirre, VI, 319).
23. Decreta Sac. Congr. S. Officii, p. 284 (R. Archivio di Stato in Roma, Fondo camerale, Congr. del S. Offizio, vol. 3).

The policy of the Roman Inquisition was wholly different. It recognized the traditional jurisdiction of the bishops and invited their coöperation. The bishop issued edicts at his discretion and could initiate prosecutions. Concurrence of course was necessary in sentences of torture and final judgement, but, if the bishop were the prosecutor, the inquisitor went to the episcopal palace for the consultations and also in other cases when the bishop acted personally and not by his Ordinary. It was all in accordance with the Clementines, except that all definitive sentences required confirmation by the Congregation.--Ibid. pp. 174-5, 177, 266-8, 272-3.

24. Archivo de Simancas, Inquisicion, Lib. 45, fol. 168.
25. Modo de Proceder, fol. 107 (Bibl. nacional, MSS., D, 122).
26. Libro XIII de Cartas (MSS. of Am. Philos. Society).
27. Benedicti PP. XIV de Synodo dioecesana, Lib. IX, cap. iv, n. 3.
28. Archivo de Simancas, Lib. 78, fol. 80.
29. Ibidem, Lib. 83, fol. 106.
30. MSS. of Royal Library of Copenhagen, 218^{b}, p. 232.
31. Archivo de Simancas, Inquisicion, Leg. 562, fol. 28.
32. Archivo hist. nacional, Inquisicion de Valencia, Leg. 100.
33. Archivo de Simancas, Inquisicion, Lib. 435^{2}; Lib. 890.
34. Páramo, p. 136.--Boletin, XV, 462.
35. Boletin, XV, 475.
36. Bulario de la Orden de Santiago, I, 37.

37. Instrucciones de 1484, § 26 (Arguello, fol. 8).
38. Archivo gen. de la C. de Aragon, Registro 3684, fol. 76, 92, 97.
39. Bulario de la Orden de Santiago, Lib. I de copias, fol. 3.--No such clause appears in later commissions.
40. Archivo de Simancas, Inquisicion, Lib. 1.
41. Ibidem, Lib. 3, fol. 27, 28, 62, 63, 72, 73, 186, 204, 242, 336.
42. Ibidem, Lib. 939, fol. 69.
43. Archivo de Simancas, Patronato real, Inquisicion, Leg. único, fol. 43.
44. Pragmáticas y altres Drets de Cathalunya, Lib. I, Tit. viii, cap. 1; Capitols concedits, § 26; Ibidem, cap. 2 (Barcelona, 1569, pp. 16,19).--Bulario de la Orden de Santiago, Lib. I de copias, fol. 219.
45. Archivo de Simancas, Inquisicion, Lib. 939, fol. 69, 118.
46. Bibl. pública de Toledo, Sala 5, Estante II, Tab. 3.
47. Archivo de Simancas, Inquisicion, Lib. 76, fol. 360; Lib. 77, fol. 30; Lib. 939, fol. 104.
48. Bibl. pública de Toledo, loc. cit.
49. MSS. penes me.
50. Córtes de Madrid del año de MDLII, Pet. lix (Valladolid, 1558, fol. xiv).
51. Archivo de Simancas, Patronato real, Inquisicion, Leg. único, fol. 76.
52. Ibidem, Visitos de Barcelona, Leg. 15, fol. 2.
53. MSS. of Library of Univ. of Halle, Yc, 20, Tom. III, XI.--Archivo de Simancas, Inquisicion, Lib. 939, fol. 69.

Yet the Ordinary's signature is appended to the sentence of acquittal of Fray Joseph de Sigüenza, in 1592.--MSS. of Halle, Yc, 20, Tom. IV.
54. MSS. of Library of Univ. of Halle, Yc, 20, Tom. VII.
55. Archivo de Simancas, Inquisicion, Lib. 82, fol. 93.
56. Archivo hist. nacional, Inquisicion de Valencia, Leg. 9, n. 1, fol. 261, 275; Leg. 9, n. 2, fol 342.
57. Archivo de Simancas, Inquisicion, Sala 39, Leg. 52, fol. 2.
58. Ibidem, Lib. 876, fol. 1, 17, 30, 41, 42, 46.--Archivo de Alcalá, Estado, Leg. 2843.
59. Discusion del Proyecto sobre la Inquisicion, p. 449 (Cadiz, 1813).
60. Archivo de Simancas, Inquisicion, Libros 559, 890.
61. Urbani PP. V, Bull. Apostolatus (Bullar. Roman. I, 261).
62. Cap. 3, 4, Extrav. Commun. Lib. V, Tit. ix.
63. Concil. Trident. Sess, XXIV, De Reform, cap. 6.--Pegnæ Comment CXLI n Eymerici Director. P. III.
64. Bulario de la Orden de Santiago, Lib. I, fol. 92.--Archivo de Simancas, Inquisicion, Lib. 926, fol. 260.
65. Instrucciones de 1484, § 5 (Arguello, fol. 4).
66. Clement. PP. VII, Bull. Cum sicut (Pegnæ Append, ad Eymerici Director.).
67. Eymerici Director. P. III, n. 59 cum Pegnæ Comment, xii.--Locati Opus Judiciale, s. v. Absolvere n. 7 (Romæ, 1570).
68. Archivo hist. nacional, Inquisicion de Toledo, Leg. 498.--"Por la presente damos licencia a qualquiera sacerdote secular ó regular para que en forma de la santa Madre Iglesia pueda absolver y absuelve á F. de la excomunion por nos puesta á pedimiento de F., imponiendole penitencia saludable á su anima y conciencia."
69. MSS. of Royal Library of Copenhagen, 214 fol.--MSS. of Bodleian Library, Arch Seld A, Subt. 15.
70. Simancæ de Cath. Institt., Tit. III, n. 5.
71. Archivo hist. nacional, Inquisicion de Valencia, Leg. 299, fol. 80.
72. Simancæ de Cath. Institt., Tit. XIII, n. 22.
73. Archivo de Simancas, Inquisicion, Lib. 939, fol. 126.
74. Corella, Praxis confessionale, P. I, Tract, i, Cap. 1, n. 8.
75. Archivo hist. nacional, Inquisicion de Toledo, Leg. 111, n. 42.
76. Ibidem, Inquisicion de Valencia, Leg. 15, n. 11, fol. 17.
77. Discusion del Proyecto sobre la Inquisicion, p. 446 (Cadiz, 1863).
78. MSS. Bibl. nacional de Lima, Protocolo 223, Expediente 5270.
79. Simancæ de Cath. Institt., Tit. XLII, n. 14.
80. Archivo de Simancas, Inquisicion, Libro 559.
81. Archivo de Simancas, Lib. 82, fol. 89; Lib. 939, fol. 126.
82. Bulario de la Orden de Santiago, Lib. III, fol. 464.--Archivo de Simancas, Inquisicion, Lib. 83, fol. 30; Lib. 939, fol. 126; Lib. 941, fol. 3.
83. See the Author's "History of Auricular Confession and Indulgences," Appendix to Vol. III.
84. Pegnæ Comment. XXV in Eymerici Director. P. II.

85. Archivo de Simancas, Inquisicion, Lib. 939, fol. 126.
86. Hinojosa, Los Despachos de la Diplomacia Pontificia, I, 330.--Danvila y Collado, La Expulsion de los Moriscos, p. 223.--Bibl. nacional, MSS, D, 118, fol. 243.--Archivo de Simancas, Inquisicion, Lib. 940, fol. 12.
87. Archivo de Simancas, Inquisicion, Lib. 54, fol. 176.--Archivo hist. nacional, Inquisicion de Valencia, Leg. 10, n. 2, fol. 39, 40, 52, 75, 114, 118.
88. MSS. of Royal Library of Copenhagen, 218^{b}, pp. 326-7, 337.
89. Danvila y Collado, La Expulsion de los Moriscos, pp. 126, 129, 181, 183, 194.
90. Lucii PP. III Epist. 171 (Migne's Patrol., CCI, 1299).
91. Ripoll, Bullar. Ord. Prædic. I, 252.--Eymerici Director. Inquis. P. III, Q, xxviii.--Hist. of Inquisition of Middle Ages, III, 71 sqq.
92. Raynald. Annal. ann. 1329, n. 70-2.
93. Pegnæ Comment. LXXVII in Eymerici Director. P. III.--Bullar. Roman. I, 420.
94. Ripoll, Bullar., IV, 22.--Wadding, Annal. Minor. ann. 1487, n. 8.
95. Bulario de la Orden de Santiago, Lib. I, fol. 94.--Archivio Vaticano, Innocent. VIII, Regist. 686, fol. 103.--Boletin, XV, 582.
96. Archivo de Simancas, Inquisicion, Lib. 939, fol. 106.
97. Wadding, op. cit. T. VIII, Regest., n. xxi.

I have not met with any special attribution of exemption to Dominicans, but a brief of Leo X, May 14, 1517, confirming all their privileges without exception, may have been construed as covering this.--Ripoll, IV, 343.

98. Archivo de Simancas, ubi sup.
99. Wadding, ann. 1524, n. xxiii.
100. Bulario de la Orden de Santiago, Lib. I de copias, fol. 115.
101. Archivo de Simancas, ubi sup.
102. Bulario de la Orden de Santiago, Lib. I de copias, fol. 79, 96.--Páramo, p. 607.

This was extended to Italy, by a brief of Jan. 15, 1530.--Clem. PP. VII, Bull cum sicut (Pegnæ Append, ad Eymerici Director. p. 107).

103. Archivo de Simancas, Inquisicion, Lib. 939, fol. 106.
104. Wadding, op. cit., Tom. VIII, Regest. pp. 225-6.
105. Fontana, Documenti Vaticani contro l'Eresia Luterana, p. 122 (Roma, 1892).
106. Pauli PP. III Bull. In Apostolici, 21 Mart. 1592 (Pegnæ Append. ad Eymerici Director. p. 109).
107. Pauli PP. IV Bull. Cum sicut nuper, 16 Apl. 1559 (Bullar. Roman. II, 48).
108. Bibl. Vaticana, MS. Ottoboniano Lat. 495, p. 7.
109. Hinojosa, Los Despachos de la Diplomacia Pontificia, I, 326, 332.
110. Bibl. Vaticana, MS. Ottoboniano Lat. 495, fol. 50.
111. Archivo de Simancas, Inquisición, Lib. 53, fol. 20; Gracia y Justicia, Leg. 621, fol. 116.
112. Bulario de la Orden de Santiago, Lib. IV, fol. 109, 111.--Páramo, p. 885.
113. Bulario de la Orden de Santiago, Lib. IV, fol. 149; Lib. V, fol. 77.
114. Bulario de la Orden de Santiago, Libro V, fol. 73, 77.
115. Ibidem, Lib. V, fol. 78.
116. A copy of this edict, printed as a broadside, is in the Bodleian Library, Arch. S, 130.
117. Archivo hist. nacional, Inquisicion de Valencia, Leg. 1, n. 4, fol. 148.
118. Cap. 16 in Sexto, V, 3.--Mich. Alberti Repertor. Inquisit. s. v. Episcopus.
119. See Vol. I, p. 147.
120. Among the leading bishops of Jewish descent, at the time, Amador de los Rios enumerates (op. cit. III, 241) Alonso of Burgos, Juan de Malvenda of Coria, Alfonso de Valladolid of Valladolid, Alonso de Palenzuela of Ciudad-Rodrigo, Pedro de Aranda of Calahorra, Juan Arias Dávila of Segovia and Hernando de Talavera of Granada.
121. Bulario de la Orden de Santiago, Lib. I, fol. 36.--Archivo de Simancas, Inquisicion, Lib. 930, fol. 18.
122. Páramo, p. 151.
123. Amador de los Rios, III, 129-30.
124. Colmenares, Historia de Segovia, cap. xxxiii, § 2; cap. xxxv, §§ 7, 13.
125. Bergenroth, Calendar of Spanish State Papers, I, xlv.
126. Coleccion de Documentos, XVIII, 290.
127. Llorente, Añales, I, 212, 242.--Boletin, XV, 578, 590.--Burchardi Diarium, II, 409, 459, 494-5; III, 13 (Ed. Thuasne).
128. Archivo de Simancas, Patronato Real, Inquisition, Leg. único, fol. 22.
129. There is a somewhat mysterious case of a summons issued, in 1516, to the "Bishop of Daroca," then in Burgos, to present himself to Ximenes, within fifteen days, under pain of loss of

temporalities and citizenship. It was enclosed to the corregidor of Burgos with instructions to serve it in presence of a notary and, if the bishop did not obey, he was to be sent to the court under secure guard. Daroca is a town near Saragossa, which never was the seat of an episcopate, but the summons was signed by Cardinal Adrian, then Inquisitor-general of Aragon, and by Calcena in the name of the governors and was countersigned by the members of the Suprema.--Archivo de Simancas, Inquisicion, Lib. III, fol. 448.

130. Dormer, Añales de Aragon, Lib. I, cap. xxvii; Lib. II, cap. xx.--Bulario de la Orden de Santiago, Lib. III, fol. 521.--Gachard, Correspondance de Charles-quint et d'Adrian VI, p. 171.--Ferrer del Rio, Comunidades de Castilla, pp. 300-2, 393, 397, 399.--Constantin v. Höfler, Don Antonio de Acuña, p. 79.

131. Bulario de la Orden de Santiago, Lib. I de copias, fol. 98.--Archivo de Simancas, Inquisicion, Libro 930, fol. 98.

132. The documents of the trial of Carranza, covering some forty thousand pages, are preserved in twenty-two folio volumes in the library of the Real Academia de la Historia and even from these there is a volume missing. The only writers whose accounts are based on these original sources are Llorente (Hist. crít. cap. xxxii-iv) and Menéndez Pelayo (Heterodoxos españoles, II, 359-415)--the one a defender of the accused and the other of the Holy Office. I have not had the opportunity of consulting these documents, but many of the more important have been printed and there are sources, aside from the inquisitorial records, which throw light on the motives which occasioned and controlled the events. These were not accessible to Llorente and appear to have escaped the attention of Menéndez Pelayo.

133. Gachard, Retraite et Mort de Charles-quint, II, 187, 188, 191, 202.

134. Gachard, op. cit., II, 195, 199, 354.

135. Gachard, op. cit., pp. 417, 418.

136. Menéndez Pelayo, Heterodoxos, II, 395.

137. In 1608 the see of Cuzco was estimated to be worth 40,000 ducats per annum.--Cabrera, Relaciones, p. 346.

138. Salazar de Mendoza, Vida de Fray D. Bartolomé de Carranza y de Miranda, cap. I-VII.-- Salazar was a penitentiary of the cathedral of Toledo and wrote this work at the request of Carranza's successor, the Inquisitor-general Quiroga. It was not printed until Valladares issued an edition in 1788. This I have not seen and my references are to a MS. copy.

139. Bzovii Annal. Eccles. ann. 1566, n. 89.--Salazar, op. cit., cap. VIII-X.

140. Salazar, cap. XI.--Coleccion de Documentos, V, 528.

141. Salazar, cap. XII.

142. Controversia de necessaria Residentia personali Episcoporum et aliorum inferiorum Pastorum. Lugduni, 1550. The first edition was of Venice, 1547; there was a third, Antwerp, 1554, and a reprint as late as 1767, in Madrid.

143. Caballero, Vida de Fray Melchor Cano, p. 624 (Madrid, 1871).

144. Philip's consulta and Cano's parecer were printed by Usoz y Rio in his "Reformistas antiguos españoles" (Dos Informaziones, Append. p. 27, Madrid, 1857) and more recently by Caballero, Vida de Melchor Cano, p. 512.

145. Caballero, pp. 502, 507, 508, 527-9, 530-2, 534-5.

146. Llorente, Hist. crít. cap. XXXII, Art. 1, n. 3.--Salazar, cap. VIII.--Menéndez Pelayo, II, 378.

147. Schäfer, Beiträge zur Geschichte des spanischen Protestantismus, III, 785-88, 791.

The Consideration in question is not, as there stated, No. 65, but No. 54, in both the original Basle edition of "Le cento e dieci divine Considerazioni" (1550) and in the Spanish version of 1558, printed by Usoz y Rio. The mistake is probably that of a copyist, confusing LIV and LXV. The Spanish version seems to have circulated among the little group of heretics in Valladolid.

148. Döllinger, Beiträge zur politischen, Kirchlichen u. Cultur-Geschichte, I, 574.--Pallavicini, Hist. Conc. Trident. Lib. XIV, cap. lii, n. 4-6.--Bzovii Annal. ann. 1566, n. 90.

149. Schäfer, Beiträge, III, 792.--See in general pp. 727-812.

150. Archivo hist. nacional, Inquisicion de Toledo, Leg. 112, n. 64, fol. 2.

151. Archivo de Simancas, Inquisicion, Sala 40, Libro 4, fol. 228.--Gachard, Retraite et Mort, II, 422.

The personage in question was a certain Juan Sánchez, of no special importance. He was arrested in Flanders, in May, 1559, and burnt alive as an impenitent in the auto of October 8, 1559.--Schäfer, op. cit., I, 254, 307, 313-14; III, 796-803.

152. Comentarios, Prologo, fol. 2^{b}.

153. The policy of the Spanish Church is forcibly expressed by the Council of Salamanca, in 1565. "The very name of heretics should be so hateful to the faithful that it should never pass our lips if it can possibly be avoided. Preachers should propound the doctrines of the faith and give the reasons and authorities for them, but should never allude to the sects of the heretics or to their arguments. In scholastic disputations no heretical, or dangerous, or erroneous assertions should be introduced, even for

the purpose of exercise, but only those approved by the customs of each university."--Concil. Salmanticens. ann. 1655, Decr. xxxii (Aguirre, V, 453).

154. Comentarios, fol. 219ª, 162ª.
155. Bzovii Annal. ann. 1566, n. 89.--Coleccion de Documentos, V, 518.
156. Gachard, op. cit., II, 427.
157. Salazar, cap. XIV, XV.--Gachard, I, 319, 321, 344, 348, 355, 356, 364, 374, 381, 385, 387, 389, 406, 410; II, 43-5, 469, 475, 477, 484, 491, 492, 494.--Sandoval, Carlos V en Juste, § xvi.--Coleccion de Documentos, V, 423.
158. Archivo de Simancas, Inquisicion, Sala 40, Lib. 4, fol. 232.--"Aunque fuesen personas constituidas en qualquier dignidad seglar ó pontifical y eclesiastica y de qualquier orden, habito y religion y estado."
159. Llorente, Hist. crít. cap. XXXII, Art. iii, n. 12.--Menéndez Pelayo, II, 386.
160. Caballero, p. 651.
161. Llorente, loc. cit.--Coleccion de Documentos, V, 518.
162. Caballero, p. 627.
163. Salazar, cap. XVII, XVIII, XXXVI.
164. Coleccion de Documentos, V, 508-17.
165. Coleccion de Documentos, V, 515, 521.
166. Llorente, Hist. crít. cap. XXV, Art. i, n. 11, 31, 57, 66, 77, 78, 95, 103; Art. ii, n. 13; cap. XXIX, Art. i, n. 4, 6, 8, 11, 12.--Cf. Danvila y Collado, Expulsion de los Moriscos, p. 156.
167. Raynald. Annal. ann. 1559, n. 19.--It is worthy of note that a copy of this brief in the archives of the Inquisition (Simancas, Lib. 930, fol. 24) extends the term of two years to three and adds to the condition of expected flight the phrase "aut alias tibi videtur expedire," thus giving Valdés full discretion to arrest. These frauds were requisite to justify his action. As Raynaldus drew from the papal registers, his version of the brief is of course correct.
168. Menéndez Pelayo, II, 386.
169. Coleccion de Documentos, V, 522.
170. Ibidem, p. 504.
171. Caballero, pp. 617-18.
172. Ibidem, pp. 616, 618, 619, 621, 624-7.
173. Ibidem, pp. 620, 621, 624.
174. Archivo de Simancas, Inquisicion, Sala 40, Lib. 4, fol. 234.
175. Döllinger, Beiträge, I, 256.
176. Ibidem, p. 254.--Caballero, p. 615.
177. Caballero, pp. 624, 625.
178. Menéndez Pelayo, II, 387.
179. The details of the arrest of Carranza are contained in an official narrative by Ambrosio de Morales, chronicler of Philip II, drawn up by order of the king to be deposited in the library of the Escorial. A recension of this, so modernized as not wholly to be trustworthy, is printed in the Coleccion de Documentos, V, 465 sqq. I have preferred to use a MS. in Bibl. nacional, Mm, 475. It will be referred to as "Morales."

Rodrigo de Castro was the son of the Count of Lemos. He proved useful and was rewarded successively with the bishoprics of Zamora and Cuenca and the archbishopric of Seville. He was made a cardinal in 1583 and died full of honors in 1600.

180. Morales, loc. cit.--Salazar, cap. XXIII.
181. Archivo de Simancas, Inquisicion, Sala 40, Lib. 4, fol. 239.
182. Morales says that Carranza heard his name in the brief. If so, it must have been interpolated, for the warrant was issued under that of January 7th, which was general in its terms.
183. Morales, op. cit.--Salazar, cap. XXI.
184. Archivo hist. nacional, Inquisicion de Toledo, Leg. 108, n. 3.
185. Salazar, cap. XXV, XXVII.--Morales, loc. cit.
186. Salazar, cap. XXIV.
187. Llorente, cap. XXXIII, Art. iii, n. 2.
188. Coleccion de Documentos, V, 415.
189. Salazar, cap. XXVI.
190. Coleccion de Documentos, V, 533-53.
191. Salazar, cap. XXI.--Menéndez Pelayo, II, 395.
192. Raynald. Annal, ann. 1560, n. 22, 23.--Döllinger, Beiträge, I, 329, 335-6.
193. Bulario de la Orden de Santiago, Lib. III, fol. 72.--Archivo de Simancas, Inquisicion, Sala 40, Lib. 4, fol. 236, 237, 239, 240, 242, 246.--Salazar, cap. XXVII.
194. Corpo Diplomatico Portugues, VIII, 248, 252.
195. Relazioni Venete, Serie I, T. V, pp. 94-5.

196. Bibl. nacional, MSS., X, 157, fol. 244.--Archivio Vaticano, Nunziatura di Spagna, Tom. I, carte 6, 8.
197. Adolfo de Castro, Protestantes españoles, p. 221.
198. Bibl. nacional, loc. cit.--Salazar, cap. XXV.
199. Coleccion de Documentos, V, 553-82.
200. Ibidem, pp. 438, 443.--Menéndez y Pelayo, II, 402-3.
201. Coleccion de Documentos, V, 424-38.
202. Ibidem, p. 523.
203. Llorente, cap. XXXIV, Art. iv, n. 1.--Döllinger, Beiträge, I, 472.
204. Pallavicini, Hist. Conc. Trident. Lib. XXI, cap. vii, n. 7.
205. C. Trident. Sess. XIII, De Reform. cap. viii; Sess. XXIV, De Reform. cap. v.
206. Lettere di Calini (Balus. et Mansi, IV, 314).--Salazar, cap. XXII.--Simancas (Adolfo de Castro, op. cit., pp. 214-15).--Raynald. Annal. ann. 1563, n. 137.--Bzovii Annal. ann. 1566, n. 91.--Coleccion de Documentos, V, 501.
207. Llorente, cap. XXXIII, Art. iv, n. 9.
208. Coleccion de Documentos, V, 495.--Archivo de Simancas, Inquisicion, Lib. 976, fol. 49.
209. Archivio Vaticano, Nunziatura di Spagna, T. I, carte 4, 5.
210. Archivio Vaticano, Nunziatura di Spagna, T. I, carte 12, 13, 14, 15.--Dépêches de M. de Fourquevaux, I, 11 (Paris, 1896).
211. Archivio Vaticano, Nunziatura di Spagna, T. I.
212. Bibl. nacional, MSS., X, 157, fol. 244.--Salazar, cap. XXVIII.--Menéndez Pelayo, II, 404.--Dépêches de Fourquevaux, I, 19, 37, 46.
213. Döllinger, Beiträge, I, 628.
214. Coleccion de Documentos, LXVIII, 456.
215. Morales (Coleccion de Documentos, V, 478).--Salazar, cap. XXIX.
216. Morales, ubi sup.
217. Laderchii Annales, ann. 1566, n. 484.--Archivio Vaticano, Nunziatura di Spagna, T. I, carte 1.
218. Morales (Coleccion de Documentos, V, 480).
219. Menéndez Pelayo, II, 405.
220. Relazioni Venete, Serie I, T. V, p. 144.
221. Salazar, cap. XXVIIbis, XXIX.
222. Coleccion de Documentoa, LXVIII, 460-2.
223. Salazar, cap. XXXI.--Llorente, cap. XXXIV, Art. 11, n. 1.--Adolfo de Castro, op. cit. p. 229. Catena, in his semi-official life of Pius simply says "la causa. condusae quasi à sentenza."--Vita del Papa Pio Quinto, p. 109 (Roma, 1587).
224. Simancas (Adolfo de Castro, p. 227).
225. Salazar, cap. XXXI.--Coleccion de Documentos, LXVIII, 465-71.--Archivo de Alcalá, Hacienda, Leg. 1049.--Bulario de la Orden de Santiago, Lib. III, fol. 158.--Llorente, cap. XXV, n. 11, 31; cap. XXIX, Art. 1, n. 4, 6, 7.--Menéndez Pelayo, II, 406.
226. Coleccion de Documentos, LXVIII, 472, 473.
227. Coleccion de Documentos, LXVIII, 478.
228. Salazar, cap. XXXIII.--Morales (Coleccion de Doc. V, 490).--Archivo de Simancas, Lib. 976, fol. 52.
229. Salazar, cap. XXXIII.--Adolfo de Castro, p. 233.
230. Theiner, Annal. Ecclesiast. II. 244.
231. Salazar, cap. XXXIV.--Simancas (Adolfo de Castro, p. 234).
232. Salazar, cap. XXXV.
233. Coleccion de Documentos LXVIII, 479.
234. Bibl. nacional, MSS. Mm, 475.
235. Salazar, cap. ult.
236. Raynald. Annal. ann. 1560, n. 23.--Pallavicini Hist. Conc. Trident. Lib. XIV, cap. 12, n. 4.
237. Bibliotheca nova, s. v. Bartholomaus Carranza.
238. El Protestantismo comparado con el Catolicismo, II, 301, 306 (Barcelona, 1844). See also Tournon, Hommes illustres de l'Ordre de Saint Dominique, IV, 438. It should be added that Menéndez Pelayo (II, 376), after an examination of the testimony, asserts that it was sufficient to justify the prosecution. This may be so, according to inquisitorial methods, but not the persistent persecution that followed.
239. Bulario de la Orden de Santiago, Lib. IV, fol. 68.
240. Hinojosa, Los Despachos de la Diplomacia pontificia, I, 303.
241. Archivo de Simancas, Inquisicion, Lib. 939, fol. 63.
242. Bulario de la Orden de Santiago, Lib. IV, fol. 91.

243. Archivo de Simancas, Inquisicion, Lib. 20, fol. 38; Lib. 52, fol. 21.
244. Archivo de Simancas, Lib. 25, fol. 66; Lib. 52, fol. 100, 125, 335.
245. Bulario de la Orden de Santiago, Lib. V, fol. 141, 144, 150.--Archivo de Simancas, Inquisicion, Legajos 418, 419, 1577.
246. Coleccion de los escritos mas importantes etc. de D. Manuel Abad Queipo, Obispo electo de Mechoacan, Mexico, 1813.--I have a copy of an edict issued by him October 8, 1810, as bishop-elect, in which he alludes to two previous ones excommunicating Hidalgo and his followers.
247. Simancæ de Cath. Institt. Tit. XXV, n. 11.--Trimarchi de Confessore abutente Sacramento Poenit., p. 172 (Genuæ, 1636).--Coleccion de Documentos tocantes á la Persecution del Obispo de Asuncion, I, ix (Madrid, 1768).--Cf. Recop. de las Indias, Lib. I, Tit. vii, ley 51.
248. Archivo de Simancas, Inquisicion, Lib. 877, fol. 266; Libro 890.--Rodrigo, Hist. verdadera, III, 492.
249. Mariana, Historia de España, Lib. XXIV, cap. xvii.
250. Eymerici Director, P. III, n. 52, 53.
251. Instrucciones de 1484, § 2 (Arguello, fol. 3).
252. Instructiones de 1500, § 12 (Arguello, fol. 13).
253. La Mantia, L'Inquisizione in Sicilia, p. 26.
254. Pragmáticas y altres Drets de Cathalunya, Lib. I, Tit. viii, cap. 1.
255. Archivo de Simancas, Inquisicion, Libro 933.
256. Ibidem, Patronato Real, Inquisicion, Leg. único, fol. 43.
257. Bibl. nacional, MSS., D, 118, p. 148. See also Llorente, Hist. crít. Append., XI.
258. Archivo hist. nacional, Inquisicion de Toledo, Leg. 498; Inquisicion de Valencia, Lib. VII de Autos, Leg. 2, fol. 61.
259. Ibidem, Inquisicion de Toledo, Leg. 251.
260. MSS. Archivo municipal de Sevilla, Seccion especial, Siglo XVIII, Letra A, Tomo IV, n. 44.--Cf. Archivo de Simancas, Inquisicion, Leg. 1475, fol. 52; Leg. 1478, fol. 106.
261. Bibl. nacional, MSS., D, 118, p. 79; S, 294, fol. 21, 74.--MSS. Archivo municipal de Sevilla, Seccion especial, Siglo XVIII, Letra A, Tomo IV, n. 43.--Archivo hist. nacional, Inquisicion de Valencia, Lib. VII de Autos, Leg. 2, fol. 64; Inquisicion de Toledo, Leg. 251.
262. Sayri Clavis Regia Sacerdotum, Lib. XII, cap. xiv, n. 32-34.
263. Archivo de Simancas, Inquisicion, Libro 939, fol. 84, 140; Visitas de Barcelona, Leg. 15, fol. 2.--Archivo hist. nacional, Inquisicion de Valencia, Leg. 2, n. 16, fol. 272.
264. Archivo de Simancas, Inquisicion, Visitas de Barcelona, Leg. 15, fol. 4,--Archivo hist. nacional, Inquisicion de Valencia, Leg. 309, Cuentas, fol. 3; Leg. 299.
265. Bordoni Sacrum Tribunal, cap. XXX, 481, 506-10 (Romæ, 1648).
266. Bulario de la Orden de Santiago, Lib. V, fol. 89.
267. Archivo hist. nacional, Inquisicion de Valencia, Leg. 9, n. 1, fol. 329; Leg. 10, n. 2, fol. 110.
268. Bibl. nacional, MSS., D, 118, fol. 261, n. 69.
269. MSS. of White Library, Cornell University, n. 616, fol. 60, 61.
270. Archivo hist. nacional, Inquisicion de Valencia, Leg. 15, n. 10, fol. 92; Leg. 16, n. 6, fol. 41; Leg. 17, n. 3, fol. 21.--Archivo de Alcalá, Estado, Leg. 2843.
271. Archivo de Simancas, Inquisicion, Visitas de Barcelona, Leg. 15, fol. 4.
272. Proceso contra Hansz Brunsvi (MSS. of Library of Univ. of Halle, Yc, 20, Tom. III).
273. Ibidem, Yc, 20, Tom. I.
274. MSS. of Am. Philos. Society.
275. Proceso contra Don Thomas Sans (MS. penes me).
276. Valladares, Semanario erudito, XXIV, 194-204.
277. Pulgar, Chronica, P. II, cap. lxxvii.
278. Of course the price for these varied according to circumstances. A contemporary document (Summaria Declaratio Bullæ Indulgentiarum Ecclesiæ Xanctonensi concessarum, 1482) tells us that the price in Rome for those in the ordinary form was nearly three florins. In Germany, early in the sixteenth century, the Beichtbriefe were sold at a quarter of a gulden apiece (Gröne, Tetzel und Luther, p. 196).
279. Archivo de Simancas, Patronato Real, Inquisicion, Leg. único, fol. 1.
In this case the papal letters appointed special persons to act under it as executors--the form known as Absolutio in vim commissionis apostolicæ.--See Formularium Instrumentorum ad usum curie Romane, fol. 2, 3 (Hain, 7276).
280. Archivo hist. nacional, Inquisicion de Toledo, Leg. 185, n. 820.
281. Sixti PP. IV, Bull. Quoniam nonnulli, §§ 4, 6.--Julii PP. III, Bull. Rationi congruit (Bullar. Roman. I, 428, 786).
When, in 1562, Pius IV reformed the Penitentiary he confined letters of absolution to the forum of conscience.--Bull. In sublimi (Bullar. II, 75).
282. Collectio Decretorum Sacræ Congregationis S^{ti} Officii, p. 245 (MS. penes me).

283. Llorente, Hist. crít., Append. n. 3.--Páramo, p. 137.--Boletin, XV, 472, 474.
284. Printed by Llorente, Append. n. 4. That this was procured, and of course paid for, by the Conversos is evident from the fact that the original was presented, January 4, 1484, to Garcia de Meneses, Bishop of Evora in Portugal, by Juan de Sevilla, who asked, as it provided that full faith should be given to all notarial transcripts, authenticated by the seal of a bishop, that he would authorize the notary, Nuñez Lorenzo, to make transcripts and attach the seal, to which the bishop assented.--Archivo de Simancas, Patronato Real, Inquisicion, Leg. único, fol. 20.

Thus the bull was brought to Spain by the Conversos; copies were needed and either they dared not trust the original to any Spanish bishop, or could find none who ventured to assist in its multiplication; it was therefore carried to Portugal, where the bishops were under no constraint.

285. Boletin, XV, 489.--Llorente, Hist. crít. cap. V, Art. iv, n. 20.
286. Archivio Vaticano, Sisto IV, Registro 677, Tom. XVIII, fol. 498.
287. Pulgar, Chronica, III, xxxviii.
288. See Vol. I, Appendix, p. 572.
289. Archivo gen. de la C. de Aragon, Regist. 3684, fol. 33
290. Archivo gen. de la C. de Aragon, Regist. 3684, fol. 45.--Páramo, p. 137.
291. Informe de Quesada (Bibl. nacional, MSS., Tj, 28).
292. Bulario de la Orden de Santiago, Lib. I, fol. 8.--Cf. Somoza de Salgado de Retentione Bullarum, P. II, cap. xxxiii, n. 85, 86.
293. Boletin, XV, 579.--Archivo de Simancas, Inquisicion, Lib. 926, fol. 260.
294. Boletin, XV, 581.
295. Somoza, loc. cit., n. 127.--Bulario de la Orden de Santiago, Lib. I, fol. 94.--Archivio Vaticano, Innoc. VIII, Regist. 686, fol. 103. (See Appendix).
296. Bulario de la Orden de Santiago. Lib. I, fol. 44.--Archive de Simancas, Inquisicion, Lib. 926, fol. 274.--Llorente, Añales, I, 146.
297. Archivo de Simancas, Inquisition, Lib. I.
298. Bulario de la Orden de Santiago, Lib. I de copias, fol. 46.
299. Somoza, op. cit., P. II, cap. xxxiii, n. 85, 86.
300. Archivo de Simancas, Patronato Real, Inquisicion, Leg. único, fol. 22.
301. Boletin, XV, 572.
302. Archivo de Simancas, Inquisicion, Lib. 1; Lib. 939, fol. 114.
303. Boletin, XV, 597.
304. Archivo de Simancas, Patronato Real, Inquisicion, Leg. único, fol. 15.--Bulario de la Orden de Santiago, Lib. III, fol. 95.--Burchardi Diarium (Ed. Thuasne, II, 491).--Villari, Niccolò Machiavelli, I, 249, 279 (Milano, 1895).
305. Llorente, Hist. crít., Appendix VII.--Nueva Recop. Lib. VIII, Tit. ii, ley 2.
306. Yet licence to return could doubtless often be had for a consideration. Compromises and commutations, as we shall see, were a recognized source of revenue and a document of this period contains an offer, from certain parties who had been absolved in Rome, of seven thousand ducats and some houses, for permission to reside in Spain and present themselves to the Inquisition for salutary penance.--Archivo de Simancas, Patronato Real, Inquisition, Leg. único, fol. 5.
307. Archivo de Simancas, Inquisicion, Libro 1.
308. Bulario de la Orden de Santiago, Lib. I, fol. 47; Lib. 3, fol. 32.--Archivo da Simancas, Inquisicion, Lib. 933.
309. Bibl. nacional, MSS., X, 157, fol. 244; D, 118, fol. 39, 41, 104.
310. Gachard, Voyages des Souverains des Pays-Bas, I, 548.
311. Bulario de la Orden de Santiago, Lib. I, fol. 13, 15.
312. Bulario, Lib. I, fol. 50.
313. Bibl. nacional, MSS., D, 118, fol. 104.
314. Somoza, op. cit., P. II, cap. xxxiii, n. 50.
315. Archivo de Simancas, Inquisicion, Lib. 3, fol. 7.--Archivo hist. nacional, Inquisicion de Valencia, Leg. 2, n. 16, fol. 296.

Somoza (op. cit., P. II, cap. xxxiii, n. 40) prints this with the date of March 17, 1510--probably a reissue.

316. Archivo de Simancas, Inquisicion, Lib. 3, fol. 71, 75, 77.
317. Döllinger, Beiträge zur politischen, kirchlichen u. Cultur-geschichte, T. III, p. 204.--Bibl. nacional, MSS., D, 118, n. 2, fol. 8.
318. Bulario de la Orden de Santiago, Lib. I de copias fol. 50.
319. Archivo de Simancas, Inquisicion, Leg. 1465, fol. 28.
320. Archivo de Simancas, Inquisicion, Libro 3, fol. 133.
321. Ibidem, Lib. 3, fol. 149, 274.
322. Bulario de la Orden de Santiago, Lib. II, fol. 19, 21.--Archivo de Simancas, Inquisicion, Lib.

72, fol. 61; Lib. 74, fol. 56, 62.

323. Llorente, Añales, II, 106.
324. Somoza, P. II, cap. xxxiii, n. 85, 86.
325. Archivo de Simancas, Inquisicion, Lib. 9, fol. 15.
326. Ibidem, Lib. 9, fol. 16.
327. Bulario de la Orden de Santiago, Lib. I de copias, fol. 59.
328. Bulario de la Orden de Santiago, Lib. I de copias, fol. 55-58.--Bibl. nacional, MSS., D, 118, n. 2, fol. 31, 104.--Archivo de Simancas, Inquisicion, Lib. 14, fol. 17, 18.--Llorente, Hist. crít. cap. XI, Art. v, n. 9.
329. Bulario de la Orden de Santiago, Lib. I de copias, fol. 23.
330. Bibl. nacional, MSS., D, 118, fol. 104.
331. Llorente, Añales, II, 181, 208, 227.--Archivo de Simancas, Inquisicion, Lib. 4, fol. 9; Lib. 9, fol. 14; Leg. 1465, fol. 28.--Bibl. nacional, MSS., D, 118, n. 54, fol. 104; fol. 177.--Archivo hist. nacional, Inquisicion de Valencia, Leg. 2, n. 16, fol. 196.
332. Bibl. nacional, MSS., D, 118, n. 54, fol. 8, 104, 177.--Archivo de Simancas, Inquisicion, Lib. 14, fol. 55-7.--Bulario de la Orden de Santiago, Lib. I de copias, fol. 65, 68, 72.--Llorente, Añales, II, 207, 216, 243.
333. Bibl. nacional, MSS., D, 118, fol. 104.
334. Ibidem, fol. 39, n. 17.
335. Bulario de la Orden de Santiago, Lib. I de copias, fol. 26, 74, 81, 83, 85.--Páramo, p. 607.
336. Somoza, op. cit., P. II, cap. xxxiii, n. 41.--Llorente, Añales, II, 334, 335.
337. Bulario de la Orden de Santiago, Lib. III de copias, fol. 133.
338. Böhmer, Francisca Hernández und Francisco Ortiz, pp. 174-5 (Leipzig, 1865).
339. Llorente, Hist. crít. cap. XIV, Art. ii, n. 4-10.
340. Somoza, op. cit., P. II, cap. xxxiii, n. 87.
341. Juan de Zuñiga, the ambassador at Rome, states that when, in 1572, the commission of Pedro Ponce de Leon as inquisitor-general was drafted, Gregory XIII had strong desire to limit his faculties so as to make the Spanish Inquisition subordinate to the Roman Congregation and that it required infinite labor to obtain it in the customary form. Possibly the case of Carranza may have suggested the innovation.--Bulario de la Orden de Santiago, Lib. IV, fol. 77.
342. Archivo de Simancas, Inquisicion, Lib. 13, fol. 21.
343. Ibidem, Lib. 79, fol. 99.--Somoza, P. II, cap. xxxiii, n. 112.
344. Bulario de la Orden de Santiago, Lib. I de copias, fol. 32, 35, 39; Libro IV, fol. 2.
345. MSS. of Royal Library of Copenhagen, 214 fol.
346. Bibl. nacional, MSS., D, 118, n. 55, fol. 175.
347. Archivo de Simancas, Gracia y Justicia, Inquisicion, Leg. 621, fol. 171.--Bibl. nacional, MSS., D, 118, n. 12, fol. 442.--Bulario de la Orden de Santiago, Lib. IV, fol. 77, 81, 83, 87; Lib. III, fol. 442.--Theiner, Annal. Ecclesiast. III, 361-2.
348. Hinojosa, Despachos de la Diplomacia Pontificia, I, 252-4, 358.
349. Archivo de Simancas, Inquisicion, Leg. 1465, fol. 28.
350. Somoza, op. cit., P. II, cap. xxxiii, n. 138.--MSS. Bibl. nacional de Lima, Protocolo 223, Expediente 5270.
351. MSS. of Library of Univ. of Halle, Yc, 20, Tom. I.
352. Zurita, Añales de Aragon, Lib. XX, cap. xlix.--Páramo, p. 151.
353. Archivo de Simancas, Inquisicion, Lib. 939, fol. 285.
354. Ibidem, Gracia y Justicia, Inquisicion, Leg. 621, fol. 139.
355. Archivo de Simancas, Inquisicion, Lib. 25, fol. 56; Lib. 52, fol. 186; Gracia y Justicia, Inquisicion, Leg. 621, fol. 102.--Bulario de la Orden de Santiago, Lib. V, fol. 51, 52.
356. MSS. of Royal Library of Copenhagen, 213 fol., p. 145.
357. Archivo hist. nacional, Inquisicion de Valencia, Leg. 1, n. 4, fol. 23.

For much of the earlier history of this case I am indebted to a MS. "Relacion sumaria de la causa que a seguido en el santo oficio de la Inquisicion del Reyno de Toledo contra Don Gerónimo de Villanueva" in the Simancas archives, Lib. 53, fol. 250-98. It bears no date but seems to have been drawn up, in 1647, as an official justification of the sentence, and presents the subject from the standpoint of the prosecution. It will be referred to as "Relacion."

The other side of the story of the convent of San Placido is given in the appeal of Doña Teresa for a reversal of her sentence. Several copies of this have been preserved. The one I have used is in the Bibl. nacional, MSS., S, 294, fol. 387. Fuller details of this curious conventual episode will be found in my "Chapters from the Religious History of Spain," pp. 309-18.

358. Two copies of the sentence of Calderon are in the Bodleian Library, Arch. Seld. 130 and A. Subt. 11. It has also been printed by Eyssenhardt, Mittheilungen aus der Stadtbibliothek zu Hamburg, 1886.

A short account of the auto de fe of 1630 will be found in the Appendix to "Chapters from the Religious History of Spain."

359. Relacion, fol. 258, 297.
360. Relacion, fol. 259-60, 290.
361. Ibidem, fol. 261-7.--"Que por lo que tocava á Don Gerónimo no tocava al santo oficio el proceder en esta causa, por no tener calidad de oficio lo contra el testificado."
362. Relacion, fol. 267-8.--Bibl. nacional, MSS., S, 294, fol. 387.--Archivo hist. nacional, Inquisicion de Valencia, Lib. VII de Autos, Leg. 2, fol. 27.
363. Pii PP. V, Bull. Inter multiplices (Lib. V, in Septimo, ii, 10).
364. Archivo de Simancas, Gracia y Justicia, Inquisicion, Leg. 621, fol. 156-60.
365. Archivo de Simancas, Inquisition, Lib. 53, fol. 54, 60.
366. Relacion, fol. 291.--Archivo de Simancas, Inquisicion, Lib. 53, fol. 81; Gracia y Justicia, Inquisicion, Leg. 621, fol. 135, 137, 171, 188.
367. Archivo de Simancas, Inquisicion, Libro 53, fol. 53, 55, 60-2.--Relacion, fol. 268-9.
368. Relacion, fol. 270-89.
369. Relacion, fol. 289.--Archivo de Simancas, Inquisicion, Lib. 53, fol. 63-4.--Pellicer, Avísos históricos (Semanario erúdito, XXXIII, 225).
370. Archivo de Simancas, Inquisicion, Lib. 53, fol. 64; Lib. 54, fol. 411.--Pellicer (Semanario, XXXIII, 231, 250).
371. Relacion, fol. 290, 291.--Cartas de Jesuitas (Memorial hist. español, XVIII, 39).--Archivo de Simancas, Inquisicion, Lib. 53, fol. 86, 92, 104.
372. Relacion, fol. 292.
373. Relacion, loc. cit.--Archivo de Simancas, Inquisicion, Libro 54, fol. 409.--Cartas de Jesuitas (Memorial hist. español, XVIII, 473).
374. Relacion, fol. 293.--Cartas de Jesuitas (Memorial, XIX, 5).
375. Relacion, fol. 293.--Martin. PP. V Bull Inter cunctas, 22 Feb. 1418 (Pegnæ Append, ad Eymeric., p. 76).--Cartas de Jesuitas (XIX, 5-7).
376. Archivo de Simancas, Inquisicion, Legajo 1495, fol. 73.
377. Ibidem, Gracia y Justicia, Inquisicion, Leg. 621, fol. 111, 131, 132.--Bibl. nacional, MSS., X, 157, fol. 244.
378. Archivo de Simancas, Inquisicion, Lib. 54, fol. 128; Gracia y Justicia, Inquisicion, Leg. 621, fol. 112. 114.
379. Bibl. nacional, MSS., S, 291, fol. 214.
380. Archivo de Simancas, Gracia y Justicia, Inquisicion, Leg. 621, fol. 115.
381. Ibidem, fol. 116.
382. Ibidem, fol. 118, 122, 130, 131, 132, 133, 151.
383. Archivo de Simancas, Inquisicion, Lib. 54, fol. 416.
384. Ibidem, Gracia y Justicia, Inquisicion, Leg. 621, fol. 154, 171.
385. Ibidem, Leg. 621, fol. 134, 135.
386. Ibidem, Gracia y Justicia, Inquisicion, Leg. 621, fol. 136, 184.
387. Ibidem, fol. 139.
388. Ibidem, Gracia y Justicia, Leg. 621, fol. 154, 197.
389. Ibidem, fol. 164, 141, 171.
390. Archivo de Simancas, Gracia y Justicia, Inquisicion, Leg. 621, fol. 155.
391. Ibidem, fol. 164-8, 181.
392. Archivo de Simancas, Gracia y Justicia, Inquisicion, Leg. 621, fol. 171.
393. Ibidem, fol. 170: Libro 54, fol. 330, 332.
394. Archivo de Simancas, Gracia y Justicia, Inquisicion, Leg. 621, fol. 172, 173, 175, 176; Inquisicion, Lib. 54, fol. 20, 342, 378.
395. Archivo de Simancas, Inquisicion, Libro 54, fol. 1, 6, 20, 26, 29, 31, 35.
396. Archivo de Simancas, Inquisicion, Libro 54, fol. 31; Gracia y Justicia, Inquisicion, Leg. 621, fol. 184.
397. Ibidem, Lib. 54, fol. 44, 54, 80.--Salazar, Inventaire general des Royaumes d'Espagne, fol. 142 (Paris, 1612).
398. Archivo de Simancas, Inquisicion, Lib. 54, fol. 44.
399. Ibidem, Lib. 54, fol. 40; Gracia y Justicia, Inquisicion, Leg. 621, fol. 186, 187.
400. Archivo de Simancas, Inquisicion, Lib. 54, fol. 61, 69, 78.
401. Ibidem, Inquisicion, Lib. 54, fol. 84, 94. Cf. fol. 294.
402. Ibidem, fol. 100, 116, 120; Gracia y Justicia, Inquisicion, Leg. 621, fol. 110.

For the intrigues connected with the Barbarino marriage see the virulent pamphlet of Gualdi Gregorio Leti. "Vita di Donna Olimpia Maldachini" pp. 185, 199. Cosmopoli Leyden., 1666.

403. Archivo de Simancas, Inquisicion, Lib. 54, fol. 128, 132, 188, 292.

404. Ibidem, Legajo 1465, fol. 73; Libro 54, fol. 230, 292, 330, 332.--Bulario de la Orden de Santiago, Lib. V, fol. 71.
405. Archivo de Simancas, Inquisicion, Lib. 25, fol. 103; Lib. 52, fol. 125.
406. Archivo de Simancas, Inquisicion, Lib. 52, fol. 335.
407. Revista crítica de Historia y Literatura, Jan.-Mar., 1900.--Memorial del Doctor Don Luis Belluga, Murcia, 1709.
408. MSS. of Trinity College, Dublin, Class 3, Vol. 27.
409. Archivo de Simancas, Inquisicion, Leg. 1465, fol. 17.
410. Concil. Plenar. Americæ Latinæ, Tit. I, cap. viii, n. 65, 66, 72 (T. I, pp. 37, 40. Romaæ, 1900).
411. Potthast, Regesta, No. 23,302.
412. Bulario de la Orden de Santiago, Lib. I de copias, fol. 118, 137.--Archivo de Simancas, Gracia y Justicia, Inquisicion, Legajo 629.
413. Archivo de Simancas, Inquisicion, Libro 72, fol. 45, 49, 80, 81, 103.
414. Ibidem, Gracia y Justicia, Inquisicion, Legajo 621, fol. 63.--Cf. Eymerici Director. P. III, Q. vi.--Simancæ de Cath. Institt. Tit. XXXIV, § 14.
415. Archivo de Simancas, Inquisicion, Lib. 50, fol. 82.--Ibidem, Sala 39, Leg. 4, fol. 57.
416. Archivo hist. nacional, Inquisicion de Valencia, Cartas del Consejo, Leg. 15, n. 11, fol. 30; Leg. 16, n. 6, fol. 33; no. 9, fol. 17, 26.
417. Arguello, fol. 9.
418. See Vol. I, Appendix, p. 578.
419. Arguello, fol. 22.
420. Arguello, fol. 9. In the Simancas copy of these Instructions (Lib. 933) it is one of the inquisitors, or the assessor, to whom the duty was assigned.
421. Ibidem, fol. 13.
422. Arguello, fol. 16, 20, 23.
423. Archivo de Simancas, Inquisicion, Lib. 933, p. 89.
424. Bulario de la Orden de Santiago, Lib. I de copias, fol. 219.
425. Archivo de Simancas, Inquisicion, Libro 72, fol. 49.
426. Archivo de Alcalá, Estado, Leg. 3137.
427. Archivo de Simancas, Inquisicion, Lib. 9, fol. 68; Lib. 72, fol. 45.

During the separation of the Inquisitions each of course had its Suprema, and even after their union under Adrian the particularist tendencies of the kingdoms kept up for some time distinct organizations. Adrian continued to sign as inquisitor-general for Aragon in all business under that crown (Archivo de Simancas, Libro 940, fol. 190). The two councils continued to keep their organizations complete, except that one relator served for both (Ibidem, fol. 188, 191; Sala 40, Lib. 4, fol. 98). Even as late as 1540 we have seen that payments for Aragon required special powers from the king (Sala 40, Lib. 4, fol. 107). To the last there were two secretaries, one for Castile and one for Aragon (Ibidem, Lib. 940, fol. 65-7).

428. Ibidem, Lib. 940, fol. 53.
429. Ibidem, Lib. 5, fol. 21.
430. Salazar y Mendoza, Crónica del Cardenal Juan Tavera, p. 217 (Toledo, 1603).
431. Páramo, p. 150.
432. Archivo de Simancas, Inquisicion, Lib. 31, fol. 34.
433. Ibidem, Gracia y Justicia, Legajo 624, fol. 181.
434. Archivo de Simancas, Inquisicion, Registro de Genealogias, n. 916, fol. 66.
435. Ibidem, Lib. 5, fol. 29; Lib. 73, fol. 52, 100, 115, 142, 143, 144, 182, 193, 240, 315; Lib. 74, fol. 116.
436. Ibidem, Lib. 76, fol. 227, 235.
437. Ibidem, Libro 939, fol. 136; Sala 40, Libro 4, fol. 104, 115.
438. Arguello, fol. 27.
439. Cabrera, Relaciones, Append. p. 571.
440. Archivo de Simancas, Inquisicion, Libro 31, fol. 34.
441. Libro XIII de Cartas (MSS. of Am. Philos. Society).
442. Archivo hist. nacional, Inquisicion de Valencia, Leg. 1, n. 4. Under Rocaberti, in 1696, there is still another formula "El ex^{mo} señor inquisidor-general con consulta de los señores del consejo."--Ibidem, fol. 194.
443. Archivo de Simancas, Inquisicion, Lib. 939, fol. 136.--MSS. of Royal Library of Copenhagen, 218^{b}, p. 320.
444. Archivo de Alcalá, Hacienda, Leg. 544^{2} (Lib. 10).--MSS. of Royal Library of Copenhagen, 218^{b}, p. 341.
445. Bibl. nacional, MSS., Pp. 28, §§ 58-88.

446. Tomás Sanchez, the supreme Spanish theologian, says "Licitum quoque est interrogare, non deprecative sed coactive, aliquam veritatem ad peculiariam Dei gloriam et astantium utilitatem quando adjurans prudenter judicaverit id expedire.... Ex levitate tamen et curiositate quadam res vanas et inutiles interrogare dæmonem in energumeno existentem est veniale propter actus imperfectionem."--In Præcepta Decalogi Lib. II, cap. xlii, n. 24, 25.

The offence of Villanueva consisted in enquiring about the future and believing the responses of the demons. This was divination, which infers denial of free-will and is therefore forbidden as heretical. This is well defined in the Edict of Faith of 1696, which restricts the offence to enquiries as to the future--"O si sabeis ... que alguna ó algunas personas ayan preguntado en los cuerpos endemoniados ó los espiritados ó lunáticos cosas por venir ocultas, preguntandolas á los demonios."

447. S. Th. Aquinat. Summæ Sec. Sec. Q. XCV, Art. iv ad 1. "Aliud autem est inquirere aliquid a dæmone sponte occurrente; quod quandoque licet propter utilitatem aliorum, maxime quando divina virtute potest compelli ad vera dicenda."

448. MSS. Bibl. nacional de Lima, Protocolo 225, Expediente 5278.

449. For most of the details of this case we are indebted to an anonymous memoir, evidently written by Folch de Cardona. It was largely circulated in MS. and finally was printed by Valladares, in 1788, under the title "Proceso criminal fulminado contra el R^{mo} P. M. Fray Froilan Díaz" and was followed by another volume of the same date "Criticos Documentos que sirven como de segunda parte al Proceso criminal etc."

Consultas by Cardona, in the name of the Suprema, are in the Bibl. national MSS., G, 61; D, 118. A review of the case from the Roman standpoint is in the library of Trinity College, Dublin, Class 3, Vol. 27. The decree of Nov. 3, 1704, is also in Simancas, Inquisicion, Legajo 1465, fol. 74.

450. Archivo hist. nacional, Inquisicion de Valencia, Leg. 1, n. 4, fol. 123, 134; Leg. 13, n. 2, fol. 13, 17, 54.

451. MSS. Trinity College, Dublin, loc. cit.
452. Bulario de la Orden de Santiago, Lib. 5, fol. 137.
453. Bibl. nacional, MSS., G, 61, fol. 208.
454. Archivo de Simancas, Inquisicion, Lib. 933, fol. 136.
455. Ibidem, Lib. 939, fol. 936.
456. Archivo de Simancas, Inquisicion, Lib. 939, fol. 105.
457. Ibidem, Lib. 1; Lib. 933.
458. Ibidem, Lib. 78, fol. 114.
459. Ibidem, Lib. 78, fol. 235, 275.
460. MS. penes me.
461. Archivo de Simancas, Inquisicion, Sala 40, Lib. 4, fol. 191; Lib. 98, fol. 144.
462. Arguello, fol. 36.
463. Archivo de Simancas, Visitas de Barcelona, Leg. 15, fol. 20.
464. Ibidem, Libro 939, fol. 121.
465. MSS. of Library of University of Halle, Yc, 20, T. I.
466. Proceso contra Mari Vaez (MS. penes me).
467. MSS. of Library of Univ. of Halle, Yc, 20, T. VIII.
468. Ibidem, Yc, 20, T. III.
469. Archivo de Simancas, Inquisicion, Legajo 1157, fol. 153-55.
470. Archivo de Simancas, Inquisicion, Libro 81, fol. 27.
471. MSS. of the Royal Library of Copenhagen, 218^{b}, p. 252.--Archivo hist. nacional, Inquisicion de Valencia, Leg. 8, n. 2, fol. 533, 547, 553, 667; Leg. 9, n. 2. fol. 234; Leg. 12, n. 2, fol. 126; Leg. 11, n. 1, fol. 247, 278.--Archivo d Sala 39, Leg. 4, fol. 23.--Libro XIII de Cartas, fol. 266, 274-5 (MSS. of Am. Philos. Society).e Alcalá, Hacienda, Leg. 544^{2}, Lib. 6, Lib. 10.--Archivo de Simancas, Inquisicion,
472. MSS. of the Royal Library of Copenhagen, 218^{b}, p. 185
473. Archivo hist. nacional, Inquisicion de Valencia, Leg. 17, n. 3, fol. 18.--Archivo de Simancas, Inquisicion, Lib. 559.
474. Archivo de Simancas, Inquisicion, Lib. 240, fol. 340.
475. Ibidem, Leg. 522.
476. Archivo hist. nacional, Inquisicion de Valencia, Leg. 10, n. 2, fol. 34.
477. Archivo de Simancas, Inquisicion, Leg. 552, fol. 52.
478. Vol. I, Appendix, p. 580.
479. Archivo de Simancas, Inquisicion, Lib. 939, fol. 105.
480. Ibidem, fol. 89.
481. Ibidem, fol. 105.--MSS. of Royal Library of Copenhagen, 218^{b}, p. 242.
482. Instrucciones Nuevas, § 5 (Arguello, fol. 28).
483. MSS. of Royal Library of Copenhagen, loc. cit.

484. Bibl. nacional, MSS., Pp. 28.
485. Bibl. nacional, MSS., Mm, 130.
486. Archivo de Simancas, Inquisicion, Libro 890.
487. Ibidem.
488. Archivo de Simancas, Inquisicion, Leg. 552.
489. Proceso contra Margarita Altamira, fol. 198-99 (MSS. of Am. Philos. Society).
490. Archivo de Simancas, Inquisicion, Libro 890.
491. Bulario de la Orden de Santiago, Lib. I de copias, fol. 219.
492. Archivo de Simancas, Gracia y Justicia, Inquisicion, Lib. 621, fol. 165.
493. Archivo de Simancas, Inquisicion, Lib. 5, fol. 24.
494. Ibidem, Sala 40, Lib. 4, fol. 99.
495. Ibidem, Lib. 77, fol. 354.
496. Ibidem, Sala 40, Lib. 4, fol. 105.
497. Archivo de Alcalá, Estado, Leg. 3137.
498. Archivo de Simancas, Inquisicion, Lib. 79, fol. 173.
499. Archivo de Simancas, Inquisicion, Lib. 939, fol. 135.
500. Ibidem, Lib. 3, fol. 225, 313.
501. Ibidem, Sala 40, Lib. 4, fol. 227; Visitas de Barcelona, Leg. 15, fol. 20.
502. MSS. of Royal Library of Copenhagen, 218^{b}, p. 212.
503. Archivo hist. nacional, Inquisicion de Valencia, Leg. 9, n. 1, fol. 7, 8, 9, 13, 19, 276, 277, 278; n. 3, fol. 142, 253, 259, 320, 323, 324, 332; Leg. 17, n. 10, fol. 47, 81, 99.--Libro XIII de Cartas, fol. 11 (MSS. of Am. Philos. Soc.).
504. Archivo de Simancas, Inquisicion, Lib. 939, fol. 132.--Archivo hist. nacional, Inquisicion de Valencia, Leg. 5, n. 2, fol. 165, 166.
505. Libro XIII de Cartas, fol. 84, 89, 114 (MSS. of Am. Philos. Society).
506. Archivo de Simancas, Inquisicion, Lib 890; Lib. 435^{2}.
507. Archivo de Simancas, Inquisicion, Lib. 5, fol. 15, 21.
508. Ibidem, Lib. 3, fol. 397, 446; Lib. 940, fol. 84; Lib. 5, fol. 6, 16, 21. Cf. Lib. 9, fol. 27, 66, 192.

For the settlement in 1502, see Lib. 2, fol. 35.
509. Archivo de Simancas, Inquisicion, Lib. 73, fol. 106, 107.
510. Ibidem, Sala 40, Lib. 4, fol. 107, 110, 113, 114, 115, 118, 137, 139, etc.--Archivo hist. nacional, Inquisicion de Valencia, Lib. VII de Autos, Leg. 2, fol. 327; Ibidem, Leg. 10, n. 2, fol. 164.
511. Archivo de Simancas, Inquisicion, Sala 40, Lib. 4, fol. 184.
512. Ibidem, fol. 124, 226; Lib. 940, fol. 41, 43, 184.
513. Archivo hist. nacional, Inquisicion de Valencia, Leg. 9, n. 2, fol. 177, 238; Leg. 14, n. 2, fol. 41.
514. Archivo de Simancas, Inquisicion, Lib. 940, fol. 43, 44.
515. Ibidem, Lib. 559.
516. Ibidem, Lib. 9, fol. 8.
517. Archivo de Simancas, Inquisicion, Lib. 78, fol. 192; Sala 40, Lib. 4, fol. 169, 239.

As a contribution to the life of one to whom all Spanish students owe a debt of gratitude, I print Zurita's petition in the Appendix. He was probably well paid for his services; in 1542 there is an order on the receiver of Aragon to pay him an ayuda de costa, or gratuity, of 600 ducats (Ibidem, Lib. 940, fol. 42).

There was a secretary of the Suprema, in 1519, named Gerónimo Zurita--probably an uncle of the historian (Arch. hist. nacional, Inq. de Valencia, Leg. 371).
518. Archivo de Simancas, Inquisicion, Lib. 5, fol. 6, 16, 21.
519. Bibl. nacional, MSS., D, 150, p. 224.
520. Archivo de Simancas, Inquisicion, Lib. 30, fol. 647, 653.
521. Archivo de Simancas, Lib. 940, fol. 205.
522. Ibidem, Lib. 31, fol. 637.--These royal perquisites were quietly left unpaid until, in 1640, Philip in his distress suddenly remembered them and ordered the receiver to render a statement of the amount due to him, until the settlement of which no other payments were to be made. To this the Suprema replied that orders had been given for its immediate settlement. This was more easily said than done, for three months later it represented that it had responded liberally to his demands; it had paid 35,000 reales of the arrearages and hoped to increase the amount to 40,000 and begged to be forgiven the balance, but the king was obdurate.--Ibidem, Lib. 21, fol. 223, 231. The crown continued to share in these perquisites. In 1670, an order for paying luminarias on the accession of Clement IX, is headed by Carlos II for the amount of 114,240 mrs.--Ibidem, Leg. 1476, fol. 7.
523. Archivo de Simancas, Inquisicion, Leg. 1480, fol. 1.
524. Ibidem, Lib. 21, fol. 252.

525. Ibidem, Leg. 1480, fol. 1, 10, 16.
526. Ibidem, Leg. 1476, fol. 7.
527. Ibidem, Leg. 1475, fol. 1, 2, 4, 19.
528. Ibidem, Leg. 1477, fol. 154.
529. Archivo de Simancas, Inquisicion, Leg. 1477, fol. 45.
530. The vellon payments were 1940 reales for erecting the staging and 100 for stretching the awning. The items in silver were
  For the companies of players 516 reales.the authors of the autos 500"the keepers of the wardrobe16"the dancers 48"three coaches for the players 24"Juan Rana32"three alguaziles 32"
  Archivo de Simancas, Inquisicion, Leg. 1475, fol. 52.
  In 1665, to reduce expenses, Philip IV ordered that these autos should not be performed separately before each royal council, but collectively before them all in the plaza.--Archivo de Alcalá, Hacienda, Leg. 544^{2} (Lib. 10).
531. Archivo de Simancas, Inquisicion, Leg. 1477, fol. 95, 100.
  The items of the account are:-- Rs. Mrs.95 lbs. Genoese sweetmeats @ 10-1/2 Rs. vellon 100832 Talavera dishes @ 5 cuartos 18 28 4 Baskets @ 7-1/2 Rs.30 6 Trays @ 2 12 4 Padlocks for the baskets @ 2-1/2 1032 Glasses @ 9 cuartos33 30 6 Venetian glasses for the members of the Council 34 2 Talavera plates 10 4 Double urinals with their covers @ 3 Rs.1230 lbs. of ordinary sweetmeats and biscuits for the attendants @ 5 Rs.150Porters to carry the sweetmeats to the houses of the officials andthe utensils to Buen Retiro 15
  Beverages:--20 Azumbres (about 10 gallons) of lemonade Rs. Mrs.10 lbs. of loaf sugar @3 Rs. 30Lemons61 oz. of scented lozenges 420 Azumbres of cinnamon water15 lbs. of sugar 45 1/2 lb. of cinnamon 20 Charcoal to boil it5 1 oz. of scented lozenges420 Azumbres of cherry water15 lbs. of sugar 4518 lbs. of cherries @ 6 cuartos 13 1 oz. of scented lozenges 410 Arrobas (250 lbs.) of snow for all the beverages @ 9 Rs.901 " sent from Retiro to keep the jars from melting9Rent of 14 garrafas (jars with ice-pails) @ 3-1/2 Rs.49Cost of one of them broken12Rent of 3 small ones for the Council33 pecks of salt to freeze the beverages @ 22 cuartos 10 172 porters for the snow and cooling-jars 108do.to take them to Retiro and return 24Labor of the official who renders the account 50 --------433 17Ornamenting and furnishing the staging 300 -------20677
  Apparently the utensils were a perquisite of the attendants as they seem to be furnished anew on each occasion.
532. Archivo de Simancas, Inquisicion, Leg. 1477, fol. 106.
533. Bibl. nacional, MSS., D, 122 (Modo de procesar, fol. 10-12); Ibidem, D, 150, fol. 1.--Archivo de Alcalá, Hacienda, Leg. 544^{2} (Lib. 9).
534. J. T. Medina, La Inquisicion en Cartagena, p. 266 (Santiago de Chile, 1899).
535. MSS. of Bibl. nacional de Lima, Protocolo 225, Expediente 5278.
536. Archivo de Simancas, Inquisicion, Lib. 31, fol. 637.
537. Ibidem, Lib. 21, fol. 231.--Bibl. nacional, MSS., D, 150, p. 224.
538. Archivo de Simancas, Inquisicion, Lib. 240, fol. 360; Lib. 559.--MSS. of Royal Library of Copenhagen, 218^{b}, p. 180.--Archivo hist. nacional, Inquisicion de Valencia, Cartas del Consejo, Leg. 16, n. 9, fol. 7.
539. Archivo de Alcalá, Hacienda, Leg. 544^{2} (Libro 10). This statement shows
  Reales. Mrs.Salaries of Suprema337,27428The three larger propinas157,290The five smaller do. 73,83632Tablados (bull-fights) 21,000Houses for officials65,156Nine luminaries 50,618 5Salaries of Madrid tribunal 24,25812Maintenance of poor prisoners (estimated) 3,000Sundry expenses of Suprema30,000Ayudas de costa and gratuities8,000To assist tribunal of Toledo and others 50,000Taxes and incumbrances on property 17,500 ------------ 837,934 9 ============
540. Archivo de Simancas, Inq., Leg. 1286, fol. 20; Leg. 1478, fol. 1-41, 61-87.
541. Archivo hist. nacional, Inquisicion de Valencia, Leg. 16, n. 9, fol. 20; Leg. 17, n. 4, fol. 7; Leg. 4, n. 3, fol. 173-258.
542. Archivo de Alcalá, Hacienda, Leg. 544^{2} (Lib. 10).
543. Llorente, Añales, I. 282.
544. Archivo gen. de la C. de Aragon, Registro 3684, fol. 68.
545. Such details as I have met with in regard to the establishment and discontinuance of the various tribunals will be found in the Appendix to Vol. I.
546. Archivo de Simancas, Inquisicion, Lib. 1.
547. Ibidem.
548. Archivo de Simancas, Inquisicion, Lib. 3, fol. 447; Lib. 4, fol. 6; Lib. 5, fol. 19; Lib. 9, fol. 65.
549. Ibidem, Lib. 3, fol. 395, 447.
550. Ibidem, Lib. 3, fol. 216, 454, 455; Lib. 9, fol. 23, 34.
551. Ibidem, Leg. 1465, fol. 105.

552. Archivo de Simancas, Inquisicion, Lib. 933; Lib. 75, fol. 25.
553. Ibidem, Legajo 787; Sala 40, Lib. 4, fol. 220.--Lib. XIII de Cartas (MSS. of Am. Philos. Society).
554. Cabrera, Relaciones, p. 489.
555. Modo de Proceder, fol. 46 (Bibl. nacional, MSS., D, 122).
556. Vol. I, Appendix, p. 572. Cf. Arguello, fol. 21.
557. Archivo gen. de la C. de Aragon, Regist. 3684, fol. 87, 92, 95.
558. Archivo de Simancas, Inquisicion, Lib. 1.
559. Vol. I, Appendix, p. 568.
560. Archivo gen. de la C. de Aragon, Regist. 3684, fol. 92, 94.
561. Archivo hist. nacional, Inquisicion de Valencia, Cartas de los Reyes Católicos, Leg. 2.
562. Archivo de Simancas, Inquisicion, Lib. 3, fol. 408.
563. Bibl. nacional, MSS., D, 118, p. 102.
564. Archivo hist. nacional, Inquisicion de Valencia, Leg. 9, n. 3, fol. 123, 166, 215, 240, 271; Leg. 10, n. 2, fol. 29, 30, 33, 76.
565. MSS. of Library of University of Halle, Yc, 20, Tom. 17.--Archivo de Simancas, Inquisicion, Lib. 33, fol. 846, 847, 851; Lib. 35, fol. 509, 567.
566. Fueros y Actos de Corte, pp. 10-11 (Zaragoza, 1647).
567. Archivo de Simancas, Inquisicion, Lib. 67, fol. 155.
568. Ibidem, Lib. 939, fol. 273.
569. Archivo de Simancas, Inquisicion, Lib. 35, fol. 106.
570. Ibidem, Leg. 1465, fol. 23.
571. Archivo hist. nacional, Inquisicion de Valencia, Leg. 9, p. 1, fol. 530, 533, 539, 547, 558, 560, 568; n. 2, fol. 210.--Archivo de Simancas, Inquisicion de Corte, Leg. 359, fol. 3; Ibidem, Inquisicion, Lib. 21, fol. 162, 317.
572. MSS. of Royal Library of Copenhagen, No. 213, fol., pp. 114, 224.
573. Archivo de Simancas, Inquisicion, Lib. 50, fol. 82; Lib. 22, fol. 10; Leg. 1465, fol. 76.--MSS. of Royal Library of Copenhagen, No. 213, fol., p. 114.
574. Archivo hist. nacional, Inquisicion de Valencia, Leg. 4, n. 2, fol. 137.
575. Archivo de Simancas, Inquisicion, Lib. 35, fol. 249.
576. Archivo hist. nacional, Inquisicion de Valencia, Leg. 3, n. 7, fol. 40; Leg. 4, n. 2, fol. 137; Leg. 9, n. 2, fol. 243.--Bibl. nacional, MSS., D, 118, fol. 146.--MSS. of Royal Library of Copenhagen, 218^{b}, pp. 300-1.
577. MSS. Bibl. nacional de Lima, Protocolo 225, Expediente 5278.
578. Archivo hist. nacional, Inquisicion de Valencia, Leg. 16, n. 5, fol. 69; n. 6, fol. 23.
579. Archivo de Alcalá, Hacienda, Leg. 544^{2} (Lib. 10); Estado, Leg. 2843.--Archivo hist. nacional, Inquisicion de Valencia, Leg. 10, n. 2, fol. 155; Leg. 12, n. 2, fol. 128; Leg. 13, n. 2, fol. 180; Leg. 14, n. 1, fol. 133; n. 2, fol. 77.
580. Censo español en el año de 1787 (Madrid, Imprenta Real).
581. Proceso contra Rosa Conejos (MS. penes me).
582. Archivo hist. nacional, Inquisicion de Valencia, Leg. 15, n. 11, fol. 31; Leg. 16, n. 6, fol. 34; n. 9, fol. 18; Leg. 17, n. 3, fol. 4. 583. Archivo hist. nacional, Inquisicion de Valencia, Leg. 4, n. 3, fol. 166, 260; Leg. 16, n. 9, fol. 34.
584. Instruccion que han de guardar los Comisarios.
585. As early as 1680 this is observable in the Toledo trial of Angela Pérez (MS. penes me). In 1728 it seems to be customary in Valencia (Archivo hist. nacional, Inq. de Valencia, Leg. 390). I have even met with a case in which the commission was merely verbal (Ibidem, Inquisicion de Toledo, Leg. 228, n. 28).
586. MSS. of Am. Philos. Society.
587. Archivo hist. nacional, Inquisicion de Valencia, Leg. 5, n. 2, fol. 27, 46, 163.
588. Arguello, fol. 13.
589. Archivo de Simancas, Inquisicion, Lib. 76, fol. 394.
590. Ibidem, Inquisicion de Canarias, Visitas, Leg. 250, Lib. 1, fol. 7, 844, 935-6.--Modo de Proceder, fol. 62 (Bibl. nacional, MSS., D, 122).
591. MSS. of Bibl. nacional de Lima, Protocolo 223, Expediente 5270.
592. Archivo de Simancas, Inquisicion, Lib. 1.
593. Ibidem, Sala 40, Lib. 4, fol. 121, 122, 128, 148, 167.
594. Archivo hist. nacional, Inquisicion de Valencia, Leg. 3, n. 17, fol. 218, 225.
595. Archivo de Simancas, Inquisicion, Sala 40, Lib. 4, fol. 165, 166.
596. Archivo hist. nacional, Inquisicion de Valencia, Leg. 5, n. 2, fol. 86, 99, 118, 128, 138.
597. Ibidem, Leg. 5, n. 1, fol. 100, 410, 414-17; Leg. 8, n. 1, fol. 15, 36, 39; Leg. 9, n. 1, fol. 349, 357, 365; Leg. 11, n. 2, fol. 98, 99, 157, 216, 218, 296-8; Leg. 372; Leg. 383.

598. MSS. of Library of Univ. of Halle, Yc, 17.
599. Archivo de Alcalá, Hacienda, Leg. 544^{2} (Lib. 10).
600. Archivo de Simancas, Registro de Genealogías, n. 916, fol. 74.
601. Archivo hist. nacional, Inquisicion de Valencia, Leg. 6, n. 2, fol. 270, 278.
602. MSS. of Royal Library of Copenhagen, 218^{b}, p 327.
603. Bibl. nacional, MSS., D, 118, fol. 56, n. 22.
604. Archivo hist. nacional, Inquisicion de Valencia, Leg. 10, n. 2, fol. 152, 157.
605. Arguello, fol. 13.
606. Archivo de Simancas, Inquisicion, Lib. 926, fol. 308.
607. Ibidem, Lib. 3, fol. 394, 395, 412.
608. Archivo de Alcalá, Hacienda, Leg. 544^{2} (Lib. 10).
609. Archivo hist. nacional, Inquisicion de Valencia, Leg. 9, n. 3, fol. 30, 60, 80, 89, 94, 157, 162, 211.--Ibidem, Lib. 7 de Autos, Leg. 2, fol. 341.--Cf. Leg. 11, n. 1, fol. 93, 198-99; 226; n. 3, fol. 167; Leg. 12, n. 1, fol. 120, 129.--Bibl. nacional, MSS., D, 118, fol. 56, n. 22.
610. Archivo hist. nacional, Inquisicion de Valencia, Leg. 10, n. 2, fol. 19.--MSS. of Royal Library of Copenhagen, 218^{b}, pp. 184, 201.
611. Archivo de Simancas, Inquisicion, Lib. 926, fol. 33.
612. Archivo de Simancas, Inquisicion, Lib. 926, fol. 18.
613. Instrucciones de 1498, § 15 (Arguello, fol. 13).--Archivo de Simancas, Inquisicion de Canarias, Expedientes de Visitas, Leg. 250, Lib. 1, fol. 6.
614. Archivo de Simancas, Inquisicion, Lib. 76, fol. 227; Visitas de Barcelona, Leg. 15, fol. 2, 20.
615. Ibidem, Lib. 926, fol. 28.
616. Ibidem, Lib. 73, fol. 84, 85, 183, 188, 201; Lib. 76, fol. 415; Lib. 933.
617. Ibidem, Lib. 77, fol. 169, 256.
618. Archivo de Simancas, Inquisicion, Lib 82, fol. 89; Lib. 939, fol. 64, 66; Lib. 941, fol. 20.
619. Ibidem, Lib. 78, fol. 272; Lib. 79, fol. 7, 239; Lib. 939, fol. 64.
620. Ibidem, Patronato Real, Inquisicion, Leg. único, fol. 28.
621. Ibidem, Lib. 1.
622. Arguello, fol. 22.--Archivo de Simancas, Inquisicion, Lib. 939, fol. 140.
623. Archivo de Simancas, Inquisicion, Lib. 1; Lib. 2, fol. 25.
624. Ibidem, Lib. 3, fol. 22, 396; Lib. 5, fol. 14.
625. Ibidem, Lib. 3, fol. 251, 316; Lib. 933.
626. Ibidem, Lib. 9, fol. 63.--Archivo hist. nacional, Inquisicion de Toledo, Hacienda, Leg. 10.
627. Archivo de Simancas, Inquisicion, Lib. 940, fol. 44, 69.
628. Archivo de Alcalá, Hacienda, Leg. 544^{2} (Lib. 10).
629. Archivo de Simancas, Inquisicion de Canarias, Expedientes de Visitas, Leg. 250, Lib. 1.
630. Modo de Proceder, fol. 60-1 (Bibl. nacional, MSS., D, 122).--MSS. of Royal Library of Copenhagen, 218^{b} fol. 301-2.
631. Proceso contra el Doctor Juan de la Camara (MSS. of David Fergusson Esq.).
632. Archivo de Simancas, Inquisicion, Lib. 36, fol. 263.
633. Archivo gen. de la C. de Aragon, Regist. 3684, fol. 68.
634. Arguello, fol. 13.--Archivo de Simancas, Inquisicion, Libro 933.--Ibidem, Vistas de Barcelona, Leg. 15, fol. 2.
635. Ibidem, Lib. 933; Lib. 942, fol. 21.
636. Modo de Proceder, fol. 62 (Bibl. nacional, MSS., D, 122). (Occasionally, however, autos particulares in the audience-chamber were held with open doors.)
637. Bibl. nacional, MSS., D, 118, fol. 84, n. 30.
638. Archivo hist. nacional, Inquisicion de Valencia, Leg. 11, n. 3, fol. 110, 114.
639. Archivo de Simancas, Inquisicion, Leg. 552, fol. 37.
640. Vol. I, Appendix, p. 578.
641. Archivo hist. nacional, Inquisicion de Toledo, Leg. 137, n. 98; Leg. 138, n. 143; Leg. 150, n. 299.
642. Fueros de Aragon, fol. 133 (Zaragoza, 1624).--Archivo de Alcalá, Estado, Leg. 3137.
643. Archivo gen. de la C. de Aragon, Registro 3684, fol. 92.
644. Archivo de Simancas, Inquisicion, Lib. 1.
645. Actos de Corte del Reyno de Aragon, fol. 94 (Zaragoza, 1664).--Bibl. nacional, MSS., D, 118, p. 102.
646. Boletin, XV, 449.--Cap. 2, Clementin. Lib. V, Tit. iii.
647. Bulario de la Orden de Santiago, Lib. I de copias, fol. 122.
648. Vol. I, Appendix, p. 572.
649. Bulario de la Orden de Santiago, Lib. I, fol. 32; Lib. I de copias, fol. 5, 8.--Bibl. nacional, MSS., D, 118, fol. 92.

650. Bulario, Lib. I, fol. 57; Lib. I de copias, fol. 11, 12.
651. Bulario de la Orden de Santiago, Lib. I de copias, fol. 10, 13, 15, 20, 23.
652. Archivo de Simancas, Inquisicion, Lib. 3, fol. 420.
653. Páramo, pp. 172, 189.
654. MSS. of Library of Univ. of Halle, Yc, 17.
655. MSS. of Royal Library of Copenhagen, 218^{b}, pp. 200, 255.
656. Archivo de Simancas, Inquisicion, Lib. 33, fol. 852.
657. MSS. of Library of Univ. of Halle, Yc, 17.--Archivo de Alcalá, Hacienda, Leg. 544^{2} (Lib. 10)--A commission appointing an inquisitor will be found in the Appendix.
658. Bulario de la Orden de Santiago, Lib. IV, fol. 131; Lib. I de copias, fol. 26, 32, 35, 39, 118. Cf. Archivo de Alcalá, Hacienda, n. 473; Archivo de Simancas, Inquisicion, Lib. 33, fol. 328.
659. Bulario, Lib. IV, fol. 137; Lib. V, fol. 117, 136, 138, 151, 199, 200, 251, 264, 295.--Archivo de Simancas, Gracia y Justicia, Leg. 629.
660. Archivo hist. nacional, Inquisicion de Valencia, Leg. 16, n. 5, fol. 42, 68.
661. Archivo gen. de la C. de Aragon, Regist. 3684, fol. 68.--Archivo de Simancas, Inquisicion, Lib. 1.
662. Archivo de Simancas, Inquisicion, Sala 40, Lib. 4, fol. 111, 159, 161; Lib. 939, fol. 62.--Bibl. nacional, MSS., Pp. 28.--Archivo de Alcalá, Estado, Leg. 2843.
663. Archivo de Simancas, Inquisicion, Lib. 939, fol. 81.--Archivo de Alcalá, ubi sup.--Bibl. nacional, ubi sup.
664. Modo de Proceder, fol. 62 (Bibl. nacional, MSS., D, 122).
665. Archivo de Simancas, Inquisicion, Lib. 76, fol. 91.
666. Instrucciones de 1498, §§ 1, 12; de 1500, § 12 (Arguello, fol. 12, 13, 14).
667. Instrucciones de 1561, § 73 (Arguello, fol. 37).
668. Archivo de Simancas, Inquisicion, Lib. 939, fol. 146.
669. MSS. of Royal Library of Copenhagen, 218^{b}, pp. 303, 304.
670. Ibidem.--Archivo de Simancas, Inquisicion, Lib. 939, fol. 140.
671. Modo de Proceder, fol. 49-59 (Bibl. nacional, MSS., D, 122).
672. Archivo de Simancas, Inquisicion, Visitas de Barcelona, Leg. 15, fol. 9.
673. Archivo de Simancas, Inquisicion, Visitas de Barcelona, Leg. 15, fol. 5, 8, 9, 20.
674. Ibidem, Sala 40, Lib. 4, fol. 225.
675. Ibidem, Lib. 942, fol. 61.
676. Ibidem, Lib. 939, fol. 140.
677. Archivo hist. nacional, Inquisicion de Valencia, Leg. 5, n. 1, fol. 379, 380; n. 2, fol. 88; Leg. 6, n. 2, fol. 106, 418; Leg. 8, n. 1, fol. 218, 278, 389; n. 2, fol. 101, 118, 119, 127, 160, 269, 281; n. 2, fol. 380, 631, 635; Leg. 9, n. 1, fol. 47, 179, 199, 324; n. 3, fol. 207, 341, 350, 393, 420; n. 2, fol. 9, 12, 132, 139, 164, 182, 187.--Libro XIII de Cartas, fol. 6, 139, 143, 217, 224, 227 (MSS. of Am. Philos. Soc.).
678. Instrucciones de 1498, § 1 (Arguello, fol. 12).--Archivo de Simancas, Inquisicion, Lib. 933; Lib. 939, fol. 63.
679. Ibidem, Lib. 45, fol. 210.
680. Archivo hist. nacional, Inquisicion de Valencia, Leg. 5, n. 1, fol. 81, 110.
681. Instrucciones de 1498 (Arguello, fol. 22).
682. Archivo de Simancas, Inquisicion, Lib. 1.
683. Archivo de Simancas, Inquisicion, Sala 40, Lib. 4, fol. 104, 111, 225.
684. Instrucciones de 1484, §§ 19, 20 (Arguello, fol. 7).--Archivo hist. nacional, Inquisicion de Toledo, Leg. 112, n. 74, fol. 15. 685. Archivo de Simancas, Inquisicion, Lib. 939, fol. 68.--MSS. of Royal Library of Copenhagen, 218^{b}, p. 185.--Bibl. nacional, MSS., D, 118, fol. 116.
686. MSS. of Royal Library of Copenhagen, loc. cit.--Bibl. nacional, loc. cit.--Archivo de Alcalá, Hacienda, No. 473.
687. MSS. of Library of Univ. of Halle, Yc, 17.--Archivo de Simancas, Inquisicion, Lib. 939, fol. 271.--MSS. of Royal Library of Copenhagen, 218^{b}, p. 184.
688. Archivo hist. nacional, Inquisicion de Valencia, Leg. 9, n. 3, fol. 83.
689. Bibl. nacional, MSS., D, 118, fol. 124, n. 44.
690. MSS. of Royal Library of Copenhagen, 218^{b}, pp. 186, 255.
691. Proceso contra Isabel de Montoya, Mexico, 1661, 1663, fol. 195, 211, 318, 328 (MS. penes me).--Archivo de Simancas, Inquisicion, Lib. 890, fol. 17.
692. Matute y Luquin, Autos de fe de Córdoba, p. 135.--Archivo hist. nacional, Inquisicion de Valencia, Leg. 112, n. 66, fol. 8.--Archivo de Simancas, Inquisicion, Leg. 1473.
693. Archivo gen. de la C. de Aragon, Regist. 3684, fol. 68.
694. Archivo de Simancas, Inquisicion, Lib. 926, fol. 23.
695. Ibidem, Lib. 21, fol. 115.--Archivo hist. nacional, Inquisicion de Toledo, Leg. 1.--MSS. of

Royal Library of Copenhagen, 218^{b}, p. 226.
    696. Arguello, fol. 22.
    697. Archivo hist. national, Inquisicion de Toledo, Leg. 251.
    698. Archivo hist. nac., Inquisicion de Valencia, Leg. 10, n. 2. fol. 33, 46, 61; Leg. 13, n. 3, fol. 42, 47.--MSS. of Royal Library of Copenhagen, 218^{b}, p. 228.
    699. Archivo gen. de la C. de Aragon, Regist. 3684, fol. 92, 94.--Arguello, fol. 22.
    700. Archivo de Simancas, Inquisicion, Lib. 3, fol. 438.--Archivo de Alcalá, Estado, Leg. 2843.
    701. Archivo de Alcalá, Hacienda, n. 473.
    702. Archivo de Simancas, Inquisicion, Lib. 83, fol. 16, 30.
    703. Archivo de Alcalá, Hacienda, n. 437.
    704. Instrucciones de 1488, § 5; de 1498 (Arguello, fol. 11, 17).--Archivo gen. de la C. de Aragon, Regist. 3684, fol. 96.--Archivo de Simancas, Inquisicion, Lib. 2, fol. 25.
    705. Archivo de Simancas, Inquisicion, Leg. 1465, fol. 105.--Matute y Luquin, Autos de fe de Córdoba, p. 137.--MSS. Archivo municipal de Sevilla, Seccion especial, Siglo XVIII, Letra A, Tomo 4, n. 50, 52.--Archivo de Simancas, Inquisicion de Corte, Leg. 351, fol. 1.
    706. Instrucciones de 1488, § 9 (Arguello, fol. 10).--Archivo de Simancas, Inquisicion, Lib. 2, fol. 7; Sala 40, Lib. 4, fol. 218.
    707. Archivo de Simancas, Inquisicion, Sala 40, Lib. 4, fol. 124, 129, 148.--MSS. of Royal Library of Copenhagen, 213 fol., p. 110.
    708. Archivo hist. nacional, Inquisicion de Valencia, Leg. 309, Cuentas, fol. 1, 4.
    709. Autos y Acuerdos del Consejo, fol. 52, 53 (Madrid, 1649).
    710. MSS. of Royal Library of Copenhagen, 218^{b}, p. 238.--Archivo hist. nacional, Inquisicion de Toledo, Leg. 228, n. 18; Inquisicion de Valencia, Leg. 4, n. 2, fol. 41, 111, 115, 205, 251; n. 3, fol. 140; Leg. 3, n. 7, fol. 103.
    711. Archivo de Simancas, Inquisicion, Lib. 1.
    712. Ibidem, Lib. 3, fol. 438.
    713. Ibidem, Sala 40, Lib. 4, fol. 110, 111, 118, 130.
    714. See Appendix.
    715. Archivo de Simancas, Inquisicion, Lib. 78, fol. 56; Leg. 1480, fol. 13.
    716. Archivo de Alcalá, Hacienda, Leg. 544^{2} (Lib. 10).
    717. Archivo gen. de la C. de Aragon, Regist. 3684, fol. 89, 92, 94.
    718. Archivo de Simancas, Inquisicion, Lib. 3, fol. 88.
    719. Ibidem, Lib. 1.
    720. Archivo hist. nacional, Inquisicion de Valencia, Leg. 6, n. 2, fol. 230.
    721. Archivo de Simancas, Inquisicion, Lib. 939, fol. 80.--Archivo de Alcalá, ubi sup.
    722. Archivo hist. nacional, Inquisicion de Valencia, Leg. 9, n. 3, fol. 447, 450.
    723. Archivo de Simancas, Inquisicion, Lib. 939, fol. 79.
    724. Archivo gen. de la C. de Aragon, Regist. 3684, fol. 64.
    725. Archivo hist. nacional, Inquisicion de Valencia, Leg. 9, n. 3, fol. 123, 166.
    726. Archivo hist. nacional, Inquisicion de Valencia, Leg. 12, n. 1, fol. 46, 48, 61, 108.
    727. Ibidem, Inquisicion de Toledo, Leg. 498; Inquisicion de Valencia, Leg. 6, n. 2, fol. 217.--Archivo de Simancas, Inquisicion, Lib. 942, fol. 64.
    728. Archivo hist. nacional, Inquisicion de Toledo, Leg. 498.
    729. Archivo de Simancas, Inquisicion, Sala 40, Lib. 4, fol. 169; Lib. 979, fol. 21, 25, 139.--Bibl. nacional, MSS., Ii, 16.--Archivo hist. nacional, Inquisition de Valencia, Cartas del Consejo, Leg. 10, n. 9, fol. 34.
    730. Bibl. nacional, MSS., D, 118, fol. 146, n. 49.
    731. Ibidem, D, 150, fol. 1.
    732. Ibidem, Mm, 130.
    733. Archivo hist. nacional, Inquisicion de Valencia, Leg. 9, n. 1, fol. 410; Leg. 309, Cuentas, fol. 4; Leg. 371; Leg. 372.
    734. Archivo de Simancas, Inquisicion, Leg. 1479, 1480.
    735. Libro XIII de Cartas, fol. 20, 21, 26, 27, 28 (MSS. of Am. Philos. Society).
    736. Vol. I, Appendix, p. 578.
    737. Arguello, fol. 22.
    738. Archivo de Simancas, Inquisicion, Lib. 1; Lib. 2, fol. 1, 15.
    739. Archivo de Simancas, Inquisicion, Lib. 3, fol. 41, 42, 308.
    740. Ibidem, fol. 397, 408, 418.
    741. Ibidem, Libro 9, fol. 140, 194.
    742. Ibidem, Sala 40, Lib. 4, fol. 106, 107, 111, 116, 124.
    743. Archivo de Simancas, Inquisicion, Sala 40, Lib. 4, fol. 227, 228, 233, 234, 237, 241, 247, 251, 253, 261, 263, 267.

744. Ibidem, Leg. 787; Leg. 552, fol. 43.--Archivo hist. nacional, Inquisicion de Valencia, Leg. 5, n. 1, fol. 41, 201, 274, 296, 407; n. 2, fol. 236, 290, 330.
745. Archivo de Simancas, Inquisicion, Leg. 1478, fol. 96; Sala 40, Lib. 4, fol. 225, 247, 265.--Archivo hist. nacional, Inquisicion de Valencia, Leg. 8, n. 2, fol. 19; Leg. 9, n. 1, fol. 190, 232.--Lib. XIII, de Cartas fol. 85, 110, 122 (MSS. of Am. Philos. Society).
746. Archivo hist. nacional, Inquisicion de Valencia, Cartas del Consejo, Leg. 17, n. 3, fol. 26.
747. Vol. I, Appendix, p. 575.--Arguello, fol. 16.
748. Instrucciones de 1488, § 7 (Arguello, fol. 10).
749. Instrucciones de 1498, § 10 (Arguello, fol. 13).
750. Arguello, fol. 14.
751. Archivo hist. nacional, Inquisicion de Toledo, Leg. 262, n. 1; Inquisicion de Valencia, Leg. 299.
752. MSS. of the Royal Library of Copenhagen, 218^{b}, p. 233.--Archivo de Simancas, Inquisicion, Libro 939, fol. 137; Lib. 83, fol. 8.
753. Archivo de Simancas, Inquisicion, Lib. 3, fol. 197.
754. Ibidem, Lib. 933.
755. Ibidem, Sala 40, Lib. 4, fol. 171, 218, 219.
756. Ibidem, Lib. 926, fol. 292.
757. Archivo de Simancas, Inquisicion, Sala 40, Lib. 4, fol. 160; Lib. 926, fol. 287.
758. Ibidem, Visitas de Barcelona, Leg. 15, fol. 2, 20.
759. Ibidem, Lib. 926, fol. 23.
760. Archivo de Simancas, Inquisicion, Libro 939, fol. 127.

Llorente says (Hist. crít., cap. XIV, art. 3, n. 16) that, in consequence of the irregularity in the arrangement of the papers of a trial, the Suprema, March 22, 1531, ordered that care should be taken to avoid it in the future. This led the tribunals to write every act on a separate sheet and not to page them, so that matters could be introduced or taken out or altered at pleasure when submitting a case to a consulta de fe or the Suprema. He tells us that there was much of this in the prosecution of Carranza and that he had himself seen it done by order of Nubla and Cevallos, inquisitors of the Madrid tribunal.

This all may be so, but the carta acordada of March 22, 1531 expressly orders that the folios shall be numbered (Archivo de Simancas, Lib. 939, fol. 137). The practice was not uniform. I have met with trials both numbered and unnumbered.

761. MSS. of Royal Library of Copenhagen, 218^{b}, p. 233.
762. Ibidem, p. 266.
763. Instrucciones de 1561, § 14 (Arguello, fol. 29).
764. Archivo de Simancas, Inquisicion, Lib. 1002; Registro de Solicitantes, A, 7, fol. 1.--Archivo hist. nacional, Inquisicion de Valencia, Leg. 66, 100.
765. Archivo de Simancas, Inquisicion, Lib. 940, fol. 175.
766. Cartas del Filosofo rancio, I, 316 (Madrid, 1824).
767. Parets, Sucesos de Cataluña (Mem. hist. español, XX, 19).--Archivo hist. nacional, Inquisicion de Valencia, Leg. 11, n. 1, fol. 168.
768. MSS. of Royal Library of Copenhagen, 213 fol., p. 136.
769. Arguello, fol. 27.
770. Archivo de Simancas, Inquisicion, Lib. 940, fol. 175, 176; Lib. 926, fol. 19.
771. Lorenzo Villanueva in "Discussion del Proyecto sobre la Inquisicion," p. 449 (Cadiz, 1813).
772. Instrucciones de 1488, § 4 (Arguello, fol. 9).
773. Archivo hist. nacional, Inquisicion de Toledo, Leg. 158, n. 431, 435.
774. Archivo de Simancas, Inquisicion, Lib. 3, fol. 3.
775. Ibidem, fol. 420, 421.
776. Archivo de Simancas, Inquisicion, Lib. 939, fol. 70.
777. Ibidem, Sala 40, Lib. 4, fol. 134.
778. Ibidem, fol. 208, 223, 252; Lib. 939, fol. 70.--Rojas de Hæret. P. 1, n. 434.
779. Modo de Proceder, fol. 17 (Bibl. nacional, MSS., D, 122).
780. Archivo hist. nacional, Inquisicion de Toledo, Leg. 498.
781. See Appendix.
782. Archivo de Simancas, Inquisicion, Lib. 3, fol. 29.
783. Ibidem, Lib. 78, fol. 168.
784. Archivo de Simancas, Inquisicion, Sala 40, Lib. 4, fol. 197.
785. Archivo hist. nacional, Inquisicion de Valencia, Leg. 299.
786. Archivo de Simancas, Inquisicion, Visitas de Barcelona, Leg. 15, fol. 2.
787. Ibidem, Lib. 939, fol. 81.
788. Ibidem, Visitas de Barcelona, Leg. 15, fol. 20.
789. MSS. of Bodleian Library, Arch. S, 130.--Actos de Corte del Reyno de Aragon, fol. 95.

790. Constitutions del Cort de 1599, cap. 26 (Barcelona, 1603).--Archivo de Simancas, Inquisicion de Barcelona, Córtes, Leg. 17, fol. 5.
791. Archivo de Simancas, Inquisicion, Lib. 939, fol. 81.
792. Bibl. nacional, MSS., D, 118, fol. 172, n. 53.
793. MSS. of Library of University of Halle, Yc, 20, Tom. VI.--Bibl. nacional, MSS., S, 294, fol. 120.--Archivo de Alcalá, Hacienda, Leg. 544^{2} (Lib. 6).
794. MSS. of Royal Library of Copenhagen, 213 fol., p. 150.--Archivo hist. nacional, Inquisicion de Valencia, Leg. 8, fol. 405.
795. Bibl. nacional, MSS., Pp, 28.
796. Archivo hist. nacional, Inq. de Valencia, Leg. 10, n. 2, fol. 170; Leg. 2, n. 18.
797. Archivo de Simancas, Inquisicion, Lib. 559.
798. Cap. 2, Clement. Lib. V. Tit. iii.
799. Archivo de Simancas, Inquisicion, Lib. 939, fol. 147.
800. Ibidem, Lib. 3, fol. 376.
801. Archivo de Simancas, Patronato Real, Inq. Leg. único, fol. 38, 39.
802. Constitutions de la Cort de Monço en lany 1547 (Barcelona, 1548, fol. xxxv).
803. Archivo de Simancas, Inquisicion, Sala 40, Lib. 4, fol. 270; Lib. 926, fol. 33; Lib. 940, fol. 172; Lib. 941, fol. 12; Lib. 942, fol. 48; Leg. 1157, fol. 182.--MSS. of Royal Library of Copenhagen, 218^{b}, p. 181.
804. Archivo de Simancas, Inquisicion, Sala 40, Lib. 4, fol. 203, 206, 208, 211.
805. Ibidem, Sala 40, Lib. 4, fol. 216; Lib. 942, fol. 20, 23, 24.
806. Bibl. nacional, MSS., D, 118, fol. 172, n. 63.--MSS. of Royal Library of Copenhagen, 218^{b}, p. 181.
807. Archivo de Simancas, Inquisicion, Lib. 20, fol. 338.
808. MSS. of Royal Library of Copenhagen, 218^{b}, p. 183.
809. Archivo de Simancas, Inquisicion, Visitas de Barcelona, Leg. 15, fol. 9.
810. Bibl. nacional, MSS. Pp, 28.--MSS. of Royal Library of Copenhagen, 318^{b}, pp. 181-8.
811. Archivo hist. nacional, Inquisicion de Valencia, Leg. 5, n. 2, fol. 91, 291, 308; Leg. 6, n. 2, fol. 217; Leg. 8, n. 1, fol. 1, 2, 6, 240, 241, 334, 431; n. 2, fol. 64, 209, 358; Leg. 9, n. 2, fol. 5, 153; Leg. 11, n. 1, fol. 3, 4, 14, 15, 59, 121, 131; Leg. 14, n. 1, fol. 86, 87, 89, 92, 98, 103.
812. Modo de Procesar, fol. 3 (Bibl. nacional, MSS., D, 122).
813. Archivo de Simancas, Inquisicion, Visitas de Barcelona, Leg. 15, fol. 2.
814. MSS. of Royal Library of Copenhagen, 218^{b}, fol. 182, 186.
815. Archivo de Simancas, Inquisicion, Lib. 688, fol. 45, 50, 56.
816. Archivo de Alcalá, Hacienda, Leg. 544^{1} (Lib. 6).
817. Ibidem, Leg. 544^{2} (Lib. 10).
818. Archivo de Simancas, Inquisicion, Lib. 14, fol. 62, 63.
819. Ibidem, Lib. 939, fol. 950.--Archivo hist. nacional, Inquisition de Valencia, Leg. 299.--Bibl. nacional, MSS., R, 128.--Modo de Proceder, fol. 7 (Bibl. nacional, MSS., D, 122).
820. MSS. Archivo municipal de Sevilla, Seccion especial, Siglo XVIII, Letra A, Tomo 4, n. 46.--Archivo hist. nacional, Inquisicion de Toledo, Leg. 498.
821. Bibl. nacional, MSS., D, 122, fol. 267; R, 128.--Matute y Luquin, Autos de fe de Córdoba, p. 155.--Olmo, Relacion del Auto general de la Fee, p. 19 (Madrid, 1680).
822. MSS. of Royal Library of Copenhagen, 213 fol., p. 149.--Royal Library of Munich, Cod. Hispan, 79 fol. 29.
823. Archivo hist. nacional, Inquisicion de Valencia, Leg. 1, n. 6, fol. 444.
824. Archivo de Simancas, Inquisicion, Lib. 559; Ibidem, Leg. 1473.--Cédulas etc. de Fernando VII, p. 317 (Valencia, 1814).
825. Amador de los Rios, III, 153.
826. I find this quoted textually in a memorial of Conversos to Philip IV (MSS. of Bodleian Library, Arch. S, 130). No such synod is contained in the conciliar collections.
827. Taronji, Estado religioso de Mallorca, pp. 237-8 (Palma, 1877).
828. Hernando de Pulgar, Epist. XXX.
829. Archivio Vaticano, Registro 685 (Innoc. VIII).--Páramo, p. 139.
830. Ripoll Bullar. Ord. FF. Prædic. IV, 125. Cf. p. 590.
831. Instrucciones de 1488, § 11 (Arguello, fol. 10).
832. Nueva Recop., Lib. VIII, Tit. iii, leyes 3, 4.--Archivo de Simancas, Inquisicion, Lib. 939, fol. 108.
833. Constitt. Collegii S. Ildefonsi, §§ 6, 7, 9, 36, 47, 48 (Gomesii de Rebus Gestis, Append.).
834. Archivo de Simancas, Inquisicion, Lib. 939, fol. 109.
835. Bulario de la Orden de Santiago, Lib. I de copias, fol. 115.
836. Archivo hist. nacional, Inquisicion de Toledo, Leg. 112, n. 74, fol. 9.

837. MSS. of Royal Library of Copenhagen, 218^{b}, p. 404.
838. Colmeiro, Córtes de los Antiguos Reinos, II, 165.
839. Ripoll, VII, 131, 134.
840. Caietani Opusc. T. I, Tract. xxxi, Respons. 6.
841. Burriel, Vidas de los Arzobispos de Toledo (Bibl. nacional, MSS., Ff, 194, fol. 46-8).
842. Ripoll, IV, 566.
843. Ibidem, p. 608.--Archivo de Simancas, Inquisicion, Lib. 939, fol. 142.
844. Nueva Recop. Lib. I, Tit. vii, ley 22.
845. Juan Gómez Bravo, Catálogo de los Obispos de Córdova, pp. 431, 435, 453, 513.
846. Burriel, op. cit. (Bibl. nacional, MSS., Ff, 194, fol. 2, 3).
847. MSS. of Library of Univ. of Halle, Yc, 20, Tom. I.--Cf. Aguirre, V, 495.
848. Salazar y Mendoza, Chronica de el Cardenal Don Juan Tavera, pp. 212, 214-15 (Toledo, 1603).
849. Burriel, op. cit. (Bibl. nacional, MSS., Ff, 194, fol. 2-68).
850. Bibl. nacional, MSS., Q, 418.
851. Relazioni Venete, Serie I, T. VI, p. 404.
852. Archivo de Simancas, Inquisicion, Libro 79, fol. 8.--Bulario de la Orden de Santiago, Lib. I, fol. 119.
853. Barrantes, Aparato para la historia de Extremadura, II, 181.
854. Döllinger, Beiträge zur politischen, kirchlichen u. Cultur-Geschichte, I, 640.
855. Archivo de Simancas, Inquisicion, Sala 40, Lib. 4, fol. 172.--Nueva Recop. Lib. IV, Tit. i, ley 18, cap. 2.
856. Archivo de Simancas, Inquisicion, Sala 40, Lib. 4, fol. 154.
857. Ibidem, Lib. 926, fol. 33.
858. Ibidem, Lib. 922, fol. 15.
859. Archivo de Simancas, Inquisicion, Sala 40, Lib. 4, fol. 170, 171, 173; Lib. 79, fol. 30.
860. Ibidem, Lib. 939, fol. 66; Sala 40, Lib. 4, fol. 172, 203, 208, 215.
861. Ibidem, Lib. 939, fol. 148.
862. Ibidem, Sala 40, Lib. 4, fol. 267; Visitas de Barcelona, Leg. 15, fol. 2, 20.
863. Danvila y Collado, Expulsion de los Moriscos, p. 169.
864. Archivo de Simancas, Sala 40, Lib. 4, fol. 226.
865. Archivo hist. nacional, Inquisicion de Valencia, Leg. 2, n. 16, fol. 226.
866. Archivo de Simancas, Inquisicion, Sala 40, Lib. 4, fol. 215; Lib. 939, fol. 148; Lib. 942, fol. 21.
867. Ibidem, Lib. 942, fol. 24; Lib. 939, fol. 141, 148.
868. Archivo de Simancas, Inquisicion, Canarias, Expedientes de Visitas, Leg. 250, Lib. 3, fol. 11.
869. Ibidem, Lib. 939, fol. 271. In spite of Philip's prohibition, dispensations were not unknown. In 1615 the Suprema orders Valencia to give his commission to Don Juan Zanoguera and "que no le obstase ser descendiente de Judios."--Archivo hist. nacional, Inquisicion de Valencia, Leg. 6, n. 2, fol. 11.
870. MSS. of Royal Library of Copenhagen, 218^{b}, p. 339.
871. Relazioni Venete, Serie I, T. VI, p. 405.
872. Juan Escobar de Corro, Tractatus bipartitus de Puritate et Nobilitate probanda, P. II, Q. iv, Art. 3, n. 1-2 (Lugduni, 1633).
873. This little work came to be known as the Tizon de la Nobleza, or Blot on the Nobility. It was largely circulated in MS. and I have a MS. translation in French, showing that it was appreciated on both sides of the Pyrenees. It was finally printed in Barcelona, in 1880.
874. Tratado de los Estatutos de Limpieza (Bibl. nacional, MSS., Q, 418).
875. MSS. of Bodleian Library, Arch. Seld. A, Subt. 11.
876. Tratado de los Estatutos de Limpieza (Bibl. nacional, MSS., Q, 418).
877. Escobar, op. cit., P. I, Q. iv, § 3, n. 55-6; Q. xii, § 2, n. 46-50; Q. xiv, § 4, n. 19; P. II, Q. ii, n. 85; Q. iii, n. 1 sqq.
878. MSS. of Royal Library of Copenhagen, 218^{b}, p. 402.
879. MSS. of Bodleian Library, Arch Seld. A, Subt. 11.
880. Archivo de Simancas, Gracia y Justicia, Inquisicion, Leg. 621, fol. 89.
881. Memorial hist. español, T. XVIII, pp. xxv, xxxii.
882. Archivo de Alcalá, Hacienda, Leg. 544^{2} (Lib. 10).--MSS. of Am. Philos. Society.--Archivo de Simancas, Inquisicion, Lib. 939, fol. 141.
883. Pedraça, Instruccion, para actuar los Comisarios (MS., Cuenca, 1667).--MSS. of Am. Philos. Society.
884. Pedraça, op. cit.--This little work appears never to have been printed. My copy is beautifully engrossed with an elaborately illuminated armorial dedication to Inquisitor-general Nithard--evidently

presented to him.

885. Archivo hist. nacional, Inquisicion de Valencia, Leg. 8, n. 1, fol. 367.

886. Libro XIII de Cartas, fol. 127-9, 187, 276 (MSS. of Am. Philos. Society). The preliminary bill of costs is as follows:--

    Diligencias y comunicacion 4 (sueldos)Auto de entrar en ellas 2Deposito y registro 4Comision, instruccion y interrogacion 12Al comisario de Cambrils, D. Tiladot, 10 dietas 200Su nuncio, las mismas 40Al Sr D. Martin Calderon (Secretario) 20 dietas 600De escriptura de 18 hojas, de letra muy metida 38.10Auto y com^{n} para las diligencias 6Seguro de deposito2Auto y remision al concejo 6Ajustar la quenta, libranza y registro 4------- 918.10 Al contador por su derecho, 2 per 100 18. 9 Al depositario" " " 18. 9 -------- 955. 8 =========

887. Ibidem, fol. 246-7, 252.

888. Archivo hist. nacional, Inquisicion de Valencia, Leg. 498.--Archivo de Simancas, Inquisicion, Lib. 559.

889. Archivo de Simancas, Inquisicion, Lib. 926, fol. 22, Lib. 942, fol. 51; Lib. 979, fol. 32.--Lib. XIII de Cartas, fol. 62 (MSS. of Am. Philos. Soc.).--Archivo hist. nacional, Inquisicion de Valencia, Leg. 3, n. 7, fol. 226, 229, 239; Leg. 9, n. 3, fol. 240; Leg. 11, n. 2, fol. 113-14.

890. Archivo de Simancas, Inquisicion, Lib. 939, fol. 142.--MSS. of Royal Library of Copenhagen, 218^{b}, p. 258.

891. MSS. of Library of Univ. of Halle, Yc, 20, T. I.

892. MSS. of Royal Library of Copenhagen, 218^{b}, pp. 398-401.--Archivo de Alcalá, Hacienda, Leg. 544^{2} (Lib. 6).

893. Defensa de los Estatutos y Nobleza españolas. Destierro de los Abusos y Rigores de los Informantes (Zaragoza, 1637).

The tract of Fray Salucio was reprinted by Valladares in the Semanario erudito, Vol. XV.

894. Novis. Recop. Lib. XI. Tit. xxvii, ley 22.--Under this law Anchias's Libro verde de Aragon shared the fate of less authoritative compilations, but a copy escaped destruction in the Biblioteca Columbina of Seville, where it was discovered by Amador de los Rios and the greater part was published by his son, Rodrigo Amador de los Rios, in the Revista de España, 1885.

895. Tratado de los Estatutos de Limpieza, cap. 1, 16 (Bibl. nacional, MSS., Q, 418).

896. MSS. of Royal Library of Copenhagen, 213 fol., p. 105; 218^{b}, p. 198.

897. Tratado de los Estatutos de Limpieza, cap. 2, 3 (Bibl. nacional, MSS., Q, 418).

898. Escobar de Purit. et Nobil. probanda, P. II, Q. 1, Gloss. viii, n. 20.

899. Cinco Excelencias del Español, fol. 98 sqq. (Pamplona, 1629)

900. Relazioni Venete, Serie I, T. V, pp. 242, 451.

901. Navarrete, Conservacion de Monarquias, pp. 51-3 (Madrid, 1626).

902. Fray Salucio does not exaggerate when he says "No hay peste en el mundo tan contagiosa, y el ayre de ella sola basta á inficionar y donde entre la mancha no es posible que salga; y poquita levadura corrompe toda la masa" (Semanario erúdito, XV, 172).

903. Francisco Santos, El No Importa de España, p. 175 (Madrid, 1668).

904. Archivo de Simancas, Inquisicion, Lib. 926, fol. 293.

905. Ibidem, Lib. 43, fol. 131.

906. Archivo de Simancas, Registro de Genealogías, n. 916, fol. 10, 22, 23, 29.

907. Archivo hist. nacional, Inquisicion de Valencia, Leg. 17, n. 4, fol. 19, 39, 101.

908. Archivo de Simancas, Inquisicion, Lib. 559.

909. Ibidem, Lib. 435^{2}.

910. Ibidem, Registro de Genealogías, n. 916. As a matter of possible interest I insert in the Appendix the certificate issued, May 24, 1816, to Fitz-James Stuart, Duke of Berwick and Alva, to enable him to take office in the Inquisition.

911. Taronji, Estado religioso etc. de Mallorca, p. 278.

912. Garau, La Fee triumfante, en quatro autos celebrados en Mallorca, por el Santo oficio de la Inquisicion, pp. 158, 161-3 (Ed. 1755).

913. Novis. Recop. Lib. XII, Tit. 1, ley 6.

914. Taronji, Estado religioso y social de la Isla de Mallorca (Palma, 1877).--Soler, Un Milagro y una Mentira (Valencia, 1858).

915. Simancæ de Cathol. Institt. Tit. IX, n. 223.

916. Constitt. 13, 15, 17 Cod. I, v; 2, 3, 4, 7, 8, 9 Cod. IX, xlix; 6, 7, 8 Cod. IX, viii.--Concil. Turon. ann. 1163, cap. 4.--Lucii PP. III, Epist. 171.

917. Partidas, P. VIII, Tit. xxxvi, ley 2.

918. Ordenanzas Reales, Lib. VIII, Tit. iv, leyes 3, 4.

919. Repertorium de Pravitate Hæret. s. v. Divisio Bonorum (Valentiæ, 1494).

920. Archivo hist. nacional, Inquisicion de Toledo, Leg. 137, n. 98; Leg. 138, n. 123; Leg. 140, n. 162; Leg. 153, n. 333; Leg. 154, n. 356.--Boletin, V, 404.

921. Instrucciones de 1484, § 20 (Arguello, fol. 7).--Archivo hist. nacional, Inquisicion de Toledo, Leg. 137, n. 98; Leg. 165, n. 551.

In Torquemada's supplementary Instructions of December, 1484, however, the system of confiscation in all its rigor is applied to those reconciled outside of the Time of Grace.--See Vol. I, p. 573.

922. Archivo gen. de la C. de Aragon, Regist. 3684, fol. 63.

923. MSS. of Bibliothèque nationale de France, fonds espagnol, 81.

924. Archivo de Simancas, Inquisicion, Lib. 3, fol. 120.

925. Pablo García, Orden de Procesar, fol. 31, 43.

926. Archivo hist. nacional, Inquisicion de Valencia, Leg. 8, n. 1, fol. 371.

927. Instrucciones de 1561, § 74 (Arguello, fol. 37).

928. Archivo de Simancas, Inquisicion, Lib. 1; Lib. 9, fol. 49; Llorente, Añales I, 363; II, 15.

929. Simancæ de Cath. Institt. Tit. ix, n. 91, 92.

930. Archivo de Simancas, Lib. 942, fol. 25.

931. Bibl. nacional, MSS., V, 377, cap. ii, § 13; cap. iii, § 9.--Archivo de Alcalá, Hacienda, Leg. 544^{2} (Lib. 6).--Archivo hist. nacional, Inquisicion de Toledo, Leg. 1.--Locati Opus judic. Inquisitor. p. 473.

932. Archivo hist. nacional, Inquisicion de Valencia, Cartas de los Reyes Católicos, Leg. 1.--Archivo de Simancas, Inquisicion, Lib. 1; Lib. 3, fol. 30, 37.

933. Ibidem, Lib. 3, fol. 389, 391; Lib. 4, fol. 8.

934. Archivo de Simancas, Inquisicion, Lib. 3, fol. 446; Lib. 5, fol. 20; Lib. 9, fol. 18, 30.

935. Ibidem, Lib. 3, fol. 427, 440.

936. Instrucciones de 1484, §§ 3, 7 (Arguello, fol. 3, 4).

937. Archivo hist. nacional, Inquisicion de Valencia, Leg. 98. 938. Instrucciones de 1484, §§ 8, 23 (Arguello, fol. 4, 8).

939. MSS. of Royal Library of Copenhagen, 213 fol., p. 132.

940. Archivo hist. nacional, Inquisicion de Toledo, Leg. 1.

941. Carbonell de Gestis Hæreticor. (Col. de Doc. de la C. de Aragon, XXVIII, 120).--Archivo hist. nacional, Inquisicion de Toledo, Leg. 1.

942. MSS. of Royal Library of Copenhagen, 213 fol., pp. 123, 130; 218^{b}, p. 389.--Modo de Proceder, fol. 65 (Bibl. nacional, MSS., D, 122).--Archivo hist. nacional, Inquisicion de Valencia, Leg. 31, 299.--Proceso contra Ana Enríquez (MS. penes me).

943. Archivo hist. nacional, Inquisicion de Valencia, Leg. 300, P. I, n. 31, 33, 35, 40.

944. Archivo gen. de la C. de Aragon, Regist. 3684, fol. 96.

945. Archivo de Simancas, Inquisicion, Lib. 1.

946. Modo de Proceder, fol. 79 (Bibl. nacional, MSS., D, 122).

947. Archivo hist. nacional, Inquisicion de Toledo, Leg. 1.--Archivo de Simancas, Inquisicion, Leg. 552, fol. 52.

948. Archivo hist. nacional, Inquisicion de Valencia, Cartas de los Reyes Catolicos, Leg. 2.

949. Archivo de Simancas, Inquisicion, Lib. 1.

950. Ibidem.

951. Ibidem, Lib. 3, fol. 23, 100, 121, 302.

952. Archivo de Simancas, Inquisicion, Lib. 933.

953. See the author's "Inquisition of the Middle Ages," I, 509, 522-4.

954. Instrucciones de 1485 (Arguello, fol. 23-4). Attributed to 1484 in Archivo de Simancas, Inquisicion, Lib. 933.

This article is in the supplementary Instructions of December, 1484, but there it draws a distinction, limiting it to the reconciled and inferring that in those condemned the rigor of the law was enforced. There is also an article exempting the debts and alienations of those reconciled within the Term of Grace. See Vol. I, p. 573.

955. Arguello, fol. 20, 22.

956. Archivo de Simancas, Inquisicion, Lib. 1; Lib. 3, fol. 42.

957. Bibl. nacional, MSS., V, 377, cap. 2, § 15.

958. Archivo de Simancas, Inquisicion, Lib. 933. This addition to § 20 is not in the Granada collection of 1537 nor in Arguello, fol. 7.

959. Archivo de Simancas, Inquisicion, Lib. 3, fol. 338.

960. Ibidem, Lib. 933.--Bulario de la Orden de Santiago, Lib. 1 de copias, fol. 219.--Pragmáticas y altres Drets de Cathalunya, Lib. I, Tit. viii, § 3.

961. Córtes de loa antiguos Reinos de Leon y de Castilla, IV, 589.

962. Simancæ de Cath. Institt., Tit. IX, n. 133, 134.

963. Padre Fidel Fita (Boletin, XV, 317-23).

964. Arguello, fol. 24.

965. Archivo gen. de la C. de Aragon, Regist. 3684, fol. 96.--Fueros de Aragon, fol. 119, 193 (Zaragoza, 1624).
966. Archivo de Simancas, Inquisicion, Lib. 1.
967. Arguello, fol. 12, 18, 20.
968. Archivo de Simancas, Inquisicion, Lib. 3, fol. 334.
969. Archivo hist. nacional, Inquisicion de Valencia, Leg. 300.
970. Archivo de Simancas, Inquisicion, Lib. 939, fol. 128.--Cf. Simancæ de Cath. Institt. Tit. IX, n. 151-2.
971. MSS. of Library of Univ. of Halle, Yc, 20, T. V.
972. Archivo de Simancas, Inquisicion, Lib. 926, fol. 22.
973. MSS. of Royal Library of Copenhagen, 218^{b}, pp. 174, 389.
974. Coleccion de los Tratados de Paz; Carlos II, Parte I, p. 11.
975. Archivo de Simancas, Inquisicion, Lib. 3, fol. 243.
976. Ibidem, Lib. 6, fol. 94.
977. Archivo hist. nacional, Inquisicion de Valencia, Leg. 300, P. I, n. 51.
978. Archivo de Simancas, Inquisicion, Lib. 3, fol. 78.
979. Archivo hist. nacional, Inquisicion de Valencia, Leg. 300, P. I, n. 46; P. II, n. 9; P. III, n. 9, 22.

In the Appendix will be found the receipt for her dower by Doña Beatriz Despuch, wife of Pere Alcañiz; she leaves the money in the hands of the receiver, awaiting decision of her claim to the ownership of certain household goods which she had bought from the confiscated estate.

980. Archivo de Simancas, Inquisicion, Sala 40, Lib. 4, fol. 178.
981. Leyes de Toro, ley lxxvii.--Hugo de Celso, Repertorio de las leyes de Castilla, s. v. Herege (Alcalá, 1540).--Nueva Recop. Lib. V, Tit. ix, ley 10.--Novís. Recop. Lib. X, Tit. iv, ley 10.
982. Archivo de Simancas, Inquisicion, Lib. 6, fol. 27.
983. Archivo hist. nacional, Inquisicion de Valencia, Leg. 300, P. III, n. 4.
984. Archivo de Simancas, Patronato Real, Inquisicion, Leg. único, fol. 40.
985. Bibl. nacional, MSS., Dd, 145, fol. 352.
986. Archivo de Simancas, Inquisicion, Lib. 78, fol. 192.
987. Simancæ de Cath. Institt. Tit. IX, n. 4.
988. Instruccion de 1484, § 22 (Arguello, fol. 8).
989. Archivo gen. de la C. de Aragon, Regist. 3684, fol. 103.
990. Archivo de Simancas, Inquisicion, Lib. 1; Lib. 3, fol. 441.
991. Coleccion de Cédulas, IV, 310 (Madrid, 1830).
992. Archivo de Simancas, Inquisicion, Lib. 3, fol. 244.
993. Ibidem, Lib. 9, fol. 195.
994. Ibidem, Lib. 3, fol. 164.
995. Archivo de Simancas, Inquisicion, Lib, 1.
996. Ibidem, Lib. 3, fol. 142.
997. Archivo de Simancas, Inquisicion, Lib. 49, fol. 58, 193.--MSS. of Bodleian Library, Arch. S, 130.
998. Arguello, fol. 20, 22, 23, 24.
999. Archivo de Simancas, Inquisicion, Lib. 78, fol. 235.
1000. Archidiaconi Gloss, super Sexto, Tit. de Hæret., cap. Cum secundum (Eymerici Director. P. II).--Bernardi Comens. Lucerna Inquis. s. v. Bona hæreticor. § 4.--Simancæ de Cath. Institt. Tit. IX, n. 29.
1001. Instrucciones de 1484, cap. 24 (Arguello, fol. 8).
1002. Archivo de Simancas, Inquisicion, Lib. 933.
1003. Archivo hist. nacional, Inquisicion de Valencia, Leg. 300, P. I, n. 26.
1004. Archivo de Simancas, Inquisicion, Lib. 933.
1005. Ibidem Lib. 1.
1006. Printed by Padre Fidel Fita, Boletin, XXIII, 393.
1007. Archivo de Simancas, Inquisicion, Lib. 9, fol. 48.
1008. Archivo hist. nacional, Inquisicion de Valencia, Leg. 300, P. I, n. 25.
1009. Ibidem, P. I, n. 67.
1010. Ibidem, P. I, n. 27.
1011. Archivo gen. de la C. de Aragon, Regist. 3684, fol. 12.
1012. Archivo de Simancas, Inquisicion, Lib. 9, fol. 61.
1013. Archivo hist. nacional, Inquisicion de Valencia, Leg. 300, P. III, n. 16.
1014. Archivo de Simancas, Inquisicion, Lib. 1.
1015. Ibidem.
1016. Ibidem.

1017. Archivo de Simancas, Inquisicion, Lib. 1.
1018. Ibidem, Lib. 3, fol. 394.
1019. Archivo de Simancas, Inquisicion, Lib. 3, fol. 93.
1020. Archivo de Simancas, Inquisicion, Lib. 3, fol. 98.
1021. Ibidem, fol. 128, 140.
1022. Archivo de Simancas, Inquisicion, Lib. 3, fol. 103.
1023. Ibidem, Lib. 9, fol. 56.
1024. MSS. of Library of University of Halle, Yc, 20, T. VI.
1025. Bibl. nacional, MSS., D, 153.
1026. Fredericq, Corpus Documentt. Inquis. Neerland., IV, 241.
1027. Colmeiro, Córtes de los antiguos Reynos, II, 179, 217, 250.--Córtes de Valladolid del año de MDLV, Pet. xii (Valladolid, 1558, fol. xxxiv).
1028. Archivo gén. de la C. de Aragon, Regist. 3684, fol. 87, 92, 95.
1029. Vol. I, Appendix, p. 573.
1030. Informe de Quesada (Bibl. nacional, MSS., Tj, 28).--Cf. Zuñiga, Annales de Sevilla, Lib. XII, año 1480.--Archivo de Alcalá, Estado, Leg. 3137.
1031. Boletin, XXIII, 293.
1032. Archivo de Simancas, Inquisicion, Lib. 1.
1033. Ibidem, Lib. 3, fol. 29, 31, 297.
1034. Discurso histórico-legal sobre la Inquisicion, p. 137 (Valladolid, 1803).
1035. Archivo de Alcalá, Estado, Leg. 3137.--Archivo de Simancas, Inquisicion, Lib. 929, fol. 294.
1036. Archivo de Simancas, Inquisicion, Lib. 3, fol. 69.
1037. Archivo de Simancas, Inquisicion, Lib. 929, fol. 295.
1038. Salgado de Somoza de Retentione Bullarum, P. II, cap. xxxiii, n. 13.
1039. Archivo de Simancas, Inquisicion, Lib. 939, fol. 303, 304, 310.
1040. Bulario de la Orden de Santiago, Lib. 1 de copias, fol. 224.
1041. Archivo gen. de la C. de Aragon, Regist. 3684, fol. 9.
1042. Archivo hist. nacional, Inquisicion de Valencia, Leg. 98; Cartas de los Reyes Católicos, Leg. 2.--Archivo de Simancas, Inquisicion, Lib. 1.
1043. Archivo de Simancas, Inquisicion, Lib. 9, fol. 63.
1044. Archivo de Simancas, Inquisicion, Lib. 1.
1045. Archivo de Simancas, Inquisicion, Lib. 2, fol. 26, 28, 29, 30; Lib. 926, fol. 211.
1046. Bulario de la Orden de Santiago, Lib. 1 de copias, fol. 219.
1047. Archivo de Simancas, Inquisicion, Lib. 1; Lib. 933; Lib. 3, fol. 181, 408, 419.
1048. Archivo de Simancas, Patronato Real, Inquisicion, Leg. único, fol. 18.
1049. Ibidem, Lib. 3, fol. 371.
1050. Archivo de Simancas, Inquisicion, Lib. 933; Lib. 3, fol. 19, 46, 65, 78, 79, 91, 107, 386, 403; Lib. 9, fol. 3.
1051. Archivo de Simancas, Inquisicion, Lib. 9, fol. 190; Lib. 3, fol. 378, 386, 400, 401, 402.
1052. Ibidem, Lib. 3, fol. 367, 372.
1053. Archivo de Simancas, Inquisicion, Lib. 3, fol. 430, 449, 450, 451, 453, 455; Lib. 927, fol. 301.
1054. Archivo de Simancas, Inquisicion, Lib. 3, fol. 403, 428, 432; Lib. 4, fol. 1-3, 5, 96; Lib. 5, fol. 17, 20, 25, 95; Lib. 9, fol. 3, 5, 28, 29, 30, 58.
1055. Archivo de Simancas, Patronato Real, Inquisicion, Leg. único, fol. 76.
1056. Instrucciones de 1498 (Arguello, fol. 18).--Bibl. nacional, MSS., D, 118, fol. 112, n. 39.
For occasional special exceptions see Archivo hist. nacional, Inquisicion de Valencia, Cartas de los Reyes Católicos, Leg. 2.--Archivo de Simancas, Inquisicion, Lib. 2, fol. 29; Lib. 3, fol. 263.
1057. Archivo de Simancas, Inquisicion, Lib. 939, fol. 128.
1058. Archivo de Simancas, Inquisicion, Lib. 926, fol. 21.
1059. Bibl. national, MSS., D, 118, fol. 167.
1060. Archivo de Simancas, Inquisicion, Lib. 3, fol. 182.
1061. Archivo hist. nacional, Inquisicion de Valencia, Leg. 300, P. II, n. 18.
1062. Archivo de Simancas, Inquisicion, Lib. 9, fol. 54.
1063. Archive de Simancas, Inquisicion, Sala 40, Lib. 4, fol. 148.
1064. Ibidem, Lib. 1.
1065. Archivo de Simancas, Inquisicion, Lib. 1; Lib. 3, fol. 67.
1066. Ibidem, Lib. 3, fol. 332.
1067. Ibidem, Lib. 5, fol. 8.
1068. Ibidem, Lib. 3, fol. 225; Lib. 933.
1069. Archive de Simancas, Inquisicion, Lib. 3, fol. 239, 294, 296, 314; Lib. 933; Lib. 940, fol.

47, 68.
1070. Ibidem, Sala 40, Lib. 4, fol. 239.
1071. Ibidem, Patronato Real, Inquisicion, Leg. único, fol. 35.
1072. Padre Fidel Fita (Boletin, XXIII, 286).
1073. Don Ramon Santa María (Boletin, XXII, 373). An abstract of a partial statement of the receipts in Valencia, during the year 1493, will be found in the Appendix. Some of the details illustrate the current business of the office.
1074. Pulgar, Letra XXV (p. 58).
1075. Archivo de Simancas, Patronato Real, Inquisicion, Leg. único, fol. 27.
1076. Ibidem, fol. 35.--It is probably to this that allusion is made, November 10, 1527, by Martin de Salinas, in a letter to Ferdinand of Austria when, in enumerating the sources from which Charles expected to carry on the war, he includes more than a million of gold offered by the New Christians, "without disturbing the Inquisition." There is no appearance that the project was successful.--A. Rodriguez Villa, El Emperador Carlos V y su Corte, p. 386 (Madrid, 1903).
1077. MSS. of Archivo municipal de Sevilla, Seccion especial, Siglo XVIII, Letra A, T. 4, n. 46.
1078. Archivo de Simancas, Inquisicion, Lib. 812, fol. 3, 4, 9.
1079. Ibidem, Gracia y Justicia, Inquisicion, Leg. 621, fol. 80-1.
1080. Bibl. nacional, MSS., S, 294, fol. 375.
1081. Ibidem, D, 150, fol. 224.--Archivo de Simancas, Inquisicion, Lib. 40, fol. 138.
1082. Archivo de Simancas, Inquisicion, Leg. 1465, fol. 30.
1083. Royal Library of Berlin, $Q^{\{t\}}$ 9548.
1084. Archivo hist. nacional, Inquisicion de Valencia, Leg. 13, n. 2, fol. 224; Leg. 14, n. 1, fol. 8.
1085. Archivo de Simancas, Inquisicion, Leg. 1479, fol. 2.
1086. Archivo hist. nacional, Inquisicion de Toledo, Leg. 1.
1087. Archive hist. nacional, Inquisicion de Valencia, Cartas del Consejo, Leg. 10, n. 9, fol. 7.--Ibidem, Leg. 100.
1088. Pulgar, Cronica, P. II, cap. lxxvii.--Zurita, Añales, Lib. XX, cap. xlix.
1089. Rodrigo, Historia verdadera, II, 53.
1090. Archive de Simancas, Inquisicion, Lib. 1.
1091. Archivo gen. de la C. de Aragon, Regist. 3684, fol. 99.--Archivo de Simancas, Inquisicion, Lib. 1.
1092. Archivo de Simancas, Inquisicion, Lib. 1.
1093. Ibidem.
1094. Córtes de los antiguos Reinos, III, 535.
1095. Archivo de Simancas, Inquisicion, Lib. 1.
1096. Instrucciones de 1488, § 13 (Arguello, fol. 11).
1097. Archivo de Simancas, Inquisicion, Lib. 1.--Ferdinand's letter asking Torquemada to lift the excommunication will be found in the Appendix.
1098. Archivo de Simancas, Inquisicion, Lib. 1.
1099. Ibidem, Lib. 2, fol. 15, 17.
1100. Ibidem, Lib. 3, fol. 50, 58, 59, 188.
1101. Coleccion de Documentos, VIII, 295, 330, 365.
1102. Archivo de Simancas, Inquisicion, Lib. 3, fol. 61. See Appendix.
1103. Archivo de Simancas, Inquisicion, Lib. 3, fol. 50, 62, 63, 80.
1104. Ibidem, fol. 91, 106.
1105. Ibidem, fol. 331. See also fol. 73, 76, 86, 87, 101, 103, 105, 112, 133, 136, 137, 138, 145, 169, etc.
1106. Archivo de Simancas, Inquisicion, Lib. 3, fol. 84, 368, 377, 378, 383.
1107. Ibidem, Lib. 2, fol. 1, 26.
1108. Ibidem, Lib. 1.
1109. Archivo de Simancas, Inquisicion, Lib. 3, fol. 33, 79.
1110. Ibidem, Lib. 1.
1111. Ibidem, Lib. 3, fol. 105.
1112. Ibidem, Lib. 1; Lib. 2, fol. 11.
1113. Archivo de Simancas, Inquisicion, Lib. 3, fol. 421, 422, 426.
1114. Ibidem, Lib. 74, fol. 90; Lib. 688, fol. 509.
1115. Archivo de Simancas, Inquisicion, Lib. 933.
1116. Pet. Mart. Epist. 622.--Bibl. nacional, MSS., D, 153.
1117. Archivo de Simancas, Inquisicion, Lib. 9, fol, 49.
1118. Archivo de Simancas, Inquisicion, Lib. 921, fol. 88.
1119. Ibidem, Lib. 9, fol. 23, 60, 70.
1120. Ibidem, Lib. 9, fol. 60, 72; Lib. 5, fol. 26; Lib. 6, fol. 74.

1121. Archivo de Simancas, Inq., Lib. 9, fol. 12, 33; Lib. 5, fol. 26; Lib. 6, fol. 95.
1122. Archivo de Simancas, Inquisicion, Lib. 9, fol. 47, 48, 51, 71.
1123. Archivo hist. nacional, Inquisicion de Toledo, Hacienda, Leg. 10.
1124. Archivo de Simancas, Inquisicion, Lib. 6, fol. 71.
1125. Joh. Friburgens. Summæ Confessor. Lib. III, Tit. xxxiv, Q. 123.
1126. In the earliest period this was expressed in the sentence, as in one on Murcia, wife of Diego González, by the Guadalupe tribunal, November 20, 1485.--"E imponemosle e damosle en penitencia en emienda y satisfacion de los dichos hereticos herrores carcel perpetua en la qual mandamos que este e haga penitencia de los dichos pecados."--Archivo hist. nacional, Inquisicion de Toledo, Leg. 133, n. 46.
1127. So in description of the Madrid auto de fe of July 4, 1642, in Archivo de Alcalá, Hacienda, Leg. 544^{1} (Lib. 6).
1128. Instrucciones de 1484, § vii (Arguello, fol. 4).
1129. Bibliothèque nationale de France, fonds espagnol, 80, fol. 169.
1130. MSS. penes me.
1131. Archivo gen. de la C. de Aragon, Regist. 3684, fol. 89.
1132. Archivo de Simancas, Inquisicion, Lib. 1; Lib. 3, fol. 176.
1133. Ibidem, Lib. 3, fol. 351.
1134. Arguello, fol. 20, 25.--Arch. de Simancas, Inq., Sala 40, Lib. 4, fol. 98.
1135. Archivo de Simancas, Inquisicion, Lib. 926, fol. 33; Lib. 939, fol. 119; Lib. 79, fol. 170; Sala 40, Lib. 4, fol. 173.
1136. Ibidem, Sala 40, Lib. 4, fol. 168.
1137. Ibidem, Lib. 942, fol. 16.
1138. Archivo de Simancas, Inquisicion, Visitas de Barcelona, Leg. 15, fol. 20.
1139. Ibidem, Lib. 933.
1140. Ibidem, Visitas de Barcelona, Leg. 15, fol. 20.
1141. Ibidem, Sala 40, Lib. 4, fol. 173, 220, 222, 229. 1142. Archivo de Simancas, Inquisicion, Sala 40, Lib. 4, fol. 163, 164, 165, 168, etc.
1143. Ibidem, Lib. 75, fol. 25; Sala 40, Lib. 4, fol. 109, 127, 277.
1144. Ibidem, Lib. 9, fol. 32; Lib. 77, fol. 354.
1145. Ibidem, Lib. 78, fol. 193. 1146. For the details see the author's "Moriscos of Spain," pp. 120-4.
1147. Archivo de Simancas, Inquisicion, Lib. 939, fol. 9; Lib. 922, fol. 15.
1148. Ibidem, Lib. 78, fol. 168.--Danvila y Collado, Expulsion de los Moriscos, pp. 183-88.
1149. Archivo hist. nacional, Inquisicion de Valencia, Leg. 2, n. 10, fol. 79.
1150. Ibidem, Leg. 98.
1151. Archivo de Simancas, Inquisicion, Lib. 78, fol. 216.
1152. MSS. of Royal Library of Copenhagen, 218^{b}, p. 234.--MSS. of National Library of Lima, Protocolo 223, Expediente 5270.--Archivo de Simancas, Inquisicion, Lib. 941, fol. 1.
1153. Archivo de Simancas, Inquisicion, Visitas de Barcelona, Leg. 15, fol. 9, 20.
1154. N. Hergueta, (Boletin, XLV, 434).
1155. Archivo de Simancas, Inquisicion, Legajo 787.
1156. Bibl. nacional, MSS, S, 121, fol. 54-67.
1157. MSS. of Library of Univ. of Halle, Yc, 20, Tom. I.
1158. Archivo hist. nacional, Inquisicion de Toledo, Leg. 1.
1159. Bibl. nacional, MSS., D, 118, p. 409.
1160. Matute y Luquin, Autos de fe de Córdova, pp. 177-8.
1161. Archivo de Simancas, Inquisicion, Lib. 20, fol. 135.
1162. Ibidem, Lib. 716.
1163. Archivo hist. nacional, Inquisicion de Valencia, Leg. 8, n. 2, fol. 279, 290, 421, 426. 1164. Ibidem, Leg. 9, n. 1, fol. 70, 72, 82, 135, 142.
1165. MSS. of Royal Library of Copenhagen, 218^{b}, p. 236.
1166. Instrucciones de 1561, § 65 (Arguello, fol. 36).
1167. Archivo de Simancas, Inquisicion de Barcelona, Leg. 15, fol. 20.
1168. Bibl. nacional, MSS., V, 377, p. 4.
1169. Archivo hist. nacional, Inquisicion de Toledo, Leg. 1.
1170. Royal Library of Berlin, Qt. 9548.
1171. Archivo de Simancas, Inquisicion, Lib. 890.
1172. Decret. Sac. Congr. S. Officii, pp. 437-8 (Bibl. del R. Archivio di Stato in Roma, Fondo Camerale, Congr. del S. Offizio, Vol. 3.)
1173. Archivo de Simancas, Inquisicion, Lib. 54, fol. 166, 176.
1174. Taxe des Parties casuelles du Boutique du Pape, p. 169 (Lyon, 1564).
1175. Archivo de Simancas, Inquisicion, Lib. 9, fol. 13.

1176. Libro verde de Aragon (Revista de España, CVI, 274).
1177. Boletin XV, 594.--Bulario de la Orden de Santiago, Lib. I de copias, fol. 51.
1178. Catálogo de las causas seguidas ante el Tribunal de Toledo, p. 139 (Madrid, 1903).--Melgares Marin, Procedimientos de la Inquisicion, I. 119 (Madrid, 1866).
1179. Archivo de Simancas, Inquisicion, Lib. 933; Lib. 939, fol. 119.
1180. Archivo de Simancas, Inquisicion, Lib. 1.
1181. See Vol. I, p. 580.
1182. Ibidem.
1183. Archivo de Simancas, Inquisicion, Lib. 3, fol. 56, 90, 405.
1184. Ibidem, Lib. 3, fol. 114.
1185. Hergenröther, Leonis X Regesta, n. 7875-6, 12507-8.
1186. Archivo de Simancas, Inquisicion, Lib. 3, fol. 103, 370, 373, 382.
1187. Ibidem, fol. 387, 403.
1188. Archivo de Simancas, Inquisicion, Sala 40, Lib. 4, fol. 100.
1189. Ibidem, Lib. 942, fol. 12; Lib. 949, fol. 68, 108, 109; Lib. 77, fol. 354.
1190. Bulario de la Orden de Santiago, Lib. 3, fol. 9.
1191. Archivo de Simancas, Inquisicion, Sala 40, Lib. 4, fol. 167.
1192. Ibidem, fol. 204.
1193. Archivo de Simancas, Inquisicion, Lib. 939, fol. 108, 115.
1194. Archivo de Simancas, Inquisicion, Sala 40, Lib. 4, fol. 213, 223, 228.
1195. Pegnæ Comment. 8 in Eymerici Director. P. III.
1196. Córtes de Madrid, año de MDLII, Pet. liii (Valladolid, 1558, fol. xiii).
1197. Decreta Sac. Congr. S^{ti} Officii, pp. 142-3 (Bibl. del R. Archivio di Stato in Roma, Fondo camerale, Congr. del S. Offizio, Vol. 3).
1198. Archivo de Simancas, Inquisicion, Lib. 1.
1199. Archivo de Simancas, Inquisicion, Sala 40, Lib. 4, fol. 98, 114, 135, 136.
1200. La Mantia, L'Inquisizione in Sicilia, p. 57.
1201. Llorente, Añales, II, 31.
1202. Archivo de Simancas, Inquisicion, Lib. 73, fol. 16, 65, 339.
1203. Ibidem, Sala 40, Lib. 4, fol. 175, 176.
1204. Archivo de Simancas, Inquisicion, Lib. 73, fol. 19.
1205. Ibidem, Leg. 1157, fol. 143, 156.
1206. Ibidem, Sala 40, Lib. 4, fol. 129.
1207. Ibidem, Sala 40, Lib. 4, fol. 182.
1208. Archivo hist. nacional, Inquisicion de Valencia, Leg. 5, n. 1, fol. 233, 254
1209. Archivo de Simancas, Inquisicion, Sala 40, Lib. 4, fol. 128. See also fol. 139, 161, 177.
1210. Ibidem, fol. 229. See also fol. 189, 233.
1211. Archivo de Simancas, Inquisicion, Sala 40, Lib. 4, fol. 238.--Cf. fol. 215, 229.
1212. Franchini, Breve Rapporto del Tribunale della SS. Inq. di Sicilia, pp. 141-45 (Palermo, 1744).
1213. Archivo de Simancas, Inquisicion, Sala 40, Lib. 4, fol. 125, 131, 163.
1214. Ibidem, Lib. 939, fol. 119.
1215. Archivo hist. nacional, Inquisicion de Valencia, Leg. 5, n. 2, fol. 282, 360, 43, 63, 69, 75, 97, 167, 100, 110, 114, 115, 121, 287.
1216. Archivo de Simancas, Inquisicion, Lib. 939, fol. 272.--Archivo de Alcalá, Hacienda, Leg. 544^{2} (Lib. 10)
1217. Informe de Quesada (Bibl. nacional, MSS., Tj, 28.)
1218. See Vol. I, p. 572.
1219. Bulario de la Orden de Santiago, Lib. I, fol. 32.
1220. Cap. 12, 13, Extra, Lib. III, Tit iv.
1221. Archivio Vaticano, Innoc. PP. VIII, Registro 685, fol. 461.
1222. Informe de Quesada, ubi sup.
1223. Ibidem.--Archivo de Simancas, Inquisicion, Lib. 1.
1224. Archivo de Simancas, Patronato Real, Inquisicion, Leg. único, fol. 24, 25.
1225. Archivo de Simancas, Lib. 1; Lib. 2, fol. 4, 5.
1226. Ibidem, Inquisicion, Lib. I.
1227. Bulario de la Orden de Santiago, Lib. I, fol. 155, 157.
1228. Archivo de Simancas, Inquisicion, Leg. 1465, fol. 28; Lib. 1.
1229. Ibidem, Lib. 1.
1230. Ibidem, Lib. 3, fol. 187; Lib. 940, fol. 200.
1231. Ibidem, Lib. 1.
1232. Ibidem, Sala 40, Lib. 4, fol. 108.

1233. Archivo de Simancas, Inquisicion, Sala 40, Lib. 4, fol. 158, 161, 164, 177.
1234. Ibidem, fol. 226, 243, 245, 247, 248, 251, 261--Coleccion de Documentos, LXVIII, 458.
1235. C. Trident., Sess. XXIII, De Reform. cap. 1.
1236. Bulario de la Orden de Santiago, Lib. 3, fol. 102.--Archivo de Simancas, Inquisicion, Lib. 939, fol. 62.
1237. C. Trident., Sess. XXIV, De Reform. cap. 12.--Bulario de la Orden de Santiago, Lib. 4, fol. 176.--Archivo de Simancas, Inquisicion, Lib. 925, fol. 228.
1238. Archivo de Simancas, Inquisicion, Lib. 939, fol. 274.
1239. Matute y Luquin, Autos de fe de Córdova, pp. 134-5.
1240. Bulario de la Orden de Santiago, Lib. I, fol. 157.
1241. Decr. Sac. Congr. S^{ti} Officii, p. 162 (Bibl. del R. Archivio di Stato in Roma, Fondo camerale, Congr. del S. Offizio, Vol. 3).
1242. MSS. of Library of Univ. of Halle, Yc, 17.
1243. MSS. of Bodleian Library, Arch. S, 130.--Bulario de la Orden de Santiago, Lib. V, fol. 59.--Archivo de Simancas, Gracia y Justicia, Inquisicion, Leg. 621, fol. 103.
1244. Archivo de Simancas, Inquisicion, Lib. 44^{2}, fol. 557.
1245. Archivo hist. nacional, Inquisicion de Valencia, Leg. 14, n. 1, fol. 137.
1246. Archivo de Simancas, Registro de Genealogias, n. 916, fol. 69.
1247. Ibidem, Lib. 559.   1248. Bulario de la Orden de Santiago, Lib. I, fol. 60.
1249. Archivo de Simancas, Inquisicion, Lib. 9, fol. 14, 15.
1250. Llorente, Añales, II, 222.
1251. Archivo de Simancas, Inquisicion, Lib. 73, fol. 240; Lib. 940, fol. 94.
1252. Archivo de Simancas, loc. cit.
1253. Sandoval, Vida del Emp. Carlos V, Vol. 2, p. 780 (Barcelona, 1625).
1254. Archivo de Simancas, Inquisicion, Sala 40, Lib. 4, fol. 231 (see Appendix to Vol. III).
See also letters from the Princess Juana to Cardinal Pacheco and the pope, in Döllinger, Beiträge zur politischen, Kirchlichen u. Cultur-Geschichte, I, 247-8.
1255. Archivo de Simancas, Inquisicion, Sala 40, Lib. 4, fol. 232.
1256. Bulario de la Orden de Santiago, Lib. III, fol. 68.--Bibl. nacional, MSS., R, 90, fol. 249.
1257. Bulario de la Orden de Santiago, Lib. III, fol. 68.
1258. Ibidem, fol. 99.--Archivo de Alcalá, Hacienda, Leg. 1049.
1259. Archivo de Simancas, Inquisicion, Sala 40, Lib. 4, fol. 234; Lab. 940, fol. 96-99.
1260. Bulario de la Orden de Santiago, Lib. IV, fol. 144.
1261. Archivo de Simancas, Inquisicion, Sala 40, Lib. 4, fol. 235, 240, 242, 249, 254.
1262. Ibidem, fol. 237, 261.
1263. Ibidem, fol. 249.
1264. Bibl. nacional, MSS., X, 157, fol. 244.
1265. Archivo de Simancas, Inquisicion, Sala 40, Lib. 4, fol. 243-6.
1266. Ibidem, fol. 100-102.--MSS. of Royal Library of Copenhagen, 213 fol., pp. 135-9.--Archivo hist. nacional, Inquisicion de Valencia, Leg. 2, n. 16, fol. 189.
1267. Libro XIII de Cartas, fol. 82, 164, 166 (MSS. of Am. Philos. Society).
1268. Archivo de Simancas, Patronato Real, Inquisicion, Leg. único, fol. 49.--"lo que ya esta comprado e consynado para ella en algunas partes, comprandolo de la manera e segund que el rey católico lo tenya mandado e començado á comprar."
1269. Ibidem, Inquisicion, Lib. 3, fol. 239, 314.
1270. Ibidem, Lib 5, fol. 15.
1271. Archivo de Simancas, Inquisicion, Lib. 3, fol. 403, 428, 430; Lib. 5, fol. 9; Lib. 9, fol. 26.
1272. Ibidem, Lib. 3, fol. 412.
1273. Ibidem, Lib. 73, fol. 144.
1274. Ibidem, fol. 186.
1275. Ibidem, Lib. 40, fol. 201.
1276. Ibidem, Sala 40, Lib. 4, fol. 238, 248, 270; Libro 940, fol. 43.
1277. Archivo de Alcalá, Hacienda, No. 473.--Archivo de Simancas, Lib. 939, fol. 128.
1278. Ibidem, Lib. 942, fol. 48.
1279. Archivo hist. nacional, Inquisicion de Valencia, Leg. 403.
The summary of income is:
   Censos de la Ciudad de Valencia, valen 6481l. 3s. --d.Censos en el Reyno de Valencia, valen 6256 6Canonicato de Valencia, valen 503 14Derecho Portugues --- -- --La canongia de Tortosa 1473La conongia de Teruel--- -- --La canongia de Xativa--- -- --La canongia de Segorbe --- -- --Los Moriscos de Valencia 1500 --Las casas valen 1500
At the end there are sundry items entered as received from the canonry of Teruel, amounting in all to 51ll. 3s. 5d. Also two payments from that of Játiva aggregating 1491l. 17s. 10d.

1280. Archivo hist. nacional, Inquisicion de Valencia, Leg. 5, n. 2, fol. 289, 332.
1281. Archivo de Simancas, Inquisicion, Libro 559.
1282. Ibidem Lib. 939, fol. 274.
1283. Archivo hist. nacional, Inquisicion de Valencia, Leg. 5, n. 2, fol. 2, 5, 36, 40, 68.
1284. Archivo de Simancas, Inquisicion, Lib. 19, fol. 100.
1285. Bibl. nacional, MSS., X, 157, fol. 244.
1286. Bleda, Cronica de los Moros de España, p. 914 (Valencia, 1618).
1287. Archivo de Simancas, Inquisicion, Lib. 26, fol. 35.
1288. Archivo gen. de la C. de Aragon, Leg. 528.
1289. Archivo hist. nacional, Inquisicion de Toledo, Contabilidad, Leg. 241, n. 33.
1290. Archivo de Simancas, Inquisicion, Lib. 926, fol. 19.
1291. Cartas de Jesuitas (Mem. hist. Español, XIX, 360).
1292. Avisos históricos (Semanario erúdito, XXXIII, 60).
1293. Archivo hist. nacional, Inquisicion de Valencia, Leg. 1, n. 1, fol 609; n. 6, fol. 331; Leg. 8, n. 2, fol. 462, 477, 578, 579, 616, 618; Leg. 9, n. 1, fol. 292; n. 3, fol. 382; Leg. 11, n. 1, fol. 94-5; Leg. 371; Leg. 377; Leg. 621, fol. 108.
1294. Archivo de Simancas, Inquisicion, Lib. 67, fol. 26.--Libro XIII de Cartas, fol. 181, 136, 146, 244 (MSS. of Am. Philos. Society).
1295. Archivo de Simancas, Inquisicion, Leg. 1465, fol. 30.
1296. Bibl. nacional, MSS., Q, 4.
1297. Archivo hist. nacional, Inquisition de Valencia, Leg. 9, n. 2, fol. 166, 199, 209, 219, 222, 228.
1298. Ibidem, fol. 173.
1299. Archivo de Alcalá, Hacienda, Leg. 544^{2} (Lib. 9). For details see Appendix.
1300. Archivo de Simancas, Inquisicion, Lib. 27, fol. 87.
1301. Bibl. nacional, MSS., Mm, 130.

The writer states that there were in Spain 1193 cathedral canonries,averaging 11,000 reales per annum, aggregating11,930,000also 3500 in collegiate churches, worth 25008,750,000 ---------- 20,680,000

As these were largely derived from tithes it shows how heavy a burden was laid on agriculture by this single feature of the church establishment.

1302. Archivo de Alcalá, Estado, Leg. 2843.
1303. Archivo hist. nacional, Inquisicion de Valencia, Leg. 15, n. 10, fol. 42, 68.
1304. Archivo hist. nacional, Inquisicion de Valencia, Leg. 16, n. 9, fol. 7.
1305. Ibidem, Leg. 4, n. 3, fol. 252, 310, 321.
1306. N. Hergueta (Boletin, XLV, 436).
1307. Código del Reinado intruso de José Napoleon Bonaparte, p. 43 (Madrid, 1845).--Coleccion de los Decretos y Ordenes de las Córtes, I, 33 (Madrid, 1820).
1308. Archivo de Alcalá, Hacienda, Leg. 544^{2} (Lib. 10).
1309. Archivo de Simancas, Inquisicion, Lib. 3, fol. 358.
1310. Archivo gen. de la C. de Aragon, Regist. 3684, fol. 77, 92, 94.--Archivo de Simancas, Inquisicion, Lib. 3, fol. 343.
1311. Instrucciones del Receptor, § 11 (Arguello, fol. 18).
1312. Archivo de Alcalá, Estado, Leg. 2843.
1313. Arguello, fol. 18.
1314. Archivo hist. nacional, Inquisicion de Valencia, Leg. 5, n. 1, fol. 18; Leg. 10, n. 2, fol. 223.--Archivo de Simancas, Inquisicion, Lib. 942, fol. 47.--MSS. of Royal Library of Copenhagen, 218^{b}, p. 247.
1315. Instrucciones del Receptor, § 10 (Arguello, fol. 18).
1316. Archivo de Simancas, Inquisicion, Lib. 1.
1317. Archivo hist. nacional, Inquisicion de Toledo, Contabilidad, Leg. 241, n. 32.
1318. Ibidem, Inquisicion de Valencia, Leg. 371.
1319. Ibidem, Leg. 309, Cuentas, fol. 1-5.
1320. Archivo de Simancas, Inquisicion, Sala 40, Lib. 4, fol. 244.
1321. Ibidem, Lib. 939, fol. 133.
1322. Archivo hist. nacional, Inquisicion de Valencia, Leg 5, n. 2, fol. 334.
1323. Archivo de Simancas, Inquisicion, Lib. 926, fol. 21.
1324. Archivo hist. nacional, Inquisicion de Valencia, Leg. 8, n. 2, fol. 327.
1325. Libro XIII de Cartas (MSS. of Am. Philos. Society).--Archivo hist. nacional Inquisicion de Valencia, Leg. 13, n. 2, fol. 52, 159, 161, 162, 165, 169, 185; Leg. 15, n. 10, fol. 11, 14, 62, 94, 109.
1326. Ibidem, Leg. 12, n. 1, fol. 29, 78, 167; n. 2, fol. 118; Leg. 13, n. 2, fol. 158, 226; Leg. 14, n. 1, fol. 128.

1327. MSS. of Am. Philos. Society.--Archivo hist. nacional, Inquisicion de Valencia, Leg. 17, n. 4, fol. 104.
1328. Archivo de Simancas, Inquisicion, Lib. 933.
1329. Archivo de Simancas, Inquisicion, Lib. 3, fol. 314-15; Lib. 933.
1330. Ibidem, Lib. 3, fol. 304.
1331. Ibidem, Lib. 3, fol. 318.
1332. Ibidem, Lib. 9, fol. 1.
1333. Archivo de Simancas, Inquisicion, Lib. 933.
1334. Ibidem, Lib. 76, fol. 235.
1335. Ibidem, Lib. 240, fol. 122.
1336. Archivo de Simancas, Inquisicion, Lib. 939, fol. 31, 130; Sala 40, Lib. 4, fol. 223.
1337. MSS. of Royal Library of Copenhagen, 218^{b}, p. 209.--Archivo hist. nacional, Inquisicion de Valencia, Leg. 5, n. 2, fol. 181; Leg. 9, n. 2, fol. 223, 249; Leg. 399.--Bibl. nacional, MSS., Pp, 28.
1338. Archivo de Simancas, Inquisicion, Lib. 979, fol. 32; Lib. 939, fol. 130, 131, 132; Lib. 942, fol. 21.--Archivo de Alcalá, Hacienda, n. 473.--Archivo hist. nacional, Inquisicion de Valencia, Leg. 5, n. 1, fol. 100.
1339. Archivo de Salamanca, Inquisicion, Lib. 926, fol. 21, 26.
1340. Archivo hist. nacional, Inquisicion de Valencia, Leg. 9, n. 2, fol. 198; Leg. 371.
1341. Libro XIII de Cartas, fol. 135, 181, 193 (MSS. of Am. Philos. Society).
1342. Archivo hist. nacional, Inquisicion de Valencia, Leg. 13, n. 2, fol. 132, 145-6; Leg. 14, n. 1, fol. 6 sqq., 56, 63-7, 110, 116, 119, 123, 138, 141, 144, 147, 150, 154; Leg. 14, n. 2, fol. 1, 4, 6, 7, 11, 13, 17, 18, 26; Leg. 14, n. 2, fol. 62, 72, 73, 79, 81, 88, 118.
1343. Ibidem, Leg. 14, n. 2, fol. 61.
1344. Instrucciones de 1484, §§ 3, 7, 8 (Arguello, fol. 3, 4).
1345. See Vol. I, p. 573.
1346. See Vol. I, p. 576.
1347. Archivo hist. nacional, Inquisicion de Toledo, Leg. 140, n. 162.
1348. Archivo hist. nacional, Inq. de Toledo, Leg. 139, fol. 145 (see Appendix).
1349. Archivo hist. nacional, Inquisicion de Toledo, Leg. 154, n. 375 (see Appendix).
1350. Ibidem, Leg. 153, n. 331.
1351. Archivo hist. nacional, Inquisicion de Valencia, Leg. 98.
1352. Albert. Albartini Repetitio nova, fol. cxlii, n. 4 (Valentiæ, 1534).
1353. Archivo de Simancas, Inquisicion, Lib. 933.
1354. Guadalajara y Xavierr, Expulsion de los Moriscos, fol. 159 (Pamplona, 1613).
1355. Clement's brief is printed in the Appendix to the author's "Moriscos of Spain."
1356. See Appendix to the author's "Moriscos of Spain."
1357. Llorente, Hist. crít. Cap. XLIV, Art. 1, n. 20.--Archivo de Simancas, Inquisicion, Lib. 559.--Archivo hist. nacional, Inquisicion de Valencia, Leg. 100; Cartas del Consejo, Leg. 17, n. 4, fol. 55.
1358. Jean Cruppi, La Cour d'Assises, pp. 132-7 (Paris, 1898).
1359. Fueros de Aragon, fol. 96-7, 150, 154-61, 163-4, 187, 195, 200-1, 204, 213-14, 236 (Zaragoza, 1624).--Observantiæ Regni Aragonum, fol. 32 (Saragossæ, 1624).
1360. Archivo hist. nacional, Inquisicion de Valencia, Leg. 61.
1361. Fueros de Viscaya, confirmados por el Rey Carlos III, Tit. xi, ley 7 (Bilbao, 1761, p. 95).
1362. Córtes de Toledo, 1436; de Madrigal, 1438 (Córtes de los Antiguos Reinos, III, 304-5, 336).--Ordenanzas Reales, VIII, i, 1, 3, 6, 10; v, 1; xi, 9.--Novís. Recop. Lib. XII, Tit. xxxiii, leyes 1-3.--Córtes de Toledo, 1480, n. 13, 38, 39, 41, 42, 44, 45, 60 (Córtes de los Reynos, etc., T. IV).--See also Montalvo's notes to the Partidas, Seville, 1491, P. III, Tit. iv, 1. 22; vi, 6, 13; viii, 7.
1363. Archivo hist. nacional, Inquisicion de Sevilla, Leg. 146, n. 243.
1364. Colmeiro, Córtes de los Reinos de Leon y de Castilla, II, 146, 159-60, 170, 177-9, 191, 198, 216, 234-7, 264, 270.
1365. Ariño, Sucesos de Sevilla, Appendice (Sevilla, 1873).
1366. Archivo hist. nacional, Inquisicion de Toledo, Leg. 233, n. 100; Leg. 110, n. 17, fol. 1-11.
1367. Concil. Toletan. ann. 1565, cap. xii, xiii, xiv (Aguirre, V, 396)
1368. Collectio Decretorum Sac. Congr. S^{ti} Officii, pp. 217, 219, 323 (MS. penes me).
1369. Archivo hist. nacional, Inquisicion de Toledo, Leg. 139, n. 145.
1370. Ibidem, Leg. 137, n. 98; Leg. 138, n. 123; Leg. 150, n. 299; Leg. 165, n. 551; Leg. 176, n. 679.
1371. Ibidem, Leg. 153, n. 331.
1372. Instrucciones de 1488, § 7 (Arguello, fol. 10).
1373. Instrucciones de Avila, (Arguello, fol. 21).
1374. Archivo hist. nacional, Inquisicion de Toledo, Leg. 158, n. 431, 435.

1375. Instrucciones de Avila, 1498, § 10 (Arguello, fol. 13).
1376. Archivo de Simancas, Inquisicion, Lib. 73, fol. 362.
1377. Proceso contra Mari Serrana, fol. xix (MS. penes me).
1378. Archivo de Simancas, Inquisicion, Lib. 926, fol. 299.
1379. MSS. of Royal Library of Copenhagen, 218^{b}, p. 335.
1380. Archivo gen. de la C. de Aragon, Leg. 528.
1381. Archivo de Simancas, Inquisicion, Lib. 69, fol. 3.
1382. Bibliotheca publica de Toledo, Sala 5, Estante 11, Tabla 3.
1383. Archivo hist. nacional, Inquisicion de Valencia, Leg. 392.
1384. Ibidem, Inquisicion de Toledo, Leg. 498; Inquisicion de Valencia, Leg. 372--Pablo García, Orden de Processar, fol. 37.
1385. Archivo de Simancas, Inquisicion, Lib. 890.
1386. Pegnæ Comment, xcvii in Eymerici Director, P. III.
1387. Modo de Proceder, fol. 55 (Bibl. nacional, MSS., D, 122). Of course there were public edicts, printed for posting on church doors. These contained penalties for defacing or removal.
1388. Archivo de Alcalá, Hacienda, Leg. 544^{2} (Lib. 6).--Archivo hist. nacional, Inquisicion de Valencia, Leg. 10, n. 2, fol. 5.--In civil cases, however, the tribunals could grant licences to print.
1389. Bibl. nacional, MSS., D, 118, p. 148.
1390. Relazioni Venete, Serie I, T. VI, p. 371.
1391. MSS. of Royal Library of Copenhagen, 214 fol. (see Appendix).

This explains why, in contrast with the voluminous Italian works on inquisitorial practice, the Spanish literature on the subject is so barren. Pablo García, secretary of the Suprema, compiled an "Orden de Processar en el Santo Oficio," but it was only intended for use in the tribunals. In 1592 there is an order on the Receiver-general of the Suprema to pay, "por la impression de los libros de procesar en el santo oficio" (Archivo de Simancas, Lib. 940, fol. 18) showing it to be a strictly official manual. It was reprinted in 1628 "en la Imprenta Real."

In 1494 there appeared in Valencia the "Repertorium perutile de pravitate hæreticorum," which commonly goes by the name of Miguel Alberto. It is based on the Old Inquisition, but contains some references to Spanish practice. Reprinted, Venice, 1588.

Something of the kind is also to be found in the two works of Arnaldo Albertino, Inquisitor of Sicily--the "Repetitio nova," Valencia, 1534, and the "De Agnoscendis Assertionibus Catholicis," printed after his death, Palermo, 1553 and Rome, 1572.

More useful is the work of Bishop Simancas "De Catholicis Institutionibus," Valladolid 1552, Venice 1573, Rome 1575 and Ferrara 1692. It has many references to Spanish practice. Still more practical is his "Theorice et Praxie Hæreseos, sive Enchiridion Judicum violatæ Religionis," first printed in 1568 and again in Venice, 1573.

Juan de Rojas, Inquisitor of Valencia, printed (Valencia, 1572) and dedicated to Inquisitor-general Espinosa his "De hæreticis una cum quinquaginta analyticis assertionibus et privilegiis Inquisitorum," containing discussions on inquisitorial practice.

Appended to Luis de Páramo's "De Origine et Progressu Officii Sanctæ Inquisitionis" (Madrid, 1598) are some dissertations on various points of practice.

There is much to be gathered from Francisco Peña's edition of the "Directorium" of Eymerich, with elaborate commentaries (Rome, 1578, and repeatedly elsewhere). A compend of these, by Fra Luigi Bariola appeared in Milan, 1610, under the title of "Flores Commentariorum R. D. Franciaci Pegnæ."

Giovanni Alberghini's "Manuale Qualificatorum S. Inquisitionis" (Saragossa, 1671, also Cologne, 1740 and Venice, 1754) is also of value for the practice of the Spanish Inquisition.

1392. Archivo de Simancas, Inquisicion, Lib. 939, fol. 273.
1393. Archivo de Simancas, Inquisicion, Lib. 943, fol. 62.--MSS. of Royal Library of Copenhagen, 218^{b}, p. 346 (see Appendix).
1394. Instruccion que han de guardar los Comisarios, Toledo, s. d.
1395. Archivo de Simancas, Inquisicion, Lib. 890.
1396. MSS. of Royal Library of Copenhagen, 218^{b}, p. 261.
1397. Ibidem, p. 250.
1398. See cases in Baluz. et Mansi Miscell. II, 289.--Fredericq, Corpus Documentt Inquisitionís Neerlandicæ, I, 330-1, 362-3, 365, 398.--Dressel, Vier Documente aus römischen Archiven, pp. 1-48 (Berlin, 1872).
1399. Archivo de Simancas, Inquisicion, Lib. 926, 927, 933.
1400. Archivo hist. nacional, Inquisicion de Toledo, Leg. 154, n. 356.--Pablo García, Orden de Processar, fol. 31.
1401. Instrucciones de 1484, § 16 (Arguello, fol. 6).
1402. Archivo hist. nacional, Inquisicion de Toledo, Leg. 139, n. 145; Leg. 140, n. 162; Leg. 148,

n. 207; Leg. 154, n. 356-375.
    1403. Arguello, fol. 13, 16.--Archivo de Simancas, Inquisicion, Lib. 933.
    1404. Archivo de Simancas, Inquisicion, Lib. 939, fol. 85
    1405. MSS. of Royal Library of Copenhagen, 218^{b}, pp. 392-7.--Archivo de Alcalá, Hacienda, Leg. 544^{2} (Lib. 6).
    1406. Simancæ de Cath. Instt., Tit. LIII, n. 5.
    1407. Fueros y Actos de Corte de Zaragoza, 1645-6 (Zaragoza, 1647, pp. 10-11).
    1408. Simancæ, op. cit., Tit. LIII, n. 10.--MS. of Royal Library of Copenhagen, 218^{b}, p. 397.
    1409. MSS. of Royal Library of Copenhagen, 218^{b}, p. 317.--Archivo hist. nacional, Inquisicion de Valencia, Leg. 31.
    1410. Instrucciones de 1561, § 16 (Arguello, fol. 29).
    1411. Páramo, p. 269.
    1412. Ledesma, Despertador Republicano, p. 96 (Mexico, 1700).--Alberghini, Manuale Qualificatorum, cap. 34 (Cæsaraugustæ, 1671).
    1413. Constt. 13, 14, 17, 18, 20, 21, Cod. IX, 1.
    1414. Simancæ de Cath. Instt., Tit. XXIX, n. 35-45
    1415. Alf. de Castro de Just. Punit. Hæres., Lib. II, cap. xxvi
    1416. Archivo hist. nacional, Inquisicion de Valencia, Seccion varios, Leg. 394, n. 25, fol. 13.
    1417. Archivo de Simancas, Inquisicion, Leg. 552, fol. 26.
    1418. Archivo hist. nacional, Inquisicion de Valencia, Leg. 10, n. 2, fol. 207.
    1419. Archivo de Alcalá, Hacienda, Leg. 544^{2} (Lib. 6).
    1420. Llorente, Hist. crít. Cap. XVIII, Art. 1, n. 11.
    1421. MSS. of Royal Library of Copenhagen, 213 fol., p, 136.
    1422. Archivo de Simancas, Inquisicion, Lib. 939, fol. 88.
    1423. Instrucciones de 1561, § 1 (Arguello, fol. 27).--Pablo García, however, says (Orden de Processar, fol. 1) that Moorish ceremonies are sometimes calificadas.
    1424. Archivo de Simancas, Inquisicion, Lib. 939, fol. 88.
    1425. MSS. of Royal Library of Copenhagen, 218^{b}, pp. 404-17.
    1426. Archivo de Simancas, Inquisicion, Lib. 939, fol. 105.
    1427. Archivo de Simancas, Inquisicion, Lib. 939, fol. 89.
    1428. Archivo hist. nacional, Inquisicion de Valencia, Leg. 372.--MSS. penes me.
    1429. Instrucciones de 1561, § 3 (Arguello, fol. 27).
    1430. Archivo hist. nacional, Inquisicion de Toledo, Leg. 138.
    1431. Archivo de Simancas, Inquisicion, Lib. 942, fol. 26, 52.
    1432. Praxis procedendi, cap. iv, n. 1 (Archivo hist. nacional, Inquisicion de Valencia).
    1433. Instrucciones de 1498, § 3 (Arguello, fol. 12).--Archivo de Simancas, Inquisicion, Lib. 939, fol. 88.
    1434. Elucidationes Sancti Officii, § 1 (Archivo de Alcalá, Hacienda, Leg. 544^{2}, Lib. 4).--Simancæ Enchiridion, Tit. xxv, n. 3; Ejued. de Cath. Instt., Tit. xvi, n. 1, 2.
    1435. Praxis procedendi, cap. 6, n. 9 (ubi sup.).--MSS. of Library of Univ. of Halle, Yc, 20, T. I.--Sousæ Aphorism. Inquisit. Lib. II, cap. 26, n. 11, 12, 15.
    1436. Archivo hist. nacional, Inquisicion de Valencia, Leg. 9, n. 1, fol. 388; Leg. 299, fol. 80.--Archivo de Simancas, Inquisicion, Leg. 552, fol. 26.
    1437. Archivo hist. nacional, Inquisicion de Toledo, Leg. 183, n. 779.
    1438. Ibidem, Leg. 114, n. 14.
    1439. Proceso contra Gil Tacis (MSS. of Am. Philosophical Society).
    1440. Archivo de Simancas, Patronato Real, Inquisicion, Leg. único, fol. 37, 38.
    1441. Actos de Corte del Reyno de Aragon, fol. 96 (Zaragoza, 1664).
    1442. Archivo hist. nacional, Inquisicion de Valencia, Leg. 12, n. 2, fol. 126.
    1443. Archivo de Simancas, Inquisicion, Leg. 552, fol. 52.
    1444. Llorente, Hist, crít., Cap. XLII, Art. 1, n. 13.
    1445. Archivo de Simancas, Inquisicion, Lib. 890, fol. 28.
    1446. Instrucciones de 1561, § 10 (Arguello, fol 28).--Instruccion y Pratica del Comisario, n. 34.--Proceso contra Angela Nuñez Marques, fol. 82 (MS. penes me).
    1447. Proceso contra Benito Peñas (MSS. of Library of Univ. of Halle, Yc, 20, T. VI.)--Pablo García, Orden de Processar, fol. 6.

    The Roman Inquisition was much more regardful of the interests of the accused. The inquisitor was instructed in no case to pledge or sell utensils, movables or tools of trade or real estate, but to restrict himself to the income or rents of the latter. The expenses of transport were thrown upon the local bishop or the papal camera, but these were usually small in view of the numerous petty tribunals, for there was one in every place of any size. Care was taken to keep down expenses and, in many places, the Inquisition consisted of a couple of rooms in the convent to which the inquisitor belonged, for he was either a Franciscan or a Dominican. The transport of those condemned to the galleys was defrayed by the towns; the maintenance of poor prisoners by the bishops, or, if they were Regulars, by the Orders to which they belonged.--Decr. Sac. Congr. S^{ti} Officii, pp. 47, 48, 178, 192, 256 sqq. (Bibl. del R. Archivio di Stato in Roma, Fondo camerale, Congr. del. S. Offizio, Vol. 3).

1448. Proceso contra Fray Estevan Ramoneda (MSS. of Am. Philosophical Society).
1449. Fueros y Actos de Corte en Zaragoza, 1645-6, pp. 4-5 (Zaragoza, 1647).
1450. Cap. 19, Tit. ii, in Sexto Lib. V.
1451. Arguello, fol. 17.--Archivo de Simancas, Inquisicion, Lib. 933.--Ibidem, Patronato Real, Inquisicion, Leg. único, fol. 44.--Ibidem, Canarias, Expedientes de Visitas, Leg. 250, Lib. 1, fol. 9
1452. MSS. of Royal Library of Copenhagen, 213 fol., pp. 19, 20. 130.--Archivo hist. nacional, Inquisicion de Valencia, Leg. 10, n. 2, fol. 37; Leg. 14, n. 2, fol. 12, 126
1453. Archivo de Simancas, Inquisicion, Leg. 1465, fol. 72.--Bibl. nacional, MSS., D, 118, fol. 112, n. 39; fol. 167.
1454. Arguello, fol. 13.--Instrucciones de 1561, § 8.--Archivo de Simancas, Inquisicion, Lib. 942, fol. 62.--MSS. of Royal Library of Copenhagen, 218^{b}, p. 228.
1455. Proceso contra Margarita Altamira, fol. 87-88 (MSS. of Am. Philos. Society).
1456. MSS. of Royal Library of Copenhagen, 213 fol., p. 129.
1457. Archivo hist. nacional, Inquisicion de Valencia, Leg. 300, P. I, n. 71.
1458. Proceso contra Margarita Altamira (ubi sup.).
1459. MSS. of Royal Library of Copenhagen, 213 fol., p. 131; 318^{b}, pp. 218, 317.
1460. Archivo de Simancas, Inquisicion, Libros 1, 2
1461. Arch. de Simancas, Lib. 40, fol. 328.
1462. Ibidem, Leg. 1480, fol. 13.
1463. Archivo gen. de la C. de Aragon, Regist. 3684, fol. 99, 100.
1464. Archivo de Simancas, Patronato Real, Inquisicion, Leg. único, fol. 44.
1465. Archivo de Simancas, Inquisicion, Lib. 942, fol. 13; Lib. 939, fol. 94.--MSS. of Royal Library of Copenhagen, 213 fol., p. 115.
1466. Instrucciones de 1561, § 76 (Arguello, fol. 37).--Pablo García, Orden de Processar, fol. 44.--Archivo de Simancas, Inquisicion, Lib. 979, fol. 30.
1467. Proceso contra Francisco Hernández (MSS. of David Fergusson, Esq.).
1468. Archivo de Simancas, Inquisicion, Leg. 1477, fol. 149.
1469. Pablo García, Orden de Processar, fol. 42.--Proceso contra Hieron. de la Madre de Dios (MSS. of Library of Univ. of Halle, Yc, 20, T. VII).--Bibl. nacional, MSS., D, 118, fol. 167.
1470. MSS. of Am. Philos. Society.
1471. Archivo de Simancas, Inquisicion, Lib. 1; Lib. 3, fol. 78.
1472. Archivo hist. nacional, Inquisicion de Toledo, Leg. 138; Leg. 112, n. 71, fol. 36.--Proceso contra Mari López de Sazeda, fol. 9 (MS penes me).--Archivo de Simancas, Inquisicion, Lib. 979, fol. 28.--Instrucciones de 1561, § 7 (Arguello, fol. 28).
1473. Pablo García, Orden de Processar, fol. 101.
1474. Proceso contra Margarita Altamira (MSS. of Am. Philos. Society).
1475. Instrucciones de 1561, § 6 (Arguello, fol. 28).
1476. Archivo de Simancas, Inquisicion, Lib. 78, fol. 96.--Instrucciones de 1561, § 61 (Arguello, fol. 35).--Pablo García, Orden de Processar, fol. 42.
1477. Instrucciones de 1561, § 6 (ubi sup.).--Archivo de Alcalá, Hacienda, Leg 544ª (Lib. 4).--Archivo de Simancas, Inquisicion, Lib. 82, fol. 132.
1478. MSS. of Royal Library of Copenhagen, 218^{b}, p. 260.
1479. Libro XIII de Cartas, fol. 17 (MSS. of Am. Philos. Society).
1480. Elucidatio Sancti Officii, § 11 Archivo de Alcalá, Hacienda, Leg. 544^{2}, (Lib. 4).
1481. Pablo García, Orden de Processar, fol. 7.
1482. Ibidem, fol. 42.
1483. Praxis procedendi, cap. vi, n. 4 (Archivo hist. nacional, Inquisicion de Valencia).
1484. MSS. of Royal Library of Copenhagen, 218^{b}, pp. 394, 417, 422.--Libro XIII de Cartas, fol. 17 (MSS. of Am. Philos. Society).
1485. Archivo de Simancas, Inquisicion, Lib. 890.
1486. Proceso de Ana de Torres, fol. 15-25, 39 (MS. penes me).
1487. Archivo hist. nacional, Inquisicion de Toledo, Leg. 231, n. 71, fol. 38.
1488. Archivo de Simancas, Inquisicion, Lib. 939, fol. 125.
1489. Bibl. nacional, MSS., V, 377, cap. i; cap. xiv, § 3.
1490. Proceso contra Angela Pérez (MS. penes me).--Archivo de Simancas, Inquisicion, Leg. 552, fol. 52; Libra 890.
1491. Partidas, P. VII, Tit. xxix, ley 11.--Novís. Recop., Lib. XII, Tit. xxxix, ley 6.
1492. Córtes de los Antiguos Reinos, IV, 599, 605.--Archivo de Simancas, Inquisicion, Lib. 21,

fol. 127.
1493. Archivo de Simancas, Inquisicion, Lib. 890.
1494. Archivo de Simancas, Inquisicion, Leg. 552, fol. 11.--Elucidationes Sancti Officii, § 30 (Archivo de Alcalá, Hacienda, Leg. 544^{2}, Lib. 4).
1495. Franchini, Breve Rapporta del Tribunale della SS. Inquisizione di Sicilia, p. 31.--Proceso contra Mari Rodriguez (MS. penes me).
1496. Archivo de Simancas, Inquisicion, Leg. 552, fol. 13.--Olmo, Relacion del Auto de la Fee de 1680, pp. 247-52.
1497. MSS. of Library of the Univ. of Halle, Yc, 17.
1498. Archivo de Simancas, Inquisicion, Lib. 940, fol. 216.
1499. Hist. crít., Cap. XLIII, Art. iii, n. 9; Art. v, n. 9.
1500. Gianbattista Confalonieri (Spicilegio Vaticano, I, 456).
1501. Orden de Processar, fol. 21.--MSS. of Library of Univ. of Halle, Yc, 20, T. V.--Archivo de Simancas, Inquisicion, Leg. 552, fol. 35.
1502. Archivo de Simancas, Inquisicion, Lib. 939, fol. 121.
1503. Miscelanea de Zapata (Mem. hist. español, XI, 202).
1504. MSS. of Library of Univ. of Halle, Yc, 20, T. VIII.
1505. Modo de Proceder, fol. 74 (Bibl. nacional, MSS., D, 122).
1506. Simancæ de Cath. Institt. Tit. XVI, n. 23; Ejusd. Adnotat. in Zanchinum, cap. 9.--Rojas de Hæret., P. II, n. 185-7.
1507. Alberghini, Manuale Qualificator., cap. xxxiii, n. 9.
1508. Archivo hist. nacional, Inquisicion de Valencia, Leg. 31.
1509. Instrucciones de 1488, § 5 (Arguello, fol. 10).
1510. Instrucciones de 1498 (Ibidem, fol. 16, 21).
1511. Archivo de Simancas, Inquisicion, Lib. 939, fol. 91, 96.
1512. Ibidem, Lib. 926, fol. 33.
1513. Archivo de Simancas, Inquisicion, Lib. 949, fol. 96.--Archivo de Alcalá, Hacienda, Leg. 544^{1} (Lib. 6).
1514. Bibl. nacional, MSS., S, 121.
1515. Instrucciones de 1561, §§ 11, 12, 58, 62, 70, 78 (Arguello, fol. 29, 35, 36, 37).--Pablo García, Orden de Processar, fol. 36
1516. Archivo de Simancas, Inquisicion, Lib. 979, fol. 22-26.--Bibl. nacional, MSS., D, 118, fol. 84, n. 40.
1517. Archivo de Alcalá, Hacienda, Leg. 544^{1} (Lib. 6).
1518. Archivo de Simancas, Inquisicion, Leg. 552, fol. 17, 40.
1519. MS. of Library of Univ. of Halle, Yc, 20, T. I.
1520. El Museo Mexicano, T. I, p. 362 (Mexico, 1843).
1521. Archivo de Simancas, Inquisicion, Lib. 890. 1522. Ibidem, Lib. 939, fol. 91.
1523. Archivo hist. nacional, Inquisicion de Valencia, Leg. 2, n. 15.
1524. Sousæ Aphorism. Lib. II, cap. 26, n. 20, 21.--Archivo de Simancas, Inquisicion, Visitas de Barcelona, Leg. 15, fol. 2.--Ibidem, Lib. 939, fol. 92.
1525. Archivo de Simancas, Inquisicion, Lib. 939, fol. 92.--Processo contra Isabel Reyner (MSS. of Library of the Univ. of Halle, Yc, 20, T. III).
1526. MSS. of Library of Univ. of Halle, Tom. VIII, X.
1527. Archivo de Simancas, Inquisicion, Lib. 939, fol. 92.
1528. Archivo de Alcalá, Hacienda, Leg. 544^{1} (Lib. 6).
1529. Archivo hist. nacional, Inquisicion de Valencia, Leg. 383.
1530. MSS. of Library of Univ. of Halle, Yc, 20, T. I.
1531. Decret. Sac. Congr. S^{ti}. Officii, p. 47 (Bibl. del R. Archivio di Stato in Roma, Fondo camerale, Congr. del S. Offizio, Vol. 3).
1532. Azpilcuetæ De Oratione, cap. xxii, n. 10 (Romæ, 1578).
1533. Proceso contra Fray Luis de Leon (Col. de Documentos, XI, 50, 52).
1534. Archivo de Simancas, Inquisicion, Lib. 939, fol. 120.
1535. Instrucciones de 1561, § 71 (Arguello, fol. 36).
1536. Archivo de Simancas, Inquisicion, Leg. 552, fol. 22.
1537. MSS. of Royal Library of Copenhagen, 218^{b}, p. 257.
1538. Archivo hist. nacional, Inquisicion de Toledo, Leg. 498.
1539. Alberghini, Manuale Qualificatorum, cap. xxxiii, n. 10.
1540. Instrucciones de 1561, § 71 (Arguello, fol. 36).
1541. Archivo de Simancas, Inquisicion, Leg. 552, fol. 28, 29.
1542. Instrucciones de 1498, § 14 (Arguello, fol. 13).
1543. Archivo de Simancas, Inquisicion, Lib. 939, fol. 77.

1544. Archivo de Simancas, Inquisicion, Lib. 666.
1545. Archivo de Alcalá, Hacienda, Leg. 544^{1} (Lib. 6).
1546. Archivo de Simancas, Inquisicion, Leg. 552, fol. 31.
1547. Ibidem, Patronato Real, Inquisicion, Leg. único, fol. 44.
1548. Archivo de Simancas, Inquisicion, Lib. 933.
1549. Bibl. nacional, MSS., D, 118, fol. 84, n. 30.--Archivo de Simancas, Visitas de Barcelona, Leg. 15, fol. 2.
1550. Instrucciones de 1488, § 5 (Arguello, fol. 10).--Archivo de Simancas, Inquisicion, Lib. 933; Lib. 76. fol. 227; Lib. 4, fol. 192; Visitas de Barcelona, Leg. 15, fol. 20.--MSS. of Royal Library of Copenhagen, 213 fol., p. 138.--Cartas de Jesuitas (Mem. hist. español, XVII, 419).--Archivo de Alcalá, Hacienda, Leg. 544^{1} (Lib. 6).
1551. Archivo de Simancas, Patronato Real, Inquisicion, Leg. único, fol. 44.
1552. Llorente, Hist. crít., Cap. XXI, Art. ii, n. 21
1553. Archivo de Simancas, Inquisicion, Sala 40, Lib. 4, fol. 147, 197.
1554. Birch, Catalogue of MSS. of the Inquisition of the Canary Islands, I, 221, 235-40; II, 975.
1555. Eduard Böhmer, Francisca Hernández, pp. 89, 91.
1556. Proceso contra Hernándo Díaz (MSS. of Library of Univ. of Halle, Yc, 20, T. III).
1557. Schäfer, Beiträge zur Geschichte der spanischen Protestantismus, III, 129.
1558. Archivo hist. nacional, Inquisicion de Toledo, Leg. 114, n. 14.
1559. Archivo de Simancas, Inquisicion, Leg. 1474, fol. 47; Leg. 1477, fol. 149.
1560. Ibidem, Lib. 933.
1561. Ibidem, Leg. 1475, fol. 134.
1562. Ibidem, Leg. 1480, fol. 110, 128.
1563. See Vol. I, p. 575.--Arguello, fol. 19
1564. Archivo gen. de la C. de Aragon, Regist. 3684, fol. 68, 86, 92, 94, 102.--Archivo de Simancas, Inquisicion, Lib. 1.--Instrucciones de 1498, § 15 (Arguello, fol. 22).
1565. Archivo hist. nacional, Inquisicion de Valencia, Legajos 377, 383.
1566. Archivo de Simancas, Inquisicion, Lib. 1.
1567. Ibidem, Patronato Real, Inquisicion, Leg. único, fol. 44.
1568. Ibidem, Lib. 3, fol. 56.
1569. Archivo de Simancas, Inquisicion, Lib. 933.
1570. Ibidem, Lib. 9, fol. 18; Lib. 926, fol. 166.
1571. Ibidem, Lib. 933; Lib. 926, fol. 167.
1572. Archivo hist. nacional, Inquisicion de Valencia, Leg. 389.
1573. Archivo de Simancas, Inquisicion, Lib. 939, fol. 92.
1574. Ibidem, Lib. 939, fol. 29.--Instrucciones de 1561, § 75 (Arguello, fol. 87).
1575. Archivo de Alcalá, Hacienda, Leg. 544^{2} (Lib. 6).
1576. MSS. of Library of Univ. of Halle, Yc, 20, T. VIII.
1577. Ibidem, Tom. VII.
1578. Archivo hist. nacional, Inquisicion de Valencia, Leg. 9, n. 1, fol. 4; Leg. 12, n. 2, fol. 126.
1579. MSS. of Library of Univ. of Halle, Yc, 20, T. VI.--Proceso contra Ana Enríquez, fol. 55 (MS. penes me).
1580. Archivo hist. nacional, Inquisicion de Valencia, Leg. 2, n. 15.--Proceso contra Antonio Adorno (MSS. of Am. Philos. Society).
1581. Archivo de Simancas, Inquisicion, Lib. 940, fol. 44, 69.
1582. Archivo hist. nacional, Inquisicion de Valencia, Leg. 5, n. 1, fol. 94.
1583. Archivo de Simancas, Inquisicion de Toledo, Leg. 428.
1584. Ibidem, Leg. 1475, fol. 134; Leg. 1480, fol. 127.
1585. Archivo hist. nacional, Inquisicion de Valencia, Cartas del Consejo, Leg. 16, n. 9.
1586. Ibidem, Leg. 9, n. 2, fol. 235; n. 3, fol. 299.--Libro XIII de Cartas, fol. 172, 174 (MSS. of Am. Philos. Society).
1587. Archivo hist. nacional, Inquisicion de Valencia, Leg. 9, n. 1, fol. 143.
1588. MSS. of Royal Library of Copenhagen, 213 fol., p. 163; 218^{b}, pp. 239, 316.
1589. MSS. of Royal Library of Copenhagen. 318^{b}, p. 397.--Archivo de Simancas, Inquisicion, Lib. 78, fol. 74.--Archivo de Alcalá, Hacienda, Leg 544^{2} (Lib. 6).
1590. MSS. of Am. Philos. Society.--Records of the Spanish Inquisition, pp. 113-48. (Boston, 1828).
1591. MSS. of Am. Philos. Society.
1592. Jacobo de las Leyes, Flores de las Leyes, Lib. II, Tit. vii, viii (Mem. hist. español, II, 230-33).
1593. Fueros de Aragon, fol. 96-7 (Zaragoza, 1624).
1594. Constt. 6, 11, 12, Cod. IV, XX.

1595. Concil. Carthag. VII, ann. 419, cap. 4.--Gratiani Decret. P. II, Caus. iv, Q. 1, cap. 1. 1596. Rojas de Hæreticis, P. II, n. 89-91.

1597. MSS. of Library of University of Halle, Yc, 20, T. 1.

1598. Archivo hist. nacional, Inquisicion de Valencia, Leg. 2, n. 10, fol. 46.

1599. Ristretto circa li Delitti più frequenti nel S. Offizio, p. 144 (MS. penes me).

1600. Archivo de Simancas, Inquisicion, Lib. 933.

1601. Padre Fidel Fita has investigated this question with his habitual thoroughness in Boletin, XXIII, 406 sqq.

1602. Simancæ Enchirid. Tit. XXXV, n. 25-6. 1603. Archivo de Simancas, Inquisicion, Leg. 552, fol. 35.

1604. Collectio Decretorum Sac. Cong. S. Officii, p. 404 (MS. penes me).

1605. Praxis procedendi, Cap. 1, n. 4 (Archivo hist. nacional, Inquisicion de Valencia).--MSS. of Royal Library of Copenhagen, 218^{b}, p. 259.--Proceso contra Angela Pérez (MS. penes me).

1606. Sousæ Aphorismi Inquisit. Lib. II, cap. xxxiv, n. 8, 9, 11, 12.

1607. Archivo de Simancas, Inquisicion, Lib. 939, fol. 86.

1608. Archivo hist. nacional, Inquisicion de Toledo, Leg. 140, n. 16; 148, n. 262.

1609. Instrucciones de 1561, § 36 (Arguello, fol. 32).--Pablo García, Orden de Processar, fol. 25.--Rojas de Hæret. P. II, n. 377-9.--Simancæ Enchirid. Tit. XXXV, n. 23, 24.--Elucidationes Sancti Officii, § 26 (Archivo de Alcalá, Hacienda, Leg, 544^{2}, Lib. 6).

1610. Archivo de Simancas, Inquisicion, Lib. 939, fol. 86.

1611. Pablo García, Orden de Processar, fol. 44.--Modo de Proceder, fol. 58 (Bibl. nacional, MSS., D, 122).

1612. Archivo de Simancas, Inquisicion, Visitas de Barcelona, Leg. 15, fol. 9.

1613. Ibidem, Lib. 890, fol. 28.

1614. Archivo de Simancas, Inquisicion, Lib. 939, fol. 72, 73.

1615. Archivo gen. de la C. de Aragon, Regist. 3684, fol. 68, 69.--Archivo de Simancas, Inquisicion, Lib. 1.

1616. Archivo de Simancas, Inquisicion, Lib. 939, fol. 95.

1617. Archivo hist. national, Inquisicion de Toledo, Leg. 132, n. 31; Leg. 140, n. 162; Leg. 148, n. 267.

1618. Proceso contra Ignacia (MSS. of Am. Philos. Society).

1619. Archivo hist. nacional, Inquisicion de Toledo, Leg. 138.

1620. Archivo de Simancas, Inquisition, Lib. 939, fol. 86, 96.

1621. MSS. of Bibl. nationale de France, fonda espagnol, n. 81.

1622. Archivo de Simancas, Inquisicion, Leg. 552, fol. 31.

1623. Libro XIII de Cartas, fol. 71 (MSS. of Am. Philos. Society).

1624. Coleccion de Documentos, XI, 273.

1625. Archivo de Simancas, Inquisicion, Lib. 979, fol. 19.--Instrucciones de 1561, §§ 36, 39 (Arguello, fol. 32).

1626. Archivo hist. nacional, Inquisicion de Toledo, Leg. 183, n. 779; Leg. 112, n. 73, fol. 18.

1627. Proceso contra Marí Gómez, fol. xlii (MS. penes me).

1628. Instrucciones de 1498, §§ 11, 16 (Arguello, fol. 13).--Archivo de Simancas, Inquisicion, Lib. 939, fol. 68.

Arguello's text says that the officiales shall not be present, a manifest misprint for fiscales, the reading in a Simancas MS. (Lib. 933).

1629. Archivo hist. nacional, Inquisicion de Toledo, Leg. 99, n. 15; Leg. 139, n. 145; Leg. 143, n. 196.

1630. Archivo de Simancas, Inquisicion, Lib. 933; Lib. 939, fol. 99.--Pablo García, Orden de Processar, fol. 46.

1631. Archivo de Simancas, Inquisicion, Lib. 716; Leg. 522, fol. 11.--Archivo hist. nacional, Inquisicion de Valencia, Leg. 2, n. 10, fol. 79.--MSS. of Library of Univ. of Halle, Yc, 20, T. I.

1632. Archivo de Simancas, Inquisicion, Lib. 939, fol. 100.

1633. Archivo de Simancas, Inquisicion, Lib. 939, fol. 100, 101.

1634. Ibidem, Visitas de Barcelona, Leg. 15, fol. 2.--Archivo hist. nacional, Inquisicion de Valencia, Leg. 299, fol. 80.--Praxis Procedendi, cap. 1, n. 8; cap. 13, n. 10 (Ibidem).

1635. MSS. of Royal Library of Copenhagen, 218^{b}, pp. 246, 407.--Praxis procedendi, cap. 13, n. 5 (ubi sup.).--Proceso contra Josepha de San Luis Beltran, fol. 116-17 (MSS. of David Fergusson, Esq.).

1636. MSS. of Royal Library of Copenhagen, 218^{b}, p. 246.--Archivo hist. nacional, Inquisicion de Valencia, Leg. 9, n. 2, fol. 243.

1637. Instruccíon y Practica del Comisario, n. 25 (Archivo hist. nacional, Inquisicion de Valencia).

1638. Archivo hist. nacional, Inquisicion de Toledo, Leg. 228, n. 24; Leg. 229, n. 42; Leg. 230, n. 60; Inquisicion de Valencia, Leg. 365, n. 42.
1639. Archivo de Simancas, Inquisicion, Lib. 939, fol. 99.--Instrucciones de 1561, § 30 (Arguello, fol. 31).--Pablo García, Orden de Processar, fol. 20.
1640. Pablo García, fol. 21.--Coleccion de Documentos, X, 32, 43, 46.
1641. Praxis Procedendi, cap. 13, n. 12; cap. 14, n. 3 (Archivo hist. nacional, Inquisicion de Valencia).
1642. Simancæ de Cath. Instt. Tit. LXVI, n. 24.
1643. Rojas de Hæret. P. II, n. 104-5, 108, 110.
1644. Bibl. nacional, MSS. V, 377, cap. xxiii, § 6.
1645. Archivo de Simancas, Inquisicion, Leg. 552, fol. 13.
1646. Cap. 20 in Sexto Lib. V, Tit. ii.--Digard, Registres de Boniface VIII, T. II, p. 412, n. 3063. A futile attempt has been made to justify this suppression by a passage in Partidas (III, xvii, 11).
1647. Archivo hist. nacional, Inquisicion de Toledo, Leg. 139, n. 145; Leg. 143, in. 196.
1648. Instrucciones de 1484, § 16 (Arguello, fol. 6).
1649. Archivo de Simancas, Inquisicion, Lib. 1.
1650. Ibidem, Lib. 926, fol. 285.
1651. Cartas de Jiménez, pp. 261-3.--Páramo, p. 159.
The authenticity of the memorial ascribed to Ximenes has been called in question, but Páramo's evidence shows that Ximenes did remonstrate with Charles on the subject and, whether he was the author or not, it unquestionably reflects the official view of the matter at the time.
The killing of the informer at Talavera probably refers to the case of Bernardino Díaz, the consequences of which caused a coolness between Leo X and the Spanish Inquisition. See above, p. 123.
1652. Proceso contra Juan Franco, fol. 15 (MSS. of Library of Univ. of Halle, Yc, 20, T. III).
1653. Archivo de Simancas, Inquisicion, Lib. 73, fol. 6.--Ibidem, Inquisicion de Canarias, Expedientes de Visitas, Leg. 250, Lib. 3, fol. 10.
1654. Archivo de Simancas, Inquisicion, Lib. 54, fol. 31, 69, 190.
1655. Boronat, Los Moriscos españoles, I, 569.--Archivo hist. nacional, Inquisicion de Valencia, Leg. 2, n. 16, fol. 269.
1656. Archivo de Simancas, Inquisicion, Leg. 552, fol. 15.
1657. Ibidem, Visitas de Barcelona, Leg. 15, fol. 9; Libro 716; Leg. 552, fol. 35.--Archivo hist. nacional, Inquisicion de Valencia, Leg. 2, n. 10, fol. 2; Leg. 372.
1658. Archivo hist. nacional, Inquisicion de Toledo, Leg. 1.
1659. Archivo hist. nacional, Inquisicion de Toledo, Leg. 110, n. 31, fol. 10.
1660. Proceso contra Pedro Flamenco (MSS. of Library of Univ. of Halle, Yc, 20, T. III).
1661. Zangeri Tract. de Quæstionibus, cap. ii, n. 49-50 (Francofurti, 1730).
1662. Boletin, XI, 94-5 (Padre Fidel Fita).
1663. Instrucciones de 1561, § 72 (Arguello, fol. 37).
1664. Archivo de Simancas, Inquisicion, Visitas de Barcelona, Leg. 15, fol. 20.
1665. Ibidem, Leg. 552, fol. 14.
1666. Decret. Sac. Congr. S^{ti} Officii, p. 68 (Bibl. del R. Archivio di Stato in Roma, Fondo Camerale, Congr. del S. Offizio, Vol. 3).
1667. Archivo hist. nacional, Inquisicion de Toledo, Leg. 112, n. 74, fol. 4.
1668. Archivo de Simancas, Inquisicion, Lib. 939, fol. 86; Leg. 552, fol. 37.
1669. Colmeiro, Córtes de los antiguos Reinos, II, 249, 275.
1670. Relacion de la Inquisicion Toledana (Boletin, XI, 293-4).--Pulgar, Crónica, P. III, cap. 54, 100.
1671. MS. Memoria de diversos Autos, Auto 27 (Vol. I, Appendix, p. 609).
1672. Instrucciones de 1498, § 8 (Arguello, fol. 13).
1673. Archivo de Simancas, Inquisicion, Lib. 1.
1674. Archivo de Simancas, Real Patronato, Inquisicion, Leg. único, fol. 43.
1675. Pragmáticas y altres Drets de Cathalunya, Lib. I, Tit. viii, cap. 1, § 12.
1676. Archivo de Simancas, Real Patronato, Inquisicion, Leg. único, fol. 47.
1677. Pragmáticas, etc., ubi sup.
1678. Leonis PP. X Const. Intelleximus (Bullar. Roman. I, 594).
1679. Córtes de Valladolid, 1523, Art. 54 (Córtes de Leon y Castilla, IV, 381).--Leyes de Toro, ley 83.
1680. See Vol. I, Appendix, p. 585.
1681. Archivo de Simancas, Inquisicion, Lib. 939, fol. 86.
1682. Simancæ de Cath. Institt. Tit. LXIV, n. 90-6; Ejusd. Enchirid. Tit. XXXVIII.
1683. Archivo de Simancas, Inquisicion, Sala 40, Lib. 4, fol. 270.--Bibl. nacional, MSS. V, 377,

Cap. XXIII, §§ 1, 2.

    1684. Archivo de Simancas, Inquisicion, Leg. 552, fol. 22-3.
    1685. Archivo hist. nacional, Inquisicion de Toledo, Leg. 111; Leg. 1, año 1656.
    1686. Ibidem, Inquisicion de Valencia, Leg. 299, fol. 80.
    1687. Archivo de Simancas, Inquisicion, Leg. 552, fol. 13.
    1688. Fueros de Aragon, fol. 205 (Zaragoza, 1624).--Nueva Recop. Lib. V, Tit. xvii, ley 7.
    1689. Archivo de Simancas, Inquisicion, Lib. 939, fol. 141, 142.
    1690. Matute y Luquin, Autos de Fe de Córdova, p. 211.--Royal Library of Berlin, Qt. 9548.--Archivo hist. nacional, Inquisicion de Valencia, Leg. 100.--Archivo de Simancas, Inquisicion, Lib. 890.
    1691. Archivo de Simancas, Inquisicion, Leg. 552, fol. 26.
    1692. Library of the Univ. of Halle, Yc, 20, T. I.--Archivo hist. nacional, Inquisicion de Toledo, Leg. 1.
    1693. Archivo de Simancas, Inquisicion, Leg. 552.
    1694. Ibidem, Lib. 876.
    1695. Archivo hist. nacional, Inquisicion de Valencia, Leg. 10, n. 2, fol. 184, 185.
    1696. Bibl. nacional, MSS., R, 128, p. 42.--Royal Library of Berlin, Qt. 9548.
    1697. Archivo de Simancas, Inquisicion, Lib. 890.
    1698. Gloss. in Cap. 2, Decreti P. II, Caus. ii, Q. 4.--Eymeric. Direct. Inquis. P. III, cap. 71.--Guid. Fulcod. Quæstiones, Q. XV (Carena de Off. SS. Inquis. Ed. 1669, p. 392).--S. Antonini Summæ P. III, Tit. xviii, cap. 2, § 5.--Summa Tabiena s. v. Inquisitor, n. 37.--Fr. Pegnæ Comment. CXX in Direct. Inquis. P. III.--Rojas de Hæret. P. II, n. 100-3.
    1699. Archivo hist. nacional, Inquisicion de Valencia, Leg. 299, fol. 80.
    1700. Archivo de Simancas, Inquisicion, Visitas de Barcelona, Leg. 15, fol. 20.
    1701. Archivo de Simancas, Inquisicion, Lib. 937, fol. 212.
    1702. Escobar de Nobil. et Purit. probanda, P. I, Q. ix, § 3, n. 18.
    1703. Simancæ Enchirid. Tit. xxxvii, n. 8.--Páramo, pp. 871-2.--Rojas de Hæret. P. II, n. 139-45.--Archivo de Simancas, Lib. 939, fol. 87.
    1704. Archivo hist. nacional, Inquisicion de Valencia, Leg. 1, n. 1, fol. 401.

In the ancient fuero of Teruel, in force from 1176 to 1597, evidence to be legal required to be of both sight and hearing--"Quia nullus pro solo visu vel pro solo auditu debet recipi in testimonio, juxta forum."--Forum Turolii, regnante in Aragonia Adefonso rege, Anno Dominice nativitatis mclxxvi, Art. 245 (Zaragoza. 1905).

    1705. Praxis Procedendi, cap. 10, n. 4 (Archivo hist. nacional, Inquisicion de Valencia).
    1706. MS. of the Library of Univ. of Halle, Yc, 20, T. I.
    1707. Archivo de Simancas, Inquisicion, Leg. 552, fol. 28, 42, 33.
    1708. Concil. Lateran. IV, ann. 1215, cap. lxx.
    1709. Memoria de diversos Autos (Appendix to Vol. I, pp. 593, 594).
    1710. Chapters from the Religious History of Spain, pp. 473, 478.
    1711. MSS. of Royal Library of Copenhagen, 213 fol., p. 148.--Archivo hist. nacional, Inquisicion de Toledo, Leg. 498.--Memoria de diversos Autos (ubi sup. p. 600).
    1712. See "Moriscos of Spain," pp. 116, 129-30.
    1713. Archivo de Simancas, Inquisicion, Leg. 552, fol. 3, 6, 31, 33.
    1714. Archivo de Simancas, Inquisicion, Leg. 552, fol. 17.
    1715. Proceso contra Mari Gómez (MS. penes me).
    1716. Archivo hist. nacional, Inquisicion de Toledo, Leg. 498.
    1717. Simancæ de Cath. Institt. Tit. xiii, n. 20.
    1718. Archivo de Alcalá, Hacienda, Leg. 544^{2} (Lib. 6).
    1719. Rojas de Hæret. P. II, Assert. 25, n. 258.--Praxis Procedendi, cap. 8, n. 22 (Archivo hist. nacional, Inquisicion de Valencia).
    1720. Archivo de Simancas, Inquisicion, Lib. 939, fol. 95.
    1721. Archivo de Simancas, Inquisicion, Visitas de Barcelona, Leg. 15, fol. 20.
    1722. MSS. of Library of Univ. of Halle, Yc, 20, T. I.
    1723. Archivo hist. nacional, Inquisicion de Valencia, Leg. 61; Leg. 299, fol. 80.--Archivo de Alcalá, Hacienda, Leg. 544ª (Lib. 4).--Bibl. nacional, MSS., V, 377, cap. 4.
    1724. Instrucciones de 1484, § 13 (Arguello, fol. 5).
    1725. Archivo hist. nacional, Inquisicion de Toledo, Leg. 133, n. 40. The artless formula of protest is "Y porque la memoria es deleznable e puede ser que algunas otras cosas aya herrado de que agora no tengo memoria, protesto ante vuestra merced que cada y de algunas otras cosas me acordare lo vendre a declarar y dezyr, desde agora pido penitencia, que por mas me aclarar e alympiar digo que si algunas personas vinieren diciendo otras cosas de mas de las desuso declaradas que ayendo tales que vuestra reverencia les debe dar fe, desde agora yo las apruevo e digo que son verdaderas y pido penitencia dellas."

1726. Boletin, XXIII, 289-312.
1727. Archivo hist. nacional, Inquisicion de Toledo, Leg. 153, n. 331.
1728. D. Manuel Serreno y Sanz, in Revista de Archivos, etc., Abril, 1902, p. 294.
1729. Simancæ de Cath. Institt. Tit. XLVIII, n. 28; Ejusd. Enchirid. Tit. LXI, § 5.--Rojas de Hæret. P. I, n. 597.
1730. Elucidationes S^{ti} Officii, § 17 (Archivo de Alcalá, Hacienda, Leg. 544^{2}, Lib. 4).--Bibl. nacional, MSS., Pp, 28; V, 377, cap. ii, § 7

This was not confined to the Spanish Inquisition, but was the current practice of the Church where it had power. See Farinacii de Hæres. Q. 187, n. 133.

1731. MSS. of Royal Library of Copenhagen, 218^{b}, p. 145.
1732. Archivo hist. nacional, Inquisicion de Toledo, Leg. 1.
1733. Ibidem.--Matute y Luquin, Autos de Fe de Córdova, p. 232--Royal Library of Berlin, Qt. 9548.
1734. Albert. Albertin. de Agnoscendis Assert. Cathol., Q. xxxvi, in fine.--Pegnæ Comment. 75 in Eymerici Direct. P. II.
1735. Bibl. nacional, MSS., Pp, 28; V, 377, cap. ii, §§ 4, 6.--Archivo hist. nacional, Inquisicion de Valencia, Leg. 299, fol. 80.--Elucidationes S^{ti} Officii, § 16 (Archivo de Alcalá, Hacienda, Leg. 544^{2}, Lib. 4).
1736. MSS. of Library of Univ. of Halle, Yc, 20, T. I.
1737. See Appendix to Vol. I, p. 580.
1738. Bibl. nacional, MSS., S. 294, fol. 243.
1739. Bibl. nacional, MSS., V, 377. fol. 53.
1740. Royal Library of Berlin, Qt., 9548.
1741. Bleda, Crónica de los Moros, p. 929.
1742. Proceso contra Manuel Díaz (MS. penes me).
1743. Instrucciones de 1484, §§ 11, 12; Instruc. de 1498, 7 § (Arguello fol. 5, 13).
1744. Bibl. nacional, MSS, PV, 3, n. 20.--Somewhat similar is the classification of Moriscos in the Toledo auto of 1594 (MSS. of Library of Univ. of Halle, Yc, 20, T. I.)
1745. Elucidationes Sti Officii, § 4 (Archivo de Alcalá, Hacienda, Leg 544^{2}, Lib. 4).--Bibl. nacional, MSS., V, 377, cap. ii, § 14.
1746. Royal Library of Berlin, Qt. 9548.--Archivo hist. nacional, Inquisicion de Toledo, Leg. 1.
1747. Instrucciones de 1484, § 15 (Arguello, fol. 6).
1748. Instrucciones de 1561, § 53 (Arguello, fol. 34)--Elucidationes S^{ti} Officii, § 22 (ubi sup.).
1749. Simancæ de Cath. Institt. T. XLVII, n. 45, 46.--Ejusd. Enchirid. Tit. LVIII, n. 14.
1750. Royal Library of Berlin, Qt. 9548.
1751. Archivo de Simancas, Inquisicion, Libro 939, fol. 342.--Elucidationes S^{ti} Officii, § 5 (ubi sup.).--Bibl. nacional, MSS., Pp, 28.
1752. MSS. of Library of Univ. of Halle, Yc, 20, T. I.--Bibl. nacional, MSS., G, 50, fol. 241.
1753. Bibl. nacional, MSS., V, 377, cap. 5, §§ 1-3.
1754. MSS. of Library of Univ. of Halle, Yc, 20, T. I
1755. Instrucciones de 1484, § 13 (Arguello, fol. 5).
1756. MSS. of Library of Univ. of Halle, Yc, 20, T. I.
1757. Archivo de Simancas, Inquisicion, Sala 40, Lib. 4, fol. 116-17, 120-1, 126, 130-4, 137, 139, 141, 161-2; Lib. 78, fol. 275, 282, 295, 322.--Archivo hist. nacional, Inquisicion de Valencia, Leg. 385.
1758. Rojas de Hæret., P. I, n. 69, 72, 75-6.--Simancæ de Cath. Institt. Tit. XLVIII, n. 25.--Arnald. Albertin. de agnoscendis Assertt. Cathol. Q. 3, n. 16.--This was inherited from the medieval Inquisition. See Eymerici Direct. P. II, Q. xxxiv and Peña's comment.
1759. MSS. of Library of Univ. of Halle, Yc, 20, T. I.--Bibl. nacional, MSS., G, 50, fol. 249.--Olmo, Relacion, etc., p. 255.--Garau, La Fee triunfante, pp. 75-8, 97.
1760. Pegnæ Comment. XLVIII in Eymerici Director., P. III.
1761. Archivo hist. nacional, Inquisicion de Valencia, Leg. 299, fol. 80.
1762. Usually the oath as to the truth of the genealogy and the limpieza of the ancestry is taken by the applicant personally, and it varies according to his taste. A few specimens will show the different formulas adopted. Some are specific and in detail as Doctor Bernardino Martinez Palomino, prebendary of Toledo, September 7, 1816.--"Los contenidos en esta genealogia son mis Padres y Abuelos Paternos y Maternos de la naturaleza que queda referida, todos legítimos y de legítimo matrimonio, limpios y de limpia sangre, sin raza de Moros, Judíos, Luteranos, Calvinistas, ni otra secta, ni procesados ni castigados por el Santo Oficio segun mi saber y entender, pues asi lo juro in verbo sacerdotis."--Ibidem, fol. 24.

Mariano Bias Garoz for himself and his wife, March 7, 1816, is specially anxious to assert his gentility--"Todos los quales son descendientes de familias ylustres, distinguidas, limpias de toda mala raza de Negros, Moros, Judíos y recien convertidos, y no han exercido oficios viles ni mecanicos y de ser asi cierto no constandome cosa alguna en contrario lo juro y firmo."--Ibidem, fol. 28.

Ramon Nieto y Herrera, July 28, 1816 contents himself with "Todos los quales juro han sido mis Padres y Abuelos Paternos y Maternos."--Ibidem, fol. 33.

1763. The document is incomplete and I have omitted a long enumeration of trivial debts collected.

1764. There is an evident error of a copyist here. The principal and accrued interest of these three censales amount to 39, 230s. 4d., or 1961 l. 10s. 4d. The receiver, who permitted such a sacrifice would scarce have dared to report it to Ferdinand.

1765. Alonso Suárez de Fuentelsaz, one of the inquisitors-general.

1766. In this collection there are two copies of this paper, one with many erasures and apparently a first draft, the other clean and final.

www.ingramcontent.com/pod-product-compliance
Lightning Source LLC
Chambersburg PA
CBHW020746160426
43192CB00006B/258